This book is dedicated to all those who practice critical thinking in their everyday lives and to those who seek to better understand public policy and criminal justice.

Acknowledgments

Every book is the product of many people, some present and some past. Each author draws upon his or her experiences, particularly with past faculty members. In this book we have drawn collectively on those faculty mentors who encouraged us to think critically. In the case of Scott Decker, those individuals included John Eigenbrodt, Russell Compton, Paul Thomas, and Robert Calvert. For Leanne Alarid those individuals include James Marquart, Dennis Longmire, Laura Myers, and Phil Reichel. Leanne also appreciates the information shared by Ken Novak, Mike Reynolds, and West Huddleston,

even though she was not able to make use of it all. For Charles Katz those individuals include Cassia Spohn, Samuel Walker, and Vincent Webb.

The editors would also like to thank the following reviewers for their suggestions: James David Ballard *(Grand Valley State University)*, Donald Bradel *(Bemidji State University)*, Philip Bridgmon *(Grand Valley State University,* Dayton Hall *(University of Houston, Victoria)*, Patricia Loveless *(Penn State University)*, Hal Nees *(Metropolitan State College, Denver)*, Ken Peak *(University of Nevada, Reno)*, and Olga Tsoudis *(Wayne State University)*. ✦

Controversies in Criminal Justice

Contemporary Readings

Scott H. Decker
University of Missouri–St. Louis

Leanne Fiftal Alarid
University of Missouri–Kansas City

Charles M. Katz
Arizona State University–West

Roxbury Publishing Company
Los Angeles, California

Library of Congress Cataloging-in-Publication Data

Controversies in criminal justice: contemporary readings / [edited by] Scott H.
Decker, Leanne Fiftal Alarid, Charles M. Katz
p. cm.
Includes bibliographical references.
ISBN 1-891487-94-9
 1. Criminal justice, Administration of—United States. I. Decker, Scott H. II.
Alarid, Leanne Fiftal III. Katz, Charles M.

HV9950 .C663 2003
364.973—dc21   2002024865

Publisher: Claude Teweles
Managing Editor: Dawn VanDercreek
Production Editor: Carla Max-Ryan
Production Assistant: Phong Ho
Typography: Synergistic Data Systems
Cover Design: Marnie Kenney

Printed on acid-free paper in the United States of America. This book meets the standards
for recycling of the Environmental Protection Agency.

ISBN 1-891487-94-9

ROXBURY PUBLISHING COMPANY
P. O. Box 491044
Los Angeles, California 90049-9044
Voice: (310) 473-3312 • Fax: (310) 473-4490
E-mail: roxbury@roxbury.net
Website: www.roxbury.net

Contents

Acknowledgments iv

About the Editors x

About the Contributors xi

Introduction 1

Part One: The Nature of American Crime

Introduction 5

**Issue I: National Drug Control Policy:
Should We Legalize Drugs?** 8

    1. **YES:** Drug Prohibition in the United States:
       Costs, Consequences, and Alternatives. 10
       Ethan A. Nadelmann

    2. **NO:** Against the Legalization of Drugs. 26
       James Q. Wilson

**Issue II: Guns and Crime: Should We
Relax Gun Permit Laws?** 36

    3. **YES:** Easing Concealed Firearms Laws:
       Effects on Homicide in Three States 38
       David McDowall, Colin Loftin, and Brian Wiersema

    4. **NO:** Firearms Costs, Firearms Benefits,
       and the Limits of Knowledge 46
       Daniel D. Polsby

Issue III: Intelligence and Crime: Do Those
     With Less Intelligence Commit More Crime? 56

  5. *YES:* The Bell Curve: Intelligence and Class
      Structure in American Life 58
      Richard J. Herrnstein and Charles Murray

  6. *NO:* Crime and the Bell Curve: Lessons
      from Intelligent Criminology 68
      *Francis T. Cullen, Paul Gendreau, G. Roger Jarjoura,
      and John Paul Wright*

Issue IV: Terrorism: Has the Government Gone
     Too Far in the Fight Against Terrorism? 83

  7. *YES:* Regarding Eavesdropping on
      Confidential Attorney-Client Communications 85
      American Civil Liberties Union (ACLU)

  8. *NO:* Big Guns, Little Guns: On the Role of
      Military and Private Gun Ownership in
      Combating Foreign Terrorism in the
      United States After 9/11 94
      Dave Klinger and Dave Grossman

Part Two: Law Enforcement and Community Policing

Introduction 101

Issue V: Police Organizations: Should Police
     Organizations Model Themselves More
     Like the 'Real' Military? 103

  9. *YES:* The Myth of the 'Military Model' of Leadership
      in Law Enforcement 105
      Thomas J. Cowper

 10. *NO:* Reenvisioning Police, Reinvigorating Policing:
      A Response to Thomas Cowper 116
      Michael E. Buerger

Issue VI: Community-Oriented Policing:
   Are We There Yet? 125

   11. ***YES:*** Community Policing: Thriving Because It Works 127
       Larry C. Plummer

   12. ***NO:*** A Response to 'Community Policing:
       Thriving Because It Works' 131
       David L. Carter

Issue VII: Zero-Tolerance Policing:
   Is It Effective in Reducing Crime? 135

   13. ***YES:*** Declining Crime Rates: Insiders' Views of the
       New York City Story. 137
       George L. Kelling and William J. Bratton

   14. ***NO:*** Zero-Tolerance Policing and the Experience
       of New York City 144
       Chris Cunneen

Issue VIII: Racial Profiling: Do the Police
   Target Minorities for Traffic Stops? 158

   15. ***YES:*** Montgomery Traffic Data Show Race Disparity 160
       Phuong Ly

   16. ***NO:*** Police Target Most Likely Criminals of All Races 162
       Jerry Oliver

Part Three: Administering Criminal Law in the Courts

Introduction 165

Issue IX: Does the Federal Grand Jury Adequately
   Perform Its Screening Role? 167

   17. ***YES:*** If It Ain't Broke, Don't Fix It 169
       Thomas P. Sullivan and Robert D. Nachman

   18. ***NO:*** Why the Grand Jury Cannot Effectively
       Screen the Prosecutor's Charging Decisions 182
       Andrew D. Leipold

Issue X: Are Drug Courts a Promising Pretrial Strategy? 190

19. ***YES:*** Looking at a Decade of Drug Courts 192
    Drug Court Clearinghouse and Technical Assistance Project

20. ***NO:*** The Drug Court Scandal 204
    Morris B. Hoffman

Issue XI: The Public as Thirteenth Juror: Should Cameras Be in the Courtroom During Criminal Trials? 228

21. ***YES:*** Time, TV, and Criminal Justice: Second Thoughts on the Simpson Trial 230
    Samuel H. Pillsbury

22. ***NO:*** The Distortion of Criminal Trials Through Televised Proceedings 247
    Taffiny S. Stewart

Part Four: Punishment of Offenders

Introduction 255

Issue XII: Lock 'Em Up: Do We Overuse Imprisonment as a Punishment Strategy? 257

23. ***YES:*** Lethal Violence and the Overreach of American Imprisonment 259
    Franklin E. Zimring (with the collaboration of Gordon Hawkins)

24. ***NO:*** Supply Side Imprisonment Policy 264
    Michael K. Block

Issue XIII: Beyond Revenge: Will the Restorative Justice Paradigm Achieve Its Intended Goals? 272

25. ***YES:*** Moving Toward Community Justice 274
    Eduardo Barajas, Jr.

26. ***NO:*** Reconsidering Restorative Justice: The Corruption of Benevolence Revisited? 280
    Sharon Levrant, Francis T. Cullen, Betsy Fulton, and John F. Wozniak

Issue XIV: For Profit or Punishment:
Should Jails and Prisons Be Privatized? 294

27. **YES:** Correctional Privatization: The Issues
and the Evidence 296
Charles W. Thomas

28. **NO:** McPrisons Are McFailures by Most If
Not All Objective Measures 308
Richard G. Hogan

Issue XV: Is It a Good Idea to House Juveniles
in Adult Correctional Facilities? 319

29. **YES:** The House of Last Resort:
Incarcerating Juveniles in Adult Prisons 321
David L. Myers

30. **NO:** Arguments Against the Confinement of
Juveniles with Adult Offenders 330
David W. Roush, Earl L. Dunlap, and Jill Rinella

Issue XVI: Megan's Law: Should Neighbors Be
Notified When a Sex Offender Is Released
Into Their Community? 343

31. **YES:** Community Notification: A Valuable
Strategy for Managing Sex Offenders
in the Community 346
Mary Ann Farkas

32. **NO:** Latent Consequences of Community
Notification Laws 353
Lisa L. Sample and Anthony J. Streveler

About the Editors

Scott **H. Decker** is Curator's Professor of Criminology and Criminal Justice at the University of Missouri–St. Louis. He received a B.A. in Social Justice from DePauw University and a Ph.D. in Criminology from Florida State University. His primary research focus has been on criminal justice policy, gangs, and violence. He is co-author of *Life in the Gang: Family, Friends and Violence* and *Confronting Gangs*. He is currently conducting an evaluation of the SafeFutures and Juvenile Accountability Incentive Block Grant programs in St. Louis and directing the evaluation of the Strategic Approaches for Community Safety Initiative (SACSI) in St. Louis.

Leanne **Fiftal Alarid** received her Ph.D. from Sam Houston State University in 1996. She is currently an associate professor and the program coordinator of criminal justice/criminology at the University of Missouri–Kansas City. She received a University faculty scholar award for excellence in research in 2001. Her research has been funded by the U.S. Department of Justice and the state of Missouri. Her areas of research expertise are institutional and community corrections, women and crime, and criminal justice policy. Dr. Alarid has authored seventeen journal articles and edited or authored three books. She recently completed *Community-Based Corrections* (2002, Wadsworth) with Paul Cromwell and Rolando del Carmen. She co-edited *Correctional Perspectives: Views from Academics, Practitioners, and Prisoners* (2002, Roxbury) with Paul Cromwell and is completing a co-edited book that is authored by an incarcerated prisoner, entitled: *Doing Time in a Modern Day Prison* (Wadsworth).

Charles **M. Katz** is an assistant professor in the Administration of Justice Department at Arizona State University West. Katz earned his Ph.D. in Criminal Justice from the University of Nebraska at Omaha in 1997. He is currently involved in two studies examining responses to community gang problems. He is the project director for a National Institute of Justice funded study of the police response to gangs in four sites: Phoenix, Arizona, Albuquerque, New Mexico, Las Vegas, Nevada, and Inglewood, California. In addition, he is working with the Office of Juvenile Justice and Delinquency Prevention and the City of Mesa, Arizona to evaluate the effectiveness of the Mesa Gang Intervention Project. Dr. Katz is also involved in two projects examining community policing at the national level. His publications include articles on community policing, policing gangs, and drugs and crime. ✦

About the Contributors

American Civil Liberties Union (ACLU) is a non-profit organization established to protect individual rights in the United States.

Eduardo Barajas, Jr., is a correctional program specialist with the U.S. Department of Justice, National Institute of Corrections, in Washington, D.C.

Michael K. Block is professor of economics and law at the University of Arizona. He is also president of the Goldwater Institute and Senior Research Fellow at the Progress and Freedom Foundation in Washington, DC.

William J. Bratton is a former police commissioner of New York City and Boston. Currently working in the private sector, he is a frequent lecturer on the issue of crime-reduction techniques, management, and leadership.

Michael E. Buerger is an associate professor at Bowling Green State University in Ohio. After nine years as a municipal police officer in New Hampshire, he has been a police researcher in a variety of settings, most recently serving as research director for the Jersey City Police Department. His current interests are problem-oriented policing initiatives, their impact on police management structures, and the resistance of police culture to reform.

David L. Carter is a professor in the school of criminal justice and director of the National Center for Community Policing at Michigan State University and specializes in policing issues. He received his Ph.D. in criminal justice administration from Sam Houston State University in Huntsville, Texas. In addition to teaching graduate and undergraduate courses at Michigan State, he is director of the Criminal Justice Overseas Study Program to England and has worked with police agencies in North America, Europe, Asia, and Africa.

Thomas J. Cowper is a captain with the New York State Police and a graduate student at Marist College. He is a former Marine officer and has served in a variety of law enforcement assignments during his 17-year police career. He was a member of the Urban Institute's site visit teams as part of the National Evaluation for the COPS program and is pursuing a research agenda on the impact of technology on government and policing.

Francis T. Cullen is distinguished research professor of criminal justice and sociology at the University of Cincinnati. He has recently coauthored *Combating Corporate Crime: Local Prosecutors at Work, Criminological Theory: Past to Present,* and *Offender Rehabilitation: Effective Correctional Intervention.*

Chris Cunneen is an associate professor of Faculty of Law at the University of Sydney in Australia.

Drug Court Clearinghouse and Technical Assistance Project (DCCTAP) is sponsored by the Drug Courts Program Office of the Office of Justice Programs, U.S. Department of Justice. The DCCTAP staff is located at American University in Washington, D.C., and Caroline S. Cooper directs the program.

Earl L. Dunlap is the executive director of the National Juvenile Detention Association at Eastern Kentucky University and project director of the Office of Juvenile Justice and Delinquency Prevention project that addresses the problem of crowding in juvenile confinement facilities.

Mary Ann Farkas is an assistant professor in the Criminology and Law Studies program at Marquette University in Milwaukee, Wisconsin.

Betsy Fulton is a Ph.D. student in the Division of Criminal Justice at the University of Cincinnati.

Paul Gendreau is a professor of psychology at the University of New Brunswick, Saint John.

Dave Grossman is a Colonel and Army Ranger as well as a psychology and military science professor at West Point. He is the author of *On Killing: The Psychological Cost of Learning to Kill in War and Society* and co-author of *Stop Teaching Our Kids to Kill: A Call to Action Against TV, Movie, and Video Game Violence* with Gloria DeGaetano. Today he is director of the Killology Research Group and, in the wake of the 9/11 terrorist attacks, is on the road almost 300 days a year, training elite military and law enforcement organizations worldwide about the reality of combat.

Gordon Hawkins is senior fellow at the Earl Warren Legal Institute at the University of California–Berkeley and co-author of the recently published *Punishment and Democracy: Three Strikes and You're Out in California*.

Richard J. Herrnstein, recently deceased, was a professor of psychology at Harvard University.

Morris B. Hoffman is a district court judge for the Second Judicial District in Denver, Colorado.

Richard G. Hogan is an assistant professor of criminal justice at the University of Tennessee, Chattanooga. His views against privatization of prisons and jails were formed from academic research and experiences in law enforcement and the federal prison system.

G. Roger Jarjoura is an assistant professor of public and environmental affairs at Indiana University, Indianapolis.

George L. Kelling is a professor in the school of criminal justice at Rutgers University and a research fellow in the Kennedy School of Government at Harvard University. He is also an Adjunct Fellow at the Manhattan Institute.

David Klinger is an associate professor at University of Missouri–St. Louis. His research includes determinants of police behavior, the community context of crime control, and the effectiveness of rapid response teams.

Andrew D. Leipold is a professor of law at the University of Illinois College of Law. He teaches and writes in the areas of criminal law and criminal procedure.

Sharon Levrant is a Ph.D. student in the Division of Criminal Justice at the University of Cincinnati.

Colin Loftin is a professor in the school of criminal justice at University at Albany.

Phuong Ly is a writer for the *Washington Post*.

David McDowall is a member of the Violence Research Group and the Department of Criminology and Criminal Justice at the University of Maryland at College Park.

Charles Murray is a fellow at the American Enterprise Institute.

David L. Myers is an assistant professor in the Department of Criminology at Indiana University of Pennsylvania. He received his Ph.D. from the University of Maryland in 1999. He recently published *Excluding Violent Youths From Juvenile Court: The Effectiveness of Legislative Waiver* and is currently involved in an assessment of treatment effectiveness for violent youths in adult correctional facilities.

Robert D. Nachman is an associate attorney at Jenner and Block law firm in Chicago. He received his J.D. from Harvard University in 1983.

Ethan A. Nadelmann served as an assistant professor of politics and public affairs at the Woodrow Wilson School of Public and International Affairs at Princeton University. From 1987–1994 at Princeton he created and chaired the Princeton Working Group on the Future of Drug Use and Alternative to Drug Prohibition. Nadelmann founded the Lindesmith Center, a leading drug policy and research institute created in 1994 with the philanthropic support of George Soross. He now serves as the Executive Director of the Lindesmith Center-Drug Policy Foundation, which merged in July of 2000.

Jerry Oliver was a 2000 commentary columnist for the *Richmond-Times Dispatch* and is Detroit's Chief of Police.

Samuel H. Pillsbury is a professor of law and Rains fellow at Loyola Law School in Los Angeles. He served as an occasional television commentator during the O. J. Simpson trial, and covered criminal courts in Florida as a newspaper reporter during one of the early cameras-in-the-courtroom experiments.

Larry C. Plummer has had responsibility for implementing community policing in Mountain View, California. He has spent 27 years in policing, the first 15 with the Berkeley Police Department, and holds a master's degree in management. He has published articles on such topics as domestic violence, honest leadership, and police and race.

Daniel D. Polsby is Kirkland and Ellis Professor of Law at Northwestern University.

Jill Rinella is a research assistant at the Center for Research and Professional Development at Michigan State University. She holds an M.S. degree in criminal justice from Michigan State University and worked on the Office of Juvenile Justice and Delinquency Prevention, Youth Gangs in the Juvenile Detention and Corrections project.

David W. Roush is an assistant professor in the School of Criminal Justice at Michigan State University, where he directs the National Juvenile Detention Association's Center for Research and Professional Development. He was past president of both the Michigan and the National Juvenile Detention Associations, editor of the *Journal of Correctional Health Care*, and compiler of *The Desktop Guide to Good Juvenile Detention Practice*, published with funding from the Office of Juvenile Justice and Delinquency Prevention.

Lisa L. Sample is an assistant professor in the Department of Criminal Justice at the University of Nebraska at Omaha. Her current research interests include the social and legal responses to crime and juvenile and criminal justice policy. She has published in the areas of disparity in the juvenile and criminal justice system and is

currently writing a book, *The Social Construction of the Sex Offender*.

Taffiny S. Stewart is an attorney in the State of Alabama.

Anthony J. Streveler is a deputy administrator with the Wisconsin Department of Corrections. Over the past several years he has played a role in the development and administration of several sex offender laws in the State of Wisconsin, including Sexual Predator Law, Polygraph Testing of Sexual Offenders, Lifetime Monitoring of Sexual Offenders, Pharmacological Interventions of Certain Child Sex Offenders, and Sex Offender Registration and Community Notification.

Thomas P. Sullivan is a partner at Jenner and Block law firm in Chicago. He was the U.S. Attorney of the Northern District of Illinois from 1977 to 1981 and received his LL.B. from Loyola University in 1952.

Charles W. Thomas received his M.A. and Ph.D. degrees from the University of Kentucky. He was professor of criminology and director of the Private Corrections Project at the University of Florida until his retirement in 1999. As a leading authority on the economic, legal, and public policy implications of correctional privatization, he continues to publish and to engage in related consulting work.

Brian Wiersema is a research associate at the University of Maryland at College Park.

James Q. Wilson is James A. Collins Professor of Management at the John E. Anderson Graduate School of Management, University of California, Los Angeles. Since the 1960s, he has chaired or served on a great number of commissions, task forces, advisory panels, and governing boards in both the public and private sectors. He is a past president of the American Political Science Association and a recipient of that association's James Madison Award for distinguished scholarship. He is well known as the author or editor of many works on crime.

John F. Wozniak is chair and associate professor of the Department of Sociology, Anthropology, and Social Work at Western Illinois University.

John Paul Wright is an assistant professor of criminal justice at East Tennessee State University.

Franklin E. Zimring is professor of law and director of the Earl Warren Legal Institute at the University of California, Berkeley. ✦

Introduction

There are two sides to every story. At least that is what most people believe. Consistent with that approach we present students with a book that provides two answers or approaches to a number of the most significant questions in criminal justice. This book examines several current controversies in criminal justice and provides two sides to each question. The authors of the chapters in this book provide contrasts to over thirty of the most important issues in this important area of public policy. In each chapter, these authors stake out a position and defend it with the best evidence and logic available. Each chapter combines two distinct elements. The first element is a logical argument. A logical argument requires that each statement in an argument be consistent with the other statements, that terms be defined in a consistent manner, and that the overall argument be logically consistent. The second element is the evidence that supports the argument. That evidence is not found in the logic of an argument; rather, it is based on external criteria. Thus each chapter combines an internal argument that can be evaluated on its own terms, independent of facts, findings, and studies with a set of facts—often the result of studies with a solid research design—that support the argument. The edi-

tors of this text believe that the process of reviewing and evaluating arguments can lead to better answers to issues in criminal justice.

The position that there are two sides—or more—to every argument is one with which the editors of this book agree. Because we endorse the scientific method, we are willing to consider that a hypothesis may receive support when it is tested. The use of a scientific method assumes that the two principles established in the paragraph above will be applied to the chapters in this book. Basically, the scientific method requires two things. The first is that a set of questions be logically consistent. The second is that questions be tested. In the sections that follow, students are encouraged to ask how well each chapter meets these two criteria. How well does the argument hold logically? Is the argument logically consistent? And what about the facts? Do they support the conclusions? Are the "facts" (scientists call them data) consistent with the argument?

Students who read the chapters in this book should also be prepared to assess whether the evidence offered was collected in a manner that was free of bias and that considers alternative explanations. The matter of alternative explanations is particularly important. One of the ways that science moves ahead is to ask the questions "What about," "What if," or "Did you consider." Each of these questions seeks to determine whether some alternative cause was responsible for the outcome of a particular study or question. This line of questioning is often identified as the search for a rival hypothesis. You might want to think about this kind of reasoning in light of the following example. It is a well-established fact that people with smaller shoe sizes are more religious. When people have smaller feet, they tend to go to church more often, express belief in a Supreme Being more often, and pray more often. Now, we don't suspect that you think having small feet is *directly* related to religious beliefs. There must be some rival hypothesis that accounts for this finding. What could it be? We encourage students to think about what those other factors could be. In the case of religious beliefs, a number of factors come to mind initially. The first would be age. It makes sense that older people are more religious, but age doesn't account for shoe size. A second factor would be height. Shorter people generally have smaller feet. But there is no logical reason why shorter people would be more religious than taller people. Another factor bears consideration. Gender may be related to the strength of religious conviction. Women are more religious than men, and, of course, women have smaller feet than men. When you think through the relationship between religiosity and shoe size, it is logical that because women have smaller feet than men, and women are more religious than men, it is gender that is responsible for the relationship.

It is this kind of thinking that we hope this book encourages; that is the primary reason we undertook to publish it. As you read each of the chapters in this book, you should critically assess the logic of the arguments and the data that each presents to support that argument. Each of the editors believes that students should be challenged to think critically about contemporary issues in criminal justice. Whether you are a criminal justice major or you are working in the criminal justice system or if this will be your first and

only criminal justice course, confronting the issues in this book is an important experience. We wrote this book with the hope that you learn at least two things from it. The first is that you will learn more about the issues that affect criminal justice on a daily basis. After all, Americans rank crime among the most serious problems they face and spend billions on public safety each year. Most cities spend more on police protection and public safety than on any other single item in their budgets. These facts combine to underscore the importance of critically considering the current controversies in criminal justice.

The second benefit we hope you gain from this book is a way of thinking. The way that the arguments are juxtaposed, the combination of facts and logic, and the structure of an argument provide examples that we hope students learn from. Arguments are more effective when they have a solid internal structure and are supported by facts. As you read these chapters you should ask yourself if the argument and facts make sense.

Finally, it is our intent that students who use this book will be able to apply the skills they learn to new problems. This will require a careful weighing of both sides of an argument and using that process to consider approaches to other issues.

There are a number of ways that students can use this book. The first is to apply critical thinking principles. We believe that the book is structured in such a way as to encourage students to use critical thinking skills in reading and responding to the issues included in the book. We also encourage students to use the Internet and contemporary news media to keep up with the issues—and the structure of arguments—raised in this book. It is certain that the facts, and perhaps the arguments regarding criminal justice issues, will change dramatically over the next few years. Unless students stay abreast of these issues, they will be unaware of such developments and consequently be in a weaker position to fully understand and consider them.

The book is organized into four parts. Part One examines the nature of criminal behavior and the law, examining such topics as drug use, legal limits on the response to terrorism, firearms laws, and the argument regarding the Bell curve and crime. Part Two examines current controversies in law enforcement and policing. Specific controversies covered in this area are community policing, the effect of zero-tolerance policing, whether racial profiling exists, and military models in law enforcement. Part Three examines the administration of the criminal law in the courts. Here we consider, for example, the role of video cameras in the courts, drug courts, and the role of the grand jury. Part Four examines the punishment of offenders. Here we include chapters that examine community notification of sex offenders moving into the area, sentencing of juveniles to adult institutions, restorative justice, and the privatization of prisons.

We do not provide conclusions for students. None of the chapters concludes with "answers." Indeed, it may be the case that we raise more questions than are answered. In our view, one question leads to other questions. That is consistent with our views about the importance of the process of examining controversies. ✦

Part One

The Nature of American Crime

Have we won the war on crime or are we ready to be hit by a crime wave? On the one hand, the FBI and other federal agencies tell us that crime is down. *Uniform Crime Report* data collected by the FBI have shown that over the past ten years crime rates have decreased for almost every major type of crime. For example, between 1993 and 1998, violent crime reports decreased by 27 percent and property crime reports decreased by 34 percent. Similar findings were reported by the *National Crime Victimization Survey,* which randomly selects respondents throughout the country and asks them whether they have been victimized in the past six months. They found that between 1993 and 1999 violent crimes decreased by 35.4 percent and property crimes decreased by almost 38 percent (Rennison 2000).

Some, however, are telling a very different story, arguing that crime is increasing and that it is only going to get worse. James Fox, a leading expert on homicide, points out that the homicide rate among teenagers has increased by over 20 percent and that because of changing birth rates the nation is facing a "ticking time bomb" (Fox 1996). Drug and gang problems are also said to be worsening.

Recent research indicates that marijuana and cocaine use by juveniles more than doubled between 1990 and 1998 (*National Household Survey on Drug Abuse: 1999* 2000) and the number of gang members doubled between 1992 and 1999 (Office of Juvenile Justice and Delinquency Prevention 2000).

The fact is that the crime problems one decides to look at, and how one decides to look at them, affects one's perceptions. When people talk broadly about crime, and changes in crime, it is difficult to figure out just what is going on. For this reason we present literature on four specific topics central to the crime controversy over the past five years.

The first issue looks at drug control policy and its effect on crime. Over the past twenty years the United States has taken a strong stance against drug use and sales. Today, about 20 percent of individuals in prison are incarcerated for a drug offense (Bureau of Justice Statistics 2000). However Western nations around the world have recently begun to decriminalize their laws concerning some drugs. Countries such as the Netherlands, Australia, and Italy rarely arrest individuals for marijuana use and almost never use incarceration to punish marijuana users. Recently, Canada has even considered decriminalizing or perhaps legalizing marijuana. U.S. officials are staunchly opposed to these changes because they believe such policies would have a dramatic impact on the availability of drugs in the United States and would increase crime rates. The two chapters presented in this section review the various forms of decriminalization and legalization that are possible and their potential influence on drug use and crime in this country.

The second issue examines controversies regarding guns, gun legislation, and crime. Today, there are about 200 million firearms in circulation, of which 70 million are handguns (Walker 2001). About 30 percent of U.S. households own a handgun, compared to about 7 percent of households in most other western nations (Messner and Rosenfeld 2001). Many anti-gun groups contend that the high amount of violence in the United States is a consequence of the large number of handguns distributed throughout the country. For example, in 1995, 68 percent of homicides were committed with a gun—most of which were committed with a handgun (Messner and Rosenfeld 2001). Some of these groups have advocated banning handguns, bullets, and the manufacturing and importation of handguns. Other organizations oppose restrictions on gun ownership and believe that individuals have the constitutional right to bear arms and that weak sentencing policies are the cause of high rates of violence. The most recent controversy surrounding guns in America has revolved around concealed handguns. Some individuals and organizations are claiming that carrying a concealed handgun reduces a persons' chance of being victimized, while others believe that concealed weapons pose a general threat to society. The two articles incorporated in this section use scientifically gathered data to debate the benefits and limitations of concealed firearm laws.

The third controversial issue examines the relative impact of intelligence on criminality. Theories attempting to explain criminality through an understanding of biology

have been around since the mid-1800s. Many of these theories focused on bumps on skulls, the size of a man's torso, and even the shape of a person's eyes. However, in the 1930s academics curtailed studying biological causes of crime because of the fear that their work might be used unethically. In the 1990s, however, there was a resurgence of interest in the connection between biology and crime. Today, researchers are examining the impact of an extra Y chromosome, testosterone, and genetics on criminality. However, one of the most controversial issues in the biology and crime debate has involved the impact of intelligence on crime. Some scientists contend that intelligence level is one of the strongest predictors of criminal behavior and that this information could be used to focus resources and personnel on those with lower intelligence in an effort to prevent future crime. Other scientists, however, argue that intelligence is unrelated to criminality and that other intervening factors such as income, ethnicity, age, gender, and peer group affiliation have greater influences on criminality. They further argue that policies based on personal characteristics and not on behavior are undemocratic and unconstitutional. The two articles included here review questions about the scientific research on intelligence and crime and discuss the possibility of factors other than intelligence that may affect criminality.

The fourth controversial issue focuses on terrorism. Since the mid-1990s, terrorism in the United States has slowly but steadily increased. Until recently, however, U.S. citizens have perpetrated most terrorist attacks. Some of these attacks included those of Ted Kaczynski (a.k.a. the Unabomber); Timothy McVeigh, who bombed the federal building in Oklahoma City; and Eric Rudolph, who is suspected of several abortion clinic bombings and the Centennial Park bombing during the 1998 Summer Olympics in Atlanta. On September 11, 2001, the most serious and devastating act of terrorism took place, with the attacks on the World Trade Center and the Pentagon, in which approximately 3,000 U.S. residents died. As a result of the attack, local, state, and federal agencies have responded through legislation, education, and beefed-up enforcement in an effort to prevent further acts of terrorism. Many of the proposals have called for sweeping new reforms, with the federal government taking on broad new responsibilities for domestic law enforcement and granting law enforcement agencies expanded powers. Many organizations have responded, arguing that the expansion of powers that the federal government has awarded itself is unconstitutional. Two chapters in this section debate the appropriateness of many of the legislative changes that have taken place since the September 11 attacks and suggest alternatives for addressing problems in the future.

References

Bureau of Justice Statistics. 2000. *Sourcebook of Criminal Justice–1999.* Bureau of Justice Statistics: Washington DC.

Fox, James. 1996. *Trends in Juvenile Violence.* Washington DC: Government Printing Press.

Messner, Steven, and Richard Rosenfeld. 2001. *Crime and the American Dream.* Belmont: Wadsworth.

National Household Survey on Drug Abuse: 1999. 2000. Washington DC: Government Printing Press.

Office of Juvenile Justice and Delinquency Prevention. 2000. *1999 National Youth Gang Survey.* Washington DC: Government Printing Press.

<http://www.ojp.usdoj.gov/bjs/prisons.htm>

Rennison, Callie. 2000. *Criminal Victimization 1999.* Washington DC: Bureau of Justice Statistics.

Walker, Samuel. 2001. *Sense and Nonsense about Crime and Drugs.* Belmont: Wadsworth. ✦

ISSUE I
National Drug Control Policy: Should We Legalize Drugs?

There are three surveys that tell the public a great deal about drug use in the United States. One survey is the *National Household Survey* (NHS), which randomly selects individuals around the country and asks them questions about their behavior. The NHS suggests that many Americans have used drugs, with about 36 percent of adults in the U.S. indicating that they have tried an illegal drug at least once. The survey also showed that about 6 percent of adults are current users, meaning that they have used an illegal drug in the past month. The *Monitoring the Future* survey annually interviews 45,000 high school students across the country about their drug use habits. The 1999 survey indicated that approximately 26 percent of high school seniors are currently using illegal drugs. Another survey, the *Arrestee Drug Abuse Monitoring* (ADAM) project, interviews recently booked arrestees in 35 cities throughout the country. As part of the project arrestees are questioned about their drug use and provide a urine sample to be tested for recent drug use. The results of the study have suggested that 60 to 70 percent of arrestees are current drug users (Walker 2001).

With all of the drug use taking place it should not be surprising that when citizens are asked about problems confronting their community, concern about drugs usually ranks somewhere near the top of their list. The public often associates drugs with crime, gangs, and many undesirable behaviors. As a consequence, the criminal justice system has played a major role in the fight against drugs. Today, for example, over 20 percent of the prison population is incarcerated as a consequence of drug-related convictions. Some critics, however, claim that the nation has gone too far in its fight against drugs. Many have pointed to the fact that in some urban areas, a young person has a better chance of going to prison because of a drug-related conviction than of going to college. On the other hand, defenders of current drug-control policies claim that many of these same communities would be devastated by problems associated with drug abuse and addiction if the nation had not taken a proactive course over the past three decades. In this section Ethan A. Nadelmann and James Q. Wilson debate the issue.

Nadelmann argues that current drug policies should be abandoned and favors the legalization of drugs. He presents evidence suggesting that current approaches to drug control are ineffective in curtailing drug use and trafficking. He also makes an argument that U.S. drug control policy is costly and counterproductive. Dr. Nadelmann recommends alternatives that he believes would reduce the costs of drug control and would specifically address the consequences of drug abuse.

Wilson, however, argues against drug legalization. He believes that if drugs were legalized, they would become less expensive and would be used increasingly in society. Although he agrees with Dr. Nadelmann that the costs of drug control policy are high, he believes that the costs of drug legalization would be even higher. The stigma attached to drug use would be removed, and the number of drug abusers and addicts would increase several fold. Dr. Wilson argues that the actual costs of drug use would escalate as a result of increased health problems, increased dependency on welfare, and increased crime.

References

Walker, Samuel. 2001. *Sense and Nonsense about Crime and Drugs.* Belmont: Wadsworth.

Critical Thinking Questions

1. What are the major advantages and disadvantages of legalizing drugs?

2. If you were a policymaker, how would you handle the issue of drug legalization?

3. What are the long-term consequences of allowing marijuana to be used for medical purposes?

Internet Websites

National Institute of Drug Abuse. <http://www.nida.nih.gov/>

Drug Enforcement Agency. <http://www.dea.gov/>

Discusses national drug policy from the point of view of the White House. <http://www.whitehousedrugpolicy.gov/>

Research on drug use, sales, and crime. <http://www.ncjrs.org/drgswww.html>

Arrestee Drug Abuse Monitoring program. <http://www.adam-nij.net/>

The Drug Reform Coordination Network. <http://www.drcnet.org/> ✦

1

Drug Prohibition in the United States

Costs, Consequences, and Alternatives

Ethan A. Nadelmann

As frustrations with the drug problem and current drug policies rise daily, growing numbers of political leaders, law enforcement officials, drug abuse experts, and common citizens are insisting that a radical alternative to current policies be fairly considered: the controlled legalization (or decriminalization) of drugs.[1]

Just as "Repeal Prohibition" became a catchphrase that swept together the diverse objections to Prohibition, so "Legalize (or Decriminalize) Drugs" has become a catchphrase that means many things to many people. The policy analyst views legalization as a model for critically examining the costs and benefits of drug prohibition policies. Libertarians, both civil and economic, view it as a policy alternative that eliminates criminal sanctions on the use and sale of drugs that are costly in terms of both individual liberty and economic freedom. Others see it simply as a means to "take the crime out of the drug business." In its broadest sense, however, legalization incorporates the many arguments and growing sentiment for de-emphasizing our traditional reliance on criminal justice resources to deal with drug abuse and for emphasizing instead drug restrictions on the availability and use of psychoactive substances and positive inducements to abstain from drug abuse.

There is no one legalization option. At one extreme, some libertarians advocate the removal of all criminal sanctions and taxes on the production and sale of all psychoactive substances—with the possible exception of restrictions on sales to children. The alternative extremes are more varied. Some would limit legalization to one of the safest (relatively speaking) of all illicit substances: marijuana. Others prefer a "medical" oversight model similar to today's methadone maintenance programs. The middle ground combines legal availability of some or all illicit drugs with vigorous efforts to restrict consumption by means other than resort[ing] to criminal sanctions. Many supporters of this dual approach simultaneously advocate greater efforts to limit tobacco consumption and the abuse of alcohol as well as a transfer of government resources from anti-drug law enforcement to drug prevention and treatment. Indeed, the best model for this view of drug legalization is precisely the tobacco control model advocated by those who want to do everything possible to discourage tobacco consumption short of criminalizing the production, sale, and use of tobacco.

Clearly, neither drug legalization nor enforcement of anti-drug laws promises to "solve" the drug problem. Nor is there any question that legalization presents certain risks. Legalization would almost certainly increase the availability of drugs, decrease their price, and remove the deterrent power of the criminal sanction—all of which invite increases in drug use and abuse. There are at least three reasons, however, why these risks are worth taking. First, drug control strategies that rely primarily on criminal justice measures are significantly and inherently limited in their capacity to curtail drug abuse. Second, many law enforcement efforts are not only of limited value but also highly costly and counterproductive. Indeed, many of the drug-related evils that most people identify as part and parcel of "the drug problem" are in fact the costs of drug prohibition policies. Third, the risks of legalization may well be less than most people assume, particularly if intelligent alternative measures are implemented.

The Limits of Drug Prohibition Policies

Few law enforcement officials any longer contend that their efforts can do much more than they are already doing to reduce drug abuse in the United States. This is true of international drug enforcement efforts, interdiction, and both high-level and street-level domestic drug enforcement efforts.

The United States seeks to limit the export of illicit drugs to this country by a combination of crop eradication and crop substitution programs, financial inducements to growers to abstain from the illicit business and punitive measures against producers, traffickers, and others involved in the drug traffic. These efforts have met with scant success in the past and show few indications of succeeding in the future. The obstacles are many: marijuana and opium can be grown in a wide variety of locales and even the coca plant "can be grown in virtually any subtropical region of the world which gets between 40 and 240 inches of rain per year, where it never freezes and where the land is not so swampy as to be waterlogged. In South America this comes to [approximately] 2,500,000 square miles," of which less than 700 square miles are currently being used to cultivate coca.[2] Producers in many countries have reacted to crop eradication programs by engaging in "guerrilla" farming methods, cultivating their crops in relatively inaccessible hinterlands, and camouflaging them with legitimate crops. Some illicit drug-producing regions are controlled not by the general government but by drug trafficking gangs or political insurgents, thereby rendering eradication efforts even more difficult and hazardous.

Even where eradication efforts prove relatively successful in an individual country, other countries will emerge as new producers, as has occurred with both the international marijuana and heroin markets during the past two decades and can be expected to

follow from planned coca eradication programs. The foreign export price of illicit drugs is such a tiny fraction of the retail price in the United States [approximately 4 percent with cocaine, 1 percent with marijuana, and much less than 1 percent with heroin][3] that international drug control efforts are not even successful in raising the cost of illicit drugs to U.S. consumers.

U.S. efforts to control drugs overseas also confront substantial, and in some cases well-organized, political opposition in foreign countries.[4] Major drug traffickers retain the power to bribe and intimidate government officials into ignoring or even cooperating with their enterprises.[5] Particularly in many Latin American and Asian countries, the illicit drug traffic is an important source of income and employment, bringing in billions of dollars in hard currency each year and providing liveable wages for many hundreds of thousands. The illicit drug business has been described—not entirely in jest—as the best means ever devised by the United States for exporting the capitalist ethic to potentially revolutionary Third World peasants. By contrast, United States-sponsored eradication efforts risk depriving those same peasants of their livelihoods, thereby stimulating support for communist insurgencies ranging from Peru's Shining Path[6] to the variety of ethnic and communist organizations active in drug-producing countries such as Colombia and Burma. Moreover, many of those involved in producing illicit drugs overseas do not perceive their moral obligation as preventing decadent gringos from consuming cocaine or heroin; rather it is to earn the best living possible for themselves and their families. In the final analysis, there is little the U.S. government can do to change this perception.

Interdiction efforts have shown little success in stemming the flow of cocaine and heroin into the United States.[7] Indeed, during the past decade, the wholesale price of a kilo of cocaine has dropped by 80 percent even as the retail purity of a gram of cocaine has quintupled from 12 to about 60 percent; the trend with heroin over the past few years has been similar if less dramatic.[8] Easily transported in a variety of large and small aircraft and sea vessels, carried across the Mexican border by legal and illegal border crossers, hidden in everything from furniture, flowers, and automobiles to private body parts and cadavers, heroin and cocaine shipments are extraordinarily difficult to detect. Despite powerful congressional support for dramatically increasing the role of the military in drug interdiction, military leaders insist that they can do little to make a difference. The Coast Guard and U.S. Customs continue to expand their efforts in this area, but they too concede that they will never seize more than a small percentage of total shipments. Because cocaine and heroin are worth more than their weight in gold, the incentives to transport these drugs to the United States are so great that we can safely assume that there will never be a shortage of those willing to take the risk.

The one success that interdiction efforts can claim concerns marijuana. Because marijuana is far bulkier per dollar of value than either cocaine or heroin, it is harder to conceal and easier to detect. Stepped-up interdiction efforts in recent years appear to have reduced the flow of marijuana into the United States and to have increased its price to the American consumer.[8] The unintended consequences of this success are twofold: the United States has emerged as one of the world's leading producers of marijuana; indeed, U.S. producers are now believed to produce among the finest strains in the world[8]; and many international drug traffickers appear to have redirected their efforts from marijuana to cocaine. The principal consequence of U.S. drug interdiction efforts, many would contend, has been a glut of increasingly potent cocaine and a shortage of comparatively benign marijuana.

Domestic law enforcement efforts have proven increasingly successful in apprehending and imprisoning rapidly growing numbers of illicit drug merchants, ranging from the most sophisticated international traffickers to the most common street-level drug dealers. The principal benefit of law enforcement efforts directed at major drug trafficking organizations is probably the rapidly rising value of drug trafficker assets forfeited to the government. There is, how-

ever, little indication that such efforts have any significant impact of the price or availability of illicit drugs. Intensive and highly costly street-level law enforcement efforts such as those mounted by many urban police departments in recent years have resulted in the arrests of thousands of low-level drug dealers and users and helped improve the quality of life in targeted neighborhoods.[9] In most large urban centers, however, these efforts have had little impact on the overall availability of illicit drugs.

The logical conclusion of the foregoing analysis is not that criminal justice efforts to stop drug trafficking do not work at all; rather, it is that even substantial fluctuations in those efforts have little effect on the price, availability, and consumption of illicit drugs. The mere existence of criminal laws combined with minimal levels of enforcement is sufficient to deter many potential users and to reduce the availability and increase the price of drugs. Law enforcement officials acknowledge that they alone cannot solve the drug problem but contend that their role is nonetheless essential to the overall effort to reduce illicit drug use and abuse. What they are less ready to acknowledge, however, is that the very criminalization of the drug market has proven highly costly and counterproductive in much the same way that the national prohibition of alcohol did 60 years ago.

The Costs and Consequences of Drug Prohibition Policies

Total government expenditures devoted to enforcement of drug laws amounted to a minimum of $10 billion in 1987. Between 1981 and 1987, federal expenditures on anti-drug law enforcement more than tripled; from less than $1 billion per year to about $3 billion.[10] State and local law enforcement agencies spent an estimated $5 billion, amount[ing] to about one-fifth of their total investigative resources, on drug enforcement activities in 1986.[11] Drug law violators currently account for approximately 10 percent of the roughly 550,000 inmates in state prisons, more than one-third of the 50,000 federal prison inmates, and a significant (albeit undetermined) proportion of the approximately 300,000 individuals confined in municipal jails.[12] The U.S. Sentencing Commission has predicted that in 15 years the federal prison population will total 100,000 to 150,000 inmates, of whom one-half will be incarcerated for drug law violations.[13] Among the 40,000 inmates in New York State prisons, drug law violations surpassed first degree robbery in 1987 as the number one cause of incarceration, account for 20 percent of the total prison population.[14] In Florida, the 8,506 drug law violators admitted to state prisons in fiscal 1987–1988 represented a 525 percent increase from fiscal 1983–1984 and 27.8 percent of all new admissions to prison in 1987–1988.[15] Nationwide, drug trafficking and drug possession offenses accounted for approximately 135,000 (23 percent) of the 583,000 individuals convicted of felonies in state courts in 1986.[16] State and local governments spent a minimum of $2 billion last year to incarcerate drug offenders. The direct costs of building and maintaining enough prisons to house this growing population are rising at an astronomical rate. The costs, in terms of alternative social expenditures foregone and other types of criminals not imprisoned, are perhaps even more severe.[17]

Police have made about 750,000 arrests for violations of the drug laws during each of the last few years.[18] Slightly more than three-quarters of these have been not for manufacturing or dealing drugs but solely for possession of an illicit drug, typically marijuana.[19] [Those arrested, it is worth noting, represent less than 2% of the 35 to 40 million Americans estimated to have illegally consumed a drug during each of the past years.[20]] On the one hand, these arrests have clogged many urban criminal justice systems: in New York City, drug law violations in 1987 accounted for more than 40 percent of all felony indictments, up from 25 percent in 1985[21]; in Washington D.C., the figure was 52 percent in 1986, up from 13 percent in 1981.[22] On the other hand, they have distracted criminal justice officials from concentrating greater resources on violent offenses and property crimes. In many cities, urban law enforcement has become virtually synonymous with drug enforcement.

The greatest beneficiaries of the drug laws are organized and unorganized drug traffickers. The criminalization of the drug market effectively imposes a de facto value-added tax that is enforced and occasionally augmented by the law enforcement establishment and collected by the drug traffickers. More than half of all organized crime revenues are believed to derive from the illicit drug business; estimates of the dollar value range between $10 and $50 billion per year.[23] By contrast, annual revenues from cigarette bootlegging, which persists principally because of differences among states in their cigarette tax rates, are estimated by between $200 million and $400 million.[23] If the marijuana, cocaine, and heroin markets were legal, state and federal governments would collect billions of dollars annually in tax revenues. Instead, they expend billions in what amounts to a subsidy of organized criminals.

The connection between drugs and crime is one that continues to resist coherent analysis both because cause and effect are so difficult to distinguish and because the role of the drug prohibition laws in causing and labeling "drug-related crime" is so often ignored. There are five possible connections between drugs and crime, at least three of which would be much diminished if the drug prohibition laws were repealed. First, the production, sale, purchase, and possession of marijuana, cocaine, heroin, and other strictly controlled and banned substances are crimes, in and of themselves, which occur billions of times each year in the United States alone. In the absence of drug prohibition laws, these activities would largely cease to be considered crimes. Selling drugs to children would, of course, continue to be criminalized, and other evasions of government regulation of a legal market would continue to be prosecuted, but by and large the connection between drugs and crime that now accounts for all of the criminal justice costs noted above would be severed.

Second, many illicit drug users commit crimes such as robbery and burglary, as well as other vice crimes such as drug dealing, prostitution, and numbers running, to earn enough money to purchase cocaine, heroin, and other illicit drugs—drugs that cost far more than alcohol and tobacco not because they cost much more to produce but because they are illegal.[24] Because legalization would inevitably lead to a reduction in the cost of the drugs that are now illicit, it would also invite a significant reduction in this drug-crime connection. At the same time, current methadone maintenance programs represent a limited form of drug legalization that attempts to break this connection between drugs and crime by providing an addictive opiate at little or no cost to addicts who might otherwise steal to support their illicit heroin habits. Despite their many limitations, such programs have proven effective in reducing the criminal behavior and improving the lives of thousands of illicit drug addicts[25]; they need to be made more available, in part by adapting the types of outreach programs for addicts devised in the Netherlands.[26] Another alternative, the British system of prescribing not just oral methadone but also injectable heroin and methadone to addicts who take drugs intravenously, persists on a small scale even today despite continuing pressures against prescribing injectables. This too merits adoption in the United States, particularly if one accepts the assumption that the primary objective of drug policy should be to minimize the harms that drug abusers do to others.[27]

The third connection between drugs and crime is more coincidental than causal in nature. Although most illicit drug users do not engage in crime aside from their drug use, and although many criminals do not use or abuse illicit drugs or alcohol, substance abuse clearly is much higher among criminals than among non-criminals. A 1986 survey of state prison inmates found that 43 percent were using illegal drugs on a daily or near daily basis in the month before they committed the crime for which they were incarcerated; it also found that roughly one-half of the inmates who had used an illicit drug did not do so until after their first arrest.[28] Perhaps many of the same factors that

lead individuals into lives of crime also push them in the direction of substance abuse. It is possible that legalization would diminish this connection by removing from the criminal subculture the lucrative opportunities that now derive from the illegality of the drug market. But it is also safe to assume that the criminal milieu will continue to claim a disproportionately large share of drug abusers regardless of whether or not drugs are legalized.

The fourth link between drugs and crime is the commission of violent and other crimes by people under the influence of illicit drugs. It is this connection that seems to most infect the popular imagination. Clearly, some drugs do "cause" some people to commit crimes by reducing normal inhibitors, unleashing aggressive and other asocial tendencies, and lessening senses of responsibility. Cocaine, particularly in the form of "crack," has gained such a reputation in recent years, just as heroin did in the 1960s and 1970s and marijuana did in the years before that. Crack cocaine's reputation for inspiring violent behavior may well be more deserved than were those of marijuana and heroin, although the evidence has yet to substantiate media depictions.[29] No illicit drug, however, is as strongly associated with violent behavior as is alcohol. According to Justice Department statistics, 54 percent of all jail inmates convicted of violent crimes in 1983 reported having used alcohol just prior to committing their offense.[30] A 1986 survey of state prison inmates similarly found that most of those convicted of arson as well as violent crimes such as murder, involuntary manslaughter, and rape were far more likely to be have been under the influence of alcohol or both alcohol and illicit drugs, than under the influence of illicit drugs alone.[31] The impact of drug legalization on this aspect of the drug-crime connection is the most difficult to assess, largely because changes in the overall level and nature of drug consumption are so difficult to predict.

The fifth connection is the violent, intimidating and corrupting behavior of the drug traffickers. In many Latin American countries, most notably Colombia, this connection virtually defines the "drug problem."

But even within the United States, drug trafficker violence is rapidly becoming a major concern of criminal justice officials and the public at large. The connection is not difficult to explain. Illegal markets tend to breed violence, both because they attract criminally minded and violent individuals and because participants in the market have no resort to legal institutions to resolve their disputes.[32] During Prohibition, violent struggles between bootlegging gangs and hijackings of booze-laden trucks and sea vessels were frequent and notorious occurrences. Today's equivalents are the booby traps that surround some marijuana fields, the pirates of the Caribbean looking to rob drug-laden vessels en route to the shores of the United States, the machine gun battles and executions of the more sordid drug gangs, and the generally high levels of violence that attend many illicit drug relationships; the victims include not just drug dealers but witnesses, bystanders, and law enforcement officials. Most law enforcement authorities agree that the dramatic increases in urban murder rates during the past few years can be explained almost entirely by the rise in drug dealer killings, mostly of one another.[33] At the same time, the powerful allure of illicit drug dollars is responsible for rising levels of corruption not just in Latin American and the Caribbean but also in federal, state, and local criminal justice systems throughout the United States.[34] A drug legalization strategy would certainly deal a severe blow to this link between drugs and crime.

Perhaps the most unfortunate victims of the drug prohibition policies have been the poor and law-abiding residents of urban ghettos. Those policies have proven largely futile in deterring large numbers of ghetto dwellers from becoming drug abusers but they do account for much of what ghetto residents identify as the drug problem. In many neighborhoods, it often seems to be the aggressive gun-toting drug dealers who upset law-abiding residents far more than the addicts nodding out in doorways.[35] Other residents, however, perceive the drug dealers as heroes and successful role models. In impoverished neighborhoods from Medellin and

Rio de Janeiro to many leading U.S. cities, they often stand out as symbols of success to children who see no other options. At the same time, the increasingly harsh criminal penalties imposed on adult drug dealers have led to the widespread recruiting of juveniles by drug traffickers.[36] Where once children started dealing drugs only after they had been using them for a few years, today the sequence is often reversed. Many children start to use illegal drugs now only after they have worked for older drug dealers for a while. And the juvenile justice system offers no realistic options for dealing with this growing problem.

Perhaps the most difficult costs to evaluate are those that relate to the widespread defiance of the drug prohibition laws: the effects of labeling as criminals the tens of millions of people who use drugs illicitly, subjecting them to the risks of criminal sanction, and obliging many of those same people to enter into relationships with drug dealers (who may be criminals in many more senses of the word) in order to purchase their drugs; the cynicism that such laws generate toward other laws and the law in general; and the sense of hostility and suspicion that many otherwise law-abiding individuals feel toward law enforcement officials. It was costs such as these that strongly influenced many of Prohibition's more conservative opponents.

Among the most dangerous consequences of the drug laws are the harms that stem from the unregulated nature of illicit drug production and sale.[37] Many marijuana smokers are worse off for having smoked cannabis that was grown with dangerous fertilizers, sprayed with the herbicide paraquat, or mixed with more dangerous substances. Consumers of heroin and the various synthetic substances sold on the street face even more severe consequences, including fatal overdoses and poisonings from unexpectedly potent or impure drug supplies. In short, nothing resembling an underground Food and Drug Administration has arisen to impose quality control on the illegal drug market and provide users with accurate information on the drugs they consume. More often than not, the quality of a drug addict's life depends greatly on his or her access to reliable supplies. Drug enforcement operations that succeed in temporarily disrupting supply networks are thus a double-edged sword: they encourage some addicts to seek admission into drug treatment programs, but they oblige others to seek out new and hence less reliable suppliers, with the result that more, not fewer, drug-related emergencies and deaths occur.

Today, about 25 percent of all acquired immunodeficiency syndrome (AIDS) cases in the United States and Europe, as well as the large majority of human immunodeficiency virus (HIV)-infected heterosexuals, children, and infants, are believed to have contracted the dreaded disease directly or indirectly from illegal intravenous (IV) drug use.[38] In the New York metropolitan area, the prevalence of a seropositive test for HIV among illicit IV drug users is over 50 percent.[39] Reports have emerged of drug dealers beginning to provide clean syringes together with the illegal drugs.[40] In England, recent increases in the number of HIV-infected drug users have led to renewed support among drug treatment clinicians for providing IV heroin addicts with free supplies of injectable methadone and heroin; this reversal of the strong preference among many drug treatment clinicians since the early 1970s for oral methadone maintenance has been spearheaded by Philip Connell, chairman of the Home Office Advisory Committee on the Misuse of Drugs.[41] But even as governments in England, Scotland, Sweden, Switzerland, Australia, the Netherlands, and elsewhere actively attempt to limit the spread of AIDS by and among drug users by removing restrictions on the sale of syringes and instituting free syringe exchange programs,[42] state and municipal governments in the United States have resisted following suit, arguing, despite mounting evidence to the contrary,[43] that to do so would "encourage" or "condone" the use of illegal drugs.[44] Only in late 1988 did needle exchange programs begin emerging in U.S. cities, typically at the initiative of nongovernmental organizations. By mid-1989, programs were under way or close to being implemented in New York City; Tacoma, Washington; Boulder, Colorado; and Portland, Oregon.[45] At the same time, drug treatment programs remain notoriously underfunded, turning away tens of thousands of addicts seeking help even as increasing billions of dollars are spent to arrest, prosecute, and imprison illegal drug sellers and users.

Other costs of current drug prohibition policies include the restrictions on using the illicit drugs for legitimate medical purposes.[46] Marijuana has proven useful in alleviating pain in some victims of multiple sclerosis, is particularly effective in reducing the nausea that accompanies chemotherapy, and may well prove effective in the treatment of glaucoma[47–49]; in September 1988, the administrative law judge of the Drug Enforcement Administration accordingly recommended that marijuana be made legally available for such purposes,[49] although the agency head has yet to approve the change. Heroin has proven highly effective in helping patients to deal with severe pain; some researchers have found it more effective than morphine and other opiates in treating pain in some patients.[50] It is legally prescribed for such purposes in Britain[50] and Canada.[51] The same may be true of cocaine, which continues to be used by some doctors in the United States to treat pain despite recently imposed bans.[52] The psychedelic drugs, such as LSD (d-lysergic acid diethylamide), peyote, and MDMA (known as Ecstasy) have shown promise in aiding psychotherapy and in reducing tension, depression, pain, and fear of death in the terminally ill[53]; they also have demonstrated some potential, as yet unconfirmed, to aid in the treatment of alcoholism.[47, 53] Current drug laws and policies, however, greatly hamper the efforts of researchers to investigate these and other potential medical uses of illegal drugs; they make it virtually impossible for any of the illegal drugs, particularly those in Schedule I, to be legally provided to those who would benefit from them; and they contribute strongly to the widely acknowledged undertreatment of pain by the medical profession in the United States.[54]

Among the strongest arguments in favor of legalization are the moral ones. On the one hand, the standard refrain regarding the immorality of drug use crumbles in the face of most Americans' tolerance for alcohol and tobacco use. Only the Mormons and a few other like-minded sects, who regard as immoral any intake of substances to alter one's state of consciousness or otherwise cause pleasure, are consistent in this respect; they eschew not just the illicit drugs but also alcohol, tobacco, caffeinated coffee and tea, and even chocolate. "Moral" condemnation by the majority of Americans of some substances and not others is little more than a transient prejudice in favor of some drugs and against others.

On the other hand, drug enforcement involves its own immoralities. Because drug law violations do not create victims with an interest in notifying the police, drug enforcement agents must rely heavily on undercover operations, electronic surveillance, and information provided by informants. In 1986, almost half of the 754 court-authorized orders for wiretaps in the United States involved drug trafficking investigations.[55] These techniques are certainly indispensable to effective law enforcement, but they are also among the least desirable of the tools available to police. The same is true of drug testing. It may be useful and even necessary for determining liability in accidents, but it also threatens and undermines the right of privacy to which many Americans believe they are morally and constitutionally entitled. There are good reasons for requiring that such measures be used sparingly.

Equally disturbing are the increasingly vocal calls for people to inform not just on drug dealers but on neighbors, friends, and even family members who use illicit drugs. Intolerance of illicit drug use and users is heralded not merely as an indispensable ingredient in the war against drugs but as a mark of good citizenship. Certainly every society requires citizens to assist in the enforcement of criminal laws. But societies, particularly democratic and pluralistic ones, also rely strongly on an ethic of tolerance toward those who are different but do no harm to others. Overzealous enforcement of the drug laws risks undermining that ethic and propagating in its place a society of informants. Indeed, enforcement of drug laws

makes a mockery of an essential principle of a free society, that those who do no harm to others should not be harmed by others, and particularly not by the state. Most of the nearly 40 million Americans who illegally consume drugs each year do no direct harm to anyone else; indeed most do relatively little harm even to themselves. Directing criminal and other sanctions at them, and rationalizing the justice of such sanctions, may well represent the greatest societal cost of our current drug prohibition system.

Alternatives to Drug Prohibition Policies

Repealing the drug prohibition laws clearly promises tremendous advantages. Between reduced government expenditures on enforcing drug laws and new tax revenue from legal drug production and sales, public treasuries would enjoy a net benefit of at least $10 billion per year and possibly much more; thus billions in new revenues would be available, and ideally targeted, for funding much needed drug treatment programs as well as the types of social and educational programs that often prove most effective in creating incentives for children not to abuse drugs. The quality of urban life would rise significantly. Homicide rates would decline. So would robbery and burglary rates. Organized criminal groups, particularly the up-and-coming ones that have yet to diversify into nondrug areas, would be dealt a devastating setback. The police, prosecutors, and courts would focus their resources on combating the types of crimes that people cannot walk away from. More ghetto residents would turn their backs on criminal careers and seek out legitimate opportunities instead. And the health and quality of life of many drug users and even drug abusers would improve significantly. Internationally, U.S. foreign policymakers would get on with more important and realistic objectives, and foreign governments would reclaim the authority that they have lost to the drug traffickers.

All the benefits of legalization would be for naught, however, if millions more people were to become drug abusers. Our experience with alcohol and tobacco provides ample warnings. Today, alcohol is consumed by 140 million Americans and tobacco by 50 million. All of the health costs associated with abuse of the illicit drugs pale in comparison with those resulting from tobacco and alcohol abuse. In 1986, for instance, alcohol was identified as a contributing factor in 10 percent of work-related injuries, 40 percent of suicide attempts, and about 40 percent of the approximately 46,000 annual traffic deaths in 1983. An estimated 18 million Americans are reported to be either alcoholics or alcohol abusers. The total cost of alcohol abuse to American society is estimated at over $100 billion annually.[56] Estimates of the number of deaths linked directly and indirectly to alcohol use vary from a low of 50,000 to a high of 200,000 per year.[57] The health costs of tobacco use are different but of similar magnitude. In the United States alone, an estimated 320,000 people die prematurely each year as a consequence of their consumption of tobacco. By comparison, the National Council on Alcoholism reported that only 3,562 people were known to have died in 1985 from use of all illegal drugs combined.[58] Even if we assume that thousands more deaths were related in one way or another to illicit drug use but not reported as such, we still are left with the conclusion that all of the health costs of marijuana, cocaine, and heroin combined amount to only a small fraction of those caused by either of the two licit substances. At the very least, this contrast emphasizes the need for a comprehensive approach to psychoactive substances involving much greater efforts to discourage tobacco and alcohol abuse.

The impact of legalization of the nature and level of consumption of those drugs that are currently illegal is impossible to predict with any accuracy. On the one hand, legalization implies greater availability, lower prices, and the elimination (particularly for adults) of the deterrent power of the criminal sanction—all of which would suggest higher levels of use. Indeed, some fear that the extent of drug abuse and its attendant costs would rise to those currently associated with alcohol and tobacco.[59] On the

other hand, there are many reasons to doubt that a well-designed and implemented policy of controlled drug legalization would yield such costly consequences.

The logic of legalization depends in part upon two assumptions: that most illegal drugs are not as dangerous as is commonly believed; and that those types of drugs and methods of consumption that are most risky are unlikely to prove appealing to many people precisely because they are so obviously dangerous. Consider marijuana. Among the roughly 60 million Americans who have smoked marijuana, not one has died from a marijuana overdose,[49] a striking contrast with alcohol, which is involved in approximately 10,000 overdose deaths annually, half in combination with other drugs.[57] Although there are good health reasons for people not to smoke marijuana daily, and for children, pregnant women and some others not to smoke at all, there still appears to be little evidence that occasional marijuana consumption does much harm at all. Certainly, it is not healthy to inhale marijuana smoke into one's lungs, indeed, the National Institute on Drug Abuse (NIDA) has declared that "Marijuana smoke contains more cancer-causing agents than is found in tobacco smoke."[60] On the other hand, the number of "joints" smoked by all but a very small percentage of marijuana smokers is a tiny fraction of the 20 cigarettes a day smoked by the average cigarette smoker; indeed, the average may be closer to one or two joints per week than one or two per day. Note, that the NIDA defines a "heavy" marijuana smoker as one who consumes at least two joints "daily." A heavy tobacco smoker, by contrast, smokes about 40 cigarettes per day.

Nor is marijuana strongly identified as a dependence-causing substance. A 1982 survey of marijuana use by young adults (18 to 25 years) found that 64 percent had tried marijuana at least once, that 42 percent had used it at least ten times, and that 27 percent had smoked in the last month. It also found that 21 percent had passed through a period during which they smoked "daily" (defined as 20 or more days per month) but that only one-third of those currently smoked daily and only one-fifth (or about 4 percent of all young adults) could be described as heavy daily users (averaging two or more joints per day).[61] This suggests in part that daily marijuana use is typically a phase through which people pass, after which their use becomes more moderate. By contrast, almost 20 percent of high school seniors smoke cigarettes daily.

The dangers associated with cocaine, heroin, the hallucinogens, and other illicit substances are greater than those posed by marijuana but not nearly so great as many people seem to think. Consider the case of cocaine. In 1986, NIDA reported that over 20 million Americans had tried cocaine, that 12.2 million had consumed it at least once during 1985, and that nearly 5.8 million had used it within the past month. Among 18- to 25-year-olds, 8.2 million had tried cocaine; 5.3 million had used it within the past year; 2.5 million had used it within the past month; and 250,000 had used it on the average weekly.[20] One could extrapolate from these figures that a quarter of a million young Americans are potential problem users. But one could also conclude that only 3 percent of those 18- 25-year-olds who had ever tried the drug fell into that category, and that only 10 percent of those who had used cocaine monthly were at risk. (The NIDA survey did not, it should be noted, include persons residing in military or student dormitories, prison inmates or the homeless.)

All of this is not to say that cocaine is not a potentially dangerous drug, especially when it is injected, smoked in the form of "crack," or consumed in tandem with other powerful substances. Clearly, many tens of thousands of Americans have suffered severely from their abuse of cocaine and a tiny fraction have died. But there is also overwhelming evidence that most users of cocaine do not get into trouble with the drug. So much of the media attention has focused on the relatively small percentage of cocaine users who become addicted that the popular perception of how most people use cocaine has become badly distorted. In one survey of high school seniors' drug use, the researchers questioned those who had used cocaine recently whether they had ever tried to stop using cocaine and found that they could not stop.

Only 3.8 percent responded affirmatively, in contrast to the almost 7 percent of marijuana smokers who said they had tried to stop and found that they could not, and the 18 percent of cigarette smokers who answered similarly.[62] Although a survey of crack users and cocaine injectors surely would reveal a higher proportion of addicts, evidence such as this suggests that only a small percentage of people who snort cocaine end up having a problem with it. In this respect, most people differ from captive monkeys, who have demonstrated in tests that they will starve themselves to death if provided with unlimited cocaine.[63]

With respect to the hallucinogens such as LSD and psilocybic mushrooms, their potential for addiction is virtually nil. The dangers arise primarily from using them irresponsibly on individual occasions.[53] Although many of those who have used hallucinogens have experienced "bad trips," far more have reported positive experiences and very few have suffered any long-term harm.[53] As for the great assortment of stimulants, depressants, and tranquilizers produced illegally or diverted from licit channels, each evidences varying capacities to create addiction, harm the user, or be used safely.

Until recently, no drugs were regarded with as much horror as the opiates, and, in particular heroin. As with most drugs, it can be eaten, snorted, smoked, or injected. The custom among most Americans, unfortunately, is the last of these options, although the growing fear of AIDS appears to be causing a shift among younger addicts toward intranasal ingestion.[64] There is no question that heroin is potentially highly addictive, perhaps as addictive as nicotine. But despite the popular association of heroin use with the most down-and-out inhabitants of urban ghettos, heroin causes relatively little physical harm to the human body. Consumed on an occasional or regular basis under sanitary conditions, its worst side effect, apart from the fact of being addicted, is constipation.[65] That is one reason why many doctors in early 20th-century America saw opiate addiction as preferable to alcoholism and prescribed the former as treatment for the latter where abstinence did not seem a realistic option.[66, 67]

It is both insightful and important to think about the illicit drugs as we do about alcohol and tobacco. Like tobacco, some illicit substances are highly addictive but can be consumed on a regular basis for decades without any demonstrable harm. Like alcohol, many of the substances can be, and are, used by most consumers in moderation, with little in the way of harmful effects; but like alcohol they also lend themselves to abuse by a minority of users who become addicted or otherwise harm themselves or others as a consequence. And like both the legal substances, the psychoactive effects of each of the illegal drugs vary greatly from one person to another. To be sure, the pharmacology of the substance is important, as is its purity and the manner in which it is consumed. But much also depends upon not just the physiology and psychology of the consumer but his expectations regarding the drug, his social milieu, and the broader cultural environment, what Harvard University psychiatrist Norman Zinberg called the "set and setting" of the drug.[68] It is factors such as these that might change dramatically, albeit in indeterminate ways, were the illicit drugs made legally available.

It is thus impossible to predict whether or not legalization would lead to much greater levels of drug abuse. The lessons that can be drawn from other societies are mixed. China's experience with the British opium pushers of the 19th century, when millions reportedly became addicted to the drug, offers one worst-case scenario. The devastation of many native American tribes by alcohol presents another. On the other hand, the decriminalization of marijuana by 11 states in the United States during the mid-1970s does not appear to have led to increases in marijuana consumption.[69] In the Netherlands, which went even further in decriminalizing cannabis during the 1970s, consumption has actually declined significantly; in 1976, 3 percent of 15- and 16-year-olds and 10 percent of 17- and 18-year-olds used cannabis occasionally; by 1985, the percentages had declined to 2 and 6 percent, respectively.[70] The policy has succeeded, as the government intended, "in making drug use boring." Finally, late 19th century America is an example of a society in which there were almost no drug laws or even drug regulations but levels of drug use were about what they are today.[71] Drug abuse was regarded as a relatively serious problem, but the criminal justice system was not regarded as part of the solution.[72]

These are however, strong reasons to believe that none of the currently illicit substances would become as popular as alcohol or tobacco even if they were legalized. Alcohol has long been the principal intoxicant in most societies, including many in which other substances have been legally available. Presumably, its diverse properties account for its popularity: it quenches thirst, goes well with food, often pleases the palate, promotes appetite as well as sociability, and so on. The widespread use of tobacco probably stems not just from its powerful addictive qualities but from the fact that its psychoactive effects are sufficiently subtle that cigarettes can be integrated with most other human activities. None of the illicit substances now popular in the United States share either of these qualities to the same extent, nor is it likely that they would acquire them if they were legalized. Moreover, none of the illicit substances can compete with alcohol's special place in American culture and history, one that it retained even during Prohibition.

Much of the damage caused by illegal drugs today stems from their consumption in particularly potent and dangerous ways. There is good reason to doubt that many Americans would inject cocaine or heroin into their veins even if given the chance to do so legally. And just as the dramatic growth in the heroin-consuming population during the 1960s leveled off for reasons apparently having little to do with law enforcement, so we can expect, if it has not already occurred, a leveling off in the number of people smoking crack.

Perhaps the most reassuring reason for believing that repeal of the drug prohibition laws will not lead to tremendous increases in drug abuse levels is the fact that we have learned something from our past experiences with alcohol and tobacco abuse. We now know, for instance, that consumption taxes are an effective method for limiting consumption rates and related costs, especially among young people.[73] Substantial evidence also suggests that restrictions and bans on advertising, as well as promotion of negative advertising, can make a difference.[74] The same seems to be true of other government measures, including restrictions on time and place of sale,[75] bans on vending machines, prohibitions of consumption in public places, packaging requirements, mandated adjustments in insurance policies, crackdowns on driving while under the influence,[76] and laws holding bartenders and hosts responsible for the drinking of customers and guests. There is even some evidence that some education programs about the dangers of cigarette smoking have deterred many children from beginning to smoke.[77] At the same time, we also have come to recognize the great harms that can result when drug control policies are undermined by powerful lobbies such as those that now block efforts to lessen the harms caused by abuse of alcohol and tobacco.

Legalization thus affords far greater opportunities to control drug use and abuse than do current criminalization policies. The current strategy is one in which the type, price, purity, and potency of illicit drugs, as well as the participants in the business, are largely determined by drug dealers, the peculiar competitive dynamics of an illicit market, and the perverse interplay of drug enforcement strategies and drug trafficking tactics. During the past decade, for instance, the average retail purities of cocaine and heroin have increased dramatically, the wholesale prices have dropped greatly, the number of children involved in drug dealing has risen, and crack has become readily and cheaply available in a growing number of American cities.[8] By contrast, marijuana has become relatively scarcer and more expensive, in part because it is far more vulnerable to drug enforcement efforts than are cocaine or heroin; the result has been to induce both dealers and users away from the relatively safer marijuana and toward the relatively more dangerous cocaine.[8] Also by contrast,

while the average potency of most illicit substances has increased during the 1980s, that of most legal psychoactive substances had been declining. Motivated in good part by health concerns, Americans are switching from hard liquor to beer and wine, from high tar and nicotine cigarettes to lower tar and nicotine cigarettes as well as smokeless tobaccos and nicotine chewing gums, and even from caffeinated to decaffeinated coffees, teas, and sodas. It is quite possible that these diverging trends are less a reflection of the nature of the drugs than of their legal status.

A drug control policy based predominantly on approaches other than criminal justice thus offers a number of significant advantages over the current criminal justice focus in controlling drug use and abuse. It shifts control of production, distribution, and, to a lesser extent, consumption out of the hands of criminals and into the hands of government and government licensees. It affords consumers the opportunity to make far more informed decisions about the drugs they buy than is currently the case. It dramatically lessens the likelihood that drug consumers will be harmed by impure, unexpectedly potent, or misidentified drugs. It corrects the hypocritical and dangerous message that alcohol and tobacco are somehow safer than many illicit drugs. It reduces by billions of dollars annually government expenditures on drug enforcement and simultaneously raises additional billions in tax revenues. And it allows government the opportunity to shape consumption patterns toward relatively safer psychoactive substances and modes of consumption.

Toward the end of the 1920s, when the debate over repealing Prohibition rapidly gained momentum, numerous scholars, journalists, and private and government commissions undertook thorough evaluations of Prohibition and the potential alternatives. Prominent among these were the Wickersham Commission appointed by President Herbert Hoover and the study of alcohol regulation abroad directed by the leading police scholar in the United States, Raymond Fosdick, and commissioned by John D. Rockefeller.[78] These efforts examined the successes and failings of Prohibition in the United States and evaluated the wide array of alternative regimes for controlling the distribution and use of beer, wine, and liquor. They played a major role in stimulating the public reevaluation of Prohibition and in envisioning alternatives. Precisely the same sorts of efforts are required today.

The controlled drug legalization option is not an all-or-nothing alternative to current policies. Indeed, political realities ensure that any shift toward legalization will evolve gradually, with ample opportunity to halt, reevaluate, and redirect drug policies that begin to prove too costly or counterproductive. The federal government need not play the leading role in devising alternatives; it need only clear the way to allow state and local governments the legal power to implement their own drug legalization policies. The first steps are relatively risk-free: legalization of marijuana, easier availability of illegal and strictly controlled drugs for treatment of pain and other medical purposes, tougher tobacco and alcohol control policies, and a broader and more available array of drug treatment programs.

Remedying the drug-related ills of America's ghettos requires more radical steps. The risks of a more far-reaching policy of controlled drug legalization—increased availability, lower prices, and removal of the deterrent power of the criminal sanction—are relatively less in the ghettos than in most other parts of the United States in good part because drug availability is already so high, prices so low, and the criminal sanction so ineffective in deterring illicit drug use that legalization can hardly worsen the situation. On the other hand, legalization would yield its greatest benefits in the ghettos, where it would sever much of the drug-crime connection, seize the market away from criminals, deglorify involvement in the illicit drug business, help redirect the work ethic from illegitimate to legitimate employment opportunities, help stem the transmission of AIDS by IV drug users, and significantly improve the safety, health, and well-being of those who do use and abuse drugs. Simply stated, legalizing cocaine, heroin, and other relatively dangerous drugs may well be the only way to reverse the destructive impact of drugs and current drug policies in the ghettos.

There is no question that legalization is a risky policy, one that may indeed lead to an increase in the number of people who abuse drugs. But that risk is by no means a certainty. At the same time, current drug control policies are showing little progress and new proposals promise only to be more costly and more repressive. We know that repealing the drug prohibition laws would eliminate or greatly reduce many of the ills that people commonly identify as part and parcel of the "drug problem." Yet that option is repeatedly and vociferously dismissed without any attempt to evaluate it openly and objectively. The past 20 years have demonstrated that a drug policy shaped by rhetoric and fear-mongering can only lead to our current disaster. Unless we are willing to honestly evaluate all our options, including various legalization strategies, there is a good chance that we will never identify the best solutions for our drug problems.

Notes

1. The terms "legalization" and "decriminalization" are used interchangeably here. Some interpret the latter term as a more limited form of legalization involving the removal of criminal sanctions against users but not against producers and sellers.
2. Statement by Senator D. P. Moynihan, citing a U.S. Department of Agriculture report, in *Congr. Rec.* 134 (no. 77), p. S7049 (27 May 1988).
3. Drug Enforcement Administration, Department of Justice, *Intell. Tends* 14 (no. 3), 1 (1987).
4. See, for example, K. Healy, *J. Interam. Stud. World Aff.* 30 (no. 2/3), 105 (summer/fall 1988).
5. E. A. Nadelmann, *ibid.* 29 (no. 4), 1 (winter 1987–88).
6. C. McClintock, *ibid.* 30 (no. 2/3), 127 (summer/fall 1988); J. Kawell, *Report on the Americas* 22 (no. 6), 13 (March 1989).
7. P. Reuter, *Public Interest* (no. 92) (summer 1988), p. 51.
8. See the annual reports of the National Narcotics Intelligence Consumers Committee edited by the Drug Enforcement Administration, Department of Justice, Washington, DC.

9. *Street-Level Drug Enforcement: Examining the Issues*, M. R. Chaiken, Ed. (National Institute of Justice, Department of Justice, Washington, DC, September 1988).

10. National Drug Enforcement Policy Board, *National and International Drug Law Enforcement Strategy* (Department of Justice, Washington, DC, 1987).

11. *Anti-Drug Law Enforcement Efforts and Their Impact* (report prepared for the U.S. Customs Service by Wharton Econometic Forecasting Associates, Washington, DC, 1987), pp. 2 and 38–46.

12. *Sourcebook of Criminal Justice Statistics, 1987* (Bureau of Justice Statistics, Department of Justice, Washington, DC, 1988), pp. 490, 494, and 518; and "Prisoners in 1987" *Bur. Justice State. Bull.* (April 1988).

13. U.S. Sentencing Commission, *Supplementary Report on the Initial Sentencing Guidelines and Policy Statements* (U.S. Sentencing Commission, Washington, DC, 18 June 1987), pp. 71–75.

14. R. D. McFadden, *New York Times*, 5 January 1988, p. B1.

15. *Annual Report, 1987–88* (Florida Department of Corrections, Tallahassee, FL, 1988), pp. 26, 50, and 51.

16. "Felony sentences in state courts, 1986," *Bur. Justice Stat. Bull.* (February 1989).

17. The numbers cited do not, it should be emphasized, include the many inmates sentenced for drug-related crimes such as violent crimes committed by drug dealers, typically against one another, and robberies committed to earn the money needed to pay for illegal drugs.

18. See the annual editions of *Sourcebook of Criminal Justice Statistics* (Bureau of Justice Statistics, Department of Justice, Washington, DC).

19. *Sourcebook of Criminal Justice Statistics, 1987* (Bureau of Justice Statistics, Department of Justice, Washington, DC, 1988), pp. 400–401.

20. *Data from the 1985 National Household Survey on Drug Abuse* (National Institute on Drug Abuse, Rockville, MD, 1987).

21. S. Raab, *New York Times*, 7 June 1987, p. A38.

22. *Drug Use and Drug Programs in the Washington Metropolitan Area: An Assessment* (Greater Washington Research Center, Washington, DC, 1988), pp. 16–17.

23. Wharton Econometric Forecasting Associates, *The Impact: Organized Crime Today* (President's Commission on Organized Crime, Washington, DC, 1986), pp. 413–494.

24. B. D. Johnson et al., *Taking Care of Business: The Economics of Crime By Heroin Abusers* (Lexington Books, Lexington, MA, 1985).

25. B. D. Johnson, D. Lipton, E. Wish, *Facts About the Criminality of Heroin and Cocaine Abusers and Some New Alternatives to Incarceration* (Narcotic and Drug Research, New York, 1986), p. 30.

26. G. F. van de Wijngart, *Am. J. Drug Alcohol Abuse* 14 (no. 1), 125 (1988).

27. A controlled trial in which 96 confirmed heroin addicts requesting a heroin maintenance prescription were randomly allocated to treatment with injectable heroin or oral methadone showed that "refusal [by doctors] to prescribe heroin is . . . associated with a considerably higher abstinence rate, but at the expense of an increased arrest rate and a higher level of illicit drug involvement and criminal activity among those who did not become abstinent." R. L. Hartnoll et al., *Arch. Gen. Psychiatry* 37, 877 (1980).

28. "Drug use and crime," *Bur. Justice Stat. Spec. Rep.* (July 1988).

29. See the discussion in P. J. Goldstein, P. A. Bellucci, B. J. Spunt, T. Miller, "Frequency of Cocaine Use and Violence: A Comparison Between Men and Women" [in NIDA (National Institute on Drug Abuse) *Res. Monogr. Ser.*, in press].

30. *Sourcebook of Criminal Justice Statistic, 1986* (Bureau of Justice Statistics, Department of Justice, Washington, DC, 1987), p. 398.

31. *Sourcebook of Criminal Justice Statistics, 1987* (Bureau of Justice Statistics, Department of Justice, Washington, DC, 1988), p. 497.

32. P. J. Goldstein, in *Pathways to Criminal Violence*, N. A. Weiner and M. E. Wolfgang, Eds. (Sage, Newbury Park, CA, 1989), pp. 16–48.

33. "A tide of drug killing," *Newsweek*, 16 January 1989, p. 44.

34. P. Shenon, *New York Times*, 11 April 1988, p. A1.

35. W. Nobles, L. Goddard, W. Cavil, P. George, *The Culture of Drugs in the Black Community* (Institute for the Advanced Study of Black Family Life and Culture, Oakland, CA, 1987).

36. T. Mieczowski, *Criminology* 24, 645 (1986).

37. C. L. Renfroe and T. A. Messinger, *Semin. Adolescent Med.* 1 (no. 4), 247 (1985).

38. D. C. Des Jarlais and S. R. Friedman, *J. AIDS* 1 267 (1988).

39. D. C. Des Jarlais et al., *J. Am. Med. Assoc.* 261, 1008 (1989).

40. S. R. Friedman et al., *Int. J. Addict.* 22 (no. 3), 201 (1987).

41. T. Bennett, *Law Contemp. Prob.* 51, 310 (1988).

42. R. J. Battjes and R. W. Pickens, Eds., *NIDA Res. Monogr. Ser.* 80 (1988).

43. D. C. Des Jarlais and S. R. Friedman, *AIDS* 2 (suppl. 1), S65 (1988).

44. M. Marriott, *New York Times,* 7 November 1988, p. B1; *ibid.,* 30 January 1989, p. A1.

45. *Int. Work. Group AIDS IV Drug Use Newsl.* 3, 3 (December 1988).

46. See, for example, P. Fitzgerald, *St. Louis Univ. Public Law Rev.* 6, 371 (1987).

47. L. Grinspooon and J. B. Bakalar, in *Dealing with Drugs: Consequences of Government Control,* R. Hamowy, Ed. (Lexington Books, Lexington, MA, 1987), pp. 183–219.

48. T. H. Mikuriya, Ed., *Marijuana: Medical Papers, 1839–1972* (Medi-Comp Press, Oakland, CA, 1973).

49. *In the Matter of Marijuana Rescheduling Petition,* Docket No. 86–22, 6 September 1988, Drug Enforcement Administration, Department of Justice.

50. A. S. Trebach, *The Heroin Solution* (Yale Univ. Press, New Haven, CT, 1982), pp. 59–84.

51. L. Appleby, *Saturday Night* (November 1985), p. 13.

52. F. R. Lee, *New York Times,* 10 February 1989, p. B3; F. Barre, *Headache* B22B, 69 (1982).

53. L. Grinspoon and J. B. Bakalar, *Psychedelic Drugs Reconsidered* (Basic Books, New York, 19779).

54. M. Donovan, P. Dillon, L. McGuire, *Pain* 30, 69 (1987); D.E. Weissman, *Narc Officer* 5 (no. 1), 47 (January 1989); D. Goleman, *New York Times,* 31 December 1987, p. B5. The Controlled Substances Act, 21 U.S.C. §801, *et seq.,* defines a Schedule I drug as one that: (i) has a high potential for abuse; (ii) has no currently accepted medical use in treatment in the United States; and (iii) for which there is a lack of accepted safety for use under medical supervision. It is contrary to federal law for physicians to prescribe Schedule I drugs to patients for therapeutic purposes.

55. *Sourcebook of Criminal Justice Statistics, 1987* (Bureau of Justice Statistics, Department of Justice, Washington, DC, 1988), p. 417.

56. "Toward a national plan to combat alcohol abuse and alcoholism: A report to the United States Congress" (Department of Health and Human Services, Washington, DC, September 1986).

57. D. R. Gerstein, in *Alcohol and Public Policy: Beyond the Shadow of Prohibition,* M. H. Moore and D. R. Gerstein, Eds. (National Academy Press, Washington, DC, 1981), pp. 182–224.

58. Cited in T. Wicker, *New York Times,* 13 May 1987, p. A27.

59. M. M. Kondracke, *New Repub.* 198 (no. 26), 16 (27 June 1988).

60. "Marijuana" (National Institute on Drug Abuse, Washington, DC, 1983).

61. J. D. Miller and I. H. Cisin, *Highlights from the National Survey on Drug Abuse, 1982* (National Institute on Drug Abuse, Washington, DC, 1983), pp. 1–10.

62. P. M. O'Malley, L. D. Johnston, J. G. Bachman, *NIDA Monogr. Ser.* 61 (1985), pp. 50–75.

63. T. G. Aigner and R. L. Balster, *Science* 201, 534 (1978); C. E. Johanson, *NIDA Monogr. Ser.* 50 (1984), pp. 54–71.

64. J. F. French and J. Safford, *Lancet,* i, 1082 (1989); D. C. Des Jarlais, S. R. Friedman, C. Casriel, A. Kott, *Psychol. Health* 1, 179 (1987).

65. J. Kaplan, *The Hardest Drug: Heroin and Public Policy* (Univ. of Chicago Press, Chicago, IL, 1983), p. 127.

66. S. Siegel, *Res. Adv. Alcohol Drug Probl.* 9, 279 (1986).

67. J. A. O'Donnell, *Narcotics Addicts in Kentucky* (Public Health Service Publ. 1881, National Institute of Mental Health, Chevy Chase, MD, 1969), discussed in *Licit and Illicit Drugs* [E. M. Brecher and the Editors of *Consumer Reports* (Little, Brown, Boston, 1972), pp. 8–10].

68. See N. Zinberg, *Drug, Set and Setting: The Basis for Controlled Intoxicant Use* (Yale Univ. Press, New Haven, C, 1984).

69. L. D. Johnston, J. G. Bachman, P. M. O'Malley, "Marijuana decriminalization: the impact on youth 1975–1980" (Monitoring the Future, Occasional Paper 13, Univ. of Michigan Institute for Social Research, Ann Arbor, MI, 1981).

70. "Policy on drug users" (Ministry of Welfare, Health, and Cultural Affairs, Rijswijk, the Netherlands, 1985).

71. D. Courtwright, *Dark Paradise: Opiate Addiction in America Before 1940* (Harvard Univ. Press, Cambridge, MA, 1982).

72. E. M. Brecher and the Editors of Consumer Reports, *Licit and Iillicit Drugs* (Little, Brown, Boston, 1972), pp. 1–41.

73. See P. J. Cook in *Alcohol and Public Policy: Beyond the Shadow of Prohibition*, M. H. Moore and D. R. Gerstein, Eds. (National Academy Press, Washington, DC, 1981), pp. 255–285; D. Coate and M. Grossman, *J. Law Econ.* 31, 145 (1988); also see K. E. Warner, in *The Cigarette Excise Tax* (Harvard Univ. Institute for the Study of Smoking Behavior and Policy, Cambridge, MA, 1985), pp. 88–105.

74. J. B. Tye, K. E. Warner, S. Glantz, *J. Public Health Policy* 8, 492 (1987).

75. O. Olsson and P. O. H. Wikstrom, *Contemp. Drug Probl.*, 11, 324 (fall 1982); M. Terris, *Am. J. Public Health* 57, 2085 (1967).

76. M. D. Laurence, J. R. Snortum, F. E. Zimring, Eds., *Social Control of the Drinking Driver* (Univ. of Chicago Press, Chicago, IL, 1988).

77. J. M. Polich, P. L. Ellickson, P. Reuter, J. P. Kahan, *Strategies for Controlling Adolescent Drug Use* (RAND; Santa Monica, CA, 1984), pp. 145–152.

78. R. B. Fosdick and A. L. Scott, *Toward Liquor Control* (Harper, New York, 1993).

Reprinted from: Ethan A. Nadelmann, "Drug Prohibition in the United States: Costs, Consequences, and Alternatives." *Science*, Vol. 245, pp. 939–947. Copyright © 1989 American Association for the Advancement of Science. Reprinted by permission. ✦

2

Against the Legalization of Drugs

James Q. Wilson

In 1972, the President appointed me chairman of the National Advisory Council for Drug Abuse Prevention. Created by Congress, the Council was charged with providing guidance on who best to coordinate the national war on drugs. (Yes, we called it a war then, too.) In those days, the drug we were chiefly concerned with was heroin. When I took office, heroin use had been increasing dramatically. Everybody was worried that this increase would continue. Such phrases as "heroin epidemic" were commonplace.

That same year, the eminent economist Milton Friedman published an essay in *Newsweek* in which he called for legalizing heroin. His argument was on two grounds: as a matter of ethics the government has no right to tell people not to use heroin (or to drink or to commit suicide); as a matter of economics, the prohibition of drug use imposes costs on society that far exceed the benefits. Others, such as the psychoanalyst Thomas Szasz, made the same argument.

We did not take Friedman's advice. (Government commissions rarely do.) I do not recall that we even discussed legalizing heroin, though we did discuss (but did not take action on) legalizing a drug, cocaine, that many people then argued was benign. Our marching orders were to figure out how to win the war on heroin, not to run up the white flag of surrender.

That was 1972. Today, we have the same number of heroin addicts that we had then—half a million, give or take a few thousand. Having that many heroin addicts is no trivial matter; these people deserve our attention. But not having had an increase in that number for over 15 years is also something that deserves our attention. What happened to the "heroin epidemic" that many people once thought would overwhelm us?

The facts are clear: a more or less stable pool of heroin addicts has been getting older, with relatively few new recruits. In 1976 the average age of heroin users who appeared in hospital emergency rooms was about 27; ten years later it was 32. More than two-thirds of all heroin users appearing in emergency rooms are now over the age of 30. Back in the early 1970s, when heroin got onto the national political agenda, the typical heroin addict was much younger, often a teenager. Household surveys show the same thing—the rate of opiate use (which includes heroin) has been flat for the better part of two decades. More fine grained studies of inner-city neighborhoods confirm this. John Boyle and Ann Bruswick found that the percentage of young blacks in Harlem who used heroin fell from 8 percent in 1970–1971 to about 3 percent in 1975–1976.

Why did heroin lose its appeal for young people? When the young blacks in Harlem were asked why they stopped, more than half mentioned "trouble with the law" or "high cost" (and high cost is, of course, directly the result of law enforcement). Two-thirds said that heroin hurt their health; nearly all said they had had a bad experience with it. We need not rely, however, simply on what they said. In New York City in 1973–1975, the street price of heroin rose dramatically and its purity sharply declined, probably as a result of the heroin shortage caused by the success of the Turkish government in reducing the supply of opium base and of the French government n closing down heroin-processing laboratories located in and around Marseilles. These were short-lived gains for, just as Friedman had predicted, alternative sources of supply—mostly in Mexico—quickly emerged. But the three-year heroin shortage interrupted the easy recruitment of new users.

Health and related problems were no doubt part of the reason for the reduced flow of recruits. Over the preceding years, Harlem youth had watched as more and more heroin users died of overdoses, were poisoned by a adulterated doses, or acquired hepatitis from dirty needles. The word got around: heroin can kill you. By 1974 new hepatitis cases and drug-overdose deaths had dropped to a fraction of what they had been in 1970.

Alas, treatment did not seem to explain much of the cessation in drug use. Treatment programs can and do help heroin addicts, but treatment did not explain the drop in the number of *new* users (who by definition had never been in treatment) nor even much of the reduction in the number of experienced users.

No one knows how much of the decline to attribute to personal observation as opposed to high prices or reduced supply. But other evidence suggests strongly that price and supply played a large role. In 1972, the National Advisory Council was especially worried by the prospect that U.S. servicemen returning to this country from Vietnam would bring their heroin habits with them. Fortunately, a brilliant study by Lee Robins of Washington University in St. Louis put that fear to rest. She measured drug use of Vietnam veterans shortly after they had returned home. Though many had used heroin regularly while in Southeast Asia, most gave up the habit when back in the United States. The reason: here, heroin was less available and sanctions on its use were more pronounced. Of course, if a veteran had been willing to pay enough—which might have meant traveling to another city and would certainly have meant making an illegal contact with a disreputable dealer in a threatening neighborhood in order to acquire a (possibly) dangerous dose—he could have sustained his drug habit. Most veterans were unwilling to pay this price, and so their drug use declined or disappeared.

Reliving the Past

Suppose we had taken Friedman's advice in 1972. What would have happened? We cannot be entirely certain, but at a minimum we would have placed the young heroin addicts (and, above all, the prospective addicts) in a very different position from the one in which they actually found themselves. Heroin would have been legal. Its price would have been reduced by 95 percent (minus whatever we chose to recover in taxes). Now that it could be sold by the same people who make aspirin, its quality would have been assured—no poisons, no adulterants. Sterile hypodermic needles would have been readily available at the neighborhood drugstore, probably at the same counter where the heroin was sold. No need to travel to big cities or unfamiliar neighborhoods—heroin could have been purchased anywhere, perhaps by mail order.

There would no longer have been any financial or medical reason to avoid heroin use. Anybody could have afforded it. We might have tried to prevent children from buying it, but as we have learned from our efforts to prevent minors from buying alcohol and tobacco, young people have a way of penetrating markets theoretically reserved for adults. Returning Vietnam veterans would have discovered that Omaha and Raleigh had been converted into the pharmaceutical equivalent of Saigon.

Under these circumstances, can we doubt for a moment that heroin use would have grown exponentially? Or that a vastly larger supply of new users would have been recruited? Professor Friedman is a Nobel Prize-winning economist whose understanding of market forces is profound. What did he think would happen to consumption under his legalized regime? Here are his words: "Legalizing drugs might increase the number of addicts, but it is not clear that it would. Forbidden fruit is attractive, particularly to the young."

Really? I suppose that we should expect no increase in Porsche sales if we cut the price by 95 percent, no increase in whiskey sales if we cut the price by a comparable amount—because young people only want fast cars and strong liquor when they are "forbidden." Perhaps Friedman's uncharacteristic lapse from the obvious implications of price theory can be explained by a misunderstanding of how drug users are recruited. In his 1972 essay he said that "drug addicts are deliberately made by pushers, who give likely prospects their first few doses free." If drugs were legal it would not pay anybody to produce addicts, because everybody would buy from the cheapest source. But as every drug expert knows, pushers do not produce addicts. Friends or acquaintances do. In fact, pushers are usually reluctant to deal with non-users because a non-user could be an undercover cop. Drug use spreads in the same way that any fad or fashion spreads: somebody who is already a user urges his friends to try, or simply shows already-eager friends how to do it.

But we need not rely on speculation, however plausible, that lowered prices and more abundant supplies would have increased heroin usage. Great Britain once followed such a policy and with almost exactly those results. Until the mid-1960s, British physicians were allowed to prescribe heroin to certain classes of addicts. (Possessing these drugs without a doctor's prescription remained a criminal offense.) For many years this policy worked well enough because the addict patients were typically middle-class people who had become dependent on opiate painkillers while undergoing hospital treatment. There was no drug culture. The British system worked for many years, not because it prevented drug abuse, but because there was no problem of drug abuse that would test the system.

All that changed in the 1960s. A few unscrupulous doctors began passing out heroin in wholesale amounts. One doctor prescribed almost 600,000 heroin tablets—that is, over 13 pounds—in just one year. A youthful drug culture emerged with a demand for drugs far different from that of the older addicts. As a result, the British government required doctors to refer users to government-run clinics to receive their heroin.

But the shift to clinics did not curtail the growth in heroin use. Throughout the 1960s the number of addicts increased—the late John Kaplan of Stanford estimated by fivefold—in part as a result of the diversion of heroin from clinic patients to new users on the streets. An addict would bargain with the clinic doctor over how big a dose he would receive. The patient wanted as much as he could get, the doctor wanted to give as little as was needed. The patient had an advantage in this conflict because the doctor could not be certain how much was really needed. Many patients would use some of their "maintenance" dose and sell the remaining part to friends, thereby recruiting new addicts. As the clinics learned of this, they began to shift their treatment away from heroin and toward methadone, an addictive drug that, when taken orally, does not produce a "high" but will block the withdrawal pains associated with heroin abstinence.

Whether what happened in England in the 1960s was a mini-epidemic or an epidemic depends on whether one looks at numbers or at rates of change. Compared to the United States, the numbers were small. In 1960 there were 68 heroin addicts known to the British government; by 1968 there were 2,000 in treatment and many more who refused treatment. (They would refuse in part because they did not want to get methadone at a clinic if they could get heroin on the street.) Richard Hartnoll estimates that the actual number of addicts in England is five times the number officially registered. At a minimum, the number of British addicts increased thirty-fold in ten years; the actual increase may have been much larger.

In the early 1980s the numbers began to rise again, and this time nobody doubted that a real epidemic was at hand. The increase was estimated to be 40 percent a year. By 1982 there were thought to be 20,000 heroin users in London alone. Geoffrey Pearson reports that many cities—Glasgow, Liverpool, Manchester, and Sheffield among them—were now experiencing a drug problem that once had been largely confined to London. The problem again was supply. The country was being flooded with cheap, high-quality heroin, first from Iran and then from Southeast Asia.

The United States began the 1960s with a much larger number of heroin addicts and probably a bigger at-risk population than was the case in Great Britain. Even though it would be foolhardy to suppose that the British system, if installed here, would have worked the same way or with the same results, it would be equally foolhardy to suppose that a combination of heroin available from leaky clinics and from street dealers who faced only minimal law-enforcement risks would not have produced a much greater increase in heroin use than we actually experienced. My guess is that if we had allowed either doctors or clinics to prescribe heroin, we would have had far worse results than were produced in Britain, if for no other reason than the vastly larger number of addicts with which we began. We would have had to find some way to police thousands (not scores) of physicians and hundreds (not dozens) of clinics. If the British civil service found it difficult to keep heroin in the hands of addicts and out of the hands of recruits when it was dealing with a few hundred people, how well would the American civil service have accomplished the same tasks when dealing with tens of thousands of people?

Back to the Future

Now cocaine, especially in its potent form, crack, is the focus of attention. Now as in 1972 the government is trying to reduce its use. Now as then some people are advocating legalization. Is there any more reason to yield to those arguments today than there was almost two decades ago?[1]

I think not. If we had yielded in 1972 we almost certainly would have had today a permanent population of several million, not several hundred thousand, heroin addicts. If we yield now we will have a far more serious problem with cocaine.

Crack is worse than heroin by almost any measure. Heroin produces a pleasant drowsiness and, if hygienically administered, has only the physical side effects of constipation and sexual impotence. Regular heroin use incapacitates many users, especially poor ones, for any productive work or social responsibility. They will sit nodding on a street corner, helpless but at least harmless. By contrast, regular cocaine use leaves the user

neither helpless nor harmless. When smoked (as with crack) or injected, cocaine produces instant, intense, and short-lived euphoria. The experience generates a powerful desire to repeat it. If the drug is readily available, repeat use will occur. Those people who progress to "bingeing" on cocaine become devoted to the drug and its effects to the exclusion of almost all other considerations—job, family, children, sleep, food, even sex. Dr. Frank Gawin at Yale and Dr. Everett Ellinwood at Duke report that a substantial percentage of all high-dose, binge users become uninhibited, impulsive, hypersexual, compulsive, irritable, and hyperactive. Their moods vacillate dramatically, leading at times to violence and homicide.

Women are much more likely to use crack than heroin, and if they are pregnant, the effects on their babies are tragic. Douglas Besharov, who has been following the effects of drugs on infants for twenty years, writes that nothing he learned about heroin prepared him for the devastation of cocaine. Cocaine harms the fetus and can lead to physical deformities or neurological damage. Some crack babies have for all practical purposes suffered a disabling stroke while still in the womb. The long-term consequences of this brain damage are lowered cognitive ability and the onset of mood disorders. Besharov estimates that about 30,000 to 50,000 such babies are born every year, about 7,000 in New York City alone. There may be ways to treat such infants, but from everything we now know the treatment will be long, difficult, and expensive. Worse, the mothers who are most likely to produce crack babies are precisely the ones who, because of poverty or temperament, are least able and willing to obtain such treatment. In fact, anecdotal evidence suggests that crack mothers are likely to abuse their infants.

The notion that abusing drugs such as cocaine is a "victimless crime" is not only absurd but dangerous. Even ignoring the fetal drug syndrome, crack-dependent people are, like heroin addicts, individuals who regularly victimize their children by neglect, their spouses by improvidence, their employers by lethargy, and their co-workers by carelessness. Society is not and could never be a collection of autonomous individuals. We all have a stake in ensuring that each of us displays a minimal level of dignity, responsibility, and empathy. We cannot, of course, coerce people into goodness, but we can and should insist that some standards must be met if society itself—on which the very existence of the human personality depends—is to persist. Drawing the line that defines those standards is difficult and contentious, but if crack and heroin use do not fall below it, what does?

The advocates of legalization will respond by suggesting that my picture is overdrawn. Ethan Nadelmann of Princeton argues that the risk of legalization is less than most people suppose. Over 20 million Americans between the ages of 18 and 25 have tried cocaine (according to a government survey), but only a quarter of a million use it daily. From this Nadelmann concludes that at most 3 percent of all young people who try cocaine develop a problem with it. The implication is clear: make the drug legal and we only have to worry about 3 percent of our youth.

The implication rests on a logical fallacy and a factual error. The fallacy is this: the percentage of occasional cocaine users who become binge users *when the drug is illegal* (and thus expensive and hard to find) tells us nothing about the percentage who will become dependent when the drug is legal (and thus cheap and abundant). Drs. Gawin and Ellinwood report, in common with several other researchers, that controlled or occasional use of cocaine changes to compulsive and frequent use "when access to the drug increases" or when the user switches from snorting to smoking. More cocaine more potently administered alters, perhaps sharply, the proportion of "controlled" users who become heavy users.

The factual error is this: the federal survey Nadelmann quotes was done in 1985, *before* crack had become common. Thus the probability of becoming dependent on cocaine was derived from the responses of users who snorted the drug. The speed and potency of cocaine's action increases dramatically when it is smoked. We do not yet know how

greatly the advent of crack increases the risk of dependency, but all the clinical evidence suggests that the increase is likely to be large.

It is possible that some people will not become heavy users even when the drug is readily available in its most potent form. So far there are no scientific grounds for predicting who will and who will not become dependent. Neither socioeconomic background nor personality traits differentiate between casual and intensive users. Thus, the only way to settle the question of who is correct about the effect of easy availability on drug use, Nadelmann or Gawin and Ellinwood, is to try it and see. But that social experiment is so risky as to be no experiment at all, for if cocaine is legalized and if the rate of its abusive use increases dramatically, there is no way to put the genie back in the bottle, and it is not a kindly genie.

Have We Lost?

Many people who agree that there are risks in legalizing cocaine or heroin still favor it because, they think, we have lost the war on drugs. "Nothing we have done has worked" and the current federal policy is just "more of the same." Whatever the costs of great drug use, surely they would be less than the costs of our present, failed efforts.

That is exactly what I was told in 1972—and heroin is not quite as bad a drug as cocaine. We did not surrender and we did not lose. We did not win, either. What the nation accomplished then was what most efforts to save people from themselves accomplish: the problem was contained and the number of victims minimized, all at a considerable cost in law enforcement and increased crime. Was the cost worth it? I think so, but others may disagree. What are the lives of would-be addicts worth? I recall some people saying to me then, "Let them kill themselves." I was appalled. Happily, such views did not prevail.

Have we lost today? Not at all. High-rate cocaine use is not commonplace. The National Institute on Drug Abuse (NIDA) reports that less than 5 percent of high-school seniors had used cocaine within the last 30 days. Of course this survey misses young people who have dropped out of school and miscounts those who lie on the questionnaire, but even if we inflate the NIDA estimate by some plausible percentage, it is still not much above 5 percent. Medical examiners reported in 1987 that about 1,500 died from cocaine use; hospital emergency rooms reported about 30,000 admissions related to cocaine abuse.

These are not small numbers, but neither are they evidence of a nationwide plague that threatens to engulf us all. Moreover, cities vary greatly in the proportion of people who are involved with cocaine. To get city-level data we need to turn to drug tests carried out on arrested persons, who obviously are more likely to be drug users than the average citizen. The National Institute of Justice, through its Drug Use Forecasting (DUF) project, collects urinalysis data on arrestees in 22 cities. As we have already seen, opiate (chiefly heroin) use has been flat or declining in most of these cities over the last decade. Cocaine use has gone up sharply, but with great variation among cities. New York, Philadelphia, and Washington, DC, all report that two-thirds or more of their arrestees tested positive for cocaine, but in Portland, San Antonio, and Indianapolis the percentage was one-third or less.

In some neighborhoods, of course, matters have reached crisis proportions. Gangs control the streets, shootings terrorize residents, and drug-dealing occurs in plain view. The police seem barely able to contain matters. But in these neighborhoods—unlike at Palo Alto cocktail parties—the people are not calling for legalization, they are calling for help. And often not much help has come. Many cities are willing to do almost anything about the drug problem except spend more money on it. The federal government cannot change that; only local voters and politicians can. It is not clear that they will.

It took about ten years to contain heroin. We have had experience with crack for only about three or four years. Each year we spend perhaps $11 billion on law enforcement (and some of that goes to deal with marijuana) and perhaps $2 billion on treatment. Large sums, but not sums that should

lead anyone to say, "We just can't afford this any more."

The illegality of drugs increases crime, partly because some users turn to crime to pay for their habits, partly because some users are stimulated by certain drugs (such as crack or PCP) to act more violently or ruthlessly than they otherwise would, and partly because criminal organizations seeking to control drug supplies use force to manage their markets. These also are serious costs, but no one knows how much they would be reduced if drugs were legalized. Addicts would no longer steal to pay black-market prices for drugs, a real gain. But some, perhaps a great deal, of that gain would be offset by the great increase in the number of addicts. These people, nodding on heroin or living in the delusion-ridden high of cocaine, would hardly be ideal employees. Many would steal simply to support themselves, since snatch-and-grab, opportunistic crime can be managed even by people unable to hold a regular job or plan an elaborate crime. Those British addicts who get their supplies from government clinics are not models of law-abiding decency. Most are in crime, and though their per-capita rate of criminality may be lower thanks to the cheapness of their drugs, the total volume of crime they produce may be quite large. Of course, society could decide to support all unemployable addicts on welfare, but that would mean that gains from lowered rates of crime would have to be offset by large increases in welfare budgets.

Proponents of legalization claim that the costs of having more addicts around would be largely if not entirely offset by having more money available with which to treat and care for them. The money would come from taxes levied on the sale of heroin and cocaine.

To obtain this fiscal dividend, however, legalization's supporters must first solve an economic dilemma. If they want to raise a lot of money to pay for welfare and treatment, the tax rate on the drugs will have to be quite high. Even if they themselves do not want a high rate, the politicians' love of "sin taxes" would probably guarantee that it would be high anyway. But the higher the tax, the higher the price of the drug, and the higher the price the greater the likelihood that addicts will turn to crime to find the money for it and that criminal organizations will be formed to sell tax-free drugs at below-market rates. If we managed to keep taxes (and thus prices) low, we would get that much less money to pay for welfare and treatment and more people could afford to become addicts. There may be an optimal tax rate for drugs that maximizes revenue while minimizing crime, bootlegging, and the recruitment of new addicts, but our experience with alcohol does not suggest that we know how to find it.

The Benefits of Illegality

The advocates of legalization find nothing to be said in favor of the current system except, possibly, that it keeps the number of addicts smaller than it would otherwise be. In fact, the benefits are more substantial than that.

First, treatment. All the talk about providing "treatment on demand" implies that there is a demand for treatment. That is not quite right. There are some drug-dependent people who genuinely want treatment and will remain in it if offered; they should receive it. But there are far more who want only short-term help after a bad crash; once stabilized and bathed, they are back on the street again, hustling. And even many of the addicts who enroll in a program honestly wanting help drop out after a short while when they discover that help takes time and commitment. Drug-dependent people have very short time horizons and a weak capacity for commitment. These two groups—those looking for a quick fix and those unable to stick with a long-term fix—are not easily helped. Even if we increase the number of treatment slots—as we should—we would have to do something to make treatment more effective.

One thing that can often make it more effective is compulsion. Douglas Anglin of UCLA, in common with many other researchers, has found that the longer one stays in a treatment program, the better the changes of a reduction in drug dependency. But he, again like most other researchers,

has found that drop-out rates are high. He has also found, however, that patients who enter treatment under legal compulsion stay in the program longer than those not subject to such pressure. His research on the California civil-commitment program, for example, found that heroin users involved with its required drug-testing program had over the long term a lower rate of heroin use than similar addicts who were free of such constraints. If for many addicts compulsion is a useful component of treatment, it is not clear how compulsion could be achieved in a society in which purchasing, possessing, and using the drug were legal. It could be managed, I suppose, but I would not want to have to answer the challenge from the American Civil Liberties Union that it is wrong to compel a person to undergo treatment for consuming a legal commodity.

Next, education. We are now investing substantially in drug-education programs in the schools. Though we do not yet know for certain what will work, there are some promising leads. But I wonder how credible such programs would be if they were aimed at dissuading children from doing something perfectly legal. We could, of course, treat drug education like smoking education: inhaling crack and inhaling tobacco are both legal, but you should not do it because it is bad for you. That tobacco is bad for you is easily shown; the Surgeon General has seen to that. But what do we say about crack? It is pleasurable, but devoting yourself to so much pleasure is not a good idea (though perfectly legal)? Unlike tobacco, cocaine will not give you cancer or emphysema, but it will lead you to neglect your duties to family, job, and neighborhood? Everybody is doing cocaine, but you should not?

Again, it might be possible under a legalized regime to have effective drug-prevention programs, but their effectiveness would depend heavily, I think, on first having decided that cocaine use, like tobacco use, is purely a matter of practical consequences; no fundamental moral significance attaches to either. But if we believe—as I do—that dependency on certain mind-altering drugs *is* a moral issue and that their illegality rests in part on their immorality, then legalizing them undercuts, if it does not eliminate altogether, the moral message.

That message is at the root of the distinction we now make between nicotine and cocaine. Both are highly addictive; both have harmful physical effects. But we treat the two drugs differently, not simply because nicotine is so widely used as to be beyond the reach of effective prohibition, but because its use does not destroy the user's essential humanity. Tobacco shortens one's life, cocaine debases it. Nicotine alters one's habits, cocaine alters one's soul. The heavy use of crack, unlike the heavy use of tobacco, corrodes those natural sentiments of sympathy and duty that constitute our human nature and make possible our social life. To say, as does Nadelmann, that distinguishing morally between tobacco and cocaine is "little more than a transient prejudice" is close to saying that morality itself is but a prejudice.

The Alcohol Problem

Now we have arrived where many arguments about legalizing drugs begin: is there any reason to treat heroin and cocaine differently from the way we treat alcohol?

There is no easy answer to that question because, as with so many human problems, one cannot decide simply on the basis either of moral principles or of individual consequences; one has to temper any policy by a common-sense judgment of what is possible. Alcohol, like heroin, cocaine, PCP, and marijuana, is a drug—that is, a mood-altering substance—and consumed to excess it certainly has harmful consequences: auto accidents, bar-room fights, bedroom shootings. It is also, for some people, addictive. We cannot confidently compare the addictive powers of these drugs, but the best evidence suggests that crack and heroin are much more addictive than alcohol.

Many people, Nadelmann included, argue that since the health and financial costs of alcohol abuse are so much higher than those of cocaine or heroin abuse, it is hypocritical folly to devote our efforts to preventing cocaine or drug use. But as Mark Kleiman of Harvard has pointed out, this comparison is quite misleading. What Nadelmann is doing

is showing that a *legalized* drug (alcohol) produces greater social harm than *illegal ones* (cocaine and heroin). But of course. Suppose that in the 1920s we had made heroin and cocaine legal and alcohol illegal. Can anyone doubt that Nadelmann would not be writing that it is folly to continue our ban on alcohol because cocaine and heroin are so much more harmful?

And let there be no doubt about it—widespread heroin and cocaine use are associated with all manner of ills. Thomas Bewley found that the mortality rate of British heroin addicts in 1968 was 28 times as high as the death rate of the same age group of non-addicts, even though in England at the time an addict could obtain free or low-cost heroin and clean needles from British clinics. Perform the following mental experiment: suppose we legalized heroin and cocaine in this country. In what proportion of auto fatalities would the state police report that the driver was nodding off on heroin or recklessly driving on a coke high? In what proportion of spouse-assault and child-abuse cases would the local police report that crack was involved? In what proportion of industrial accidents would safety investigators report that the forklift or drill-press operator was in a drug-induced stupor or frenzy? We do not know exactly what the proportion would be, but anyone who asserts that it would not be much higher than it is now would have to believe that these drugs have little appeal except when they are illegal. And that is nonsense.

An advocate of legalization might concede that social harm—perhaps harm equivalent to that already produced by alcohol—would follow from making cocaine and heroin generally available. But at least, he might add, we would have the problem "out in the open" where it could be treated as a matter of "public health." That is well and good, *if* we knew how to treat—that is, cure—heroin and cocaine abuse. But we do not know how to do it for all the people who would need such help. We are having only limited success in coping with chronic alcoholics. Addictive behavior is immensely difficult to change, and the best methods for changing it—living in drug-free therapeutic communities, becoming faithful members of Alcoholics Anonymous or Narcotics Anonymous—require great personal commitment, a quality that is, alas, in short supply among the very persons— young people, disadvantaged people—who are often most at risk for addiction.

Suppose that today we had, not 15 million alcohol abusers, but half a million. Suppose that we already knew what we have learned from our long experience with the widespread use of alcohol. Would we make whiskey legal? I do not know, but I suspect there would be a lively debate. The Surgeon General would remind us of the risks alcohol poses to pregnant women. The National Highway Traffic Safety Administration would point to the likelihood of more highway fatalities caused by drunk drivers. The Food and Drug Administration might find that there is a non-trivial increase in cancer associated with alcohol consumption. At the same time the police would report great difficulty in keeping illegal whiskey out of our cities, officers being corrupted by bootleggers, and alcohol addicts often resorting to crime to feed their habit. Libertarians, for their part, would argue that every citizen has a right to drink anything he wishes and that drinking is, in any event, a "victimless crime."

However the debate might turn out, the central fact would be that the problem was still, at that point, a small one. The government cannot legislate away the addictive tendencies in all of us, nor can it remove completely even the most dangerous addictive substances. But it can cope with harms when the harms are still manageable.

Science and Addiction

One advantage of containing a problem while it is still containable is that it buys time for science to learn more about it and perhaps to discover a cure. Almost unnoticed in the current debate over legalizing drugs is that basic science has made rapid strides in identifying the underlying neurological processes involved in some forms of addiction. Stimulants such as cocaine and amphetamines alter the way certain brain cells communicate with one another. That alteration is complex and not entirely understood, but in simplified form it involves modifying the way in which a neurotransmitter called dopamine sends signals from one cell to another.

When dopamine crosses the synapse between two cells, it is in effect carrying a message from the first cell to activate the second one. In certain parts of the brain that message is experienced as pleasure. After the message is delivered, the dopamine returns to the first cell. Cocaine apparently blocks this return, or "reuptake," so that the excited cell and others nearby continue to send pleasure messages. When the exaggerated high produced by cocaine-influenced dopamine finally ends, the brain cells may (in ways that are still a matter of dispute) suffer from an extreme lack of dopamine, thereby making the individual unable to experience any pleasure at all. This would explain why cocaine users often feel so depressed after enjoying the drug. Stimulants may also affect the way in which other neurotransmitters, such as serotonin and noradrenaline, operate.

Whatever the exact mechanism may be, once it is identified it becomes possible to use drugs to block either the effect of cocaine or its tendency to produce dependency. There have already been experiments using desipramine, imipramine, bromocriptine, carbamazepine, and other chemicals. There are some promising results.

Tragically, we spend very little on such research, and the agencies funding it have not in the past occupied very influential or visible posts in the federal bureaucracy. If there is one aspect of the "war on drugs" metaphor that I dislike, it is its tendency to focus attention almost exclusively on the troops in the trenches, whether engaged in enforcement or treatment, and away from the research-and-development efforts back on the home front where the way may ultimately be decided.

I believe that the prospects of scientists in controlling addiction will be strongly influenced by the size and character of the problem they face. If the problem is a few hundred thousand chronic, high-dose users of an illegal product, the chances of making a difference at a reasonable cost will be much greater than if the problem is a few million chronic users of legal substances. Once a drug is legal, not only will its use increase but many of those who then use it will prefer the drug to the treatment: they will want the pleasure, whatever the cost to themselves or their families, and they will resist—probably successfully—any effort to wean them away from experiencing the high that comes from inhaling a legal substance.

If I Am Wrong . . .

No one can know what our society would be like if we changed the law to make access to cocaine, heroin, and PCP easier. I believe, for reasons given, that the result would be a sharp increase in use, a more widespread degradation of the human personality, and a greater rate of accidents and violence.

I may be wrong. If I am, then we will needlessly have incurred heavy costs in law enforcement and some forms of criminality. But if I am right, and the legalizers prevail anyway, then we will have consigned millions of people, hundreds of thousands of infants, and hundreds of neighborhoods to a life of oblivion and disease. To the lives and families destroyed by alcohol we will have added countless more destroyed by cocaine, heroin, PCP, and whatever else a basement scientist can invent.

Human character is formed by society; indeed, human character is inconceivable without society, and good character is less likely in a bad society. Will we, in the name of an abstract doctrine of radical individualism, and with the false comfort of suspect predictions, decide to take the chance that somehow individual decency can survive amid a more general level of degradation?

I think not. The American people are too wise for that, whatever the academic essayists and cocktail-party pundits may say. But if Americans today are less wise than I suppose, then Americans at some future time will look back on us now and wonder, what kind of people were they that they could have done such a thing?

Note

1. I do not here take up the question of marijuana. For a variety of reasons—its widespread use and its lesser tendency to addict—it presents a different problem from cocaine or heroin. For a penetrating analysis, see Mark Kleiman, *Marijuana: Costs of Abuse, Costs of Control* (Greenwood Press, 217 pp.).

ISSUE II
Guns and Crime:
Should We Relax Gun Permit Laws?

The issue of guns and crime is one of the most debated in the country and has played a major role in both local and national elections. Today the number of crimes that are committed with guns is staggering—about 1.2 million annually. The handgun problem is probably most pronounced among juveniles and young people. Between 1985 and 1994, for example, while the number of adult homicides decreased substantially, the number of homicides committed by young people (18 to 24 years old) more than doubled. The primary weapon of choice was the handgun. While the number of juvenile homicides committed with other weapons remained constant over this time period, the number of juvenile homicides committed with a handgun more than doubled (Dunworth 2000).

Most of the debate has surrounded the extent to which the government should control handguns. Gun control advocates believe that if the number of guns in society were reduced, there would be a decline in the number of homicides and firearms-related assaults. By contrast, those opposed to gun control argue that fewer guns would not have an impact on crime and might actually increase crime. In the next section the authors discuss the impact of gun permit laws.

David McDowall, Colin Loftin, and Brian Wiersema argue that laws to "encourage" the issuance of gun permits might inadvertently increase gun crime. The authors examine data obtained from the state of Florida between 1973 and 1992 to test their hypothesis. The analysis revealed that in all five areas studied, firearm homicides increased after "shall issue" laws were passed. In conclusion, McDowall and his associates suggest that one strategy to reduce gun crime might be to disarm both civilians and the police.

In response, Daniel D. Polsby maintains that the liberalization of gun laws has resulted in a general deterrent effect on violent crime. Polsby notes that the analyses by McDowall's team are problematic for three reasons. First, he argues that if McDowall et al. had examined data for a longer period of time, they would have found that firearm violence in these areas declined rather than increased. Second, he maintains that the authors examined trends in violence only in a few cities in Florida and, as a result, reached erroneous conclusions. Third, Polsby argues that the authors' basic hypothesis is incorrect and that criminals are actually deterred from carrying firearms when they are aware that civilians and police officers carry them.

Reference

Dunworth, Terence. 2000. *National Evaluation of the Youth Firearms Violence Initiative*. Washington DC: National Institute of Justice.

Critical Thinking Questions

1. Should we encourage citizens to carry guns? Why?

2. How have gun laws had an impact on violence?

3. How do you interpret the Second Amendment? Does it give the right to bear arms to individuals or only to individuals in the "militia"?

Internet Websites

Several firearms-related studies conducted by the University of Chicago. <http://www.lib.uchicago.edu/~llou/guns.html>

A Website that contains several links to firearms sites. <http://www.gunscholar.com/data.htm>

Federally funded research on firearms. <http://www.ojp.usdoj.gov/firearms/publications.htm>

The Johns Hopkins Center for Gun Policy and Research. <http://support.jhsph.edu/departments/gunpolicy/> ✦

3
Easing Concealed Firearms Laws

Effects on Homicide in Three States[*]

David McDowall
Colin Loftin
Brian Wiersema[**]

Introduction

Restrictions on carrying concealed weapons are among the most common gun control policies.[1] These statutes limit who may have a deadly weapon—usually a handgun—hidden on their person when outside the home. By reducing access to guns in public, concealed weapons laws seek to make firearms less available for violence.[2]

Details of concealed weapons laws vary greatly among localities, but most approaches fall into two categories. One of these is a discretionary system, sometimes called "may issue" licensing.[3] Under this policy, legal authorities grant licenses only to those citizens who can establish a compelling need for carrying a gun.

The other approach is a non-discretionary, or "shall issue," system.[4] Here the authorities *must* provide a license to any applicant who meets specified criteria. Because legal officials are often unwilling to allow concealed weapons, adopting a shall issue policy usually increases the number of persons with permits to carry guns.[5]

In 1985, the National Rifle Association announced that it would lobby for shall issue laws.[6] Several states, including Florida, Mississippi, and Oregon, have since changed from may issue to shall issue systems. Advocates of shall issue laws argue that such laws will both prevent crime and reduce homicides.[7]

This article examines the frequency of homicides in the large urban areas of Florida, Mississippi, and Oregon, before and after their shall issue laws began. The analysis provides no support for the idea that the laws reduced homicides; instead, it finds evidence of an increase in firearm murders.

The Laws

On October 1, 1987, Florida adopted a shall issue law that greatly expanded eligibility to carry a concealed weapon.[8] The new statute required the state to grant a concealed weapon license to any qualified adult who had taken a firearms safety course. Those persons with a history of drug or alcohol abuse, a felony conviction, mental illness, physical inability, or who were not Florida residents were disqualified from obtaining a license.

Prior to the passage of the Florida shall issue law, county officials set their own standards for concealed carry. Throughout the state, about 17,000 persons held permits, including 1,300 in Dade County (Miami) and 25 in Hillsborough county (Tampa).[9] The number of licenses rose steadily after the passage of the new law, reaching 141,000 in September 1994.[10]

Mississippi adopted a shall issue law on July 1, 1990.[11] The Mississippi law was similar to the Florida law, except that it did not require firearms safety training. Mississippi's earlier law was highly restrictive, generally allowing only security guards to have concealed weapons.[12] In contrast, the new law is more lenient; by November 1992, the state had issued 5,136 new licenses.[13]

Oregon adopted a shall issue law on January 1, 1990, in a compromise between supporters and opponents of stricter gun control measures.[14] Oregon's new law required county sheriffs to provide a concealed handgun license to any qualified adult who had taken a firearms safety course. People who could not obtain a license included: those with outstanding arrest warrants, those on pretrial release, those with a history of mental illness, or those with a felony or recent misdemeanor conviction.

In addition to easing laws on concealed carrying, Oregon's new law also tightened standards for buying a gun. While the old law barred convicted felons from owning handguns, the new law prohibited convicted felons from owning any type of firearm. Oregon's new law also lengthened the waiting period for handgun purchases and required more detailed background checks. It further prohibited most persons ineligible for a concealed handgun license from obtaining any firearm.

Before the passage of the new law in 1991, Oregon's sheriffs issued concealed handgun licenses at their discretion. In 1989, there were fewer than 500 licensed carriers in Clackamas, Multnomah, and Washington counties, the core of the Portland metropolitan area.[15] By October 1993, the number of licenses in these counties grew to 16,000.[16]

Possible Effects of Shall Issue Licensing on Crime

While the shall issue policies clearly increased the number of persons licensed to carry concealed weapons in Florida, Mississippi, and Oregon, their effects on crime are less obvious. There are grounds to believe that crime might increase, decrease, or remain the same after a shall issue law is passed.

Shall issue licensing might reduce crime by deterring criminal offenders. Criminals generally wish to avoid victims who may be carrying guns.[17] Knowledge that many citizens have concealed weapons could discourage attempts at crime, especially crimes against strangers and crimes in public areas.

On the other hand, shall issue licensing also might raise levels of criminal violence. This is so because shall issue laws increase the number of persons with easy access to guns. Zimring and Cook argue that assaults are often impulsive acts involving the most readily available weapons.[18] As guns are especially deadly weapons, more firearm carriers might result in more homicides.

Advocates of shall issue licensing cite figures showing that few legal carriers misuse their guns.[19] Yet greater tolerance for legal carrying may increase levels of illegal carrying as well. For example, criminals have more reason to carry firearms—and to use them—when their victims might be armed.[20] Further, if permission to carry a concealed weapon is easy to obtain, citizens and law enforcement officials may be less apt to view illegal carrying as a serious offense.

Still, shall issue licensing may be irrelevant to crime. Even in areas with shall issue policies, only a small fraction of adults have licenses to carry guns. Many citizens keep guns in their homes, and police officers often carry guns when off-duty and in plain clothes. The increase in available firearms due to shall issue licensing may be of little consequence.

Existing Evidence on the Effects of Shall Issue Licensing

Most empirical discussions of shall issue licensing compare homicides in Florida before and after the beginning of its law. Homicide is the most accurately recorded crime, reducing the influence of measurement error on the comparison. Florida adopted its law earlier than did the other states, providing more time to day the effects.

All existing comparisons of Florida homicide rates before and after the passage of the Florida shall issue law found that Florida homicides decreased after the shall issue law. The National Rifle Association, for example, notes that Florida's homicide rate fell by 21 percent when comparing 1987 with 1992.[21]

Although the Florida experience appears to support a deterrent effect, the existing comparisons suffer from several weaknesses. First, these studies all use Uniform Crime Report data compiled by the Federal Bureau of Investigation (FBI). In 1988, the FBI did not publish crime counts for Florida. Evaluations based on the FBI data thus must ignore 1988 or use estimates of the 1988 total. This is important because 1988 was the first full year after the law's passage.[22]

Second, the existing evaluations use short time series of annual data. Even in Florida, there are few annual observations after the law began, and most comparisons only include those years immediately prior to the law's passage. Because crime increases and decreases over time due to the operation of many factors, comparisons using short time series are highly prone to the influence of chance events that briefly push homicides above or below their average levels.

Third, the existing comparisons examine total homicide rates for the entire state. If some areas respond differently to the laws than do others, a statewide analysis may miss important effects. For example, the influence of shall issue laws may be greater in urban settings where crime is most prevalent. If this were true, including rural areas in an analysis would make it more difficult to detect changes in violence. Similarly, combining firearms and other weapon homicides might mask effect unique to one type of murder.

Fourth, most existing studies compare homicide levels before the shall issue law only with levels in 1991 or later. In February 1991, Florida adopted background checks of handgun buyers, and in October 1991, it began a waiting period for handgun purchases.[23] Comparisons that use only 1991 or later years cannot separate the effects of the shall issue law from those of the other two laws. The reductions in homicides that these studies claim may as easily be due to the other policies as to shall issue licensing.

In short, current evaluations leave much room for doubt about the effects of the Florida law. The shall issue laws in Mississippi and in Oregon have not received even this limited attention. A more detailed analysis using data from all three states would allow stronger inferences about the impact of the policies.

Research Design

Study Design and Data

Similar to existing evaluations of shall issue licensing, this study used an inter-rupted time series design to estimate average homicide levels before and after shall issue policies began.[24] We studied patterns in Florida, Mississippi, and Oregon. In addition, we analyzed monthly homicide counts and examined only large urban areas within the three states. To find if the laws influenced gun deaths differently, firearm homicides were separated from homicides by other means.

We conducted analyses for Dade (Miami), Duval (Jacksonville), and Hillsborough (Tampa) counties in Florida, and for Hinds (Jackson) county in Mississippi. Because there were relatively few homicides in Multnomah county (Portland), we combined Clackamas, Multnomah, and Washington counties in Oregon. For each area, we used death certificate data compiled by the National Center for Health Statistics (NCHS) to count monthly homicides through December 1990.[25] Health departments in Florida, Mississippi, and Oregon provided additional cases from January 1991, to December 1992.

For all areas except Miami, we studied the period between January 1973 and December 1992 (240 months). We confined our Miami analysis to January 1983 through December 1992 (120 months) because of an unusually sharp increase in homicide rates in May 1980 after an influx of Cuban refugees. In later 1982 the rates appeared to stabilize.[26]

In total, there were 177 months before the shall issue law in Jacksonville and Tampa, and 57 months before the shall issue law in Miami. For all three Florida cities there were 63 months after the law. In Mississippi there were 210 pre-law months and 36 post-law months. In Oregon there were 204 pre-law months and 36 post-law months.

To remove the effects of systematic variation from each time series, we developed autoregressive integrated moving average (ARIMA) noise models.[27] The noise models allow for variables, such as poverty or age structure, which influenced homicides both before and after the legal changes. If not controlled, these variables may bias inferences about the laws.

After developing suitable noise models, we added intervention models to measure changes in homicides following the shall issue laws.[28] We considered three intervention models: an abrupt permanent change model, a gradual permanent change model, and an abrupt temporary change model.[29] For each series, the abrupt permanent change model provided the best fit to the data.[30]

Our analysis avoids the major problems of previous comparisons. The NCHS data collection system is independent of the FBI, allowing us to use 1988 Florida homicide counts.[31] The long monthly time series provides more stable estimates of homicide patterns before and after the shall issue laws began. By studying firearms and other weapon murders separately in several areas, we can more precisely isolate any changes due to the laws.

Threats to Validity and Supplementary Analysis

Interrupted time series studies are among the strongest non-experimental research designs.[32] Still, as is true with any design, time series studies do not eliminate all threats to valid inference.

Perhaps the most important threat to the design's validity is "history," the possibility that a permanent change in another variable produced an observed effect.[33] For example, suppose that each area adopted other policies that influenced crime when they began their shall issue laws. These policies then would be confounded with the laws, and they would be historical threats to validity.

The major method we used to avoid historical threats was replication of the analysis in five metropolitan areas. An unnoticed historical event may have increased or decreased homicides in any single area after its shall issue law began. Yet if similar outcomes occur in several different places after the laws, historical events become a less plausible explanation of the change.[34] With a consistent set of results, an historical explanation would require that each area witness permanent changes in other causes of homicide at about the time its law began. These changes would have to influence homicides in the same way in each area, increasing them in all five areas or decreasing them in all five areas.

The areas in our study are geographically separated and demographically diverse, and they adopted their laws at three different times. While the replications cannot entirely rule out history, a consistent set of results would greatly narrow the range of historical events that could account for an effect. On the other hand, a varied pattern of results, with large increases or decreases in only one or two areas, would support an historical explanation.

Beyond replication, we used two additional methods to assess historical threats. First, we searched for other legal changes, especially changes in firearms laws, which might affect homicides. The most significant laws we found were Florida's background check, adopted in February 1991, and waiting period, adopted in October 1991.[35]

Florida's waiting period and background check laws began more than three years after shall issue licensing, leaving little data to estimate their effects. Still, we included these laws in a supplementary analysis to verify that they were not confounded with the licensing policy. Because the waiting period followed the background checks closely in time, we considered them as a single law that began in February 1991.

As a second check on historical threats, we estimated models that included homicide counts for the entire United States as an additional independent variable. This analysis studied whether homicide changes in the five areas simply mirrored national pattern; that is, homicide levels may have changed after the laws only because of events common to the nation as a whole. If this were true, the shall issue laws would not influence homicides net of the national counts.

We could obtain national homicide counts only through the end of 1991.[36] This limits the amount of data after the shall issue laws, especially in Mississippi and Oregon. Still, the national analysis provides an idea of whether broad historical events can explain any observed local changes.

Besides considering historical threats, we also conducted a supplementary analysis that used homicide rates instead of homicide counts. The population of all five areas grew over the study period, especially in the

Florida cities. Homicide counts thus may have changed after the laws in part because of increases in the populations at risk.

To remove the influence of population, we estimated models for homicide rates per 100,000 persons. Only annual population figures were available, so we aggregated homicides in each area by year.[37] Because the annual data provided few cases to study changes in rates, we next pooled all five areas using a fixed effects analysis of variance model.[38] This created a single set of data, with seventy observations before the laws and twenty after the laws.[39] As in the main analysis, we then estimated separate equations for firearm homicides and for homicides by other methods.

In the pooled equations we first removed the mean homicide rates for each area and year. This controls for constant rate differences between the areas and for events that similarly influenced rates across all areas in a given year.[40] We then included intervention variables to measure the effects of the shall issue and (for the Florida cities) background check and waiting period laws.

Results

Estimates of the effects of the shall issue laws on the monthly homicide counts are presented here. To simplify the presentation, we report only the means before the laws and the changes in homicides after the laws began.[41]

The results show that firearms homicides increased in four of the five areas in the post-law period. Except the increase in Miami and the decrease in Portland, these changes were statistically significant ($p < .05$). Expressed as percentages, the changes varied from a decrease of 12 percent (Portland) to an increase of 75 percent (Jacksonville).[42] Considering each area as a replication of the same experiment, gun homicides increased by an average of 26 percent. An inverse normal combined test of statistical significance easily rejected the null hypothesis of zero overall change.[43]

In contrast to gun homicides, homicides by other means did not show a consistent pattern of effects. Homicides without fire-arms increased in Tampa and Jacksonville, but they fell in the other three areas. Across all five areas, the average change in homicides without guns was an increase of less than 1 percent. In combination, this change was statistically insignificant.

The analysis for the Florida cities includes the state's waiting period and background check laws. These results provide no evidence that the original estimates were due to confounding between the other laws and shall issue licensing. Adding the other laws slightly increased the coefficients for the shall issue policy, but it did not alter their statistical significance.

Although not central to our study, it is worth noting that the levels of each Florida firearms series decreased after the waiting period and background checks began. Yet homicides without guns also fell in two cities, and the policies should influence only firearm crimes. The results do not point to any strong conclusions about the waiting period and background check laws.

Analysis that adds national homicide counts to control for patterns in the United States as a whole are presented as well.[44] In each area, there was a positive relationship between local homicide patterns and patterns in the nation. Still, including the national counts only modestly changed the estimates for shall issue licensing.

Finally, we report the results for the annual homicides rates. Here the coefficient for the shall issue policies is the average effect across all five cities. Gun homicides increased on average by 4.5 per 100,000 persons, a value significantly different from zero. In contrast, murders without guns decreased insignificantly. Gun homicides fell insignificantly following Florida's waiting period and background check laws, while other weapon homicides increased.

Discussion

Across the five areas, firearms homicides increased in the aftermath of the shall issue laws. In contrast, homicides without guns remained steady. These findings were little altered when we considered other laws, controlled for variations in national homicide counts, and allowed for population change.

The pattern of results leads us to two conclusions, one stronger than the other. The stronger conclusion is that shall issue laws do not reduce homicides, at least in large urban areas. If there were such a decrease, other events would have to push murders up strongly enough to mask it in all five areas that we studied. Such events are possible, of course, but we believe that they are extremely unlikely.

The weaker conclusion is that shall issue laws raise levels of firearms murders. Coupled with a lack of influence on murders by other means, the laws thus increase the frequency of homicide. This interpretation is consistent with other work showing that policies to *discourage* firearms in public may help prevent violence. For example, studies by Pierce and Bowers and by O'Carroll et al. found that laws providing mandatory sentences for illegal gun carrying reduced firearms crimes in Boston and Detroit.[45] Similarly, Sherman et al. found that gun crimes fell during a Kansas City program that confiscated firearms from people who carried them outside their homes.[46]

Despite this evidence, we do not firmly conclude that shall issue licensing leads to more firearms murders. This is so because the effects varied over the study areas. Firearms homicides significantly increased in only three areas, and one area witnessed an insignificant decrease. In combination, the increase in gun homicides was large and statistically significant. Yet we have only five replications, and two of these do not clearly fit the pattern.

The statistical significance of the combined results aside, the analysis implies that shall issue policies do not *always* raise levels of gun murder. Sometimes, at least, local conditions operate to blunt any effects. The areas without significant increase, Portland and Miami, may be unusual, but we lack the data to examine whether this is true.

Stated in another way, we cannot completely dismiss historical events as an explanation of the increases in firearms murders. One would need a complex theory to explain how history could mask a *decrease* in homi-

cides after the laws. Historical accounts of the apparent *increase* might be much simpler. One would then be left with the hypothesis that the effects of the laws are nil.

A more definitive analysis should be possible in the future. Besides Mississippi and Oregon, six other states have adopted shall issue laws based on the Florida model. Four of these—Alaska, Idaho, Montana, and Wyoming—have small populations and low levels of criminal violence.[47] As a result, it would be difficult to perform a statistically meaningful analysis of changes in homicides after their laws began.

Yet, two more populous states, Arizona and Tennessee, enacted shall issue licensing in 1994.[48] Given several years of experience with the laws in these areas, future research could provide more certain estimates of the effects on firearms violence.

Between January 1995 and March 1995, the legislatures of Arkansas, Utah, and Virginia sent shall issue laws to their Governors for signature.[49] Similar laws were pending in an additional fourteen states, including California, Illinois, and Texas.[50] Given this level of interest, it is likely that shall issue licensing will continue to receive attention in the future.

While our analysis does not allow a firm conclusion that shall issue licensing increases firearms homicides, it does suggest caution about these laws. Some observers consider strict limits on firearms outside the home to be among the most effective forms of gun control.[51] Beyond any influence on violence, the policies are easy to enforce and they do not inconvenience most gun owners. When states weaken limits on concealed weapons, they may be giving up a simple and effective method of preventing firearms deaths.

Notes

*This research was supported by grant R49-CCR-306268 from the U.S. Public Health Service, Centers for Disease Control and Prevention.

**Members of the Violence Research Group and Department of Criminology and Criminal Justice, University of Maryland at College Park.

1. *See* James D. Wright et al., UNDER THE GUN: WEAPONS, CRIME, AND VIOLENCE IN

AMERICA 243–72 (1983); Gary Kleck & E. Britt Patterson, *The Impact of Gun Control and Gun Ownership Levels on Violence Rates*, 9J. QUANTITATIVE CRIMINOLOGY 249 (1993).

2. *See, e.g.,* Franklin E. Zimring, *Firearms, Violence, and Public Policy*, 265 SCI. AM. 48 (1991).

3. Gary Kleck, POINT BLANK: GUNS AND VIOLENCE IN AMERICA 411–14 (1991).

4. *Id.*

5. Paul H. Blackman, Carrying Handguns for Personal Protection: Issues of Research and Public Policy (presented at the Annual Meeting of the American Society of Criminology (Nov. 1985)).

6. *Id.; see also* G. Ray Arnett, *Sincerely, GRA*, 133 AM. RIFLEMAN 7 (1985).

7. *See, e.g.,* Wayne LaPierre, GUNS, CRIME, AND FREEDOM, 29–39 (1994); David B. Kopel, *Hold Your Fire: Gun Control Won't Stop Rising Violence*, 63 POL'Y REV. 58 (1993).

8. FLA. STAT. ch. 790.06 (1992). *See* Richard Getchell, *Carrying Concealed Weapons in Self-Defenses: Florida Adopts Uniform Regulations for the Issuance of Concealed Weapon Permits*, 15 FLA. ST. U. L. REV. 751 (1987).

9. *See* Lisa Getter, *Accused Criminals Get Gun Permits*, MIAMI HERALD, May 15, 1988, at 1A; Stephen Koff & Bob Port, *Gun Permits Soar Through Loopholes*, ST. PETERSBURG TIMES, Jan. 7, 1988, at A1.

10. FLORIDA DEPARTMENT OF STATE, DIVISION OF LICENSING, CONCEALED WEAPONS/FIREARM LICENSE STATISTICAL REPORT FOR PERIOD 10/10/87 TO 09/30/94 (1994).

11. MISS. CODE ANN. § 45-9-101 (1991).

12. David Snyder, *New Miss. Gun-Permit Law Raises Visions of Old West*, TIMES-PICAYUNE (New Orleans), Aug. 13, 1990, at A1.

13. Grace Simmons, *Police Want Concealed Guns Banned From Cars*, CLARION-LEDGER (Jackson), Nov. 11, 1992, at A1.

14. OR. REV. STAT. § 166.291-§ 166-295 (1991). *See also*, Rhonda Canby, *1989 Oregon Gun Control Legislation*, 26 WILLAMETTE L. REV. 565 (1990).

15. Bill MacKenzie, *Packin' the Heat*, OREGONIAN (Portland), Nov. 4, 1993 at A1.

16. *Id.*

17. *See, e.g.,* James D. Right & Peter H. Rossi, ARMED AND CONSIDERED DANGEROUS: A SURVEY OF FELONS AND THEIR FIREARMS 141–59 (1986).

18. Franklin Zimring, *Is Gun Control Likely to Reduce Violent Killings?*, 35 U. CHI. L. REV. 721 (1968), Philip J. Cook, *The Technology of Personal Violence*, in 14 CRIME & JUS.: ANN. REV. RES. 1 (Michael Tonry ed., 1991).

19. *See, e.g.,* LaPierre, *supra* note 7, at 36–38; Jeffrey R. Snyder, *A Nation of Cowards*, 113 PUB. INTEREST 40 (1993). *See also* FLORIDA DEPARTMENT OF STATE, *supra* note 10.

20. In a survey of prison inmates, Wright and Rossi found that a majority of gun-carrying criminals cited armed victims as an important motivation for their actions. Wright & Rossi, *supra* note 17, at 150. Of course, criminals rarely will know with certainty if a potential victim has a concealed gun. Even unarmed victims may therefore be more vulnerable to harm.

21. NATIONAL RIFLE ASSOCIATION, INSTITUTE FOR LEGISLATIVE ACTION, FACT SHEET: CARRYING CONCEALED FIREARMS (CCW) STATISTICS (1994). *See also* LaPierre, *supra* note 7, at 33; Kopel, *supra* note 7, at 63; George F. Will, *Are We 'A Nation of Cowards'?*, NEWSWEEK, Nov. 15, 1993, at 92–93.

22. In addition, from 1988 through 1991 Florida did not report data to the FBI that distinguished firearms homicides from homicides by other means. Existing comparisons use only total homicide counts.

23. FLA. STAT. chs. 790.065, 790.0655 (1992).

24. *See* Thomas D. Cook & Donald T. Campbell, QUASI-EXPERIMENTATION: DESIGN AND ANALYSIS ISSUES FOR FIELD SETTINGS 207–32 (1979).

25. Department of Health and Human Services, National Center for Health Statistics, Inter-University Consortium for Political and Social Research, Mortality Detail Files, 1968 to 1990 (1993).

26. Still, we reached similar conclusions when we analyzed all 240 months of Miami data.

27. George E. P. Box et al., TIME SERIES ANALYSIS: FORECASTING AND CONTROL (3d ed. 1994).

28. *Id.* at 462–69.

29. *See* David McDowall et al., INTERRUPTED TIME SERIES ANALYSIS 83–85 (1980).

30. *Id.* at 83–85 (discussing criteria for selecting the best-fitting model).

31. For a description of the FBI and NCHS data collection systems, *see* Marc Riedel, *Nationwide Homicide Data Sets: An Evaluation of the*

Uniform Crime Reports and the National Center for Health Statistics Data, in MEASURING CRIME: LARGE-SCALE, LONG-RANGE EFFORTS 175 (Doris Layton MacKenzie et al. eds., 1990)

32. *See* Donald T. Campbell & Julian C. Stanley, EXPERIMENTAL AND QUASI-EXPERIMENTAL DESIGNS FOR RESEARCH 37–43 (1963).

33. Cook & Campbell, *supra* note 24, at 211.

34. Campbell & Stanley, *supra* note 32, at 42 (pointing out that the natural sciences heavily rely on time series designs, and use replications to rule out rival hypotheses).

35. FLA. STAT. chs. 790.065, 790.065 (1992). As we noted earlier, Oregon changed several other features of its firearms laws when it adopted shall issue licensing. Because these other changes began with the shall issue policy, we cannot separately estimate their effects.

36. Department of Health and Human Services, National Center for Health Statistics, Inter-University Consortium for Political and Social Research, Mortality Detail Files, 1968 to 1991 (1994).

37. For 1973–1978 we used county-level population estimates from U.S. DEPARTMENT OF COMMERCE, BUREAU OF THE CENSUS, STATISTICAL ABSTRACT OF THE UNITED STATES (various years). For 1980–1992 we used unpublished Census Bureau estimates. The Census Bureau did not estimate county populations in 1979, and we interpolated values for that year.

38. *See* Cheng Hsiao, ANALYSIS OF PANEL DATA (1986).

39. Florida and Mississippi began their laws in the middle of the year. In the annual analysis we placed the interventions for these states at the first full year after the laws, 1988 for the Florida cities and 1991 for Jackson. Oregon's law began in January 1990, so we placed Portland's intervention at 1990.

40. Hsiao, *supra* note 38, at 138–40.

41. An appendix that describes the analysis in more detail is available from the authors.

42. The NCHS data include civilian justifiable homicides, in which private citizens killed criminals during attempted felonies. We thus cannot dismiss the possibility that part of the rise in firearms murders was due to permit holders who shot offenders in self-defense. Still, justifiable homicides are rare, and it is not plausible that they could account for the bulk of the increase. According to FBI data for 1992, there were 262 justifiable handgun homicides in the entire United States, 1.7% of the 15,377 firearm murders. *See* FEDERAL BUREAU OF INVESTIGATION, CRIME IN THE UNITED STATES, 1992, at 15–22 (1993).

43. *See* Larry V. Hedges & Ingram Olkin, STATISTICAL METHODS FOR META-ANALYSIS 39–40 (1985). The test assumes that the replications are independent. Because we include three cities from the same state in the analysis, this is probably only approximately correct.

44. Because the national counts were not stationary in level, we used their first differences in this analysis. *See* Box, *supra* note 27, at 89–130 for a discussion of nonstationary time series models.

45. Glenn L. Pierce & William J. Bowers, *The Bartley-Fox Gun Law's Short-Term Impact on Crime in Boston,* 455 ANNALS AM. ACAD. POL. & SOC. SCI. 120, 120–37 (1981); Patrick W. O'Carroll et al., *Preventing Homicide: An Evaluation of the Efficacy of a Detroit Gun Ordinance,* 81 AM. J. PUB. HEALTH 576 (1991).

46. Lawrence W. Sherman et al., *The Kansas City Gun Experiment,* NATIONAL INSTITUTE OF JUSTICE RESEARCH IN BRIEF (Jan. 1995). Sherman and associates note that about 20 percent of the seized firearms were legally carried.

47. ALASKA STAT. §§ 18.65.700-8.65.720 (1994); IDAHO CODE § 18-3302 (1993); MONT. CODE ANN. § 45-8-321 (1993); WYO. STAT. § 6-8-104 (1994).

48. ARIZ. REV. STAT. ANN. § 13-3112 (1994); TENN CODE ANN. § 39-17-1315 (1994).

49. Roger Worthington, *Support Mounting for Concealed Guns,* CHI. TRIB., Mar. 6, 1995, at A1.

50. Sam Howe Verhovek, *States Seek to Let Citizens Carry Concealed Weapons,* N.Y. TIMES, Mar. 6, 1995, at A1.

51. *See* Mark H. Moore, *The Bird in Hand: A Feasible Strategy for Gun Control,* 2 J. POL'Y ANALYSIS & MGMT. 185 (11983); Samuel Walker, SENSE AND NONSENSE ABOUT CRIME: A POLICY GUIDE 179–198 (2d ed. 1989).

Reprinted from: David McDowall, Colin Loftin, and Brian Wiersema, "Easing Concealed Firearms Laws: Effects on Homicide in Three States." *Journal of Criminal Law & Criminology,* Vol. 86, No. 1, pp. 193–206. Copyright © 1995 by Northwestern University School of Law. Reprinted by permission. ✦

4

Firearms Costs, Firearms Benefits, and the Limits of Knowledge

Daniel D. Polsby

America's intensifying dismay about violent crime has become so pervasive that one may well affirm that there is something of a "national crime crisis." Yet there is something of a puzzle as well. Overall crime rates in the United States have been falling for nearly twenty years. Violent crime, declining on a national basis for the last three years, has not changed dramatically since 1980, especially in comparison to the startling run-up in serious crime that coincided with the maturation of the post-war birth cohort. The homicide rate has fluctuated to some extent, but despite recent increases it is still below the levels of the late 1970s and indeed, below the rates recorded through most of the 1920s.

To some extent the growth of public apprehension concerning violent crime can be explained by its cumulative nature: "[w]e experience the crime wave not as separate moments in time but as one long descending night."[1] When serious crime touches oneself or one's family, it is an event that is more or less present throughout one's life. The direction of crime rates should be less important, therefore, than changes in the number of people whose lives have been touched by crime. This number may constantly increase through a generation or more though the crime rate falls. It should be obvious, however, that cumulative enlargement of the circle of people who have been victimized by crime can be at best an incomplete explanation for the change in public attitude that is taking place. Public attitudes about crime have changed much more rapidly than the size of its population of victims. "The crime crisis" is a crisis of confidence in the ability of the public sector to address the crime problem constructively. As such it is very much a part of the tide of skepticism about the role of government that has been an expanding feature of partisan political discourse in recent years. Liberalized carry concealed laws are essentially a response to intensifying doubt about the capacity of government—the police, the court, and the corrections system—to deliver adequate levels of public or personal security. Serious questions remain, however, concerning the ability of private sector practices to deliver the goods where the public sector has failed.

Because the techniques of social science are clumsy, the information generated is often nebulous and hard to interpret. Seldom do social researchers have the luxury enjoyed by Rutherford or Michaelson, of performing a crucial experiment and then proclaiming that a definite increment in human understanding has been attained. Social scientists must sort through literatures filled with hints and intimations in order to get an idea of what is definitely known, and even then gains in knowledge are most often of the null variety, as we fail to find good evidence to support a hypothesis. The problem is ingrained in firearms research, because few if any criminologists believe that guns are the sole factor promoting anti-social behavior. It is not guns themselves, but guns plus additional variables, that lead to trouble. Getting much beyond that generality has been frustrating, and has often seemed something akin to biologists investigating microbes with binoculars. Firearms effects on crime rates—what good do guns do and what harm do they do—seem to be at most quite marginal, and of course available investigative techniques are of seriously limited power. Still, the game is worth the candle if undertaken with proper circumspection, for though accessions to knowledge from any given study may be small, the matter ultimately under scrutiny, that of personal and collective security, is of perennial concern.

In recent years a number of states, including Alaska, Arizona, Florida, Georgia, Idaho, Mississippi, Montana, Oregon, Pennsylvania, Tennessee, Texas, Virginia, West Virginia, and Wyoming, have relaxed their laws regulating civilians' carrying of concealed firearms, thus joining Connecticut, Indiana, Vermont, and Washington in adopting regimes significantly more permissive than those typical in the rest of the country. A number of other states currently have similar modifications under consideration. The two questions that these amendments beg—and indeed that they may eventually help to answer—are: (1) whether widely permitted civilian handgun carriage risks turning every argument between strangers into a wild west shoot-'em-up, or, conversely; (2) whether increasing the prevalence of concealed handguns drives the crime rate down. These are the questions David McDowall, Colin Loftin, and Brian Wiersema seek to measure with interrupted time series analysis, looking at the experience in the largest urban areas of Florida (Miami, Jacksonville, and Tampa), Mississippi (Jackson) and Oregon (Portland). What they found was statistically significant enlargements in firearms homicides in three of the five cities and insignificant changes in Portland and Miami.

In order properly to evaluate the findings of studies like this one, it is useful to bear in mind the theoretical reasons that might be adduced either to believe or to doubt whether liberalizing civilian access to firearms actually will enhance either the general security of the public or (what is a distinct question) the private security of the person who arms himself. The argument in favor of liberalized gun laws would point to their usefulness as a means of deterring attackers. There is no *a priori* reason to believe that firearms should be any less useful to civilians, at least those properly trained to use them, than to police officers. Open carrying of a

side arm tends to create a private security good (i.e., by "hardening" a particular target), whereas concealed carrying, if it is believed to be reasonably widespread, should tend to create a public security good because it will not be evident to a predator which potential victims or bystanders might have the means to resist attack.

There are also theoretical reasons for skepticism. One is that if an argument blows up between two people, resort to a handgun would confer what is sometimes called a "first mover" advantage. Hostile confrontations between latent antagonists, each of whom estimates that the other is (with some probability) armed, may catastrophically degenerate into gunplay as each recognizes the advantage of beating the other to the draw and the detriment of being beaten. Environments in which "first movers" possess a strategic edge—what in international arms reductions talks would be called a "first strike capability," are well understood to be intrinsically unstable.[2] Another theoretical reason that points in the same direction was suggested separately by Frank Zimring[3] and Philip Cook[4], who explained why higher levels of civilian armaments (what is called in jargon "gun density") would be associated with higher levels of homicide. This theory is based on the observation that many homicidal assaults are not accompanied by a specific intention to kill but rather are mercurial outbursts whose lethality will depend on the virulence of the weapons at hand. Guns are much more lethal, wound for wound, than other weapons.[5] When the ratio of firearms to non-firearms weapons increases, one should expect to see increases in the rate of homicide, and conversely, holding all else constant.

McDowall, Loftin, and Wiersema do not actually test the Zimring-Cook hypothesis, because their study focuses on the relationship between the liberalization of carry concealed weapons laws and, not murder rates, but firearms murder rates. Hence, their study does not measure the size of the margin in which homicidally tending persons will substitute non-firearms weapons when firearms become more difficult to get. But it does reach conclusions consistent with those in a number of studies over the past decade that find connections between firearms laws and rates of homicide and suicide. The most widely publicized contributions have appeared in the *New England Journal of Medicine,* authored by John Sloan and collaborators,[6] Arthur Kellermann and collaborators,[7] and Loftin, McDowall, and Wiersema themselves.[8] Taken together, these papers have affected to establish not only that restricting civilian access to firearms saves lives (i.e., is a sound public health measure analogous to abating a disease vector from the environment), but also—a special theme of Dr. Kellermann's—that firearms do not increase the personal security of those who possess them but, on the contrary, actually constitute a "risk factor" for becoming a homicide victim. Such results have received wide media coverage and have considerably gratified those who disdain firearms, the "gun culture," and the people and artifacts taken to be associated with them. However, the actual results of this research look far more modest if one actually reads the text of the monographs rather than the many press notices that accompanied their publication. As a threshold point, it is seriously debatable whether either the Sloan or the Kellermann results should be credited at all, because the data on which their work rests was neither deposited with the *New England Journal* nor otherwise made available to independent researchers.[9]

Even if one takes the papers at face value, however, they do not make a trustworthy case either for the Kellermann et al. "victimization-risk factor" hypothesis or for the Sloan et al. "firearms density relates to homicide" hypothesis. Kellermann et al. should not have been surprised to find that homicide victims are armed in disproportionate numbers: a large and growing proportion of victims are criminals themselves;[10] it is rational (if not usually legal) for people who might be embarrassed to call upon official police services to arm themselves, especially if, as is true of the narcotics *demi-monde,* the risk of being killed by competitors, creditors and others in the business are great[11] and no doubt known to be great. It is unpersuasive to maintain that homicide victimization follows handgun ownership in a causal sequence, as though possession of a weapon could somehow magnetize murderers to ones' doorstoop. Sloan et al. made a great deal out of differences in firearms murder and suicide rates in the assertedly matched cities of Seattle, Washington, with its relatively slack gun control laws, and Vancouver, B.C., with its relatively strict laws. Among several important questions discounted by this methodology is whether and to what extent the state of the law is a satisfactory proxy for the actual density of firearms. There are, of course, large conceptual and practical distinctions between "how has the law changed" and "how has gun-possession behavior changed." The second of these questions cannot be answered by assumption rather than with data. At least one researcher, moreover, has expressed doubts that the assumption is correct.[12]

It is noteworthy that the authors of *Concealed Firearms Laws* stop short of making the claim that relaxing concealed carry laws "will" lead to higher rates of firearms homicides. They do, however, end their paper with a warning against repealing restrictive carry concealed laws. The benefit of this form of gun control is discretely characterized as the weaker of two conclusions that emerge from the analysis (the stronger being that liberalized concealed carry laws do not have a measurable crime-fighting effect), but the result can hardly be thought a strong foundation upon which to build public policy.

The issue, in brief, is what is called the specification problem, a chronic pitfall of time series studies. It is often difficult to know how to interpret findings when the direction taken by a dependent variable (e.g., the homicide rate) exhibits great sensitivity to the time period selected for examination.[13] McDowall, Loftin, and Wiersema's own previous work on the 1976 District of Columbia gun control law illustrates the objection clearly.[14] The authors' conclusion there—that the gun control law prevented an average of forty-seven deaths per year from homicides and suicides—seems doubtful because not only did they fail to give a measure of firearms density that was independent of the ordinance itself, but, to their professed surprise, the numbers seemed to them to indicate that the law had operated virtually instantaneously to suppress the rate of homicides by firearms. In other words, their study finds a beneficial effect from simply implementing the law, that shows up in the homicide statistics before it could possibly have had an appreciable effect on the actual distribution of firearms in the jurisdiction. It is not clear why this should be the case, but the effect is plain to see in the data.[15]

Or is it? In the D.C. study, for example, the authors looked at a number of years in which homicides and suicides by firearms were generally declining. If different periods had been selected for measurement—the D.C. study stopped in 1988—it would have been necessary to explain the long-term association between restrictive gun control laws and *increased* homicide rates as the District's numbers, both for homicide and firearms homicide, climbed steadily higher in the later 1980's. Currently these rates much exceed those in any state notwithstanding the District's more stringent gun control laws.[16] Or, had one chosen to measure firearms homicides from mid-1974 through mid-1980— a period in which the rates were trending lower (though with plenty of month to month variance)—it might have seemed more natural to associate the decline in the murder rate with some event more nearly coincident with its beginning—for example, the resignation of President Nixon or the election of the 94th Congress—rather than with a variable like the gun control law, that commenced some two years after the decline in the murder rate had begun. The null hypothesis actually fits the facts rather exactly: the murder rate in a given jurisdiction and the state of its statute law relating to firearms possession have little or nothing to do with one another.

"Easing Concealed Firearms Laws" exhibits specification difficulties similar to those of the earlier effort. For example, in four of the five cities studied, 1973 was used as the baseline for beginning the study, but in Miami, 1983 was used as the baseline because "of an unusually sharp increase in homicide rates in May 1980 after an influx of Cuban refugees. In late 1982 the rates appeared to stabilize."[17] Had Miami been treated uniformly with the other jurisdictions studied rather than given its own time period, evidently it would have exhibited a statistically significant *decrease* in homicides instead of no significant change. The authors might justify this special treatment as an appropriate effort at noise reduction in the data, but because the outcome in this sort of inquiry is so sensitive to changes in the time period being studied, the exercise is bound to awaken qualms in the minds of skeptics, and to further weaken a conclusion that the authors concede to be weak to begin with. This is not at all meant as a reproach to the authors, but rather a cautionary appeal to those unaccustomed to the limitations of this kind of research about the quality of information that it is capable of generating.[18] It is often difficult to tell the difference between a spurious and a meaningful association among data.

There is, however, at least one reason that is not indwelling in methodology to be restrained about basing policy conclusions on "Easing Concealed Firearms Laws." The paper selects for study three cities in Florida—but why so? The change in the concealed carry law, after all, was statewide, and during the period studied, the murder rate for the state as a whole declined.[19] If it increased somewhat in two of the state's most populous cities and held constant in a third, it must have decreased considerably elsewhere in the state. Is it the case that concealed carry laws "caused" matters to get worse in some places while "causing" them to get better in others? Here one must punt. It is not impossible for one and the same variable to produce a certain effect in some circumstances and the opposite effect in other circumstances. But, it is just as plausible to think that the independent variable (that is, the change in the state's concealed carry law) was actually "causing" nothing as to think that it was causing both of two antithetical effects at once.

There is one quite startling result from the Florida experience that is given little credence by the authors but that deserves some notice. It appears that not a single one of the homicides studied by McDowall, Loftin, and Wiersema was committed by someone who had obtained concealed carry permits under liberalized laws but would have been denied such permits under prior law. In other words, the authors concede that the increase in the population entitled to carry concealed did not contribute directly to *any* of the excess firearms mortality found by the study. In that case, then, why was there any increased killing at all? *Easing Concealed Firearms Laws* proposes that "greater tolerance for legal carrying may increase levels of illegal carrying as well. For example, criminals have more reason to carry firearms—and to use them—when their victims might be armed."[20]

Possibly so—but not obviously so. Indeed, the authors' reasoning points to the far-fetched conclusion that legal carrying of firearms by police officers would increase illegal carrying by criminals. It also implies that increasing the police presence on the streets would lead to higher levels of firearms crime. Surely not. In principle, the expected value of the sort of street crime that is facilitated by brandishing a firearm should decrease as the chances of being shot by a victim, a Good Samaritan or a police officer, increases. The use of a firearm confers a decisive tactical advantage on a criminal predator whether his victim is armed or not, but from the predator's point of view, use of a firearm would undoubtedly have greater net utility in a world in which he had the only gun than it would in a world where some potential targets were secretly armed. Increasing the chances that a predator may encounter armed prey—or may have to deal with an armed Good Samaritan—might very well diminish the value of a firearm to him rather than increase it.

When discussing the effects of concealed carry laws, one should not overlook the evident fact that such laws are capable of putting the Zimring-Cook hypothesis to a practical test. This hypothesis is undoubtedly the most important conjecture in the literature connecting increasing firearms availability with exacerbated rates of mortality from interpersonal violence. Indeed, precisely because the Zimring-Cook argument is a co-

gent one, it calls for explanation why it is not borne out more convincingly in the data. One would certainly expect that legalizing concealed carriage would increase by some amount—probably a large amount—the number of people who actually do carry firearms on their persons in public. A number of states have had permissive concealed carry laws for several years now, and hundreds of thousands of people have applied for and received legal authority to carry guns in these jurisdictions. There must certainly be, in a sample so large over a period so long, many hundreds of cases (and indeed, many tens of thousands) where people legally carrying guns got drunk, lost their tempers, were in traffic accidents, had domestic quarrels, and in short, experienced all of the psychological *sturm und drang* which modern life is capable of dishing out—yet so far as a diligent Nexus search discloses, there seems to be not a single case, anywhere in the country, of someone who was legally carrying a concealed handgun using that weapon in a criminal homicide. Thus, the best direct evidence currently available that bears on the Zimring-Cook hypothesis seems to be inconsistent with it.

Perhaps this experience points to nothing more exciting than the fact that the most extreme categories of social violence are still quite rare in the general population. On the other hand, more interesting game may be afoot. Suppose, counterbalancing the Zimring-Cook effect, there were something that might be called the Robert Heinlein effect, after the science-fiction author who coined the aphorism "an armed society is a polite society."[21] There are plenty of historical examples,[22] and a sophisticated theory to organize them,[23] that demonstrate the ability of heavily armed populations to live together in peace.[24] Furthermore, what if there were also something that might be called the Gary Kleck effect—the principle that while firearms wounds are more serious than those inflicted by other weapons, hostile confrontations that are mediated by firearms are less likely to lead to woundings in the first place—true, whether the person with a gun is a predator or a defender. In this case, the extra lethality of firearms wounds might be negated by the fact that fewer wounds were inflicted in the first place.[25]

The proposition that private firearms may possess some such compensating utility has provoked massive public controversy in recent years. This comes as a result of the fact that the program of the American gun control movement, to restrict private firearms to recreational activities and de-legitimatize them as a means of self-defense, will seem misguided. It is not too grandiose to claim that if one could verify the compensating utility hypothesis, or falsify it, one would possess the *passe-partout* to national firearms policy. On the firing line of this controversy Kleck and his co-author Marc Gertz find that privately owned firearms are used in as many as two and one-half million annual instances of lawful self defense. This estimate is twenty or thirty times higher than the figure given by the Justice Department's National Household Victimization Survey, which for most purposes is considered to be the best available measure of American crime statistics. Which estimate is the better? Kleck and Gertz's argument against too heavy a reliance on survey numbers is sensible enough: in a world in which defending oneself and one's property is increasingly stigmatized as barbaric—if not tortuous or criminal—there is good reason to suppose that survey respondents might not account for themselves honestly, especially not to a government auditor.

To some extent it is an inherent limitation of survey research that one can never be sure that self-reported instances of using firearms in defense of self or property have been correctly or even defensibly tallied by respondents. Nor can one be certain of how many correctly self-reported cases involve criminals defending their contraband inventory from other criminals.[26] Nor can we be confident that cases in which some sort of self defense might be privileged were also cases in which the use of a firearm would be sanctioned.[27] Kleck and Gertz have made every effort to design their survey around the resulting problems, but a more fundamental objection to their project remains. Even if such survey research instruments could be made perfect—so that every respondent ac-

curately self-reported necessitous defensive firearms use—it is questionable what information one would have acquired. It is far from evident that counting self-defensive uses of firearms is a meritorious index of private firearms' crime-suppressive utility. Surely the real question is how much predatory behavior is discouraged assuming a given diffusion of private firearms. The focus of concern should not be the number of times a firearm was displayed, let alone how often one was discharged, and certainly not how often someone was wounded or killed. What one should really want to know is the number of times overt threats were made unnecessary because the existing distribution of firearms set up an implicit threat potent enough to make explicit threats unnecessary.[28] In other words, one must ask what distribution of private arms is optimal in society. Of course this question presents variables one cannot count (e.g., how many times did a burglary or a rape or a murder not-happen), and asks one to value these non-events in relation to how money might be invested alternatively in firearms in order to produce comparable levels of personal security. As no one can possibly perform this calculation, abstruse even if it were not beset with unknowns, one is consigned to trying to count instances in which "good guys" used guns to run off "bad guys" who were threatening them unlawfully. One is reminded here of that ancient joke about the man who lost his keys in a dark alley but looked for them under a lamp post because there the light was better.

The connection between the data concerning the dispersion of firearms on the one hand, and the homicide statistics on the other is strikingly irregular. For example, we know that firearms ownership correlates positively with household income,[29] and recent figures from a survey of Chicago and its suburbs show a marked inverse correlation between the density of handgun ownership in a given neighborhood and the rates of homicide and other serious crimes.[30] To generalize about the American population as a whole, homicide has been trending downward over the past decade or so;[31] the rebound of the homicide rate to its very high, later-1970's level of nine or greater in 100,000 looks to be essentially explainable by the rapid increase in rates of both commission and victimization of homicide among populations of urban, African-American, teenage boys. It is not widely appreciated that this spike in the statistics dates only from the mid-1980's and is not at all associated either with the relaxation of firearms regulation laws or with increases in the supply or practical availability of firearms. Something changed around 1984 or 1985—but what? Alfred Blumstein pins the rap just where it chiefly belongs, namely, on changes in the retail market for drugs and in law enforcement efforts to control the drug market. Not only did the bull market for crack cocaine greatly multiply the number of illegal retail transactions that occurred (this being the point in the distribution chain that is most vulnerable to police intervention), but it also seems to have involved a new and younger class of distributors, taking advantage, perhaps, of the relative lenity of the juvenile justice system.[32] Juveniles' debut in this marketplace demanded a gun for protection of self, remittances, and inventory, and for sustaining a reputation that would facilitate treating one's elders on terms of proper respect.[33] To this parvenu class of criminals, the economic opportunities in the cocaine market were perceived to be greater, and may actually have been greater, than those that were available in the straight world, notwithstanding the enormous risks to life, limb, and liberty that resulted.[34]

With respect to the firearms side of this problem, it cannot be emphasized too strongly that *one is dealing with a demand-led rather than a supply-led phenomenon*—young men *demanding* guns as a means of self defense and self-realization. These young men are not merely using guns because large numbers of them are floating around, as mayors and police chiefs insinuate when they tell reporters that "there are too many guns out there." Recognizing this problem as a demand-side situation predicts the limited usefulness (if not futility) of public policies that seek to "dry up" the supply of guns. The most ludicrous policies of this type are "turn-in-your-gun days" or rules that prohibit police departments from selling surplus weapons. But many kinds of regulatory interventions that place burdens on legal markets embrace the same faulty premise.

Nevertheless, optimists remain who believe that supply-reduction techniques might hold the key to the reduction of gun violence. Among these people, none is more incorrigibly optimistic than Philip Cook. Along with his collaborators Stephanie Molliconi and Thomas Cole, Cook concedes the difficulties of trying to regulate the possession and use of the two-hundred-plus million firearms already in place in the United States. He reasons that because guns used in crimes will tend to have been recently acquired, "[a]n effective transfer-regulating scheme that prevents guns from going to dangerous people would be nearly as successful [in suppressing the homicide rate] as a much more intrusive scheme targeted at current gun owners."[35]

Indeed, this premise is almost tautologically true, but the trick is: how does one successfully regulate a market for a commodity for which there exist no satisfactory substitutes and which is demanded by people whose disposition to comply with the law is less than that of average citizens, and whose willingness to take risks is greater? Despite the hopefulness of Cook et al. on this score, it is by no means clear that introducing additional restrictions into (currently legal) firearms markets—cutting down on sales through classified ads or gun shows or the like—will have much effect disarming those prone to firearms abuse. For illustration: it has been widely noticed that the effectiveness of local gun control laws can be defeated by gun runners, who load up on guns in low regulation jurisdictions and sell them—illegally—in high regulation jurisdictions. Several years ago it was widely noticed that many of the guns seized from criminals by Washington, D.C. police had originally been procured in Virginia. Public indignation led to Virginia enacting a law that would allow only one gun per month to be purchased legally by a given individual.[36]

This exercise damaged the Capital's illicit gun market little if at all; the gun runners simply moved a few states south, to Georgia, where no such rationing is practiced. Of course it is easy to turn this observation into a plea for Georgia now to do something (which would move the action to Texas or Arkansas) and thence into a polemic for a national firearms law; but that sort of twist in the argument tends to obscure the source of the difficulty, which does not lie in the disuniformities or inadequacies of various states' firearms laws but in the fundamental economics of the crime business. Of course gun runners will seek the least cost and most convenient source of supply, whatever it may be, legal markets, if available, but if they cannot deliver what is demanded, the turn to illegal markets, of smuggled guns or guns manufactured in cottage industry, is a simple operation. The acquisition behavior of illicit retail customers should be discouraged modestly at best by piling costs on gun runners. These customers are seeking to invest in capital plant for which there exist no ready substitutes. Licit buyers, on the other hand, usually are shopping for items of personal consumption, for which a number of obvious substitutes (e.g., archery; B-B guns; and for that matter, going to the movies) evidently exist. The implication of this situation, though usually ignored, is very important: *The price sensitivity of firearms buyers will diminish as their motive for owning a firearm becomes more sinister. The price sensitivity of buyers will increase as their motive for owning a firearm becomes more innocuous.*

The expectation that the sorts of market interventions described by Cook et al. would have a beneficial effect on the homicide rate embeds the assumption of monotonicity, that is, that there are constant returns (in the form of lowered homicide rates) to reductions in the number of firearms in private hands. Those who in any degree credit the possibility of Heinlein or Kleck effects operating, however, and who understand the implication of the distinction between "firearm as capital" and "firearm as toy," will regard this assumption as rather naive. Such students of the problem will consider the question of how firearms are distributed in society as much more important than how many there are. They will also reject as inherently

counter-productive efforts to adopt policies that aim at reducing the number of arms in the hands of criminals by imposing regulatory costs in licit markets.[37]

Notes

*Kirkland & Ellis Professor of Law, Northwestern University. Grateful acknowledgement is made to the Kirkland & Ellis Research Fund and the William M. Trumbull Research Fund, each of which partly subsidized the preparation of this paper. The research assistance of James K. Fitzpatrick, M.D., is also acknowledged with thanks. None of the above are to be held responsible for any of the ideas or attempted ideas expressed herein.

1. Adam Walinsky, *The Crisis of Public Order,* 276 ATLANTIC MONTHLY, July 1995, at 41, 44.

2. Jerome H. Kahan, SECURITY IN THE NUCLEAR AGE 273 (1975); Herman Kahn, ON THERMONUCLEAR WAR (1969); Herman Kahn, THINKING ABOUT THE UNTHINKABLE IN THE 1980's (1984); Thomas C. Schelling, THE STRATEGY OF CONFLICT 232 (1960); Thomas C. Schelling, ARMS AND INFLUENCE 224–25 (1966); Wolfgang K. H. Panofsky, *The Mutual Hostage Relationship Between America and Russia,* 52 FOREIGN AFFAIRS 109 (1973); Albert Wohlstetter, *The Delicate Balance of Terror,* 37 FOREIGN AFFAIRS 211 (1959).

3. Frank Zimring, *Is Gun Control Likely to Reduce Violent Killings?,* 35 U. CHI. L. REV. 721, 735 (1968).

4. Philip Cook, *The Technology of Personal Violence,* 14 CRIME & JUST. 1, 13 (1991).

5. Gary Kleck, POINT BLANK: GUNS AND VIOLENCE IN AMERICA 164 (1991).

6. John H. Sloan et al., *Firearm Regulation and Rates of Suicide,* 322 NEW ENG. J. MED. 369, 373 (1990); John H. Sloan et al., *Handgun Regulations, Crime, Assaults, and Homicide: A Tale of Two Cities,* 319 NEW ENG. J. MED. 1256, 1261 (1988).

7. Arthur L. Kellermann et al., *Gun Ownership as a Risk Factor for Homicide in the Home,* 329 NEW ENG. J. MED. 1084, 1090 (1993); Arthur L. Kellermann & Donald T. Reay, *Protection or Peril?: An Analysis of Firearm-Related Deaths in the Home,* 314 NEW ENG. J. MED. 1557, 1559 (1986).

8. Colin Loftin et al., *Effects of Restrictive Licensing of Handguns on Homicide and Suicide in the District of Columbia*, 325 NEW ENG. J. MED. 1615, 1620 (1991).

9. Brandon Centerwall notes that Sloan has not made his data available. Brandon Centerwall, *Homicide and the Prevalence of Handguns: Canada and the United States, 1976-1980*, 134 AM. J. EPIDEMIOLOGY 1245, 1246 (1991). Professor Henry Schaeffer of the North Carolina State University Genetics Department made a telephone request and Professor Lawrence Southwick of the SUNY-Buffalo School of Management Sciences a written request to Dr. Kellermann to inspect the data on which his 1993 study was based. Neither was honored.

10. Chicago Police Department reports show that the percentage of Chicago homicide victims with police records has been as high as 65 percent in recent individual years. *See, e.g.,* DETECTIVE DIVISION, CHICAGO POLICE DEPARTMENT, MURDER ANALYSIS 23 (1992) (65.53 percent of homicide victims in 1992 had criminal records). In the early 1970s, the corresponding figures were 40–45 percent. *Id.*

11. Peter Reuter & Mark A. R. Kleiman, *Risks and Prices: An Economic Analysis of Drug Enforcement*, 7 CRIME & JUST.: ANN. REV. RES. 289, 305 (1986).

12. Robert J. Mundt, *Gun Control and Rates of Firearms Violence in Canada and the United States*, 32 CAN. J. CRIMINOLOGY 137, 137–54 (1990).

13. Gary Kleck et al., The Emperor has No Clothes: Using Interrupted Times Series Design to Evaluate Social Policy Impact (Oct. 30, 1993) (unpublished manuscript, presented to the American Society of Criminology).

14. Loftin et al., *supra* note 8, at 1619–20.

15. Glenn Pierce and William Bowers found something similar in their study of Massachusetts' gun control law, and proposed that some sort of "announcement effect" may have been at work to produce this result. Glenn Pierce & William Bowers, *The Bartley-Fox gun Law's Short-Term Impact on Crime in Boston*, 455 ANNALS AM. ACAD. POL. & SOC. SCI. 120, 130–31 (1981). As this proffer amounts to the proposition that publicity about the new gun law discouraged murderers from shooting people, a bit of skepticism is warranted.

16. The authors believe that the growth of the crack cocaine market and other intervening variables eventually overcame the benefits of the gun control law, and of course, no one can say for sure if matters would have been worse had the District's gun control law not been toughened. The fact remains, however, that neither crack cocaine nor other social ills were unique to Washington, D.C.: what was unique was its strict gun control law and a homicide rate that in recent years has been as high as 80 in 100,000 of population per year— a rate nearly five times higher than that in the next most-sanguinary American jurisdictions, gun-loving Texas and Louisiana. Loftin et al., *supra* note 8, at 1620.

17. David McDowall et al., *Easing Concealed Firearms Laws: Effects on Homicide in Three States*, 86 J. CRIM L. & CRIMINOLOGY 193, 198 (1995).

18. Claims about what this study demonstrates, many of which are plainly more intrepid than any made by its authors, have received wide currency in the newspapers. Among the 83 mentions of this study in the Nexis data base, for example, was a column by Chicago Sun-Times editorial writer Cindy Richards, bearing the headline: "Legalizing Hidden Guns Will Increase Slaughter." Cindy Richards, *Legalizing Hidden Guns Will Increase Slaughter*, CHI. SUN-TIMES, March 12, 1995, at 36.

19. Clayton E. Cramer & David B. Kopel, *"Shall Issue": The New Wave of Concealed Handgun Permit Laws*, INDEPENDENCE INST. 15 (Oct. 1994) (on file with author).

20. McDowall et al., *supra* note 17, at 196.

21. James P. Pinkerton, *Column Right: Nullification: Wrong in 1832 and in 1995*, L.A. TIMES, October 12, 1995, at 9 (quoting Robert Heinlein).

22. Roger D. McGrath, GUNFIGHTERS, HIGHWAYMEN AND VIGILANTES (1984); Robert Day, *"Sooners" or "Goners," They Were Hell Bent on Grabbing Free Land*, 20 SMITHSONIAN 192, 202 (1989).

23. John Umbeck, *Might Makes Rights: A Theory of the Formation and Initial Distribution of Property Rights*, 19 ECON. INQUIRY 38, 40–46 (1981).

24. Daniel D. Polsby, *Equal Protection*, REASON MAG., Oct. 1993, at 34, 37.

25. Kleck, *supra* note 5, at 163–64.

26. So far as the law is concerned, criminals have just as much right to defend themselves from unlawful force as anyone else, but it seems

safe to suggest that as far as public policy is concerned, this interest of criminals should be lightly regarded. Thought-experimental proof: if the *only* utility of firearms were to allow criminals to use them in lawful self-defense, we should have no difficulty embracing and trying to enforce a universal gun ban because *ex hypothesis*, the only people who would be made worse off thereby would be criminals.

27. Defenders are never privileged to use deadly weapons when it would be reasonable to use non-deadly weapons or none at all. Furthermore, a number of states follow the Model Penal Code rule that certain circumstances require retreat before deadly force may lawfully be used.

28. Some scholars have taken a crack at pondering the imponderable. For example, David Kopel writes:

Only for one category of violent crime, namely, burglary, does the British rate exceed the American rate. Burglary is a more socially destructive crime in Britain because most British burglars attack houses when a victim is present. A 1982 survey found 59 percent of attempted burglaries take place against an occupied home, compared to just 13 percent in the United States. Fear of being shot convinces most American burglars to strike empty targets. [citations omitted.]
David Kopel, THE SAMURAI, THE MOUNTIE AND THE COWBOY 92, 127 (1992).

29. Kleck, *supra* note 5, at 23.

30. Metro Chicago Information Center, *Summary of Neighborhood Crime Perceptions,* in 1991–1995 MCIC METRO SURVEY (1995).

31. *E.g.,* BUREAU OF JUSTICE STATISTICS, UNITED STATES DEPARTMENT OF JUSTICE, SOURCEBOOK OF CRIMINAL JUSTICE STATICS 1993, at 388, figure 3.7 (1994).

32 Jean Rimbach, *Crime Without Punishment— Many Youths See System as "a Joke,"* BERGEN COUNTY REC. (NJ), Feb 2, 1994, at A1.

33. Elijah Anderson, *The Code of the Street,* 273 ATLANTIC MONTHLY, May 1994, at 81.

34. Reuter & Kleiman, *supra* note 11, at 303.

35. Philip Cook et al., *Regulating Gun Markets,* 86 J. CRIM. L. & CRIMINOLOGY 59, 63 (1995).

36. *E.g.,* Rene Sanchez, *Building an Arsenal One Gun at a Time,* WASH. POST, Nov. 3, 1993, at A1; Donald Baker, *Wilder Signs Gun Control Bill,* WASH. POST, Mar. 24, 1993, at C1.

37. Daniel D. Polsby, *The False Promise of Gun Control,* 273 ATLANTIC MONTHLY, Mar. 1994 at 57.

ISSUE III
Intelligence and Crime: Do Those with Less Intelligence Commit More Crime?

Prior to the 1900s, biology played a major role in the explanation of criminal behavior. Many scientists made the claim that crime was the consequence of personal defects such as a person's race, hereditary background, or feeblemindedness. There was also a popular "scientific" belief that body type had an impact on criminality. Body type theories hypothesized that particular physical features (called somatotypes) were predictors of criminality. For example, ectomorphs were persons who were small, frail, and shy; mesomorphs were individuals who were larger and had more aggressive personalities; and endomorphs were persons who were overweight and had a happy-go-lucky personality. It was hypothesized that mesomorphs were the most likely to engage in crime (Williams and McShane 1994).

Over the last three decades, however, less and less emphasis has been placed on the idea that personal defects influence criminality. Instead, scientists today look to other psychological and sociological explanations for criminality. However, there are still a small number of scientists who examine biological influences on crime. Many of these scientists examine the impact of brain dysfunctions, genetic traits, and intelligence on criminality. The insistence that biology is linked with criminality is why the best-selling book, *The Bell Curve*, caused such an uproar among the public and academics.

In their book, Herrnstein and Murray (1994) hypothesize that a person's intelligence is a strong predictor of whether that person will commit crime. They used data obtained from the *National Longitudinal Survey of Youth* (NLSY), which surveyed 12,686 respondents ages 14 to 22. The survey collected information on both intelligence and crime. The authors found that the more "cognitively challenged" a person is, the more likely he or she is to commit crime, fail at school, have children out of wedlock, and be unemployed. They suggest that legislators who develop crime-control policies need to keep in mind that most criminals have a low IQ.

Francis T. Cullen and his colleagues refute the work of Herrnstein and Murray, arguing that while intelligence does have a role in predicting criminality, its impact is relatively small when compared to other factors. To illustrate their point, the authors reanalyze Herrnstein and Murray's data and review prior studies examining the relationship between intelligence and crime. They demonstrate that Herrnstein and Murray's conclusions are misleading and claim that their work is based on ideology rather than on scientific evidence.

References

Williams, Frank and McShane, Marilyn. 1994. *Criminological Theory*. Englewood Cliffs: Prentice Hall.

Herrnstein, Richard J. and Charles Murray. 1994. *The Bell Curve: Intelligence and Class Structure in American Life*. New York: Free Press.

Critical Thinking Questions

1. Does IQ have an impact on criminality? If so, how great is that impact?

2. What factors other than IQ have an influence on criminality?

3. How should criminal justice officials treat those who have a low IQ and have committed a crime?

Internet Websites

Website dedicated to the understanding of genetics and crime. <http://www.crime-times.org/>

Research article on the connection between mental illness and crime. <http://pages.nyu.edu/~er26/toxicmind.html>

Contains links to other sites that focus on biology and crime. <http://www.molbio.princeton.edu/courses/mb427/2000/projects/0011/references1.htm> ✦

5

The Bell Curve

Intelligence and Class Structure in American Life

Richard J. Herrnstein
Charles Murray

Crime

Crime can tear a free society apart, because free societies depend so crucially on faith that the other person will behave decently. As crime grows, society must substitute coercion for cooperation. The first casualty is not just freedom but the bonds that make community life attractive. Yes, it is always possible to buy better locks, stay off the streets after dark, regard every stranger suspiciously, [and] post security guards everywhere, but these are poor substitutes for living in a peaceful and safe neighborhood.

Most Americans think that crime has gotten far too high. But in the ruminations about how the nation has reached this state and what might be done, too little attention has been given to one of the best-documented relationships in the study of crime: As a group, criminals are below average in intelligence.

As with so many . . . other problems . . . , things were not always so bad. Good crime statistics do not go back very far in the United States, but we do not need statistics to remind Americans alive in the 1990s of times when they felt secure walking late at night, alone, even in poor neighborhoods and even in the nation's largest cities. In the mid-1960s, crime took a conspicuous turn for the worse . . . , [particularly, for] the kind of crime that worries most people most vis-

cerally: violent crime, which consists of robbery, murder, aggravated assault, and rape.

. . . From 1950 through 1963, the rate for violent crime was almost flat, followed by an extremely rapid rise from 1964 to 1971, followed by continued increases until the 1980s. The early 1980s saw an interlude in which violent crime decreased noticeably. But the trend-line for 1985–1992 is even steeper than the one for 1963–1980, making it look as if the lull was just that—a brief respite from an increase in violent crime that is now thirty years old.[1]

There is still some argument among the experts about whether these numbers . . . , [which were] drawn from the FBI's *Uniform Crime Reports*, mean what they seem to mean. But the disagreement has limits. Drawing on sophisticated analyses of these numbers, the consensus conclusions are that victimization studies, based on interviews of crime victims and therefore including crimes not reported to the police, indicate that the increase in the total range of crimes since 1973 has not been as great as the official statistics suggest, but that the increase reflected in the official statistics is also real, capturing changes in crimes that people consider serious enough to warrant reporting to the police.[2]

Depraved or Deprived?

The juvenile delinquents in Leonard Bernstein's *West Side Story* tell Officer Krupke that they are "depraved on account of we're deprived," showing an astute grasp of the poles in criminological theory: the psychological and the sociological.[3] Are criminals psychologically distinct? Or are they ordinary people responding to social and economic circumstances?

Theories of criminal behavior were mostly near the sociological pole from the 1950s through the 1970s. Its leading scholars saw criminals as much like the rest of us, except that society earmarks them for a life of criminality. Some of these scholars went further, seeing criminals as free of personal blame, evening up the score with a society that has victimized them. The most radical theorists from the sociological pole argued that the definition of crime was in itself ideological, creating "criminals" of people who were doing nothing more than behaving in ways that the power structure chose to define as deviant. In their more moderate forms, sociological explanations continue to dominate public discourse. Many people take it for granted, for example, that poverty and unemployment cause crime—classic sociological arguments that are distinguished more by their popularity than by evidence.[4]

Theories nearer the psychological pole were more common earlier in the history of criminology and have lately regained acceptance among experts. Here, the emphasis shifts to the characteristics of the offender rather than to his circumstances. The idea is that criminals are distinctive in psychological (perhaps even biological) ways. They are deficient, depending on the particular theory, in conscience or in self-restraint. They lack normal attachment to the mores of their culture, or they are peculiarly indifferent to the feelings or the good opinion of others. They are overendowed with restless energy or with a hunger for adventure or danger. In a term that was in common use throughout the nineteenth and early twentieth centuries, chronic offenders may be suffering from "moral insanity."[5] In other old-fashioned vocabularies, they have been called inhumane, atavistic, demented, monstrous, or bestial—all words that depict certain individuals as something less than human. In their most extreme form, psychological theories say that some people are born criminal, destined by their biological makeup to offend.

We are at neither of these theoretical poles. Like almost all other students of crime, we expect to find explanations from both sociology and psychology. The reason for calling attention to the contrast between the theories is that public discussion has lagged; it remains more nearly stuck at the sociological pole in public discourse than it is among experts. In this chapter, we are interested in the role that cognitive ability plays in creating criminal offenders. This by no means requires us to deny that sociology, economics, and public policy might play an important part in shaping crime rates. On the contrary, we assume that changes in those domains are likely to interact with personal characteristics.

Among the arguments often made against the claim that criminals are psychologically distinctive, two are arguments in principle rather than in fact. We will comment on these two first, because they do not require any extensive review of the factual evidence.

> Argument 1: Crime rates have changed in recent times more than people's cognitive ability or personalities could have. We must therefore find the reason for the rising crime rates in people's changing circumstances.

When crime is changing quickly, it seems hard to blame changing personal characteristics rather than changing social conditions. But bear in mind that personal characteristics need not change everywhere in society for crime's aggregate level in society to change. Consider age, for example, since crime is mainly the business of young people between 15 and 24.[6] When the age distribution of the population shifts toward more people in their peak years for crime, the average level of crime may be expected to rise. Or crime may rise disproportionately if a large bulge in the youthful sector of the population fosters a youth culture that relishes unconventionality over traditional adult values. The exploding crime rate of the 1960s is, for example, partly explained by the baby boomers' reaching adolescence.[7] Or suppose that a style of child rearing sweeps the country, and it turns out that this style of child rearing leads to less control over the behavior of rebellious adolescents. The change in style of child rearing may predictably be followed, fifteen or so years later, by a change in crime rates. If, in short, circumstances tip toward crime, the change will show up most among those with the strongest tendencies to break laws (or the weakest tendencies to obey them).[8] Understanding those tendencies is the business of theories at the psychological pole.

Argument 2: Behavior is criminal only because society says so. There cannot be psychological tendencies to engage in behavior defined so arbitrarily.

This argument, made frequently during the 1960s and 1970s and always more popular among intellectuals than with the general public, is heard most often opposing any suggestion that criminal behavior has biological roots. How can something so arbitrary, say, as not paying one's taxes or driving above a 55 mph speed limit be inherited? the critics ask. Behavior regarding taxes and speed limits certainly cannot be coded in our DNA; perhaps even more elemental behaviors such as robbery and murder cannot either.

Our counterargument goes like this: Instead of crime, consider behavior that is less controversial and even more arbitrary, like playing the violin. A violin is a cultural artifact, no less arbitrary than any other man-made object, and so is the musical scale. Yet few people would argue that the first violinists in the nation's great orchestras are a random sample of the population. The interests, talents, self-discipline, and dedication that it takes to reach their level of accomplishment have roots in individual psychology—quite possibly even in biology. The variation across people in any behavior, however arbitrary, will have such roots. To that we may add that the core crimes represented in the violent crime and property crime indexes— murder, robbery, and assault—are really not so arbitrary, unless the moral codes of human cultures throughout the world may be said to be consistently arbitrary in pretty much the same way throughout recorded human history.

But even if crime is admitted to be a psychological phenomenon, why should intelligence be important? What is the logic that might lead us to expect low intelligence to be more frequently linked with criminal tendencies than high intelligence is?[9]

One chain of reasoning starts from the observation that low intelligence often translates into failure and frustration in school and in the job market. If, for example, people of low intelligence have a hard time finding a job, they might have more reason to commit crimes as a way of making a living. If people of low intelligence have a hard time acquiring status through the ordinary ways, crime might seem like a good alternative route. At the least, their failures in school and at work may foster resentment toward society and its laws.

Perhaps the link between crime and low IQ is even more direct. A lack of foresight, which is often associated with low IQ, raises the attractions of the immediate gains from crime and lowers the strength of the deterrents, which come later (if they come at all). To a person of low intelligence, the threats of apprehension and prison may fade to meaninglessness. They are too abstract, too far in the future, too uncertain.

Low IQ may be part of a broader complex of factors. An appetite for danger, a stronger-than-average hunger for the things that you can get only by stealing if you cannot buy them, an antipathy toward conventionality, an insensitivity to pain or to social ostracism, and a host of derangements of various sorts, combined with low IQ, may set the stage for a criminal career.

Finally, there are moral considerations. Perhaps the ethical principles for not committing crimes are less accessible (or less persuasive) to people of low intelligence. They find it harder to understand why robbing someone is wrong, find it harder to appreciate the values of civil and cooperative social life, and are accordingly less inhibited from acting in ways that are hurtful to other people and to the community at large.

With these preliminaries in mind, let us explore the thesis that, whatever the underlying reasons might be, the people who lapse into criminal behavior are distinguishable from the population at large in their distribution of intelligence.

The Link Between Cognitive Ability and Criminal Behavior: An Overview

The statistical association between crime and cognitive ability has been known since intelligence testing began in earnest. The British physician Charles Goring mentioned a lack of intelligence as one of the distinguishing traits of the prison population that he described in a landmark contribution to modern criminology early in the century.[10] In 1914, H. H. Goddard, an early leader in both modern criminology and the use of intelligence tests, concluded that a large fraction of convicts were intellectually subnormal.[11]

The subsequent history of the study of the link between IQ and crime replays the larger story of intelligence testing, with the main difference being that the attack on the IQ/crime link began earlier than the broader attempt to discredit IQ tests. Even in the 1920s, the link was called into question, for example, by psychologist Carl Murchison, who produced data showing that the prisoners of Leavenworth had a higher mean IQ than that of enlisted men in World War I.[12] Then in 1931, Edwin Sutherland, America's most prominent criminologist, wrote "Mental Deficiency and Crime," an article that effectively put an end to the study of IQ and crime for half a century.[13] Observing (accurately) that the ostensible IQ differences between criminals and the general population were diminishing as testing procedures improved, Sutherland leaped to the conclusion that the remaining differences would disappear altogether as the state of the art improved.

The difference, in fact, did not disappear, but that did not stop criminology from denying the importance of IQ as a predictor of criminal behavior. For decades, criminologists who followed Sutherland argued that the IQ numbers said nothing about a real difference in intelligence between offenders and nonoffenders. They were skeptical about whether the convicts in prisons were truly representative of offenders in general, and they disparaged the tests' validity. Weren't tests just measuring socioeconomic status by other means, and weren't they biased against the people from the lower socioeconomic classes or the minority groups who were most likely to break the law for other reasons? they asked. By the 1960s, the association between intelligence and crime was altogether dismissed in criminology textbooks, and so it remained until recently. By the end of the 1970s, students taking introductory courses in criminology could read in

one widely used textbook that the belief in a correlation between low intelligence and crime "has almost disappeared in recent years as a consequence of more cogent research findings,"[14] or learn from another standard textbook of "the practical abandonment of feeblemindedness as a cause of crime."[15]

It took two of the leading criminologists of another generation, Travis Hirschi and Michael Hindelang, to resurrect the study of IQ and criminality that Sutherland had buried. In their 1977 article, "Intelligence and Delinquency: A Revisionist View," they reviewed many studies that included IQ measures, took into account the potential artifacts, and concluded that juvenile delinquents were in fact characterized by substantially below-average levels of tested intelligence.[16] Hirschi and Hindelang's work took a while to percolate through the academy (the author of the 1982 edition of one of the textbooks quoted above continued to make no mention whatever of IQ),[17] but by the end of the 1980s, most criminologists accepted not just that an IQ gap separates offenders and nonoffenders, but that the gap is genuinely a difference in average intellectual level or, as it is sometimes euphemistically called, "academic competence." Criminology textbooks now routinely report the correlation between crime and intelligence, and although some questions of interpretation are still open, they are narrower than they used to be because the correlation itself is no longer in dispute.[18]

The Size of the IQ Gap

How big is the difference between criminals and the rest of us? Taking the literature as a whole, incarcerated offenders average an IQ of about 92, 8 points below the mean. The population of nonoffenders averages more than 100 points; an informed guess puts the gap between offenders and nonoffenders at about 10 points.[19] More serious or more chronic offenders generally have lower scores than more casual offenders.[20] The eventual relationship between IQ and repeat offending is already presaged in IQ scores taken when the children are 4 years old.[21]

Not only is there a gap in IQ between offenders and nonoffenders, but a disproportionately large fraction of all crime is committed by people toward the low end of the scale of intelligence. For example, in a twenty-year longitudinal study of over five hundred boys in an unidentified Swedish community, 30 percent of all arrests of the men by the age of 30 were of the 6 percent with IQs below 77 (at the age of 10) and 80 percent were of those with IQs below 100.[22] However, it stands to reason (and is supported by the data) that the population of offenders is short of very low-scoring persons—people whose scores are so low that they have trouble mustering the competence to commit most crimes.[23] A sufficiently low IQ is, in addition, usually enough to exempt a person from criminal prosecution.[24]

Do the Unintelligent Ones Commit More Crimes—or Just Get Caught More Often?

Some critics continue to argue that offenders whose IQs we know are unrepresentative of the true criminal population; the smart ones presumably slipped through the net. Surely this is correct to some degree. If intelligence has anything to do with a person's general competence, then it is not implausible that smart criminals get arrested less often because they pick safer crimes or because they execute their crimes more skillfully.[25] But how much of a bias does this introduce into the data? Is there a population of uncaught offenders with high IQs committing large numbers of crimes? The answer seems to be no. The crimes we can trace to the millions of offenders who do pass through the criminal justice system and whose IQs are known account for much of the crime around us, particularly the serious crime. There is no evidence for any other large population of offenders, and barely enough crime left unaccounted for to permit such a population's existence.

In the small amount of data available, the IQs of uncaught offenders are not measurably different from the ones who get caught.[26] Among those who have criminal records, there is still a significant negative correlation between IQ and frequency of offending.[27] Both of these kinds of evidence

imply that differential arrests of people with varying IQs, assuming they exist, are a minor factor in the aggregate data.

Intelligence as a Preventative

Looking at the opposite side of the picture, those who do not commit crimes, it appears that high cognitive ability protects a person from becoming a criminal even if the other precursors are present. One study followed a sample of almost 1,500 boys born in Copenhagen, Denmark, between 1936 and 1938.[28] Sons whose fathers had a prison record were almost six times as likely to have a prison record themselves (by the age of 34–36) as to sons of men who had no police record of any sort. Among these high-risk sons, the ones who had no police record at all had IQ scores one standard deviation higher than the sons who had a police record.[29]

The protective power of elevated intelligence also shows up in a New Zealand study. Boys and girls were divided on the basis of their behavior by the age of 5 into high and low risk for delinquency. High-risk children were more than twice as likely to become delinquent by their mid-teens as low-risk children. The high-risk boys or girls who did not become delinquent were the ones with the higher IQs. This was also true for the low-risk boys and girls: The nondelinquents had higher IQs than the delinquents.[30]

Children growing up in troubled circumstances on Kauai in the Hawaiian chain confirm the pattern. Several hundred children were followed in a longitudinal study for several decades.[31] Some of the children were identified by their second birthday as being statistically "vulnerable" to behavioral disorders or delinquency. These were children suffering from two or more of the following circumstances: they were being raised in troubled or impoverished families; had alcoholic, psychologically disturbed, or unschooled (eight years or less of schooling) parents; or had experienced prenatal or perinatal physiological stress. Two-thirds of these children succumbed to delinquency or other psychological disturbances. But how about the other third, the ones who grew up without becoming delinquents or disturbed psychologically? Prominent among the protective factors were higher intellectual ability scores than the average for the vulnerable group.[32]

The Link Between Cognitive Ability and Criminal Behavior: White Men in the NLSY

In the United States, where crime and race have become so intertwined in the public mind, it is especially instructive to focus on just whites. To simplify matters, we also limit the NLSY sample to males. Crime is still overwhelmingly a man's vice. Among whites in the sample, 83 percent of all persons who admitted to a criminal conviction were male.

Interpreting Self-Report Data

In the 1980 interview wave, the members of the NLSY sample were asked detailed questions about their criminal activity and their involvement with the criminal justice system. These data are known as self-report data, meaning that we have to go on what the respondent says. One obvious advantage of self-reports is that they presumably include information about the crimes of offenders whether or not they have been caught. Another is that they circumvent any biases in the criminal justice system, which, some people argue, contaminate official criminal statistics. But can self-report data be trusted? Criminologists have explored this question for many years, and the answer is yes, but only if the data are treated gingerly. Different racial groups have different response patterns, and these are compounded by differences between the genders.[33] Other issues are discussed in the note.[34]

Our use of the NLSY self-report data sidesteps some of the problems by limiting the analysis to one ethnic group and one gender: white males. Given the remaining problems with self-report data, we will concentrate in this analysis on events that are on the public record (and the respondent knows are on the public record): being stopped by the police, formal charges, and convictions. In doing so, we are following a broad finding in crime research that official contacts with the law enforcement and criminal justice system are

usefully accurate reflections of the underlying level of criminal activity.[35] At the end of the discussion, we show briefly that using self-report data on undetected crimes reinforces the conclusions drawn from the data on detected crimes.

IQ and Types of Criminal Involvement

The typical finding has been that between a third and a half of all juveniles are stopped by police at some time or another (a proportion that has grown over the last few decades) but that 5 to 7 percent of the population account for about half the total number of arrests.[36] In the case of white males in the NLSY, 34 percent admitted having been stopped at some time by the police (for anything other than a minor traffic violation), but only 3 percent of all white males accounted for half of the self-reported "stops."

Something similar applies as we move up the ladder of criminal severity. Only 18 percent of white males had ever formally been charged with an offense, and a little less than 3 percent of them accounted for half the charges. Only 13 percent of white males had ever been convicted of anything, and 2 percent accounted for half of the convictions. Based on these self-reports, a very small minority of white males had serious criminal records while they were in this 15 to 23 age range.

Like studies using all races, the NLSY results for white males show a regular relationship between IQ and criminality. . . . [In particular,] those who reported they had never even been stopped by the police (for anything other than a minor traffic violation) were above average in intelligence, with a mean IQ of 106, and things went downhill from there. Close to a standard deviation separated those who had never been stopped by the police from those who went to prison.

A similar pattern emerges when the criminal involvements are sorted by cognitive classes: Class I, described as very bright, through Class V, described as very dull. Involvement with the criminal justice system rises as IQ falls. Then we reach Class V, with IQs under 75. Class Vs are stopped, charged, and convicted at lower rates than the Class IVs but are sentenced to correctional facilities at rates almost exactly the same rate. We noted earlier that people at the lowest levels of intelligence are likely to be underrepresented in criminal statistics, and so it is in the NLSY. It may be that the offenses of the Class Vs are less frequent but more serious than those of the Class IVs or that they are less competent in getting favorable treatment from the criminal justice system. The data give us no way to tell.

In addition to self-reports, the NLSY provides data on criminal behavior by noting where the person was interviewed. In all the interviews from 1979 to 1990, was the young man ever interviewed in a correctional facility? The odds that a white male had ever been interviewed in jail were fourteen times greater for Class V than for white males anywhere in the top quartile of IQ.

Being incarcerated at the time of the interview signifies not just breaking the law and serving time but also something about the duration of the sentence, which may explain the large increase at the bottom of the ability distribution. The NLSY sample of white males echoes the scientific literature in general in showing a sizable IQ gap between offenders and nonoffenders at each level of involvement with the criminal justice system.

The Role of Socioeconomic Background

We will use both self-reports and whether the interviewee was incarcerated at the time of the interview as measures of criminal behavior. The self-reports are from the NLSY men in 1980, when they were still in their teens or just out of them. It combines reports of misdemeanors, drug offenses, property offenses, and violent offenses. Our definition of criminality here is that the man's description of his own behavior put him in the top decile of frequency of self-reported criminal activity.[37] The other measure is whether the man was ever interviewed while being confined in a correctional facility between 1979 and 1990. . . .

Both measures of criminality have weaknesses but different weaknesses. One relies on self-reports but has the virtue of including uncaught criminality; the other relies on the workings of the criminal justice system

but has the virtue of identifying people who almost certainly have committed serious offenses. For both measures, after controlling for IQ, the men's socioeconomic background had little or nothing to do with crime. In the case of the self-report data, higher socioeconomic status was associated with higher reported crime after controlling for IQ. In the case of incarceration, the role of socioeconomic background was close to nil after controlling for IQ, and statistically insignificant. By either measure of crime, a low IQ was a significant risk factor.

The Role of a Broken Home

When people think about the causes of crime, they usually think not only of the role of juvenile delinquent's age and socioeconomic background but also of what used to be called "broken homes." It is now an inadequate phrase, because many families do not even begin with a married husband and wife, and many broken homes are reconstituted (in some sense) through remarriage. But whatever the specific way in which a home is not intact, the children of such families are usually more likely to get in trouble with the law than children from intact families.[38] This was true for the NLSY white males. An intact family consisting of the biological mother and father was associated with better outcomes for their children than any of the other family arrangements. Was the young man ever stopped by the police? Thirty-two percent of white males from intact families compared to 46 percent of all others. Booked for an offense? Fifteen percent compared to 29 percent. Convicted of an offense? Eleven percent compared to 21 percent. Sentenced to a correctional facility? Two percent compared to 7 percent.

Although family setting had an impact on crime, it did not explain away the predictive power of IQ. For example, a young man from a broken family and an average IQ and socioeconomic background had a 4 percent chance of having been interviewed in jail. Switch his IQ to the 2d centile, and the odds rise to 22 percent. (Switch his socioeconomic background to the 2d centile instead, and the odds rise only from 4 to 5 percent.)

The same conclusions apply to the measure of self-reported crime.

The Role of Education

Scholars have been arguing about the relationship of education to crime and delinquency for many years without settling the issue. The case of the NLSY white males is a classic example. Of those who were ever interviewed in jail, 74 percent had not gotten a high school diploma. None had a college degree. Clearly something about getting seriously involved in crime competes with staying in school. Low IQ is part of that "something" in many cases, but the relationship is so strong that other factors are probably involved—for example, the same youngster who is willing to burglarize a house probably is not the most obedient of pupils; the youngster who commits assaults on the street probably gets in fights on the school grounds; the youngster who is undeterred by the prospect of jail time probably is not much motivated by the prospect of getting a high school degree; and so forth. Does high school dropout actually cause the subsequent crime? Many people assumed so until Delbert Elliott and Harwin Voss published a study in 1974 that concluded the opposite: Crime diminished after school dropout.[39] Since then, everyone has agreed that eventual dropouts tend to have high levels of criminal activity while they are in school, but disputes remain about whether the rates fall or rise after the dropout occurs.[40]

For our purposes, it makes little sense to examine the continuing role of IQ in our usual educational samples when the action is so conspicuously concentrated among those who fall neither in the high school nor the college graduate samples. Running our standard analysis on white males who did not get a high school diploma did not shed much more light on the matter.[41] Given the restriction of range in the sample (the mean IQ of the white male dropout sample was 91, with a standard deviation of only 12.5), not much can be concluded from the fact that the ones at the very bottom of the cognitive ability distribution were less likely to report high levels of criminal activity. For these school dropouts, the likelihood of having been interviewed in jail rose as IQ fell, but the relationship was weaker than for the unrestricted sample of white males.

Crime, Cognitive Ability, and Conscience

By now, you will already be anticipating the usual caution: Despite the relationship of low IQ to criminality, the great majority of people with low cognitive ability are law abiding. We will also take this opportunity to reiterate that the increase in crime over the last thirty years (like the increases in illegitimacy and welfare) cannot be attributed to changes in intelligence but rather must be blamed on other factors, which may have put people of low cognitive ability at greater risk than before.

The caveats should not obscure the importance of the relationship of cognitive ability to crime, however. Many people tend to think of criminals as coming from the wrong side of the tracks. They are correct, insofar as that is where people of low cognitive ability disproportionately live. They are also correct insofar as people who live on the right side of the tracks—whether they are rich or just steadily employed working-class people—seldom show up in the nation's prisons. But the assumption that too glibly follows from these observations is that the economic and social disadvantage is in itself the cause of criminal behavior. That is not what the data say, however. In trying to understand how to deal with the crime problem, much of the attention now given to problems of poverty and unemployment should be shifted to another question altogether: coping with cognitive disadvantage. . . .

Notes

1. The proportional increases in property crime tracked more or less with the increases in violent crime until the late 1970s. Since then, property crime has moved within a narrow range and in 1992 was actually lower than it had been ten years earlier. This divergence between violent and property crimes is in itself a potentially significant phenomenon that has yet to be adequately explored.

2. For citations of the extensive literature on this subject, see Chaiken and Chaiken 1983; Wilson and Herrnstein 1985. The official statistics may have understated the increase in these "crimes that people consider serious enough to warrant reporting to the police," insofar as many burglaries, assaults, and street robberies that would have been reported in the 1950s (when there was a reasonable chance that the police would conduct a genuine investigation) are no longer reported in urban areas, where it is taken for granted that they are too minor to compete for limited police resources.

3. A more traditional way to sort the theories is to contrast classical theories, which depict crime as the rational behavior of free agents, based on costs and benefits, with positive theories, which look for the causes of crime in society or in psychological makeup (for discussion of criminological theory, see, for example, Gottfredson and Hirschi 1990; Wilson and Herrnstein 1985). We are distinguishing only among positive theories, because the notion of criminals as rational agents seems to fit few actual criminals and the role of costs and benefits can readily be absorbed by a positive theory of criminal behavior (see Wilson and Herrnstein 1985, Chap. 2). A distinction similar to ours between psychological and sociological theories is one between "psychiatric" and "criminological" theories in Wessely and Taylor 1991.

4. Freeman 1983; Mayer and Jencks 1989; Wilson and Herrnstein 1985, Chaps. 11, 12.

5. Cleckley 1964; Colaizzi 1989.

6. Wilson and Herrnstein 1985.

7. Wilson and Herrnstein 1985.

8. In fact, within criminological theory, the distinction between being disposed to break the law and being disposed to obey it has some resonance, as illustrated in, for example, Gottfredson and Hirschi 1990. This is a fine point of theory, which we cannot elaborate on here.

9. For more extended discussion of the logic of the link between IQ and committing crime, see Gottfredson and Hirschi 1990; Hirschi 1969; Wilson and Herrnstein 1985.

10. Goring 1913.

11. Goddard 1914.

12. Murchison 1926. We know now that this was a peculiarity of a federal prison like Leavenworth, which had relatively few of the run-of-the-mill offenders typical in state prisons.

13. Sutherland 1931.

14. Haskell and Yablonsky 1978, p. 268.

15. Reid 1979, p. 156.

16. Hirschi and Hindelang 1977.

17. Reid 1982.

18. A balanced, recent summary says, "At this juncture it seems reasonable to conclude that the difference [between offenders and nonoffenders in intelligence] is real and not due to any of the possible methodological or confounding factors that have been noted in the literature" (Quay 1987 p. 107ff.).

19. The gap between offenders and nonoffenders is typically larger on verbal than on performance (i.e., nonverbal) intelligence tests (Wilson and Herrnstein 1985). It has been suggested that this is because the essential difference between offenders and nonoffenders is the difference in g; it is well known that verbal scores are more dependent on g than performance scores (Gordon 1987; Jensen and Faulstich 1988). Another, not necessarily inconsistent, interpretation is that verbal intelligence scores do better at measuring the capacity for internalizing the prohibitions that help deter crime in nonoffenders (Wilson and Herrnstein 1985). Multiple offenders, as distinguished from offenders in general, also have significant deficits in logical reasoning ability per se (Reichel and Magnusson 1988). Whatever the reason for these patterns of differences, the methodological implications are clear: The rare study that fails to find much of an association between IQ and offending may have used nonverbal scores or scores that, for one reason or another, minimize individual differences in g.

20. E.g., Blumstein et al. 1985; Denno 1990. National studies of convicts who get rearrested after release also show that those with low levels of education (which are presumably correlated with low test scores) are at higher risk for recidivism (Beck and Chipley 1989).

21. Lipsitt et al. 1990.

22. Reichel and Magnusson 1988.

23. Hirschi 1969; Wilson and Herrnstein 1985.

24. Nicholson and Kugler 1991.

25. The evidence in fact suggests that smart offenders pick crimes with lesser likelihood of arrest and larger payoffs (Wilson and Herrnstein 1985).

26. Moffitt and Silva 1988; Hindelang et al. 1981; Hirschi and Hindelang 1977; Wilson and Herrnstein 1985.

27. Richel and Magnusson 1988.

28. Kandel et al. 1988.

29. In this sample, there was no significant correlation between IQ and socioeconomic status, and IQ remained a significant predictor of offending even after the effects of parental SES and the sons' own level of education were entered as covariates in an analysis of covariance.

30. White et al. 1989.

31. Werner and Smith 1982.

32. Werner 1989; Werner and Smith 1982.

33. The most serious problem is the established and pronounced tendency of black juveniles to underreport offenses (Hindelang 1978, 1981).

34. Not surprisingly, the most serious offenders are the ones who most often underreport their crimes. Serious offenders are also the ones most likely to go uninterviewed in survey research. At the other extreme, minor offenders brag about their criminal exploits. They inflate the real level of "crime" by putting minor incidents (for example, a schoolyard fist fight, which can easily fit the technical definition of "aggravated assault") in the same category with authentically felonious attacks.

    Since we are focusing on the role of intelligence, self-report data pose a special problem, for it has been observed that people of low intelligence are less candid than brighter respondents. This bias would tend to weaken the correlation between IQ and crime in self-report data.

35. The authoritative source on self-report data for juveniles is still Hindelang et al. 1981. See also Hindelang 1978, 1981; Smith and Davidson 1986.

36. Wolfgang, Figlio, and Sellin 1972; Wilson and Herrnstein 1985.

37. This represents the top decile of white males. To use the same index across racial groups is inadvisable because of the different reporting characteristics of whites and blacks.

38. For a review of the literature, see Wilson and Herrnstein 1985.

39. Elliott and Voss 1974.

40. Thornberry et al. 1985 uses the Philadelphia Cohort Study to demonstrate rising crime after dropout for that well-known sample.

41. The sample includes those who got a GED—most of whom had gotten it at the correctional institution in which they were incarcerated at the time of their interview.

6

Crime and the Bell Curve

Lessons from Intelligent Criminology

Francis T. Cullen
Paul Gendreau
G. Roger Jarjoura
John Paul Wright

In the aftermath of the publication of *The Bell Curve: Intelligence and Class Structure in American Life* (Herrnstein and Murray 1994), Charles Murray has remained remarkably calm amid a storm of criticism that has accused him of being stupid about intelligence and, still worse, of giving solace to racists (see, e.g., Jacoby and Glauberman 1995; "Race" 1994). Critics have not read his book (at least not carefully), responds Murray, but if they would, they would learn that the judicious conclusions set forth in *The Bell Curve* are based on hard facts. Murray repeatedly informs interviewers that he simply is being a good social scientist who is conveying unpleasant truths that can be ignored only at the nation's long-term peril (see also DeParle 1994; Murray and Herrnstein 1994).

At least with regard to crime, we claim otherwise; Murray's social science is misleading, and his message is erroneous. He needs a boost in his criminological intelligence. The apparent persuasiveness of *The Bell Curve*, which Murray coauthored with the late Richard Herrnstein, is that it purports to show that IQ has *powerful* and largely *immutable* effects across a range of

behaviors. If "cognitively disadvantaged," a person is going to commit crimes, fail at school, be unemployed, end up on welfare, produce illegitimate kids, and be a lousy citizen. But if these effects do not in fact exist, or if these effects are in fact amenable to reversal, then the foundation on which Herrnstein and Murray's (1994) thesis is built crumbles.

We evaluate *The Bell Curve* only with regard to claims made about crime and, in turn, about crime-related policies. If Herrnstein and Murray are wrong about crime, then their science elsewhere in the book may be equally suspect—a fact other social scientists have attempted to demonstrate (see, e.g., Dorfman 1995; Goldberger and Manski 1995; Hauser 1995; Sternberg 1995a; see also Morin 1995). In any case, crime is an area about which the authors of *The Bell Curve* should have special knowledge. Herrnstein, for example, coauthored (with James Q. Wilson) the widely read *Crime and Human Nature* (Wilson and Herrnstein 1985), whose cover carries the descriptive phrase, "The Definitive Study of the Causes of Crime." Murray wrote about crime in *Losing Ground* (Murray 1984) and in an earlier book (coauthored with Louis A. Cox, Jr.), *Beyond Probation* (Murray and Cox 1979). And both authors of *The Bell Curve* contributed chapters to Wilson and Petersilia's (1995) *Crime*, a volume advertised on the front cover as showing how "twenty-eight leading experts look at the most pressing problem of our time."

We also should note that the initial wave of reviews of *The Bell Curve* primarily criticized Herrnstein and Murray for employing a narrow, outdated conceptualization of "intelligence," for claiming that IQ is difficult to boost, and for implying that African Americans are intellectually inferior (Gould 1994; Jacoby and Glauberman 1995; "Race" 1994). Although valuable, these critiques do not directly address the adequacy of the empirical analyses in *The Bell Curve*. As Hauser (1995) observes, "Many . . . critics have lacked either the time or the expertise to identify more than a few of the factual or scientific errors and distortions in the text" (p. 149). In this regard, our main goal is *not* to repeat existing challenges to *The Bell Curve*—challenges about the nature of IQ that date to the 1970s (Chomsky 1972); see also Neisser, Boodoo, Bouchard, Boykin, Brody, Ceci, Halpern, Loehlin, Perloff, Sternberg, and Urbina 1996)—but rather to take seriously Hauser's admonition to examine the "guts" of Herrnstein and Murray's analysis.

Toward this end, we reanalyze the data on crime reported in *The Bell Curve* and show that the effects of IQ on criminal involvement are, at best, modest. We then supplement this reanalysis by summarizing previous meta-analyses and studies of the predictors of crime. We show, again, that IQ is a weak to modest risk factor in offending and that its criminogenic effects are dwarfed by a range of factors, many of which are amenable to change.

Building on these points, we contend that Herrnstein and Murray's policies to control crime, especially among the cognitively disadvantaged, have virtually no empirical support and, on their face, are certainly preposterous. These policy proposals might be treated as merely amusing—something to provide criminologists with a good laugh—were it not for the fact that the hardback edition of *The Bell Curve* had an early printing of 400,000 copies (Kamin 1995) and was on *The New York Times Book Review's* "Best-Sellers" list for nearly four months. We consider these policy proposals as dangerous not so much because they may be implemented but because they reinforce—persuasively, we must admit—a way of thinking about crime that is seductive, simplistic, and punitive. Indeed, Murray has been called "the most dangerous conservative" (DeParle 1994) precisely because he weaves together citations to research, graphs, and judiciously presented argumentation to convince his audience that he is a "reasonable" social commentator. We believe that it is important to use "intelligent criminology" to deconstruct his "science" and to unmask the ideology underlying *The Bell Curve*.

We proceed to take the additional step of conveying how IQ might be used responsibly in correctional interventions. The role of individual differences as risk factors in offending has mounting empirical support (see e.g., Andrews and Bonta 1994; Caspi, Moffitt, Silva, Stouthamer-Loeber, Krueger, and Schmutte 1994; Farrington 1994, 1995; Gendreau, Little, and Goggin 1996; Loeber and Dishion 1983). We see no reason for criminologists to treat these finds as undesirable, although we understand historically how depictions of offenders as immutably criminal have been missed to justify repressive, social Darwinist policies that acquit the social order of any complicity I crime (cf. Gould 1981). With regard to IQ, we contend that cognitive differences among offenders should not be ignored but rather taken into account when dispensing treatments—a far different perspective from that of Herrnstein and Murray, who dismiss a treatment agenda. We also suggest that criminologists should remain attentive to efforts within psychology to reconceptualize IQ, which in turn may lead to even more constructive methods of delivering effective services to offenders.

Crime and the Bell Curve: A Reassessment

Analysis in *The Bell Curve*

In *The Bell Curve*, Herrnstein and Murray (1994) use data from the National Longitudinal Survey of Youth (NLSY). The NLSY, initiated in 1979, surveyed 12,686 respondents ages 14 to 22 years. The study oversampled minorities and low-income groups; however, with weighted scores, the data provide nationally representative estimates. In 1980, the NLSY added a measure of cognitive ability, the Armed Forces Qualification Test (AFQT). Herrnstein and Murray claim that the AFQT is a psychometrically valid and reliable test that correlates well with standard IQ tests and measures general intelligence (the so-called "g factor").

In their analyses, Herrnstein and Murray standardize the raw scores of the AFQT so that they can be read as typical IQ scores. The authors also employ standardized measures (z scores) of age and socioeconomic status (SES), the two main control variables in their multivariate analyses. Their analyses use weighted estimates and are confined to White males in the NLSY, purportedly to eliminate measurement biases that race and gender might have introduced.

The NLSY contains several measures of crime. In 1980, the respondents were asked to complete a standard 20-item self-report delinquency scale. The sample members also self-reported the extent of their "penetration" into the criminal justice system, that is, whether they had been "stopped by the police but not booked, booked but not convicted, convicted but not incarcerated, [or] sentenced to a correctional facility" (Herrnstein and Murray 1994, p. 246). The NLSY also can determine whether respondents ever were interviewed n jail when the annual NLSY survey was conducted between 1979 and 1990.

Herrnstein and Murray devote a full chapter of *The Bell Curve* to crime. Their general strategy is to show the salience of IQ in crime causation. In using the NLSY data, they first establish that those with lower AFQT scores have higher odds of penetrating the criminal justice system. They then show that even with SES controlled, the IQ-crime relationship holds both for self-reported crime and for being interviewed while in jail; in fact, SES effects are minimal and, if anything, are positive. They also report that being from a "broken home" increases the risk of crime, but it too does not eliminate IQ's criminogenic influence. They offer a convoluted discussion of the "role of education" in which they show that poor educational performance is associated with being interviewed in jail. Strangely, however, how IQ is implicated in the school-crime relationship is not pursued empirically or theoretically (cf. Lynam, Moffit, and Stouthamer-Loeber 1993; Ward and Tittle 1994).

Herrnstein and Murray (1994) conclude the chapter with the reminder of "the importance of the relationship of cognitive ability to crime" (p. 251). Their policy agenda then becomes clear. "Many people," they observe, "tend to think of criminals as coming from the wrong side of the tracks. They are correct insofar as that is where people of low cogni-

tive ability disproportionately live" (p. 251). It follows, they claim, that in dealing "with the crime problem, much of the attention now given to problems of poverty and unemployment should be shifted to another question altogether: coping with cognitive disadvantage" (p. 251).

Reanalysis of the NLSY Data

We attempt to show below that Herrnstein and Murray's (1994) analysis of the NLSY data misleads about the relationship between IQ and crime. In investigating these data, we are prepared, for the sake of argument, to accept their much-contested assumption that general intelligence exists and can be measured through a single IQ score. Furthermore, we are prepared to ignore white-collar crime, a domain of lawlessness peculiarly suited to the cognitive elite. Instead, our goal is to demonstrate that even on their own terms, Herrnstein and Murray's claims about crime are based on questionable science and, as Gardner (1994) points out, furnish a "shaky bridge to policy" (p. 78).

Explained Variation

The existing research suggests that intelligence is a risk factor in juvenile and adult crime (see, e.g., Farrington 1994, 1995; Gendreau, Little, and Goggin 1996). The key issue, however, is whether the *magnitude* of IQ's effects on criminal behavior is small or large. Small effects would discourage making intelligence a major determinant of social policy, whereas large effects would suggest that crime control policies should be reformulated to focus directly on cognitive disadvantage—which, of course, is Herrnstein and Murray's (1994) position.

A common way in which to assess the importance of a theoretical variable (in this case, IQ) is to see how much variation the variable can explain in the dependent variable (in this case, crime). As readers familiar with statistics know, the term R^2 typically is used to measure the amount of explained variation. Herrnstein and Murray do not report the R^2s for their analyses in the text of *The Bell Curve* but instead confine them to an appendix. As several critics note, the amount of variance that IQ explains across many outcomes is weak to modest (see e.g., Gould 1994; Morin 1995; Taylor 1995). Crime is no exception to this pattern.

In Appendix 4 of *The Bell Curve* (Herrnstein and Murray 1994, pp. 620–621), the authors provide the logistic regression analyses for only two measures of crime: being in the top decile on the self-report crime scale and having been interviewed in a correctional facility between 1979 and 1990. With the AFQT score, age, and SES in the equation, the analysis explains 1.5 percent of the variation in self-reported crime and 9.6 percent of the variation in being interviewed in jail (see also Taylor 1995, p. 157).

We are interested in assessing the amount of explained variation in the different measures of crime that could be attributed solely to the AFQT. Therefore, we re-estimate the Herrnstein and Murray models after removing SES.[1] . . . Here we consider criminal involvement as operationalized in five different ways by Herrnstein and Murray. For consistency of interpretation, we report the results of ordinary least squares regression. In the case of non-interval-level dependent variables (i.e., in the top decile of self-reported crimes, ever interviewed in jail, penetration of the criminal justice system), the pseudo R^2s from the appropriate analyses confirmed the results. . . . The results are reported based on both the 1980 and 1990 sample weights.[2]

For the three measures of self-reported crime, less than 1 percent of the variation is explained. Regardless of whether the 1980 or 1990 sample weights are used, the R^2 climbs at most to 2.6 percent for ever interviewed in jail and 3.4 percent for penetration into the criminal justice system (i.e., none to being sentenced to a correctional facility). Again, we would not dismiss these findings on IQ as being unimportant. We question, however, whether explaining less than 4 percent of the variation in crime warrants an 845-page book whose underlying goal ostensibly is to use science to justify dismantling social welfare approaches to crime and other societal problems.[3]

Misspecified Models

As noted, Herrnstein and Murray (1994) seek to establish the causal significance of IQ by showing how AFQT scores are related more strongly to crime than to social class with age controlled in the analysis. Other factors—family structure and education—are considered haphazardly. This methodological approach, which characterizes much of *The Bell Curve*, obviously is flawed. As Massey (1995) observes, "Herrnstein and Murray misspecify their models by failing to include other independent variables that are clearly relevant to the outcomes they are investigating and likely to be confounded with intelligence" (p. 752).

In a normal scientific approach, Herrnstein and Murray would have first identified the known predictors of crime and then sought to demonstrate that IQ could explain variation above and beyond these criminogenic risk factors. The factors are identified in the readily available literature including Herrnstein's own work (Herrnstein 1995; Wilson and Herrnstein 1985). By limiting their analysis primarily to three factors—IQ, SES, and age—they risk misspecifying their model and inflating the effects of IQ (cf. Lynam, Moffitt, and Stouthamer-Loeber 1993). We will return to this issue when we summarize meta-analyses on the predictors of crime, but here we show the limits of their approach using NLSY data.

The NLSY data set is not ideal for studying crime causation because it was not designed to operationalize the major psychological or sociological theories of criminality. For illustrative purposes, however, we more fully specified Herrnstein and Murray's model by including urban-rural residence, family structure (living with mother and father at age 14), frequency of religious participation, internal locus of control (youth reports having little influence over things that happen to him), and a range of items that might be seen as indicators of conventional bonds and attitudes (youth would shoplift if unable to support family, would choose to work if he could live comfortably without working, and expects to be working in five years; highest grade youth would like to complete). Like Herrnstein and Murray (1994), pp. 620–621), we use logistic analysis to assess two crime measures: being in the top decile of self-reported crime and being interviewed in a correctional facility at least once between 1979 and 1990.

. . . The Herrnstein and Murray three-variable model suggests that IQ is significantly related to self-reported crime. In the more fully specified model, however, IQ no longer retains statistical significance. By contrast, a number of social variables have a significant impact on crime. Thus, being in the top decile on the 20-item self-report scale is positively related to urban residence and social class and is negatively related to living with one's father at age 14, frequency of religious participation, commitment to a work ethic, and academic aspirations.[4]

. . . Next, we learn that in the fully specified model, IQ's effects on being interviewed in a correctional facility are reduced but not eliminated. Even so, the crime measure is related negatively to living with one's father at age 14, religious participation, expectations of being able to work, and academic aspirations.

These analyses are not simply an exercise in statistical gymnastics but rather make a telling point: The effects of the sociological variables are not eliminated by IQ and, in fact, outweigh the causal importance of intelligence. We do not dispute that IQ might have indirect effects on crime through some of these social variables (see Lynam et al. 1993; Ward and Tittle 1994), but this remains a possibility that Herrnstein and Murray do not systematically consider. Instead, their analysis pits IQ against a sociological variable, SES, long known to be a weak predictor of crime (Andrews and Bonta 1994; Gendreau, Little, and Goggin 1996; Tittle and Meier 1990; Tittle, Villemez, and Smith 1978). On this basis, they dismiss social welfare interventions and urge that social policy be driven by the overriding reality that people differ in their cognitive abilities.

In their own data, however, the potential importance of social factors could easily have been demonstrated. But to do so would have raised two disturbing—to Herrnstein

and Murray—policy implications. First, IQ is merely one of many predictors of crime and, thus, is hardly in a position to dictate the future of crime control policy. Second, because factors such as religious participation, attitudes, conventional bonds, or even living at home with one's father are not immutable, the NLSY data provide a basis for designing programs that target criminogenic risk factors for change (see also Menard and Morse 1984).

Crime or Detection?

In both Herrnstein and Murray's (1994) and our analysis of the NLSY data, IQ is weakly related or unrelated to self-reported crime but is more strongly related, albeit modestly, to measures of crime that depend on a respondent being processed by the criminal justice system such as being in jail or penetrating into the system (we refer to these as "system measures of crime"). Herrnstein and Murray's explanation for this finding, of course, is that the cognitively disadvantaged are more involved in crime. An alternative explanation, however, is that individuals' levels of intelligence affect not their criminality but rather the likelihood that, if they break the law, they will be caught and processed by the justice system; in short, smarter criminals are better at avoiding detection. The research on this topic is limited, but previous studies tend to suggest that such a detection effect does not exist or that, if it does exist, it is not substantively meaningful (Herrnstein 1995, pp. 51–52; Herrnstein and Murray 1994, p. 242; Moffitt and Silva 19888; Raine 1993, p. 234). This conclusion usually is made on the grounds that IQ is related to both self-report and official measures of crime in roughly similar magnitudes.

We hasten to point out that this is not the case in the NLSY data, a fact that Herrnstein and Murray ignore. As seen in the more fully specified equations. . . , IQ is not statistically related to self-reported crime but is related to being interviewed in a correctional facility. Furthermore, IQ explains different amounts of variation in self-report and system measures of crime. . . .

More illuminating, however, is the analysis . . . which examines the impact of IQ on system processing—that is, being interviewed in a jail and penetration into the criminal justice system—with a control introduced for the number of self-reported crimes committed. If the detection effect is wrong, then we should expect two relationships. First, self-reported crime should be positively related to the system measures because those who commit more crimes should penetrate deeper into the criminal justice system. . . .

Second, once self-reported crime is introduced, the relationship between IQ and the system crime measures should be eliminated or greatly reduced. In essence, the effects of IQ should be "contained" in self-reported crime and thus no longer should have any impact on being in jail or in the system; that is, IQ should cause self-reported crime and thus have only indirect effects, not direct effects, on measures of system penetration. Notably, this does *not* occur; the relationship of IQ to being jailed or in the system is virtually unchanged after self-reported crime is entered into the equation. Thus, it appears that, independent of their actual levels of crime, "cognitively disadvantaged" offenders are more likely to be jailed and processed in the system.

We recognize that self-report and system measures of crime differ in the domains of crime they tap and, especially, in their ability to assess serious crimes (Sykes and Cullen 1992). This methodological consideration may partially confound the analysis we report. Even so, at a minimum, the data suggest that at least part of, and potentially a good portion of, the variation in the system processing crime measures is accounted for by a detection effect. If so, then the case for the criminogenic effects for IQ put forth in *The Bell Curve* is further undermined.[5]

The Relative Importance of IQ as a Criminogenic Risk Factor

In addition to analyzing NLSY data, Herrnstein and Murray (1994), pp. 241–244) provide a selective review of previous empirical studies that illustrate the negative rela-

tionship of IQ to crime. Their review of this research is not so much wrong as it is misleading; although they discuss the IQ-crime link, they remain silent on how powerfully IQ is associated with criminal behavior versus other potential risk factors. Remember, the critical issue is not whether IQ is related to crime but rather whether it is, as Herrnstein and Murray claim, the *overriding* factor. Resolving this criminological question is critical because it is the basis for evaluating Herrnstein and Murray's policy claims. Only if IQ is a powerful risk factor in crime should cognitive differences be allowed to play a salient role in formulating crime control and related social policies.

Perhaps the best method to assess the relative importance of causal variables is through a quantitative research synthesis or meta-analysis, a technique that dates back more than 50 years (Snedecor 1946) and that has gained increasing use in medicine and in the social sciences, including criminology, over the past two decades (Andrews, Zinger, Hoge, Bonta, Gendreau, and Cullen 1990; Gendreau and Andrews 1990, pp. 178–182; Glass 1976; Glass, McGaw, and Smith 1981; Hunt 1997). Meta-analytic techniques are especially useful in providing a relatively precise quantitative assessment of how strongly two variables are associated when their relationship is calculated across a number of studies in which the two variables appear.

Fortuitously, there recently have been four meta-analyses on the predictors of recidivism for various types of adult male offenders (Bonta, Law, and Hanson forthcoming; Gendreau, Goggin, and Law forthcoming; Gendreau, Little, and Goggin 1996; Hanson and Bussiere 1996) and one on male and female juvenile offenders (Simourd and Andres 1994). Taken together, these meta-analyses encompass almost 500 studies and 4,000 effect sizes or correlations between predictors and crime. From these, we abstracted 86 effect sizes or correlations between IQ and recidivism based on studies that assess a total of 42,831 offenders. . . .

[From these analyses] we found that two major conclusions can be drawn. . . . First, the effect size or correlation between IQ and crime is weak to modest in magnitude with no effect size in the meta-analyses for adults exceeding .10. For juveniles, the correlation climbs upward but only to a high of .17. Second, in the relative ranking of predictors, IQ generally is among the weakest of the risk factors assessed in the meta-analyses. For example, across all the meta-analyses, IQ is in the top half of the predictors only once. On average, approximately 80 percent of the competing risk factors rank as more powerful predictors than intelligence when examining the unweighted effect sizes; the comparable mean score across the weighted effect sizes is about 70 percent. It appears, therefore, that IQ is hardly the preeminent determinant of crime that Herrnstein and Murray claim it to be.

A further comparison is equally instructive in revealing the modest importance of intelligence as a source of illegal conduct. IQ typically is assessed by a composite measure that combines scores on several academic achievement subtests. What occurs, then, when composite IQ scores are compared not with single risk factors but rather with a composite index of risk factors? Recall that in the meta-analyses . . . , the IQ effect sizes range from .00 to .17. By contrast, the correlations between crime and composite risk indexes reviewed in these same meta-analyses range from .22 to .45. Recent individual studies, which employ similar composite risk measures, demonstrate equivalent, if not stronger, relationships (rs = .43 to .53) (Coulson, Ilacqua, Nutbrown, Guilekas, and Cudjoe 1996; Rice and Harris 1995; cf. Simourd 1997).[6]

We also should note that among the most powerful predictors is a class of risk factors that Andrews and Bonta (1994) call "criminogenic needs": attitudes, values, beliefs, and behaviors (e.g., having delinquent associations) that support an antisocial lifestyle (see also Gendreau, Goggin, and Paparozzi 1996; Simourd 1997). Across the meta-analyses . . . , these factors typically have effect sizes ranging from .10 to .40. In fact, criminogenic needs usually have larger effect sizes than even the best results in favor of IQ, which come from a series of well-conducted studies on juvenile offenders (Caspi

et al. 1994; Lynam et al. 1993; Moffitt, Lynam, and Silva 1994; cf. Block 1995). In this research, the correlations of IQ and recidivism range from .06 to .31. The correlations of indexes of criminogenic need and recidivism in these studies, nonetheless, are higher (rs = .17 to .48).

Criminogenic need factors not only are robust predictors of crime but also are "dynamic" in nature; that is, they can change and, thus, are amenable to correctional treatment (Gendreau, Little, and Goggin 1996). This reality contravenes the bell curve paradigm put forth by Herrnstein and Murray, which sees crime as rooted in the supposedly immutable trait of low IQ. An approach that stresses criminogenic needs leads to a progressive correctional agenda based on intervention and offender rehabilitation. As we will see, Herrnstein and Murray, by embracing the bell curve paradigm and ignoring the scientific evidence on criminogenic needs and rehabilitation, ultimately draw the "logical" but misguided conclusion that punishing the cognitively disadvantaged is the best means of achieving a safer society.[7]

The Bell Curve and Crime Control Policy

By itself, Herrnstein and Murray's (1994) discussion of IQ and crime might be seen as provocative and as a useful, albeit exaggerated, corrective to those who dismiss out of hand the idea that criminal behavior could be linked to cognitive ability. In the end, however, the agenda of *The Bell Curve* is not science but rather social policy. On the broadest level, Herrnstein and Murray seek to provide an intellectual foundation for government neglect of social problems, especially those that are stratified by race and class. Their antipathy toward progressive approaches is seen most readily in their opposition to affirmative action, welfare, and programs that target "cognitively disadvantaged" (and poor) children. This stance also informs their discussions of crime policy.

The Dangers of Bell Curve Thinking

In devising their crime policies in *The Bell Curve*, Herrnstein and Murray (1994) were not criminological virgins; they already had gone on record in earlier writings as being sympathetic to deterrence-based approaches to crime control (Murray 1984; Murray and Cox 1979; Wilson and Herrnstein 1985). In these works, they either studiously ignored or did not take seriously the existing research showing the limits of deterrence and the promise of treatment interventions. Unsurprisingly, this slanted scholarship is reproduced in *The Bell Curve* (cf. Andrews et al. 1990; Lipsey 1992; Lipsey and Wilson 1997).[8]

As supposed friends of the cognitively disadvantaged, Herrnstein and Murray warn that American society increasingly is being socially and physically segregated by intelligence. They offer the dire prediction that unless this trend is reversed, we will head toward a "custodial state" in which the cognitively advantaged will use their brains, affluence, and political power to have the state isolate, monitor, coercively punish, and generally neglect the well-being of stupid Americans. In Herrnstein and Murray's (1994) scenario, fed up with the dangerous and profligate behaviors of low-IQ citizens, the cognitive elite will use their influence to create "a high tech and more lavish version of the Indian reservation for some substantial minority of the nation's population, while the rest of America tries to go about its business" (p. 526).

How might we reverse "the way we are headed"? Herrnstein and Murray's (1994) solution is to recreate a society, much like small towns used to be in the 1950s, in which "everyone has a valued place" in local communities and in which life is governed by "simple rules" uncomplicated by unnecessary government interference. And how, then, might this approach solve America's enduring crime problem? In the kinder and gentler society that Herrnstein and Murray envision, steps would be taken to "make it easier to live a virtuous life" (pp. 543–544). Thus, the rules about violating the law would be made "simpler" and highlighted with a bold magic marker so that even the cognitively disadvantaged would understand them. "People of limited intelligence can lead moral lives in a society that is run on the basis of 'Thou shalt not steal'," observe Herrnstein and Murray, but such people "find it much harder to lead moral lives in a society that is run on the basis of 'Thou shalt not steal unless there is a really good reason to'" (p. 544).

Of course, these simple crime rules become clear and morally vivid only if violating them has consequences. Legal transgressions would have to trigger unambiguously administered *punishments* that give short shrift to personal excuses or social circumstances. This is the way it once was, Herrnstein and Murray (1994) claim, back in the 1950s when the United States was morally uncomplicated and crime was commensurately lower (cf. Coontz 1992). Accordingly, the "policy prescription is that the criminal justice system should be made simpler. The meaning of criminal offenses used to be clear and objective, and so were the consequences. It is worth trying to make them so again" (p. 544).

One might have expected that in advancing this policy proposal, Herrnstein and Murray would have made some attempt to show that it was based on scientific evidence rather than on pure speculation. For example, they might have tried to show that because the United States was "simpler" in the 1950s, the relationship of IQ to crime was much lower in that era than it is in today's complex society where victim ideology and the "abuse excuse" supposedly make moral messages weak and unclear (see Dershowitz 1994). Or, they might have marshaled cross-cultural data showing that in "simpler" or more communal societies—say, New Zealand—IQ does not predict crime. If they had undertaken these comparative analyses, however, then they would have learned that the data do not support these suppositions (Hirschi and Hindelang 1977; Moffitt and Silva 1988).

They also might have tried to cite data showing that maximally effective punishment-based strategies work better with dull people or dull criminals than with smart ones (see Matson and DiLorenzo 1984, p. 3).

Again, there are no data to support this idea either in the experimental or the clinical punishment literature (Masters, Burish, Hollon, and Rimm 1989; Matson and DiLorenzo 1984; Walters and Grusec 1977). In fact, in one of the rare well-controlled laboratory studies on the effectiveness of punishment on a sample of high-risk offenders, it was the brightest subjects who produced the best performances by far in response to a punishing stimulus (Gendreau and Suboski 1977; see also Wilson and Herrnstein 1985, pp. 379–380). Because the logic underlying Herrnstein and Murray's policy proposals cannot be substantiated, perhaps that is why they make no effort in the discussion of their crime control policies to introduce even a shred of supportive scientific evidence.

The danger is not that legislators will rush off to write simpler laws but rather that *The Bell Curve*—and other works like it—will help to legitimize a way of thinking about crime that will both be ineffective and contribute to a what Clear (1994) calls the "penal harm movement." This mind-set typically combines three features. First, it reduces the complex phenomenon of crime and its control to a simple equation. For Herrnstein and Murray, the equation is that because IQ causes crime, the panacea is to make simple laws. Second, offenders are seen to have some immutable trait, in this case low intelligence. Third, although this trait cannot be changed through the delivery of social services, offenders still can be induced to conform through punishment, that is, by seeing that bad acts have "consequences."[9] Therefore, logic dictates that the solution to crime is to inflict pain on offenders. Indeed, whether in the "custodial state" or in the "virtuous society," Herrnstein and Murray see stupid people who break the law as ending up in jail.

The scientific poverty of this thinking is readily apparent. IQ is at best a modest predictor of crime; many other factors, which are amenable to change, are much stronger criminogenic risk factors; and deterrence-based interventions generally have been shown to be ineffective in reducing, if not positively related to, offender recidivism (e.g., see Gendreau, Goggin, Cullen, Andrews, and Bonta 1997). In light of this scientific knowledge base, to propose formulating simple rules backed up by punishment as the main solution to crime control strains credulity. Such a proposal could come only from those who are criminologically challenged or intellectually duplicitous.

We should add the caveat that Herrnstein and Murray, or their advocates, might point to sections of *The Bell Curve* that take a more judicious stand on crime. Herrnstein and Murray (1994) note, for example, that IQ cannot explain gender differences in crime or account for large swings in crime rates (pp. 239, 245). These qualifications, however, remain at the periphery of their thinking and, thus, do not cause them to revise their theorizing about IQ and crime or to revise their policy recommendations. In the end, they still ignore other known predictors of crime and do not hesitate to trumpet a policy agenda that ultimately seeks to lock up stupid people (see also Dorfman 1995).[10]

The Responsible Use of IQ

Although we are highly critical of Herrnstein and Murray's (1994) slanted analysis of IQ and crime, we believe that criminologists should not "throw the baby out with the bath water" and ignore the role of intelligence in crime and corrections. Both the NLSY data and meta-analyses reveal that IQ is a criminogenic risk factor and, thus, is an individual difference that must be included in theories of crime causation (see also Gibbons 1994, pp. 128–150). Here we suggest two additional considerations regarding IQ that have implications for developing more effective offender treatment interventions: the "responsivity principle" and the concept of "practical IQ."

The Responsivity Principle

As presented by Andrews and Bonta (1994), the responsivity principle states that services designed to reduce offender recidivism will be enhanced if the style and modes of service are matched to the learning styles and abilities of offenders. We should note that the main focus of treatment interventions is to change those criminogenic factors most closely associated with recidivism such as antisocial values. Still, the ability to change these criminogenic factors will be inhibited if the treatment is not delivered in a way that takes into account a ranger of other responsivity factors that, although weakly related or unrelated to recidivism, do affect offenders' receptivity to intervention. Anxiety, depression, mental disorder, and IQ are examples of factors that are weak predictors of recidivism but potentially important considerations in the delivery of treatment (Bonta et al. forthcoming; Gendreau, Little, and Goggin 1996; Simourd and Andrews 1994).

Thus, having intimate knowledge of an offender's intellectual capacity and aptitude is advantageous in designing treatment modules (see, e.g., Hoge and Andrews 1996) For example, offenders who have low IQs would perform more effectively than higher functioning offenders in an instructional format that requires less verbal and written fluency and less abstract conceptualizations. In addition, they would likely profit from a more extensive use of tangible reinforcers and from repeated, graduated behavioral rehearsal and shaping of skills. Moreover, therapists should be selected who relate optimally to offenders' styles of intellectual functioning and to the content of the treatment modules.

We are not proposing that merely designing "simpler treatments" for offenders, as opposed to designing "simpler laws" as Herrnstein and Murray contend, is the panacea for crime among the cognitively disadvantaged; rather, we take the more complex position in which IQ is seen as only one among many factors that should be considered in the classification and treatment of offenders. Again, the main focus of correctional interventions should be on the strongest predictors of recidivism—that is, criminogenic factors that generally would not include intelligence—whose changes in the treatment process have been found to produce reduced recidivism (see, e.g., Andrews et al. 1990; Gendreau and Goggin 1996). Even so, IQ and similar responsivity variables are relevant to the extent that they influence the ability of treatment interventions to reach the criminogenic factors targeted for transformation.

Assessing IQ: Practical Intelligence

Although a complete review is beyond the scope of our present work, we believe that it is important to note, and to explore the policy implications of, the emerging movement in psychology to broaden the conceptualization of IQ to include "practical intelligence" (see, e.g., Gardner 1994; Neisser 1976; Sternberg, Wagner, Williams, and Horvath 1995). Conventional "academic" intelligence, which is based on school-oriented linguistic, mathematical, and performance (e.g., block design) tasks, has dominated the measurement of IQ. Founding researchers on IQ, however, recognized some 70 years ago that intelligence also involves the capacity to learn from experience and to adapt to the surrounding environment—functioning that "goes beyond getting high scores on tests or good grades in school. It includes . . . how you manage your life in general" (Sternberg 1995b, p. 382; see also Wechsler 1974).

Although certainly not discounting the importance of conventional academic IQ and its powers to predict outcomes in some social domains (Schmidt and Hunter 1981), psychologists promoting practical intelligence place more emphasis on a person's ability to learn and profit from experience, to monitor effectively one's own and others' feelings and needs, and to solve everyday problems (Gardner 1983; Sternberg 1985a). Most important, these scholars maintain that in contrast to conventional IQ, which is seen as difficult to boost, practical intelligence is modifiable. They present preliminary evidence demonstrating impressive gains in academic achievement through programs that train schoolchildren in practical intelligence skills (see, e.g., Sternberg et al. 1995, p. 923).

The conceptualization and measurement of practical intelligence are in the preliminary stages of development, and the ultimate viability of the construct, although promising, remains to be determined (Lubinski and Benbow 1995; Sternberg et al. 1995). With these caveats in mind, we suggest that practical IQ potentially may have special relevance for modifying offender behavior and, in turn, for designing more effective correctional interventions.

Thus, it is possible that offenders, faced with challenging social environments and/or personal propensities, lack the practical IQ to cope effectively, reacting instead with aggression, hostility, substance abuse, the pursuit of immediate gratification, and rationalizations for criminal behavior. If so, then efforts to work with offenders to boost their practical intelligence may reduce their risk for recidivism by enhancing their ability to solve daily problems, to monitor their own and others' feelings, and to learn from positive experiences.[11] Although not directly comparable to studies of practical IQ, this view gains a measure of support from research on cognitive-behavioral treatment interventions. These investigations show that cognitive-behavioral programs, which target thinking patterns, values, and behaviors for change—that is, risk factors encompassed or affected by practical IQ—have been particularly effective in lowering offender recidivism (see, e.g., Andrews et al. 1990; Gendreau and Goggin 1996; Henning and Frueh 1996).[12]

Again, Herrnstein and Murray (1994) favor an approach to IQ that stresses the immutability of cognitive ability and the ineffectiveness of government-run interventions aimed at improving people's lives (other than, of course, building a "simpler" society). By contrast, we see IQ as information that can be used to design and deliver more effective treatment interventions. In the end, when people violate the law, Herrnstein and Murray's policy agenda offers punishment and incapacitation. Our agenda offers the hope, rooted in scientific criminology, that positive behavioral change is possible and can be made more likely when treatment interventions take into account people's individual differences including their intellectual competencies (see also Lynam et al. 1993).

Conclusion: Intelligent Criminology

Close scrutiny of *The Bell Curve* reveals both the lack of and the important role to be played by intelligent criminology. We argue that Herrnstein and Murray (1994) are "cognitively challenged" criminologists. Their analysis exaggerates the causal importance of intelligence in criminal behavior and ignores an enormous body of research on competing predictors of crime. Their failure to consider alternative criminogenic risk factors is inexcusable not only because the research documenting their salience is readily available but also because doing so leads them to justify ill-conceived, repressive crime policies. By portraying offenders as driven into crime predominantly by cognitive disadvantage, Herrnstein and Murray mask the reality that stronger risk factors not only exist but also are amenable to effective correctional intervention.

We hope, however, that we have illuminated how positivist criminology can be valuable in deconstructing bell curve "science" and in revealing its ideological base. In this instance, we tried to move beyond the type of broad, ideologically inspired condemnation found in many review of Herrnstein and Murray's work. Instead, our goal was to show that the best way in which to fashion an intelligent criminological response to *The Bell Curve* was to draw on the discipline's empirical knowledge base. To the extent that we have achieved this goal, we trust that we have provided a more general lesson in the power of a scientific approach to criminology to combat mean-spirited ideology and to justify confronting crime with a more progressive policy agenda (see also Currie 1985; Harland 1996; Howell, Krisberg, Hawkins, and Wilson 1995).

Notes

1. Herrnstein and Murray (1994) argue that the AFQT may be influenced by the age of the youths, which ranged from 16 to 24 years at the time of the test. For this reason, age is included with the AFQT in these models. Our own analyses show that age, by itself, explains a very minimal amount of variation in the dependent variables. A table of the results is available from the authors on request.

2. Herrnstein and Murray (1994) focus their analysis on a subsample of cases for which they had complete information on all vari-

ables used in their book. This required them to restrict their sample to those men still in the sample in 1990 (the 12th wave of the NLSY). For our purposes, we are examining only variables generated from the first 2 waves of the NLSY. For the remaining analyses, we are using the 1980 weighted sample.

3. In analyzing the effect size in prediction research, it is common to square the correlation coefficient (Pearson's r) because R^2 is the proportion of variation in the dependent variable (in this case, typically crime or recidivism) explained by the independent variable(s). In a contrary view, Rosnow and Rosenthal (1993) contend that R^2 "has its uses in a number of situations, but it is a poor indicator of the effect size because . . . it underestimates the practical importance of the observed outcome" (p. 248). In prediction, the magnitude of the correlation coefficient (r) approximates the percentage of difference between individuals who have more or less of a particular characteristic. Therefore, "weak" r values of .10 can be important in corrections where the aim is to predict involvement in potentially serious behaviors (David Farrington, personal communication, February 17, 1995; see also Gendreau, Goggin, and Paparozzi 1996, p. 64; Gendrau, Little, and Goggin 1996, p. 588). In the NLS, the correlations between the AFQT and the outcome measures were as follows: log of number of self-reported crime (-.072), in top decile of self-reported crime (-.071), decile of self-reported crime (-.066), ever interviewed in jail (-.156), penetration of criminal justice system (-.156). These correlations suggest that IQ makes a contribution in predicting offender recidivism. The issue at hand, however, is not whether low intelligence is a risk factor—which we fully concur it is—but rather whether low IQ is so criminogenic that it surpasses the effects of other risk factors and should be the chief determinant of criminal justice policy.

4. Although many of the variables are self-explanatory, others need to be clarified by listing the items used to measure the concepts in question: strong work ethic = youth would choose to work if he could live comfortably without working; stake I conformity = youth expects to be working in five years; academic aspirations = highest grade youth would like to complete; locus of control = youth reports having little influence over things that happen to him; rationalization favoring crime = youth would shoplift if unable to support

family. With the exception of academic aspirations, which is coded by the grade selected, the items were coded 1 = *yes* and 0 = *no*.

5. We checked the robustness of the findings by introducing the variables controlled in the full model reported [earlier] (e.g., frequency of religious participation, academic aspirations). The results remained constant; IQ was significant in these analyses even with self-reported crime in the equation.

6. An example of a composite index is the Level of Supervision Inventory–Revised (Andrews and Bonta 1995). The inventory contains 54 items that are subdivided into 10 subscales (e.g., criminal history, education/employment, companions, attitudes/orientation).

7. As this article was being finalized for publication, we received a meta-analysis of the predictors of violent and serious delinquency by Lipsey and Derzon (1997), which covers 793 effect sizes, 18 of which concern IQ. Those authors examine whether variables measured during two age periods (6 to 11 years and 12 to 14 years) are predictors of delinquency at ages 15 to 25 years. They divide these predictors into five groups, rank-ordering them according to the magnitude of their effect on delinquency. Confirming the results . . . , IQ is in the fourth lowest group of predictor variables for both age categories, with the r values of IQ ranging from .11 to .12. By contrast, sociological variables are stronger predictors. Most revealing is that antisocial peers and weak socialites have r values in the 12 to 14 years age category of .37 and .39, respectively. Furthermore, Lipsey and Derzon (1997) point out, "It is especially noteworthy that the strongest predictors from both the ages 6–11 and 12–14 periods represent relatively malleable factors . . . that can be addressed by intervention programs" (p. 14).

8. In fairness, some discussions in these previous works are arguably balanced in their review of the evidence on offender interventions (see, e.g., Wilson and Herrnstein 1985, pp. 374–403). Even here, however, the treatment literature is not thoroughly reviewed, and the evidence in favor of punishment is more optimistically assessed. More telling is that this scholarship does not inform Herrnstein and Murray's (1994) assessment of crime control policy in *The Bell Curve*.

9. We are not aware of any learning research that demonstrates that an organism, human or otherwise, can respond only to punishment.

10. Particularly problematic for the bell curve paradigm is that correctional interventions that adhere particularly well to the principles of effective treatment typically achieve reductions in recidivism of 20 percent to 50 percent with high-risk offenders, who presumably are an especially dull lot of lawbreakers (see Andrew et al. 1990; Gendreau 1996; see also Lipsey and Wilson 1997). Of course, Herrnstein and Murray (1994) do not cite this research and do not address theoretically why change is possible for high-risk offenders who have penetrated the criminal justice system.

11. See also the work of Goleman (1995) on the related, if not partially overlapping, concept of "emotional intelligence" (see also Gibbs, Puzzanchera, and Giever 1997).

12. For a review of assessment tools in this domain that are roughly analogous to some of the definitions of practical IQ, see Gendreau, Goggin, and Paparozzi (1996) and Simourd (1997).

References

Andrews, D. A. and James Bonta. 1994. *The Psychology of Criminal Conduct*. Cincinnati, OH: Anderson.

——. 1995. *LSI-R: The Level of Service Inventory–Revised*. Toronto: Multi-Health Systems.

Andrews, D. A., Ivan Zinger, Robert D. Hoge, James Bonta, Paul Gendreau, and Francis T. Cullen. 1990. "Does Correctional Treatment Work? A Clinically-Relevant and Psychologically-Informed Meta-Analysis." *Criminology* 28: 369–404.

Block, Jack. 1995. "On the Relation Between IQ, Impulsivity, and Delinquency: Remarks on the Lynam, Moffit, and Stouthamer-Loeber (1993) Interpretation." *Journal of Abnormal Psychology* 104: 395–398.

Bonta, James, Moira Law, and Karl Hanson. Forthcoming. "The Prediction of Criminal and Violent Recidivism Among Mentally Disordered Offenders; A Meta-Analysis." *Psychological Bulletin*.

Caspi, Avshalom, Terrie E. Moffitt, Phil A. Silva, Magda Stouthamer-Loeber, Robert F. Krueger, and Pamela S. Schmutte. 1994. "Are Some People Crime-Prone? Replications of the Personality-Crime Relationship Across Countries, Genders, Races, and Methods." *Criminology* 32: 163–194.

Chomsky, Noam. 1972. "The Fallacy of Richard Herrnstein's IQ." *Social Policy* 3: 19–25.

Clear, Todd R. 1994. *Harm in American Penology: Offenders, Victims, and Their Communities*. Albany: State University off New York Press.

Coontz, Stephanie. 1992. *The Way We Never Were: American Families and the Nostalgia Trap*. New York: Basic Books.

Coulson, Grant, Giorgia Ilacqua, Verna Nutbrown, Diana Giulekas, and Francis Cudjoe. 1996. "Predictive Utility of the LSI for Incarcerated Female Offenders." *Criminal Justice and Behavior* 23: 427–439.

Currie, Elliott. 1985. *Confronting Crime: An American Challenge*. New York: Pantheon.

DeParle, Jason. 1994. "Daring Research or 'Social Science Pornography'?" *New York Times Magazine*, October 9: 48–52, 62, 70–71, 74, 78, 80.

Dershowitz, Alan M. 1994. *The Abuse Excuse: And Other Cop-Outs, Sob Stories, and Evasions of Responsibility*. Boston: Little, Brown.

Dorfman, Donald D. 1995. "Soft Science with a Neoconservative Agenda." *Contemporary Psychology* 40: 418–421.

Farrington, David P. 1994. "Human Development and Criminal Careers." Pp. 511–584 in *The Oxford Handbook of Criminology*, edited by M. Maguire, R. Morgan, and R. Reinder. New York: Oxford University Press.

——. 1995. "The Development of Offending and Antisocial Behaviour from Childhood: Key Findings from the Cambridge Study in Delinquent Development." *Journal of Child Psychology and Psychiatry* 360: 929–964.

Gardner, Howard. 1983. *Frames of Mind: The Theory of Multiple Intelligence*. New York: Basic Books.

——. 1994. "Cracking Open the IQ Box." *The American Prospect* 20: 71–80.

Gendreau, Paul. 1996. "The Principles of Effective Intervention with Offenders." Pp. 117–130 in *Correctional Options That Work: Defining the Demand and Evaluating the Supply*, edited by A. T. Harland. Thousands Oaks, CA: Sage.

Gendreau, Paul and D. A. Andrews. 1990. "Tertiary Prevention: What the Meta-Analyses of the Offender Treatment Literature Tell Us About 'What Works'." *Canadian Journal of Criminology* 32: 173–184.

Gendreau, Paul and Claire E. Goggin. 1996. "Principles of Effective Correctional Programming." *Forum on Corrections Research* 8: 38–41.

Gendreau, Paul, Claire E. Goggin, Francis T. Cullen, D. A. Andrews, and James Bonta. 1997. "The Effectiveness of 'Get Tough' Strategies on Offender Recidivism." Unpublished manuscript, Centre for Criminal Justice Studies, University of New Brunswick, Saint John.

Gendreau, Paul, Claire E. Goggin, and Moira A. Law. Forthcoming. "Predicting Prison Misconducts." *Criminal Justice and Behavior.*

Gendreau, Paul, Claire E. Goggin, and Mario Paparozzi. 1996. "Principles of Effective Assessments for Community Corrections." *Federal Probation* 60 (September): 64–70.

Gendreau, Paul, Tracy Little, and Claire E. Goggin. 1996. "A Meta-Analysis of the Predictors of Adult Offender Recidivism: What Works!" *Criminology* 34: 575–607.

Gendreau, Paul, and Milton D. Suboski. 1971. "Age and IQ Discrimination Conditioning of the Eyelid Response." *Journal of Experimental Psychology* 89: 379–382.

Gibbons, Don C. 1994. *Talking About Crime and Criminals.* Englewood Cliffs, NJ: Prentice Hall.

Gibbs, John J., Charles M. Puzzanchera, and Dennis Giever. 1997. "Emotional Intelligence and Criminal Behavior: A Conceptual Framework and Empirical Test." Paper presented at the annual meeting of the Academy of Criminal Justice Sciences, Louisville, KY, March.

Glass, Gene V., Barry McGaw, and Mary Lee Smith. 1981. *Meta-Analysis in Social Research.* Beverly Hills, CA: Sage.

Goldberger, Arthur S. and Charles F. Manski. 1995. "Review Article: The Bell Curve by Herrnstein and Murray." *Journal of Economic Literature* 33: 762–776.

Goleman, Daniel. 1995. *Emotional Intelligence.* New York: Bantam.

Gould, Stephen Jay. 1981. *The Mismeasure of Man.* New York: Norton.

——. 1994. "Curveball." *The New Yorker,* November 28: 1339–1349.

Hanson, R. Karl and Monique T. Bussiere. 1996. *Predictors of Sexual Offender Recidivism: A Meta-Analysis.* Ottawa: Solicitor General of Canada.

Harland, Alan T., ed. 1996. *Choosing Correctional Options That Work: Defining the Demand and Evaluating the Supply.* Thousand Oaks, CA: Sage.

Hauser, Robert M. 1995. "Symposium: The Bell Curve." *Contemporary Sociology* 24: 149–153.

Henning, Chris R. and B. Christopher Frueh. 1996. "Cognitive-Behavioral Treatment of Offenders: An Evaluation of the Vermont Department of Corrections Cognitive Self-Change Program." *Criminal Justice and Behavior* 23: 523–541.

Herrnstein, Richard J. and Charles Murray. 1994. *The Bell Curve: Intelligence and Class Structure in American Life.* New York: Free Press.

Hirschi, Travis and Michael J. Hindelang. 1977. "Intelligence and Delinquency: A Revisionist Review." *American Sociological Review* 42: 571–587.

Hoge, Robert D. and D. A. Andrews. 1996. *Assessing the Youthful Offender: Issues and Techniques.* New York: Plenum.

Howell, James C., Barry Krisberg, J. David Hawkins, and John J. Wilson, eds. 1995. *Serious, Violent, and Chronic Juvenile Offenders: A Sourcebook.* Thousand Oaks, CA: Sage.

Hunt, Morton. 1997. *How Science Takes Stock: The Story of Meta-Analysis.* New York: Russell Sage.

Jacoby, Russell and Naomi Glauberman, eds. 1995. *The Bell Curve Debate: History, Documents, Opinons.* New York: Times Books.

Kamin, Leon. 1995. "Lies, Damned Lies, and Statistics." Pp. 81–105 in *The Bell Curve Debate: History, Documents, Opinions.* New York: Times Books.

Lipsey, Mark S. and James H. Derzon. 1997. "Predictors of Violent or Serious Delinquency in Adolescence and Early Adulthood: A Synthesis of Longitudinal Research." Paper prepared for the OJJDP Study Group on Serious and Violent Juvenile Offenders, March.

Lipsey, Mark S. and David B Wilson. 1997. "Effective Intervention for Serious Juvenile Offenders: A Synthesis of Research." Paper prepared for the OJJDP Study Group on Serious and Violent Juvenile Offenders, January.

Loeber, Rolf and T. Dishion. 1983. "Early Predictors of Male Delinquence: A Review." *Psychological Bulletin* 94: 68–99.

Lubinski, David and Camilla P. Benbow. 1995. "An Opportunity for Empiricism: A Review of Multiple Intelligence: The Theory in Practice." *Contemporary Psychology* 40: 935–937.

Lynam, Donald, Terrie Moffitt, and Magda Stouthamer-Loeber. 1993. "Explaining the Relation Between IQ and Delinquency: Class, Race, Test Motivation, School Failure, or Self Control?" *Journal of Abnormal Psychology* 102: 187–196.

Massey, Douglas S. 1995. "Review Essay: The Bell Curve." *American Journal of Sociology* 3: 747–753.

Masters, John C., Thomas G. Burish, Steven D. Hollon, and David C. Rimm. 1989. *Behavior Therapy: Techniques and Empirical Findings.* San Diego: Harcourt Brace Jovanovich.

Maston, Johnny L. and Thomas M. DiLorenzo. 1984. *Punishment and Its Alternatives: A New*

Perspective for Behavior Modification. New York: Springer.

Menard, Scott and Barbara Morse. 1984. "A Structuralist Critique of the IQ-Delinquency Hypothesis: Theory and Evidence." *American Journal of Sociology* 89: 1347–1378.

Moffitt, Terrie E., Donald R. Lynam, and Phil A. Silva. 1994. "Neuropsychological Tests Predicting Persistent Male Delinquency." *Criminology* 32: 277–300.

Moffitt, Terrie E., and Phil A. Silva. 1998. "IQ and Delinquency: A Direct Test of the Differential Detection Hypothesis." *Journal of Abnormal Psychology* 97: 330–333.

Morin, Richard. 1995. "An Army From Academe Tries to Straighten Out 'The Bell Curve'." *Washington Post,* January 16: A3.

Murray, Charles. 1984. *Losing Ground: American Social Policy, 1950-1980.* New York: Basic Books.

Murray, Charles A., and Louis A. Cox, Jr. 1979. *Beyond Probation: Juvenile Corrections and the Chronic Delinquent.* Beverly Hills, CA: Sage.

Murray, Charles A. And Richard J. Herrnstein. 1994. "Race, Genes and IQ: An Apologia." *The New Republic,* October 31: 27–37.

Neisser, Ulric, Gwyneth Boodoo, Thomas J. Cbouchard, Jr., A Wade Boykin, Nathan Brody, Stephen J. Ceci, Ciane F. Halpern, John C. Loehlin, Robert Perloff, Robert J. Sternberg, and Susana Urbina. 1996. "Intelligence: Knowns and Unknowns." *American Psychologist* 51: 77–101.

"Race." 1994. *The New Republic,* October 31. (Issue devoted to *The Bell Curve*)

Raine, Adrian. 1993. *The Psychopathology of Crime: Criminal Behavior as a Clinical Disorder.* San Diego: Academic Press.

Rice, Marnie E. and Grant T. Harris. 1995. *Cross-Validation of Actuarial Predictions.* Research report, Vol. 12, No. 2 Penetanguishene, Ontario: Mental Health Centre.

Rosnow, Robert L. and Robert Rosenthal. 1993. *Beginning Behavioral Research: A Conceptual Primer.* New York: Macmillian.

Schmidt, Frank L. and John E. Hunter. 1981. "Employment Testing: Old Theories and New Research Findings." *American Psychologist* 36: 1128–1137.

Simourd, David J. 1997. "The Criminal Sentiments Scale—Modified and Pride in Delinquency Scale: Psychometric Properties and Construct Validity of Two Measures of Criminal Attitudes." *Criminal Justice and Behavior* 24: 52–70.

Simourd, Linda and D. A. Andrews. 1994. "Correlates of Delinquence: A Look at Gender Differences." *Forum on Corrections Research* 6: 26–31.

Snedecor, George W. 1946. *Statistical Methods.* 4th ed. Ames: Iowa State College Press.

Sternberg, Robert J. 1985. *Beyond IQ: A Triarchic Theory.* New York: Cambridge University Press.

———. 1995a. "For Whom the Bell Curve Tolls: A Review of *The Bell Curve*." *Psychological Science* 6: 257–261.

———. 1995b. *In Search of the Human Mind.* Fort Worth, TX: Harcourt Brace.

Sternberg, Robert J., Richard K. Wagner, Wendy M. Williams, and Joseph A. Horvath. 1995. "Testing Common Sense." *American Psychologist* 50: 912–927.

Sykes, Gresham M. and Francis T. Cullen. 1992. *Criminology.* Fort Worth, TX: Harcourt Brace Jovanovich.

Taylor, Howard F. 1995. "Symposium: The Bell Curve." *Contemporary Sociology* 24: 153–158.

Tittle, Charles R. and Robert F. Meier. 1990. "Specifying the SES/Delinquency Relationship." *Criminology* 28: 271–299.

Tittle, Charles R., Wayne J. Villemez, and Douglas A. Smith. 1978. "The Myth of Social Class and Criminality." *American Sociological Review* 43: 643–656.

Walters, Gary and Joan Grusec. 1977. *Punishment.* San Francisco: Freeman.

Ward, David A. and Charles R. Tittle. 1994. "IQ and Delinquency: A Test of Two Competing Explanations." *Journal of Quantitative Criminology* 10: 189–212.

Wechsler, David. 1974. *The Measurement and Appraisal of Adult Intelligence.* Baltimore: Williams & Wilkins.

Wilson, James Q. and Richard J. Herrnstein. 1985. *Crime and Human Nature.* New York: Simon & Schuster.

Wilson, James Q. and Joan Petersilia, eds. 1995. *Crime.* San Francisco: ICS Press.

ISSUE IV

Terrorism: Has the Government Gone Too Far in the Fight Against Terrorism?

Shortly after the September 11 attacks, anti-terrorism legislation was passed. The legislation granted the federal government sweeping powers to address and respond to terrorism in the United States. First, the legislation allowed law enforcement officials more latitude in investigating financial transactions such as counterfeiting, smuggling, and money laundering. It also made it easier for the government to seize the financial assets of known terrorists. Second, the anti-terrorism legislation authorized greater freedom to agencies to share intelligence. Third, the legislation allows for the surveillance of all communications used by terrorists, such as e-mail, telephones, cellular phones, and the Internet. Fourth, restrictions on the jurisdictional validity of warrants were lifted. In particular, warrants under the new legislation are valid across county, district, and state lines (Office of the Press Secretary 2001). Last, the new legislation permitted the use of military tribunals, rather than traditional courts, to try and convict members of terrorist organizations.

The American Civil Liberties Union (ACLU) argues that the anti-terrorism legislation passed by Congress and signed by President Bush goes too far and that elements of the legislation are unconstitutional. In particular, the ACLU points out that the legislation authorizes the Department of Justice to eavesdrop on conversations between suspected terrorists and their attorneys without a warrant. The ACLU believes that the legislation is inconsistent with attorney-client privilege, violates the Sixth Amendment right to the assistance of counsel, violates prisoners' rights to access to the courts, and violates the Fourth Amendment, which prohibits unreasonable searches and seizures. They also claim that the law is vague and provides for no oversight or review of the Attorney General's decisions.

Dave Klinger and Dave Grossman argue that the legislative response to terrorism may not be enough to effectively address future terrorist attacks. In particular, they believe that military-style terrorist attacks led by foreign nationals will most likely take place in the near future. The authors point out several examples of military-style attacks that have already taken place in the United States and how current local and national policies are not effective. They argue that the most effective and legal means of addressing foreign-led terrorism is to employ the use of the United States military. In their chapter they discuss the legal barriers to implementing this strategy and how these barriers might be overcome.

Reference

Office of the Press Secretary. 2001. "President signs anti-terrorism bill." Remarks by the President at signing of the Patriot Act, anti-terrorism legislation. (October 26, 2001). <http://www.whitehouse.gov/news/releases/2001/10/20011026-5.html>

Critical Thinking Questions

1. Discuss the constitutionality of using the military to respond to terrorism within the United States.

83

2. Discuss the rights of individuals regarding eavesdropping on confidential attorney-client communications and whether the Attorney General has gone too far (or not far enough) in the war against terrorism.

3. If you were the President, how would you have responded to the September 11 attacks?

Internet Websites

Central Intelligence Agency. <http://www.cia.gov>

Federal Bureau of Investigation–Denver office. <http://www.fbi.gov/contact/fo/denver/inteterr.htm>

Office of Homeland Security. <http://www.whitehouse.gov/homeland/>

Government Accounting Office. <http://www.gao.gov/new.items/d0115.pdf>   ˙

National Association of Defense Attorneys. <http://www.nacdl.org/public.nsf/freeform/terrorism1?OpenDocument&ExpandSection=5,3#_Section5> ✦

7

Regarding Eavesdropping on Confidential Attorney-Client Communications

66 Fed. Reg. 55062
(October 31, 2001)
Submitted December 20, 2001

American Civil Liberties Union

Introduction

On October 31, 2001, the Attorney General promulgated an amendment to 28 C.F.R. Parts 500 and 501. See 66 Fed. Reg. 55062 (October 31, 2001). The regulation became effective immediately, without the usual opportunity for prior public comment. It allows the Department of Justice, unilaterally, without judicial oversight, and with no meaningful standards, to eavesdrop on the confidential attorney-client conversations of persons in custody whom the Justice Department itself may be seeking to prosecute.

This regulation is an unprecedented frontal assault on the attorney-client privilege and the right to counsel guaranteed by the Constitution. It is especially disturbing that these provisions for monitoring confidential attorney-client communications apply not only to convicted prisoners in the custody of the federal Bureau of Prisons (BOP), but to all persons in the custody of the Department of Justice, including pretrial detainees who have not been convicted of crime and are presumed innocent, as well as material witnesses and immigration detainees, who are not accused of any crime. 28 C.F.R. § 501.3(f) (as amended). The regulation is also unnecessary, as existing law permits the monitoring of attorney-client communications when a judge issues a warrant upon a showing of probable cause. The undersigned organizations call on the Attorney General to rescind this regulation immediately.

The Regulation

The regulation vests the Attorney General with unlimited and unreviewable discretion to strip any person in federal custody of the right to communicate confidentially with an attorney. In any case in which the Attorney General believes that there is "reasonable suspicion" that a person in custody "may" use communications with attorneys or their agents "to further or facilitate acts of terrorism," the Justice Department "shall . . . provide appropriate procedures for the monitoring or review of communications between that inmate and attorneys or attorneys' agents who are traditionally covered by the attorney-client privilege." 28 C.F.R. § 501.3(d) (as amended).

Except in the case of prior court authorization, the Department "shall provide written notice to the inmate and to the attorneys involved, prior to the initiation of any monitoring or review," that "all communications between the inmate and attorneys may be monitored, to the extent determined to be reasonably necessary for the purpose of deterring future acts of violence or terrorism." 28 C.F.R. § 501.3(d)(2) (as amended).

The Department "shall employ appropriate procedures to ensure that all attorney-client communications are reviewed for privilege claims and that any properly privileged materials . . . are not retained during the course of the monitoring." The intercepted attorney-client communications are to be reviewed by a "privilege team." "Except in cases where the person in charge of the privilege team determines that acts of violence or terrorism are imminent, the privilege team shall not disclose any information unless and until such disclosure has been approved by a federal judge." 28 C.F.R. § 501.3(d)(3) (as amended).

The Regulation Is Inconsistent with the Attorney-Client Privilege

As the United States Supreme Court has recognized:

> The attorney-client privilege is the oldest of the privileges for confidential communications known to the common law. 8 J. Wigmore, Evidence § 2290 (McNaughton rev. 1961). Its purpose is to encourage full and frank communication between attorneys and their clients and thereby promote broader public interests in the observance of law and administration of justice. The privilege recognizes that sound legal advice or advocacy serves public ends and that such advice or advocacy depends upon the lawyer's being fully informed by the client. As we stated last Term in *Trammel v. United States*, 445 U.S. 40, 51, 100 S.Ct. 906, 913, 63 L.Ed.2d 186 (1980): "The lawyer-client privilege rests on the need for the advocate and counselor to know all that relates to the client's reasons for seeking representation if the professional mission is to be carried out." And in *Fisher v. United States*, 425 U.S. 391, 403, 96 S.Ct. 1569, 1577, 48 L.Ed.2d 39 (1976), we recognized the purpose of the privilege to be "to encourage clients to make full disclosure to their attorneys." This rationale for the privilege has long been recognized by the Court, see *Hunt v. Blackburn*, 128 U.S. 464, 470, 9 S.Ct. 125, 127, 32 L.Ed. 488 (1888) (privilege "is founded upon the necessity, in the interest and administration of justice, of the aid of persons having knowledge of the law and skilled in its practice, which assistance can only be safely and readily availed of when free from the consequences or the apprehension of disclosure").

—*Upjohn Co. v. United States*, 449 U.S. 383, 389, 101 S. Ct. 677, 682 (1981).

Indeed, so well-established is this privilege, and so compelling the societal interest in unobstructed communication between clients and their attorneys, that the Supreme Court has held that the privilege survives even after the client's death. *Swidler & Berlin v. United States*, 524 U.S. 399, 410, 118 S. Ct. 2081, 2088 (1998).

> Knowing that communications will remain confidential even after death encourages the client to communicate fully and frankly with counsel. While the fear of disclosure, and the consequent withholding of information from counsel, may be reduced if disclosure is limited to posthumous disclosure in a criminal context, it seems unreasonable to assume that it vanishes altogether.

524 U.S. at 407, 118 S. Ct. at 2086. Consistent with the fundamental importance of the attorney-client privilege in our system of justice, federal courts have zealously protected the confidentiality of privileged communications between prisoners and their attorneys. See, e.g., *Gomez v. Vernon*, 255 F.3d 1118, 1135 (9th Cir. 2001), cert. denied, 70 U.S.L.W. 3291 (December 10, 2001) (affirming imposition of monetary sanctions on assistant attorneys general who acquired and read privileged communications from prisoners' attorneys).[1]

The core purpose of the attorney-client privilege—to encourage full and frank disclosure by the client of information that may be embarrassing or damaging, and a thorough discussion between attorney and client of legal strategy and options—simply cannot be served when both attorney and client know that the very government agency that is prosecuting the client is listening in.

This concern is not allayed by the regulation's provision that "properly privileged materials" will not be retained during the course of the monitoring. The chilling effect on attorney-client communication does not require that privileged information, or indeed any information, actually be intercepted and turned over to prosecutors. Rather, the attorney-client relationship is fatally compromised as soon as attorney and client are informed that henceforth, all their communications are subject to government monitoring.

Moreover, under the regulation, the determination of what constitutes "properly privileged materials" is made not by a neutral and disinterested judge, but unilaterally by the Justice Department itself. It will therefore be impossible for detainees and their counsel to know in advance what portions of their intercepted communications the Justice Department will ultimately deem to be "properly privileged materials." This uncertainty renders the privilege worthless. "[I]f the purpose of the attorney-client privilege is to be served, the attorney and client must be able to predict with some degree of certainty whether particular discussions will be protected. An uncertain privilege, or one which purports to be certain but results in widely varying applications . . . , is little better than no privilege at all." Upjohn, 449 U.S. at 393, 101 S. Ct. at 684.

In some limited circumstances, attorney-client communications lose their privileged status pursuant to the "crime-fraud exception" to the privilege. See U.S. v. De La Jara, 973 F.2d 746, 748 (9th Cir. 1992) ("[i]n order to successfully invoke the crime-fraud exception to the attorney-client privilege, the government must make a *prima facie* showing that the attorney was retained in order to promote intended or continuing criminal or fraudulent activity"). However, it hardly follows from this narrow exception that the Justice Department may eavesdrop on all of a detainee's attorney-client communications, and then determine, unilaterally and after the fact, that some of these communications fell within the crime-fraud exception.

Rather, the Supreme Court has made clear that the determination whether an attorney-client communication falls within the crime-fraud exception is to be made by courts, not prison officials or prosecutors. Indeed, even to obtain in camera review of an allegedly privileged communication to determine whether the crime-fraud exception applies, the government must first provide the court with "a factual basis adequate to support a good faith belief by a reasonable person" that in camera review may reveal evidence to establish the exception's applicability. *United States v. Zolin*, 491 U.S. 554, 572, 109 S. Ct. 2619, 2631, 105 L.Ed.2d 469 (1989). This showing must be made using non-privileged evidence. Id., 491 U.S. at 574, 109 S. Ct. at 2632. See also De La Jara, 973 F.2d at 749 (district court erred by conducting in camera review of allegedly privileged communication without first requiring prosecution to make prima facie showing supporting such review).

The Regulation Violates the Sixth Amendment Right to the Assistance of Counsel

A person facing criminal charges is entitled, under the Sixth Amendment to the Constitution, to the assistance of counsel for his defense. *Gideon v. Wainwright*, 372 U.S. 335, 339–40, 83 S. Ct. 792, 794 (1963). This right is not limited to the trial itself, but includes the assistance of counsel in investigation and preparation of a defense. Indeed, the Supreme Court has recognized that "to deprive a person of counsel during the period prior to trial may be more damaging than denial of counsel during the trial itself." *Maine v. Moulton*, 474 U.S. 159, 170, 106 S. Ct. 477, 485, 88 L.Ed.2d 481 (1985). See also *Johnson-El v. Schoemehl*, 878 F.2d 1043, 1051 (8th Cir. 1989) (where defendants' right to communicate effectively with counsel is "inadequately respected during pre-trial confinement, the ultimate fairness of their eventual trial can be compromised"). This right to counsel includes the right to confer with one's lawyer.

Geders v. United States, 425 U.S. 80, 88–91, 96 S. Ct. 1330, 1335–37, 47 L.Ed.2d 592 (1976). "Free two-way communication between client and attorney is essential if the professional assistance guaranteed by the sixth amendment is to be meaningful." *United States v. Levy*, 577 F.2d 200, 209 (3d Cir. 1978).

More specifically, "the essence of the Sixth Amendment right is, indeed, privacy of communication with counsel." *United States v. Rosner*, 485 F.2d 1213, 1224 (2d Cir. 1973). As the Justice Department itself has stated, "the

Sixth Amendment's assistance-of-counsel guarantee can be meaningfully implemented only if a criminal defendant knows that his communications with his attorney are private and that his lawful preparations for trial are secure against intrusion by the government, his adversary in the criminal proceeding." *Weatherford v. Bursey*, 429 U.S. 545, 554 n. 4, 97 S. Ct. 837, 843 n. 4, 51 L.Ed.2d 30 (1977) (quoting Brief for United States as *Amicus Curiae*). In Weatherford, the Supreme Court specifically acknowledged that the effective assistance of counsel is threatened by a reasonable "fear that the government is monitoring [attorney-client] communications through electronic eavesdropping." Id.

Under the regulation, the defendant and his counsel are confronted not just by "the fear that the government is monitoring [their] communications," but by the certain knowledge that it is doing so. Unlike the defendant in Weatherford, the defendant cannot ensure confidential communications with his attorney merely by excluding third parties from such communications. Rather, he has been told that none of his communications with his attorney will be confidential—that all such communications, whether conducted in person, by mail, or by telephone, are subject to government monitoring.

The devastating effect of such a policy on the right to counsel was recently recognized by the United States Court of Appeals for the Seventh Circuit, speaking through Chief Judge Richard A. Posner:

We put to the government at oral argument the following example. The government adopts and announces a policy of taping all conversations between criminal defendants and their lawyers. It does not turn the tapes over to the prosecutors. It merely stores them in the National Archives. The government's lawyer took the position that none of the defendants could complain about such conduct because none could be harmed by it, provided the prosecutors never got their hands on the tapes. We are inclined to disagree, although for a reason that will become apparent shortly we need not attempt to resolve the issue definitively. *The*

hypothetical practice that we have described would, because of its pervasiveness and publicity, greatly undermine the freedom of communication between defendants and their lawyers and with it the efficacy of the right to counsel, because knowledge that a permanent record was being made of the conversations between the defendants and their lawyers would make the defendants reluctant to make candid disclosures. (Totalitarian-style continuous surveillance must surely be a great inhibitor of communication.)
—*United States v. DiDomenico*, 78 F.3d 294, 299 (7th Cir. 1996).

The Regulation Violates Prisoners' Constitutional Right of Access to the Courts

Separate and distinct from the Sixth Amendment rights of persons facing criminal charges, "[i]t is . . . established beyond doubt that prisoners have a constitutional right of access to the courts." *Bounds v. Smith*, 430 U.S. 817, 821, 97 S. Ct. 1491, 1494, 52 L.Ed.2d 72 (1977). This right is not limited to pretrial detainees facing criminal charges, or those appealing criminal convictions, but extends to convicted prisoners who may wish to seek a writ of *habeas corpus* or file an action challenging the conditions of their confinement. Indeed, "[b]ecause a prisoner ordinarily is divested of the privilege to vote, the right to file a court action might be said to be his remaining most fundamental political right, because preservative of all rights." *McCarthy v. Madigan*, 503 U.S. 140, 153, 112 S.Ct. 1081, 1091, 117 L.Ed.2d 291 (1992).[2] This right of access to the courts "means that inmates must have a reasonable opportunity to seek and receive the assistance of attorneys. Regulations and practices that unjustifiably obstruct the availability of professional representation . . . are invalid." *Procunier v. Martinez*, 416 U.S. 396, 419, 94 S.Ct. 1800, 1814, 40 L.Ed.2d 224 (1974).[3]

Federal courts have uniformly recognized that the right to receive the assistance of counsel includes the right to communicate confidentially with counsel. As one federal court of appeals has stated:

Citation of authority is hardly needed for the proposition that an inmate's right of unfettered access to the courts is as fundamental a right as any other he may hold. All other rights of an inmate are illusory without it, being entirely dependent for their existence on the whim or caprice of the prison warden. The judiciary, moreover, has not been content merely to keep free the lines of communication between the inmate, the courts, and agencies of correction. Whether as a vital concomitant of the prisoner's right to petition the bench or as a distinct requirement of his right to effective counsel guaranteed by the Sixth Amendment, a right of access by an inmate to counsel has been perceived by a number of courts. *Johnson v. Avery*, 393 U.S. 483, 89 S.Ct. 747, 21 L.Ed.2d 718 (1969), for example, required that prison authorities allow inmates ready access to jailhouse lawyers. In the same vein, prison officials have been prohibited from interfering with postal communications between an inmate and his counsel which relate to the legality of either his criminal conviction or the conditions of his incarceration, even where the lawyer is not the inmate's counsel of record. *The final phase of this development has been a recognition that the effective protection of access to counsel requires that the traditional privacy of the lawyer-client relationship be implemented in the prison context.*
   —*Adams v. Carlson*, 488 F.2d 619, 630–31 (7th Cir. 1973) (citations omitted, emphasis added).

See also *Bach v. People of the State of Illinois*, 504 F.2d 1100, 1102 (7th Cir. 1974) ("We think that contact with an attorney and the opportunity to communicate privately is a vital ingredient to [a prisoner's] effective assistance of counsel and access to the courts"); *Smith v. Robbins*, 454 F.2d 696, 697 (1st Cir. 1972) ("[T]he prisoner has a right to have the confidence between himself and his counsel totally respected"); *Bieregu v. Reno*, 59 F.3d 1445, 1456 (3d Cir. 1995) ("the right of court access guarantees the privacy of attorney-client communications").
   For these reasons, it is well established that attorney-client mail may not be read by prison officials. See Bieregu, 59 F.3d at 1456 ("[o]f all communications, attorney mail is

the most sacrosanct"); *Adams*, 488 F.2d at 631; *Smith*, 454 F.2d at 696-97; see also *Muhammad v. Pitcher*, 35 F.3d 1081, 1083 (6th Cir. 1994) (prisoner "has a fundamental interest in maintaining the confidentiality" of correspondence from the state Attorney General's office; failure to treat such mail as confidential is unconstitutional).
   Similarly, courts agree that prisoners must be allowed confidential in-person consultations with attorneys. See *Ruiz v. Estelle*, 679 F.2d 1115, 1154–55 (5th Cir. 1982) (affirming injunction prohibiting censorship of attorney-client mail and ensuring confidential attorney-client interviews); *Dawson v. Kendrick*, 527 F. Supp. 1252, 1314 (S.D.W. Va. 1981) (prisoners' right of access to courts "carries with it the right to seek, obtain and communicate privately with counsel;" attorney-client interview area that does not provide privacy is inadequate); see also *Williams v. Price*, 25 F.Supp.2d 623, 630 (W.D. Pa. 1998) (prison officials' failure to provide facilities for confidential attorney-client conversation violates prisoners' First Amendment free speech and Fourteenth Amendment privacy rights).
   Once again, it is no answer to say that under the regulation, "properly privileged materials" will not be retained. The violation of the prisoner's right to counsel does not require that privileged communications be affirmatively used against the prisoner in a criminal prosecution, or even that such communications be intercepted. Rather, the violation occurs as soon as the prisoner and his lawyer are informed that their confidential attorney-client communications will henceforth be monitored by government agents.
   Indeed, courts have explicitly rejected the argument that the prisoner's rights are not violated as long as confidential communications are not actually intercepted. In *Muhammad v. Pitcher*, 35 F.3d 1081 (6th Cir. 1994), a prisoner challenged the prison's policy of opening mail addressed to him from the state Attorney General's office. Prison officials argued that because the actual piece of mail they opened was not itself confidential, the prisoner's rights had not been violated. The court rejected this argument, noting that it "overlooks the chilling effect that

the challenged policy has on inmates who desire to correspond confidentially with the state Attorney General." Id. at 1083. As the court noted, "[i]t is well-settled that a chilling effect on one's constitutional rights constitutes a present injury in fact." Id. at 1084. Other courts have similarly recognized that monitoring of attorney-client communications has an impermissible chilling effect on those communications, regardless of what, if anything, is actually intercepted. See *Smith*, 454 F.2d at 697 (noting that "a prisoner, and possibly some attorneys, may feel, if only to a small degree, that someone in the chain of command may not be trusted, and that the resulting fear may chill communications between the prisoner and his counsel. . . . [W]e see no reason to leave such possible apprehensions on such an important matter as right to counsel in the minds of the prisoner or his attorney"); *Taylor v. Sterrett*, 532 F.2d 462, 469 (5th Cir. 1976); *Bieregu*, 59 F.3d at 1452.

The Regulation Violates the Fourth Amendment

The Fourth Amendment to the Constitution prohibits "unreasonable searches and seizures." Although the Fourth Amendment rights of incarcerated persons are diminished, they are not non-existent, and the warrantless interception of attorney-client communications contemplated by the regulation violates these rights.

In *Hudson v. Palmer*, 468 U.S. 517, 530, 104 S. Ct. 3194 (1984), the Supreme Court held that the Fourth Amendment does not apply to searches of prisoners' cells. The Court reasoned that prison security requires that prison officials have "[u]nfettered access" to prisoners' cells to search for contraband. 468 U.S. at 527, 104 S. Ct. at 3200. However, even after Hudson, "[t]he door on prisoner's rights against unreasonable searches has not been slammed shut and locked." *United States v. Cohen*, 796 F.2d 20, 23 (2d Cir. 1986). For example, if a cell search is initiated by prosecutors for law enforcement purposes, rather than by prison officials for prison security purposes, prisoners

do retain Fourth Amendment rights, and a warrant must be obtained. Id. at 24.

Moreover, courts have recognized that in contexts other than cell searches, "a convicted prisoner maintains some reasonable expectations of privacy while in prison." *Cornwell v. Dahlberg*, 963 F.2d 912, 916 (6th Cir. 1992). For example, because of the common understanding that one has a privacy interest in one's naked body, strip searches and body cavity searches of prisoners must be justified under the Fourth Amendment. See, e.g., *Covino v. Patrissi*, 967 F.2d 73, 78 (2d Cir. 1992) ("we have little doubt that society is prepared to recognize as reasonable the retention of a limited right of bodily privacy even in the prison context").

The confidentiality of attorney-client communications is one of the strongest expectations of privacy known to our society. For centuries these communications have been universally recognized as confidential, even after the client's death, because of the importance of "encourag[ing] the client to communicate fully and frankly with counsel." *Swidler & Berlin v. United States*, 524 U.S. 399, 410–11, 118 S. Ct. 2081, 2088 (1998). If this confidentiality survives death, it surely survives incarceration, and incarcerated persons retain a reasonable expectation of privacy in these communications. Thus, any interception of these communications must be justified under the Fourth Amendment.

Determining whether a search is reasonable under the Fourth Amendment "requires a balancing of the need for the particular search against the invasion of personal rights that the search entails." *Bell v. Wolfish*, 441 U.S. 520, 559, 99 S. Ct. 1861 (1979) (involving pretrial detainees). The warrantless interception of attorney-client communications cannot pass this test.

As explained above, the invasion of the attorney-client privilege is total; all such communications are subject to interception. Moreover, the warrantless searches that courts have approved in the prison context, such as cell searches and strip searches, have been based on the need to maintain prison security (for example, by preventing the smuggling of drugs or weapons), and courts have granted great deference to the expertise of prison officials in that area. *See Hudson, supra.* By contrast, interception of attorney-client communications under the regulation is done for general law enforcement purposes, not prison security reasons, and is in no way based on the special expertise of prison officials. These searches therefore require more stringent scrutiny under the Fourth Amendment. *See Cohen, supra.*

Thus, under the Fourth Amendment, attorney-client communications cannot be intercepted without a warrant based on a finding of probable cause. As the Supreme Court has stated:

> The presence of a search warrant serves a high function. Absent some grave emergency, the Fourth Amendment has interposed a magistrate between the citizen and the police. This was done not to shield criminals nor to make the home a safe haven for illegal activities. It was done so that an objective mind might weigh the need to invade that privacy in order to enforce the law. The right of privacy was deemed too precious to entrust to the discretion of those whose job is the detection of crime and the arrest of criminals.
>
> —*McDonald v. United States*, 335 U.S. 451, 455–56, 69 S. Ct. 191, 193, 93 L.Ed. 153 (1948).

In this case, given the paramount privacy interests at stake, the Fourth Amendment does not permit the Attorney General to decide, unilaterally and without judicial oversight, to eavesdrop on the confidential attorney-client communications of persons he is seeking to prosecute.[4]

The Regulation Is Vague, Contains No Meaningful Standards, and Provides No Oversight or Review of the Attorney General's Decision to Eavesdrop on Attorney-Client Communications

The regulation allows monitoring of attorney-client communications whenever the Attorney General believes there is "reasonable suspicion" that a person in federal custody "may" use communications with attorneys or their agents "to further or facilitate acts of terrorism." However, there is no provision for judicial review of the Attorney General's determination, which is apparently effective indefinitely. No definition of "reasonable suspicion" or "acts of terrorism" is provided. There is no requirement of a finding that the attorney in question would be likely to cooperate with the detainee in furthering "acts of terrorism."[5]

Once the Attorney General makes this determination, the client and his attorneys are to be notified that "all communications between the inmate and attorneys may be monitored, to the extent determined to be reasonably necessary for the purpose of deterring future acts of violence or terrorism." The term "acts of violence or terrorism" is not defined, but this provision appears to be more expansive than that set forth in the previous paragraph, which allows monitoring of attorney-client communications only upon a finding that the detainee may use such communications to further or facilitate "acts of terrorism." Moreover, the regulation does not specify the standards used to determine the extent of monitoring that is "reasonably necessary," nor identify the person who makes that determination.

Intercepted attorney-client communications are to be reviewed by a "privilege team" to ensure that "properly privileged materials . . . are not retained." The "privilege team" may disclose intercepted information if "the person in charge of the privilege team determines that acts of violence or terrorism are imminent." However, there is no indication of the identity or qualifications of members of the "privilege team," except that they are "not involved in the underlying investigation." There is no review of the "privilege team's" determination as to which of the intercepted attorney-client communications are privileged. Similarly, there are no standards for, and no review of, the determination by the "person in charge of the privilege team" that "acts of violence or terrorism are imminent." Such vague, standardless language invites arbitrary, inconsistent, and discriminatory application of the regulation. More fundamentally, to have the Attorney

General determine, unilaterally and without judicial oversight or review, when to eavesdrop on the attorney-client communications of a person whom he may be seeking to prosecute is completely inconsistent with our adversarial system of justice.

The Regulation Is Unnecessary Because Existing Law Allows Monitoring of Attorney-Client Communications Upon a Showing of Probable Cause and Issuance of a Warrant

Finally, the regulation is entirely unnecessary. If federal officials have probable cause to believe that a detainee is using communications with his attorney to further a criminal purpose, existing law allows them to obtain a search warrant to intercept these communications. Indeed, the Supreme Court has even approved searches of an attorney's law office, provided a warrant has first been obtained from a neutral and detached magistrate. See *Andresen v. Maryland*, 427 U.S. 463, 479-80, 96 S. Ct. 2737, 2748, 49 L.Ed.2d 627 (1976) (approving search of law office pursuant to a warrant based on probable cause); *National City Trading Corp. v. United States*, 635 F.2d 1020, 1026 (2d Cir. 1980) (same).

Thus, if prison officials have reason to believe that a particular prisoner is using legal mail, or any other privileged mail, to violate the law or threaten security, "they may, upon a showing of probable cause, obtain a search warrant to read and open the mail." *Guajardo v. Estelle*, 580 F.2d 748, 759 (5th Cir. 1978). See, e.g., *Benjamin v. Kerik*, 102 F.Supp.2d 157, 178 (S.D.N.Y. 2000), aff'd, 264 F.3d 175 (2d Cir. 2001) (New York City jail system "does not read or censor ingoing or outgoing inmate mail except pursuant to a lawful search warrant"). Similarly, if the government has probable cause to believe that a prisoner is using attorney-client conversations to further criminal activity, it may obtain a warrant from a federal judge to intercept those communications. See *United States v. Harrelson*, 754 F.2d 1153, 1168–69

(5th Cir. 1985) (approving court-authorized electronic surveillance of conversations between federal prisoner and attorney).

Conclusion

Existing law strikes an appropriate balance between legitimate law enforcement needs and the right of clients to communicate confidentially with their attorneys. This regulation, which gives the Attorney General unfettered authority to strip clients and their counsel of this ancient and fundamental right, is unconstitutional, dangerous, and entirely unnecessary. It should be rescinded immediately.

Submitted this 20th day of December, 2001.

*Comments of the following

American Civil Liberties Union
David C. Fathi, Staff Counsel
Amy B. Fettig, Litigation Fellow
733 15th St. N.W., Suite 620
Washington, DC 20005
(202) 393-4930

Steven R. Shapiro, Legal Director
125 Broad Street
New York, NY 10004
(212) 549-2500

Laura W. Murphy, Director,
Washington National Office
Rachel King, Legislative Counsel
122 Maryland Ave. N.E.
Washington, DC 20002
(202) 544-1681

Notes

1. In an October 12, 2001 memorandum to the heads of all federal departments and agencies, the Attorney General cautioned against release of privileged documents pursuant to the Freedom of Information Act. Ironically, in this memorandum the Attorney General specifically recognized the importance of the attorney-client privilege and the "sound policies underlying" that privilege. See Ashcroft

FOIA Memorandum, available at <http://www.usdoj.gov/oip/foiapost/2001foiapost19.htm>

2. The importance of a prisoner's right to challenge his conditions of confinement is illustrated by reports of mistreatment of those held in the wake of the September 11 attacks. See Benjamin Weiser, "Jordanian Student Held in U.S. Says Police Abused Him in Jail," *N.Y. Times,* December 5, 2001, at B8.

3. In *Lewis v. Casey,* 518 U.S. 343, 349, 116 S. Ct. 2174, 135 L.Ed.2d 606 (1996), the Supreme Court held that a prisoner's right of access to the courts is not violated unless the prisoner shows "actual injury." However, Lewis does not apply to prison officials' affirmative interference with a prisoner's access to counsel; nor does it apply to the Sixth Amendment rights of pretrial detainees. *Benjamin v. Fraser,* 264 F.3d 175, 185 (2d Cir. 2001).

4. As explained below, it is already possible under existing law to intercept prisoners' attorney-client communications when a warrant has been issued based upon a finding of probable cause that criminal activity is occurring.

5. The regulation appears simply to presume that attorneys, who are officers of the court and who undergo extensive background checks before they are admitted to the bar, would willingly cooperate in criminal or terrorist activity. Federal courts have been unwilling to make this presumption. See, e.g., *Adams v. Carlson,* 488 F.2d 619, 631-32 (7th Cir. 1973) (before requiring that attorney-client visits take place in a room divided by a glass barrier, "a prison warden must come forward with facts which tend to support a reasonable suspicion not only that contraband is being smuggled to inmates . . . , but that their attorneys are engaged in the smuggling") (emphasis added).

Signatories to the ACLU comments are:

American Immigration Lawyers Association

Arab American Institute

Asian American Legal Defense Education Fund

Center for Democracy & Technology

DC Prisoners' Legal Services Project

Electronic Privacy Information Center

Equal Justice Program, Howard University School of Law

Friends Committee on National Legislation

Lawyers Committee for Human Rights

Legal Action Center

Legal Aid Society of New York

Libertarian Party

The Multiracial Activist

National Association for the Advancement of Colored People

National Black Police Association

Unitarian Universalist Association of Congregations

Washington Council of Lawyers

World Organization Against Torture

Reprinted from: American Civil Liberties Union online comments <http://www.aclu.org/safeandfree/122001_comments.pdf> ✦

8

Big Guns, Little Guns

On the Role of Military and Private Gun Ownership in Combating Foreign Terrorism in the United States After 9/11

Dave Klinger
Dave Grossman

When foreign terrorists slammed hijacked airliners into the World Trade Center towers and the Pentagon on September 11, 2001 (9/11), it was the first time since British troops invaded our shores during the War of 1812 that foreign nationals carried out a successful attack on U.S. soil. The attacks of 9/11 shocked our nation and prompted many changes in the way America approaches terrorism. We now have armed soldiers standing guard at our nation's airports; security at nuclear plants and other vulnerable targets has been beefed up; and military jets are patrolling our skies in order to intercept and possibly shoot down hijacked jets before they can be smashed into their intended targets. Much has also changed on the legal front. New laws have been instituted that expand the power of the police to spy on people, for example, and the President has announced that suspected terrorists who are not U.S. citizens may be tried in special military tribunals.

These and other changes have come about because government officials have decided that such changes are needed to protect our nation from the sorts of terrorist attacks that they believe are most likely to occur or would

be most disruptive to our way of life (e.g., airline hijackings and attacks on nuclear facilities). A look at the situation we currently face, however, suggests that we should make some other changes that would allow us to deal more effectively with a potential threat that we have so far overlooked: military-style attacks by well-trained terrorist cells in public spaces such as schools, shopping malls, churches, and sports arenas.

The responsibility for dealing with attacks of this sort currently rests solely with the police, but consideration of the matter indicates that the police would be quickly overmatched should a group of terrorists conduct a military-style assault. This chapter shows why the police may not be capable of dealing effectively with military-style assaults by terrorist cells and argues that we should allow the U.S. military to take on terrorists under certain conditions. It will also discuss how a successful military-style terrorist assault might damage public confidence in the government's ability to protect its citizens and how this loss of confidence might affect the way that Americans view private gun ownership.

The Threat of Military-Style Attacks

We are concerned about military-style assaults in the United States because they are a tactic that Islamic terrorists have used extensively overseas. Palestinian gunmen have carried out such attacks against Israelis for decades, and other Islamic terrorists have conducted military-style assaults against other targets as well. A notable attack of this type occurred in 1981, when a group of Islamic fundamentalist Egyptian soldiers assassinated President Anwar Sadat as he was reviewing troops during a parade. Egypt was also home to another notable military-style terrorist attack when, in 1997, a group of Islamic fundamentalists killed 58 foreign tourists and four Egyptians at the Temple of Hatshepsut in Luxor. Similar attacks have long occurred in other parts of the Islamic world and have continued since 9/11; the most visible one was in October of 2001, when Islamic militants armed with assault rifles killed a Muslim security guard and 15 worshipers attending services at an Anglican Church in Bahawalpur, Pakistan. Given this history, we would be unwise to believe that terrorist groups that have conducted military-style attacks in other nations would not be willing to do so within our borders.

Although the United States has so far avoided military-style terrorist attacks by foreign nationals, the last 35 years have seen numerous cases in which Americans have executed well-planned large-scale attacks on their fellow citizens. The first, and one of the bloodiest, of these occurred on August 1, 1966, when a former Marine named Charles Whitman went on a rampage for more than an hour with two rifles and a shotgun at the University of Texas at Austin. From a tower, he shot more than 40 people before being killed by the police.

One reason Whitman's attack lasted so long is that the Austin police, like every other police department in the mid-1960s, did not have the equipment, the organization, or the training needed to effectively deal with an assault by a heavily armed adversary. That Whitman was able to hold police at bay for more than an hour led many law enforcement agencies to develop specially trained and equipped units that could rapidly resolve similar situations. These units came to be known as SWAT teams (for Special Weapons and Tactics). Today, nearly all large law enforcement agencies and many small ones in the United States have some sort of SWAT team.

In the years since Whitman's rampage, SWAT teams have been called upon to deal with many sorts of special threat situations besides crazed people firing at innocents (hostage situations, for example). As SWAT teams developed a base of experience, the notion that SWAT should rush into crisis situations gave way to a different sort of police doctrine. It was found that the most effective and safest thing that SWAT could do in the vast majority of situations they handled was to slow things down, contain whatever problem was afoot, gain control of the problem location, and work to de-escalate the situa-

tion through negotiations or some other nonlethal means. As experience showed that patient SWAT action was a sound way to deal with many sorts of critical incidents, the notion of taking things slow during dangerous situations became the norm in other realms of police work. Indeed, until quite recently, it was widespread police doctrine that patrol officers who found themselves in special threat incidents should not attempt to resolve them, but rather should seek to contain the situation and call for the SWAT team, which would then patiently work to resolve the situation.

The doctrine that patrol officers should handle all critical incidents by standing by and calling for SWAT and that SWAT should move slowly toward resolution was called into question in the 1990s, when a wave of school shootings in which one or two students viciously attacked their classmates swept across the country. Prior to the spring of 1999, all of these shootings had ended by the time the first police officers arrived on the scene, so little thought was given to the standard police response of waiting and taking things slowly in ongoing special threat situations. Then, on April 20, 1999, two students from Columbine High School in Jefferson County, Colorado, invaded their school with a cache of guns and homemade explosives and killed 15 people (including themselves).

What made Columbine different from previous school shootings is that police officers were on the scene throughout the rampage; one police officer even exchanged gunshots with the two students before they entered the school. Within minutes, moreover, other officers had arrived at the school. Rather than immediately going into the school to halt the shooting, however, these officers followed the standard police doctrine of containing the location and calling for SWAT. SWAT officers did not enter the school until some 35 minutes after the two gunmen shot their last victim (and 10 minutes after they had killed themselves). SWAT then slowly moved through the building and methodically evacuated students, staff, and faculty, taking some four hours to complete the process.

The officers who responded to the Columbine massacre were roundly criticized from many quarters for waiting outside the school while the killers executed students inside and for moving slowly through the building once they went in. Among the many lessons that American law enforcement took from Columbine was that time was not always on their side when dealing with armed intruders—that waiting to negotiate with people who have no interest in doing so only increases the odds that innocents will die. This realization has led to a change in police doctrine regarding the proper response to critical incidents. Since Columbine, law enforcement officials have come to realize that the "take it slow" model is not appropriate for all special threat situations—that there are times when police officers need to move fast in order to protect innocents from murderers who are interested in quickly killing as many people as possible.

This realization has led to enhanced law enforcement training designed to provide patrol officers with the tools needed to stop killers who are in the process of actively shooting other people. The training, in what has come to be known as "rapid response" tactics, often includes simulation exercises with paintball guns and other types of weapons whose projectiles leave some sort of mark when they strike a person or object, and it often takes place in real schools. Police officers are trained to ignore the wounded and to move rapidly toward "the sound of the guns" in order to stop the killings as quickly as possible.

Limitations and a Proposed Solution

Although "rapid response tactics" and the mindset behind them are a welcome step forward in police preparedness for dealing with active shooters, they are not adequate for dealing with large-scale, well-coordinated terrorist attacks. Rapid response tactics were designed to deal with one or two disturbed individuals carrying run-of-the-mill weapons, not well-trained foreign terrorist cells equipped with military ordnance. Consequently, the first police officers responding to a military-style terrorist attack would

quickly find themselves outgunned, and it would then be up to SWAT to save the day. The problem is that SWAT also could well be outgunned, for SWAT teams are trained and equipped to deal with conventional criminals, not foreign terrorists. They simply do not have the capabilities to match the explosives, armor, and support systems that well-equipped terrorists could use in an attack. Because the police are not prepared to effectively deal with attacks by groups of terrorist shooters, we believe that the nation needs to set up a system that will allow the U.S. military to respond to such situations on short notice.

As a general rule, we are opposed to the use of the U.S. military for law enforcement purposes on U.S. soil. When terrorists from abroad take or plan to take violent actions on U.S. soil, however, they are not merely violating laws, they are committing acts of war. Because combating war is what the military is designed to do, when foreign nationals (and U.S. citizens aiding and abetting them) wage war on U.S. soil, they should not be viewed as criminals who should be arrested under the aegis of the Fourth Amendment of the Constitution, which requires that police officers show substantial restraint when they seize citizens. Rather, they should be treated as enemy soldiers who fall under the wholly different legal strictures of warfare.

No one objected when the federal government announced in the wake of 9/11 that military aircraft with the assignment to shoot down hijacked jetliners would be patrolling U.S. air space for the indefinite future. No one objected because it was apparent to all that there is no way to prevent terrorist suicide jets from completing attacks other than having military jets fire missiles into them. There is simply no other way to accomplish the task of protecting targets on the ground from sky-borne assaults. In the same way, we believe that the time has come for U.S. military personnel to be on standby to respond should foreign terrorists (or U.S. residents acting as soldiers for a foreign interest) launch a ground-based attack. Because such an attack would quickly overwhelm police capacity to protect life, the law enforcement officials in charge should be able to quickly call for military assistance.

Indeed, we believe that the police should be able to obtain military support in other sorts of situations in which it is reasonable to believe that the people they are dealing with are foreign terrorists (or U.S. residents acting as soldiers for a foreign interest). We argue for this because there are other situations besides active shooter assaults where police capabilities would not match up with the threat posed by terrorists. One situation of this sort would be when law enforcement officials locate terrorists who are planning an attack at a location such as a safe house. Just as police officers are not well prepared to stop terrorist attacks that are in progress, they are ill prepared to deal with terrorists who would be willing to use extreme violence to defeat an attempt to arrest them.

The history of American policing is full of cases in which officers were outgunned by the criminal suspects they went to arrest. In many such cases both officers and innocent citizens were wounded or killed as the police exchanged gunfire with suspects. And these cases involved rag-tag criminals and mentally disturbed individuals, not dedicated terrorists. A group of well-trained terrorists equipped with top-notch military hardware could easily carry the fight to the police who came to get them and cause large numbers of casualties among both the police and citizens in the immediate area.

Under our proposed model, in order to prevent the loss of innocent life that almost surely would come in a protracted shoot-out between the police and a terrorist group, the local civilian authorities (e.g., the mayor) would inform a military officer (designated beforehand) that the police had located a terrorist cell and requested assistance. The house would be surrounded by a combination of local SWAT officers and U.S. military forces. If the terrorists inside surrendered when the demand to do so was issued, they would be taken into custody using standard law enforcement procedures. If, on the other hand, the terrorists did not surrender to the police, the military would be there to destroy the house and all inside with whatever ordnance was proper as soon as the first shot

rang out from inside the location. No hour-long gun battle, no police officers firing small arms as they were attacked with explosives and automatic weapons, no unnecessary risk to thousands of innocent civilians living within the range of aggressive gunfire—just swift, sure death to those who invaded (albeit on a small scale) our nation.

America has begun to grasp that things have indeed changed since 9/11. But if Americans don't think ahead and prepare for the worst-case scenario—for the next terrorist step—then we are sure to experience additional potentially preventable deaths, perhaps not on the scale of 9/11, but a large number nonetheless. A large well-armed and disciplined terrorist cell that attacked a large school, a sports arena, or any other of the many sorts of places where thousands of Americans congregate could kill vast numbers of people before the police could stop them. Because the police have very limited capacity to deal with threats of this sort, we need to get the military working, within the framework of the Constitution, with civilian law enforcement to protect innocent U.S. citizens from the future acts of war that our adversaries have promised to visit upon us.

The Legal Barrier

Our proposal that the military be utilized to deal with terrorists on U.S. soil runs smack up against Federal law, which generally prohibits military involvement in civilian law enforcement activities. The relevant Federal law is the *Posse Comitatus Act*, which Congress passed in 1878 because of concerns about some of the ways that military units were used during Reconstruction. The Act reflects a long-standing American tradition that the military and civilian realms of society be kept separate and that the use of the Army in civilian law enforcement activity be outlawed "except in cases and under circumstances expressly authorized by the Constitution or Act of Congress." (By extension, the Air Force is included because it was originally a branch of the Army.) The Act does not cover the Navy or the Marines, but the Department of Defense has issued regulations that extend it to these branches of the armed forces as well. Thus, the *Posse Comitatus Act* and subsequent regulations substantially restrict the legal capacity of any of the four branches of the military to act directly against anyone in the United States who would try to commit terrorist acts.

Because the *Posse Comitatus Act* allows Congress to authorize the military to enforce specific laws in specific cases and circumstances, however, these restrictions are not set in stone. Presently, the largest exception to the Act that Congress has carved out concerns enforcing drug laws. As the so-called "War on Drugs" heated up during the 1980s, Congress authorized the military to assist the anti-drug efforts of civilian police agencies by providing them with training, equipment, and help in conducting surveillance operations. These "Drug War Exceptions" to the *Posse Comitatus Act* do not allow servicemen and servicewomen to take direct action against civilians, however, which speaks volumes about America's reluctance to let soldiers deal with people who engage in illegal behavior on U.S. soil.

Given the existence of the *Posse Comitatus Act* and our nation's deep-seated social sentiment that the military should stay out of law enforcement, our proposal that military units engage terrorists in combat must overcome both legal and cultural barriers. The first barrier is, in theory, rather simple to surmount: Congress can create a terrorist exception to the Act (similar to the drug-war exception) that allows members of the military to directly engage terrorists. The second barrier might not be so easy to overcome, for it may prove difficult to get the American public to support legislation that runs against our long-standing aversion to military action against civilians. America quickly acceded to armed troops standing guard in airports and other locations around the country in the wake of 9/11, but these GIs are simply providing security. We believe that Americans would not so quickly agree to give the military wide-ranging powers to take offensive action against people here in the United States (nor do we believe that they should do so).

It seems to us that the cultural barrier can be overcome through the legislative process that is necessary to overcome the legal one. If Congress were to create an exception to the *Posse Comitatus Act* that would limit military action to only those sorts of terrorist threats that law enforcement clearly is not designed to handle, they could craft a narrow law that would allow the military to respond when needed, while at the same time retaining strict limits on military powers. Legislation that would restrict military activity to those situations in which probable cause exists that the individuals plotting or engaging in terrorist activity are foreign nationals (or American citizens working on behalf of a foreign power) would be such a law. With this approach, the civilian authorities could call for military assistance only if probable cause is established; if not, the police would handle the situation.

This probable cause standard would set a bright line that civilian authorities could look to when in the midst of a situation that could involve foreign (or foreign-sponsored) terrorism. The standard would also provide the same bright line for military commanders who would have to sign off on the deployment of military forces when their civilian counterparts request assistance. If military assets were to be committed in a situation in which the probable cause threshold were not met, then the civilian authorities and military commanders in charge would be subject to the penalty provisions of the *Posse Comitatus Act* (which consist of unspecified fines and up to two years of imprisonment). This threat should be sufficient to preclude precipitous deployment of military assets in regular police matters.

On the other hand, the probable cause standard would allow for mistakes made in good faith that might arise during quickly evolving situations. Take, for example, a replay of the May, 1995, case in which a deranged man stole a tank from a National Guard armory and went on an extended joyride through San Diego, California, destroying much in his path before the police were able to kill him when the tank suffered a mechanical failure. We would argue that in the current climate, it would be eminently reasonable to believe that a tank rolling through an American city is somehow connected to foreign terrorism and that it would therefore be reasonable to use military assets (an anti-tank missile fired from an Army helicopter, perhaps) to stop its rampage. If it turned out that the situation was utterly unrelated to foreign terrorism (as was the case in the San Diego incident), those who called for and authorized the military strike would not be criminally liable because the decisions to employ the military would have been based on probable cause that there was a foreign terrorist link.

A terrorist exception to the *Posse Comitatus Act* could even help clarify the circumstances under which military action would be authorized by setting out specific conditions that would constitute the necessary probable cause. The law could state, for example, that the use of military hardware such as tanks and armored personnel carriers in attacks constitutes the probable cause necessary to call out the military. The list of specific circumstances would be a short one, but it would provide helpful guidance for civilian authorities and military commanders when violent incidents erupt.

Crafting a sound terrorism exception to the *Posse Comitatus Act* will require substantial thought and careful consideration of many factors by our legislators. We believe that Congress should go through the deliberative process necessary to come up with a bill that will allow the military to deal directly with foreign terrorism. If they do not, Americans will continue to stand naked against the threat of violence that law enforcement is simply not equipped to deal with. As David Gergen, Editor at Large for *U.S. News and World Report* put it: "Whatever the nature of the next attack, if another 'big one' comes and the government is woefully unprepared or incompetent, public confidence will collapse at home and the war effort will be badly crippled."

Private Gun Ownership

The crisis of confidence that would follow governmental failure in the face of another "big one" would likely have substantial re-

percussions in another realm of legislation: gun laws. A look around the globe indicates that western nations have adopted two basic responses to terrorism: the British model, which combines restrictive gun laws with extensive public surveillance, and the Israeli or Swiss model, in which large numbers of citizens are armed and trained how to use their weapons. Thus, there are two competing models that our nation can turn to for how we should respond in the face of growing terrorist threats: reduce civil liberties and restrict individuals' access to firearms, or maintain civil liberties and perhaps even expand individuals' access to firearms. Although 9/11 raised the visibility level of many safety-related issues, access to guns has so far received minimal attention, perhaps because the men who hijacked all four planes used blades, not bullets, to perpetrate their crimes. Because a military-style assault would, by definition, involve guns, on the other hand, it would likely focus considerable attention on the gun law issue.

It can be argued that the original application of the Second Amendment was that "the people" referred to the general population, and "a well ordered militia" also referred to the general American public and its ability to protect itself from raids by Indians and invasions by foreigners. This original intent can be observed in the militia enactments, passed by the U.S. Congress in 1792, which required that "every able-bodied male citizen between the ages of 18 and 45 be enrolled [in the militia] and equip himself with appropriate weaponry. . . ." In 1903, new legislation "divided the class of able-bodied male citizens between 18 and 45 years of age into an 'organized militia' to be known as the National Guard of the several States, and the remainder of which was then described as the 'reserve militia,' and which later statutes have termed the 'unorganized militia.' " Today, faced with a new threat from abroad, this meaning is likely to reassert itself.

Indeed, this interpretation has been reaffirmed in a recent opinion from the Fifth Circuit Court of Appeals. In *U.S. vs. Emerson*, the Court held that "All evidence indicates that the Second Amendment, like other parts of the Bill of Rights, applies to and protects individual Americans. We find that the history of the Second Amendment reinforces the plain meaning of its text, namely that it protects individual Americans in their right to keep and bear arms whether or not they are a member of a select militia or performing active military service or training."

Applications for concealed gun permits have skyrocketed since the 9/11 attacks—despite the fact that it is difficult, if not impossible, to conceive of a scenario in which civilians' carrying of weapons could prevent an airline hijacking (since such weapons cannot be carried on aircraft). If Americans have responded to crimes in the air (where they cannot carry firearms) by arming themselves, then the demand for gun permits would probably be quite dramatic in the wake of a military-style terrorist attack on the ground (where citizens would be allowed to carry their guns), even though pistols would have very limited value in the sort of case that prompted the demand.

Conclusion

The possibility of a military-style terrorist attack is very high because: (1) it is consistent with the Middle Eastern terrorist *modus operandi* (MO) and is salient in their minds from recent events, and (2) it is an effective and simple means of creating mass casualties and terror. We cannot expect authorities to prevent every single attack of this sort that is in the offing, so we must think hard about how best to reduce the loss of innocent life once such an attack commences. Because

the military has the assets to accomplish this goal by stopping such attacks in short order, we need to immediately reconsider the role of the military in domestic terrorist situations and lay the groundwork for them to support law enforcement forces in active terrorist attacks.

Finally, in the face of the threat posed by terrorists from abroad, we foresee that there will likely be a significant reassessment of gun laws and the interpretation of the Second Amendment. If we had been told a year ago that 18-year-old soldiers with loaded weapons would be in every airport in America, it is unlikely that anyone would have believed it. Similarly, the new realities associated with military-style terrorist attacks might result in changes that few would believe today. Among those changes may be a more traditional application of the Second Amendment and the concept of the "unorganized militia."

The authors sincerely hope that we are wrong in our belief that military-style attacks by foreign terrorists loom on the horizon. We also hope that if our fears are realized, our nation will have taken steps that can minimize the damage while at the same time honoring the legal and social traditions that make our nation worth defending in the first place.

Part Two

Law Enforcement and Community Policing

The police have an extremely complex role. They are responsible for many of the problems that other agencies cannot handle or are unwilling to handle. The responsibilities arise largely because the police are one of the few government agencies that is available to the public 365 days a year, seven days a week, 24 hours a day. Police agencies serve the public in a variety of ways. First, they are responsible for enforcing laws—making arrests for violent crimes, such as robbery and assault, and property crimes, such as auto theft and burglary. Second, they deal with and attempt to resolve problems in maintaining order. For example, police officers respond to complaints about arguments and disputes, loitering youths, and other types of disturbances. Third, police officers are responsible for handling service-related issues. The citizenry often call the police for medical assistance, animal control problems, and to help them with problems that they otherwise could not handle by themselves (Walker and Katz 2002).

For most of the twentieth century, with the exception of some technological innovations, policing did not change. Organizationally, the police were structured much like the military. Officers wore uniforms; the command structure was hierarchical; and there was an authoritarian rank structure. Strategically, the police relied on reactive approaches in the control of crime, such as random preventative patrol, criminal investigations, and rapid response to calls for service. The police remained distant from the community, particularly minority communities. By the beginning of the 1980s, policing in the United States began to undergo a metamorphosis. Police organizations adopted organizational structures and strategies that attempted to behave proactively to control crime and disorder. They also attempted to embrace the public, particularly traditionally disenfranchised groups, and to integrate their needs into the priorities of the police.

The changes that have taken place over the past twenty years have resulted in the police implementing new types of organizational structures and operational activities. With this change, however, has come a great deal of controversy. In Part Two, we discuss four of the most significant controversies involving police organizations and the strategies they use.

The first controversy in this section focuses on the organizational structure of police departments. Some suggest that if the police are to improve, they need to more closely resemble the military in terms of hierarchy, leadership, and management. Critics, however, contend that the police function is so different from that of the military that modeling the police after the military would be foolhardy. Two police experts debate the topic through a review of the literature and by providing anecdotes of their own experiences as police officers.

The second issue in this section examines the community policing literature and discusses changes in the role of the police over time. Some critics of community policing claim that the movement lacks substance and is only an attempt by the police to better market themselves. Supporters of community policing, however, contend that the change is real and that community policing (1) is resulting in greater contact between the police and the public; (2) has led to the police being more proactive; and (3) has focused police attention on addressing the root causes of crime. To further examine this controversy, the contributors discuss the attributes of community policing, the extent to which agencies have adopted this approach, and the impact of community policing on police effectiveness.

The third issue examines the effectiveness of zero-tolerance policing. Zero-tolerance policing focuses enforcement efforts on order maintenance problems within a community. Supporters of zero-tolerance policing argue that by focusing police resources and time on disorder and minor forms of crime, order will be restored, which will eventually result in less crime. Critics of this strategy, however, argue that zero-tolerance policing results in increased conflicts between the police and the public and results in more incidents in which the police use excessive force. Two chapters in this section review zero-tolerance policing as it is used in New York City, explain the effect the strategy has had on crime, and discuss its impact on poor and minority communities.

The fourth controversial issue in this section focuses on racial profiling—otherwise known as "driving while black." Some civil rights organizations are claiming that the police are stopping and searching African-American drivers because of their ethnicity, not because they are suspected of criminal activity. This problem, or the perception of it, has led to an even deeper divide between the police and minority communities. The police have argued that they only stop those who match a suspect's description or those who otherwise look suspicious. Those in the minority community, however, claim that the only thing that makes some drivers look suspicious is the fact that they are black. The two chapters included in this section explain the phenomenon known as driving while black and debate the nature and extent of the problem.

Reference

Walker, Samuel, and Charles M. Katz. 2002. *The Police in America: An Introduction,* Fourth Edition. McGraw-Hill: Boston. ✦

ISSUE V
Police Organizations:
Should Police Organizations Model Themselves More Like the 'Real' Military?

American police departments are organized along quasi-military lines. They wear uniforms, have comparable rank structures, are organizationally authoritarian, and are permitted to use force. This model was adopted because it was believed to be the most effective and efficient model for controlling employees and distributing workloads. As the quasi-military organizational style of management became engrained in police culture, police agencies became more centralized, bureaucratic, and authoritarian in nature. These attributes over time led to police organizations being viewed as ineffective because they were too rigid and inflexible, unable to adapt to change. As a consequence, since the 1980s, administrators in many police agencies have attempted to move away from the quasi-military style of organization. In particular, they attempted to reduce the number of rules and regulations within the organization and tried to create an organizational environment that is much less formal. In other words, they have tried to transform police agencies into organizations that allow officers greater discretion. Thus, officers will have more flexibility to solve problems, and they will feel empowered to proactively address problems.

Thomas Cowper, a 17-year police veteran and captain with the New York State Police, and Michael Buerger, professor and former police officer, debate this issue. Cowper argues that while the police have attempted to model themselves after the military, they have done so according to myths about the military model rather than according to the "real" military model. This error, he argues, has led to police organizations being highly autocratic, centralized, and intellectually rigid. He argues that participatory management, decentralization, and creative and innovative problem solving characterize the real military model, which account for the military's success over the years. He contends that because the mission and objectives of the police and military are similar, the police should adopt the real military model to improve effectiveness and efficiency.

In response, Buerger argues that the mission and objectives of the police are vastly different from the military's in that their responsibilities are much more varied, complex, and difficult to perform. He maintains that if we are to improve the police, we must change the way we view them as a profession and as employees. First, Buerger explains that the role of the police includes law enforcement, order maintenance, and service. As such, modeling the police after the military does not accurately portray the mission or duties of the police. Second, if the police are to improve, Buerger argues, they must change their hiring practices. Police departments will need to move beyond hiring individuals who are simply interested in a secure city job and must hire people who have the capacity to solve complex problems and who can work with a diverse population.

Critical Thinking Questions

1. What are three major differences between the police and the military?

2. What are the major problems in the field of policing and which "model" would be most suited to address such problems?

3. Briefly discuss how the military model has influenced policing today.

Internet Websites

Federally funded research examining the police. <http://www.ojp.usdoj.gov/bjs/lawenf.htm>

Monograph discussing police organization and structure. <http://www.ncjrs.org/pdffiles1/nij/187083.pdf>

Information about the Military Police. <http://www.militarypolice.com/>

Federally funded research examining the police. <http://www.ojp.usdoj.gov/nij/lawedocs2001.html>

Website that offers links to research on the police. <http://virlib.ncjrs.org/LawEnforcement.asp> ✦

9

The Myth of the 'Military Model' of Leadership in Law Enforcement

Thomas J. Cowper

It is a commonly accepted law enforcement notion that police agencies of the free world today are designed on the "military model" of organization and leadership. Modern analogies either lionize that model or deride it as utterly inappropriate for a civil police force. Neither view is correct: There are two military models, each based on a largely symbolic, limited, and inaccurate understanding of military doctrine and practice. One is a vicious parody, combining absurdist fiction such as Joseph Heller's *Catch-22* with a narrow view based on individual military experiences. The other is an imaginary (and inflated) heroic vision, wrapped in the flag of a different category of fiction, from the cinema accounts of Sergeant York and Audie Murphy to the *Rambo* and *Delta Force* genre. Both do a grievous disservice to both the military and the police: Each in its own way makes the military a scapegoat for the ineptitude, structural absurdities, bad management, and outright criminality in police work that are the legacies of the politicization of the American police throughout their history.

This article will not attempt to justify or defend every military practice policy or procedure throughout history as either good or applicable to policing. Clearly, the military has had more than its share of abusive commanders and unenlightened organizational policies. What it will attempt to do is dispel the notion of a single military leadership model that needs to be rejected—a stereotypical model based on authoritarian, centralized control of mindless subordinates conditioned to shoot first and ask questions later (Kopel & Blackman, 1997). This fallacious notion is causing many progressive police decision makers to ignore or reject a vast body of knowledge and experience—organizational structures, training and development philosophies, methods of operation, and practical leadership—that could radically improve the way law enforcement agencies conduct the business of policing. In fact, police commanders, who understand strategic and tactical decision-making and can incorporate effective operational planning techniques as well as organizational command and control methodologies into the conduct of police operations will increase our ability as peacekeepers to successfully resolve crisis situations without the use of military assistance, ordnance, heavy weaponry, and excessive violence.

A number of superficial similarities lend themselves to the military comparison. Police departments tend to be organized with rank structures and uniforms and incorporate many of the various accoutrements of the armed forces, designed in large measure to set cops apart from mere civilians and signal obvious membership in an organization that wields the immediate force of government. Many police executives desire for their agencies strict uniformity, respect for the chain of command, and the sharp, professional appearance of parade ground soldiers patterned after military style organization and discipline. Many individual officers themselves enjoy the apparent status and prestige afforded by a traditional association with the elite warrior class in society. Proponents of this model are quick to use symbolic "war on crime" rhetoric to justify its strict, top-down command-and-control style as essential to both the police crime suppression mandate and the requirement to control armed police officers. On the other hand, critics of the model deride it as being excessively rigid, centrally controlled by micromanaging bureaucrats, autocratic, secretive, intellectually and creatively constraining, and highly resistant to any initiative that would allow employee participation in the operational decision making process of the organization. Furthermore, many behaviorists, modern management scientists, and civil libertarians assert that the military model, this conflict-oriented, overly rigid, and centrally controlled bureaucratic organizational structure, fosters aggressive and confrontational behavior by police officers toward the public (Weber, 1999).

Time and again, the military model is held up as portraying the absolute antithesis of an enlightened, progressive, people-oriented approach to organizational management and structure. Chains of command are derided as too restrictive and rank structures as too authoritarian; uniform appearances and strict discipline are criticized for creating rigid and inflexible mind-sets. Many cops themselves purge terms such as *tactics* and *operations* and *doctrine* from their vocabulary at every opportunity, lest they acquire the bankrupt trappings of militaristic brutes through mere word association. And yet, proponents of the military model continue to uphold the paramilitary tradition, imposing control and commanding authority with strict discipline and reveling in many of the customs and courtesies that have been a part of the martial lifestyle for centuries.

During the years, progressive chiefs of police have gone to great lengths to distance themselves and their agencies from the contamination of militarism. Attempts were made to substitute traditional military style uniforms with blazers and ties or non-threatening colors such as white and beige; formal titles and positions have been eliminated in some agencies, replaced with the less Spartan, more civilian appellations such as "police agent"; and the black and white full-sized patrol car has at times been traded in for less traditional, less aggressive colors and styles.[1] And yet, despite the critics, many within the policing community still desire the look and feel of strict militarism and work to maintain the appearance of policing as a sort of Spartan brotherhood of domestic warriors keeping America safe for democracy.

The community-oriented policing (COP) phenomenon has only added fuel to the fire, as many COP proponents assume that military thinking is incompatible with the philosophy of empowerment necessary for today's free-thinking and free-acting line officers. Many attempts to depart from the military model by creating new forms of organizational benevolence and workplace democracy were miserable and obvious failures. If others failed to create revolutionary new methods for running police departments, they at least succeeded in curtailing the more egregious pathologies attributed to the military model—an abusive workplace environment, top-down micro-management, and overly aggressive, narrowly thinking, enforcement-oriented officers (Trojanowicz & Bucqueroux, 1990). And through it all, the uniforms and the mannerisms and the supposed authoritarian military style of doing business continues to be a popular organizational model for police departments.

The fundamental [questions that have never been asked are], Do these so-called attributes, rejected out of hand by some and desperately clung to by others, truly reflect any model used or practiced by the military? Does the centralized control, micromanagement, and an authoritarian boot camp style of leadership come from actual military practice and policy? Did it ever? If so, then the efforts to distance policing from the originators and proponents of such conventions is a wise one. But if our perception of the military and its so-called model are flawed, then we are advocating a move that, at best, disregards a significantly large category of experience and learning from our collective consideration and potential benefit. At worst, it causes us to reject the very model of organization and leadership that we should be striving to emulate, because at least conceptually, organized policing and organized war fighting should be approached in very similar manners.

Both advocates and opponents of the military model base their positions on faulty assumptions and limited knowledge. The modern military is not the top-down, centrally controlled monolith that many traditional police managers cherish and forward-thinking police progressives decry. American military officers are not trained to be the arrogant martinets that generations of police supervisors have aspired to emulate, and their doctrine does not demand the blind obedience of mindless brutes commonly attributed to military culture by its many detractors. A careful and open-minded examination of current military theory and practice will reveal an approach to organization and leadership that is radically different from what both advocates of the military model and its critics within law enforcement currently believe. What is found instead is a thoroughly professional approach based on careful analysis of the arena in which they operate and a comprehensive understanding of the theories and doctrines that create success. Instead of accepting or rejecting supposed military methods and leadership models based on insufficient or inaccurate knowledge and a distorted notion of reality, we need to thoroughly examine the profession we claim to emulate.

Police organization and military organization attempt to accomplish very similar ends. Both involve the application of governmentally sanctioned force, in the ultimate sense, in the form of a combined use of men and materials organized and structured to solve a myriad of problems concerning conflicts with and resistance to that government's determined will. Both use a variety of means other than direct force to accomplish their respective missions while maintaining continuum of force options as a last resort. Both employ a wide assortment of specialists and units against multiple opponents simultaneously. Both engage in operations such as peacekeeping, humanitarian relief, and life saving, as well as the direct and forcible intervention in the affairs of others. Both must deal effectively with the civilian populations in and around their areas of operation and solve problems to succeed. And both are constrained in their efforts by exter-

nally applied rules of engagement that limit the amount of force they can apply at a particular time and place based on the totality of existing operational and political circumstances as perceived and determined by civilian decision makers and the law.[2]

Table 9.1

Conceptual Similarities Between Military and Policing Professions

Military/Policing

Application of Government Force to Societal Conflicts

Apply Organizational Resources to Resolve Crises

Use of Problem Solving Strategies, Tactics, Techniques

Employ Specialized Units and Individual Experts

Continuum of Force Options with Rules of Engagement

The Historical Perspective

Although it may be true that the world's military forces have produced their share of abusive autocrats and micromanaging dictators, it is equally true—but usually overlooked—that throughout history, the military has worked diligently to eliminate them from its ranks. Like businesses, the military must create atmospheres conducive to creative thinking, individual initiative, and even audacious independent action on the part of subordinates in combat, because it is essentially those human qualities that give one army the advantage over an equally formidable—sometimes a much more formidable—force. As far back as 1000 B.C., military theorists and generals wrote in great detail about what motivates men to fight and die and win in combat. No doubt that some of that writing could lend itself to the typical view of abusive and autocratic military leadership. But discounting the cultural attitudes, societal conventions, and historical realities of their day, even the early writings of ancient philosophers such as Sun Tzu indicate an understanding of leadership that goes far beyond micromanaging autocrats and sending hoards of mindless serfs in mass formations blindly to their collective deaths on the mere whim of the general.

On the contrary, many of these early military philosophers reflect a keen understanding of human nature and the elusive psychological factors within groups of human beings that compels them to endure hardship and display inordinate courage in the face of almost-certain death based solely on the inspiration of their leader and devotion to his cause or vision (San Tzu, trans. 1971). In 350 B.C., modern concepts such as personal and positional power, expert power, knowledge power, and information power, as opposed to reward power, coercive power, and connection power, were articulated in the writings of the Greek historian and acclaimed military commander Xenophon (as cited in Heinl, 1966), who said,

> The leader must himself believe that willing obedience always beats forced obedience, and that he can get this only by really knowing what should be done. Thus he can secure obedience from his men because he can convince them that he knows best, precisely as a good doctor makes his patients obey him.

In the declarative statement, "willing obedience always beats forced obedience," Xenophon, a military leader, identified the basic sources of power as they relate to leaders and followers in organizations. And he did so more than 2,500 years before the advent of modern research techniques and enlightened management theories.

Within military circles, this was not an isolated insight. In more modern times, the Earl of Essex wrote in a letter on September 24, 1642, "I shall desire all and every officer to endeavor by love and affable carriage to command his soldiers, since what is done for fear is done unwillingly, and what is unwillingly attempted can never prosper" (as cited in Heinl, 1966, p. 170). Clearly, then, not all of military history and culture has advocated or relied on forced and strict obedience of mindless subordinates. And in fact, the most successful military leaders and their organizations throughout history have embodied, to some extent, many of the tenets of modern democratic, participative leadership theory. General Creighton W. Abrams, aside from

being a highly skilled U.S. combat officer in three wars, was most notable as a leader who encouraged his subordinates to openly question his policies and procedures and offer their own alternatives as a means to achieve employee "buy-in" and improved morale. As a tank battalion commander, he encouraged dissent among his subordinates during discussions concerning policy and procedures. Taylor and Rosenbach (1996) stated,

> Abrams made sure that his young officers were not inhibited in these discussions. In fact, stimulated by his challenges, they argued with him constantly. Usually, he would let them persuade him to do it their way. Maybe that way was not always as good as the way he would have done it, but having argued so strongly for their own solutions they were committed to making them work. Abrams, of course, knew this full well. (p. 122)

Perhaps, due to the life-and-death nature of the military profession, the modern armed forces of the First World nations have focused their attention heavily on leadership and its impact on structure and operations. In doing so, the modern military, particularly the American military, has radically improved the way it organizes its personnel and applies its resources to solve the various problems and accomplish the various missions necessitating its employment. Contrary to the popular notion of autocratic martinets demanding blind and unquestioning obedience from witless and uncreative followers, the modern military has continued to learn and build on the lessons learned from both historical and contemporary research regarding organization and leadership.

The Real Military Model

. . . A careful analysis of today's military reveals a radically different picture of leadership and organization. Much more than do civilian corporations and enterprises, military organizations understand the criticality of studying the field of leadership, of developing their leaders, and of understanding the complex and dynamic nature of the arena in which that leadership will be tested—conflict and crisis. Such an endeavor requires not mindless robots centrally controlled by authoritarian dictators, with no discretion to act and incapable of creative thought, but independent and audacious teams led by innovative, knowledgeable, and dynamic leaders.

The *Marine Corps' Doctrinal Publication (MCDP)-1 Warfighting* (1997),[3] written to all Marines, not simply to senior commanders and generals, states,

> An even greater part of the conduct of war falls under the realm of art, which is the employment of creative or intuitive skills. Art includes the creative, situational application of scientific knowledge through judgment and experience, and so the art of war subsumes the science of war. The art of war requires the intuitive ability to grasp the essence of a unique military situation and the creative ability to devise a practical solution.

This "employment of creative or intuitive skills" applies every bit as much to the Lance Corporal/Fire Team Leader as it does to the Captain/Company Commander or Commandant of the Marine Corps. But its value does not flow simply from the authority and willingness of subordinates to depart from established orders or procedures. The value of this ability to devise practical solutions is derived from the fundamental doctrines of the profession, a thorough understanding of unit and organizational missions, and the comprehensive knowledge base and developed experience of the practitioner on which the "art" is based. Egon Bittner's analysis of the police as "a mechanism for the distribution of non-negotiably coercive force employed in accordance with the dictates of an intuitive grasp of situational exigencies" (Kappeler, 1970/1999) attempts to grapple with the same essence. So does the problem-oriented policing movement, although we have been somewhat more successful at articulating the underlying science than in achieving its artful application on the street.

For decades, the modern military has actively and purposely worked to develop leaders who can think independently, take action without detailed supervision, and create solutions to complex and rapidly changing problems. In fact, despite the overall degradation of leadership during the Vietnam and the post-Vietnam era, even the doctrine of that day touted the knowledge and creative ability of noncommissioned officers and junior officers as our major advantage over our more centrally controlled and absolutely rigid Soviet adversaries, which we were likely to meet *en masse* on the plains of Europe or, in the case of the Marine Corps, on the frozen tundra and mountains of Norway or the southern flank of NATO.

Modern doctrine has evolved much further. Again, from the *MCDP-1 Warfighting* (1997),

> First and foremost, in order to generate the tempo of operations we desire and to best cope with the uncertainty, disorder, and fluidity of combat, command and control must be decentralized. That is subordinate commanders must make decisions on their own initiative, based on their understanding of their senior's intent, rather than passing information up the chain of command and waiting for the decision to be passed down.

Military commanders and leaders down to the lowest levels are mandated to take action to solve problems and accomplish any and all assigned missions without detailed orders and with little or no supervision. In addition, this mandate to take action, to take risk, is backed by a doctrinal admonition against a "zero-defects" mentality that viciously condemns and punishes even the slightest mistake, which is a common practice in most rigid and highly authoritarian organizations (*FM 100-14: Risk Management*, 1998).

But the military does not simply talk about leadership. To achieve this kind of individual skill and level of leadership development within its ranks, the military services have implemented structural and operational methods that directly encourage independent and creative action. They have proactively, rationally, and purposely developed organizational systems that foster decentralization and participative decision-making. Concepts such as mission tactics (telling subordinates what needs to be done, not how to do it) and commander's intent (a device designed to help subordinates understand the larger context of their actions, allowing them to depart from the original plan in the heat of battle in a way that is consistent with the aims of the higher commander) are specific operational methodologies designed to prevent micromanagement and over supervision of subordinates while supporting initiative at the lowest possible level.[4] *Marine Corps' Doctrinal Publication 6, Command and Control (MCDP-6,* 1997) supports the principles articulated in Warfighting (**MCDP-1,** 1997), officially defining the command and control process as "a dynamic, interactive process of cooperation" that occurs vertically within and laterally outside the chain of command.

That the authoritarian, centrally controlled concept of the military still persists in the minds of both advocates and critics, in spite of concrete operational practices and detailed and comprehensive official documentation to the contrary, is puzzling. It may be indicative of widespread animosity toward and ignorance of things military resulting from the Vietnam era. Or it may be something else entirely. Whatever the cause, this misunderstanding of military organizational and leadership doctrine has significantly affected the structure and leadership of modern policing in America.

The Result of Wrong Assumptions

The primary result of this mistaken view of military leadership has been the philosophical assumptions made concerning appropriate organizational and operational methods of policing as opposed to the military. Certainly, there is the assumption of a boot-camp style of leadership, as the military model has caused many police leaders and line officers alike to assume the manner or at least the outlook of a drill sergeant, the "Yes, Sir. No, Sir. Three bags full, Sir!" arrogant expectation of autocratic micro-managers. This style of leadership (not even a true representation of leadership by boot camp drill instructors) has done within policing exactly what its critics decry: created organizations that are centrally controlled and highly inflexible, characterized by top-

down order transmission and bottom-up reporting; less creative and more intellectually rigid individual officers bound to tradition and regulations, unable to deal effectively with both the dynamics of modern policing theories and the communities they serve; and a more combat/enforcement-oriented force, with a resulting increase in isolation from and hostility between police and citizens. It has been justly criticized and should be replaced, as it was by the military decades ago.

The adoption of this grossly inaccurate model of leadership and organization, mistakenly attributed to the military, has obviously distorted police perceptions and leadership methodologies. Confronted with complex organizational situations and relying only on their personal experience at the lowest levels of the military hierarchy, police leaders with limited organizational training and career development use the military model as a means to obtain immediate and absolute obedience to orders without question. With limited leadership and operational training to fall back on and routinely confronted with dangerous crisis situations in their communities, many police supervisors and managers depend on an organizational structure that supports top-down decision making and total submission to ensure their authority and status within the hierarchy and retain operational control. Coupled with a faulty assumption about the military, the assertion of paramilitary status by police agencies reinforces the poor leadership practices assumed to be an essential element of that profession.

Inaccurate assumptions and mistaken beliefs about how military organizations perform have caused the police profession to ignore and neglect important organizational concepts and structures that could radically improve their ability to enhance public safety. First, the misguided rejection of the military model (or the slavish adherence to the incorrect one) has contributed to the belief that the "crime-fighter" police officer is an independent operative. Fed by media images, most spectacularly the figure of "Dirty Harry" Callahan, this is the belief that the typical street-level police officer or investigator is considered the primary crime fighter, a "lone ranger" on patrol, operating apart and in isolation from his peers and wholly removed from the ever-watchful eye of his supervisors. Working within such a model, neither the officer nor the police department benefits from the very thing that makes organizations effective—the cooperative effort of multiple agents acting in concert that produces a more effective result than the sum of the individual agents acting alone: synergy.

This model also unnaturally separates the supervisor and upper management officers from the policing mission from the moment they are promoted. Police supervisors tend to monitor (from varying distances) the activities of individually operating subordinates who are engaged in crime fighting, but they are rarely involved in the direct application of their personnel and resources to the crime-fighting effort. Instead of an organizational outlook, police officers view themselves as individual crime fighters only to the point that they become supervisors, managers, administrators, and executives within the police department. To a greater or lesser extent (depending on the agency), all those above the lowest street-level ranks merely oversee and support the individual operational functions of line level officers. They do not contribute, in any operational sense, to the organized policing or law enforcement effort—to actual crime fighting.

Table 9.2

Actual Contrasts Between Military and Policing Professions

Military	Policing
Combined Arms	Isolated Units/Functions
Team Philosophy	Individual Philosophy
Leadership	Supervision/Management
Cohesive Doctrine	Detailed Policies
Proactive Operations	Reactive Operations
One Method of Operation	Two Methods of Operation

This individualized concept of organization is anathema to military professionals who view themselves as (and are by doctrine considered) "war fighters," whether they are on the front lines or on the general staff. The terms *supervisor* and *manager*, as occupational positions distinct from the war fighter, are not found in American military manuals, because supervision and management are considered merely individual components of effective leadership. All components and levels of the military hierarchy are engaged in the battle or conflict, each one planning, organizing, coordinating, and leading at his or her appropriate level or position but all working together to accomplish the operational war-fighting mission. Military personnel are either commanders or subordinates, fulfilling operational or support roles, in a line or a staff position. Not everyone is a "trigger puller," but everyone is a war fighter. And everyone up the chain of command actively participates in the war-fighting effort, not simply in supervising or managing the people involved in it.

There are numerous concepts or doctrines within the military that support and encourage this organizational war-fighting mentality that are almost completely missing in policing. The military actively employs concepts such as combined arms, which views successful war fighting as the highly coordinated employment of every organizational function or specialty in a mutually supporting manner and actively integrates all of the actions of an organization's resources and personnel to best operational advantage. Command and control, which gathers, collates, analyzes, and develops intelligence from all available information related to the war fighting effort, orchestrates operational planning and facilitates decision making based on the generated intelligence information and then coordinates and directs the timely and effective employment of those same resources toward a common goal. The concept of the commander himself, a person with extensive tactical, operational, and organizational leadership training, development, and experience in both line and staff positions, is the one person ultimately responsible for creating teamwork and the organizational and operational environment conducive to success. All of these distinctly military concepts increase the performance of organizations by improving the combined actions of the independent and creative individuals within them.[5]

Second, by automatically rejecting and/or fundamentally misunderstanding military theory and doctrine, policing has developed two completely divergent and incompatible modes of operation: the routine or daily mode of individual patrol and investigatory action, and the crisis mode of multiple unit response to serious and large-scale incidents. As previously stated, the common view of operational policing is that of the lone ranger on patrol, randomly operating in near isolation from his or her peers and largely removed from the directing/coordinating influence of his or her supervisor. This is the predominant method of operation in most departments, because crises tend to occur relatively infrequently, particularly in the smaller, suburban, and rural departments that make up the majority of American police agencies. With line-level officers operating independently and supervisors and managers doctrinally removed from the operational arena, untrained and unskilled in the art of employing personnel and resources in a combined and coordinated fashion, crisis situations have traditionally presented police departments with overwhelming challenges.

Correct use of military operational principles such as combined arms, command and control, and commandership could have significantly improved police responses during the Attica prison uprising, the MOVE confrontation in Philadelphia, the siege at the Branch Davidian compound in Waco, the Los Angeles Police Department response to the Rodney King riots, or the World Trade Organization riots in Seattle. Realizing this, the police officers themselves are beginning to learn the lessons of these and other less notable incidents by attempting to improve their own organizational response protocols. Although the police have attempted to adapt the Incident Command System (ICS) (a concept first developed by the Fire Service) to police use, it is often little more than a belated effort to organize resources during a crisis. The rudimentary police application of this process ignores the very methods of operation and leadership developed and refined over centuries by military organizations essentially for the same reasons. ICS is one method of organization that has been evolving over the past 20 years, with perhaps 10 years of significant police participation. But it suffers from structural inconsistencies and ignores fundamental organizational and operational doctrines, which tends to diminish its effectiveness and which, as already experienced by the military, could take many decades or longer to significantly improve and refine.[6]

But aside from its inherent imperfections, ICS's major flaw is that it is only used during a crisis. Because of the relative rarity of its employment, most police supervisors and managers do not generally understand how to function within it or use it properly. The traditional police dual-mode methodology imposes a dangerous dichotomy between everyday operations and crisis operations. The policing solution to this dilemma (particularly in light of the police organizational methodology of removing supervisors and managers from the routine day-to-day crime fighting) has not been for sergeants and lieutenants and more senior police leaders to learn and understand ICS, the accepted system of organization and operation during larger emergencies. The predominant response has been to train one or a few specialists in the department, many times significantly junior people, to implement the ICS process at a critical incident. Senior police officials, those commanders who are ultimately responsible for the success or failure of these life-and-death situations and who receive the pay and recognition commensurate with their status, remain largely ignorant of the organizational and operational doctrine being used during a crisis. They simply and dangerously rely on operational specialists to advise them how to plan, operate, and employ their resources. The collective signal that this method of dealing with critical incidents sends throughout the profession is that if it is not important enough for our senior commanders and executives to study and understand, then it is not important.

In contrast, military organizations have one structure and one method of operation. Whether in garrison or in the field, during high intensity conflict or operations other than war, units are organized and operations are carried out in the same manner. Commanders are always commanders; they are always involved in operations, and they always understand the operational principles governing them and their units. Individuals are intimately familiar with operational procedures because they operate, conceptually speaking, the same way day in and day out, whether it is routine training, humanitarian relief, peacekeeping, or all-out war. Police organizations could dramatically improve both their routine and crisis operations under the same type of consistent methodology.[7]

The rejection of things military by the policing profession has also drastically hindered our ability to create improvements in our current doctrine and operational methods. ICS has already been mentioned. But an even more recent "innovation" in police operations has been the concept of the COMPSTAT Process (Safir, n.d.)—the use of crime data and statistics to direct police response to crime trends and patterns and hold jurisdictional commanders responsible for efforts to reduce and eliminate them. COMPSTAT is a highly simplified form of military operational planning that uses tactical and strategic intelligence data to drive operations. It is comparatively elementary in that it fails to seek and understand the theories and concepts behind the method—the differences between tactical and strategic information/data; principles such as unity of command and combined arms operations; and the interaction and relationships between commanders, their staffs, and their operational units. It fails to address the organizational structures and operational practices (such as those mentioned above and others) that contribute to successful resolution of the identified problems. COMPSTAT is an attempt to produce genuine results by treating organizational symptoms (lack of accountability, intradepartmental coordination, bottom-up information flow) in isolation from the wider systemic factors and issues in the department that actually drive operations.

The military, philosophically accomplishing the same types of missions with the same types of resources, has developed and has been developing the theories and methods to do its job for centuries. The doctrines are sound and the methodologies are effective, albeit ever changing and improving. The philosophical concepts are directly applicable to law enforcement, with only minor and insignificant modification. Many of the operational and structural techniques are largely appropriate to our profession. Yet, it is the leadership, the kind of leadership that creates the esprit and morale and professionalism found in today's armed forces, that today's police forces should be most emulating.

Conclusion

The modern military has centuries of history, traditions, and lessons on which are based current doctrines and operational methodologies. Today's military leaders continually glean the best examples and messages from ancient historians and warfare theorists, incorporating what has been proven over the course of time to be successful into contemporary situations and practices, modifying and building on changeable ideas, and rejecting those that are or are becoming antiquated and outdated. The U.S. armed forces have an active and integrated "Lessons Learned" program that incorporates existing doctrine with detailed and open after-action critique designed to speed improvement in operational and structural methodologies. The modern military profession has solid operational and leadership doctrine on which its entire existence and methodologies are based—doctrine that is constantly being improved upon and that has directly contributed to its tactical and strategic victories over the past 20 years.

There is no doubt that the combination of the military with police in the United States would and does meet with severe opposition among the citizenry, and rightly so. This article in no way advocates the militarization of policing in America in the sense of heavy-handed storm troopers and "jack-booted thugs" usurping fundamental constitutional freedoms through combat oriented actions. The unbridled use of total war tactics and highly destructive weaponry must be avoided within our borders, against our citizens. Military forces and police forces should always be completely separate and different organizations in a free society. In fact, the military customs, courtesies, traditions, and accoutrements, the "Yes, Sir. No, Sir. Three bags full, sir!" historic trappings of warrior poets that authoritative police managers treasure far more than substantive military practices, hold no relevance to policing and should be abandoned.

But there is also no doubt that conceptually, our missions and objectives are strikingly similar. Furthermore, our adversaries are becoming increasingly sophisticated and tactically adept, requiring a much more organized and capable operational response on the part of civilian police agencies if we intend to be successful without direct military support or intervention. Without dramatic improvement in the tactical and strategic organization of American law enforcement agencies, a reliance on armed military units to supplement police could be an inevitable result. As such, we should study and adopt the particular organizational and operational doctrines and methodologies that the military has developed that are applicable to our profession. A correct view of the military and the incorporation of specific military theories and practices into policing will improve the way we do business, give us a distinct strategic and tactical advantage over any criminal adversary within our borders, and make our operations safer and less prone to violent resolution. It can only benefit America's police departments, and ultimately the citizens we serve, if we look at the military model as it truly is: a highly professional and organizationally mature profession and not as the aberration that many think it is—the rigid dinosaurs of wars long lost.

Notes

1. E-mail discussion with Dr. Michael Buerger, associate professor of criminal justice at North-eastern University, Boston, Massachusetts; and Alberto Melis, now chief in Waco Texas. In referring to the "police agent" concept, Buerger referenced *The Task Force Report on the Police of the President's Commission on Law Enforcement and Administration of Justice* (1967). Departments mentioned as experimenting with various other nonmilitary modes and methods include Lauderhill, Florida; Aspen, Colorado; and San Jose, California.

2. See *FMFRP 12-41* (1989). Although not difficult to see the obvious similarities between a SWAT team conducting a hostage rescue at a failed bank robbery and the British Special Air Service conducting a hostage rescue at the Iranian Embassy in London, it is perhaps a bit more abstract to view routine police operations, particularly community policing efforts, in light of military tactics and operational leadership. But the analogy remains strikingly viable. War fighting and crime fighting philosophies are not mutually exclusive.

3. *Marine Corps' Doctrinal Publication (MCDP)-I Warfighting* (1997) is the Marine Corps' foundational document concerning fundamental doctrine, that is, the philosophical framework for the way the Marine Corps conducts its business. It is required reading for all Marines and is the nexus of all other doctrinal publications. Most current Marine Corps doctrinal publications may be found on the Internet at <http://www.doctrine.quantico.usmc.mil/>.

4. Mission tactics is the process of assigning subordinates specific missions and leaving the manner of accomplishing those missions completely in their hands. The use of mission tactics by an organization relies on the exercise of initiative and creative thinking by subordinates and allows them the freedom to take whatever steps are necessary to solve problems and accomplish their mission based on their own available resources and the unique and rapidly changing situations that they face. To allow widely divergent subordinates this decentralized freedom of decision and action and still attain a common organizational goal in the most effective manner possible, there must be a means of focusing and coordinating the various independent subordinate efforts. Commander's intent allows subordinates to exercise their own initiative based on the immediate and uniquely changing circumstances confronting them in a way that is consistent with the higher commander's aims in accomplishing the overall mission. There are two components to any mission: the task to be accomplished and the reason behind it. Every mission

has an intended purpose or the reason for accomplishing the task. With an understanding of the intent of a particular mission, responsible and free-thinking subordinates are allowed to exercise informed initiative in harmony with the commanders original desires. Situations routinely change, making accomplishment of specific tasks obsolete and perhaps even counterproductive, whereas the original intention can continue to guide actions.

5. From *MCDP-6, Command and Control* (1997): "The aim is not to increase our capacity to perform command and control. It is not more command and control that we are after. Instead, we seek to decrease the amount of command and control that we need. We do this by replacing coercive command and control methods with spontaneous, self-disciplined cooperation based on low-level initiative, a commonly understood commander's intent, mutual trust, and implicit understanding and communications."

6. The military, like policing, is organized along line and staff functions. As such, it has developed an organizational doctrine and a structure to support it that, like the Incident Command System (ICS), attempts to aid the planning and conduct of operations along with the commander's decision-making process. ICS has no fundamental organizational doctrine on which it is based and is a process and structure that does not correspond with normal police operations. Its structure tends to blur the distinctions between command and staff functions. The role and purpose of the commander, chain and unity of command, and the functional relationships between the staff, the operational units, and their mutual commander are ambiguous and confusing, particularly when implemented rarely, during crises.

7. The military views mobilized operations—for example, war, humanitarian relief, peacekeeping, nation building, and so forth—as an extended form of everyday or peacetime operations. Commanders and their units, composed of a functional staff along with the subordinate operational units that in the same manner all the time. The tempo and urgency of operations will change with the level of crisis, but the structure and managerial/command relationships of the organization remain constant. Civilian ICS, as a separate and distinct form of organization only employed during a crisis, is inherently at odds with the basic method of daily police operations and its standard organizational structures and command relationships.

References

FMFRP 12-41: Professional knowledge gained from operational experience in Vietnam, 1967. (1989). Washington, DC: Department of the Navy, United States Marine Corps.

FM 100-14: Risk Management. (1998). Washington, DC: Department of the Army.

Heinl, R. D., Jr. (1966). *Dictionary of military and naval quotations.* Annapolis, MD: U.S. Naval Institute.

Kappeler, V. E. (Ed.). (1999). *Police and society: Touchstone readings* (2nd ed.). Prospect Heights, IL: Waveland Press. (Reprinted from *The functions of the police in modern society,* by E. Bittner, 1970, Chevy Chase, MD: National Institute of Mental Health).

Kopel, D. B., & Blackman, P. M. (1997). Can soldiers be peace officers? The Waco disaster and the militarization of American law enforcement. *Akron Law Review,* 619–659. Littleton, CO: Fred B Rothman & Company.

Marine Corps' Doctrinal Publication (MCDP)-I, Warfighting (1997). Washington, DC: Department of the Navy, Headquarters United States Marine Corps.

Marine Corps' Doctrinal Publication (MCDP)-6, Command and Control (1997). Washington, DC: Department of the Navy, Headquarters United States Marine Corps.

Safir, H. (n.d.). *The COMPSTAT process.* New York: NYC Office of Management Analysis and Planning.

Sun Tzu. (1971) *The art of war* (S. B. Griffith, Trans.). London: Oxford University Press.

The task force reports on the police of the president's commission on law enforcement and administration of justice. (1967). Washington, DC: U.S. Government Printing Office.

Taylor, R. L., & Rosenbach, W. E. (Eds.). (1996). *Military leadership: In pursuit of excellence* (3rd ed.). Boulder, CO: Westview.

Trojanowicz, R., & Bucqueroux, B. (1990). *Community policing.* Cincinnati, OH: Anderson.

Weber, D. C. (1999). *Warrior cops: The ominous growth of paramilitarism in American police departments* (CATO Institute Briefing Papers No. 50). Washington, DC: CATO Institute.

10
Reenvisioning Police, Reinvigorating Policing

A Response to Thomas Cowper

Michael E. Buerger

In the [previous article] Thomas J. Cowper proposed that the American police look to the American military for substance rather than secondhand symbolism, tradition, and trappings and secondhand respect. Were we to take his recommendations to heart, we would witness a radical transformation of the police commensurate with those envisioned by the Progressive reformers or the President's Commission of earlier eras.

And, we would be in for the battle of our lives. The proposal calls for nothing less than forsaking calcified bulwarks of selfishness and ego that have long constituted the dark underbelly of the professional ethic. The police establishment would need to be overhauled in important internal dimensions, to be sure, but as Cowper noted, many progressive reform efforts have run aground on the shoals of the police subculture. For reforms to have meaning, corresponding changes will be required in the external political and social environments that support and direct the police.

The core of Cowper's argument, it seems to me, is this: Although both institutions rely on the ability of their lower-ranked personnel to make decisions autonomously, only the military instills this decision-making process within a common understanding of doctrine.

Policing does in fact have a doctrine and has since the promulgation of the Metropolitan Police Act of 1829. That doctrine is embodied in Robert Peel's Nine Principles (Lee, as cited in Fyfe, Greene, Walsh, Wilson, & McLaren, 1997):

1. The basic mission for which the police exist is to prevent crime and disorder as an alternative to their repression by military force and severity of legal punishment.

2. The ability of the police to perform their task is dependent on public approval of their existence, actions, behavior, and on the ability of the police to secure and maintain public respect.

3. The police must secure and maintain the respect and approval of the public as well as the cooperation of the public in the task of observance of laws.

4. To recognize always that the extent to which the cooperation of the public can be secured diminishes, proportionately, the necessity for the use of physical force and compulsion for achieving police objectives.

5. To seek and to preserve public favor, not by catering to public opinion, but by constantly demonstrating absolutely impartial service to law, in complete independence of policy, and without regard to the justice or injustice of the substance of individual law; by ready offering of individual service and friendship to all members of the public without regard to their wealth or social standing; by ready offering of sacrifice in protecting and preserving life.

6. To use physical force only when the exercise of persuasion, advice and warning is found to be insufficient to obtain public cooperation to an extent necessary to secure observance of law or to restore order; and to use only the minimum degree of physical force which is

necessary on any particular occasion for achieving a police objective.

7. To maintain at all times a relationship with the public that gives reality to the historic tradition that the police are the public and that the public are the police; the police being only members of the public who are paid to give full-time attention to duties which are incumbent on every citizen in the interests of community welfare and existence.

8. To recognize always the need for strict adherence to police executive functions, and to refrain from even seeming to usurp the powers of the judiciary or avenging individuals or the state, and of authoritatively judging guilt and punishing the guilty.

9. To recognize always that the test of police efficiency is the absence of crime and disorder, and not the visible evidence of police action in dealing with them. (p. 8)

Similar to Chesterton's view of Christianity, however, the American political establishment did not examine Peel's tenets and find them wanting. It found them difficult (or unsatisfactory for the Age of Patronage) and never tried them.

As a result, "professionalization" of the American police has been a bootstrap movement conducted by a few lonely reformers whose ideas, until recently, have been honored more in the breach than the observance. Bittner's (1970/1991) observations about policing as a "tainted profession" and one in which "police . . . can, with very few exceptions, accomplish something *for* somebody only by proceeding *against* someone else" remain true today, as does his observation that "the ecological distribution of police work . . . reflects a whole range of public prejudices" (pp. 36–37). Other than the public exhortations of the community-policing movement—which to date has primarily resulted only in limited, largely symbolic special-unit successes and is in danger of being perverted into zero tolerance and mutated police-community relations units under the guise of citizens' academies—little has been

done to alter that equation within the occupation itself.

Whereas Cowper correctly noted that both the police and the military "engage in operations such as peacekeeping, humanitarian relief and life saving, as well as the direct and forcible intervention in the affairs of others" the circumstances under which they do so are different. The military's direct and forcible interventions are a matter of feast or famine: Either the substance has met the rotating blade, or it has not. Military life is composed of long stretches of preparation time in between episodes of intense combat. That time is filled with training, retooling, study, and more training, trying to anticipate and prepare for the next conflict. Humanitarian relief and life saving are usually little more than interludes in this ongoing state of preparing, although the modern military seems to be adapting to the incorporation of such "soft" missions much better than the police. (Although in truth, the movement, protection, and disbursement of large quantities of food or medicine are not so remote from the movement of war material that it would not be considered practice, and peacekeeping in volatile zones shares much in common with control of invaded territories in wartime.)

For the police, however, direct and forcible intervention in the affairs of others is a constant. Viewed from one perspective, the police are much more of an occupying army than the occupying Army itself, and the application of force is interspersed with the other duties and responsibilities. In many respects, the overlapping responsibilities make policing the more complex and difficult task and the more worthy of professional status, especially in light of the accompanying and ever-present restrictions on civil interventions. In policing, there is no hill to be taken, no territory to be gained and controlled, only an endless swell of human misery and debauchery to be quelled or controlled. The clarity of *win* and *lose* that attends the military occupation will forever elude policing.

Cowper's mention of "the life and death nature of the military profession" deserves note too because one of the symbolic flags that the American police wrap themselves in is just that "life and death" imagery. From Peter Manning's (1997) description of the "symbolization of police work" to John Crank's (1998) analysis of police culture to the literal bloody shirt of the case of *People of the State .of IL v. Murray Blue* (2000), the image of sudden death at the hands of a human adversary dominates the "sacred canopy" (Manning, 1997, p. 21) over police work. The American police do face death in the line of duty, although it is sporadic and often tainted with error that requires expungement by dramaturgy. In the words of one correspondent (M. Sleeves, personal communication, December 1, 1998),

> The amazing thing is that the job gets done as well as it does, but it is by no means done as well as it should be. And I know of no other "profession" where one can die stupidly as a result of poor tactics and/or the "Beagle Reflex," quite possibly killing off a few bystanders in the process and yet be so thoroughly lionized by one's peers as a result. Or accept unethical or downright criminal behavior, while self-righteously claiming "professional courtesy" or "don't criticize."

But regardless of the circumstances of death, it is the Fact of Death that so closely links the police with their military cousins. The American public has always reserved its greatest sympathy and honor for the citizen soldier, plucked from their lives and their communities to answer their country's call. The death of the conscript or of the volunteer—each in their own way an Everyman—resonates more distinctly than the death of a career military officer despite the respect and honor afforded to military professionals. Nevertheless, Noble Sacrifice is an extremely thin doctrine on which to organize the ethic of policing; it has been so persistent more because of a default of positive leadership than a rational choice in its own right.

So, too, is the Noble Cause in which the police imagine themselves as a Thin Blue Line (itself a borrowed metaphor from the Thin Red Line of the 93rd Highlanders of the British Army in Crimea). Perhaps the most egregious misuse of the military metaphor is the accompanying denigration of the "enemy," who in fact are citizens of the nation. The police descriptive vocabulary is ripe and rich with exclusionary language (*scum, dirtbags, animals,* and the like) that closely parallels the denigrating terms used in times of war to dehumanize The Enemy (*Hun, Nip, slope, gook,* etc.) and that has historical precedence in the dehumanization of entire peoples marked for extermination (such as the Nazis' use of *vermin, germ, insect,* and the like to identify the Jews as Other). Add to that the overt racism of earlier eras, when the police enforced Jim Crow laws, de facto segregation, and social mores most charitably described as White supremacist, and the Noble Cause of "Protect and Serve" strikes a discordant chord.

Important structural differences between the military and the police are often ignored in discussions about the "military model" regardless of which unrealistic model is being promoted. The military is not a single point-of-entry, up-through-the-ranks organization whose command levels empathize with the worldview of their subordinates. Although giving due adulation to those from the enlisted ranks who do make the grade (whether through Officer Command School or by battlefield promotion), the military command ranks are staffed with career officers educated at the nation's military service academies. They have a career track (as Cowper noted) that provides them with multiple opportunities to succeed, or fail, and through which they undergo constant observation and assessment—a career path that lies in the shadow of an "up-or-out" promotion system not found in policing. It is unlikely that we would find many proponents for such a model among police practitioners, although a modified form is conceivable.

Neither is the military unionized. The single most salient difference between the two organizations may lie here in the contrast between the military as a career and policing as "the Job." The adoption of a 19th-century model of private sector union organizing, with its hackneyed socialist rhetoric and antagonistic relationships with employers, makes no more sense for an occupation aspiring to be a profession than does the *Platoon/Apocalypse Now* or *Sands of Iwo Jima/*

Hellcats of the Navy "military" images that Cowper so rightly spurned.

Yet we cannot forget that the private-sector dictum that "management gets the union it deserves" applies with vigor to police unionism. (Although it is not without a sense of irony that we note the role played by seniority—one of unionism's sacred bovines—in the creation of the autocratic, capricious, dunderheaded, know-nothing, and often vicious police "leadership" of the bygone eras.) The opening chapters of Dorothy Guyot's (1991) *Policing as Though People Matter* is a convenient, although relatively benign, reminder of how far the police establishment has come in the last quarter century. What is at issue is whether the parties to the struggle recognize the changes that occur in the environment and whether they respond appropriately.

Similar to the American police establishment itself, police unionism should not be symbolized by its most egregious examples. Police unionism is similarly fragmented, representing primarily local concerns. Although national organizations of the Fraternal Order of Police, the International Union of Police Associations, and others exist, their sphere of influence is generally that of the national political scene. Despite their reputation in some venues, not every union is villainous, not every union-management relationship venomous. There are numerous locales where union and management have common cause on most issues, and there are progressive union leaders just as there are progressive chiefs of police. Neither can we simply sweep away the history and legal precedents that govern the employer-employee relationship.

Rather than wish for magic bullets and philosophers' stones or graft piecemeal and largely unrealistic "solutions" to the existing framework, it is in our best interest to adopt Cowper's call for creation of a policing doctrine. To do so, I propose, we collectively need to undertake two distinct but conceptually linked tasks. The first will be to replace the present patchwork of labor laws, arbitration precedents, and arcanae such as the "Police Officers' Bill of Rights" with a comprehensive doctrine of public employment.

Second, we need to reexamine our understanding of police departments as organizations, as Cowper suggested toward the end of the article with his "warfighting" analogy.

A Doctrine of Public Employment

Without extensively rehearsing the foundations of American labor law (particularly the harlequin patchwork of cases from completely different political eras, the Roaring Twenties, and the Great Depression), I offer that the original exemption of governmental employees from laws designed for employer-employee relations in the private sector was wiser than the later decision to apply those laws to public-sector relationships. To make such a claim does not assert that public-sector employees should have no rights at all but proffers instead the view that public employment is sufficiently different in its aspect that an appropriate set of rules be devised for the employer-employee relationship.

The first step toward such a goal would be a national debate over what standards are appropriate for public employment, including a discussion of whether there are multiple layers of expectations: Do sewer workers face ethical dilemmas comparable to those of police officers or rescue personnel (probably not, despite the common metaphor)? Are clerical positions with access to sensitive data (criminal history, victimization, public health records, etc.) comparable to other clerical positions (again, probably not)? Where ethical situations are concerned, what conduct is cause for dismissal? For lesser punishments? What standards of proof are acceptable evidence for deprivation of "property" (i.e., suspension without pay or dismissal)? What is the balance between the traditional "property right" of employment at public expense and obligations to the public trust? What obligations should police officers be under to report misconduct by fellow officers, and how is a CRASH Rampart "I don't remember" defense to be treated?

Conversely, what are the privileges of public employment? What rights attach to those who undertake police service? What is the status of second jobs, both type and quantity? What legal rights balance the public responsibilities inherent in the new model? Does status as an Agent of the State demand surrender of any of the normal protections afforded private citizens under the law (or the current equivalents such as the *Garrity* requirements), or does it provide greater protection (such as the union-negotiated "48-hour rule" before officers must give statements to investigators in shooting incidents)? Is an officer under investigation responsible to civilian review or only to the so-called paramilitary chain of command? Is there a right to answer only to a sympathetic audience of persons who have "walked a mile in your shoes," or does public employment require public defense of one's conduct before a potentially hostile public?

In the final analysis, the question is "Who owns the job?" As many scholars of the police have noted (most recently and cogently Crank, 1998), "professionalism" among the police rank and file throughout the 20th century has translated into a desire to be autonomous, as free of external oversight (and as free to exercise what they quaintly—and inaccurately—term professional courtesy) as they perceive doctors and lawyers to be. Embedded in this model are all the arcane contractual, arbitration-built, and subterranean rules of police subculture that have been constructed on a deep and often justified distrust of management. They range from the 6-month wait before a transfer takes effect in Newark, New Jersey (Buerger, 1998), to the 48-hour rule, to the Blue Wall of Silence and social ostracism for "ratting" on a "brother" officer. The polar opposite of this legacy is Florida's Sun Shine Law, which treats every police record—including Internal Affairs investigations—as a public document open to anyone who asks for it. The understanding that promotes a Sun Shine Law is that policing is a public job done in public fashion, conducted on behalf of the public, and paid for by public funds (B. H. Levin, personal communication, July 14, 1998); its very nature demands greater accountability from employees than that required in private-sector contracts. Although public entities do not hold a monopoly on employment per se (and hence the property right does not protect refusals to enforce the law based on an employee's religious beliefs, such as a North Dakota police chief dismissed for refusing to guard an abortion provider or an Indiana state trooper fired for refusing to work on a riverboat casino), they do hold a monopoly on the police power.

Traditionally the employer of last resort in some instances (a curious evolution of the political patronage device), what obligations incur when municipalities are forced to accept less-than-ideal candidates for positions requiring skill and trust? (Witness the current employment problems encountered in major cities such as New York and Los Angeles as relatively low-paying police jobs fail to attract sufficient numbers of qualified candidates and fail to keep trained incumbents [Flynn, 2000] or those in Washington, D.C., and Miami in the wake of large-scale forced hirings.) In light of the demands laced on the police individual and collectively, what are the responsibilities of the hiring agencies to ensure adequate training, equipment, and leadership? How are these responsibilities to be balanced across jurisdictions with extremely disparate resource bases? What responsibilities lie within state and federal government systems to aid, sustain, coordinate and promote change across the spectrum of agencies under their umbrella?

Ultimately, the public debate ought to deal with the mission and function of the police in modern society and society's realistic expectations of them. Are the police to be only "law enforcers" (that is, agents of retribution) as the police themselves continue to plead, or must they embrace the larger mission of fostering law compliance as envisioned by Peel, Rowan, and Mayne?[1] If we are to replace the agglutinated golem that is modern policing, a Marley's ghost dragging the chains of its past, with a recognized profession driven by doctrine, we must answer that question first. The other questions then chip away at the encrustations until we arrive at the model that we desire for policing in the 21st century. And at that point we, like the modern military that Tom Cowper recommended to us, must reshape the organization to maintain and promote that model.

Reenvisioning Police Organizations

Police organizations retain much the same character that they had in the 19th century when the job was merely a patronage position: With only a few exceptions, every task is done by someone wearing a blue uniform regardless of their actual qualifications for the work. Work is performed serially, with no innate capacity to compensate for overloads and with only a marginal support network. Positions are replaced serially, with no overlap or transference of information, as though policing were merely an assembly line, with any marginally trained worker capable of learning quickly and performing the repetitive task of any given station. Promotions are made on the merest of evidence, unrelated to and woefully unprepared for the new task responsibilities, with rote memorization still the key to advancement in too many jurisdictions.

Police institutions are still encrusted with the old notions of control, which repeated demonstrations of the lack of professional attainment in some quarters make necessary. Once a new doctrine of public employment has been agreed on, with a mission for the modern police, transforming the basic police organization into something approaching Cowper's "true military" model will still require a series of subordinate steps. It will not be achieved overnight, and it will not be a panacea. The American federalist system all but guarantees there will be considerable variations on the basic themes (as well as backwater pockets where the old ways persist). Unions and other organizations almost certainly will continue to exist to promote the interests of their memberships; the notion that a revamping of police service will produce one big happy family is just silly. There still will be cases of individual police misconduct and misjudgments, "bad shoots" and raids of the wrong houses, corruption and sexual misconduct, and abuse of sick time. Those are human problems and predilections, and it is not the role of doctrine to eliminate them (and although

some of the problems should be reduced by the measures discussed next, people still change over time, make mistakes under pressure despite the best of preparations, and react impulsively to unexpected threat or provocation; even good cops can have bad days). The acid test lies not in individual failings but the improvement in the overall effectiveness of the police in their role as a part of the community.

A complete overhaul of screening, hiring, and training of employees will be a mandatory first step. Unless the public debate decides that traditional "law enforcement" focused on collaring miscreants is the only true calling of the public police, discarding the facades of community policing and problem solving, the "new New Police" will not have the luxury of merely deciding who they like best among the candidates who present themselves for employment with visions of high-speed chases and shoot-outs dancing in their heads. Police agencies will need to actively recruit for those with the skills to handle people from all walks of life (we get some of those folks by the current method and build some through experience and the good fortune of competent mentors, but the continuing problem of police estrangement from the minority and disenfranchised communities—the modern versions of "the dangerous classes"—demonstrates that we have far fewer than we need).

The current recruitment efforts by major departments experiencing a hemorrhage of trained officers to retirement, other departments, and other employment is but a pale version of the effort that will be needed to revamp the police. A true renaissance requires more than warm bodies with a vague interest in tracking down serial killers or warm bodies interested primarily in a secure City Job—assured salary and benefits just for showing up and opportunities for ample overtime. A profession requires professional skills, professional ethics, and professional education and training.

(In that vein, we should anticipate subsidiary changes as well. Those of us resting smug in our ivory towers may quickly find that our traditional criminal justice curricula, teaching the outlines of the criminal justice systems and the sociology of crime, become irrelevant once the police establishment figures out what it really needs. Federal agencies already consider the criminal justice degree a "generalist degree" on a par with English, history, education, geology, and many others. If a truly professional vision is developed for policing, we may well find ourselves losing ground to multidisciplinary studies—beyond our own current conceit of what constitutes "multidisciplinary"—that embrace professional training in communications, human services, perhaps teaching, and [dare we speak it?] social work as core skills necessary for police service.)

Simultaneously, radical changes will be needed in the way promotions are handled, including the abandonment of the seniority system, radical revision of civil service, and an effective way of integrating into the selection process both past performance and success in training for the new position. Civil service was a 19th-century answer to a 19th-century problem, but failure to adapt to changing conditions and expectations has made it an anachronism, an obstacle to true professionalization and reform. The minimal system now in place in far too many jurisdictions is a perversion of the notion of "merit," a political compromise skewed toward the concept of promotion as a benefit that should be equally open to all employees. The opposite legacy, of using promotions and assignments as a way of supporting friends and supporters (and denial of same as a punishment for adversaries), is equally pernicious to the well-being of the organization, but correcting a mistake by imposing its mirror opposite usually does not work well. If we adopt the military approach favored by Cowper, promotion is decidedly not a level playing field: It is a meritocracy in two parts, exemplary past performance and promising aptitude for new responsibilities. At present, the American police generally are ill equipped to meet either mandate.

(This is in some sense a circular argument because the evaluating supervisor is generally—although hardly exclusively—a weak link in the assessment of officer performance; creating better supervisors through performance evaluations will have to overcome that hurdle. However, a comparable challenge faced the post-Vietnam military and was met.)

Equally important is Cowper's observation that the military has a robust and coordinated organization behind every "trigger-puller" (a most unfortunate term, given the instant discussion). Policing by contrast is wafer thin in important aspects. Despite the modest advances of civilianization (and the fictional advances of redeployment through technology), the end result has been to "put more cops on the street" in old deployment patterns without a thought or care for actual effectiveness.

For all our collective rhetoric, we have hardly begun to scratch the surface of true proactive policing, whether Goldstein's "problem-oriented" approach or Sherman's "evidence-based" model. Information systems have largely been transferred from paper files to computer files, but our databases are still driven by the most easily coded boxes, suitable for counting and compiling but seriously limited for any form of useful analysis. We can track calls for service more readily, "account" for more of police activities, and display them with multifarious colors and symbols in electronic layers galore, but we are still no closer to devising credible responses to problems than were our pin-mapping counterparts of the 1950s. The credentials of the line officers are but one aspect of this and their attitude toward unbadged ("civilian") employees merely another. Police agencies still staff according to ancient workload formulae based on calls for service received: Every other activity is a robbery of Peter to pay Paul. A similar conundrum afflicts supervision and middle management, where administrative demands are foisted on badge-wearing individuals whose primary functions of supervision and leadership languish, the bastard stepchildren of paperwork.

Because we are in no position to provide each serving officer with a *True Witness* (Heinlein, 1961), the next best thing would be to provide each officer with an amanuensis capable of report writing and data entry. Paperwork alone deprives the nation of innumerable hours of officer time: An arrest is 2 hours (off the street) and is a mathematical fact of life in urban police departments and arrests for offenses under state oversight (driving under the influence, domestic violence, etc.) may consume even more time. Manual compilation of statistics and reports by supervisors blinds the organization to important parts of the "low-visibility" work of the streets and makes the line officer much more of a lone ranger than is envisioned in the textbooks that rehearse "span of control" mantras from the 1950s. The most important knowledge generated by the police goes unexamined because marginal (and most often antiquated) police computer systems are not set up to code for nuance. Even at that, the vast quantum of police work that does not generate an offense or incident report slips into oblivion, save for fragments and distortions of the participants' memories and an abstract date-time-place category record in the CAD system.

At the same time, a parallel source of information is woefully undernourished as the supervisory and managerial cadres of policing are increasingly diverted from the coaching, instruction, and evaluation functions—for which we need trained, experienced minds—in favor of compilations and memoranda that in other organizations are clerical functions. The notion that a police agency must be "lean" and comprised primarily of uniformed gun toters is a relic of the past.

Similarly lugubrious—almost as much as the "equivalencies" of redeployment through technology efficiencies—is the idea that proactive work can somehow be accomplished during "uncommitted time." The small fragments of time "freed" by using a computer to enter reports are essentially string too short to save. Although it will be a substantial tax burden, providing overlap of functions, (as some police departments already do, and as Chicago and other split-force agencies have done to create community policing in their jurisdictions) and enhancing the team approach is a necessary precursor to proactive police work. Too many agencies already work at a union-determined "minimum-staffing" level geared mostly to officer safety, not to department ef-

fectiveness. This is not a call for more cops for the sake of more cops or for more cops to do more effective zero tolerance street sweeps. It is a recognition of the need for nonpatrol time that is never the less "crime-fighting" time: team meeting and analysis time, community mobilization, and canvassing time that are done as regular duties—not when there is a lull in "regular duties."

Similarly, training in all aspects of police work must be a regular and consistent element of "regular duties," as it is in Cowper's ideal military. To think that a single recruit academy supplemented by an annual ordeal of 40 or 80 hours of classroom-based boredom constitutes adequate training for a profession is simply ludicrous. Skills atrophy, details and nuances are forgotten; and pre-planning is relegated to the province of special units. An overhaul of police training, or better yet an intelligent fusion of training and education (both physical and mental), is long overdue. It will stress municipal budgets, yes—especially out in Smallville. But when combined with better recruitment and selection processes, it is a necessary investment in public policing to reduce the current negatives and promote an effective police profession for the coming century.

Doctrine? An excellent beginning . . . but only the beginning.

Note

1. Sir Robert Peel is widely regarded as the founder of the modern police, the London Metropolitan Police of 1829; Charles Rowan and Richard Mayne were the first two commissioners of the force.

References

Bittner, E. (1991). The function of police in modern society: A review of background factors, current practices, and possible role models. In C. B. Klockars & S. D. Mastrofski (Eds.), *Thinking about police: Contemporary readings* (pp. 35–51). New York: McGraw-Hill. (Reprinted from *Crime and delinquency issues. National Clearinghouse for health information*, 1970, Chevy Chase, MD: National Institute of Mental Health.)

Buerger, M. E. (1998). [Field notes]. Unpublished raw data.

Cowper, T. J. (2000). The myth of the "military model" of leadership in law enforcement. *Police Quarterly, 3*, 228–246.

Crank, J. P. (1998). *Understanding police culture.* Cincinnati, OH: Anderson.

Flynn, K. (2000, November 25). Behind the success story, a vulnerable police force. *The New York Times* [Online]. Available: <http://www.nytimes.com/2000/11/25/nyregion/25POLI.html>.

Fyfe, J. J., Greene, J. R., Walsh, W. F, Wilson, O. W., & McLaren, R. C. (1997). *Police administration* (5th ed.). New York: McGraw-Hill.

Guyot, D. (1991). *Policing as though people matter.* Philadelphia: Temple University Press.

Heinlein, R. (1961). *Stranger in a strange land.* New York: G. P. Putnam.

Manning, P. K. (1997). *Police work: The social organization of policing* (2nd ed.). Prospect Heights, IL: Waveland.

People of the State of IL v. Murray Blue (2000). [Online]. Available: <http://caselaw.lp.findlaw.com/scripts/getcase.pl?court=il&vol=sc%5c2000%5c84046&involv=3>

ISSUE VI
Community-Oriented Policing: Are We There Yet?

In 1994, President Clinton signed the Violent Crime Control and Law Enforcement Act into law. The Crime Act, as it later became known, allocated approximately $8.8 billion for the implementation of community policing in the United States and established the Department of Justice's Office of Community-Oriented Policing Services (COPS). Since its implementation, the COPS office has provided almost $8 billion to over 12,000 state and local law enforcement agencies. Despite the fact that most police departments have implemented at least some form of community policing, many academics and police officials question whether it works. In the following sections Larry C. Plummer, a 27-year police veteran, and David L. Carter, professor and director of the National Center for Community Policing, debate the issue.

Plummer argues that community policing is thriving across the country because it works. He maintains that community policing returns policing to its roots, where the police are intimately connected to their communities, and offers a simple philosophy as to what policing should be about. As a result, there is increased community support for the police in general, which has given police leaders a clearer vision of what policing should look like in the future. Plummer argues that community policing is also successful because it encourages creativity and accepts differences between people and communities. This change, he believes, allows the police to be more effective and equitable in designing organizational structures and operational strategies. Additionally, community policing is results oriented, asking the police to show real evidence of their success.

Carter responds to Plummer's argument and concludes that police agencies may not have come as far as Plummer believes. First, he points out that community policing does not "return the police back to their roots," as Plummer claims, and that such statements are misleading. Instead, Carter argues that in the past policing was primarily reactive in nature, whereas community policing is proactive in nature, requiring much more from the police. Second, Carter contends that community policing is not as simple as Plummer suggests. Not only are the police required to change their organizational structure to fit into the framework of community policing, but this approach also requires an intellectual and cultural shift on the part of police officers. Third, Carter argues that community policing may not be "thriving" as Plummer suggests. He maintains that many police agencies only claim to implement community policing so that they can receive the federal funds that have been allocated for such efforts. In reality, however, they have made no basic changes.

Critical Thinking Questions

1. Describe community policing and give three examples of community policing tactics.

2. Has community policing been implemented and what is its future in the United States?

3. How effective is community policing? Use evidence from the chapters to support your position.

Internet Websites

Community-Oriented Policing Services Office. <http://www.usdoj.gov/cops/>

Information on the state of community policing today. <http://www.webdevgroup.org/nij/cp1997.htm>

Contains basic information about community policing. <http://www.concentric.net/~Dwoods/>

Police Executive Research Forum. <http://www.policeforum.org/>

Police Foundation. <http://www. policefoundation.org/> ✦

11
Community Policing

Thriving Because It Works

Larry C. Plummer

Despite many obstacles, the movement by police agencies to operationalize community policing in communities nationally and internationally has progressed demonstrably through the span of several decades and is thriving.

It is axiomatic that the implementation of change in policing, in any form, faces many hurdles, and the major philosophical and operational shifts required to implement community policing present even more challenges. However, our efforts to evolve to community policing have and will continue to be aided by a variety of factors that will support continued growth of the movement.

It Is Natural

Community policing makes sense. It has a historical base and is a natural process for our police personnel. Furthermore, it serves needs expressed by our communities and works well with our governmental and private partners.

Unlike nouveau programs and systems previously tried and abandoned in policing, community policing is not new or foreign to our business. It is not a buzzword, a brainchild, or a strict or slick management or marketing tool with limited application or a finite lifespan.

Community policing or, simply, policing with and as part of the community is a philosophy that originated in old England. Following his establishment of the London Met-

ropolitan Police, Sir Robert Peel established principles to guide the activities and behaviors of his constables. One of these, often relayed by Mr. Chris Braden, "the police are the public and the public are the police," is viewed by many as perhaps the original seed or thought from which modern community policing has evolved. Although not labeled as such at the time and not utilized by Peel to develop a strict community policing model in London, Peelian principles and Peel's basic policing model were eventually used as a model for the development of policing in the United States and elsewhere.

Recommitting ourselves to a community-policing philosophy represents a natural return to these very basic roots and now, a (root) system that has been extended by the work and leadership of such people as Herman Goldstein, George Kelling, and Chris Braden, and by our own significant experience with its practice. Together, these provide us with an ever-expanding foundation for continuing our efforts to sustain and enhance the growth of community policing.

More natural than our return to community policing itself is the draw that our commitment to it presents to police personnel, community members, and our governmental and private partners. The community policing philosophy highlights the critical importance that human relationships and cooperation play in successful problem solving, and a noteworthy by-product of the process is the great personal rewards it pays to all involved.

Police personnel are, in part, like all people, naturally altruistic. And although many motives draw them to policing, the opportunity to work with and to help people is particularly appealing. Community policing offers our members the opportunity to solve problems and see the results. Over the course of time, the fulfilling nature of the environments created by this type of activity can help to sustain and motivate them throughout their careers.

Community members share responsibility for solving problems with the police and have a great appetite to know more about and be involved with the police. Likewise, our governmental and private partners, who for so long have been shut out of our business, have a strong need to be informed, involved, and to play a role in problem-solving initiatives. Our implementation of community policing provides both groups with the venue for finally becoming real, involved partners in the job of policing and the hands-on work of crafting safer communities.

The multidisciplinary involvement provided in community policing environments is both an attribute and catalyst. The inclusive nature of community policing ensures that growth and evolution will be self-sustaining because different perspectives bring new energy to the problem-solving table. Societal problems no longer are the exclusive province of the police to resolve—everyone can participate, and the inclusion and ownership of others provides constant infusion of different perspectives, energy, and solutions.

It Is Simple

The complicated, confining, and foreign nature of so many of the programs and systems imported into police work over the past several decades has contributed to their short lifespan.

In contrast, community policing is abjectly simple. Its premises about people, partnerships, and problem solving present us all with the unique ability to convey and implement the philosophy using a language that is common and easily understood.

This is not to say that the leap between philosophy and practice is not a great one. Implementing community policing is an extremely difficult task. Creating cultural, systematic, and operational shifts, and then adjusting these shifts to accommodate transitional stages, the environment, and roadblocks—while at the same time maintaining operational stability—is not simple.

However, despite biases and other obstructions that must be understood and overcome, the simplicity of the philosophy itself has and will continue to support our ability to explain, be advocates of, and sustain the growth of community policing.

It Encourages Creativity

Law enforcement agencies committed to traditional philosophies certainly offer themselves and their members the opportunity to express their creativity. However, most often, creativity must be displayed through traditional enforcement-type activities and within very narrow boundaries. Such boundaries are designed specifically to define and guide traditional organizations and their members, and are usually focused almost exclusively on enforcement and reactive activities. Accordingly, the traditional toolbox has very few implements for police officers to use in the construction of creative and long-lasting solutions.

Although traditional roles and activities must remain an integral part of any community policing environment, community policing agencies are defined quite differently. They are driven by their emphasis on the utilization of a broad array of means and participants to resolve problems and carry out their missions, with traditional methods and systems being but one part of the whole.

Community policing agencies place great value on creativity and autonomy and can finally encourage their members to go "beyond the dots" in developing partnerships and problem-solving schemes. Members have a greater opportunity to exhibit their altruistic talents and to fulfill personal needs and community expectations. Our governmental and community partners share in the creative processes. This pool of creative expression couples with successes to energize our members, partners, agencies and communities, and to build a sustaining base of vitality for community policing initiatives.

In a much broader sense, the nature of transition processes being designed to implement community policing further invigorates community policing environments. Whereas traditional agencies view the future by delineating very specific, short-term destinations and generally construct very linear processes to reach their goals, community policing futures are viewed as constantly evolving. They are really ongoing, circular works-in-progress.

The understanding that agencies will constantly be evolving to meet the demands of their communities becomes an end in and of itself, with no specific ending point. Transition processes are constructed in painstaking, detailed fashion, but emphasis is placed on creativity, involvement by many stakeholders, flexibility, and the evolutionary nature of the process itself.

It Implies an Appreciation for Diversity

Community policing implies appreciation for diversity in the way we look, think, and act, and our willingness to accept diversity as expressed in our communities.

Policing has been notoriously slow to embrace and display an appreciation for diversity, and recent events have again turned the focus of our communities to this critical issue. However, community policing has also provided the public with the opportunity to notice what is good and can be better about policing and to build new support for policing.

Because successfully policing with partners in our communities requires that we cultivate relationships with our communities, transition efforts pay great attention to building a mutual trust with communities, both as precursor to and as a result of relationship-building processes.

Many things go into building trust. Access, dialogue, feedback, and respect for others are key components of the equation. However, most critical to the formula and, without a doubt, a prerequisite to success is the exhibition by policing agencies that we appreciate diversity. Community policing agencies highlight the need for mutual respect, ethical conduct, and the reflection of the demographics of their communities. Community policing agencies appreciate diverse opinions and different thinking. Diversity and the various shades of life in our communities are recognized as a means to support and enhance the staying power of community policing.

It Requires Paying Attention to Our Environments

Traditional environments focus on singular incidents of crime, crime trends, arrests, and bringing closure to problems for the short term.

As agendas shift to real problem solving—addressing the multitude of factors that combine to cause or promote disorder and crime for the long term—community policing agencies place a much higher priority on making connections with and assessing the ever-changing natures of their environments.

Agencies have found that understanding the nature and disposition of our communities is essential to building of trust, partnerships, and effective problem solving initiatives. Having a strong grasp of and relationship with our rapidly changing environments provides us with a much greater opportunity to succeed in serving our communities.

It Is Results Oriented

During the past decade, more and more has come to be expected from policing agencies. The success we have had in advancing community policing into our communities and culture has increased those expectations. Specifically, our communities now demand more of our time and, ultimately, real results.

The demand and pressure for results is good however, and community policing provides the most appropriate vehicle for us to become more accountable and effective in responding to our communities. Community policing agencies produce by transforming themselves into multidimensional service providers, hubs and facilitators for collective action, and by addressing problems in a more thorough fashion.

It Is Bolstering Community Support

Community policing bolsters community support in the form of physical participation, fundraising, the creation of a vocal base of public support, and political will for increased budgetary appropriations.

The public and our governing bodies appear to have grown tired of our never-ending demands for more and more money to fight crime in the same traditional ways. The adoption of community policing philosophies and the associated positive results have given our communities a better chance to see and be involved with what they pay for. Inclusion of others and the fruits of our communal efforts have clearly provided community policing agencies with a windfall of renewed support.

It Has Unified Police Leadership and Direction

Although the dangers posed by changes in leadership and the practice of dishonest leadership still merit our strong attention, they have been diminished by the successes of community policing and by the strong base of leadership responsible for advancing the movement.

Initially championed by a handful of practitioners, researchers, academicians, and institutions such as the Police Executive Research Forum, community policing's base of leadership has grown dramatically over the years. This base is now expansive and strong and includes municipal, state, national, and international organizations and governing bodies, community entities, a growing section of the public at large, and a growing number of police chiefs, sheriffs, and personnel in their charge.

The base is also significantly marked by its potential. Looking to the future, it seems easy to project a further strengthening of the leadership body committed to advancing community policing. Our current stock of leaders will expand and grow exponentially as more of our members are raised in the environment and new converts are persuaded to believe in the philosophy.

Conclusion

Community policing is not a gimmick or shallow program. It is a mindset and philosophy fueled by inclusion, tolerance, and good old-fashioned police work. Our communities enjoy the inclusion, those with diverse world views now have a forum, and police officers are able to exercise their altruistic desires to serve and to make a difference. Whereas once we focused on our most basic mission, that of apprehending criminals, we now work under an umbrella philosophy that requires that we not only invite but mandate that communities participate with us in solving social and criminal problems.

Although not all police agencies are involved in community policing, most have it or are implementing it in some form. We all struggle with its implementation, and resistance still abounds, but it remains the focus of dialogue and mission in policing.

Community policing has been resilient and is standing the test of time so often failed by other programs and systems. Indeed, the constancy of our purpose and efforts serves both as an important key to and measure of our success with community policing.

Community policing is in fact thriving because it works! It serves a multitude of needs and stakeholders. Creating closer ties to our communities and creating partnerships to solve problems just makes sense. The dynamics created in community policing environments combine and can develop to ensure that they not only endure, but grow even stronger.

As we look to the future, we all share the opportunity, perhaps even the responsibility, to help those we serve (including our co-workers) to better understand community policing's strengths and attributes so that we can pull together to overcome obstacles and foster its continued growth.

Reprinted from: Larry C. Plummer, "Community Policing: Thriving Because It Works." *Police Quarterly*, Vol. 2, No. 1, Mar 1999, pp. 96–102. Copyright © 1999 by Sage Publications, Inc. Reprinted by permission. ✦

12

A Response to 'Community Policing

Thriving Because It Works'

David L. Carter

Plummer's enthusiasm and optimistic support of community policing is an encouraging sign of the concept's growth. As more practitioners—particularly middle managers—embrace the philosophy, the more we will learn about training, deployment, and resource management to maximize the concept's utility. Having said this, there are some points on which we disagree.

A Perspective on History

It is common to hear references to community policing as a "return to our roots" or a "back to basics" approach to policing as practiced in England 170 years ago following Peelian reform. Not only is this misleading, it does a disservice to the body of research on policing over the past three decades and the conceptual innovations promulgated by such people as Herman Goldstein, Robert Trojanowicz, James Q. Wilson, and George Kelling, among others.

There is no doubt that Peelian reform was a significant development in policing and that many of Peel's principles continue to provide good guidance. However, policing under Peelian reform was not the same as community policing today. The constables of the London Metropolitan Police following Home Secretary Peel's restructuring were generally reactive: They patrolled beats on foot reacting to calls from citizens and requests for service. Just as in the case of American reform policing, constables also initiated contacts with people and situations where there was potential criminality or disorder. Yet, the predominant practice remained reactive (albeit on foot).

Peel's principles and vision of policing used neither crime analysis nor problem solving. Police administrators did not employ needs assessments of the community, nor was the scientific method applied to police work. Moreover, classical management practices—typically autocracy—was the norm compared to quality management principles that are so predominant in the community policing environment of today.

The propositions of Sir Robert Peel did not reflect a philosophy of policing, but a practice of behavior for constables. It was not viewed with a broad conceptual foundation incorporating attitudes, values, and beliefs about the fundamental purpose and operational environment of policing, but a regimen of good practice in accordance to Peel's principles (or guidelines). Similarly, Peelian policing asked the public to cooperate with the police, whereas community policing seeks partnership with the public.

There is doubt of the positive influence produced by Peelian reform—it was a substantial step forward in the professional practice of policing. However, for the current discussion, the important point to note is that policing under Peelian reform was different from community policing. As such, the suggestion that law enforcement is returning to its roots is misleading. Indeed, the current community policing initiatives in England and Wales are consistent with the philosophical vision of community policing and problem solving as found in the United States, most frequently under the rubric of restorative justice—particularly as found in the Thames Valley Police.

The Nature of Police Personnel

Plummer explained that police personnel are for the most part naturally altruistic and are attracted to police work by the opportunity to work with and help people. We like to believe this, but evidence and experience suggest that this may not be wholly accurate. Historically, people were drawn to law enforcement for job stability and a decent pension. Law enforcement was not viewed as a calling nor as a profession; it was more typically viewed as low-skilled blue collar work for people who could not get a better job.

This visage of policing changed—notably beginning in the late 1960's—for a wide variety of reasons related to social evolution that are far too involved to discuss here. The point to note is that the prestige associated with being a police officer has steadily increased, leading to a growth of higher quality personnel in the police ranks. However, these individuals were not necessarily drawn to law enforcement out of an altruistic commitment to help one's fellow man. Perceptions of excitement, the ability to work outside the trappings of an office, and the ability to exercise authority were among the motivators for people to join the police.

With higher educational levels and better recruiting methods, an increasingly higher caliber of personnel was enticed into police ranks. These changing personnel processes made a systematic contribution to the inculcation of community policing in American police organizations. Yet, this remains a transitional process. The caveat is to recognize that the transition continues. To assume that the attitude and character of most American police officers reflects this altruistic nature may be premature.

It Is Not Simple

Perhaps the point on which I have the greatest disagreement with Plummer (2000) is his statement that "community policing is abjectly simple" (p. 84). In my view, there is nothing simple about it. Successful implementation of community policing requires a complete philosophical change in organizational culture. This includes policy changes in a wide range of areas such as deployment, assignment, supervision, personnel evaluation, response alternatives to calls, call management, and a host of related changes to the infrastructure.

Beyond organizational issues is the need to change the occupational attitudes, values, and beliefs of officers. We are asking officers to challenge conventional wisdom and perform tasks they have historically not been asked to do—in some cases, tasks they have been explicitly told to avoid. Because of the natural dogmatism humans experience, this intellectual shift is extraordinarily difficult. Officers experience dissonance in daily tasks while trying to assimilate cultural changes in the organization. This is complicated by the fact that authority and responsibility are significantly decentralized, requiring more accountability of officers in a wide range of duties. Moreover, we ask officers to be creative in identifying and responding to problems within the community. Creative thought is extraordinarily difficult, particularly in organizations that have traditionally inhibited creativity.

Although describing community policing as simple may be aesthetic, it is nonetheless misleading. It belies the complex nexus of management and social-psychological adaptation required of personnel at all levels.

The Fragility of Community Policing

Plummer states that community policing is strong and resilient. Indeed it is common to hear rhetoric about how community policing is the accepted form of policing today and how it has become institutionalized. Common conversations at professional meetings of both police administrators and academics speak of the inculcation of community policing and its positive effects on communities. Unfortunately, these observers are far too often advocates or represent special interests, lacking any objective view or seeing community policing from a narrow breadth of vision.

I would argue that community policing is still an extremely fragile concept, that its acceptance is tentative and its institutionalization in standard police practice remains superficial. One simply has to go to virtually any city and talk with the average uniformed officer. In many cases, the officer will not be able to completely explain the concept and/or will state that the department "is not really doing community policing." This should not be viewed as a failure. Rather, it is a reasonable reaction to a philosophical change in policing.

Yes, community policing and problem-solving experimentation have been in the literature for nearly two decades. However, widespread implementation of the concept has only occurred in the last few years (and was largely fueled by the Office of Community-Oriented Policing Services [COPS] hiring incentives). Because it is a major philosophical change in the practice of policing coupled with the need to tailor to a community and, importantly, the need to resocialize police personnel, it is only natural that uncertainty remains.

Other evidence supporting the notion that community policing has not been fully accepted is the widespread use of community policing units and other forms of piecemeal implementation. Similarly, the difficulty of defining the application of community policing to specialized units such as investigations and traffic further lend credence to the notion that community policing is still evolving within police organizations.

With uncertainty, incomplete socialization, a lack of full institutionalization, and the natural dogmatism of humans, one will find that the institutionalization of community policing as the accepted mode of policing in the United States remains fragile. Changes in political leadership or a crime-related crisis are examples of factors that can undermine the change process, leading an organization back to a reactive framework. Forward progress toward change necessitates that police leaders move gingerly across a complex landscape of policy, politics, special interests, empirical research, experimentation, complex social issues, and diverse motivations of key participants. This must necessarily be done with caution as a socio-behavioral infrastructure is built to support the change toward community policing.

Recognition of this fragility is important so that practitioners and researchers who support community policing can remain vigilant in their efforts to further the change process. To mislead ourselves by inferring that community policing has become solidified in policing practice is to mask the dynamics of this evolutionary process.

A Unifying Force?

Increasingly, police leadership is being unified around the community policing philosophy. However, the motivation for that unity is based in several different factors. First, there are many police leaders who have sincerely embraced the concept in the belief that community policing affords them the means to provide the best possible service and safety to a community. They have committed resources and taken risks to explore new avenues of police service delivery in furtherance of this ideal. Although the number of police leaders in this category has grown dramatically over recent years, one could still argue that is not the norm.

In the second category, one finds police executives who have adopted the concept for a variety of ancillary reasons. Some have tried community policing because it was a trend, some because they perceived current approaches were not working, and some because the language and practice of community policing is "what is expected" of a contemporary police leader. In these cases there is experimentation, but not full commitment. Many remnants of reform/reactive policing remain. More important, there is no real commitment to immerse the organization in the philosophy. Although there are certainly risks associated with such immersion—risks I do not have to take while sitting at my computer writing this—we know that true organizational reacculturalization will not likely occur in such environments. Instead, there will be pockets of people within the organization who have adopted the change to community policing whereas others remain on the traditional course. The result is organizational conflict, inconsistent goals, and mixed signals to personnel regarding the organization's missions. In the end, inefficiency and ineffectiveness are the most likely products with the community being the loser.

A third group of police leaders has adopted the community policing philosophy in name, far more than spirit, largely to get their share of federal funds afforded through hiring incentives, special program funds, and/or cost-free training. Either on their own initiative or as a result of political mandates in their jurisdictions, their true commitment goes little beyond lip service and their intent is centered on gaining resources in any way possible. To balance the risk of sounding too cynical on this point, I have been told by police managers that they will "play the federal game" to "get a piece of the pie." For such agencies, community policing will never have a reasonable chance to work simply because there is no commitment.

Finally, there are police executives who philosophically do not believe that community policing is an appropriate model for law enforcement. Their perspective centers on traditional policies and practices with no engagement in a charade of community policing. In some cases, this is reinforced by communities that simply want a reactive police force. Although we may be in disagreement, there is integrity in this position.

The significant point to note in these observations is that there is a continuum of support for the community policing concept with some significantly disparate approaches to the inculcation of the philosophy. We are a long way from unity in police management.

Conclusion

I applaud Plummer's efforts and enthusiasm. Indeed, I support his efforts and willingness to stand at the forefront of change in the community policing movement. Commitment such as his is essential for the change process to occur. My caution, however, is to view all aspects of the process with an objective and critical eye. Every idea will have strengths and weaknesses, proponents and opponents, planned and unplanned consequences, and debate about successes and failures. These dichotomies demand a pragmatic strategy for the change process. That is the challenge that continues.

Reference

Plummer, L. C. (2000). "Community Policing: Thriving Because It Works." *Police Quarterly*, 2, 83–88.

Reprinted from: David L. Carter, "A Response to 'Community Policing: Thriving Because It Works.'" *Police Quarterly*, Vol. 2, No. 1, Mar 1999, pp. 96–102. Copyright © 1999 by Sage Publications, Inc. Reprinted by permission. ✦

ISSUE VII
Zero-Tolerance Policing:
Is It Effective in Reducing Crime?

Over the past two decades, police agencies across the nation have been adopting a variety of community policing strategies, including several that are focused on the aggressive enforcement of disorder offenses. These aggressive strategies are popularly known as quality-of-life policing, and they target social and physical disorder rather than crime per se. By aggressively policing social and physical disorder, agencies believe they can make community members more inclined to care for their neighborhoods. In turn, the greater care will restore orderliness, eventually lead community members to feel safer, and signal to potential criminals that lawbreaking is not tolerated. Although some agencies have adopted quality-of-life policing as part of a department-wide strategy, it is also employed in specific neighborhoods identified as having serious problems with crime and disorder. Only a few researchers across the country have begun to examine the impact of quality-of-life policing on crime. In the following section the authors discuss their views on quality-of-life policing.

George L. Kelling and William J. Bratton argue that the reduction of disorder and crime in New York City was the result of implementing quality-of-life policies. The authors discuss the "broken windows" metaphor and how it helped police design this strategy. They describe how quality-of-life policing was first tested in the subway system and show how it contributed toward the substantial reduction of serious crime in New York City.

Chris Cunneen, on the other hand, argues that crime has not necessarily been reduced in New York City because of quality-of-life policing. In fact, this strategy has been accompanied by a number of injustices. First, it has led to the suppression of dissent. This suppression, in large part, the author argues, is the result of the police attempting to limit "bad" disorder in the city but actually limiting constitutional disorder. Second, he argues that quality-of-life policing has led to an increase in excessive force. For example, there are many complaints that relatively minor offenses by citizens are being met with unacceptable levels of police brutality. Third, the author argues that quality-of-life policing has led to a deterioration of community policing in New York City. The hard line approach of the police has led to a breakdown in police-community relations. In conclusion, Cunneen suggests that quality-of-life policing is more about public relations than about good policing.

Critical Thinking Questions

1. What is the theoretical basis for zero-tolerance policing?

2. What have been the three major problems associated with zero-tolerance policing?

3. Is zero-tolerance policing effective? Use evidence from the chapters to support your argument.

Internet Websites

Basic information on Broken Windows Theory. <http://eagle.onr.com/onpatrol/cs.brokwin.html>

Article on the problems with Broken Windows Theory. <http://chronicle.com/free/v47/i22/22a01401.htm>

Baltimore Police Department and zero-tolerance policing. <http://www.baltimoremd.com/indepen/barefoot.html>

New York Times article on the legality of zero-tolerance arrests. <http://www.city-journal.org/html/9_2_what_weve_learned.html>

Article on the failure of zero-tolerance policing. <http://www.cjcj.org/jpi/windows.html>

Article on the constitutionality of arresting and confining individuals for petty offenses. <http://www.crimelynx.com/divjust.html> ✦

13
Declining Crime Rates

Insiders' Views of the New York City Story

George L. Kelling
William J. Bratton

Introduction

Something dramatic happened in New York City in 1994: a lot of people stopped committing crimes, especially violent ones. The reduction in the number of persons committing murders, for example, while not unprecedented,[1] was extraordinary. Since 1994, a debate has raged about why this happened. Putting our position up front, we believe the police played an important, even central, role in getting people to stop committing crime in New York City. Despite arguments to the contrary,[2] no evidence exists that the substantial drops in crime in New York City, especially the initial ones when one of the authors of this paper, William Bratton, was commissioner, were the result of economic change, changes in drug use patterns, or demographic changes. Arguably, New York City's economy, drug use patterns, and demography might be different now in 1998. Unemployment was at 10 percent the month Bratton took over the New York City Police Department (NYPD) (January 1994) and at 8.7 percent when he resigned (April 1996)—hardly a booming economy.[3] And remember as well, the initial reductions in crime were so steep that by August of 1995—three years ago, but only twenty months after Bratton took office—

New York magazine declared in a cover story, "The End of Crime As We Know It."[4]

Readers should understand that this debate about the origins of crime reductions in the United States, especially in New York City, are not just academic in the sense that detached scholars are searching objectively for some "truth" lurking out there somewhere in the data. In fact criminological and political ideologies have shaped a good portion of this debate and are barely beneath the surface of even the most "detached" presentations. We do not pretend to be free from strong points of view about what happened in New York City. We were there and our presence belies any "detached objectivity." Yet, we are not alone in having important vested interests in the outcome of the debate.

Aside from the lack of any competing explanations, our confidence that the police played an important role in New York City has three origins:

(1) We had a guiding "idea" about how to prevent crime; put another way, we had a theory of action;

(2) We applied this idea in New York City's subway and, without anticipating it, the subway experiences became the "pretest" for what was to happen later citywide;

(3) Bratton, most importantly, but Kelling as well, had been struggling with issues of how to improve policing through police leadership, management, and administration for over two decades—principles developed in the context of organizational and policy literature and experience.

In the three sections that follow, we will be brief. We have written elsewhere about these issues and will not repeat our arguments here in detail.

The 'Idea'—Broken Windows

The "broken windows" metaphor had its origin in an *Atlantic Monthly* article by James Q. Wilson and Kelling.[5] It argued that, just as a broken window left untended was a sign that nobody cares and leads to more and severe property damage, so disorderly conditions and behaviors left untended send a signal that nobody cares and results in citizen fear of crime, serious crime, and the "downward spiral of urban decay."[6] The article also argued that whenever crime and communities verged on being out of control in the past, residents and authorities in neighborhoods moved to reassert controls over youth and over disorderly behavior.

The implications of this point of view are that minor offenses have serious consequences for the life of neighborhoods and communities. Citizens, city leaders, and police ignore them at their peril. This point of view is at odds with the reigning crime control policy view that had been developing throughout the 1950s and 1960s and made explicit by President Johnson's Crime Control Commission.[7] Police, in this view, are "law enforcement officers," the front end of the criminal justice system whose business is serious crime—arresting offenders. For a variety of reasons police got out of the business of minor offenses. These reasons went beyond the utilitarian view that scarce police resources should best be concentrated on "serious" crimes. They included an understanding of how police abused loitering and vagrancy ordinances in the past; a desire for the less intrusive policing and a more judicious use of the police authority in a democracy; and, a view that many of the offenses, like prostitution, are victimless.

Nonetheless, we argued that the links between disorder, fear, and crime went something like the following:

Disorder → Citizen Fear → Withdrawal (Physical & Social) → Increased Predatory Behavior → Increased Crime → Spiral of Decline.[8]

According to this model, waiting until serious crimes occur to intervene is too late: dealing with disorderly behavior early, like successful communities have in the past, prevented the cycle from accelerating and perpetuating itself.[9]

Moreover, experiences in the subway taught us that many chronic, serious offenders also behave in a disorderly fashion and commit minor offenses like farebeating. Police order maintenance activities also give police the opportunity to make contact with and arrest serious offenders for minor offenses.

We never claimed that order maintenance alone is the sole means of preventing crime. Solving crimes, incarceration, social change, deterrence by other means, police presence and persuasion, citizen vigilance, reduction of opportunities, environmental design, and other factors play a role as well. In New York City's subway, however, we argue that order maintenance was an especially significant part of reclaiming the subway and reducing crime.

The Subway

In April of 1989, Robert Kiley, Chairman of New York State's Metropolitan Transportation Authority (MTA) asked Kelling to assist the MTA in solving a problem in the New York City Transit Authority's subway (NYCTA). Kiley believed that the subway was in deep trouble—passenger usage of the subway was in rapid decline. New York City's late 1980s economic slump partially explained this decline. But marketing surveys suggested a more complicated problem: "homelessness" was frightening passengers and causing them to abandon the subway in droves. This was after $8 billion dollars had been poured into the subway to upgrade trains and tracks during the early and mid-1980s.

The NYCTA had already largely solved the problem of subway graffiti—a problem considered so intractable that its eradication was considered by some to be one of the most successful urban policy "wins" on record.[10] Yet, despite this achievement the frightening and intimidating behavior of a large group of miscreants overmatched whatever advantages accrued from graffiti elimination.

For those who have not experienced New York's subway during the late 1980s, its nightmarish circumstances are hard to describe. "In your face" panhandlers confronted riders throughout the system, from station entrances to trains. A quarter of a million passengers a day were "farebeaters," going over, under, and around turnstiles. Youths deliberately blocked turnstiles, held open emergency gates, and extorted fares from passengers. Platforms, trains, and passageways reeked from public urination and defecation. Young men stalked tollbooths planning to rob them if by any chance their doors were opened. These same tollbooths—literally under siege—had already been firmly secured, including being equipped with special automatic fire extinguishers that would be activated if youths poured gasoline into the money window and lit it to force toll-takers to open booth doors. Drug and alcohol abusers and the emotionally disturbed, often one and the same, sprawled throughout the entire system—at times taking over entire cars on a train. Robberies of passengers were increasing.

For the Transit Police Department (TPD), at this time an independent police department of some 4,000 officers, it was business as usual. They shared the common view held by every one from homeless advocates, to the New York City Civil Liberties Union, to the New York Times.[11] The problem was "homelessness" and homelessness was not the TPD's problem. Robberies consumed its attention. For example, the TPD was eager to restart an earlier discredited decoy unit. When confronted by Kiley about the subway's "homelessness" problems, TPD's administration at first balked. Later, under pressure, it proposed massive cleaning crews armed with high-powered hoses supported by a special police unit that would eject the "homeless" as they "interfered" with or got in the way of cleaning.

The story of reclaiming the subway by the police has been told elsewhere and need not be repeated here.[12] Summarizing, a large scale problem-solving exercise was conducted, the problem in the subway was properly understood as illegal disorderly behavior, policies were developed and officers trained to deal with disorder. The legal battles over police activities to rein in panhandling were fought and ultimately won; TPD leadership, however, was recalcitrant and the effort flagged. Bratton was recruited as Chief of the TPD in April of 1990; he pro-

vided leadership and implemented a large-scale effort to restore order. Following these actions, serious crime began an immediate and steep decline.

Disorder and crime are no longer serious problems in New York's subway—it is among the safest in the world. It feels, smells, and "tastes" different. Indeed, the culture was so different that by the mid-1990s the Transit Authority initiated a civility campaign, encouraging citizens to queue before boarding trains—a campaign that would have been a joke in the late 1980s. Returning ex-New Yorkers are stunned by the changes.

We highlight the subway experience because it has been lost in the bigger New York City disorder and crime story, especially since the TPD was absorbed by the New York City Police Department (NYPD) in 1995. Yet, it is an important story. It is probably one of the largest problem-solving exercises on record. The police tactics, organizational change, and administrative processes implemented in the TPD foreshadowed charges in the New York City Police Department. Still and all, the reclamation of the subway stands as a major event in public policy—certainly on a par with graffiti eradication—that raised and managed complex policy, constitutional, legal, and moral issues.

From our point of view and within the context of this discussion, it is especially important because it is hard to attribute the changes in the subway to anything other than police action. To be sure, the NYCTA implemented major efforts to deal with the genuinely homeless who were attempting to use the subway as a surrogate shelter. Graffiti had been eliminated and trains and tracks upgraded. Attempts had been made to target-harden the tollbooths and token-boxes (youths had been able to "spring" their doors with large screwdrivers and steal hundreds of tokens at a time), and some areas had been blocked off to the public. Moreover, subway officials were implementing a "station manager" program that focused on restoring a sense of station "ownership" and concern for passengers. But the subway environment was spinning out of control despite subway improvements and attempts at target hardening. Moreover, post-hoc explanations used to explain the later citywide reductions in crime—changes in drug use patterns, improved economy, declines in the number of youths, etc.—simply do not apply. Drug selling was not a major issue in the subway; unemployment was increasing during the time in question; and there was no evidence of a decline in the youth population.

The question is raised, "But isn't the subway a simpler system and easier to reclaim than city streets and public spaces?" This is the point of the subway story. It is a simpler system. People pay to enter it. There are few private spaces, only trains, platforms, passageways, and entrances and exits. One would expect that if police action, in this case to restore order, were to have an impact in any setting, it would be in such a restricted environment. From our standpoint it was an ideal place to test the broken windows hypothesis: that is, one way to reduce fear of crime and prevent serious crime is to restore order. The subway is a system in which the potentially confounding variables cited by social scientists are controlled.

Certainly, we cannot aver with scientific certainty that the crime reductions in the subway are the result of the police intervention. We put forward the following, however:

1. In response to a growing problem, the TPD developed a specific set of interventions that included police tactics and changes in organizational structure and administrative processes;

2. The TPD "called its shots," predicting that order could be restored and that crime would be reduced;[13]

3. Immediately following the intervention, crime began a steep decline.

The "after, therefore because of" fallacy? Perhaps. We doubt it. No other explanation seems plausible. Did graffiti elimination play a role? Target hardening? Social services for the genuinely homeless? Other factors? Of course. But action by the TPD achieved a "tipping point." We will return to the idea of "tipping point."

A final point in this introduction: no explanation of what happened in New York City can ignore the subway experience. While originally not conceived of as such, it became the pretest to what happened in the city.[14]

Leadership and Management

The New York City story is more complicated than the subway story. New York City is an intricate political, social, economic, and cultural entity in its own right. It has elaborate linkages to state, national, and international institutions and forces. Crime is more complicated in the city than in the subway. For example, the serious crime problem in the subway is largely robbery, with most of them being "grab and run"—crimes that, while not trivial, are less ominous than many of the confrontational robberies on city streets. Crime varies in other respects as well.

Moreover, more complex control systems operate in the city—from the "small change" of neighborhood life,[15] to schools, churches, family, workplace, business improvement districts, community groups, and others. Potentially confounding influences are not naturally controlled.

The NYPD is more complicated than the TPD was, and, frankly, it was in deep trouble when Bratton assumed control in 1994. Its troubles with abuse and corruption during the early 1990s were well known, largely as a result of newspaper revelations and the subsequent work of the Mollen Commission.[16] But there was another story in the NYPD, as least as dark as the abuse and corruption accounts, but far less well known—the lack of quality policing. Since the 1970s Knapp Commission,[17] the NYPD had been preoccupied with corruption. So much so that it was widely understood, but only partially true, that the "business" of the NYPD had become "staying out of trouble." And, of course, the most certain way to stay out of trouble was "to do nothing." Surely this is an overstatement, but nonetheless, it had considerable basis in fact. Most symptomatic of this "stay out of trouble by doing nothing" orientation was that line patrol officers were restrained by policy from making drug arrests, even if dealing was conducted right in front of their noses.[18] In respects it was the worst of all possible scenarios: too much abuse and corruption, too much corruption control, and not enough quality policing.[19] Bratton described the NYPD administrative world in *Turnaround*:

[T]he New York City Police department was dysfunctional.

First, it was divided into little fiefdoms, and some bureau chiefs didn't even talk to each other. OCCP didn't talk to patrol, patrol didn't get along with the Detective Bureau, and nobody talked to internal affairs. . . .

. . . . Each bureau was like a silo: Information entered at the bottom and had to be delivered up the chain of command from one level to another until it reached the chief's office. . . .

. . . When Maple [a key Bratton advisor who had been a lieutenant in the TPD and who was a deputy commissioner under Bratton] analyzed the bureaus, the news got worse. How was the NYPD deployed? The Narcotics Bureau, he discovered, worked largely nine to five or five to one, Monday through Friday. The warrant squad was off weekends. Auto-crimes squad, off weekends. Robbery squads? Off weekends. The community-policing officers—those six thousand baby-faced twenty-two-year-olds who were going to solve all the neighborhoods' problems—off weekends. Essentially, except for the detectives, patrol officers, and some other operations going round the clock, the whole place took Saturdays and Sundays off.[20]

Leading and managing such troubled organizations had become Bratton's stock-in-trade. The NYPD had been the fifth police organization he had headed that was in organizational trouble. His conviction that leading, inspiring, and directing middle-management was the key to improving police organizations was evident in a paper he published with Kelling[21] and was apparent in his work with the TPD.[22] His closest organizational advisors, Robert Wasserman (a police leader and consultant for over 30 years) and Robert Johnson (President of First Security—a Boston-based private security firm) had

struggled with management issues for decades. Wasserman, who had been an advisor to previous NYPD Commissioner Lee Brown, knew where the strengths of the NYPD were buried. Johnson had struggled to find leadership and management methods in the private sector to maintain core values and technologies in highly decentralized and geographically dispersed organizations. Other key advisors included John Linder, who had developed methods to do quick scans on organizational problems and opportunities, and Jack Maple, who is perhaps one of the savviest, street wise, and creative cops around. The ideas for Compstat—an organizational method both for holding precinct commanders accountable and for developing anti-crime tactics—grew directly out of the private sector management experiences of Johnson and the street sense of Maples.

This too has all been discussed previously.[23] We summarize it here to make the following point: Bratton approached his commissionership in New York City with a clear plan. He had an idea about how to prevent crime; he had an organizational strategy he wanted to implement; and he had pretested both with great success in New York City's subways. Again as in the subway, he called his shots—both by demanding that mid-level managers be held accountable for crime reduction and by producing plans for dealing with specific problems such as guns, youth violence, domestic violence, quality of life, auto crimes, and others. One of the hallmarks in social science is that research should be guided by theory. Bratton's strategy was, in effect, management guided by theory. Innovations were implemented and crime dropped. A lot.

Conclusion

What happened in New York City? We, of course, will never know with scientific certainty. No credible alternatives, however, have been put forward to contradict our belief that police action played a pivotal role. In the final analysis, we believe that we have seen New York City do what cities and communities have traditionally done when confronted by disorder, crime, and mayhem: it has moved to reassert control over disorderly behavior, fear, and crime.

The move to reassert control has been discernible in New York City since the late 1970s. Communities organized, business improvement districts organized, graffiti was eliminated from the subway, additional police were recruited and hired, prosecutors turned to communities for guidance (especially in Brooklyn), order was restored in the subway, and Mayor Rudolph Giuliani was given a political mandate to restore order and help bring crime under control. But, there were limits to what could be accomplished without an active police presence. Things had been allowed to deteriorate for so long, aggressive youths had been so emboldened—indeed in the absence of an active police presence, they virtually dominated public spaces in many communities— that traditional control measures were simply not robust enough to restrain their predatory behavior. And, in the midst of the "crack" epidemic, their violence spun out of control. Thus, the pattern described in Fagan et al.'s "Tale of Two Trends"[24] comes as no surprise to us. They compare non-gun homicides with gun homicides. That non-gun homicides should be declining over an extended period of time is consistent with our view of how New Yorkers have been reclaiming their city over the long haul. Fagan et al.'s assertion that "The rate of lethal violence broke important new ground only after 1995 or 1996"[25] is consistent with our interpretation as well. This was the exact period during which police were reinvigorated and their impact started to be felt. Likewise, we have no quarrel with Curtis' basic thesis,[26] that poor people are capable of helping themselves. We have never asserted otherwise: it has been basic to Bratton's practice and it is explicit in both the original "Broken Windows"[27] and "Fixing Broken Windows."[28]

Our basic premise is this: the restoration of assertive policing in 1994 and 1995 interacted with community forces to achieve an unprecedented "tipping point" in violent and other forms of crime.[29] Community forces, although formidable, could not do it alone. History and research gives us evidence that police cannot do it alone.[30] To assert that both the community and police played significant roles demeans neither. Can we ever be more specific in attributing causality? We doubt it. . . .

Notes

1. See Jeffrey Fagan et al., *Declining Homicide in New York City: a Tale of Two Trends in U.S. Homicide Rates*, 88 J. Crim. L. & Criminology 1277 (1998).

2. *See generally,* Alfred Blumstein & Richard Rosenfeld, *Explaining Recent Trends in U.S. Homicide Rates*, 88 J. Crim. L. & Criminology 1175 (1998).

3. New York City Police Department, New York City Crime Control Indicators & Strategy Assessment 41 (1998).

4. Craig Horowitz, *The Suddenly Safer City*, New York, Aug. 14, 1995, at 20.

5. James Q. Wilson & George L. Kelling, *Broken Windows: The Police and Neighborhood Safety*, Atlantic Monthly, Mar. 1982, at 29.

6. Wesley Skogan, Disorder and Decline: Crime and the Spiral of Urban Decay in American Neighborhoods 84 (1990).

7. President's Commission on Law Enforcement and the Administration of Justice, the Challenge of Crime in a Free Society (1967).

8. *See* Skogan, *supra* note 6 at 77; George L. Kelling & Catherine M. Coles, Fixing Broken Windows: Restoring Order and Reducing Crime on Our Communities 20 (1996).

9. *See* Wilson & Kelling, *supra* note 5, at 33.

10. Nathan Glazer, *On Subway Graffiti in New York*, Public Interest, Winter 1978, at 3–11; Maryalice Sloan-Howitt & George L. Kelling, *Subway Graffiti in New York City: Gettin' Up' vs. Meanin' It and Cleanin' It*, 1 Security J. 131 (1990).

11. Kirk Johnson, *Officials Debate How to Get Homeless out of Subways*, New York Times, Sept. 5, 1988 § 1, at 23.

12. *See generally* William J. Bratton, Turnaround: How America's Top Cop Reversed the Crime Epidemic (1998); Kelling & Coles, *supra* note 8, at 108–156.

13. The TPD's slogan under Bratton was "Disorder, farebeating, and robbery are one problem—deal with one and you deal with all."

14. Although, frankly, at least once over dinner, Bratton, Robert Wasserman, and Kelling played the mind game of how such tactics

and policies could be implemented in New York City and, oh, if only they could. Moreover, Kelling had some hope that broken windows ideas might be incorporated into New York City. Prior to Mayor Giuliani's 1993 campaign for mayor, Kelling had met with Giuliani and his staff on one occasion and with Giuliani alone on another to discuss the implications of broken windows for New York City. Likewise, Bratton met with him during this period to discuss the turnaround in the subway.

15. Jane Jacobs, The Death and Life of Great American Cities 73 (1961).

16. The Mollen Commission investigated corruption and abuse in the New York City Police Department during the early 1990s.

17. The Knapp Commission investigated corruption and abuse in the New York City Police Department during the early 1970s.

18. Marcus Felson, Kelling's colleague at the Rutgers School of Criminal Justice, has suggested in a personal conversation that a major crime prevention mechanism would be to "get people to do their jobs"—police, prosecutors, zoning officials, etc.—at one level, just what Bratton did with the NYPD.

19. *See, e.g.,* Frank Anechiarico & James B. Jacobs, The Pursuit of Absolute Integrity: How Corruption control Makes Government Ineffective 157–170 (1996).

20. Bratton, *supra* note 12, at 208–209.

21. George L. Kelling & William J. Bratton, *Implementing Community Policing. The Administrative Problem,* in Perspectives on Policing 4 (National institute of Justice ed., 1993).

22. Bratton, *supra* note 12, at 157–160.

23. *Id.,* at 233–239; Kelling & Coles, *supra* note 8 at 146–149.

24. Fagan et al., *supra* note 1 at 12–13.

25. *Id.* at 12.

26. Richard Curtis, *The Impossible Transformation of Inner-City Neighborhoods: Crime, Violence, Drugs and Youth in the 1990s,* 88 J. Crim. L. & Criminology 1233, 1263 (1998).

27. Wilson & Kelling, *supra* note 5.

28. Kelling & Coles, *supra* note 8.

29. Malcolm Gladwell, *The Tipping Point,* New Yorker, June 3, 1996, at 32.

30. For a summary of this history and research, see Kelling & Coles, *supra* note 8, at 70–107.

14
Zero-Tolerance Policing and the Experience of New York City[1]

Chris Cunneen

In recent years there has been considerable lauding of the New York experience in reducing crime through zero-tolerance policing approaches. This paper is a critical examination of some of the issues that have emerged in relation to zero-tolerance policing in New York.

The concept of zero tolerance is ambiguous. As one commentator noted, it is a sound byte term regularly used by the media and politicians (Burke 1998, 12). It has been defined as a generic expression to cover a variety of proactive, confident, assertive policing strategies (Burke 1998, 12). Of course such a definition is itself so overly generalized as to be virtually useless. Some of the advocates of what is referred to as a zero tolerance approach, such as George Kelling and William Bratton, have, in fact disassociated themselves from the term "zero tolerance" (Wadham 1998, 49). Zero tolerance policing is no doubt favored as a political slogan precisely because of its populist appeal and inherent ambiguity.

Zero-tolerance policing is said to [have begun] in New York during the 1990s under Police Commissioner Bratton and Mayor Giuliani. Giuliani was elected Mayor in 1993 and Bratton was appointed as Commissioner soon after. Giuliani's electoral campaign had centered around "reclaiming the streets" of New York.

As Greene (1999) has noted "reclaiming the streets" was only one of six crime strategies that Bratton developed. The others involved reducing youth violence, domestic violence, auto-related crime, drug dealing and the numbers of guns on the streets. However, "cracking down hard on the most visible symbols of urban disorder proved to be a powerful political tool for bolstering Giuliani's image as a highly effective mayor" (Greene 1999, 3). Reclaiming the streets through a focus on "quality of life" offenses became the hallmark of how zero-tolerance policing was understood in New York.

An important element in zero-tolerance policing has been the use of CompStat—a computerized managerial system. According to Bratton, it is based on four principles: accurate and timely intelligence; rapid deployment of personnel and resources; effective tactics; and relentless follow-up and assessment. The current Police Commissioner, Safir, has described CompStat as a "crime management tool that uses weekly crime statistics, computer mapping and intensive strategy sessions to direct the implementation of crime fighting strategies" (cited in Burke 1998, 20). There is clearly considerable pressure placed on borough and precinct commanders to achieve reductions in crime within their areas.[2] Nicholl (1997) has noted however, that the performance by which commanders are judged are "numbers": the number of street searches, the number of high rise searches (verticals), the number of summons[es], the number of arrests, the number of warrants executed, and so forth.

A further component of zero-tolerance policing has been significant increases in police strength. Between 1990 and 1996 the number of officers in the NYPD grew significantly from around 30,000 to over 38,000. There is a proposal to increase the department by a further 1,900 officers during the 1998/1999 fiscal year, which would bring the total strength to 40,210 officers—a 25 percent increase over the number of officers in 1990 (IBO 1998).

The NYPD emphasized more minor "quality of life" crimes, such as graffiti, vagrancy, begging, "squeegee" windshield washing, subway turnstile-jumping, illegal vending, street level drug dealing and street prostitution. These offenses were pursued to demonstrate "control" of the streets. Bratton had previously been Chief of the New York Transit Police and embarked on a "quality of life" policing program that had seen large-scale arrests of people for fare evasion. As Greene (1999) has noted, what Bratton embarked on as Police Commissioner was, in some ways, a traditional law enforcement crack down on local crime: arrest and gaoling of low-level drug offenders, picking up school-age youth for truancy, aggressive use of stop and search powers, warrant checks and arrest of those caught violating even minor public order laws.

During the initial period of zero-tolerance policing between 1993 and 1996 arrests increased by 23 percent. The type of arrests reflected the strategy of targeting low-level public order offenses and minor drug offenses—arrests for misdemeanors rose by 40 percent and arrests for misdemeanor drug offenses rose by 97 percent. By way of contrast, arrests for more serious offenses (felonies) rose by 5 percent during the same period (Greene 1999).

A significant part of zero-tolerance policing has also involved attempts at regulating various aspects of public expression. In particular, this has involved refusals to permit processions, marches and rallies. There have been a number of Federal court cases challenging Police Commissioner Safir (who replaced Bratton) over violations of the First Amendment. These include successful challenges to allow a protest procession by taxi drivers in May 1998. There was an attempt to prevent food vendors from marching against a curtailment of their stands, and a declaration that no more than 30 people could assemble at any one time on the steps of City Hall. In October 1998, the October 22 Coalition, who were planning a protest against police brutality, were refused a permit to march. The decision was overturned by a

Federal Court judge. The judge ruled that the refusal of the permit was a suppression of their First Amendment Rights and that the decision to refuse the permit had more to do with the protesters' message than any likely excessive traffic congestion (Kit Roane "Federal Judge Orders City to Allow a Rally Against Police Brutality", *New York Times*, 22 October 1998, B1). The City appealed the decision. However, three Federal court judges upheld the right to hold the march (Kit Roane "Permitted By Court, 1,000 March Against Police Brutality", *New York Times*, 23 October 1998, B3). In August 1998, a permit was refused to hold the Million Youth March in Harlem. A Federal Court judge ruled that the refusal was unconstitutional and that the rules in relation to granting permits were "breathtaking in their lack of standards" (Abby Goodnough, "Judge Rejects Effort to Block Harlem March", *New York Times*, 27 August 1998, B1). A later Federal court appeal upheld the right of the rally to take place (Dan Barry "Harlem Rally to Take Place Within Limits", *New York Times*, 2 September 1998, B1).

The policing of demonstrations and marches in the city has also been the subject of complaints about police concerning violence, provocation, the refusal to negotiate with organizers and widespread arrests. Immediately prior to the Million Youth March in Harlem the Police Commissioner announced plans to "saturate the site" with police and to promptly clear the streets at 4pm. The rally ended in violence when a police helicopter swooped low over the crowd and police in riot gear stormed the stage to shut down the meeting three minutes after the allotted time for the event had expired. The event had attracted 6,000 attendees and 3,000 police. Numerous policing experts criticized the police handling of the event, particularly the aggressive tactics and refusal to negotiate. Professor Lawrence Sherman described the tactics as the application of zero-tolerance policing to crowd control (Kit Roane, "Huge Deployment of Police Planned for Harlem Rally", *New York Times*, 5 September 1998, A1; Abby Goodnough, "Giuliani and Organizers of

Rally Clash Over Use of Force by Police", *New York Times*, 7 September 1998, A1, B4).

A march and vigil over the killing in Wyoming of gay college student Matthew Shepard resulted in the arrest of more than 100 people in October 1998. Police defended the arrests by saying that the organizers had failed to get a permit. Rally organizers said the police refused to talk or negotiate with them. In fact the rally's organizers and marshals were arrested at the beginning of the march. As the march continued, demonstrators were batoned by police and charged by mounted police (Michael Cooper, "60 Arrested in Rally Against Bias Crimes", *New York Times*, 20 October 1998, B3; John Kifner, "Protesters Say Police Created Havoc at Rally", *New York Times*, 21 October 1998, B5).

Zero tolerance policing has also involved the use of various ordinances such as New York's City Parks Department regulations. The New York Civil Liberties Union successfully argued that summons[es] for violating regulations issued against three Socialist Worker's Party members for "unlawful solicitation" and "unlawfully assembly, meeting and exhibition" violated their First Amendment rights. The three party members had been collecting signatures for a petition in a City park. Besides issuing them with summons, the NYPD also seized political literature and other material. The court dismissed the summons and ordered the police to return the material ("New York Mayor No Friend to First Amendment, NYCLU Says at Independence Day Rally", *ACLU News*, 4 July 1998, <www.aclu.org/news/nO7O498a.html>).

Similar regulations were used to prosecute members of the All Saints Lutheran Church who were distributing condoms as part of their HIV/AIDS education program in the South Bronx. The court held that the prosecutions violated the First Amendment. Three members of the National Organization of Women were prosecuted for "unlicensed general vending" for distributing and selling various pro-choice and feminist material during the annual Gay Pride Parade ("New York Mayor No Friend to First Amendment, NYCLU Says at Independence Day Rally", *ACLU News*, 4 July 1998, <www.aclu.org/news/nO7O498a.html>).

Police strategies have included greater use of CCTV. This has occurred in various public areas such as Washington Square where it was aimed at deterring small-scale drug-dealing, as well as in some housing estates ("New York City Residents Rally against Video Cameras", *New York Times*, 2 February 1998). In addition to the use of CCTV, police tactics in Washington Square have involved completely sealing off the park during operations, thus detaining all people there at the time. After a legal challenge by the Civil Liberties Union, the NYPD has adopted a policy whereby they will no longer completely seal off city parks but at least leave one exit open. The sealing off of particular areas has not only included parks and squares, but also involved neighborhood areas. In these instances, mobile command posts have been established (using police from outside the precinct) to allow for police "sweeps" through the area. Residents are forced to remain in doors. This strategy is referred to as "barricading"—in which an entire block is laid siege to for weeks on end (Asche 1998, 4). These types of operations have generally required a greater level of police surveillance, including an increased use of police helicopters.

The greater control of street offenses has seen the movement of some illegal behavior into new domains. For example, the crackdown on the selling of drugs at the street level has resulted in greater drug dealing in private premises. As the drug market has reorganized itself to deal with police pressure, the exchange of drugs is more likely to occur indoors. One result has been the development of more intimate relationships between buyers and sellers, which has also made the work of undercover police far more difficult.

A further result of this has been a dramatic increase in the number of police raids on houses. And a result of more raids on private apartments and houses has been an increase in the number of raids on the wrong premises. Between 1994 and 1997 there was a 50 percent increase in the number of people who required reimbursement for damage caused as the result of wrongful police raids. One of the more disturbing aspects of these bungled raids has been the refusal of the Police Commissioner to apologize to the victims and to acknowledge that the raids were errors. The Administration's view has been that if the police raid a house or apartment identified by an informer, and it turns out to be the wrong house, then the police have acted correctly.[3]

The pressure on police to maintain arrest rates for drugs which were set in the mid 1990s has intensified the concentration on minor drug dealing, as well as turning attention to the customers. Researchers noted one heroin user, who had never been arrested for drug-related offenses since beginning use in the 1970s, was arrested five times for drug possession between November 1996 and May 1997. Other innovations in drug distribution have involved the use of delivery services where an order is placed by telephone and a bicycle messenger delivers the drugs (Hamid, et al 1997, 383–384).

Sex work has also changed since the introduction of zero-tolerance policing. The police crackdown on street prostitution began in 1994 with more than 9,500 prostitutes and clients arrested. Since that time there are significantly fewer street workers. However, the sex trade has moved largely onto the Internet where agencies and individual workers can operate with relative safety from police intervention. According to the operator of Redlightnet, an online clearinghouse for the sex trade, the decline of crime in New York and the rapid growth in tourists and conventions had meant an even bigger market for prostitution (Kit Roane, "Prostitutes on Wane in New York Streets But Take to Internet", *New York Times*, 23 February 1998, A1).

It appears that it is the pro-arrest strategy for minor offenses that is causing a great deal of resentment among a cross section of New Yorkers.[4] The pro-arrest strategy has been stepped-up under Police Commissioner Safir, particularly during 1997 and 1998. Individuals on bicycles are being stopped, searched, handcuffed and arrested for offenses relating to their bicycles such as riding without a bell, or without a headlight or taillight, or on the footpath. They often remain in police custody for over 24 hours before appearing in front of the court. Similarly, men and women have been arrested and held in custody for having open containers of alcohol at neighborhood weekend basketball games or for selling such things as peeled oranges (Jim Dwyer, "The No-Bell Losers. Jail for You if that Cop Feels Like It", *Daily News*, 25 October 1998). Others have been caught up in the pro-arrest strategy for minor traffic offenses such as failing to wear a seatbelt. They also can spend well over 24 hours in custody before being brought before a court (Jim Dwyer, "Zero Tolerance, Zero Sense", *Daily News*, 31 July 1997).

In the majority of these minor offenses no other charges are laid, nor are outstanding warrants found. Yet part of the strategy behind zero-tolerance policing is that by intervening in less serious offenses there is likelihood that more serious matters will be uncovered. During the ongoing controversy over the arrest of bicycle riders in late 1998, an analysis was conducted of 73 people arrested and detained for matters relating to their bicycles. It was found that 17 people were in possession of drugs and four were carrying firearms. Over two thirds of the people detained had no other matter before the court except the one relating to their bicycle (Jim Dwyer, "Apple's Now Suspect City", *Daily News*, 1 November 1998).

It is claimed that the most beneficial outcome of zero-tolerance policing has been the decline in the level of crime in New York City. According to the Mayor's Office there has been a 60 percent drop in murders, a 12 percent drop in rapes, a 48 percent drop in robberies and a 46 percent drop in burglaries. Between 1993 and 1997 reported serious offenses fell by 44 percent (Greene 1999, also IBO 1991). Some of the possible reasons for this, as well as comparative data, will be discussed further below.

The Torture of Abner Louima

Abner Louima, a 30-year-old Haitian immigrant, was arrested on 9 August 1997 outside a Brooklyn nightclub following a dispute between police and clubgoers.

Witnesses told the *New York Times* that Louima was arrested while trying to break up a fight. He was allegedly assaulted twice while being transported to the police station. At the station he was allegedly subjected to racist abuse. In the washroom of the station, one officer then shoved a wooden stick (believed to be a broom or toilet plunger handle) into Louima's rectum and mouth. The officer then borrowed gloves from another officer and reportedly carried the stick covered in excrement and blood around the police station.

Other inmates in the cell where Louima had been placed complained that he was bleeding. He was held for three hours before being transported to hospital. Louima claimed that officers threatened to kill him if he made any complaint. Doctors confirmed serious internal injuries and broken front teeth which were consistent with his allegations of assault. Louima was hospitalized for two months. The police charges against him were dropped.

No police officer at the station reported the attack. A nurse who treated Louima and reported the incident to the Internal Affairs Bureau (IAB) did not have her report recorded. The first officially recorded complaint came from Louima's parents some 36 hours after the attack. The IAB did not attend the police station where the attack occurred until 48 hours after the incident.

During the two weeks following the attack, fourteen officers were suspended or placed on modified duties. Many of these officers had been the subject of previous complaints of police brutality. Two officers were charged with aggravated sexual assault, and another two officers were charged with assault. The officer directly responsible for sodomizing Louima was also charged with assaulting another Haitian male on the same night as the attack on Louima. A sergeant was charged with attempting to conceal both assaults.[5]

It would be simplistic to argue that the torture of Abner Louima was the result of zero-tolerance policing. However, it is *indicative* of the types of severe problems within the NYPD that a strategy of zero-tolerance policing has exacerbated: aggressive public order policing; the routine use of violence and, in extreme cases, torture; and the targeting of minority groups. Certainly the widespread use of violence against members of minority groups is a major issue. The New York City Public Advocate claimed that the police torture of Louima was part of a "pattern of police abuse, brutality and misconduct" (Human Rights Watch 1998, 382; Greene 1998).

The Police-Community Relations Inquiry 1997–1998

A task force to review police-community issues was established by the Mayor of New York following the alleged beating and torture of Abner Louima. The Mayor's Task Force on Police-Community Relations comprised 31 members including clergy, the director of the New York Civil Liberties Union, members of the City council, community leaders, a retired police chief and lawyers.

The recommendations of the task force were rejected by the Mayor in March 1998. He criticized the Task Force's majority report and failed to mention the torture of Louima which been the catalyst for establishing the Task Force. "Some of the things we've already done. Some of the things I've opposed in the past, I'll continue to oppose them. And some of the things are unrealistic and make very little sense" (Dan Barry, "Giuliani dismisses police proposals by his task force", *New York Times*, 27 March 1998, 1). The Mayor complained that the Task Force had ignored the drop in crime in the city.

Among the recommendations in the majority report were the elimination of the forty-eight hour delay allowed for officers under investigation; the creation of an auditor position to review the performance of the Civilian Complaint Review Board (CCRB) and to improve cooperation by the police department with the CCRB; better screening of police recruits; bilingual or multi-lingual receptionists in precincts that have a large number of residents who do not speak English; and requiring officers to live in the city in an effort to improve diversity, and cultural awareness, on the force.

There was also a minority report, authored by three members of the Task Force who reportedly believed the Task Force's majority report was inadequate. Among other recommendations, the minority report called for the creation of an independent special prosecutor's office (Human Rights Watch 1998, 270; Dan Barry, "Giuliani dismisses police proposals by his task force", *New York Times*, March 27, 1998).

What Can Be Learned from the New York City Example?

The Suppression of Dissent

The introduction of zero-tolerance policing has been accompanied by an attempt to control dissent, including the desire to ban a range of demonstrations as outlined above. Norman Siegel, the Director of the New York Civil Liberties Union, noted the following:

> I've been here 13 years and my legal director has been here even longer, and we've never filed as many cases involving one administration. The Mayor's vision of a new New York is a vision that is more authoritarian and repressive, a vision that is antithetical to our rich tradition of tolerance for protest and dissent ("New York Mayor No Friend to First Amendment, NYCLU Says at Independence Day Rally", *ACLU News*, 4 July 1998, <www.aclu.org/news/n070498a.html>).

Demonstrations and marches have occurred because of the intervention of the Federal court that has over-ruled the refusal of permits by the Police Commissioner. However, the policing strategies which have then been used to control marches and processions have reflected a hardline, non-negotiated approach. The lessons concerning crowd control learned from the demonstrations of the 1960s have been ignored and there is now far greater likelihood of serious public disorder directed against police.

Police Brutality, Particularly Against Racial and Ethnic Minorities

Police corruption and the use of excessive force have long been recognized as a prob-

lem in the NYPD. The Mollen Commission of Inquiry into corruption in the NYPD in 1994 found police officers were involved in drug dealing, robberies, assaults, perjury and falsification of records. It also found a failure by the NYPD to discipline officers accused of brutality.

A 1996 Amnesty International investigation after the Mollen Commission found that some steps had been taken to tackle corruption within the NYPD. However, police brutality remained a serious problem. Importantly, Amnesty noted that local community and civil rights groups reported that aggressive zero-tolerance policing policies "had been accompanied by unacceptable levels of brutality, especially toward racial minorities". There were many cases "where police officers had used excessive force in response to minor incidents, including assaulting bystanders for taking photographs or criticizing police treatment of others" (Amnesty International 1996).

The Amnesty report noted that

> The evidence suggests that the large majority of the victims of police abuses are racial minorities, particularly African-Americans and people of Latin American or Asian descent. Racial disparities appear to be especially marked in cases involving deaths in custody or questionable shootings, an issue Amnesty International believes should be the focus of particular inquiry (Amnesty International 1996).

Certainly the police precincts with the highest number of reported complaints against police are in neighborhoods with higher proportions of African-American and Latino residents (Greene 1999). Amnesty reports have continued to draw attention to the high level of police killings and the apparent failure to respond to police who are responsible for the deaths. For example, an unarmed African-American was shot dead in a New York supermarket on 25 December 1997 by police who said they mistook the keys he was carrying for a gun. The officer who shot him had been involved in eight prior shootings but had not been placed on any monitoring program (Amnesty International 1998, 27).

Statistics published by the CCRB indicate that minorities are disproportionately the victims of police abuse—particularly African-Americans. Half the people who lodged complaints with the CCRB from January to June 1995 were African-American (50 percent), a quarter were Latino (26 percent), while the remainder were either white (21 percent) or "other" (3 percent), including Asian. The CCRB semiannual report for the first half of 1997 noted a similar trend where African-Americans and Latinos lodged 78 percent of complaints against police. The 1996 investigation by Amnesty International also revealed that more than two thirds of the cases of police brutality were African-American or Latino. Most of the police officers involved were white. Nearly all of the victims in the cases of deaths in custody (including shootings) reviewed by Amnesty were members of racial minorities.

Similarly, Human Rights Watch noted in a 1998 report that the cost of zero-tolerance policing was revealed by

> citizen complaints against more aggressive NYPD officers during the past several years and continuing impunity for many officers who commit human rights violations despite the recent reorganization of both the civilian review board and the police department's internal affairs bureau . . .
>
> There is often a racial or ethnic component to police abuse cases in New York City, with many incidents also fuelled by language barriers and miscommunication in the culturally diverse city (Human Rights Watch 1998, 268–269).

In November 1998 the New York City Council's Public Safety Committee issued a report arguing for stronger policies to control police brutality. The Committee's chairperson noted that

> The Department has perpetuated a police culture in which officers may be emboldened to conduct themselves in a manner that runs contrary to departmental policy, the law and public interest. . . . It is not a stretch to suppose that officers—such as those implicated in the Louima incident—felt that they could get away

with it (Michael Cooper, "Stronger Policies Are Needed to Stem Police Brutality", *New York Times,* 10 November 1998, B1).

Increased Complaints Against Police and Increased Deaths in Police Custody

Despite reforms following the Mollen Commission, complaints against the police registered with the CCRB have risen sharply since 1993. The CCRB reported 4,920 new complaints in 1994, an increase of 37 percent over the previous year. While complaints cover a range of alleged abuses from discourtesy to deaths in custody, the largest proportion (1,670 complaints) were for excessive force. These had also risen proportionately since 1993. A further increase of 32 percent was noted for the first six months of 1995 compared to the first six months of 1994. Complaints against police recorded by the CCRB continued to rise in 1996. During early 1997 there was a slight decline in the number recorded. However, it was later revealed that complaints were being undercounted by the CCRB by around 20 percent as a result of a "clerical error" (Michael Cooper, "New York Undercounted Civilian Complaints about Police", *New York Times,* 11 December 1997, B1). After the Louima incident in the later half of 1997 there was again an increase in the number of complaints lodged. The most recent figures for the first half of 1998 revealed a 20 percent increase in complaints compared to the same period in the previous year (Michael Cooper, "Complaints Against Police in '98 Grow 20 Percent", *New York Times,* 11 June 1998, B7).

During the specific period between 1993 and 1996 when Bratton was the Police Commissioner complaints concerning police misconduct rose by 65 percent ("ACLU Warns of 'Dark Side' of NY Police Plan", *The Philadelphia Inquirer,* 16 December 1997). In the four years up to 1998 the filing of civil rights claims against police for abusive conduct had increased by 75 percent and they were continuing to increase (Greene 1999).

There is little doubt that the increase in complaints is associated with the introduction of zero-tolerance policing. According to

Amnesty International, police have suggested that the sharp increase in complaints arose as a result of increased arrests and police activity during the intensive anti-crime drive (known as the "quality of life initiative" before attracting the title of "zero tolerance"). According to police, many complaints arose from more effective policing and an increase in arrests, rather than genuine abuses. However, the CCRB noted that most of the complaints arose from encounters with police that did not involve arrests or persons receiving summonses. Most complainants had no prior complaint history, so could not be characterized as "chronic" complainers.

In 1996 the Amnesty delegation were told by several sources, including officials from the CCRB, that more aggressive policing had led to an increase in complaints of ill treatment. This view was certainly reflected in the complaints statistics noted above. In addition deaths in custody increased. The NYPD statistics for 1993 and 1994 show a rise in both the number of civilians who died from police shootings (an increase of 35 percent) and in the number of people who died in police custody (an increase of 53 percent).

Failure to Deal with Complaints Against Police

The CCRB is an independent board responsible for dealing with complaints against police. However, it has no power to take action against police officers—all matters relating to the disciplining of police officers are conducted by the NYPD. The New York Task Force on police-community relations reported in March 1998 that the NYPD had taken either no action, or imposed minimal discipline, in a large proportion of complaints found to be substantiated by the CCRB. The task force found that 57 percent of substantiated cases resulted in no disciplinary action at all; in other cases disciplinary measures were "slight". The CCRB report for 1997 revealed that action was taken in less that one third of cases (89 of a total 276) referred to the police department for disciplinary action (Amnesty International 1998, 45).

The situation of disciplining officers found to have engaged in misconduct was made even more farcical when, in September 1998, it was revealed that the CCRB had failed to pass on to the NYPD 108 substantiated cases of police misconduct (Michael Cooper, "Police Say Panel Withheld Findings Against 108 Officers", *New York Times*, 2 September 1998, B3).

The failure of the police department to deal with issues of brutality and corruption has been a constant source of criticism of the City's administration. Some, such as councilor and chair of the Public Safety Committee, Shelden Leffler, have argued that while zero tolerance of offending is demanded of the public, there is no zero tolerance approach to police misconduct ("Got a Police Problem? Keep it to Yourself", *New York Times*, 29 March 1998; Bob Herbert "The Stone Wall of Silence", *New York Times*, 23 July 1998, A25).

The Demise of Community Policing and the Further Marginalization of Ethnic and Racial Minorities

Some criminologists have commented that although Bratton was not antagonistic to the basic principles of community policing including a commitment to crime prevention, problem-solving and closer community partnerships, the effect of the changes he commenced in the NYPD has been to undermine community policing approaches (Greene 1999, 4). While managerial changes devolved power to the local command level, the enforcement strategies which were embarked upon were those of a traditional "law and order" crackdown, and were not developed in partnership with local communities.

Both the general police crackdown in neighborhoods and the hardline taken against demonstrations and marches shows that there is *no negotiation* of who is arrested or what they are arrested for. The failure to negotiate and the failure to develop partnerships with communities in relation to their policing needs reflects a substantial departure from community policing principles.

The NYPD does not reflect the ethnic and racial composition of New York City where a little over 40 percent of the population are white, 29 percent black, 24 percent Latino and the remainder predominantly Asian American. The large majority of NYPD officers are white. In 1995 the racial distribution of the NYPD was 72 percent white, 15 percent Latino, 11 percent African-American and 2 percent of other ethnicities. The NYPD is also comparatively non-representative by United States standards—in a 1992 study New York was ranked last among 50 cities surveyed to see how well police departments reflected the racial make-up of their populations.

The separation of police officers from the community they police is further accentuated when it is noted that most NYPD officers live in the suburbs outside the city. Amnesty International (1996) has noted that some critics of the department allege that this has contributed to a sense of alienation and tension between the police and the inner-city communities in which they work.

The cultural and spatial separation of police from the communities in which they work is further reflected in the lack of confidence, which minority groups have in the police. A *New York Times* poll in October 1997 found that 82 percent of blacks and 71 percent of Hispanics felt the police did not treat whites and blacks in New York City with equal fairness. The poll reflected the findings of other studies and was taken several years after the introduction of zero-tolerance policing in the city.

Value for Money?: The Relationship Between Policing Levels and Crime Reduction

Zero tolerance policing is a resource intensive policing strategy. It requires high staffing levels to achieve the necessary level of direct law enforcement on the streets. Therefore, it is fair to ask whether citizens get value for money from the increased number of police necessary to operate a zero-tolerance policing strategy. Does the increase in resources actually lead to a reduction in the crime rate?

As noted previously the size of the NYPD increased dramatically during the first half of the 1990s. The city also experienced a 46 percent reduction in the crime rate during the same period (1990–1996). San Diego is a city with a similar crime index rating as New York.[6] During the same period it achieved over 40 percent reduction in the crime rate with a 1 percent increase in its per capita police staffing levels (IBO 1998). San Diego restructured its police department along a community policing model, which stressed problem solving, and police community partnerships for reducing crime. In contrast to the New York experience the drop in crime rates in San Diego was achieved at the same time as the number of arrests between 1993 and 1996 actually *declined* by 15 percent. Complaints against police for misconduct also fell. San Diego police also made greater use of new technologies in crime mapping and police intelligence in locating consistent areas of high crime. However, they were able to utilize the new technologies within a context of community policing (Greene 1999).

The Independent Budget Office (IBO) for the City of New York provided comparative analysis to the City Council's Committee on Public Safety on differing rates of policing and crime rates in the 25 largest United States cities. The IBO found that many other cities achieved significant reductions in the crime rate with either much smaller per capita police staff levels or with actual reductions in police staff levels.

- San Diego achieved a 40 percent drop in the crime rate with a 1 percent increase in per capita police staffing levels.
- Dallas achieved a 39 percent drop in the crime rate with a decline in the per capita police staffing levels of between 2 and 3 percent.
- Pittsburgh achieved a 36 percent drop in the crime rate with a 6 percent increase in per capita police staffing levels.
- El Paso achieved a 33 percent drop in the crime rate with a 5 percent increase in per capita police staffing levels.
- Miami achieved a 28 percent drop in the crime rate with a decline in the per capita police staffing levels of over 11 percent.

- Seattle achieved an 18 percent drop in the crime rate with a decline in the per capita police staffing levels of 6 percent (IBO 1998).

Based on the 1996 FBI Crime Index figures, New York had the third lowest crime rate of the 25 largest United States cities. However, it had the second highest (after Washington) per capita police staff levels. The two big cities with lower crime rates than New York are Indianapolis and San Jose. By way of comparison with New York, these two cities also have the lowest per capita police staff levels of the 25 largest cities. In Indianapolis there are 13 police officers for every 10,000 residents, and in San Jose there are 16 police officers for every 10,000 residents. In New York there are 53 police officers for every 10,000 residents. In San Diego where there was dramatic reduction in crime rates and a small increase in the policing levels, the per capita policing level is 17 per 10,000—less than a third of New York's (IBO 1998).

The relationship between the level of policing and the level of crime in a community is by no means clear. Some cities have both low crime rates and low per capita policing levels. Others have high crime rates and high police staffing levels. In addition some cities have achieved significant reductions in crime without embarking on a zero-tolerance policing strategy with the associated increase in police staff levels.

Has Zero-Tolerance Policing Reduced Crime?

As noted above, proponents of zero-tolerance policing point to the decline in the crime rate in New York as proof of the success of the strategy. However, there are doubts that the falling crime rate in the city during this period was simply attributable to zero-tolerance policing given that many other large United States cities experienced similar declines, although using different policing strategies and with dramatically different levels of policing. Nationally the incidence of serious violent crime and property crime declined in the United States during the first half of the 1990s. National victimization surveys show a decline in rape, robberies, aggravated assaults and property crime. Not all large cities or states recorded a fall. However, there appears to be no correlation between whether zero-tolerance policing strategies were introduced, or, indeed, whether "three strikes" legislation and mandatory minimum prison terms were introduced, and the decline in crime rates (Greene 1999).

A range of demographic, social and economic factors, as well as some law enforcement strategies such as greater control on handguns, have likely contributed to the declining levels of particular types of violent crime. Economic growth, reduced levels of unemployment and greater community-based activities to reduce crime are likely to have had an effect on crime levels (IBO 1998; Greene 1999). There have also been significant changes in the pattern of drug use including the decline in the use of crack-cocaine. An ongoing study by Hamid, et al, (1997) of heroin use in New York has found that young African-Americans are avoiding both heroin and cocaine. Even licit drugs are viewed with disfavor.[7] Others have argued that there is a direct connection between the drop in the murder rate in New York and the decline in the crack cocaine epidemic (Dixon 1998, 97).

Local Accountability, Crime Reduction and the Falsification of Records

Zero tolerance policing has relied on new information technologies which provide localized assessment of the nature and incidence of crime and provide for the targeting of police resources at the local level. They also provide the opportunity for police managers to place considerable pressure on local area police commanders to demonstrate results in reducing crime or increasing the number of arrests.

The experience in the United States appears to be an upsurge in falsifying crime reports designed to demonstrate a reduction in the number of crimes being committed in particular areas. Recent media reports have suggested manipulation of crime data (usually by downgrading the nature of the crime when it is recorded) in a number of cities where commanders have felt the pressure to show ever-decreasing crime rates (Fox Butterfield, "As Crime Falls, Pressure Rises to Alter Data", *New York Times*, 3 August 1998).

Nicholl (1997) provides a selection of quotes from NYPD officers which reflect the distorting influence which zero-tolerance policing and CompStat have had on policing:

> CompStat is the tail wagging the dog. I am trying to build relationships with my community so my crime rates are increasing because there is more confidence in reporting crime to us. But I then get beaten over the head at CompStat.

> Robbery patrol hours and the number of verticals are more important than dealing with domestic violence and rape.

> You try reporting a crime to the station—they don't answer the phone, so their numbers are distorted because people just give up.

> I am not accepting this as an assault report—no one gets their ribs cracked by a hairbrush. Get rid of it.

> We have to find more larceny reports—if we only have three this week, they will expect us only to have two next week.

And from a lieutenant, "I spend all my time counting crime reports and checking we are not recording too many. I don't get to go out on patrol with my officers any more" (Nicholl 1997, 5).

She adds,

> These are quotes from real cops in NYPD who have had to operate to CompStat and under the fear of being caught out with high crime figures. It strikes me this is wholly predictable—the consequence of a police department driven by fear of being embarrassed if they do not reduce the levels of crime. Crime statistics are notoriously unscientific. They are made even harder to make sense of if there is tomfoolery going on with the way crime figures are recorded (Nicholl 1997, 5).

Conclusion

There are highly divergent views within police services concerning the merits of zero-tolerance policing—it would be highly misleading to view all senior police as favorably disposed to the idea of zero-tolerance policing. To a greater extent it has been the overtly political use of the concept of zero-tolerance policing which is alarming. Many of the proponents of zero-tolerance policing present a naive and public relations-inspired view of policing in New York City. The purpose of this paper has been to raise questions around such a sanitized view.

In addition the experience of New York also provides a useful framework for considering criminological arguments against zero-tolerance policing. These augments can be summarized as follows.[8]

- There is a lack of evidence of any direct causal link between zero-tolerance policing and declining crime figures. In some United States jurisdictions the same reduction in levels of crime are being achieved through other policing strategies. The pressure placed on local commanders to show ongoing reductions in crime has lead to concern about falsification of crime statistics.

- Zero tolerance policing is resource intensive. It requires either increased police numbers or the allocation of existing resources away from other areas of enforcement. Thus zero-tolerance policing strategies are seen as invariably short-term and expensive. Zero tolerance policing emphasizes offenses in public places—street offenses. It is apparently not concerned with other and potentially more major areas of violence such as domestic violence, nor other facets of property crime such as fraud. The notion of "quality of life" is itself defined to only include a narrow section of "public" life. Corporate crime and environmental crime, for example, have large scale effects on "quality of life". Crimes which occur in the private sphere (such as domestic violence) are not seen as "quality of life" issues at all.

- Zero tolerance policing represents a return to pro-active policing strategies (common in Britain prior to the inner city riots of the early 1980s, and common in parts of Australia during the 1980s and early 1990s, particularly with the use of tactical response police). Zero tolerance policing may increase the level of public disorder because it is proactive. It contradicts the results of major inquiries into public disorder such as the Scarman inquiry in the UK, which stressed policing based on community consent, trust and participation. It will also worsen relations between particular communities and police.

- Zero tolerance policing undermines principles of community policing including commitments to crime prevention, problem-solving and closer community partnerships. In this sense, zero-tolerance policing is antithetical to policing by consent—the supposed hallmark of policing in a democracy. Policing priorities are defined external to the community.

- Zero tolerance policing strategies have been consistently implicated with violations of civil and political rights.

- By targeting street offences, zero-tolerance policing is aimed at essentially the poor and the homeless. Racial and ethnic minorities are also concentrated in these groups. Zero tolerance policing will lead to greater discrimination—either directly through the targeting of minorities or indirectly through their greater presence among those arrested.

- Zero tolerance policing will lead to far greater levels of criminalization. In particular, minority groups that already have large proportions of their male population with criminal records will see even greater degrees of criminalization. This will further compound social and economic marginalization.

- Zero tolerance policing will bring about an increase in complaints about police misconduct and brutality particularly from minority groups.

- Zero tolerance policing will require greater court resources to deal with increased arrests; it will impact eventually on the prison population (through greater criminalization, increased fine defaulters and sentences of imprisonment).

- Zero tolerance policing rests on a spurious assumption that the law is neutral and can be enforced in all situations—that complete enforcement is a possibility. However, public order and the actions which constitute disorder are broadly defined and open to constant interpretation and discretionary decisions by police. By pretending that zero tolerance is possible, the more important question of *who* gets arrested is obscured.

The experience of zero-tolerance policing in New York shows that these issues and arguments are matters of very real concern, and go to the heart of the nature of relationship between police and the social and political communities, which are the subjects of policing.

Notes

1. Research assistance was provided by Zena Dabboussy. Thanks to Penny Andrews, Rick Curtis, Judith Greene, Sid Haring and Rebecca Peters in New York City. Sections of this paper were part of a larger report prepared for the Law and Justice Section of Aboriginal and Torres Straight Islander Commission (ATSIC).

2. "CompStat operates by the police commanders . . . giving periodical briefings to the senior management of the NYPD. These take place in the central command room of the Department, which is set out like a wartime operations center. The management team sits around a horseshoe-shaped desk while the borough commander stands in the middle. The crime statistics for the borough are displayed on screens behind the commander whether they want them or not. The statistics . . . are selected by the management team. . . . There is one CompStat meeting a week and the borough commanders do not know which

of them are going to be called to give a brief-ing. . . . There is little doubt that these often 'brutal' periodical interrogations . . . by NYPD senior management in an environment that resembles a wartime operations center have provided sufficient motivation to achieve success in the fight against crime" (Burke 1998, 20). See also Silverman (1998, 59).

3. John Marzulli "Cops Delay Reporting Botched Raid". *Daily News,* 3 March 1998; Kit Roane, "Bronx Man Recounts Abuse by Police in Mistaken Raid". *New York Times,* 4 March 1998; Kit Roane, "Once Again Police Raid Wrong Apartment", *New York Times,* 21 March 1998; John Marzulli "Cop Raid Targets Cry Foul", *Daily News,* 8 May 1998; Jim Dwyer, "Safir Not Sorry for Bad Raids", *Daily News,* 10 August 1998; Juan Gonzalez, "Cops Trampling Families and Rights", *Daily News,* 19 November 1998.

4. According to Silverman (1998) summons[es] are used if an individual is carrying a Govern-ment-issued photo identification and has no outstanding warrants.

5. For a further discussion of the Louima inci-dent see Human Rights Watch 1998, 286–289; "Abuse Charge Rocks New York Police Department" *ACLU News,* 14 August 1997, <www.aclu.org/news/w08l497c.html>.

6. An index based on the rate of serious offenses, which compares and ranks 189 of the largest United States cities.

7. "Equally profound changes have occurred in other aspects of their lives. For example, they commit far fewer crimes or acts of violence than formerly. . . . At the same time, they have redoubled their efforts to complete their edu-cation, find jobs and participate in commu-nal activities" (Hamid, et al 1997, 378).

8. Some of these points can be found in various articles including (Burke 1998; Dixon 1998; Greene 1999; Nicholl 1997; Palmer 1997; Pol-lard 1997: Wadham 1998).

References

Amnesty International (1996) *United States of America: Police Brutality and Excessive Force in the New York City Police Department,* Am-nesty International Report, AMR 51/36/96 <http://www.amnesty.org/ailib/aipub/1996/AMR/25103696.htm>

Amnesty International (1998) *United States of America: Rights for All,* Amnesty International Report, AMR 51/35/98 <http://www.rightsforall-usa.organizations>.

Asche, A. (1998) *Zero Tolerance Policing,* Prelimi-nary Report, Report to the Legislative Assem-bly, Darwin, 18 August 1998.

Bratton, W. (1998) *Turnaround,* Random House, New York.

Burke, R. (ed) (1998) *Zero Tolerance Policing,* Perpetuity Press, Leicester.

Burke, R. (1998) "A Contextualization of Zero-Tolerance Policing Strategies" in Burke, R. (ed) *Zero Tolerance Policing,* Perpetuity Press, Leicester.

Dennis, N. (ed) (1997) *Zero Tolerance: Policing in a Free Society,* Institute of Economic Affairs, London.

Dixon, D. (1998) "Broken Windows, Zero Toler-ance and the New York Miracle", *Current Is-sues in Criminal Justice,* vol 10, no 1, pp 96–106.

Gibbons, S. (1996) "Reclaiming the Streets", *Po-lice Review,* vol 104, no 5386, 13 September, pp 18–21.

Gibbons, S. (1997) "Zero Tolerance", *NSW Police News,* vol 77, no 7, pp 25–26.

Greene, J. (1999) "Zero Tolerance: A Case Study of Police Policies and Practices in New York City", *Crime and Delinquency,* (forthcoming).

Hamer, J. (1997) "Zero Tolerance Policy in the USA", *New Law Journal,* vol 147, no 6792, 16 May, pp 737–738.

Hamid, A., Curtis, R., McCoy, K., McGuire, J. (1997) "The Heroin Epidemic in New York City: Current Status and Prognoses", *Journal of Psychoactive Drugs,* vol 29, no 4, pp 375–391.

Henderson, C., and Reder, R. (1997) "Zero Toler-ance Policing in Hillsborough County", *Police Chief,* vol 63, no 2, February 1997, pp 54–55.

Howe, S. (1997) "Kelling's Law", *Policing Today,* vol 3 no 4, pp 17–19.

Human Rights Watch (1998) *Shielded from Jus-tice: Police Brutality and Accountability in the United States,* Human Rights Watch, New York.

Independent Budget Office (IBO), City of New York (1998) Correspondence with the New York City Council Committee on Public Safety, 16 March 1998, 11 May 1998. On file with author.

Kelling, G., and Coles, C. (1997) *Fixing Broken Windows,* Touchstone, New York.

Morgan, R., and Newburn, T. (1997) "Tough on Zero Tolerance", *New Statesman,* vol 126, no 4336, 30 May, p 14.

Nicholl, C. (1997) "Zero Tolerance", Paper pre-sented at a conference in Manchester, 24 March 1997, unpublished.

Palmer, D. (1997) "When Tolerance Is Zero", *Alternative Law Journal,* no 22, pp 232–236.

Pollard, C. (1997) "Zero Tolerance: Short Term Fix, Long Term Liability" in Dennis, N. (ed) *Zero Tolerance: Policing in a Free Society,* Institute of Economic Affairs, London.

Potter, K. (1996) "Zero Tolerance", *Police Review,* vol 104, no 5378, 19 July 1996, pp 18–20.

Rutherford, A. (1997) "The Government, Crime and Public Order", *New Law Journal,* vol 147, no 6797, 20 June, pp 932–933.

Silverman, E. (1998) "Below Zero Tolerance: The New York Experience", in Burke, R. (ed) *Zero Tolerance Policing,* Perpetuity Press, Leicester.

Wadham, J. (1998) "Zero Tolerance Policing: Striking the Balance, Rights and Liberties" in Burke, R. (ed) *Zero Tolerance Policing,* Perpetuity Press, Leicester.

Wilson, J., and Kelling, G. (1982) "Broken Windows", *The Atlantic Monthly,* vol 249, no 3, March 1982 pp 29–38.

ISSUE VIII
Racial Profiling: Do the Police Target Minorities for Traffic Stops?

Concern over disproportionate enforcement of the law is not new. In recent years, there has been increased attention to one specific form of disproportionate enforcement of the law—racial profiling. There has long been concern over the fact that minority drivers receive a disproportionate number of traffic tickets, are searched more often than white drivers, and end up being arrested more often than white drivers, a pattern sometimes called "driving while black." A good deal of the attention being paid to this issue is a consequence of a suit filed by the U.S. Justice Department against the State of New Jersey, specifically the New Jersey Division of State Police, in 1999. This suit resulted in a consent decree, an agreement between the State of New Jersey and the U.S. Justice Department, that the New Jersey State Police had engaged in inappropriate targeting of minorities for traffic stops.

Despite the fact that a majority of Americans, regardless of race, believe that racial profiling exists, there is controversy over the issue. One of the points of controversy is how to establish whether, in fact, such behavior exists. Some argue that the disproportionate number of traffic stops of minority drivers is in itself evidence of racial profiling. Others argue that it is impossible to establish the intent of an officer without examining every stop and every officer individually. More than a dozen states have conducted studies of traffic stop patterns. These studies have generally concluded that black and Hispanic drivers are stopped at rates that are similar to or modestly higher than rates for white drivers. However, the largest disparities between white and minority drivers occur for decisions to search a driver and take such drivers under arrest. There is concern on the part of some in law enforcement that increased attention to racial profiling will lead to "de-policing," the under-enforcement of the law in minority communities, many of which are plagued by high crime rates. Others argue that the overrepresentation of minorities in traffic stop data is indicative of the higher levels of crime in minority communities.

Because of its importance to issues of due process, equal protection under the law, and crime control, the topic of racial profiling is not likely to vanish from public debate. Understanding this issue is important for students of criminal justice.

In the first chapter in this section Phuong Ly examines traffic data from Montgomery County, Maryland. The author argues that the data show racial disparity in the number of traffic stops by the police. In particular, he reports that when compared to Caucasians, African-American drivers were much more likely to receive oral and written warnings, were more likely to be interrogated by the police in the field, and were three times more likely to be asked if their vehicle could be searched. The author discusses the possibility of whether the police discriminate in their decision to stop a vehicle.

Jerry Oliver, the former Chief of Police in Richmond, Virginia, argues that there may be several explanations other than discrimination to account for why the police are more likely to stop African-American drivers. He points out that in several communities across the country the police are being asked by the community to aggressively attack crime, drugs, and disorder. As a consequence of the use of aggressive tactics, Oliver believes tensions have flared between the police and minority communities and these tensions have resulted in charges of police racism. He then points out that those who are arrested, prosecuted, and convicted of crimes in these communities are more likely to be African American; he argues that it would be unreasonable to believe that the statistics reflecting traffic infractions and stops would be any different.

Critical Thinking Questions

1. Is there evidence suggesting that the police engage in racial profiling?
2. Should the police be permitted to profile if it is effective?

3. What types of problems might result from racial profiling?

Internet Websites

Missouri Attorney General's Office. <http://www.ago.state.mo.us/>

Police Executive Research Forum. <http://www.policeforum.org/>

San Diego Police Department. <http://www.sannet.gov/police/>

Basic information on Driving While Black. <http://www.wolfenet.com/~jneedlel/BLACK1.HTM>

American Civil Liberties Union. <http://www.aclu.org/profiling/>

Report on profiling by the National Organization of Black Law Enforcement Officers. <http://www.noblekids.org/profiling.htm> ✦

15
Montgomery Traffic Data Show Race Disparity

Phuong Ly

Black drivers were stopped at a disproportionate rate by Montgomery County police when compared with the number of blacks who live in the county. . . . The reasons black and Hispanic drivers were stopped and the treatment they received also were strikingly different from those in stops of white drivers, the data show.

Police Chief Charles A. Moose said at a news conference that he thinks black drivers are being stopped at a fair rate and that police are not racially profiling drivers. He pointed to statistics showing that black drivers account for 26.2 percent of stops resulting from the use of radar or laser devices or from red-light violations—actions in which police have little control over the drivers stopped. Of the total number of stops, black drivers accounted for 27.3 percent. Blacks make up 15.1 percent of the county's population.

"There's consistency," Moose said. "The skews aren't very dramatic. . . . We don't have any evidence of racial profiling."

But leaders of the county chapter of the NAACP—whose complaints about police prompted the agreement with the U.S. Justice Department that produced the statistics—said they continue to believe that minority drivers are targeted in Montgomery. NAACP leaders said police officers cannot be trusted to log data correctly. Neither race nor ethnicity is listed on driver's licenses, and police officials said there is no way to determine whether officers record the correct information for each person stopped.

The statistics on American Indians may show how demographic data in the study is based on impressions or decisions by individual officers. The American Indian category is simply labeled "Indian" on the handheld computers the officers carry. About 460 American Indians were stopped, according to police, but census numbers show that only about 2,500 American Indians live in the county and that there is no large population of them region-wide.

"I think there's room for concern," said Mary Betters, co-chairwoman of the NAACP's criminal justice committee. "I don't believe there's a department policy of racial profiling, but I wouldn't say that there isn't profiling on the part of individual officers."

The statistics are the first look at data the Justice Department has required Montgomery County to keep since Sept. 1, 2000. Yesterday, police released information on the 32,743 traffic stops made from October 2000 to March 2001. Officials had predicted that the first data would be released early this year, and they said the delay was caused by technical problems.

The Justice Department's nearly four-year probe of Montgomery County police—during which two traffic stops within two weeks ended in the fatal shootings of two blacks—did not find that civil rights were violated. But Justice officials said that county police issued 21 percent of traffic tickets to black drivers in 1997–1998; at the time, blacks accounted for 12 percent of the county's population.

Police leaders have argued that relatively high numbers of blacks may be getting stopped because there are also nonresident black drivers who travel through Montgomery, particularly from the District and Prince George's County. The traffic stop data did not show a dramatic difference when only drivers from Montgomery County were tallied. Black drivers who live in Montgomery County accounted for about 23 percent of all stops of county residents. The 160-page report also noted differences in how minority drivers were treated:

- A higher percentage of black drivers received oral and written warnings and field interrogations. Hispanic drivers received a significantly higher number of equipment repair orders, civil and criminal citations and arrests.

- Blacks drivers were about three times as likely as whites to be asked if their vehicles could be searched. Of 450 searches, 197, or 43.8 percent, were of black drivers; 150 were of whites; and 78 were Hispanics. In the searches, contraband was found more than 30 percent of the time for each of the three groups. The statistics do not include searches made after an arrest or a stop made in connection with suspected criminal activity.

- Blacks and Hispanics were less likely to be stopped when radar surveillance or red-light violations were involved. About 8.8 percent of the stops on radar/red-light violations were of Hispanic drivers; Hispanics accounted for 11.4 percent of total stops. The figures for black drivers were 26.2 percent and 27.3 percent, respectively.

In contrast, for white drivers, a higher percentage of stops were for radar/red light violations—56.3 percent—compared with 52.7 percent for all stops. . . .

Amy Farrell, a researcher at Northeastern University who is studying traffic stop data, said statistics on searches in Montgomery and other jurisdictions seem to provide some support for minority drivers who complain that police hold them longer than white drivers. "Now, there may be legitimate reasons," she said. "But that seems to be something we need to do more research on."

Data collection at other police departments, such as in San Jose and St. Paul, MN, have also shown black drivers stopped at a rate disproportionate to the black population.

. . . Montgomery police officials said there were several problems they want to correct for subsequent data collections. During the six months, about 30 motorist records were lost because some officers did not download the data from their pocket computers regularly. The numbers of citations and stops do not match because multiple citations could be made for one stop. Officers also have filled in some fields such as "arrest" and "no action" incorrectly, officials said, and there is not yet a way to capture the demographics of passengers. Police officials said the data collection did not appear to create a chilling effect or "de-policing" by officers. Last year, when data were not collected, 58,000 traffic citations were issued. So far this year, 73,000 citations have been issued.

Reprinted from: Phuong Ly (with contributions by staff researcher, Bridget Roeber), "Montgomery Traffic Data Show Race Disparity." *Washington Post*, November 2, 2001, p. B01. Copyright © 2001 by *The Washington Post*. Reprinted by permission. ✦

16

Police Target Most Likely Criminals of All Races

Jerry Oliver

Is it blatant acts of bigotry or the demand for high box scores in crime reduction efforts that are fueling the latest tempest in police/community relations? Whether widespread racial profiling by police departments on our country's highways and street—commonly referred to as "Driving While Black"—actually occurs is still very much open to debate.

Led by prominent African-American, civil rights, and political leaders, along with the American Civil Liberties Union's (ACLU) Police Practices Project out of Northern California, there have been countless complainant interviews and numerous studies commissioned across the U.S. to research this "differential hassling" of motorists by police. Legislation also has been introduced in Congress and in various statehouses, including Virginia, to pass Traffic Stop Statistical Study Acts. These Acts, if passed, would allow for the study and banning of racial profiling on any federally or state-funded highway and in any drug interdiction program. They would even bar traffic stops as a crime-fighting tactic.

The issue has been highlighted by recent national attention on police misconduct and abuse involving African-Americans in local police departments in New York, Baltimore, Washington D.C., Los Angeles, and Riverside, California, and in both the New Jersey and Maryland State Police Departments. Many in the black community believe these are clear examples of escalating bigotry and discrimination by police officers in enforcing criminal and traffic laws.

As an African-American police leader, I suggest that there is another point of view in need of serious consideration by racial-profiling investigators. Over the past several years, there has been constant and intense political pressure placed on police agencies nationwide, particularly in urban areas, to reduce violent crime, respond effectively to the war on drugs, and address citizen demands for safe neighborhoods.

These pressures have caused police leaders in increasing numbers to adopt proactive, aggressive crime reduction strategies. These strategies use a variety of legal, but confrontive or intrusive, techniques to create a safe environment, reduce crime, and ensure job security for the police leader. At the insistence of local officials or governing bodies, police chiefs have adopted high-tech, high-presence, and high-pressure initiatives to reduce the incidence of, and the opportunities for, disorder, misconduct, and mischief.

These aggressive enforcement tactics have exacerbated the concerns of the racial-profiling camp and have helped generate charges of disparate treatment of black citizens by police. Take Richmond, for example: In order to meet or exceed the City Council's mandated public-safety goal to reduce violent crime in our city by 30 percent by the year 2000, the Richmond Police Department had to recharge its enforcement efforts with more assertive, proactive engagement on the corners and streets of Richmond.

These efforts, including strict enforcement strategies such as Project Exile, Operation R.I.P., and Blitz to Bloom, seek to balance crime-control strategies with democratic principles. They are directed toward illegal behavior known to contribute to the homicide rate, gun violence, and various other elements of confusion and chaos in our city. Not surprising to me, however, those arrested in Richmond were overwhelmingly black.

Richmond's population is majority African-American. It is an indisputable fact that African-Americans, for historical, sociological, and economic reasons, are disproportionately represented in our violent crime (homicides, aggravated assaults, rapes, and robberies) statistics both as victims and as perpetrators. For instance, of the 74 homicides that occurred in our city in 1999, 87 percent of the victims were black and 89 percent of the known suspects were black. The numbers are similar in each crime category.

Thus, if we are to have effective violent crime-reduction strategies in our community, there will be disproportionate stops, public contacts, arrests, prosecutions, and incarcerations of African-Americans by police. I maintain that it is the presence of criminals on our streets—African-Americans or otherwise—and the pressure from our constituencies to address crime and disorder respectfully but aggressively that are more at the core of the racial-profiling debate than bigotry.

Perhaps our black leadership and the ACLU can spend as much time, energy, and resources seeking to prevent black criminality as they have spent in preventing cops from racially profiling suspects.

Reprinted from: Jerry Oliver, "Police Target Most Likely Criminals of All Races." *Richmond Times-Dispatch*, January 2, 2000, p. G3. Copyright © 2000 by *Richmond Times-Dispatch*. Reprinted by Permission. ✦

Part Three

Administering Criminal Law in the Courts

The courts perform a pivotal role in the criminal justice system. Prosecutors, defense attorneys, and judges—known as the "courtroom workgroup"—are the key players within the courtroom. Although individuals in the courtroom workgroup sometimes have competing goals, they must also work together to move cases along in an efficient manner. The players in the justice system typically follow a certain sequence of events when an alleged crime has been committed. For example, after the police apprehend someone suspected of committing a crime, the prosecutor must decide if there is enough evidence to charge the suspect. If probable cause exists, the prosecutor then screens the case to decide which crime(s) to charge. Shortly after the defendant's first appearance in court, for most felony cases (about 95 percent) the prosecution and the defense agree on a plea bargain; that is, the defendant agrees to plead guilty in exchange for a lesser charge, which may carry a lighter sentence.

For felony crimes that may go to trial, the prosecutor must ensure that there is probable cause to believe that the defendant may have committed the crime he or she is being charged with. The prosecutor cannot make

that decision alone, however. The grand jury is considered to be the second screening device to ensure that a case is not being brought haphazardly against an individual by the government. The grand jury is composed of between 16–23 citizens and functions as a second opinion within the federal system and in about half of all states. The first controversial issue in this section asks whether the federal grand jury adequately performs its role in inspecting cases brought before it by the prosecutor. (The federal grand jury is the focus here because state grand juries vary widely, and it is not practical to generalize the workings of the federal system to that of the state systems.) All grand juries provide an opinion as to whether enough evidence exists in the case to warrant taking it further in the criminal justice process. If the grand jury votes to indict the defendant, its members agree with the district attorney that enough evidence exists to move forward with the prosecution of the case. For states that do not have the grand jury system, the case is scrutinized by the prosecutor's office through a process known as an "information."

Another recent development in the court system has been the increase in the number of drug-related cases and subsequent convictions. As an interdependent entity, the court is greatly affected by police enforcement and arrest patterns. When there are police crackdowns on the possession and sale of drugs, aimed at both major drug operations and small-time dealing, drug caseloads escalate and cause a backlog in the courts, which increases case processing time.

Furthermore, many drug offenders are addicted to drugs and/or alcohol and do not get proper treatment for their addiction in prison. Drug offenders return to the criminal justice system at high rates through relapse (return to drug or alcohol abuse), recidivism (return to criminal behavior), or both. A proposed solution to these problems is the creation of "drug courts" to process the high numbers of drug offenders. The object is to allow drug users the chance to enter drug and alcohol treatment centers in the community and divert them from prison. Unlike most other criminal courts, drug courts are a type of specialty court that serves as a pre-trial diversion strategy. Pre-trial diversion means that if offenders successfully complete treatment and other conditions of their sentence, the conviction can be deleted or expunged from their record.

In sum, the goals of drug courts include expediting case processing time, offering community drug treatment, and diverting drug addicts from jail and prison (saving prison bed space for violent offenders). The issue of the effectiveness of drug courts is discussed in detail.

For the small percentage of cases that actually go to trial, there is a long-standing debate concerning media presence in the courtroom. Goldfarb (1998, 156) believes that there is a trend toward increased public demand for greater knowledge of government's decision-making power. To this end, the latest controversy is whether video cameras should be permitted to record live court proceedings for the television-viewing public. Trials in adult criminal court have always been open to journalists and the general public. A small number of high-profile criminal cases have had limited press coverage in court, beginning with the kidnapping and murder of aviator Charles Lindbergh's son in the 1930s. Since that time, court opinions in the matter have varied greatly, from no restrictions to limiting the number of cameras, the type of cameras, and the placement of cameras while court is in session. The issue resurfaced during the 1996 televised criminal trial of O. J. Simpson, after which live coverage became a debatable issue for the courts. After the Simpson trial, many television shows have appeared that show actual court cases. The issue addresses whether cameras interfere with the justice process (e.g., whether the behavior of trial participants is changed) or whether there is a right to report court hearings as they occur in a process of "open government" (Goldfarb 1998).

Reference

Goldfarb, Ronald L. 1998. *TV or Not TV: Television, Justice, and the Courts.* New York: New York University Press. ✦

ISSUE IX
Does the Federal Grand Jury Adequately Perform Its Screening Role?

Following the felony arrest of a suspect, the prosecutor must decide whether to charge the suspect with a crime. If the prosecutor believes there is probable cause that the defendant committed the crime, the prosecutor must use the grand jury as a screening device in federal felony cases and in 19 states. Six states require a grand jury for capital crimes only, while a grand jury is optional in 25 states (Emerson 1983). The way a grand jury is selected varies by state, but the selection process is conducted using names from voter registration records and driver's licenses.

The federal grand jury is controlled by Congress but functions as an "arm of the court" or as an independent check of the prosecutor. Since the prosecutor represents the government, the grand jury system was created to ensure that the government would not or could not indiscriminately bring criminal charges against an individual citizen without adequate burden of proof. In other words, the grand jury stands between the accuser and the accused. Since the 1980s, the use of the federal grand jury has increased and is the preferred method for complex federal cases and white-collar crimes (Brenner and Lockhart 1996).

The grand jury has two main functions: an investigatory function and a screening (or accusatory) function. The investigatory function includes the power of the grand jury to subpoena witnesses or evidence for further consideration. In its screening or accusatory role, the grand jury serves (in theory) as an independent institution, beyond the power of the courts, to prevent the government from abusing its power. In the eyes of the prosecutor, use of the grand jury is appealing because grand juries are unconstrained by the rules of Miranda and the exclusionary rule, and they can issue summonses to call up witnesses and examine illegally gathered evidence. The prosecutor acts as a legal advisor and directs the secretive grand jury process. If the grand jury agrees with the prosecutor and believes that probable cause exists, it votes to indict (called a "true bill"). If the grand jury believes that the case lacks the strength to go to trial, it refuses to indict by issuing a "no true bill" (Blank 1993; Brenner 1995).

Both of the following selections agree that the grand jury does an adequate job in its *investigatory* role. The controversy is whether the grand jury sufficiently performs its accusatory or screening role. First, Thomas Sullivan and Robert Nachman declare that there is nothing wrong with the way the grand jury performs its screening role. The authors do not believe that the government has abused its authority in its relationship with federal grand juries. They oppose any reforms (e.g., giving the defendant the right to have a judge review the sufficiency of a grand jury indictment) that the American Bar Association is recommending. Allowing for judicial review of the grand jury's decision would increase costs and delay cases within the criminal justice system, they say. Moreover, judicial review would negate the independent authority of the grand jury.

Andrew Leipold argues that grand juries do a poor job of assessing the evidence brought forth by the prosecutor in deciding whether to indict. Thus, grand juries are not independent bodies that protect citizens from the government. Rather, grand juries are merely rubber stamps for the prosecutor, even if the prosecutor should supply a case with questionable evidence. Leipold discusses the differences between the accused person's rights denied at a grand jury hearing compared to the rights afforded a defendant at a trial. He concludes that grand jurors are not allowed to (or are not informed that they may) find and weigh competing facts, yet they are asked to determine whether facts that the prosecutor sets before them satisfy the legal standard of probable cause. Most citizens are not trained to know when probable cause has been achieved, and therefore jurors simply agree with the prosecutor.

References

Blank, Blanche Davis. 1993. *The Not So Grand Jury: The Story of the Federal Grand Jury System*. Lanham, MD: University Press of America.

Brenner, Susan W. 1995. "The Voice of the Community: A Case for Grand Jury Independence." *Virginia Journal of Social Policy and the Law* 3: 67–131.

Brenner, Susan W., and Gregory G. Lockhart. 1996. *Federal Grand Jury Practice*. St. Paul, MN: West.

Emerson, Deborah. 1983. *Grand Jury Reform: A Review of Key Issues*. Washington, DC: Department of Justice, National Institute of Justice.

Critical Thinking Questions

1. How could the grand jury system be reformed to improve the current practices?

2. How involved should the prosecutor be when working with the grand jury? How far should a grand jury be able to go to challenge a prosecutor's decision on a case?

3. Should the grand jury proceedings be made available to the accused after an indictment has been filed? (They are currently kept secret.)

4. Should the grand jury system be abolished altogether? If so, what would be an adequate replacement?

Internet Websites

State grand jury sites. <http://www.udayton.edu/~grandjur/links/state.htm>

Ex-New York state grand juror recommends reforms. <http://www.udayton.edu/~grandjur/recent/gjafr.htm>

Deputy district attorney of Kings County in Brooklyn, NY, describes how state grand juries work. <http://www.udayton.edu/~grandjur/recent/hnygjw.htm>

General information on the federal grand jury. <http://www.pawd.uscourts.gov/Public/Jury/fgj.htm>

Federal grand jury reform report and bill of rights. <http://www.criminaljustice.org/public.nsf/freeform/grandjuryreform?open document>

Discusses whether the administration of the federal grand jury secrecy provisions adhere to due process concepts. <http://www.law.fsu.edu/journals/lawreview/frames/241/kaditxt.html>

Handbook of the structure and inner workings of the federal grand jury. <members.tripod.com/~jctMac/fgj.html> ✦

17

If It Ain't Broke, Don't Fix It

Thomas P. Sullivan
Robert D. Nachman

The federal grand jury system has emerged relatively unscathed from the stormy attacks of the 1970s, when critics, decrying the political abuse of the grand jury by the Nixon administration, called for radical changes to the system. The 95th Congress considered several different reform bills,[1] including no less than four alternative constitutional amendments to abolish all or part of the fifth amendment requirement that grand jury indictments initiate federal prosecutions. In addition, the American Bar Association (hereinafter "A.B.A.") approved an authoritative position paper advocating significant changes (hereinafter "A.B.A. Principles").[2]

This reforming fervor has produced few tangible results. In 1979, Congress amended Rule 6 of the Federal Rules of Criminal Procedure to require the recording of all grand jury proceedings, except the jurors' deliberations and voting.[3] Congress amended the rule further in 1983 to clarify certain matters concerning the secrecy of grand jury proceedings.[4] In 1980, the Department of Justice issued new, comprehensive guidelines governing the work of United States attorneys (hereinafter "Department of Justice guidelines").[5] These new legislative and executive responses to widespread criticism of the grand jury have fallen short of the wishes and expectations of many reformers; nonetheless, for the time being, at least, the federal grand jury as an institution appears to be relatively stable.

The federal grand jury is a powerful body.[6] It may summon practically anyone it wants, and, through the statute providing for the immunization of witnesses,[7] it may compel a summoned person to testify or risk going to jail for contempt. It conducts its business through secret proceedings which are largely unreviewable by the courts.[8] It may indict any person or entity, and thus require that defendant to stand trial for the alleged crime.[9]

Knowledgeable observers recognize and concede that federal grand juries do not protect citizens from unwarranted accusations by the government.[10] Rather, federal grand juries usually adopt the prosecutor's suggestions, and readily return indictments against the persons and upon the charges the prosecutor recommends.[11]

The tremendous power of federal grand juries, and the occasional abuse of authority by prosecutors who control that power, has led to calls for the abolition of the grand jury,[12] or for substantial reform of its proceedings,[13] in order to make the grand jury more independent of the prosecutor. This Article examines the accusatory [screening] function of the federal grand jury system in light of these proposals. It explores whether the system is working as intended, and to the extent it is not, which proposals hold the best chances for effecting meaningful change without crippling the law enforcement process.

This article concludes that the grand jury should, with a few minor changes, remain as the body to initiate federal prosecutions, because the grand jury, by and large, adequately fulfills an appropriate accusatory function. Although overzealous or overreaching federal prosecutors can manipulate the federal grand jury, by and large the Department of Justice has not abused its authority. Furthermore, no current proposal for reform of the federal grand jury system can eliminate the possibility of abuse without unduly obstructing federal law enforcement and federal courts, and adding substantial cost and delay to the federal criminal justice system. Thus, the protection of citizens is best left in the hands of the conscientious prosecutors who occupy the offices of the United States Attorney and their assistants throughout the country. The last part of this Article discusses reforms aimed at ensuring that conscientiousness.

The Dominance of the Prosecutor Over the Grand Jury, and Two Critical Responses

Critics of the grand jury begin with the observation that grand juries no longer perform an independent screening function, but instead merely "rubber stamp" indictments tendered by prosecutors.[14] We believe this is true in most instances. Federal prosecutors and their assistants, in cooperation with the federal investigative agencies, decide upon the persons and subject matters to investigate, the witnesses to call, and the documents to subpoena. They decide which targets to pursue and which witnesses to immunize. They often orchestrate the investigations of other independent federal agencies. They act as counsel to the grand jury, advising it on legal issues, and in effect, represent the grand jury in hearings on grand jury matters before the federal judiciary. Given this role of federal prosecutors, it is understandable that the members of the grand jury come to rely upon the prosecutors to summon and produce appropriate witnesses and documents, and come to trust the prosecutors' judgment as to which cases they should pursue, and whom they should indict.

When a federal prosecutor seeks an indictment from the grand jury, almost invariably the grand jury returns a true bill.[15] Indeed, "no bills" are so rare that prosecutors regard them as freak occurrences.[16]

Experienced federal defense lawyers understand the prosecutor's near total control of the grand jury. When they seek to avoid indictment of their clients, these defense attorneys rarely ask to have their clients appear before the grand jury. Rather, the defense lawyers address their arguments and pleas to the prosecutor, and sometimes have their clients submit to interviews with the prosecutor and the investigating agents, because they assume that the prosecutor, not the grand jury, will determine who will be indicted, and for what. These experienced practitioners treat the grand jury's vote simply as a formality.[17]

Critics have responded in two ways to the erosion of the grand jury's traditional role as an independent buffer between the state and the citizenry. Some critics have called for a total abolition of the grand jury system. They suggest that the grand jury be replaced by a system in which the prosecutor commences prosecution by means of an information, and the target of prosecution has a right to a full preliminary hearing before a neutral magistrate.[18] States which have abolished the grand jury system use systems similar to that proposed.[19] Other critics, notably the A.B.A., advocate retaining the grand jury but reforming certain aspects of grand jury practice in order to curb prosecutorial power and return the grand to its role as a screening device, designed to separate worthy from unworthy prosecutions.[20]

Either abolition or extensive reform of the grand jury's accusatory function would add extra steps to the process of criminal prosecution, and foreseeably, would change other aspects of the criminal justice system as well.[21] . . .

The Grand Jury's Accusatory Function Needs No Major Reform

The A.B.A. proposals to reform the grand jury's accusatory function assume that grand juries indict individuals who should not be indicted. The proposals lay the blame for this at the feet of overzealous, sometimes unscrupulous prosecutors, who are unchecked by an independent grand jury.[22] The reformers argue that the grand jury insulates the prosecutor from public scrutiny and thereby inadvertently abets prosecutorial abuse.[23] In order to stop unwarranted indictments, the A.B.A. seeks to transform the grand jury from a prosecutorial "puppet" to an independent screening body. This transformation involves two steps. First, a judge should be required to tell grand jurors that they must carefully screen cases, and second, prosecutors should be required to support their requests for indictment with evidence of the type that they will be required to produce at trial.[24] The A.B.A. proposals include, among others: (1) requiring that the judge inform the grand jury of its duty to screen out unworthy prosecutions;[25] (2) giving the target of a grand jury the right to testify before the grand jury;[26] (3) requiring the prosecutor to present all available exculpatory evidence;[27] (4) forbidding the use of evidence which would be constitutionally inadmissible at trial to support an indictment;[28] and (5) prohibiting the use of hearsay testimony to support an indictment, except under narrowly defined circumstances.[29] To put teeth into these new rules, the Model Act [Model Grand Jury Act] provides for a post-indictment, pre-trial hearing to test the validity of the indictment.[30] At the hearing, a judge or magistrate will review the transcript of grand jury proceedings to ensure that the proceedings complied with Model Act procedures, and to weigh independently the evidence presented to the grand jury for legal sufficiency.[31]

Most of the proposed rules for grand jury procedure strike us as sensible, and most are consistent with Department of Justice policy.[32] But we believe that it is a mistake to grant each defendant a right to challenge the sufficiency of the evidence supporting a grand jury indictment. In complex cases involving lengthy testimony and numerous documents, "sufficiency" hearings would place substantial burdens on the judiciary. We believe that this additional burden on the federal system is not warranted, for there is no hard evidence that prosecutors, federal or state, engage in the kinds of misconduct which these proposals are designed to prevent.[33] Rather than making the encounter between the government and the target a fairer one, these proposals will add substantial time and expense to what is already a slow, cumbersome, and costly process.

Before taking drastic steps which embrace such troubling consequences, a legislative body must satisfy itself that a serious problem with the current system exists. The A.B.A. proposals to reform the accusatory function of the federal grand jury begin with the link between prosecutorial power and abuse of the system: "The most obvious defect [of the grand jury system] is the grand jury's complete dependence on the prosecutor for all its information, advice, and direction."[34] This observation precedes a catalogue of the enormous powers of the prosecutor in a grand jury proceeding compared to the powerlessness of the citizens whom the grand jury chooses to investigate: the grand jury can subpoena someone within its jurisdiction virtually at will; it can conduct fishing expeditions without first establishing any likelihood of wrongdoing; it can strip individuals of the fifth amendment right against self-incrimination by granting them immunity; and it may jail them for failure to comply after being granted immunity.[35] In short, reformers argue that the omnipotent government can, and often does, take advantage of the hapless, defenseless citizen, who does not even have the benefit of counsel within the grand jury room.[36]

As we have observed above, we believe that many of the reformers' perceptions about the prosecutor's domination over the grand jury are accurate. However, merely detailing the prosecutor's power over the grand jury and painting the citizen-grand jury confrontation in David and Goliath terms does not make a case for the need to reform grand jury accusatory proceedings. Instead, a meaningful call to reform the grand jury's accusatory function must begin with sound proof that, under the current system, the grand jury indicts people who should not be indicted. If this is not the case, it will be counter-productive to add more steps to the accusatory process. In other words, "If it ain't broke, don't fix it."

To determine whether grand juries indict inappropriate people, one must first define whom the grand jury properly should indict. Justice Department Principles, the A.B.A. proposals, and common sense all suggest that the likelihood of conviction at trial should be the chief standard of indictability.[37] The standard should also give weight to the nature and seriousness of the offense, the wishes of the victim, and the background of the target.

A grand jury indictment represents the decision of a grand jury to cause the government to try someone for the alleged commission of a crime. An indictment should not be used as a form of punishment. A prosecutor who is convinced that a person has committed an offense, but believes that the government probably will be unable to prove guilt beyond a reasonable doubt at trial, should not seek an indictment. The Department of Justice guidelines are also in agreement:

> The attorney for the government should commence or recommend federal prosecution if he believes that the person's conduct constitutes a federal offense and that the admissible evidence will probably be sufficient to obtain and sustain a conviction.[38]. . .

A comment to this principle clarifies the standard:

> [A]s a matter of fundamental fairness and in the interest of the efficient administration of justice, no prosecution should be initiated against any person unless the government believes that the person probably will be found guilty by an unbiased trier of fact.[39]

The Model Grand Jury Act suggests a similar "probability of conviction" standard.[40]

A prosecutor working with a grand jury has a strong incentive to seek indictments only in those cases in which there is a substantial probability of securing a conviction at trial. Prosecutors pride themselves on winning a high percentage of their cases.[41] And since the prosecutor who secures an indictment will be identified with the case, that prosecutor is unlikely to press for an indictment when evidence appears insufficient to convict.[42] Even when a prosecutor will not personally handle the case beyond the indictment stage, he is loathe to "saddle one of his cohorts with the trial of a 'turkey.'"[43]

Department of Justice statistics indicate that federal prosecutors indict only when there is a strong likelihood of conviction. Over the last decade, federal prosecutors convicted the great majority of defendants who were prosecuted—65.2 percent by plea of guilty or, in a few instances, *nolo conten-*

dere, and 12.5 percent by conviction at trial.[44] Only 3.5 percent of all defendants were acquitted at trial.[45]

The remaining defendants—18.8 percent of the total—are listed as "dismissed."[46] Since "dismissed" is a catchall category, covering a wide variety of situations, a precise interpretation of this category is impossible.[47] Some dismissals result from plea agreements under which the prosecutor dismisses a felony indictment and then files an information on a lesser charge to which the defendant pleads guilty; this is listed as one dismissal and one guilty plea.[48] In other cases the prosecutor dismisses a case against a convictable defendant in exchange for cooperation in other investigations, or in exchange for the defendant's confession of guilt and agreement to enter a pre-trial diversion program.[49] Other dismissals reflect a procedural step such as when a prosecutor, upon receiving new evidence or when faced with a deficiency in an already returned indictment, dismisses one indictment and presents a superseding indictment to the grand jury against the same defendant or a case is transferred to another district pursuant to Rule 20 of the Federal Rules of Criminal Procedure.[50] Available statistics do not distinguish these cases from those in which the prosecutor dismisses an indictment due to insufficient evidence.[51]

Conservatively assuming that prosecutors dismissed only half of these defendants for strategic or technical reasons unrelated to the strength of the government's cases, prosecutors have a conviction rate of over 85 percent.[52] The federal conviction rate is more likely 90 percent or greater.[53] This surely does not indicate any widespread error or abuse in the federal prosecutors' decisions as to whom to indict.

Since the A.B.A. reformers did not have statistical support, they relied on a mixture of speculation and anecdote to suggest that prosecutor-dominated grand juries return unwarranted indictments.[54] In one argument, they contended that many prosecutors believe it is proper to try to convict without trial someone whom they believe has committed a crime, even though the suspect's legal guilt probably cannot be proven beyond a reasonable doubt at trial because the admissible evidence is only marginally sufficient.[55] Generally, the reformers assumed that prosecutors think they can indict doubtfully convictable defendants, and still retain their high conviction rates by pressuring these defendants to plead guilty to the indicted offense or some lesser charge.[56] Thus, Professor Arenella argued:

> While most prosecutors claim that they would not seek an indictment unless there was a high probability of securing a conviction at trial, recent studies of *state* prosecutorial practices suggest otherwise. Foremost among the reasons for defective screening of legal guilt is the possibility of conviction through plea-bargaining. Many state prosecutors find nothing wrong with charging and convicting a defendant whom they believe is factually guilty even though the government lacks sufficient admissible evidence to convict at trial. Not surprisingly they view the doctrine of legal guilt as a technicality that interferes with their own view that justice is done when criminal sanctions are applied to defendants they believe to be factually guilty. Others accept the doctrine's validity but equate it with the exclusionary rule and the trial's formal proof requirements. In their view, defendants waive its requirements when they plead guilty because the doctrine applies only to the criminal trial itself.
>
> Thus, a prosecutor may seek an indictment when the evidence of guilt is marginal and then offer an attractive bargain to induce a guilty plea. Moreover, the absence of any effective limits on prosecutorial discretion in filing charges the prosecutor to enhance the government's plea-bargaining position by charging the defendant with more serious crimes than the evidence or the facts of a particular case warrant. To prompt a plea in weak cases, some prosecutors engage in bluffing tactics where they puff the strength of the case before offering an attractive bargain. These prosecutors regard this practice as legitimate and skillful bargaining even in cases where the prosecutor knowingly lacks sufficient evidence of legal guilt to reach the jury.[57]

Although Professor Arenella asserted the existence of the practice and its widespread use, he tendered no supporting evidence, other than a single study which reflected the views and practices of unidentified state prosecutors.[58] Even if the study's authors are correct in their assertions about *state* prosecutors, this does not establish the need for widespread reform of the *federal* grand jury system. There does not appear to be any evidence that federal prosecutors seek indictments in cases where they know the evidence is insufficient and then offer an attractive plea bargain to the defendants.[59]

Moreover, there is no persuasive evidence to support Professor Arenella's other charges of prosecutorial abuse. To support his claim that federal prosecutors may indict unconvictable defendants, Professor Arenella cited one article by a former Assistant United States Attorney who, more than 20 years ago, served for four years in the Northern District of California.[60] Yet the article he cited stated that "prosecution would almost never be commenced unless the chances of success seemed better than fair," and "most assistants felt it was not right to use the prosecutional system just to harass an individual, however guilty he might be and hence, unless the case could be won, it was morally wrong to prosecute it."[61]

Professor Arenella also alleged that prosecutors may seek to indict unconvictable defendants for political reasons, and cited the practices of the Nixon administration as evidence.[62] Clearly, prosecutorial excesses such as are attributed to the Nixon administration's Department of Justice cannot be justified. However, our experience, encompassing many years in active federal criminal practice, both defending and prosecuting, and our observations of the federal criminal justice system as it operates throughout the country, indicates strongly that today the government seldom uses or abuses federal grand juries for political purposes.[63]

We believe that the A.B.A. reform proponents have failed to establish the existence of problems significant enough to justify the drastic changes they propose. Unnecessary tinkering with working machinery usually leads to trouble. The federal grand jury system "ain't broke" and therefore doesn't need fixing.

Even if it is true that, as Professor Arenella assumed, federal prosecutors seek indictments in cases in which the evidence is insufficient, or trump up indictments for political reasons,[64] it is highly questionable whether the proposed solutions will alleviate the problem. Professor Arenella's theory is that the grand jury will reliably adjudicate the appropriateness of a defendant's going to trial if it is provided with evidence similar to that which will be placed before a petit jury at the actual trial.[65] Professor Arenella admits that this is an untested theory.[66] Indeed, there is good reason to doubt that it will be effective.

The fact that the grand jury will hear certain evidence it may not have heard without these reforms does not guarantee a better screening process. The "reformed" grand jury will probably hear more of the government's actual prospective trial witnesses, and fewer federal agents giving summaries of trial witnesses' testimony. However, there will still be no cross-examination, without which accurate assessment of a witness' credibility cannot be made.

Furthermore, even though a judge may admonish the grand jury to screen out weak cases,[67] the grand jury will still look only to the prosecutor for guidance. Prosecutors will still decide which cases or individuals to investigate, which witnesses to call, and what evidence to present. They will still be the ones who interpret laws for the grand jury. If prosecutors are at all sensitive, they will establish rapport with the grand jury. Prosecutors will still communicate to the grand jury, however subtly, their belief that the grand jury should indict the suspect. Thus, even with the reforms, when a grand jury is straddling the fence on the question of probable cause, it will almost certainly accede to the prosecutor's judgment, as it does in the present system.

The only real check on the initiation of prosecution, then, will be the court's review of the grand jury transcript. Professor Arenella apparently hoped that the prospect of such a review would deter the prosecutor from asking the grand jury to return indictments against defendants who have a questionable likelihood of conviction. This does not appear likely. The Model Act's standards are not difficult to meet, though they force prosecutors to jump through several hoops and burden courts with the time consuming task of applying them.[68] Marginal cases will pass this review, and thus the Model Act will not deter prosecutors from prosecuting them. At best, the review process will discourage prosecutors from pursuing egregiously weak cases, however, the reformers have not established that prosecutors present such cases for indictment to federal grand juries today.

While the benefit of these proposals is negligible, the added burden they would impose on the system is certain to be great. Prosecutors will have to spend additional time and taxpayers' money preparing for more intricate grand jury proceedings. They have to bring nearly all witnesses before the grand jury, which necessitates not only added preparation time, but also added transportation expense. The review process will surely necessitate substantial judicial time and expense as well. As five members of the Criminal Justice Council who filed a minority report criticizing the Act stated:

> The drafters of the proposed Act have created a process which is calculated to burden the criminal justice system with an additional level of review in every case. It can be expected with some confidence that the motion for review will be the norm; indeed, it will verge on ineffective representation not to make such a motion.[69]

The minority report ultimately rejected the concept of judicial review in all cases, as did the A.B.A. House of Delegates at its January 1982 meeting.[70] We share the minority report's opinion as to the failure of the Model Act's drafters to make the case for reform:

> The drafters suggest that such a revolution [providing for judicial review of the sufficiency of every indictment] is necessary because the grand jury will otherwise be unable effectively to serve its screening function and because prosecutors now rely on their ability to bring criminal charges and to coerce guilty pleas without providing the defendant

[with] a forum in which to test the legitimacy of these charges. But we suggest that, whatever the value of an academic debate on the merits of our present criminal justice system, there has been no showing of a flaw in the grand jury process sufficient to justify the A.B.A.'s proposing . . . such a revolution.[71]

Thus, a defendant should not have the right to have a court review the sufficiency of an indictment which is valid on its face.

Safeguarding Against Prosecutorial Abuse in the Federal Grand Jury

We have argued that the federal grand jury functions well as an accusatory body, and should not be subjected to radical change. Nonetheless, we realize that the grand jury system gives the federal prosecutor an awesome amount of power. As Justice Jackson said, while he was Attorney General, "The prosecutor has more control over life, liberty and reputation than any other person in America. His discretion is tremendous."[72]

After all is said and done, the best safeguard against grand jury abuse is the appointment and training of intelligent, experienced compassionate people to serve as prosecutors. Since even highly capable and experienced persons can make errors of judgment, it is also important that each prosecutorial office institute a review system, regarding the decision to indict. For example, for many years, the federal prosecutor in the Northern District of Illinois has utilized a tiered process to review proposals to indict.[73] An Assistant U.S. Attorney ("Assistant") who wishes to submit an indictment to the grand jury must first submit a "prosecution memorandum" and a draft copy of the indictment to both the chief and deputy chief of his division. The memorandum contains the names of the prospective defendants, the specific statutes under which they will be charged, the specific counts of the contemplated indictment, the agents and agency which helped to prepare the case, a summary of the evidence available against each defendant, and an analysis of possible defenses, evidentiary problems, and other matters which might affect the successful prosecution of the case. The division chief and/or deputy meet with the Assistant in conference to discuss the prosecution memorandum. They also discuss foreseeable problems with the prosecution of the case. Often, they will ask the Assistant to do more preparation before proceeding with the approval process. If and when the division chief approves the indictment at the indictment conference, the memorandum and draft indictment are sent to the First Assistant U.S. Attorney, who reviews them and either sends them back for further clarification or approves them and forwards them to the U.S. Attorney. The U.S. Attorney performs one final review, signs the indictment, and sends back so that the Assistant can submit the case to the grand jury. Only prospective indictments which have passed all three levels review are submitted to the grand jury.[74]

Similar systems of review are in place in many other U.S. Attorneys' offices and within the Department of Justice.[75] We believe the Department of Justice should amend the U.S. Attorneys' Manual[76] to mandate such a review process in every federal prosecutorial office before a prosecutor may present an indictment to the grand jury. The review will guard against an individual prosecutor's misjudgment or overreaching.

There are other adjustments which profitably may be made to the grand jury system. We support several of the fine-tunings suggested by the A.B.A. Principles and the Model Grand Jury Act, but for reasons different from those of the authors of those documents. We welcome most of the A.B.A.'s principles, but not because they will empower the grand jury to make independent judgments. We believe that every grand jury inevitably will approve almost every indictment presented by the prosecutor, even in marginal cases. The A.B.A.'s changes will benefit the system by reminding the prosecutor of his or her duty and by allowing the grand jury to better aid the prosecutor in his or her exercise of judgment. While we believe these changes to be beneficial, we do not believe them to be vital to the proper functioning of the system. Accordingly, though we support many of the A.B.A. Principles regarding prosecutorial duties as *guidelines* for federal prosecution, we do not believe a violation should be cause to dismiss the indictment.

We support the A.B.A. Principles concerning *the court's and the prosecutor's charge to the grand jury.* We believe that the court and prosecutor should clearly advise grand juries of their duties and responsibilities. Additionally, the grand juries should be told the elements of the alleged crimes.[77] The better informed the grand jury, the more it will help the prosecutor in screening cases.

The U.S. Attorneys' Manual already contains provisions reflecting several of the other proposed reforms. Regarding *exculpatory* evidence, the Manual provides,

> When a prosecutor conducting a grand jury inquiry is personally aware of substantial evidence which directly negates the guilt of the subject of the investigation, the prosecutor must present or otherwise disclose such evidence to the grand jury before seeking an indictment against such a person.[78]

Regarding *unconstitutionally obtained evidence*, the Manual provides,

> [A] prosecutor should not present to the grand jury for use against a person whose constitutional rights clearly have been violated evidence which the prosecutor personally knows was obtained as a direct result of the constitutional violation.[79]

Apart from differing enforcement mechanisms, the Department of Justice and the A.B.A. are in accord regarding the prosecutor's duty with respect to exculpatory evidence and constitutionally inadmissible evidence.[80]

Hearsay presents a more difficult problem. At its 1984 mid-year meeting, the American Bar Association approved a new Grand Jury Reform Principle about hearsay: "Absent some compelling necessity, the prosecutor should not present the grand jury with a hearsay version of critical eyewitness testimony as a substitute for such testimony when it is available."[81] The Model Act's version of the hearsay provision, which the A.B.A. rejected, is much more stringent.[82]

The U.S. Attorneys' Manual, on the other hand, eschews even the broad, rather vague standards approved by the A.B.A. The Manual sets no hard and fast rule, except that prosecutors should present hearsay evidence for what it is, rather than as first-hand testimony.[83] Other than this provision, it leaves the whole question of hearsay evidence to the discretion of the individual prosecutor:

> Each United States Attorney should be accountable to himself in this regard and to the grand jurors. . . . The question should not be so much whether to use hearsay evidence, but whether, at the end, the presentation was in keeping with the professional obligations of attorneys for the government, and afforded the grand jurors a substantial basis for voting upon an indictment.[84]

We believe that the current Department of Justice position on hearsay is basically correct. In the abstract, the general principle, "whenever possible, present first person testimony," is appealing, but in practice, the question of whether to use first person or hearsay testimony is often a question of available time and resources—time and money to transport the witness, and time to prepare the witness to testify. Since, in reality, the prosecutor rather than the grand jury performs the effective screening function, we are not troubled by leaving this decision up to the prosecutor's discretion. We propose, however, adding two sentences to the U.S. Attorneys' Manual's provision on hearsay[85] to the effect that, (1) the key government witnesses, such as accomplices, eyewitnesses, and victims, should, if possible, testify before the grand jury; and (2) if U.S. Attorneys or Assistants entertain serious doubts about a witness' credibility, they should, if possible, present this witness to the grand jury for scrutiny.[86]

Several A.B.A. Principles concern the *rights of witnesses before the grand jury.* Both the U.S. Attorneys' Manual and the A.B.A. Principles agree that targets of grand jury investigations should have the opportunity to testify before the grand jury,[87] that the government should tell targets that they are possible indictees,[88] and that all witnesses should know of their privilege against self-incrimination.[89]

The *right of witnesses to be accompanied by attorneys into the grand jury* room has caused a great deal of controversy. The Department of Justice disapproves of the practice, while the A.B.A. favors it.[90] When attorneys were first allowed into grand jury rooms in state court systems, opponents feared that attorneys would disrupt grand jury proceedings. In practice, counsel have been able to behave themselves while in the grand jury room.[91] Therefore, there is no overriding reason for barring counsel from the grand jury room, so long as counsel clearly understand that their role is limited to advising the client quietly, and that counsel are not permitted to address the grand jurors or otherwise take an active part in the proceedings before the grand jury.

Whether or not witnesses are allowed to bring counsel into the grand jury room, we believe that Congress should amend Federal Rule of Criminal Procedure 6(e) to provide that witnesses are entitled to a transcript of their own testimony before the grand jury provided that they make appropriate arrangements to reimburse the government for its costs.[92] This is a logical extension of Rule 6(e)(1)'s requirement that grand jury proceedings be recorded, and Rule 6(e)(2)'s exemption of witnesses from the grand jury rule of secrecy. Transcripts would be especially helpful to witnesses who appear at grand jury hearings without attorneys and later seek legal representation on an issue related to their testimony. At present many courts require witnesses to show a compelling necessity before allowing them access to their own testimony.[93]

We also believe that Congress should amend the so-called *"Jencks Act,"*[94] to provide defendants with earlier access to grand jury testimony and other prior statements of prospective witnesses, unless there is a risk of physical harm or intimidation to a witness or other good cause. The government should have the burden of proof to show cause for withholding the material. Earlier access will give the defense more time to prepare its case properly. It may also aid defendants in deciding whether or not to seek or accept a plea bargain. As Professor Arenella pointed out, defendants often are forced to make their plea-bargaining decisions in the dark, without a good idea of the strength of the prosecution's case.[95] If a defendant knew what kind of case the government had against him, he could make a more intelligent plea bargaining decision.

We also propose one more reform that has not been addressed by the A.B.A. We suggest that *the size of the grand jury be reduced* from twenty-three people to a smaller number, perhaps seven, nine or eleven. This reduction in size will eliminate many logistic problems currently posed by twenty-three person grand juries, at no cost to the effectiveness of the system. The chief benefit of the grand jury—having citizens from the outside observe and participate in the investigation and charging process—can be accomplished just as well with fewer than twenty-three persons. Many states now successfully utilize grand juries with fewer than twenty three people.[96] Typically, states using smaller grand juries have created a "super majority" requirement for the approval of indictments.[97] We believe that these requirements effectively compensate for whatever lack of diversity might result from the reduction in the number of grand jurors. On an eleven-person grand jury, for example, we propose that no indictment be returned unless approved by a vote of at least seven members.

Conclusion

Because the grand jury already functions well as an accusatory body, it should remain the primary charging vehicle in the federal system, and should not be subjected to the widespread reforms proposed by the American Bar Association and the Model Grand Jury Act. Specifically, defendants should not routinely have the right to judicial review of the sufficiency of evidence before the grand jury. Since the grand jury has such vast power, and since the prosecutor has so much influence over the grand jury, some form of oversight and guidance of federal prosecutors is necessary. We believe that a tiered system of review of the decision to seek an indictment will provide the needed oversight, and will help to eliminate whatever abuse currently exists. The other reforms which we have proposed or approved will further fine-tune the system to make it more efficient and equitable overall.

Notes

1. *See Grand Jury Reform: Hearings on H.R. 94 Before the Subcomm. on Immigration, Citizenship, and In'l Law of the House Comm. on the judiciary,* 95th Cong., 1st Sess. 484 (197 7) [hereinafter cited as *House Hearings*]; *The Grand Jury Reform Act of 1978: Hearings on S. 3405 Before the Subcomm. on Admin. Practice and Procedure of the Senate Comm. on the judiciary,* 95th Cong., 2d Sess. 154 (1978).

2. For a list of these principles, *see* ABA GRAND JURY POLICY AND MODEL ACT 4-5 (2d ed. 1982) [hereinafter cited as *ABA Pamphlet*).

3. Order Amending FED. R. CRIM. P. 6, 441 U.S. 985 (1979).

4. Order Amending FED. R. CRIM. P. 6, 461 U.S. 1117 (1983).

5. U.S. Department of Justice, Principles of Federal Prosecution, 27 CRIM. L. REP. 3277 (1980).

6. . . . Subsequent to the Revolution, the fifth amendment to the United States Constitution formally incorporated the requirement that a grand jury initiate felony prosecutions. Many states incorporated similar provisions into their own constitutions. However, in Hurtado v. California, 110 U.S. 516 (1884), the Supreme Court refused to incorporate the fifth amendment's grand jury requirement into the fourteenth amendment's concept of due process of law. Thus, the states remain free to proceed with felony prosecutions by means other than grand jury indictments. For the history of the grand jury, *see generally* M. FRANKEL & G. NAFTALIS, THE GRAND JURY: AN INSTITUTION ON TRIAL 6–17 (1977); Calandra v. United States, 414 U.S. 338, 342 n.3 (1974) and sources cited therein. . . . For a survey of state practices, *see* J. VAN DYKE, JURY SELECTION PROCEDURES 264–270 (1977).

7. 18 U.S.C. sec. 6001-05 (1976).

8. *See* FED. R. CRIM. P. 6(d), (e).

9. *See generally* U.S. CONST. amend. V; FED. R. CRIM. P. 6.

10. *See, e.g.,* Arenella, *Reforming the Federal Grand Jury and the State Preliminary Hearing to Prevent Conviction Without Adjudication,* 78 MICH. L. REV. 463 (1980).

11. *See, e.g.,* United States v. Mara, 410 U.S. 19 (1973). . . .

12. *See, e.g.,* Campbell, *Eliminate the Grand Jury,* 64 J. CRIM. L. & CRIMINOLOGY 174 (1973).

13. *See, e.g.,* Arenella, *supra* note 10.

14. *See, e.g.,* Arenella, *Reforming the State Grand Jury System A Model Grand Jury Act,* 13 Rutgers L.J. 1, 9 (1981); Campbell, *supra* note 12.

15. When federal prosecutors decide that a case, including cases in which the grand jury has reviewed evidence, should not result in an indictment, they do *not* present the case to the grand jury for return of a no bill. Rather, they fill out a form called a "Declination" in which they set forth the reasons why the case has been terminated without presentation to the grand jury for indictment.

16. During the fiscal year ending September 30, 1984, grand juries returned 17,419 indictments and only 68 "no true bills." Statistical Report of U.S. Attorneys' Offices, Fiscal Year 1984 (Report 1–21), introductory material, p. 2.

17. That is not to say that the grand jury is not at times helpful to the prosecutor. *See infra text* accompanying notes 18–21.

18. *See, e.g.,* Campbell, *supra* note 12.

19. California, among other states, utilizes preliminary hearings in many instances. For a state by state survey of grand jury responsibilities, *see* J. VAN DYKE, *supra* note 6 at Appendix B.

20. *See* Arenella, *supra* note 14.

21. *See infra* notes 80–82 and accompanying text.

22. *See supra* notes 12–16 and accompanying text

23. *See* Arenella, *supra* note 10; Campbell, *supra* note 12.

24. A.B.A. Principles 6 and 29; Model Grand Jury Act § 100.

25. A.B.A. Principles 22 and 27; Model Grand Jury Act § 204.

26. A.B.A. Principle 5; Model Grand Jury Act § 102.

27. A.B.A. Principle 3; Model Grand Jury Act § 101.

28. A.B.A. Principle 6; Model Grand Jury Act § 100.

29. A.B.A. Principle 31, relating to hearsay, was enacted by voice vote in the February 1984 Mid-Year Meeting (reported in 52 U.S.L.W.

2473 (1984). *See* A.B.A. 1984 Midyear Meeting, Reports with Recommendations to the House of Delegates 108B (hereinafter cited as 1984 *Mid-Year Meeting Report*]; Model Grand Jury Act § 100.

30. This provision, intended to give effect to A.B.A. Principle 25, is found in Model Grand Jury Act § 105. It reads as follows:

Section 105: MOTION TO DISMISS IN-DICTMENT ON GROUND OF INSUF-FICIENCY OF GRAND JURY EVIDENCE

1. After arraignment upon an indict-ment, the court may, upon motion of the defendant made within [30] days after receipt of the grand jury tran-script or as the court otherwise pro-vides, dismiss such indictment or any count thereof upon the ground that the evidence before the grand jury was not legally sufficient to establish the offense charged or any lesser in-cluded offense.

2. The evidence presented to the grand jury is legally sufficient if, viewed in the light most favorable to the State, it would constitute probable cause as to each element of the crime. The court's review of the evidence shall be a review of the grand jury transcripts (either written or electronically re-corded) and exhibits, without further testimony.

3. In evaluating the legal sufficiency of the evidence presented to the grand jury, the court can only consider evi-dence which would be admissible at trial except for hearsay testimony ad-mitted under § 100(2)–(4). The fact that the grand jury considered evi-dence which would have been ex-cluded at trial does not invalidate the indictment as long as the remaining competent evidence is legally suffi-cient to constitute probable cause as to each element of the crime; except in those cases where the nature, ex-tent, and prejudicial effect of the in-competent evidence presented to the grand jury provides strong grounds for believing that the grand jury would not have indicted the defen-dant if it had only considered the le-gally admissible evidence presented to it.

4. The validity of an order denying any motion made pursuant to this section is not reviewable upon an appeal from a judgment of conviction fol-lowing trial based upon legally suffi-cient evidence.

31. *Id.*

32. *See infra* notes 88–91, 101–104, 106, & 107 and accompanying text.

33. *See infra* notes 56–65 and accompanying text.

34. Arenella, *supra* note 14, at 9.

35. *Id.*

36. *Id.* at 9–10.

37. A.B.A. Principle 4; U.S. Department of Jus-tice, Principles of Federal Prosecution, Part B.2, 27 CR. L. REP. at 3277, 3278–79 (1980) [hereinafter Principles of Federal Prosecu-tion, Part B.2].

38. Principles of Federal Prosecution, Part B.2.

39. *Id.* at 3279. The comment makes clear that the standard to be used is that of an *unbiased* trier of fact. Where bias makes conviction un-likely, the prosecutor may still proceed. . . .

40. *See* Model Grand Jury Act § 105(2) and Com-mentary.

41. Kaplan, *The Prosecutorial Discretion—A Com-ment*, 60 Nw. U. L. Rev. 174, 180 (1965).

42. *Id.*

43. *Id.*

44. FEDERAL OFFENDERS IN U.S. DISTRICT COURTS 1982, Table 3 [hereinafter *Federal Offenders*].

    The statistics on which these figures are based reflect all defendants terminated in a given year in the U.S. District Courts, regard-less of whether their prosecutions were begun by indictment, information, or otherwise. The federal government does not keep fig-ures as to the dispositions of criminal cases begun solely by grand jury indictment. None-theless, since well over half of all federal criminal cases are initiated by indictment (*see Federal Offenders*, *supra* note 44, Table 1), these figures are probably representative of the terminations of indicted defendants.

45. *Federal Offenders*, *supra* note 44, Table 3.

46. *Id.*

47. Conversation with C. Madison Brewer, Direc-tor of the Office of Management Information and Support of the Executive Office for U.S. Attorneys, whose office is responsible for compiling such statistics.

48. *Id.*

49. *Id.*

50. *Id.*

51. *See Federal Offenders, supra* note 55, Table 3.

52. Since the "dismissed" category incorporates more than just those cases for which the prosecutor had insufficient evidence, one half of all "dismissed" defendants—9.4 percent of the total group—must be eliminated from the sample base. Assuming an initial sample base of 1000 defendants, the adjusted base is 906 defendants, of whom 777 are convicted. The conviction rate is thus 777/906, or 85.8 percent.

53. This is the authors' estimate and is based on trial practice experience.

54. *See Arenella, supra* note 10.

55. *Id.* at 503–05.

56. *Id.*

57. *Id.* at 503–05 (footnotes omitted).

58. *See* H. MILLER, W. McDonald & J. CRAMER, PLEA BARGAINING IN THE UNITED STATES (1978), *cited* in Arenella, *supra* note 10 at 471 n.26.

59. Department of Justice guidelines forbid the practice of striking a plea bargain when the prosecutor lacks sufficient evidence to reach the jury . . . *[see]* Principles of Federal Prosecution, Comment to Principle D.2(f), 27 CR. L. REP. at 3284.

60. Kaplan, *supra* note 41, *cited* in Arenella, *supra* note 10, at 505.

61. Kaplan, *supra* note 41, at 180. . . .

62. Arenella, *supra* note 10, at 505–06.

63. *See also* Kaplan, *supra* note 41, at 181. Former Assistant U.S. Attorney Kaplan states that "it was generally felt that where the public eye would be on the prosecution, the criticism would be all the more-severe if the case were lost. As a result, it was often stated that, 'if you go after a big one, you must be pretty sure you can get him.' " *Id.*

64. *See* Arenella, *supra* note 10, at 503–05.

65. *Id.* at 540 n.387; *see also* Arenella, *supra* note 14 at 13.

66. *See* Arenella, *supra* note 10, at 540 n.387.

67. *See* Model Grand Jury Act §204 (elements of the charge to the grand jury).

68. For example, the reform proposal's ban on hearsay will force prosecutors to bring several witnesses before the grand jury, rather than relying on one federal agent's summation of these witnesses' testimony.

69. Arenella *supra* note 14, at 50.

70. *Id.* At 57.

71. *Id.* At 51.

72. Jackson, *The Federal Prosecutor,* 24 J. Am. JUDICATURE SOC'Y 18 (1940).

73. These procedures have never been formalized in writing. These procedures were in effect during the period of 1977–81 when author Thomas P. Sullivan was U.S. Attorney for the Northern District of Illinois.

74. The grand jurors do not know of this review process, nor do they see the copy of the indictment signed by the U.S. Attorney until after they have voted a true bill.

75. It is interesting to observe that no such review system was in place during Kaplan's term as an Assistant in the Office of the U.S. Attorney for the Northern District of California. Kaplan, *supra* note 41, at 176.

76. The U.S. ATTORNEYS' MANUAL, a Department of Justice publication contained in a series of looseleaf notebooks which are updated periodically, reflects the current state of the law, and official Department of Justice policy. Citations are to the Manual current as of May 1, 1984.

77. *See* A.B.A. Principles 22 and 27. In advocating these principles, we do not mean to suggest that defense attorneys may use an allegedly faulty grand jury instruction as a basis for quashing an indictment.

78. U.S. ATTORNEYS' MANUAL, Paragraphs 9–11.334.

79. U.S. ATTORNEYS' MANUAL, Paragraphs 19–11.331.

80. Compare U.S. ATTORNEYS' MANUAL, Paragraphs 19–11.334 *with* A.B.A. Principle 3; *compare* U.S ATTORNEYS' MANUAL, Paragraphs 19)11.331 *with* A.B.A. Principle 6.

81. *See* 1984 Mid-Year Meeting Report, *supra* note 39, at 108B.

82. *See* Model Grand Jury Act § 100. . . .

83. U.S. ATTORNEYS' MANUAL, paragraphs 9–11.332.

84. *Id.*

85. *Id.*

86. We believe the prosecutor should not withhold a witness from the grand jury simply because he is reluctant to make a record which might later be used to impeach that witness.

87. *Compare* A.B.A. Principle 5 *with* U.S. ATTORNEYS' MANUAL, paragraphs 9–11.252.

88. *Compare* A.B.A. Principle 2 *with* U.S. ATTORNEYS' MANUAL, paragraphs 19–11.250.

89. *Id.*

90. *Contrast* A.B.A. Principle 1 *with* U.S. ATTORNEYS' MANUAL, paragraphs 19–11.356.

91. *See House Hearings, supra* note 1, at 1571, 1574. "[N]o public prosecutor of any of the more populous districts of those states which to any extent authorize the presence of counsel, and of whom inquiry was made, has reported any actual disruption of the grand jury's proceedings by reason of the presence of counsel for the witness." *Id.*

92. *See* Wing & Cushman, *Grand Jury Taping: Should a Witness Be Allowed to Record Testimony?*, NAT. L.J., March 5, 1984, at 15.

93. *See, e.g.,* United States v. Clavey, 578 F.2d 1219 (7th Cir. 1978) (per curiam) (en banc), *vacating,* 565 F.2d 111 (7th Cir. 1977), *cert. denied,* 439 U.S. 954 (1978) . . .; Bast v. United States, 542 F.2d 893, 896 (4th Cir. 1976), a cases cited therein. *But see* Judge Wyzanski's dissent in *Bast,* 542 F.2d at 897–99.

94. 18 U.S.C. sec. 3500.

95. Arenella, *supra* note 10, at 311.

96. Twenty-one states currently allow 12 or fewer people to constitute a grand jury; four of these states allow 7 or fewer people to serve as a grand jury. *See* J. Van Dyke, *supra* note 6, at 264–70.

97. For example, Iowa requires 5 of 7 grand jurors in order to indict and Ohio requires 7 of 9 grand jurors to indict. *Id.*

18
Why the Grand Jury Cannot Effectively Screen the Prosecutor's Charging Decisions

Andrew D. Leipold

A grand jury is a group of citizens called together by a court to decide whether criminal charges should be filed against a suspect. Unlike a trial jury, the grand jury never passes on the question of guilt or innocence; its role is to decide whether there is enough evidence to justify putting a person on trial at all. If the grand jury decides that the prosecutor has presented enough evidence to justify a criminal charge, it votes to return a "true bill," which when signed by the prosecutor and filed with the court becomes an "indictment," the formal criminal charge the government must later prove at trial.

The Fifth Amendment to the United States Constitution provides that "No person shall be held to answer for a capital, or otherwise infamous, crime unless on a presentment or indictment of a Grand Jury," except in certain cases involving the military. The theory behind this provision is that before the government can accuse someone of a serious crime, there should be citizen review of the evidence to prevent the prosecutor from filing weak or malicious charges. In practice, however, grand juries have come to serve a second, equally important, function. Under the prosecutor's direction, grand juries have enormous investigative power, allowing them to gather evidence of criminal activity in cases where traditional law enforcement efforts might be inadequate. Through the use of subpoenas—orders by the court commanding witnesses to appear or to produce physical evidence—the grand jury can compel people to reveal to prosecutors evidence of criminal activity. The grand jury thus serves as both a "sword" and a "shield": it acts as a sword in the prosecutor's hands when it investigates crimes, and as a shield for the accused when it evaluates the government's evidence to decide whether the accused should be indicted (LaFave, Israel, and King 1999, vol. 3 §8.1a).

The grand jury's performance of these two roles has long been criticized. Critics complain that the grand jury is *too* effective a tool when it comes to investigating crimes; there are few restrictions on what a prosecutor and grand jury can demand when gathering evidence, and some have complained that this power is used to harass suspects and witnesses. In contrast, others complain that grand juries are entirely ineffective in screening the prosecutor's cases and that they therefore fail to protect the accused from weak, unfounded accusations. This essay looks at the second part of the criticism and concludes that grand juries in fact do a poor job of evaluating the prosecutor's decision to file criminal charges.

The Operation of a Federal Grand Jury

The operation of a typical federal grand jury is straightforward. A group of 23 citizens are chosen at random and asked to serve for an indefinite period not to exceed eighteen months. A trial judge administers the oath and gives the jurors general instructions about their duties, but otherwise plays almost no role in the process. The judge will not sit in the grand jury room and has no say in the decision whether to indict.

Perhaps the most striking feature of grand jury hearings is their secrecy. Not only are the press and public barred from the proceedings, so is the person who is suspected of committing the crime and his or her lawyer. According to Rule 6e of the Federal Rules of Criminal Procedure, attendance in the grand jury room is limited to the prosecutor, the jurors, the court reporter, and the single witness who is being questioned. Those who participate in the hearing are sworn to secrecy, and the court may use its contempt powers to ensure that the prosecutors and the jurors (but not the witnesses) maintain this silence even after the case is finally resolved (United States Supreme Court 2000; Goldstein 1998).

Once in session, the grand jury's task is to review the cases submitted by the government. The prosecutor calls and questions witnesses, and presents to the jurors documentary evidence related to the crime in question. Unlike trial jurors, the grand jurors may question the witness and may discuss the case with the prosecutor as evidence is being submitted. After the prosecutor has presented the case, he or she recommends that the jurors vote to return an indictment, accusing a defendant of a specific crime that the prosecutor believes is supported by the evidence. The jurors then deliberate in private. Unlike a trial jury, they are not required to find that the defendant should be indicted "beyond a reasonable doubt," nor is there a requirement that the jurors be unanimous. If at least twelve agree that the evidence shows "probable cause" to believe the suspect committed the crime, the person is charged with the crime, and the case then moves on to a trial. If the jury determines that the prosecutor's case is too weak—that the evidence does not show probable cause to believe that the suspect committed the crime—the jury informs the prosecutor of this fact, and the prosecutor is prevented from taking the suspect to trial.

A federal grand jury is allowed to consider virtually any kind of evidence that the prosecutor decides to present. The prosecutor is not required by the Constitution to inform the grand jury of evidence that favors the suspect, even if that evidence is exculpatory.

Jurors are allowed to consider hearsay, illegally obtained evidence, tips, rumors, or even their own knowledge of the alleged crime. The Federal Rules of Evidence do not apply to grand jury proceedings, so the prosecutor can ask leading questions, can ask witnesses to speculate about facts about which they have no direct knowledge, and can pursue other matters that would be considered irrelevant or inappropriate if presented at trial (Beale, et al. 1997). The decision of which evidence to present is almost entirely in the prosecutor's hands: the suspect has no right to testify in his own defense, and those witnesses who are called to testify are not allowed to bring counsel with them into the grand jury room. The suspect may not present contrary evidence and is not given access to the testimony of his or her accusers until the trial begins. In short, the grand jurors hear only what the prosecution wants them to hear—the most inculpatory version of the facts, regardless of whether this version is based on evidence that will later be considered when the suspect goes to trial.

Assessing the Grand Jury's Screening Function

Critics are nearly unanimous in concluding that grand juries do not protect innocent suspects from being indicted, nor do they prevent a suspect who is guilty of only a lesser crime from being indicted for a more serious crime (Leipold 1995). Instead, critics believe that the grand jurors do whatever the prosecutor tells them to, a claim that has been repeated so often it has become a cliché: If asked, the saying goes, "a grand jury would indict a ham sandwich" (*In re Grand Jury Subpoena [Stewart]* 1989). Nevertheless, Congress and the Supreme Court have been unmoved by these criticisms and continue to decide cases and pass rules that assume the effectiveness of the grand jury's screening function.

Those who claim that grand juries merely "rubber stamp" the prosecutor's charging decision typically point to statistics to support their view. Most commonly, they note that an extremely high percentage of cases submitted to grand juries result in indictments. The numbers are impressive: in one 12-month period, for example, federal grand juries returned over 17,000 indictments and refused to indict only 68 times, an astounding 99.6 percent success rate for prosecutors (Sullivan and Nachman 1984). (Statistics from other years are slightly lower, but similar.) For some critics, these numbers are apparently persuasive evidence of the grand jury's ineffectiveness.

Even brief reflection shows how unhelpful these figures are. The fact that grand juries return true bills in nearly all cases may indeed demonstrate that jurors simply approve whatever charge the government asks for. But the numbers may also show that grand juries are a great success. A review of the prosecutor's decision-making process leading to the request for the indictment shows why.

Federal prosecutors know that their charging decisions must be approved by the grand jury. In deciding which charges to bring, the prosecutor thus determines not only which accusations can be proven at trial, but also which accusations will result in an indictment. If we assume that prosecutors will decline to present charges to a grand jury that they think will be rejected, then we would expect prosecutors to submit only those cases that are sufficiently strong to survive a grand jury's review. If a case looks weak, a reasonable prosecutor will never present the evidence and the case will be dismissed before it reaches the grand jury room. So, under either view of the grand jury—the jurors do whatever the prosecutor says, or they effectively spot weak cases, thereby discouraging prosecutors from presenting the evidence in the first place—we would expect a high percentage of the cases presented to lead to indictments. The percentage of indictments returned therefore provides little useful information.

Indeed, contrary to the suggestion of critics, there would be cause for concern if grand juries *refused* to indict in a high percentage of cases. A high rejection rate would mean either that the prosecutor was terrible at evaluating cases (i.e., he or she could not determine in advance whether a case was

strong or weak) or that the grand jury was so unpredictable that prosecutors could not anticipate when an indictment would be returned. In the former case, we might conclude that the grand jury was fulfilling its role (although we would be troubled by the prosecutor's performance); but in the latter case, we would hardly conclude that the higher percentage of rejected cases was a sign that the grand jury was serving as an effective screen.

The more relevant number might be the percentage of indictments that result in guilty pleas before trial or guilty verdicts following a trial. If a high percentage of indictments later resulted in judgments of guilt, this would be evidence that grand juries are not returning indictments when the prosecutor's case was weak or frivolous. The argument would be that even if grand juries were allowing weak cases to go forward to trial, the *trial* juries would discover the flaws in the case and find the defendant not guilty. Stated differently, the fact that a defendant must be found guilty beyond a reasonable doubt by a trial jury could be seen as proof that the decision to indict (on the basis of probable cause) was proper.

This reasoning also has its limits. Although conviction at trial of the crime charged in the indictment is strong evidence that the grand jury acted correctly, a guilty plea—the procedure by which the overwhelming number of convictions are obtained—is weaker evidence. A significant number of guilty pleas result from a bargain between the prosecution and defense, and a frequent part of that bargain is that some charges are reduced or dropped. It is hard to evaluate a grand jury's decision when the defendant pleads guilty to a lower charge than the one set forth in the indictment: It might be that the grand jury simply accepted the prosecutor's recommendation on the higher charge even though the evidence would support only a lesser offense. The grand jury's duty to shield is surely not limited to protecting the completely innocent; it also encompasses the duty to protect lesser criminals from unduly high charges. When a defendant pleads guilty to a lesser charge than the one presented to the grand jury, however, it is difficult to know whether the shield worked.

The premise that underlies the use of statistics to measure effectiveness is that any screening that occurs takes place *in the grand jury room*. But that premise is erroneous. In almost every case, the prosecution knows whether the evidence is sufficient to obtain an indictment before the grand jury votes: The prosecutor has complete control over the evidence submitted, runs no risk of being surprised by bad judicial rulings on the evidence or by clever cross-examination by the defense counsel, and has enough experience (personally or institutionally) to know how most jurors will react to the evidence (Leipold 1995). So, if the prosecutor believes that the grand jury will not indict, in most cases he or she will simply dismiss the case before it reaches the grand jury room.

The extent to which this prosecutorial "self-screening" occurs is impossible to quantify. When a prosecutor decides not to pursue an indictment, that decision is not recorded in any public document, and even if it were, the documentation would not be helpful. Few prosecutors would admit that they would have pursued a weak case were it not for the existence of a grand jury—this could be an admission of poor judgment or even an ethical violation (U.S. Department of Justice 1997). Yet it is precisely such a case that has been "screened" by the grand jurors, even though the case was never presented to them.

In short, the grand jury is most likely to act as a shield when its *presence* convinces a prosecutor, in advance of a request for an indictment, that there is nothing to be gained by pursuing the case. Critically, however, the extent to which any screening takes place in the prosecutor's office depends on the degree to which a prosecutor is convinced that a request for an indictment would be fruitless; this in turn depends on the degree to which the prosecutor believes that if a weak case *were* submitted, it would be rejected by the grand jurors.

The Problem Lies in What We Ask Grand Jurors to Do

If statistics cannot adequately measure grand jury effectiveness, the question remains: How can we tell whether grand juries really screen cases effectively? The answer is found in the capabilities of the jurors themselves. By focusing on the task grand jurors are asked to perform, we may be able to predict the probability that weak cases will be identified, and thus predict the likelihood that the prosecutor will refrain from presenting these cases for indictment.

The barriers to a grand jury's ability to screen cases are not obvious because its task seems so simple. Jurors listen to the prosecutor's case and then are asked to answer a single question: Is there a "probable cause" to believe that the suspect committed the specified crime?

The core problem is that grand jurors are not qualified to answer this question. Whether probable cause exists is ultimately a *legal* determination about the sufficiency of the evidence: Has the prosecutor put forth enough accurate information to get above the legal threshold established by the probable cause standard? In submitting a case to the grand jury, we are asking nonlawyers with no experience in weighing evidence to decide whether a legal test is satisfied, and to do so after the only lawyer in the room, the prosecutor, has concluded that it has been. Because jurors lack any experience or expertise in deciding if probable cause exists, it becomes not only predictable but also logical that the grand jurors will indict, not because they are a rubber stamp, but because they have no benchmark against which to evaluate the evidence. Thus, they have no rational justification for rejecting the prosecutor's recommendation.

The point can be made most easily by comparing the role of grand jurors to that of trial jurors. It could be argued that trial jurors make a similar "sufficiency of the evidence" decision when they decide whether the prosecution has proved its case "beyond a reasonable doubt." But a grand jury's determination of probable cause is qualitatively different than a trial jury's verdict, and these differences are crucial to the ability (or inability) of the two panels to perform their respective functions.

One of the main justifications for having nonlawyers serve on trial juries is that ordinary citizens are believed to be at least as good as judges at sifting through the facts and deciding which of the competing versions of the case is correct. Indeed, the adversary system that governs a trial is premised on the idea of presenting two "biased" versions of the same events and letting a neutral decision maker (the jury) decide where between the competing views the truth lies. Jurors are well-suited for this: Although they have less experience in evaluating witnesses and evidence than a judge does, assessing witness credibility and spotting flaws in testimony do not require any special *legal* skill; it turns much more on life experiences and common sense (*Duncan v. Louisiana* 1968). Thus, we believe that the conclusions of lay people will, in most trials, result in an accurate finding of whether the defendant committed the crime.

Once jurors find the facts, they must decide if those facts establish guilt beyond a reasonable doubt, a task that is superficially similar to that made by the grand jury in its probable cause determination. Note, however, our discomfort in allowing trial juries to make this decision. If at any point the court determines that the facts are not in dispute and that the prosecutor cannot prove guilt beyond a reasonable doubt, the court bypasses the jury and enters a judgment of acquittal. Judges also can overrule the jury's finding of guilt after trial or on appeal, but only if the facts that *could* have been found by the jury will not support a conviction. Judges will not reconsider facts that might have been found by the jury, but are free to redetermine the legal question of whether those facts satisfy the reasonable doubt standard (*United States v. McCall* 1972). In short, with limited exceptions, we let the trial jury make the ultimate legal decision about guilt *only* when that determination might be affected by the resolution of a factual dispute.

Contrast the trial jury's role with that of the grand jury. Unlike at trial, where the adversary system is designed to present con-

flicting facts, a grand jury hearing is carefully structured to *avoid* conflicting facts. The prosecutor is not obligated to present contrary evidence, and the suspect has no right to testify or challenge the evidence. Instead, the grand jurors are presented with a single version of the events surrounding the crime, and then asked to apply a legal standard to those facts.

In virtually every other context such decisions are left to judges, and the few times we allow nonlawyers to make analogous determinations are instructive. The closest parallel to the grand jury decision is when a police officer makes an arrest without having first obtained an arrest warrant. An arrest warrant is a document that gives prior judicial authorization to make an arrest. The police can arrest someone only if they have probable cause to believe that a person committed a crime, so in some respects, their decision is similar to the one made by the grand jurors. In both cases, the decision to accuse a person is made by nonlawyers, and both the grand jurors and the police officer make decisions based on information that has not been tested by the adversary process, increasing the risk that the data are erroneous or incomplete. Because police are routinely allowed to make such decisions—most arrests are made without a warrant—it could be argued that the grand jury's probable cause decisions should be entitled to equal respect.

On closer examination, however, the analogy to police decisions to arrest highlights the incongruity of the grand juror's role. As with trial jurors, we trust the police to decide when the appropriate legal standard has been satisfied, but we do not trust them for long. The police must either obtain a warrant before making an arrest or, more commonly, must promptly submit that decision to a magistrate (a lower-level judicial officer) for review after the fact. In either situation, there is quick and routine judicial oversight of the police officer's probable cause decision.

The contrast to the grand jury is stark. Once the indictment is returned, the issue of probable cause is conclusively determined. There are few legal challenges that can be raised to the indictment, none of which addresses directly the accuracy of the grand jury's probable cause determination.

In sum, the decision to entrust grand jurors with this legal determination is an anomaly in the law. Grand jurors are not permitted to perform the one task for which they are qualified (finding and weighing competing facts) and are required to perform the one task for which they are not qualified (determining whether a single set of facts satisfies a legal standard). In these circumstances, jurors will inevitably defer to the prosecutor's conclusion on the legal question. More to the point, prosecutors can expect this deference and may bring forward weak, unfounded, or malicious charges. The grand jury therefore fails to provide the screening that traditionally has justified its existence.

The True Screening Role of the Grand Jury

Just because grand jurors are not qualified to make the probable cause determination does not mean they fail to screen in *any* respect. There are at least three ways a grand jury might restrain the prosecutor's charging decision, quite apart from its assessment of the evidence. First, it might conduct its own investigation and uncover exculpatory evidence. Second, it might convince the prosecutor to drop the charges by spotting previously undiscovered weaknesses in the case. Third, it might refuse to allow a case to go forward for policy reasons, even though there is plenty of evidence of guilt (Leipold 1995). The first two possibilities are of dubious merit, however, and the third may actually undermine the values the institution is designed to protect.

Uncovering Flaws in the Government's Case

Although normally the prosecutor decides what evidence will be submitted to a grand jury, the jurors always have the authority to demand more. They are free to question the witnesses themselves, require that more witnesses be called, or subpoena additional documents. This power, one could argue, means that a prosecutor cannot be certain that the grand jury will be satisfied with seeing only one side of the case. A prosecutor who wants to indict a suspect despite weak evidence, and who plans to do so by presenting an incomplete set of facts, should be worried that the jurors will look beyond the government's presentation of evidence and uncover the flaws in the case.

The argument is valid in theory, but it is doubtful that a prosecutor feels this pressure in practice. Grand jurors rarely ask questions or take control of the proceedings in any meaningful way, probably because institutional pressures discourage them from doing so (Brenner 1995; LaFave, Israel, and King 1999). Typically jurors are required to hear a large number of cases, most of which are prepared in advance by the prosecutor and may take only a short time to present. Given many grand jurors' lack of understanding about the legal question they are asked to decide, it would take an unusual and suspicious juror to challenge the prepared evidence and demand that more time be spent on a case (Leipold 1995). If jurors do not know what they are looking for (*i.e.*, the quantum of evidence that satisfies the probable cause standard), it is unlikely that they will spend much energy on the search.

The incentives to accept the government's evidence at face value are increased when it becomes clear to jurors that their powers to investigate are subject to prosecutorial oversight. When witnesses are subpoenaed, they are often interviewed by the prosecutor before testifying; when documents are produced, they are first reviewed by the prosecution and put into a manageable form before being presented to the jury. As sensible as these steps are for administrative reasons, they hardly encourage the jurors to think of themselves as directing the investigation. Any screening that flows from the jurors' exercise of their investigatory powers is therefore likely to be by accident rather than by design.

Helping the Prosecutor Find Weak Cases

A second possibility assumes a more benign prosecutor. Sometimes the prosecution is truly undecided about whether charges should be filed and looks to the grand jury to help make that decision. In some cases, the prosecutor will be uncertain whether a crime was in fact committed, or how serious a charge is warranted, perhaps because he or she is not certain which witness is telling the truth. Here the prosecutor might welcome the chance to present the conflicting evidence to jurors, hoping that they can determine what really took place. The jurors' reactions to the evidence can then guide the prosecution in making its charging decision.

Here the prosecutor is using the jurors to their best advantage, finding facts and weighing credibility. In these cases, the grand jurors are truly screening cases and will prevent the government from bringing charges by convincing the prosecutor that a trial jury would be unlikely to convict. The obvious drawback to this type of screening is that it has nothing to do with restraining the prosecution from overreaching. Here the grand jury can screen only when the prosecutor allows it to—when the government is looking for assistance on a difficult question and, most importantly, when it goes beyond its normal obligations and presents a full view of the evidence, both favorable and unfavorable. Because there is no *requirement* that more than one side of the case be presented, however, a prosecutor who wishes to charge a suspect with a weak case—perhaps to harass or perhaps to force a plea bargain before all the facts are known—remains free to do so. The prosecution will thus be restrained by the grand jury only when it is willing to be restrained. And while *allowing* the prosecution to have its case reviewed prior to trial may be an idea with independent merit, it is hard to argue that this is what the framers of the Fifth Amendment had in mind.

Shielding the Guilty

The better view is that the grand jury serves only one meaningful screening function. Given the nature of the question asked and the evidence presented, the grand jury is qualified to screen only cases that it believes should not be brought to trial *regardless* of the strength of the evidence. In effect, the grand jury can serve only as a pretrial "nullification" device, eliminating those cases where the jury believes that an otherwise guilty defendant is not worthy of prosecution.

The parallel to trial juries is again instructive. A trial jury has the power to find a defendant not guilty for any reason it wishes, no matter how clear the evidence of guilt, and that decision is conclusive because the prosecution is barred by the double jeopardy clause of the Constitution from appealing the acquittal. The trial jury's power to nullify is based on a belief that valid laws are not always fair, and that even fair laws can be unfairly applied (Weinstein 1993). A jury, as the disinterested representative of the community, can put this belief into operation by refusing to convict in cases where technical guilt is clear. Thus, for example, a defendant may be clearly guilty of possessing a small amount of drugs, but if the jury believes that the law is too harsh, or the defendant deserves another chance, or the prosecutor behaved improperly in bringing the charges, the trial jury can end the case by refusing to convict.

The grand jury can perform this nullification function in the pretrial context. Although the jurors have no expertise in deciding whether the evidence is legally sufficient, they presumably retain a rough sense of right and wrong and thus have some ability to decide as a policy matter if this defendant should be charged with a crime. Regardless of the strength of the evidence, the jurors are free to decide that a suspect is not worthy of condemnation, that the law itself is unfair, or that the charges are too high considering the harm done. In such cases, the grand jury can refuse to return an indictment as a way of voicing its disagreement with the prosecutor's decision to charge.

If the grand jury is viewed as a pretrial nullification device, its ability to screen cases becomes more meaningful. Now a prosecutor weighing the charging options does not just ask whether the jurors can be convinced that the evidence is sufficient; instead, the question becomes whether the jurors will decide that the prosecutor is acting appropriately in trying to enforce a particular law against this suspect—a vague but decidedly nonlegal question that a jury is perfectly capable of resolving. A prosecutor who is confident of his or her ability to convince a jury to indict in a weak case may have less confidence that a jury can be convinced to indict in an "unfair" case.

The grand jury's nullification power is a mixed blessing at best. There undoubtedly have been cases where the grand jury refused to indict, despite strong evidence of guilt, because the defendant appeared to act properly, the prosecution seems politically motivated, or the law in question is anachronistic or unpopular. This exercise of power is seen by many as desirable, and it is perhaps enough to justify the grand jury's reputation as a shield. A refusal to indict may also, however, be based on prejudice against the crime victim, bias in favor of the target, or other illegitimate reasons. The danger in giving the power to nullify to a group of unelected, anonymous, and unaccountable citizens is that they are free to use that power in illegitimate ways, precisely because they are answerable to no one. The power to nullify is, at least in the particular case, the power to frustrate the apparent will of the electorate to enforce the criminal law when evidence shows a crime has occurred.

The problems of allowing the grand jury to nullify charges are compounded by the secrecy of the process. At trial, the evidence of the defendant's criminal behavior is revealed in open court, so that even if a jury nullifies there is a public record of what has occurred. Not so with the grand jury. If it refuses to indict a popular suspect (for example, a police officer) who is accused of violating the civil rights of an unpopular victim (a convicted felon), there is no way to know whether the suspect was innocent, was guilty but the prosecutor failed to present sufficient evidence, or was guilty but the grand jurors refused to indict because of their sympathy for the police or antagonism for the victim.

Reasonable minds can disagree about whether the grand jury's nullification power is desirable, but it seems clear that this function best describes and explains the grand jury's screeni10ng role. More importantly, these are the terms on which grand jury reform should be debated: whether the power to nullify is consistent with the constitutional command and whether it is a desirable part of a rational criminal justice system.

Note

A more extensive version of this article can be found in Andrew D. Leipold, (1995) "Why Grand Juries Do Not (and Cannot) Protect the Accused." *Cornell Law Review*, 80: 260–324. The ideas set forth in this chapter are used with permission of the Cornell Law Review.

References

Beale, Sara Sun, William C. Bryson, James E. Felman, and Michael J. Elson. 1997. *Grand Jury Law and Practice*, 2nd ed., Vol. 1. St. Paul, MN: West Group.

Brenner, Susan W. 1995. "The Voice of the Community: A Case for Grand Jury Independence." *Virginia Journal of Social Policy and The Law* 3: 67–131.

Goldstein, Howard W. 1998. *Grand Jury Practice*. New York: Law Journal Seminars Press.

LaFave, Wayne R., Jerold H. Israel, and Nancy J. King. 1999. *Criminal Procedure*, Vols. 3 and 5. St. Paul, MN: West Group.

Leipold, Andrew D. 1995. "Why Grand Juries Do Not (and Cannot) Protect the Accused." *Cornell Law Review* 80: 260–324.

Sullivan, Thomas P. and Robert D. Nachman. 1984. "If It Ain't Broke, Don't Fix It: Why the Grand Jury's Accusatory Function Should Not Be Changed." *Journal of Criminal Law and Criminology* 75: 1047–1069.

U.S. Department of Justice. 1997. *United States Attorneys' Manual*, paragraphs 9–27.300, Washington, DC: U.S. Department of Justice.

United States Supreme Court. (Amended Dec. 1, 2000). *Federal Rules of Criminal Procedure*. Washington, DC: Government Printing Office. Accessed: <http://www.law.ukans.edu/research/frcrilll.htm>

Weinstein, Jack B. 1993. "Considering Jury 'Nullification': When, May, and Should a Jury Reject the Law to Do Justice?" *American Criminal Law Review* 30: 239–254.

Court Cases

Duncan v. Louisiana, 391 U.S. 145, 156 (1968).

United States v. McCall, 460 F.2d 952, 956–57 (D.C. Cir. 1972).

In re Grand Jury Subpoena (Stewart), 575 N.Y.S.2d 974, 977 n.1 (Sup. Ct.), *aff'd as modified*, 548 N.Y.S.2d 679 (App. Div. 1989). ✦

ISSUE X
Are Drug Courts a Promising Pretrial Strategy?

The latest trends in American courts are specially trained judges and courtrooms for specific defendants. Known as "specialty courts," there are now mental health courts, domestic violence courts, and drug courts, which have been developed nationwide to address particular types of problems that lead to law-breaking behavior. Since the first two types of courts are very recent developments and thus have little documented research, this section addresses only drug courts.

The concept of drug courts began in the 1980s in response to the increased number of drug offenders who were being arrested and funneled through the court system. Many of these drug cases involved people who were in possession of small amounts of illegal drugs, were drug-addicted, or both. Studies found that for addicts who committed crime to support their drug habits, drug treatment reduced both drug use and incidents of crime (Hubbard et al. 1988). However, prisons did not offer enough drug treatment programs to fill the demand that incarcerated drug offenders were creating. By the mid-1990s, prisons overflowed with nonviolent drug offenders, who were released with an untreated drug habit.

Drug courts are different from traditional criminal courts in that they are dedicated only to drug cases. Most drug courts do not hear motions or conduct trials. Rather, judges take a more personal interest in the progress of high numbers of drug offenders. Some drug courts focus on diversion from prison by allowing drug users the chance to enter drug and alcohol treatment in the community while they live at home. Through a combination of diversion, treatment, and expediting cases, drug courts purport to lighten the load on traditional district courts, which can then focus on nondrug felony crimes (Inciardi et al. 1996).

The Drug Court Clearinghouse and Technical Assistance Project (DCCTAP) compiles information on the nearly 400 adult, juvenile, and tribal drug court programs nationwide. Tribal drug courts are present on Native American reservations and function in the same manner as other drug courts. DCCTAP has written a favorable summary of the results of drug courts over the first decade of their existence, including the benefits achieved in the areas of cost-effectiveness; treatment and services provided; high employment retention rates; babies born to drug-free mothers; reduction of recidivism; family reunification; and long-term sobriety. The report details the accomplishments and impact of many drug courts around the United States.

Morris B. Hoffman, a district judge in Denver, Colorado, writes a scathing piece criticizing the theory and practice of drug courts from his perspective as a drug court judge. Some of his arguments are that drug courts have been embraced without our really knowing whether they are effective and that drug courts change the role of judges from enforcers of the law to glorified probation officers. He also argues that drug courts end up sending to prison drug offenders who fail treatment and they do not result in speedy case processing. In practice, drug cases clog the court system more than ever before, resulting in an enormous caseload. The stress leads to frequent judicial rotations and the institutionalization of one judge's sentencing philosophy as long as he or she presides over all drug cases.

References

Hubbard, Robert L., James J. Colling, J. Valley Rachal, and Elizabeth R. Cavanaugh. 1988. "The Criminal Justice Client in Drug Abuse Treatment." Pp. 57–80 in Carl G. Leukefeld and Frank M. Tims, Eds., *Compulsory Treatment of Drug Abuse: Research and Clinical Practice*, National Institute of Drug Abuse Monograph 86. Washington, DC: U.S. Department of Health and Human Services, National Institute of Drug Abuse.

Inciardi, James A., Duane C. McBride, and James E. Rivers. 1996. *Drug Control and the Courts*. Newbury Park, CA: Sage.

Critical Thinking Questions

1. Is the trend toward specialty courts (drug courts, mental health courts, domestic violence courts) a good use of criminal justice resources?

2. Is punishment or treatment the best approach for drug offenders?

3. Do drug courts actually help keep offenders out of the system?

Internet Websites

Drug Courts Program Office, Office of Justice Programs. <http://www.ojp.usdoj.gov/dcpo/>

National Association of Drug Court Professionals. <http://www.drugcourt.org>

National Drug Court Institute. <http://www. ndci. org/aboutndci.htm>

National Criminal Justice Reference Service. <http://www.ncjrs.org>

National GAINS Center for People with Co-Occurring Disorders in the Justice System. <http://www.prainc.com/gains/index.html>

National Institute on Drug Abuse (NIDA). <http://www.nida.nih.gov>

Office of Justice Programs Drug Court Clearinghouse and Technical Assistance Project (DCCTAP). <http://www.american.edu/justice> ✦

19

Looking at a Decade of Drug Courts

Drug Court Clearinghouse and Technical Assistance Project

Introduction

What began in 1989 as an experiment by the Dade County (FL) Circuit Court to call upon the authority of a sifting judge to devise—and proactively oversee—an intensive, community-based treatment, rehabilitation, and supervision program for felony drug defendants in an effort to halt rapidly increasing recidivism rates has become a national movement during the decade that has followed. "Drug court" activity is now underway in 49 of the 50 states, as well as in the District of Columbia, Puerto Rico, Guam, a number of Native American Tribal Courts, and two federal district courts.

The appeal of the drug court lies in many sectors: more effective supervision of offenders in the community; more credibility to the law enforcement function (arrests of drug offenders are, indeed, taken seriously, even by court systems that are inundated with cases); greater accountability of defendants for complying with conditions of release and/or probation; greater coordination and accountability of public services provided, including reduced duplication of services and costs to the taxpayer, and more efficiency for the court system through removal of a class of cases that places significant resource demands for processing, both initially and with probation violations and new

offenses that otherwise would undoubtedly occur. Dramatic as these benefits may be, however, they do not explain the tremendous personal impact that drug courts have on all who have been involved with them—even the casual observer of a drug court session.

What has made the drug court movement so powerful and infectious is its human element. Close to 140,000 drug-dependent offenders have entered drug court programs since their inception and more than 70 percent are either still enrolled or have graduated—more than double the rate of traditional treatment program retention rates. Drug court participants reflect all segments of the community. Approximately two-thirds are parents of minor children. Approximately 10 percent are veterans. Men participate at more than twice the rate of women, although the percentage of female participants is rising. Most drug court participants have been using drugs for many, many years; many are polydrug users. Most have never been exposed to treatment, although a large majority have already served jail or prison time for drug-related offenses.

Unlike traditional treatment programs, becoming "clean and sober" is only the first step toward graduating from drug court. Almost all drug courts require participants (after they have become clean and sober) to obtain a high school or GED certificate, maintain employment, be current in all financial obligations—including drug court fees and child support payments, if applicable—and have a sponsor in the community. Many programs also require participants to perform community service hours—to "give back" to the community that is supporting them through the drug court program. One drug court requires prospective graduates to prepare a 2-year "life plan" following drug court graduation for discussion with a community board to assure the court that the participant has developed the "tools" to lead a drug-free and crime-free life.

The original goals for drug courts—reductions in recidivism and drug usage—are being achieved, with recidivism rates substantially reduced for graduates and, to a lesser but significant degree, for participants who do not graduate as well. Drug-usage rates for defendants while they are participating in the drug court, as measured by the frequent, random urinalysis required of all participants, are also substantially reduced, generally to well under 10 percent, dramatically below the rate observed for non-drug court offenders.

The "outcomes" that drug courts are achieving go far beyond these original goals, however: the birth of more than 750 drug-free babies to drug court participants; the re-unification of hundreds of families, as parents regain or are able to retain custody of their children; education and vocational training and job placements for participants, to name a few. Most significantly, many of the judges who have served as "drug court judges" have requested an extension of their assignment, and many have taken on the drug court duty in addition to their other docket responsibilities.

The following sections of this publication highlight the background of the drug court "movement," the major areas in which drug courts differ from traditional adjudication processes, and salient accomplishments to date.

Background

Since the mid-1980's, many state and local criminal justice systems have been inundated with felony drug cases. Court dockets became overloaded with drug cases and drug-involved offenders, leaving fewer resources available to adjudicate serious, violent felonies. During this same period, it became increasingly clear that: (1) incarceration in and of itself does little to break the cycle of illegal drug use and crime, and offenders sentenced to incarceration for substance-related offenses exhibit a high rate of recidivism once they are released; and (2) drug abuse treatment is demonstrably effective in reducing both drug addiction and drug-related crime if participants remain in treatment for an adequate period of time.

In the early 1990's, a number of jurisdictions began to rethink their approach to han-

dling defendants charged with drug and drug-related offenses and explored ways of adapting the "drug court" concept introduced by Dade County in 1989. Defendants targeted for the "drug court" have generally been nonviolent offenders whose current involvement with the criminal justice system is due, primarily, to their substance addiction. Defendants eligible for the drug court are identified as soon as possible after arrest and, if accepted, are referred immediately to a multiphase outpatient treatment program entailing multiple weekly (often daily) contacts with the treatment provider for counseling, therapy, and education; frequent urinalysis (usually at least weekly); frequent status hearings before the drug court judge (biweekly or more often at first); and a rehabilitation program entailing vocational, educational, family, medical, and other support services.

Drug court programs are currently operating in 42 states, the District of Columbia, Puerto Rico, and one federal district, and programs are planned or about to be implemented in Guam, one additional federal district, and seven additional states, including several Native American Tribal Courts. Over 350 programs have been implemented, and 225 additional programs are about to start or are being planned. In addition, since 1995, 14 states have either enacted or have under consideration legislation dealing with the establishment of or funding for drug courts, and one state (Delaware) has implemented a statewide drug court program. The scope of drug court activity underway extends to state, local, Native American tribal courts, and federal districts.

Initially most drug courts focused on first offenders, but, increasingly, jurisdictions are targeting more serious offenders for several reasons: (1) recognition of the apparent futility of traditional probation and/or incarceration sentences that have already been imposed on many of these defendants and have failed to prevent continued drug use and criminal activity; and (2) a policy decision to use the limited resources available to the drug court for persons with serious substance addiction problems, rather than those with less severe problems who might be served through other programs.

Effectiveness of the Approach

Reduction in Drug Use

Traditional Adjudication Process. Drug Use Forecasting (DUF) data collected on defendants in 35 cities indicate that 36 to 78 percent of arrested males and 20 to 67 percent of arrested females were under the influence of at least one illicit drug[1] at the time of arrest. Defendants convicted of drug offenses are either sentenced to a period of incarceration or referred for probation supervision, with few jurisdictions requiring frequent drug testing to monitor drug use after conviction. Jurisdictions that do have the capacity to monitor defendants on pretrial release or probation generally note significant drug usage rates, but are unable to respond promptly to positive tests. Few jails or prisons provide any comprehensive treatment services for inmates, and none provide long-term rehabilitation support once the defendant is released. In jurisdictions that require, as a condition of probation, completion of a treatment program, there is generally no follow-up monitoring of whether defendants who complete such programs actually cease or reduce their use of drugs. This situation, coupled with available recidivism data (see below), has led many justice system officials to conclude that the traditional case disposition process lacks the capacity to bring about any significant reduction in drug usage and criminal activity by persons convicted of drug offenses.

Drug Court Experience. Because drug court programs test defendants for drug use on a regular basis (usually at least weekly), information regarding drug use by defendants under drug court supervision is available and known to the court on an ongoing basis, and is responded to promptly with appropriate sanctions. Consequently, the drug use of defendants participating in drug court programs is substantially reduced and significantly lower than that reported for non-drug court defendants, and for participants who graduate from the programs (ranging from 50 to 65 percent) is eliminated alto-gether for most participants. Recidivism among graduates also appears to be very low (see below).

Reduction in Recidivism

Traditional Adjudication Process. Most criminal justice system professionals estimate that well over 50 percent of defendants convicted of drug possession will recidivate with a similar offense within 2 to 3 years.[2] The more frequently a defendant has been arrested for a drug offense, the more likely he or she is to recidivate. A high percentage of defendants convicted of drug possession are also arrested for property offenses during the period when they are using illicit substances, and a substantial percentage have either committed violent offenses or are considered likely to do so, particularly as their addictions progress. Defendants in drug court programs report spending at least $50–$100 per day on drugs before entering the drug court, and many report spending considerably more. The money to maintain their drug habits is usually derived from theft and other criminal activity, whether reported or not.

Drug Court Experience. In comparison, drug court programs are experiencing a significant reduction in recidivism among participants. Depending upon the characteristics of the population targeted and the degree of social dysfunction and other problems they present (employment status, family situation, medical condition, etc.), recidivism among all drug court participants has ranged between 5 and 28 percent and less than 4 percent for graduates. The drastic reduction in drug use by drug court participants, and the consequent criminal activity associated with drug use, is confirmed by urinalysis reports for drug court defendants, usually well over 90 percent negative.

Intensive Supervision

Intensive supervision is provided where little existed before.

Traditional Adjudication Process. Under the traditional adjudication process, supervision of defendants released before trial usually consists of a weekly call-in and periodic reporting to a pretrial service agency during the pretrial period (usually 60 to 120 or more days following arrest); after conviction, supervision usually consists of monthly reporting to a probation officer. Urinalysis is generally conducted only periodically, and treatment services provided only if available. The court's involvement occurs only when probation violations are reported—generally when new crimes are committed. Bench warrants may be issued for defendants who fail to appear for court hearings, but their actual execution (e.g., the defendant's arrest) may not occur for months and is often triggered only by a new arrest.

Drug Court Experience. Defendant supervision and monitoring—as well as treatment services—in all of the drug court programs are significantly more immediate and intensive than would have been provided to the typical drug court defendant before the program began. Drug court defendants come under the court's supervision very shortly after arrest, and throughout a typical 12- to 15-month period are required to attend treatment sessions, undergo frequent and random urinalysis, and appear before the drug court judge on a regular and frequent basis. Almost all of the drug courts have instituted procedures for immediate execution of bench warrants (often within hours) for defendants who fail to appear at any court hearing.

Capacity to Promptly Address Relapse and Its Consequences

Traditional Adjudication Process. It is particularly common for defendants on probation for drug offenses to fail to comply with probation conditions entailing attendance at treatment programs or abstinence from drug use. Frequently, their failure to comply is evidenced by a new arrest for a drug or drug-related offense, generally becoming known to the justice system months after the defendant's drug use has resumed—if it ever ceased in the first place. This new arrest usually triggers: (1) a probation violation hearing, which generally results in imposition of the original sentence suspended when the defendant was placed on probation, and (2) conviction for the new offense,

often resulting in an additional sentence of incarceration. It is common for this cycle to continue indefinitely once the defendant is released, with an enhanced incarceration sentence imposed each time to reflect the defendant's lengthening criminal history. At least 60 percent of offenders incarcerated in 1997 were imprisoned for drug or drug-related offenses and more than 75 percent of the correctional population had substance abuse problems.[3]

Drug Court Experience. Recognizing that substance addiction is a chronic and recurring disorder, the drug court program maintains continuous supervision over the recovery process of each participant, through frequent court status hearings, urinalysis, and reports from the treatment providers to the supervising judge. Drug usage or failures to comply with other conditions of the drug court program are detected and responded to promptly. Immediate responses—such as enhanced treatment services, more frequent urinalysis (daily, if necessary), imposition of community service requirements, and "shock" incarceration—are some of the options drug court judges use to respond to program noncompliance. In appropriate situations, particularly where public safety is at issue or participants willfully fail to comply with program conditions, they are terminated from the drug court and referred for traditional adjudication, with standard penalties are applied. Data reported by the 200 oldest drug courts indicate that drug use is being reduced for most participants, not just drug court graduates.

Integration of Drug Treatment with Other Rehabilitation Services

Integration of services is promoting long-term recovery.

Traditional Adjudication Process. Although there are strong correlations between drug abuse and other attributes of social dysfunction exhibited by drug users, such as poor reading skills, dysfunctional family relationships, and low self esteem, most courts do not address these problems when sentencing drug-using offenders. At best, they refer them to a treatment program and/or a special skills class, with no regular follow-up monitoring of their participation or its results, absent a violation of probation filed by the probation officer (see above).

Drug Court Experience. In contrast, a fundamental premise of the drug court approach is that cessation of drug abuse requires not only well-structured treatment services but coordinated and comprehensive programs of other rehabilitation services to address the underlying personal problems of the drug user, and promote his or her long-term reentry into society. While sobriety is a primary objective of the drug court program, no participant can successfully complete the program without also addressing needs relating to his/her long-term rehabilitation. In addition to sobriety, most drug courts require participants to obtain a high school or GED certificate; obtain or maintain employment; and develop mentor relationships within the community to sustain them after they leave the drug court program.

Summary Results: The First Decade

Retention Rates

Programs report high participant retention rates.

Despite their rigorous requirements, drug court programs are retaining a significant percentage of the defendants enrolled, and consequently, are having a more significant impact on participants' lives than traditional pretrial and/or probation supervision. Data from the 200 oldest drug courts (confirmed by a 1997 U.S. General Accounting Office study) reflect an average retention rate of more than 70 percent (the total of graduates plus active participants), despite the difficult populations that most programs target. These retention rates can be contrasted with the significantly lower rates generally acknowledged for traditional drug treatment programs dealing with criminal defendants, with slightly higher rates for individuals not involved with the criminal justice process. It has also been noted that, in many cases, defendants may be terminated from a drug court program because they fail to meet the stringent requirements imposed by the court but have nevertheless made significant progress in terms of reducing drug use and im-

proving their employment status, educational development, and family relationships. These people often eventually succeed in subsequent treatment programs in which they enroll.

The Nature and Extent of Addiction Being Addressed

The nature and extent of addiction among drug court participants varies widely but generally tends to be severe.

Most drug court participants, even first offenders, appear to have significant histories of substance addiction, frequently 15 or more years. Based on information provided by the 200 oldest drug courts, the primary drug used most frequently by drug court participants is crack/cocaine, although many are polydrug users. Sixty percent of the drug courts also report heroin use among participants and more than one-half report methamphetamine addiction, notably in the central and eastern regions of the country as well as the West, where it had previously appeared to be concentrated. Marijuana and alcohol use, in conjunction with other substances, was also reported by most of the programs. Increasing prevalence of the abuse of prescription drugs and, among juveniles, toxic inhalants is also being reported.

Judicial Supervision

Participants note judges' supervision, coupled with drug court treatment services and strict monitoring, is key to their success.

Responses from two recent surveys of 400 drug court participants in the final phases of participation in more than 50 different programs[4] indicated that the close supervision—and encouragement—provided by the drug court judge, coupled with the programs' intensive treatment and rehabilitation services and ongoing monitoring, were critical in promoting their success in the program. More than one-fourth of the respondents had been in at least one treatment program during the previous three years which they had left unsuccessfully.

Cost-Effectiveness

The average cost for the treatment component of a drug court program ranges between $1,200 and $3,500 per participant, depending upon the range of services provided and whether any of these services are provided by existing agencies. Savings in jail bed days alone have been estimated to be at least $5,000 per defendant—which does not factor in the value of the added capability (see below) to incarcerate the more serious offenders that many jurisdictions are also deriving from these programs. Similarly, prosecutors are reporting that the drug court programs have reduced police overtime and other witness costs, as well as grand jury expenses for those jurisdictions with an indictment process, that would otherwise be required if these cases proceeded in the traditional manner. Most programs also report that a substantial percentage of the participants who came into the program unemployed and on public assistance have become employed while in the program and are now self-supporting. In addition, many participants who are employed at the time of program entry are able to maintain their employment, despite their arrest, because of their program participation.

Benefits for Families and Children

Approximately two-thirds of the drug court participants are parents of minor children. Many of these parents have lost or are in danger of losing custody of their children because of their drug use. Drug court participation has resulted in many of these litigants' retaining or regaining custody upon completing the drug court. More than 750 drug-free babies have been reported born to female drug court participants while enrolled in drug court programs, thus obviating the substantial medical and social service costs (estimated at a minimum of $250,000 per baby) required to care for a drug-addicted infant, let alone the resultant societal impact. Almost all drug courts provide family counseling and parenting services, and at least half provide aid with housing, food, and clothing. An increasing number are providing child care services and facilities while parents attend drug court treatment sessions and hearings.

Criminal Justice Resources

Criminal justice resources are freed up for violent and other serious criminal cases.

In addition to cost savings, all components of the justice system report that the drug court programs are enabling their agencies to allocate criminal justice resources more efficiently. Staff and services, which had heretofore been consumed by the less serious but time-consuming drug cases now targeted for drug court assignment, can be directed to more serious cases and to those offenders who present greater risks to community safety. Some prosecutors and indigent defense counsel report that the case preparation and court appearance time freed up by drug court programs is equivalent to one or more FTE attorney positions. The caseloads assumed by the drug court judges have also freed up other judges' docket time for other criminal matters as well as civil cases which, in many jurisdictions, have been given secondary priority because of the drug caseload. In jurisdictions where jail space has been freed up, this space is now being used to house more serious offenders and/or to assure that they serve their full sentences.

Benefits to Prosecutors and Police

Prosecutors and police in many jurisdictions report that the drug court has significantly enhanced the credibility of the law enforcement function, provides their agencies with a more effective response to substance abuse, and is a significant alternative to the "revolving door" syndrome that frequently results from the traditional case process. Defendants are no longer released back into the community—and back to using drugs—shortly after arrest but, rather, placed in a rigorous, court-supervised treatment program that carries an important message to the community regarding the seriousness of illegal drug use. A recent poll of 318 police chiefs found that almost 60 percent advocate court-supervised treatment programs over other justice system options for drug users.[5] In a number of jurisdictions, prosecutor and/or police agencies have contributed asset forfeiture funds to the local drug court and have campaigned with the judiciary for community support.

Adult Model Being Adapted for Juvenile and Family Matters

Over 80 juvenile drug courts, addressing both delinquency and dependency matters, have been implemented and 50 more are being planned in both state courts and Native American Tribal Courts. Juvenile drug courts use the rigorous and ongoing judicial supervision, treatment and community resources of their adult counterparts, but in addition, shape the program's treatment and rehabilitation services to also focus on the juvenile's developmental needs, family situation, and peer environment as well as the *juvenile.*

Highlights of National Drug Court Survey Findings

The 1997 *Drug Court Survey Report,* recently published by the Office of Justice Programs Drug Court Clearinghouse and Technical Assistance Project at American University, provides a comparative profile of the 95 oldest drug court programs and includes operational information and comments from drug court judges, prosecutors, defender offices, law enforcement agencies, corrections departments, and treatment providers involved with the operation of the drug courts in their respective jurisdictions. The *Survey Report* also includes comments from 256 participants in the final phases of 55 drug court programs in 23 states and the District of Columbia.

The following are the most salient observations that emerge from the survey and subsequent follow-up data. . . .

Primary Services Being Provided

Comprehensive, Individualized Treatment Services. Many drug courts are diversifying the treatment services being provided to address the multitude of needs and backgrounds of participants. Many of the treatment program components, for example, are developing differentiated "tracks" to address the diversity of treatment needs pre-sented by drug court clients. Special components are also being developed for the special ethnic and/or cultural groups represented, and other "special populations" including pregnant women, mothers, fathers, persons who have been sexually abused, and others.

Physical and Mental Health Services. Drug courts are providing a range of physical and mental health services to participants, as well as substance-abuse treatment. Almost all of the drug courts provide public health services, including HIV and TB screening and referral. An increasing number of programs are also developing special services to address the needs of dually diagnosed participants who have mental health problems, frequently as a result of their substance abuse, and, in many jurisdictions, comprise a significant percentage of the drug court-eligible populations. A number of drug courts routinely utilize the services of a physician and/or nurse.

Education, Job Training, Employment, and Other Rehabilitation Services. The range of support and rehabilitation services being delivered by drug courts is expanding significantly. Many of the early drug courts focused primarily upon treatment services, with ancillary support for education, job training, and placement. Most of these early drug courts, and their numerous progeny, have expanded their treatment and rehabilitation services significantly, recognizing the diversity of both treatment and other needs presented by the drug court populations. The expanded services being developed also reflect, in large part, a growing recognition that the drug court must treat not only the participant's addiction but the numerous associated personal problems most participants encounter—physical, mental, housing, family, employment, self-esteem, etc.— if long-term sobriety and rehabilitation is to be achieved and future criminal activity is to be significantly reduced.

Offenders Targeted: Focus on Long-Term Drug Users

Drug courts are increasingly targeting the chronic recidivists as well as first offenders. Many drug courts that began as pretrial diversion programs are expanding their focus to target individuals with more extensive criminal histories who require the rigid supervision and monitoring of the drug court and can benefit from the treatment and rehabilitation services provided. Less than 20 percent of presently operating drug courts restrict their services to first offenders. Although generally not eligible for diversion because of their more extensive criminal history, defendants with more extensive criminal histories are generally offered some incentive to complete the drug court, such as suspension of a jail or prison term, or a reduction in the period of their probation.

Most programs report that participants are presenting moderate to severe crack/cocaine addiction with other drug usage and alcohol addiction as well. Crack/cocaine addiction is prevalent among most drug court participants. In addition, approximately 75 percent of the drug courts report moderate to severe marijuana addiction and 53 percent of the programs report moderate to severe heroin addiction. Approximately one-third of the programs also report moderate to severe methamphetamine addiction presented by participants. Since the first comprehensive Drug Court Survey in 1995, a notable prevalence of methamphetamine has been reported by programs in the central and eastern regions of the country, as well as in the West, where it had previously appeared to be concentrated. Two-thirds of the responding programs also report moderate to severe alcoholism presented by their clients. Over 60 percent of the programs routinely test for alcohol consumption as well as illegal drug use. All of the drug courts either prohibit or strongly discourage the use of alcohol by drug court participants. For juvenile drug courts, the most prevalent drugs reported had, until recently, been alcohol and marijuana. However, increasing prevalence of crack/cocaine, methamphetamine, and toxic inhalants is being noted. The average age at first use in juvenile drug courts is 10 to 12 years, and some programs report usage as early as 8 years.

Who Is the Drug Court Client?

Close to 140,000 individuals have enrolled in drug courts to date, and approximately 70 percent have graduated or are still participating. A profile of 256 drug court participants in the final phases of 55 drug courts in 23 states and other data reported by operating programs indicates the following:

Participant Enrollment and Performance. Significantly more males than females are enrolling in drug court programs; in some programs, females who participate in drug courts are more heavily involved with drugs than males by the time they become involved in the criminal court process. Where day care, special women's groups, and other special services are offered, females are graduating at a higher rate than their male counterparts. For voluntary programs, a high percentage of defendants offered the opportunity to participate in the drug court accept it despite its more rigorous requirements compared with the traditional sanction to which they are exposed.

Participant Demographics. The average age of drug court participants is generally over 30; the average age of *graduates* in individual programs is often older than the average age for all *participants* in the program. In a number of programs, the average age for female participants is younger than for male participants.

Most participants who responded to the 1997 survey were single, divorced, or widowed. Twenty-five percent were currently married. Men were more frequently single or never married (56 percent vs. 41 percent). More women were currently married (28 percent vs. 21 percent). . . . Approximately 16 percent of the 256 participants surveyed in 1997 were either veterans (13 percent) or in the active military (3 percent). The percentage of veterans participating in drug courts in 1999 was approximately 10 percent, with almost no participants in the active military.

Drug Usage of Participants. Most drug court participants have been using drugs for at least 15 years, and generally much longer. Most are using multiple illegal drugs at the time of program entry, and are also using alcohol. Some have also abused prescription drugs. Approximately one-fourth of drug court participants have participated unsuccessfully in at least one—and often more—prior treatment programs. Many drug court participants have served time in prison for prior drug offenses.

Educational Status of Participants. Almost all of the drug court programs require a high school or GED certificate in order to graduate. The educational profile of the 256 participants surveyed in 1997 revealed that 5 percent had less than an eighth grade education, 25 percent had some high school, 36 percent were high school graduates or had a GED certificate, 9 percent had post high school technical training, 15 percent had 2 years of college, 6 percent had 3 to 4 years of college, 2 percent held an undergraduate college degree, and 3 percent had completed some postgraduate study.

Children of Participants. Many drug court participants are parents. About 60 percent of the 256 drug court participants surveyed were parents of minor children, many of whom were in foster care at the time the parent entered the drug court. More recent information from 100+ drug courts indicates that a similar percentage of participants in these programs are parents of minor children, with an estimated 50,000 children represented among drug court parents.

Participant Retention. The retention rates for drug courts remain high, generally between 65 and 85 percent, despite the difficult populations most programs are targeting, the rigid participation requirements of these programs, the rapid proliferation of drug courts nationally, and their expansion to more complex caseloads. The rapid proliferation of drug courts does not appear to have had a negative impact on the high retention rates (total graduates plus active participants divided by total number ever enrolled) experienced by early programs. Moreover, retention rates do not appear to be decreasing over time. Retention rates for programs begun during the period of 1989–1992 are similar to those of the more recently implemented programs. The retention rates also do not appear to be influenced by the population size of the jurisdiction served. Drug courts in large metropolitan areas (e.g., with populations over 750,000) appear to retain participants at a rate similar to drug courts in smaller jurisdictions with populations under 200,000 and in rural areas.

Impacts Being Achieved

Recidivism. Recidivism rates continue to be significantly reduced for graduates as well as for participants who do not complete the program. Recidivism rates reported by drug courts continue to range between 2 and 20 percent, depending upon the characteristics of the population targeted. In almost all jurisdictions, recidivism is substantially reduced for participants who complete the drug court program and to a considerable, although generally lesser, degree for those who do not complete the program as well. Less than 3 percent of the recidivism rates for drug court graduates involve violent offenses, and almost all of the small number of violent offenses reported have been misdemeanors. Most of the recidivism reported involves new drug possession charges or traffic violations arising out of driving license suspensions resulting from the initial drug court charge.

Drug Use. Drug usage, as measured by the percent of negative urine samples for drug court participants during the frequent, random urinalyses conducted, is being reduced for most *participants*, not just graduates, despite the substantial drug usage of these defendants when entering the drug court. Examples of the rate of clean urine samples reported for participants while in the drug court are [between 84 percent and 98 percent clean].

Justice System Cost Savings. Drug courts are continuing to achieve cost savings for the justice system, particularly in the use of jail space and probation services. A number of jurisdictions report reducing and/or more efficiently using jail space and probation services as a result of the drug court, which frees up these resources so that they can focus on other offenders who present greater public safety risks. Savings are also reported in prosecutor and law enforcement functions, particularly in regard to court appearance costs. All sectors of the justice system have also noted "cost avoidance" results from the reduced recidivism of drug court participants and graduates. Among the jurisdictions reporting specific annual justice system cost savings as a result of the drug court are:

- Albuquerque, NM-Met $612,000/yr. based on 90 day jail sentences @ $68/day.

- Kalamazoo, MI-male $100,485/yr. based on 4,785 jail days @ $21/day.

- Pittsburgh, PA. $2,073,643 based on 33,120 jail days saved @ $62.61/day.

- Los Angeles, CA-Mun $2.5 million (jail/prison costs saved based on 2 yr. aver. sentence @ $25,000/year).

- Philadelphia, PA. $2,835,000 based on 1,350 months saved @ $70/day.

- San Joaquin Co., CA $1,834, 950 (based on 28,230 jail days saved plus $1,220,000 (based on 12,200 prison days saved).

- Washington DC: $4,065–$8,845 per client in jail costs (amount fluctuates, depending upon use of jail as a sanction while the defendant is enrolled in the drug court); and $102,000 in prosecution costs.

Employment for Participants. Many individuals participating in the drug court are able either to *retain their jobs or to obtain employment* as a result of drug court participation. While a small percentage of drug court participants have steady jobs at the time of program entry, a substantial number (generally more than 65 percent) are unemployed or employed only on a sporadic basis. Many of the individuals who are employed at the time of program entry report that they were able to retain employment by demonstrating participation in the drug court, and a high proportion of unemployed individuals obtain employment while enrolled.

A number of drug courts (Portland and Las Vegas, for example), have a job counselor on site dedicated to working with drug court participants. Almost all of the drug courts provide vocational training and job development services. Many judges also work with local employers to personally guarantee daily supervision of persons they employ in order for them to either retain or obtain employment. . . .

Long-Term Sobriety. Drug courts are developing close working relationships with a broad base of community organizations to promote the long-term sobriety and rehabilitation of participants. Almost all drug courts are working closely with community groups to provide support services for participants, both during and following drug court participation. Through both community networks and involvement with local AA and NA groups, participants are often linked with community mentors shortly after entering the drug court. Drug courts are also developing close working relationships with local chambers of commerce, medical providers, community service organizations, the local educational system, the faith community, and other local institutions to provide a broad-based network of essential services that can be drawn upon to serve the needs of drug court participants.

Alumni Groups.Drug court graduates are forming alumni groups and serving as mentors for new participants in many jurisdictions. In many of the older programs, particularly (Jacksonville, Las Vegas, Portland, Rochester, and San Bernardino, for example), drug court graduates are, at their own initiative, forming alumni groups, continuing the network of support they developed during drug court participation, as well as serving as mentors for new participants. Several alumni groups (Rochester, Grants Pass, Oregon, and Tulare Co, California/juvenile) publish periodic newsletters.

Family Reunification and Other Family Services. Drug courts are resulting in family reunification in many instances. In many programs, parents who have lost custody or may lose custody of their children because of their drug use have regained it upon completion of the drug court program.

In Pensacola, for example, the first two graduates of the family (dependency) drug court established in early 1996 illustrate the impact of the drug court on the families of these women: one of the women had four minor children, the other had five minor children. Both had a long history of drug usage; one had been in state prison for 3 years, having been sent to prison by the drug court judge when he presided over her previous case. She was a long-term crack addict; the other was primarily alcohol- and marijuana-addicted. Neither had any permanent residence or work history. Their cumulative total of 9 children were living in foster care. Both now have a home (one rents; one owns); one is working; both families are re-united; neither mother currently uses drugs, and both have been clean for over one year.

In Portland, almost all of the more than 100 female participants who lost custody of their minor children due to their substance abuse regained custody of their children at the conclusion of their participation in the drug court.

In Kalamazoo, at least 15–20 percent of the women in the female drug court program at any one time are also involved with pro-bate court proceedings regarding loss of cus-tody of their children; almost all of them re-gain custody of their children following completion of the drug court. Participants in the newly established male drug court, while not as extensively involved with the loss of custody of their children, have brought in letters from their children and wives ex-pressing their gratitude at having their fa-thers and husbands "back" from drugs.

In Las Vegas, at least 40 women who have lost custody of their children have regained them after completing the drug court pro-gram.

Drug courts are providing a wide array of family services. Almost all of the drug courts provide family counseling, and at least half provide assistance with housing, food, and clothing. Most of the programs also provide parenting classes, including special seg-ments on stress and anger management.

Birth of Drug-Free Babies. Birth of drug-free babies is an unplanned program impact. Well over 750 drug-free babies have been re-ported born to drug court participants, in-cluding one set of twins in Rochester; a num-ber of pregnant women are currently participating in drug court programs across the country.

Other Justice System Benefits

Support from Law Enforcement Agencies. Increased collaboration is devel-oping among drug courts and law enforce-ment agencies. Many drug courts are devel-oping close relationships with local law enforcement agencies and community polic-ing activities. Much effort is being made by drug court judges to explain the drug court process to line officers who are generally the arresting officers in many drug court cases. The police departments in several drug court jurisdictions (New Haven and San Diego, for example), have assigned an officer full-time to the drug court to assist with monitoring and supervising participants and to immedi-ately execute bench warrants for any partici-pants who fail to appear in court or are oth-erwise noncompliant with drug court orders. A number of drug courts provide ar-resting officers with updated information on the progress of their arrestees in the drug court, and many drug courts invite the ar-resting officer to participants' graduation ceremonies.

Adaptation of the Drug Court Model to Other Justice System Initiatives. Many ju-risdictions are adapting the adult drug court model to juvenile populations and family matters. More than 80 juvenile and/or family drug courts have been implemented and an-other 50 are being planned. Using the adult drug court model of intensive, ongoing judi-cial supervision and the development of a structured system of sanctions and rewards, juvenile and family drug courts are focusing on both delinquency cases and dependency matters. There is also increasing recognition among the adult drug court judges that chil-dren and other family members who live with an adult substance abuser are at partic-ular risk for becoming substance-involved. Consequently, a number of adult drug courts are developing special prevention-oriented components for children and other family members of adult drug court participants, whether or not they are already involved with the adult or juvenile justice system.

The drug court experience appears to be providing a model for other community-based justice system initiatives that focus on chronic repeat offenders whose criminal ac-tivity is aggravated by coexisting substance abuse and/or related problems. A number of jurisdictions are developing special dockets, modeled after the drug court approach, to handle other classes of chronic criminal of-fenders whose criminal activity is aggra-vated by coexisting substance abuse and/or related problems and for whom the conventional sanctions available to the criminal justice system are inadequate. Domestic violence matters, for example, with their special offender supervision, coordination, and follow-up needs, and the multiple ramifications that these cases often generate for the "system" (custody, support, medical, housing, etc.) are considered particularly appropriate for the drug court approach. Many jurisdictions are also looking to the drug court "model" to apply to the high volume of "quality of life" crimes (ordinance violations, loitering, etc.) which, although less serious in terms of criminal sanction, can seriously erode the life of many communities.

The drug court experience is evolving daily, from both a national perspective and the local perspectives of the 575+ communities in which drug court activity is underway or being planned. While the full impact of drug courts probably will not be evident for some time, the experience of the first decade demonstrates the remarkable achievements drug courts have spurred in all segments of the justice system and the community. While we may not have a definitive assessment of drug court impact over the long term, the short-term impact is significant and touches many segments of the community: public safety, criminal activity, drug use, public health, child welfare, employment, education, to name a few. Unequivocally, judges involved with drug court programs during this first decade maintain that the drug court approach is far more effective than the traditional criminal case process for the signifi-cant number of offenders who seriously desire to address their substance addiction and turn their lives around. Most of the judges who take this position have been dealing with criminal caseloads for many years, and many of them are former prosecutors.

Notes

1. U.S. Dept. of Justice, National Institute of Justice. *1997 Drug Use Forecasting: Annual Report on Adult and Juvenile Arrestees. 1997.*

2. See also *Corrections Facts at a Glance: Criminal Offender Statistics, 1997.* U.S. Dept. of Justice, Bureau of Justice Statistics.

3. U.S. Dept. of Justice, Bureau of Justice Statistics. *Special Report: Substance Abuse and Treatment: State and Federal Prisoners, 1997.* 1999.

4. State Justice Institute. 1995 National Symposium on the Implementation and Operation of Drug Courts. *Drug Courts: Participant Comments.* OJP Drug Court Clearinghouse and Technical Assistance Project at American University. *1997 Drug Court Survey: Participant Perspectives.*

5. Police Foundation and Drug Strategies. *Drugs and Crime Across America: Police Chiefs Speak Out.* 1996.

Reprinted from: Drug Court Clearinghouse and Technical Assistance Project, *Looking at a Decade of Drug Courts* (revised 1999). Office of Justice Programs Drug Court Clearinghouse and Technical Assistance Project, American University, Washington, DC. Available at: <http://www.american.edu/justice/publications/decade1.htm> ✦

20
The Drug Court Scandal

Morris B. Hoffman

Drug courts are sweeping the country, a contagion fueled by federal grants and sparked by well-intentioned state and local trial judges frustrated by the lost war on drugs. These specialized courts are changing the criminal justice landscape in fundamental ways. They are affecting the arrest policies of officers on the street, the charging policies of prosecutors, and the very nature of the judicial function. They are changing the way judges deal with prosecutors, defense lawyers, defendants, and each other. They are increasing the already unhealthy interdependency of the judicial branch and the burgeoning cottage industry of private treatment providers. They are significantly altering the allocation of limited judicial resources. They are filling our state prisons with drug users, despite promising to do just the opposite. They are inviting comprehensive federal involvement, thereby risking comprehensive federal meddling, in the day-to-day operations of state and local courts. And they are doing all of this with nary an intellectual shot being fired.[1]

The scandal of America's drug courts is that we have rushed headlong into them—driven by politics, judicial psychopharmacology, fuzzy-headed notions about "restorative justice" and "therapeutic jurisprudence,"[2] and by the bureaucrats' universal fear of being the last on the block to have the latest administrative gimmick. We have embraced the drug court panacea without asking, let alone resolving, even the most basic of questions: What is the purpose of drug courts? Do drug courts work? Are the costs of drug courts, including their costs in de-individualized justice, worth their benefits? Should the sentencing philosophy of a single drug court judge or group of drug court judges be institutionalized?

Beyond these basic questions, we have yet to examine several shifts implicit in creating drug courts: Should judges be making drug policy simply because elected officials lack the political will to do so? Do we really want to stimulate the prosecution of low-level possession and sales cases to such a great degree that we fill our state prisons with those who cannot be treated successfully? Is it an efficient use of limited judicial resources to have drug court judges serving as glorified probation officers?

These are the kinds of hard, fundamental questions that, in a less hysterical environment, careful judges, careful court administrators, and, indeed, a careful body politic would insist on examining before committing to such a serious undertaking. They are questions we all should insist on asking before a single new drug court is created or a single existing one is continued. . . .

It is tempting to view drug courts as a magic solution to the ancient dilemma about drugs. Indeed, this temptation, fueled by an enormous injection of federal money, may have much to do with the great popularity of drug courts. I submit, however, that the drug court as a public policy solution to the drug dilemma is no solution at all, but rather a conflicted, and some would say cynical, appeasement of two powerful political forces—the law enforcement community and the treatment community.

If drug use is truly uncontrollable, then refusal to take advantage of treatment is also uncontrollable. Indeed, the treatment community teaches us that recovery is a continuing process of failures and successes. Yet, to appease the law enforcement community, drug courts typically impose an arbitrary number and quality of excusable failures before the drug defendant is treated like any other criminal defendant and sentenced accordingly. If drug addiction is truly a disease

that manifests itself in uncontrollable behavior until treated, why is the criminal law
involved at all as a backup to failed treatment? Do we give cancer patients three tries
at chemotherapy before sending them to the
penitentiary? Or, perhaps more analogously,
do we give insane criminal defendants three
tries at being cured before we forget about
the requirement of *mens rea* and move them
from the state hospital to the state penitentiary? I suggest that the reason most of us are
against the outright legalization of all drugs
is that we do not really believe, with the kind
of breadth and depth required of such matters, that much, if any, drug use is really the
involuntary product of a disease mechanism.

Even if we believe some drug use is involuntary, why not at least make efforts to separate those few who may really be diseased
from those who simply choose to take drugs?
I suspect the answer is that we recognize the
complex and fundamentally intractable
problem of separating voluntary from involuntary drug use. At what point does the mere
desire to disengage from life's pains by taking drugs become an uncontrollable compulsion? Despite all of our modern bluster
about how much is known about the biological bases of addiction, the answer to this fundamental moral question is unknown, and
might be unknowable. For all its weaknesses
as the precursor to the disease model of addiction, at least the Alcoholics Anonymous
model recognized this central moral component to addiction.

Drug courts, whatever their benefits, do
not serve this function of moral screening.
On the contrary, their unstated central assumption is that modern treatment modali-
ties are so effective that if a defendant fails
them three or four times, it must be the defendant's "fault," and that particular defendant therefore must be one of those "volunteer" addicts against whom the sword of the
criminal law may morally swathe and not a
truly "diseased" addict. We compassionate
judges can then sentence that defendant to
prison, smug with the knowledge that our
experts, by the simple device of offering
treatment a certain arbitrary number of

times, can separate the diseased from the
criminal.

Everyone is satisfied, except the incorrigi-
ble drug user. We satisfy the experts because
they get paid for the failed treatment; we satisfy the law enforcement community because we take a hard approach to the
incorrigibles; and we satisfy our own internal sense of justice by reminding ourselves
that our experts have performed the
Solomonic miracle of separating out the diseased unintentional drug user from the
criminally intentional drug user.

But of course this whole approach is a
charade. Our treatment efforts are hardly so
effective that a mere three or four failures indicate some kind of intentional failing.[3] In
any event, a case can be made that if addiction is really a disease, then the most diseased defendants are precisely the defendants most likely to fail many, and perhaps
even all, treatment attempts. Drug courts
thus may be performing a kind of reverse
moral screening—those defendants who do
not respond to treatment, and therefore may
be the most diseased, go to prison, while
those defendants who respond well and
whose use of drugs truly may have been voluntary, escape prison.

This half-crime approach to drug use also
makes no sense at the crime end of the dis-
ease-crime axis. Once we have made the social decision that crack, for example, is such
an addictive, dangerous drug that smoking it
should be a crime, it makes little moral sense
to excuse that crime for a certain number of
times in order to try to treat it. We do not do
that with shoplifting or with sexual assault
on a child, despite the psychiatric labeling of
some extreme forms of those behaviors as
"diseases."[4] Instead, we have made the social
choice that shoplifting and sexual assaults
are behaviors that we simply will not tolerate, regardless of their etiology. Issues related to kleptomaniacal or pedophilial compulsion are left to be dealt with where they
should be—at sentencing. We should treat
drug crimes no differently.

By existing simply to appease two so dia-
metric and irreconcilable sets of principles,
drug courts are fundamentally unprincipled.
By simultaneously treating drug use as a

crime and as a disease, without coming to grips with the inherent contradictions of those two approaches, drug courts are not satisfying either the legitimate and compassionate interests of the treatment community or the legitimate and rational interests of the law enforcement community. They are, instead, simply enabling our continued national schizophrenia about drugs.

There is another philosophical problem with drug courts, related both to the doctrinal schizophrenia discussed above and to some of the institutional issues discussed below:[5] courts simply should not be in the business of forcing medical treatment on people convicted of crimes as a condition of a favorable sentence. They most certainly should not be in the business of forcing treatment on defendants who have not yet been convicted as a condition of being released on bond. Yet that is exactly what drug courts are all about.

One of the principal purposes of the judicial branch, and of all the procedural and evidentiary protections attached to that branch, is to insure that the force of the criminal law is wielded soberly. I sympathize with drug court proponents who see the filing of criminal charges as a special opportunity to "get the attention" of drug users and intervene meaningfully in their lives. Of course, it is precisely because drug defendants face the wrath of the criminal law that we may be in the best position to "get their attention" and force treatment that will benefit everyone if it is successful. But we are judges, not social workers or psychiatrists. We administer the criminal law because the criminal law is its own social end. It is not, or at least ought not be, a means to other social ends. . . .

In a jurisprudential context, these battles are part of a larger war about so-called "restorative justice," or what some commentators have called "therapeutic jurisprudence."[6] These ideas emanate from the proposition that the judiciary can be a powerful force for social change, not just in the traditional way of applying the law in individual cases, or even by pushing the existing law to new enlightened boundaries, but by actively intervening in the day-to-day lives of litigants in an infinite variety of non-traditional ways.[7] A full discussion of these broad and controversial ideas is beyond the scope of this Commentary. Suffice it to say that, if they are intended to free judges not only from the constraints of the separation-of-powers doctrine but even from the limits of our own expertise, they are dangerous ideas indeed. I cannot imagine a more dangerous branch than an unrestrained judiciary full of amateur psychiatrists poised to "do good" rather than to apply the law.[8]

Unexamined Effectiveness: Do Drug Courts Work?

Perhaps the most startling thing about the drug court phenomenon is that drug courts have so quickly become fixtures of our jurisprudence in the absence of satisfying empirical evidence that they actually work. Although many studies and many kinds of studies have examined drug courts, none has demonstrated with any degree of reliability that drug courts work.

There are three kinds of drug court studies.[9] The most common evaluate operational processes and deal with statistics like filings, drop-out rates, and other data shedding light on the actual drug court process.[10] The second type of study is the cost-savings analysis, which aims to compare the operational and sentencing costs of drug courts to the operational and sentencing costs of traditional courts.[11] The third, and for our purposes the most meaningful, studies have been the so-called "impact evaluations," which attempt in some fashion to assess the impact of drug courts, most often by comparing recidivism rates between some drug court population and some non-drug court population.[12]

Impact evaluations have taken three forms: (1) informal surveys of a single drug court conducted by that drug court's personnel;[13] (2) formal studies of a single drug court conducted by outside professionals, but commissioned by that particular drug court; and (3) formal studies of one or more drug courts conducted by outside professionals and not commissioned by the drug courts being studied, though often funded by the federal Drug Courts Program Office. The informal impact surveys done by drug court personnel typically make outlandish and unsupportable claims of massive reductions in recidivism rates. The formal studies—both commissioned and noncommissioned—provide quite different and rather mixed results. Most have concluded that drug courts are effective in speeding drug cases through the system, but that drug courts have only a marginal impact, if any, in reducing recidivism. . . .

Formal Impact Studies

There also have been dozens of formal, academic studies of drug court effectiveness. These studies range from independent national studies covering many different jurisdictions to studies of individual drug courts commissioned by the very drug court to be studied. Most of these studies, although considerably more formal than informal surveys, are not published in peer-reviewed or other professional journals.[14] Despite the dozens of formal studies, and despite congressional directives in the mid-1990s for more comprehensive and meaningful impact studies,[15] only a handful have made the proper comparison between all drug court defendants—rather than only drug court graduates—and all traditional drug defendants. The recidivism results in that handful of studies are substantially less promising than the wild claims regularly made in informal surveys, as the following summary of those studies illustrates.

1991 American Bar Association Study. The American Bar Association (ABA) sponsored the first significant independent study of drug court effectiveness and published it in 1991.[16] This study examined four urban drug courts:(1) Cook County (Chicago), Illinois; (2) Milwaukee; (3) Philadelphia; and (4) Dade County (Miami), Florida. The first three are DCM-based models, and, of course, Dade County is treatment-based.

Not surprisingly, the ABA study found that the DCM-based courts achieved significant reductions in case-processing times, but no reductions in recidivism. The ABA study also concluded that the savings in case-processing time could be achieved without isolating drug cases. In other words, the study found that because it is how the

drug case is managed rather than *where* it is managed, the benefits of DCM-based drug courts can be achieved without having special drug courts, simply by identifying drug cases (or any cases, for that matter) and managing them accordingly.

The most significant, and troubling, finding of the ABA study was that the Dade County treatment-based drug court was no more effective than traditional courts in reducing arrest recidivism. It found that over a one-year follow-up period drug court defendants suffered a 32 percent recidivism rate compared to the 33 percent recidivism rate suffered by drug defendants before implementation of the drug court.[17]

The ABA study also confirmed the suspicions of many prosecutorial critics of the drug court experiment: drug courts result in more lenient sentences.[18] In theory, neither treatment-based drug courts nor DCM-based drug courts should have any impact on the lengths of sentences that defendants eventually receive. Treatment-based drug courts should involve fewer defendants receiving jail or prison time, and the time they do receive may be dribbled out at the front end in the form of short jail stays for violating bond or probation conditions.[19] But for drug court defendants who violate their probations and eventually are sentenced, the fact that they came through a treatment-based drug court ought to have no bearing on the length of the sentences they ultimately receive. DCM-based drug courts also should have no impact on sentencing. They are just traditional courts processing drug cases in an accelerated fashion. Yet the 1991 ABA study found that both in Cook County and Philadelphia, quicker dispositions resulted in reductions in the average length of prison sentences.[20]

1994 Maricopa County Study. The impact study of the Maricopa County (Phoenix), Arizona, drug court compared traditional court drug defendants given probation to drug court defendants over a thirty-six month follow-up period. Because the Maricopa County Drug Court is post-adjudicative, and because the control group was therefore limited to probationers, the Maricopa County study arguably understates the traditional recidivism rate.[21] Even so, the results were moderately more encouraging than the 1991 ABA study: 43.7 percent traditional court recidivism versus 33.1 percent drug court recidivism.[22]

1994 Dade County Study. In 1994, evaluators studied the Dade County Drug Court a second time to see if they could improve on the dismal results from the 1991 ABA Study.[23] Over an eighteen-month follow-up period, traditional recidivism was measured at 48.7 percent, compared to drug court recidivism measured at 33.2 percent.[24] There was, however, a remarkable, and unaccounted for, difference in failure-to-report rates—with drug court defendants failing to report 52 percent of the time, compared to 9 percent for drug defendants in traditional courts.[25] More significantly, the target groups were not randomly assigned.[26]

1996 Baltimore Study. Evaluators examined both the county and district drug courts in Baltimore, using a very short follow-up period of six months. They reported modest drops in recidivism in both courts: from 27.1 percent to 22.6 percent in district court, and from 30.4 percent to 26.5 percent in county court.[27] The short time period used for this study significantly decreases its reliability.[28] . . .

Post-1996 Studies: The General Accounting Office and Belenko Meta-Studies. Since the time of the [1997] Sherman Report, only six additional impact studies have been conducted. Like the previous research, the studies had quite mixed results, ranging from huge drops in recidivism rates reported out of the drug court in Riverside, California, (33 percent to 13 percent)[29] to statistically insignificant differences reported out of the drug court in Denver (58 percent to 53 percent).[30]

In addition to evaluations of particular drug courts or groups of drug courts, the literature is becoming increasingly filled with so-called "meta-studies"—studies of drug court studies. The most significant meta-study to date is probably the one delivered to Congress in July 1997 by the United States General Accounting Office (GAO).[31] The GAO report is based on twenty evaluations done through March 1997, covering sixteen different drug courts. After expressing several concerns about the design and scope of many of the evaluations,[32] the GAO concluded that there was insufficient data and research to definitively determine whether drug courts were effective in reducing recidivism and drug relapse.[33]

One of the most recent meta-studies of which I am aware is Steven Belenko's June 1998 review of thirty evaluations representing twenty-four different drug courts.[34] The Belenko study is by far the most optimistic meta-study done to date. But even Belenko concedes that most drug court evaluators continue to target drug court graduates instead of all drug court participants, that only a few studies have tracked recidivism for more than a one-year follow-up period, and that only two of the studies used a random method of identifying target drug court defendants.[35]

Treatment-based drug courts have been in existence now for eleven years—more than enough time to generate reliable data on the $64,000 question of whether they work. Despite an enormous reservoir of data, enormous federal financial incentives to prove effectiveness, and an express congressional directive to undertake meaningful effectiveness studies, the evidence on drug court effectiveness remains breathtakingly weak.[36]

. . . The post-pilot burden should now be squarely on the proponents of drug courts to demonstrate their effectiveness in reducing recidivism. So far, they have failed to meet that burden, and on that basis alone we should consider abandoning the experiment. But drug courts not only do no demonstrable good, I believe there are cogent arguments that they are inflicting serious injuries to the institution of the judiciary and to the way in which that institution relates to the other two branches of government.

Unexamined Operational Concerns: How Do Drug Courts Really Work, and What Impact Are They Having on the Rest of the Judicial System?

Having witnessed the birth and development of the Denver Drug Court firsthand,[37] I also have witnessed firsthand a whole series of what I will loosely call operational problems. I do not know whether these problems are anything but anecdotal, because the self-generated literature in this area, as discussed above, tends not to be very soul-searching.[38] Nevertheless, I suspect that several of these problems are so systemic in nature that they are likely to crop up, and likely have cropped up, in many jurisdictions. . . .

The Popcorn Effect

In Denver, we grossly underestimated the enthusiasm with which our police and prosecutors would embrace the idea of the drug court. As a result, our projections of the number of drug filings in the new drug court were woefully understated.[39] We expected that the drug court would stimulate some modest increases in the number of drug filings, but instead of modest increases, we got massive increases. Filings nearly tripled after the drug court's first full year and have remained at that many-fold level since.

There were 1,047 drug cases filed in the Denver District Court in 1993, the last full year before implementation of the drug court.[40] In 1995, the first full year of the drug court, that number jumped to 2,661.[41] The following year, drug filings increased to 3,017.[42]

This increase in drug filings was not merely a reflection of an overall increase in criminal filings. On the contrary, from the moment the drug court was created, the percentage of drug cases filed in our court has exploded. In 1993, the first full year before the drug court, drug filings represented 28.6 percent of all criminal filings.[43] In 1995, the first full year after the drug court, that percentage skyrocketed to 51.5 percent and has remained at that high level.[44]

It is clear that there is a significant feedback phenomenon going on between the arrest and prosecution end of the process on the one hand and the adjudicatory end on the other hand. The very presence of the drug court, with its significantly increased capacity for processing cases, has caused police to make arrests in, and prosecutors to file, the kinds of ten-and twenty-dollar hand-to-hand drug cases that the system simply would not have bothered with before, certainly not as felonies. It is not just a matter of intensifying existing arrest and charging policies; since the adoption of the drug court, the Denver police have engaged in an extensive unprecedented campaign of undercover "buy-bust" operations.[45]

This is not at all to say that these cases are not deserving of felony prosecution, or even that efforts focused on these low-level possession cases are not paying larger social dividends in terms of cleaning up our streets.[46] Nevertheless, it is clear that the mere presence of the Denver Drug Court has stimulated a demand that will probably always outpace our capacity to deal with it. This popcorn effect—called "net widening" in some of the literature—is a well-recognized phenomenon whenever law enforcement resources are targeted at designated kinds of cases:

> [A] number of 1970s-era reform efforts [have] followed this pattern: Legislatures created a low-cost case-processing mechanism with the idea of diverting some offenders from the more expensive prison system; prosecutors then used the low-cost mechanism not to reallocate existing categories of cases (as intended), but to add new cases to the system—to widen the system's net.[47]

The popcorn effect caused by the Denver Drug Court has had a real and deleterious impact on our bench, both in and out of the drug court itself.

The sheer number of defendants run through the drug court mill every day is taking an enormous toll on the drug court judge, the drug court staff, sheriffs, prosecutors, and public defenders. In 1997 and 1998, there were an average of ninety-one defendants on the drug court docket each day, with a high of 140 per day in January 1997 and a low of about eighty-eight per day in April 1998.[48] By contrast, non-drug court felony courtrooms in Denver handle an average of eight to twelve defendants per day.[49] Even our county and municipal courts do not see daily numbers anywhere approaching the numbers seen in the drug court.[50]

Except for its Herculean founder, no judge has been able to remain in the Denver Drug

Court for more than one year, and even then it has been necessary for them to take regular and substantial breaks. The stresses on staff are just as bad. At the time of this writing, in an effort to avoid burnout by drug court judges and their staffs, our court is considering a formal rotation system of substitute drug court judges to relieve the drug court judge at regular intervals throughout the year.

It seems to me that no judge, and no judge's staff, should be expected to deal effectively with the kinds of numbers we are seeing. Pretending that they can will only lead to demoralized and ineffective drug courts.[51]

. . . The popcorn effect also has affected the rest of us on the Denver District Court. When the drug court was first approved, the idea was that other judges on our bench would assist in handling drug court trials when the drug court needed that assistance. But before the ink was dry on the drug court's formation, it became clear that the enormous number of drug filings would make it necessary for all drug trials to be tried outside of drug court. A similar, though slower developing, result has occurred with respect to motions. By the end of 1998, the lion's share of all drug court motions also were being heard outside of the drug court. Although the 1999 drug court judge was hopeful that the addition of a second magistrate would free him up to hear motions,[52] that has not been the case.[53]

In transferring drug court trials and motions hearings, resort is made first to other criminal courts. If no criminal courts are available, resort is made to the civil courts and then to the domestic courts. Thus, all divisions of the Denver District Court have been impacted by the drug court's inability to handle its own trials and motions.

As a result, the rest of us have less time to devote to our regular dockets, because we are doing all the drug court trials and many of the drug court motions hearings. I do not mean to suggest that we are all so overworked that we cannot occasionally devote some time to drug court matters, but the problem is a problem of institutional accountability and of sheer volume.

A drug court that neither conducts trials nor hears motions is not really a court,[54] and a drug court that is too busy to conduct trials or hear motions should suggest to us that there is something terribly wrong with the whole arrangement. Moreover, when we consider the broad question of whether drug courts are working—especially their speed in processing cases—we artificially inflate their efficiency if we ignore the fact that the most time-consuming and inefficient aspect of any true court—the job of conducting trials—is not even being performed in the drug court. All of us could process a lot more cases a lot faster if we did not have to bother with those troubling trials.

Nor is it a matter simply of the rest of us now trying the same number of drug cases we used to try before the drug court took them from us. Again, it is a matter of the popcorn effect. Because the drug court itself has stimulated a many-fold increase in the number of drug cases filed, there has been a corresponding increase in the number of drug trials, causing non-drug courts to try significantly more drug cases than they were trying before the adoption of the drug court.[55]

The impacts of the Denver Drug Court on the rest of this bench are not limited to the inconvenience of taking transfers of drug trials or motions hearings. The drug court's inability to do its own trials and motions has had a dramatic impact on the heretofore generous willingness of judges on this bench to accept transfers from other judges. We have a long tradition of helping each other out when one of us has more than one matter set to begin on the same day, and that tradition has always cut across criminal, civil, and domestic lines. We have kept statistics on these transfers, and, prior to drug court, our chief judges have always proudly announced with regularity that the likelihood of litigants in need being able to find a transfer court hovered around 80 percent.[56] Since the implementation of the drug court that number has plummeted, to roughly 50 percent.[57] As a result, both civil and criminal litigants in Denver are substantially more likely than they were five years ago to have their trials continued, simply because the drug court cannot handle its own docket.

The situation has gotten so bad that, as of mid-1999, drug cases are no longer even set for trial until the deadline for disposition passes. Then, they are simply assigned to one of the regular criminal courtrooms without waiting for a reluctant volunteer.[58]

These impacts on the colleagues of a drug court judge can be profound and are something that all judges should consider carefully before deciding whether to cross the drug court Rubicon.

Trying to Deal with the Popcorn Effect

Even after sloughing off all of its trials and most of its motions hearings, the Denver Drug Court still could not keep its head above the rising tide of filings. So other solutions were contemplated.

Two and one-half years after the drug court's inception, Judge John Coughlin, Bill Meyer's successor in the drug court, decided that the increased filings required a drastic cutback in the drug court's jurisdiction. In an attempt to reduce drug court cases by 25 percent, Judge Coughlin decided, effective February 18, 1997, to exclude from drug court all cases in which the defendant was either a two-time felon (and, therefore, under Colorado law, ineligible for probation without the district attorney's consent)[59] or was a non-citizen against whom there was an existing hold by the Immigration and Nationalization Service (INS). It appears that these cutbacks reduced drug court filings by approximately 25 percent,[60] and it also appears that these reductions have been permanent.[61] But the cutbacks were made only at the drug court level—by district attorneys filing the excluded cases in regular courtrooms rather than in drug court. No change was made at either the street level in terms of who was arrested or at the charging level in terms of who was prosecuted. The nets stayed wide, and 25 percent of the catch was thrown over to the traditional courts. So even though the drug court enjoyed a 25 percent reduction in filings, total drug filings continued to accelerate without any reduction, with there regular non-drug court courtrooms now bearing the brunt of 25 percent of the popcorn.

Moreover, trying to reach an arbitrary 25 percent reduction by slashing so broadly as to exclude all two-time felons and illegal aliens drastically changed the original "all-comers" philosophy of the Denver Drug Court. Every two-time felon is not an unacceptable drug court risk; indeed, before February 1997 two-time felons were regularly given drug court dispositions if they were otherwise deemed appropriate.[62] The original concept of the Denver Drug Court as an "all-comers" court, as is the case with a handful of other ambitious drug courts, was to reach the hardcore addict who, more often than not, has been through the revolving doors of prison on many other drug or drug-driven convictions, and who is therefore quite likely to have two or more prior felony convictions.[63] Excluding all two-time felons from drug courts in order to help achieve a 25 percent reduction in cases makes no more sense, and arguably makes considerably less sense given the goal of reaching hardcore addicts, than excluding people whose last names begin with letters from the first quarter of the alphabet. . . .

Exploding Prison Populations

One of the most disturbing aspects of the Denver Drug Court is that, despite the crucial reformist promise that drug courts will assist in reducing the numbers of people incarcerated for drug offenses, in Denver more drug defendants are being sentenced to prison than ever before, by a factor of more than two. In 1993—the last full year before the Denver Drug Court—265 drug defendants were sentenced to prison out of the entire Denver District Court, representing nearly 86 percent of the total number of defendants convicted of drug offenses that court in that year.[64] In 1995—the first full year after the Denver Drug Court—434 defendants received prison sentences in the Denver Drug Court, representing nearly 80 percent of all drug convictions in the Denver Drug Court that year.[65] In 1997, 625 drug court defendants received prison sentences, again representing roughly 80 percent of all drug convictions in the Denver Drug Court that year.[66] In other words, although the *percentage* of drug defendants receiving prison sentences has remained remarkably constant, both before and during the drug court era, the raw numbers of drug defendants going to prison has more than doubled.[67]

The apparent paradox of more drug defendants going to prison out of courts designed specifically to send fewer drug defendants to prison is not surprising at all. It is a direct and predictable consequence of dismal recidivism results coupled with massive net-widening. Although in theory drug courts should reduce the number of prison sentences meted out for drug offenses—both by the successful treatment of drug defendants and at the very least by delaying the imposition of prison sentences while defendants attempt to complete treatment—this theory assumes, quite incorrectly, that treatment will be moderately successful and that drug court dollars will be used to treat defendants already in the system rather than to triple the size of the intake.

Moreover, it is precisely because drug courts are designed to get defendants into treatment quickly that they accelerate the day on which the decision is made that treatment has failed and that defendants should go to prison. Drug court defendants are monitored closely and are given a finite number of relatively closely spaced opportunities to fail. When they exhaust all their chances, they go to prison. As a result, particularly with the poor recidivism results achieved by most drug courts, drug court defendants are, by the very nature of the process, more likely to end up in prison than their traditional cohorts and are certainly more likely to end up there sooner. . . .

Cookie Cutter Sentences

Another by-product of the popcorn effect is that drug court judges simply do not have the time to impose individualized sentences. Even if they did, the very presence of a fixed array of dispositional and treatment regimens begins to drive a one- or maybe three-size(s)-fit(s)-all philosophy. The dispositional algorithm in the Denver Drug Court, at least for defendants charged with simple possession, is fairly rigid: (1) if you have two or more prior felony convictions you do not even get into drug court;[68] (2) if

you have no prior felonies, and you were arrested with a small so-called "personal use" amount of drugs,[69] then you get a deferred judgment; (3) otherwise, you get probation.[70] This is not sentencing, it is triage.

Drug court proponents resist the charge of cookie cutter sentencing by protesting that a drug court judge has substantially more information about a defendant at sentencing than a traditional court usually has. It is true that a pre-sentence report in the Denver Drug Court has a whole host of detailed information about a defendant's drug use garnered during the pre-adjudicative phase of treatment—including specific levels of drugs in his system at regular intervals of time, his general reaction to the treatment regimen, and an expert's guesses about amenability to treatment—that traditional pre-sentence reports do not contain. But having detailed information is one thing; having the time and institutional inclination to use it to fashion individualized sentences is quite another. The drug court judge uses this information primarily to decide the dispositional track and treatment level in which to place the defendant. That is, this detailed individualized information is used simply to pick from a few different cookie cutters.

I do not fault drug court judges, prosecutors, or public defenders for falling into fixed sentencing algorithms. Much like traffic courts, drug courts simply do not have the time to spend on each defendant to fashion a sentence responsive to individual circumstances. Instead, we have a few pigeonholes into which we put defendants depending not on difficult issues like a defendant's character or the particular circumstances of a crime, but rather on objective and easily determined factors. In traffic court, we are forced by volume to look at easily measurable things like the defendant's driving record and how fast he was going. In drug court, we are forced by volume to look at easily measurable things like the number of prior felonies and the quantity and type of drugs used. In both kinds of courts, we then mete out sentences generally based only on those few variables and generally falling into only a few categories and ranges. The difference, of course, is that a defendant in traffic court faces modest penalties; a defendant in drug court faces a felony conviction and substantial incarceration.

This willingness to use the threat of prison as a club to induce treatment, and then to follow through on the threat when defendants dare not to respond to our enlightened treatment efforts, is one of the most tragic consequences of drug courts. In our unbridled enthusiasm to treat defendants, we focus all our energies and all our sentencing discretion on a single factor—a defendant's amenability to treatment. Then, when all the ebbs and flows of treatment are tallied up and labeled as an overall failure, which they are for a depressingly large percentage of all drug court defendants,[71] all of the failures are lumped together and the automatic prison machine kicks into gear. Deferred sentences are revoked, suspended sentences are reinstated and diverse drug defendants, who may share nothing but a common and entirely predictable failure to respond to treatment, are sent to prison with virtually no further judicial inquiry.

It is as if our dismal treatment efforts are clearing our consciences about sending drug users to prison. There is a certain tortured logic to this sort of "equal" treatment of incorrigibles, once one adopts the flawed drug court axiom that drug abuse is fundamentally a disease and not a crime, and therefore that when we sentence defendants to prison we are punishing them for their failed treatment rather than for their unlawful drug use. . . .

Changing Judges

I read with bemusement an announcement in a recent federal drug court publication that drug courts work so well and drug court judges are so satisfied at the good work they are accomplishing that "[m]any of the judges who have served as a 'drug court judge' have requested an extension of their assignment."[72] This certainly has not been the case in the Denver Drug Court. . . .

The annual rotation of drug court judges is particularly problematic when one considers that the judge and the regular three person staff (a division clerk, a reporter, and a bailiff or law clerk) are rotating into a permanent and, at least by individual courtroom standards, rather large sixteen-person drug court staff. This permanent staff consists of two magistrates,[73] one drug court coordinator, nine staff members in the drug court coordinator's office, and four permanent courtroom personnel.[74] This permanent bureaucracy is not only permanent in the sense that it remains in place as drug court judges come and go, but also permanent in the sense that the presiding drug court judge does not have the power to hire or fire its members. The drug court magistrates and drug court coordinator are hired and fired by the chief judge. The nine permanent staff members are hired and fired by the drug court coordinator. Thus, the at-will employment powers that district judges traditionally have enjoyed regarding the hiring and firing of our staff are substantially curtailed in drug court.

Quite apart from the fact that the drug court judge cannot hire or fire permanent staff, the presence of this large permanent bureaucracy presents a very different, and substantially more complex, organizational challenge than that faced by the traditional trial judge. The size alone is a problem. The drug court judge's division clerk, who is used to presiding over a three-person staff, is suddenly confronted with being the titular head of an eighteen-person bureaucracy. The permanence of that bureaucracy, particularly in the face of an annual parade of different presiding judges and division clerks, risks creating a sort of shadow court, not answerable to the particular temporary occupant of the drug court bench and resistant to an attempts by that temporary occupant to effect changes.

To be fair, it does not appear that the Denver Drug Court has suffered from this kind of bureaucratic inertia. On the contrary, the first few drug court judges have been quite willing and able to move the bureaucracy in significant directions, so much so that the way in which the drug court worked in the first few years has varied in significant respects from year to year.[75] Whether this flexibility will continue as the permanent staff becomes more entrenched remains to be seen. . . .

Unexamined Institutional Concerns: Should Judges Be Making These Fundamental Policy Decisions, and Should Their Talents Be Wasted Implementing Them?

There is a kind of institutional double-whammy to drug courts. On the one hand, their mere adoption trumps a whole array of deep and difficult public policy questions that judges have no business trumping. On the other hand, their implementation forces judges to engage in day-to-day work for which they are not suited.

Separation of Powers

There is no better measure of the institutional impropriety of drug courts than their own proponents' expressed ideas about their purpose. The chief district attorney assigned to the Denver Drug Court put it as bluntly as anyone by explaining that the purpose of drug courts is "the cost-effective curtailment of drug abuse."[76] I respectfully submit that no court's "purpose" should be to curtail a perceived social problem, no matter how lofty the curtailers' motives or how scurrilous the perceived problem. Our function is to ensure that the rule of law is justly enforced. The job of curtailing a particular crime, or of achieving any other particular social end, is a legislative and executive function, not a judicial one. Only the legislative and executive branches have the imprimatur of public consensus. Judges, no matter the strength nor even the accuracy of our views about policy, have no right to make policy. Yet drug courts are the living embodiment of judge-created policy.

There is a palpable, day-to-day face to this unholy drug court alliance between the branches of government. The entire drug court milieu is constructed as a single, unified institutional response to the problem of drugs. Prosecutors, defense lawyers, and judges are meant to meld together as a kind of single public service institution designed to do what is best for drug defendants, or

"clients," as they are referred to in the drug court new-speak. Indeed, it is *de rigeur* that drug courts cannot operate successfully without the "cooperation" of the judge, prosecutors, police, sheriffs, and defense lawyers. The very instant this "cooperation" is achieved, the protections inherent in the adversary nature of our system are put at risk.[77]

In the Denver District Court, this unholy alliance has evolved into a daily ritual, euphemistically called "staffing." At these staffing sessions, the judge, prosecutor, public defender, probation officers, and sometimes a staff person from the drug court coordinator's office meet together in chambers to discuss all of that day's dispositional, sentencing, and revocation hearings. The judge, after hearing from everyone, reaches a presumptive decision. Defendants are not present and the staffing meetings are not on the record. Quite apart from obvious constitutional concerns,[78] these staffing sessions symbolize what is wrong with the drug court institution: substantive decisions about a felony defendant are being made by some inter-branch committee acting more like a support group than a court.

It is one thing for defendants facing a few days or weeks in county jail for drunk driving or misdemeanor domestic violence to be confronted by an alliance of prosecutors, defense lawyers, and judges unified in an effort to re-educate and treat them. But it is quite another thing when the defendants face felony charges that can put them in the penitentiary for decades. We may be willing to sacrifice age-old traditions of judicial independence and adversariness for the former, but should not be for the latter. If we are going to continue to treat some drug use as a felony, punishable by many years in prison, then we should treat drug cases seriously—not like parking tickets in a mill in which the judge, prosecutor, and defense lawyer spend their days together trying to push as many people through as possible.

Impinging on the Legislative Function. Drug courts are an attempt to answer one of the most beguiling public policy questions of our time, indeed of any time. Their very existence represents a policy determination that involuntary treatment efforts should be undertaken, at least for some defendants,[79] before the full fury of the criminal law is unleashed. Not only does the exasperating question of drug policy contain within it a whole host of difficult scientific, legal, and cultural sub-issues, but the drug court solution raises as many public policy issues as it purports to answer. Regardless of one's position on complex issues like the scope of the drug problem, the disease theory of addiction, or the legalization of some drugs, surely these are public policy questions that must be answered by elected lawmakers after open and vigorous public debate, not by judges operating in the cloak of pseudoscience. Rather than restraining themselves until public consensus congeals on these terribly important and difficult policy issues, many drug court proponents seem to relish their role as courageous truth merchants stepping into a void left by frightened legislators unwilling to take the tough political stands necessary to deal with this issue. I cannot imagine a more elitist, institutionally tone-deaf, or dangerous expansion of the judicial function.

There are two possible responses to this institutional criticism: Congress itself has given its legislative blessing to drug courts, and drug courts are not exercising any powers—bond with conditions, deferred judgments, or probation with conditions—that traditional courts do not already have. These responses are disingenuous.

Neither Congress nor any state legislature of which I am aware has altered any substantive drug laws in their rush to appropriate money for drug courts. Appropriating money to one branch so that that branch may usurp the legislative function does nothing to cure the separation-of-powers problem. It is precisely because drug courts raise such touchy public policy questions in such an ultimately ambiguous way that the legislative branch is so keen on passing the bucks, literally, to them.

Moreover, drug courts are not simply using the traditional powers of bond conditions, deferred judgment, and probation conditions. They are using these traditional judicial powers in a way that is not only nontraditional, but in fact not even judicial. The very purpose of the drug court is not to resolve criminal liability, but to use the threat of criminal liability to coerce defendants into treatment. Again, maybe this approach is entirely sensible, but it is still an approach that is fundamentally legislative. If it is such a good idea, Congress and state legislatures should redefine the crime of drug use to be use plus a failure to take advantage of a certain number and quality of treatment opportunities. They have not done so because there is no public consensus for such an approach.

Impinging on the Executive Function. Providing medical treatment to persons convicted of crimes, or even to persons in custody awaiting trial, is an executive function, not a judicial one. By mechanically imposing treatment conditions on all criminal defendants before they have even entered a plea, drug courts blur the fundamental distinction between the accused and the convicted, and therefore between the judicial function of determining guilt and the executive function of carrying out sentences and treating prisoners.

Courts—whose very function is to determine whether the State has met its burden of proving whether any criminal conduct has occurred—are an entirely inappropriate forum to be focusing on whether defendants have been "cured" of their addictions and whether for that reason punishment should not be imposed. We are trained as judges and lawyers to apply the rules of procedure and evidence to adversarial proceedings. The product of those proceedings should be a verdict about guilt or liability, not whether Joe Smith should be treated at Acme House or Metropolis Hospital.

This critique does not simply rest on judges being untrained in these areas or their judicial talents being wasted, though it certainly includes these concerns;[80] it is a matter of defining the judicial function. We are the third branch of government and are given sobering powers designed to protect citizens not only from one another, but also from the abuses of the other two branches. We ought not become robed therapeutic administrators just because we have convinced ourselves we are acting for the public good.

If we are truly serious about treatment, sufficient resources could and should be directed to the executive branch's corrections facilities—at both the pre-conviction (county jail) and post-conviction (state prison) levels. That is where the push for treatment—voluntary and semi-voluntary—belongs. Mark Kleiman, whose work on "coerced abstinence" is often cited in support of the drug court notion that drug use must be detected early and punished quickly, actually focused his ideas as much on parole conditions as probation conditions.[81] In other words, treatment and punishment should not be viewed as mutually exclusive weapons in the war against drugs. If we continue to believe that possession of some drugs is serious enough to warrant incarceration, then that incarceration should be imposed without further therapeutic hand-wringing, but it should be coupled with intense drug treatment programs in jail or prison and with Draconian parole conditions. Parole eligibility and the threat of parole revocation can serve an important and entirely appropriate coercive role in giving inmates and parolees an incentive to take part in treatment programs after they have been found by judges to be deserving of some punishment.

I realize that prison is exactly what well-intentioned drug court proponents want drug defendants to avoid, but that just gets us back into the crime-disease soup. Besides, as discussed above, drug courts are very likely sending more drug users to prison than ever before.[82] I also realize that there may be substance to the drug court mantra that early intervention is better than late intervention, but that proposition is not without constitutional, institutional, and common-sense limits.[83]

In addition to impinging on the corrections function of the executive branch, drug courts tread on, and in large measure demolish, the traditional executive functions of the prosecutor. It is a time-honored and jealously guarded right of prosecutors to decide whether to offer a particular defendant a plea bargain and what bargain to offer.[84] In drug courts, that powerful and sobering prosecutorial power is reduced to a few different sizes of cookie cutter pleas.[85] The decision of whether to offer any plea bargain at all—and even the decision about what particular cookie cutter to use—is driven entirely by a few objective criteria, not by the exercise of any meaningful prosecutorial discretion.[86] The very reason drug courts need prosecutors to "get on board" is that by doing so prosecutors are abdicating their prosecutorial discretion to this amorphous multi-branch thing we call "drug court."[87] Even if prosecutors retain theoretical control over their power to offer dispositions, the sheer volume and pace of drug court renders that theoretical control functionally meaningless. Prosecutors are no more able to make intelligent charging and dispositional decisions in an unmanageable ocean of cases than judges are able to make intelligent dispositional and sentencing decisions.[88]

Federal Intrusion. Drug courts provide the federal government with an attractive vehicle through which to interfere unduly with the traditional role of state and local governments in dealing with crime. It is not much a case of blatant federal interference[89] as a matter of indirect influences exerted through the lure of federal dollars. We have already seen this phenomenon at work. As a condition of obtaining federal drug court funds, newly proposed drug courts are now encouraged to meet a host of design and implementation criteria set by Department of Justice bureaucrats in Washington.[90]

Drug courts—born in the laboratories of individual states and municipalities—have become increasingly federalized and homogenized. It is a dangerously short distance from the federal government telling us what our drug courts must look like to telling us how they should be operated.[91]

Intra-Branch Problems

Even as a matter within the judiciary, and ignoring the extent to which they usurp the legislative and executive functions and invite federal intrusion, drug courts present daunting institutional problems. They turn judges into glorified probation officers and institutionalize a single judge's sentencing philosophy.

Glorified Probation Officers. Drug court judges spend much of their time doing things that could and should be done by probation officers. I do not mean this criticism to denigrate the efforts of probation officers or to overvalue the efforts of judges. On the contrary, our roles have become muddled in drug court not because judges have stepped into a vacuum created by incompetent probation officers, but rather because the very purpose of drug courts is to blend the adjudicative and probationary functions.[92] It is a blending that not only violates basic notions of adversariness, but one that makes no practical organizational sense.

Probation officers are trained, and in my experience most are very skilled, in performing all of the challenging probation functions that we demand of them, even though we generally refuse to give them the necessary resources. Drug courts have crowned the drug court judge as a kind of chief probation officer, one with direct probationary responsibility over thousands of defendants rather than with supervisory responsibility over dozens of other probation officers. This kind of probationary micro-management makes no organizational sense whatsoever, even ignoring the fact that the crowned chief probation officer is by definition an amateur.

I recognize that it is an article of faith central to drug courts that defendants pay more attention to a judge telling them, in a courtroom, what they must do to avoid imprisonment than they do to a probation officer telling them the same thing over the telephone or in a probation office or home visit. A related article of faith is that a hands-on approach by judges gives them a working knowledge of each defendant, which becomes invaluable in making decisions about that specific defendant. With all due respect to the drug court believers, the sheer volume of defendants pushed through the drug court mill each day—not to mention dismal recidivism benefits—belies these articles of faith.

Judges would have to be blessed with photographic memories, or egos bordering on narcissism, to believe they have a working knowledge of the thousands of defendants who appear in drug court each month. Conversely, drug defendants no doubt are keenly aware of the irony that a single drug court judge is even less able to retain a hands-on knowledge of the thousands of defendants in the system than a probation officer is able to maintain a hands-on knowledge of hundreds of defendants.

Proponents respond, correctly, that the drug court system as a whole keeps much closer track of defendants than traditional courts do.[93] I submit, however, that that success has more to do with the enormous probation resources poured into drug courts than the ethereal and, I must say, self-important notion that defendants pay more attention to judges than to probation officers. I suspect that traditional courts had the probation resources of drug courts they could be just as effective in keeping track of defendants and just as ineffective in reducing recidivism.[94]

Even if there were an inherent value in a judge, rather than a probation officer, performing probation functions in drug court, we must all recognize that we pay an institutional price for that added value. Judges, trained in the nuances of procedure, evidence, and substantive law and allegedly appointed for their intellectual abilities as well as their sense of proportion, compassion, and justice, spend much of their day in drug court looking at urine sample results and how many days of jail time to impose on the reluctant patient. Is this really the kind of work the judicial branch wants its judges doing? Is it really the kind of work most judges want to be doing?[95]

Institutionalizing a Single Judge's Sentencing Philosophy. There are many reasons we do not ordinarily organize our multi-judge criminal courts so that we have specialized burglary judges, sexual assault judges, or forgery judges, and one of the most compelling of these reasons is to avoid enshrining a single judge's sentencing philosophy.[96] The act of sentencing a defendant is a complex event, in which many factors are brought to bear and filtered through a particular judge's persona. It is an intensely personal act. Not only are some judges harsher sentencers in general than others, but many judges, consciously or unconsciously, develop sentencing patterns that vary by type of crime or by sentencing alternative. Some judges treat so-called white-collar crimes much more harshly than do others, but treat drug crimes much less harshly. Some of us believe drug dealers, as opposed to drug users, should almost always go to prison; some of us recognize many drug dealers deal in order to make money to use drugs. Some of us are more enamored than others of probation or other alternatives to prison, such as community corrections. Some of us often impose short county jail sentences as conditions of probation; others seldom do.

Of course, these differences result in inconsistent sentences on an individual judge-by-judge and defendant-by-defendant basis. By continuing to give judges some meaningful sentencing discretion, most state legislatures have made the judgment that sentencing inconsistency is a price worth paying for a system that, at least in theory, has the capacity to make individual adjustments when necessary in order to achieve a just result. Within limits, one person's sentencing inconsistency is another's justice.

I believe that an important feature of the awesome sentencing power with which we are invested is to spread around the sentencing duties in multi-judge courts—either by ensuring that all judges do all kinds of cases (the integrated approach) or, in specialized courts, by ensuring that judges regularly rotate from one specialty to another. Otherwise, our gain in sentencing consistency is paid for with an unacceptable concentration of sentencing power in a single judge.

Drug courts are the worst of both of these worlds. They fix a single judge's sentencing philosophy for a long period of time, and then the entire bureaucracy must adjust to a new sentencing philosophy when the drug court judge changes. It is true that traditional courts face this same challenge whenever there is a change of judge. But the problem is exacerbated in drug courts, not only because the judges may tend to change frequently and may tend to get burnt out quickly,[97] but more importantly because drug courts, unlike most other felony-level criminal courts, occupy an entire criminal field. For the whole period that Judge Jones sits on the Metropolis Drug Court, every criminal defendant charged with a drug crime in Metropolis faces Judge Jones and is subjected to Judge Jones's particular sentencing philosophy. This arrangement is a dangerous concentration of judicial power, and one that, in any other context, most multiple-judge courts are specifically designed to avoid.

Moreover, judicial power is, by its very nature, more sharply exercised in drug courts than in traditional courts. The purpose of drug courts is to coerce treatment, and drug court judges are the chief coercers. Their powers are not only grounded in the inherently intrusive act of forcing people to undergo certain kinds of quasi-medical treatment, but those powers are brought to bear much more frequently than in traditional courts. Drug court judges are, and are meant to be, a regular and unpleasant force in the daily lives of drug court defendants. As a consequence, the particular sentencing peccadilloes of any given judge are much more likely to express themselves in drug court than in traditional court.

Conclusion

We have succumbed to the lure of drug courts, to the lure of their federal dollars, to the lure of their hope, and to the lure of their popularity. Drug courts themselves have become a kind of institutional narcotic upon which the entire criminal justice system is becoming increasingly dependent. Our police and prosecutors cannot give them up because they see in them the magic promise of an end to a drug-tolerant culture, not to mention the somewhat less magical political allure of skyrocketing rates of arrest, prosecution, and imprisonment. Our treatment community cannot give them up because they see in them the magic promise of a world in which drug addiction is treated instead of punished—and the somewhat less magical economic allure of millions of treatment dollars. Judges and politicians cannot give them up because they see in them the magic promise of finally being able to reconcile these two irreconcilable views about drugs.

As with drugs themselves, however, the promises of drug courts do not measure up to their harsh reality. They are compromising deep-seated legal values, including the doctrine of separation of powers, the idea that truth is best discovered in the fires of advocacy, and the traditional role of judges as quiet, rational arbiters of the truth-finding process. In their mad rush to dispose of cases, drug courts are risking the due process rights of defendants and turning all of us—judges, staff, prosecutors, and public defenders alike—into cogs in an out-of-control case-processing machine.

And what have they delivered in exchange? Reductions in recidivism are so small that if they exist at all they are statistically meaningless. Net-widening is so large that, even if drug courts truly were effective in reducing recidivism, more drug defendants would continue to jam our prisons than ever before.

It is time for all of us to take a much harder look at drug courts, at their awkward placement straddled among the three branches, at their true effectiveness, and at their real operational and institutional costs. It is time, especially for judges, to resist the lemming-like dash toward a society in which bedrock legal principles that have served us for generations are sacrificed for the immediate gratification of the latest political fad.

In his wonderfully balanced and insightful book, *Against Excess: Drug Policy for Results*, Mark Kleiman summarizes the extremism that has come to dominate the public policy debate about drugs:

> A spirit of fanaticism is evident in much of what is now done publicly and privately to combat the menace of drug abuse: more and more extreme efforts with less and less clarity about why they are undertaken or what benefits they are expected to produce. Reporters scurry around, writing stories on the panacea-of-the-month: using the army, random drug testing, legalization, the death penalty for drug dealers, boot camps, getting tough with source countries, treatment on demand.[98]

I am afraid that drug courts are the latest panacea-of-the-month, that judges are be-coming the latest conscripts in the failed war on drugs, and that the fanatic popularity of drug courts does not reflect their potential value as one small tool in an attempt to cope with an extremely complex problem, but just the latest in a long history of thoughtless excesses. An observation Mark Kleiman made at the beginning of his book is particularly apropos to drug courts, and particularly to the Chicken Soup aspects of our mad dash to them: "Fanaticism consists of redoubling your efforts when you have lost sight of your aim."[99] We should spend less time feeding the fanaticism of drug courts and more time in an honest debate about the deep moral and social issues inherent in drug use, drug abuse, and drug control.

Notes

1. Despite the fact that hundreds of drug courts have spread to jurisdictions all over the United States and hundreds more are scheduled to spread . . . they have been the object of almost no serious legal scholarship. Bar journals, judicial journals, and, to a lesser extent, law reviews are filled with short articles about drug courts, usually about recently adopted drug courts and often written by the judges who founded the courts. *See, eg.,* Susan Gochros, *Hawaii Drug Court, Ho 'Ola Hou (Renewed Life),* RAW. B.J., Mar. 1998, at 32 passim; Judge Stephen L. Henriod, *Drug Court in the Third District,* UTAH B.J., Aug. 1997, at 35 *passim;* Hon. William D. Hunter, *Drug Treatment Courts: An Innovative Approach to the Drug Problem in Louisiana,* 44 LA. B.J. 418 passim (1997); Judith S. Kaye, *Special Report: The State of the Judiciary,* N.Y. ST. B.J., May/June 1998, at 50 *passim;* Claire McCaskill, *Combat Drug Court: An Innovative Approach to Dealing with Drug Abusing First Time Offenders,* 66 UMKC L. REV. 493 *passim* (1998); Hon. Sheila M. Murphy, *Drug Courts: An Effective, Efficient Weapon in the War on Drugs,* 85 ILL. B.J. 474 *passim* (1997). Most of these articles are long on anecdote and self-congratulation, but painfully short on analysis. The one exception I came across was a refreshingly restrained and thoughtful piece written by William Keesley, who is a South Carolina Circuit Court judge. *See* Hon. William P. Keesley, *Drug Courts,* S.C. LAW., July/Aug. 1998, at 32.

The few scholarly treatments addressing drug courts are aimed at broader issues of "restorative justice" or "therapeutic jurisprudence," and their discussions of drug courts tend to be quite clipped. E.g., Hon. Peggy Fulton Hora et al., *Therapeutic Jurisprudence and the Drug Treatment Court Movement— Revolutionizing the Criminal Justice System's Response to Drug Abuse and Crime in America*, 74 NOTRE DAME L. REV. 439 *passim* (1999); David B. Wexler, *Reflections on the Scope of Therapeutic Jurisprudence*, 1 PSYCHOL. PUB. POVY & L. 220 *passim* (1995). I am aware of only four scholarly pieces discussing drug courts at length. Two of them can be described as fairly pro-drug court, though both recognize and address some of the difficult empirical and institutional issues raised in this commentary. *See* James R. Brown, Note, *Drug Diversion Courts: Are They Needed and Will The Succeed in Breaking the Cycle of Drug-Related Crime?* 23 NEW ENG. J. ON CRIM. & CIV. CONFINEMENT 63, 98 (1997); William D. McColl, Comment *Baltimore City's Drug Treatment Court: Theory and Practice in an Emerging Field*, 55 MD. L. REV. 467, 518 (1996). The other two are mildly anti-drug court and focus on the ethical challenges that drug courts pose to defense lawyers. *See* Richard C. Boldt, *Rehabilitative Punishment and the Drug Treatment Court Movement*, 76 WASH. U. L.Q. 1205, 1216, 1999); *Developments in the Law-Alternatives to Incarceration for Drug-Abusing Offenders*, 111 HARV. L. REV. 1863, 1898 (1998).

2. *See, e g.,* Hora et al., *supra* note 1, at 440; Wexler, *supra* note 1, at 220.

3. On the contrary, compulsory treatment efforts in the drug court context have been embarrassingly ineffective.

4. Kleptomania is a recognized mental disorder, and its diagnostic criteria are currently set forth in DSM-IV, [American Psychiatric Association, Diagnostic and Statistical Manual of Mental Disorders, 4th ed. 1994]. Pedophilia is a recognized mental disorder, and its diagnostic criteria are currently set forth in id. [the DSM-IV].

5. *See infra* text accompanying notes 76-88.

6. Eg., Hora. et al., *supra* note 1, at 440; Wexler, *supra* note 1, at 220.

7. The idea behind the growing movement of "therapeutic jurisprudence" is that because the experience of coming before our courts is having therapeutic consequences for defendants, our courts should capitalize on the moment when a person is brought before us and use it as a starting point for improving the defendant's overall lifestyle. *See* Sheila M. Murphy, *Therapeutic Jurisprudence: Its Time Has Come*, TRIAL JUDGES NEWS, Winter 1997/1998, at 3, 3.

8. Actually, these ideas are attempts to repackage and revive what criminologists have described generally as "the rehabilitative ideal," in which the focus of the criminal law was to change the attitude and, ultimately, the behavior of convicted criminals. FRANCIS A. ALLEN, THE DECLINE OF THE REHABILITATIVE IDEAL 2-3 (1981). The rehabilitative ideal gained popularity between the World Wars and remained pre-eminent through the 1970s. . . . By 1980, however, as criminologists began to take a closer empirical look at the whole issue of the effectiveness of rehabilitation, many began to repudiate the rehabilitative ideal, replacing it with penal notions that put more emphasis on retribution and on the short-term protection of society than on rehabilitation. . . . Drug courts represent a quaint, and some would say naive, attempt to revive long-repudiated notions that state criminal power can efficiently change the behaviors, let alone the attitudes, of individuals. *See generally* Boldt, *supra* note 1, at 1035–36 (arguing that some aspects of drug courts represent a dangerous return to the rehabilitative ideal at the expense of due process).

9. *See* Steven Belenko, *Research on Drug Courts: A Critical Review,* 1 Nat'l Drug Ct. Inst. Rev, 1, 3 (1998).

10. *See id.* at 11, 17.

11. *See id.* at 17–18. As of June 1998, there had been no completed cost-savings analyses done for any drug court. *See id.* at 18. Since then, there have been only two studies of which I am aware that include some cost-savings analysis—the 1999 study of the Riverside (California) drug court and the Portland County (Maine) drug court. *See* Michelle Shaw & Kenneth Robinson, *Reports on Recent Drug Court Research*, 2 NAT'L DRUG COURT INST. REV. 107, 116 (1999) (reviewing the 1999 study of the Riverside drug court, which was conducted by Dale K. Sechrest & David Schicor); *id.* at 119 (reviewing the 1999 study of the Portland County drug court, which was conducted by Donald F. Anspach & Andrew S. Ferguson).

12. *See* Belenko, *supra* note 9, at 16–17.

13. These surveys often are called "internal impact surveys."

14. *See* Belenko, *supra* note 9, at 8.

15. *See* Violent Crime Control and Law Enforcement Act of 1994, Pub. L. 103–322, §50002, 108 Stat. 1796, 1958–59 (codified at 42 U.S.C. §3796ii (1994)) (repealed 1996).

16. *See* BARBARA E. SMITH ET AL., AMERICAN BAR ASS'N, STRATEGIES FOR COURTS TO COPE WITH THE CASELOAD PRESSURES OF DRUG CASES (1991); *see also* STEVEN BELENKO & TAMARA DUMANOVSKY, BUREAU OF JUSTICE ASSISTANCE, U.S. DEPT. OF JUSTICE, SPECIAL DRUG COURTS: PROGRAM BRIEF 2 (1993). (Sup. Docs No. J26.31:D84/2);, at 13–15 (describing and discussing this study in detail).

17. *See* Robert Granfield & Cindy Eby, *An Evaluation of the Denver Drug Court: The Impact of a Treatment-Oriented Drug Offender System* 10 (1997), at 11 (describing the 1991 ABA Study). These dismal results from Dade County improved in a subsequent study done in 1994. *See infra* text accompanying notes 23–26.

18. *See* BELENK0 & DUMANOVSKY, *supra* note 16, at 13. Belenko and Dumanovsky observe:

The ABA study also concluded that more lenient sentences were associated with quicker dispositions. In Philadelphia, shorter average prison sentences were imposed more often after the introduction of the DCM system. Similarly, Chicago has an increase in the use of probation sentences and a decrease in prison sentences. Only Milwaukee showed no evidence of changes in sentencing patterns with the introduction of the speedy trial drug court.

This has certainly not been the experience in the Denver Drug Court, where substantially more drug defendants are going to prison and are going there for a longer period of time than before drug court. *See infra* text accompanying notes 65–69.

19. Although the percentage of prison sentences may go down as a result of some drug courts, the actual raw numbers of prison sentences, and even the total amount of prison time given, may well go up if drug courts stimulate large increases in case filings. *See infra* text accompanying notes 64–67.

20. *See* SMITH ET AL., *supra* note 16, at 4, 10–11. One explanation for more lenient drug court sentences is that judges who volunteer for drug court may just be easier drug sentencers than their traditional counterparts, though I am aware of no studies confirming such a hypothesis. If this hypothesis is true, it highlights the general concerns, articulated below, that drug courts dangerously institutionalize the sentencing philosophy of a single judge or group of judges. *See infra* text accompanying notes 97–98.

21. *See supra* note 9 at 21. *Also see* Lawrence W. Sherman et al., University of MD, National Institute of Justice, A Report to the United States Congress: Preventing Crime: What Works, What Doesn't, What's Promising 9-51 (n.d.) [hereinafter *The Sherman Report*].

22. *See* Belenko, *supra* note 9, at 31. The Sherman Report later characterized this reduction as statistically "non-significant." THE SHERMAN REPORT, *id.*, at 9–51.

23. *See supra* text accompanying notes 16–20.

24. *See* Belenko, *supra* note 9, at 30.

25. *See* THE SHERMAN REPORT, *supra* note 21, at 9–52.

26. *See supra* note 29 (discussing the problem of non-random assignment).

27. *See* Belenko, *supra* note 9, at 31.

28. *Id.* at 29-34.

29. But the evaluation of the Riverside Drug Court did not use random controls. The control subjects, though initially selected at random, were then screened as "possible candidates for drug court had it existed at that time." Belenko, *supra* note 9, at 29. . . . In addition, the Riverside study used a longer follow-up period for the control group than for the target group, inflating control group recidivism. . . .

30. *See* Belenko, *supra* note 9, at 29; Granfield & Eby, *supra* note 17, at 26. Granfield and Eby also examined the more sophisticated measure of average number of arrests, . . . and the results were even less promising: defendants suffered an average of 0.8 arrests in the one-year follow-up period regardless of whether they came out of regular courtrooms or out of the drug court. *See* Granfield & Eby, *supra* note 17, at 25. To be fair to the Denver Drug Court, it is, or at least was at its inception and at the time of the Granfield and Eby study, a drug court that does not screen or exclude participants, which probably goes a long way toward explaining its dismal recidivism per-

formance. The recidivism results for all six studies are summarized in the following table:

City	Recidivism %	
	Traditional Court	Drug Court
Denver, CO	58.0	53.0
Multnomah County, OR (Portland)	1.53*	0.59*
Oakland, CA	1.33*	0.75*
Riverside, CA	33.0	13.4
Travis County, TX (Austin)	41.0	38.0
Wilmington, DE	51.1	33.3

*Expressed not as a percentage, but rather as the average number of arrests suffered during the follow-up period. *See*Belenko, *supra* note 9, at 29–31.

31. U.S. GEN. ACCOUNTING OFFICE, DRUG COURTS: OVERVIEW OF GROWTH, CHARACTERISTICS, AND RESULTS (1997) (Sup. Docs. No. GA1.13:GGD-97-106).

32. The GAO study details a number of problems found in the evaluations, including concerns regarding short observation periods, flawed recidivism data, a lack of comparison groups, and different target populations and treatment services, all of which make it difficult to accurately compare different drug courts. *See id.* at 7–8.

33. *See id.*

34. *See* Belenko, *supra* note 9.

35. *See id.* at 34–36. The most recent meta-study of which I am aware is a 1999 compilation of studies funded by Correctional Counseling, Inc. (CCI), a private criminal justice research organization based in Alexandria, Virginia. *See* Shaw & Robinson, *supra* note 11, at 107–19. The CCI summary examined five drug court studies. The three new studies suffer from the same frailties as all the other studies: they target the wrong group—graduates instead of all drug court defendants; they involve selection criteria that render the control group not random; and two of them (Salt Lake City and Portland) use unacceptably short follow-up periods.

36. As one of the most recent formal impact evaluations noted, research on recidivism rates is ambiguous and conflicting, necessitating further research. *See* Granfield & Eby, *supra* note 17, at 12.

37. I was appointed to the Denver District Court in December 1990. The Denver Drug Court began operations on July 1, 1994. I served in one criminal division from January 1995 through January 1998, and, although I have never volunteered to be the drug court judge, like most of my colleagues, I have taken many transfers of drug court trials and motions hearings.

38. See *supra* note 1. . . .

39. In Denver, one example of our submission to the temptations of accounting is the misleading manner in which our clerk's office counts the number of drug filings. *See infra* note 40.

40. Denver District Court's Criminal Filings Statistics for 1991–98 from Miles M. Flesche, Clerk of the Denver District Court, to the Judges of the Denver District Court 1 (May 10, 1999) [hereinafter Criminal Filings Statistics for 1991–98] (on file with the *North Carolina Law Review*). It is important to recognize that the case filing figures from our clerk's office are higher (up to 30%) than the figures published by the district attorney's office and given by the district attorney's office to other agencies studying the Denver Drug Court. Though there was initially some confusion about this difference, we now realize that the clerk's figures include all drug arrests from the first advisement in county court, even if those cases are dismissed without ever having actually been filed in district court. This has the effect of dramatically boosting district court filings, perhaps in response to the siren of accounting discussed above. *See supra* text accompanying note 256. In any event, even the more conservative filing figures from the district attorney's office reflect a more than two-fold explosion in filings between 1993 and 1995.

41. *See* Criminal Filings Statistics for 1991–98, *supra* note 40, at 1.

42. *See id.*

43. The following table depicts the number of criminal cases filed in the Denver District Court from 1991 through 1998, the number of drug cases filed in that same period and the percentage of the total number of criminal cases that the number of drug cases represented:

Year	Criminal Cases	Drug Cases	% Drug Cases
1991	3795	958	25.2
1992	3790	1014	26.7
1993	3762	1047	27.8
1994	3907	1260	32.2

Year	Criminal Cases	Drug Cases	% Drug Cases
1995	5154	2661	51.6
1996	5814	3017	51.9
1997	5458	2825	51.8
1998	5089	2585	50.8

See id.

44. *See id.*

45. As the Denver District Attorney noted, "[The explosion in drug filings is] not because drug usage has increased but because law enforcement has stepped up efforts to address the community concerns." A. William Ritter, *Denver Looks to Hire Drug Czar*, DENV. POST, Apr. 1, 1999, at 38.

46. As mentioned earlier, drug court proponents insist that drug courts are having dramatic impacts in reducing crime, not necessarily by curing addicts, but rather by decreasing the frequency of their criminal activities. Such alleged benefits, even if real, are of course the result of making the kinds of low-level arrests that were not made before the days of drug courts; they are not the result of drug courts themselves. That is, these alleged clean-up benefits presumably would be enjoyed if we arrested all the same people who are now being funneled into drug court, but handled them traditionally. It is the fact of their arrest, and not any claimed treatment successes, that arguably accounts for these collateral benefits.

   To a great extent, these claimed collateral benefits are a special version of the broader and much-popularized "broken windows" theory of crime prevention. The broken windows theory holds that visible disorder breeds crime and that by re-asserting visible order by fixing broken windows, cleaning up trash, removing graffiti, and removing people who look like gang members or drug dealers—crime will necessarily be reduced. *See* James Q. Wilson & George L. Kelling, *Broken Windows*, ATLANTIC MONTHLY, Mar. 1982, at 29, 29–31; *see also* Dan M. Kahan, *Social Influence, Social Meaning, and Deterrence*, 83 VA. L. REV. 349, 367–73 (1997) (discussing the application of the theory in New York City). The broken windows theory is not without its critics. *See, e.g.* Albert W. Alschuler & Stephen J. Schulhofer, *Antiquated Procedures or Bedrock Rights?: A Response to Professors Meares and Kahan*, 1998 U. CHI. LEGAL F. 215, 215–44; Bernard E. Harcourt, *Reflecting on the Subject: A Critique of the Social Influence Conception of Deterrence, the Broken Windows Theory, and Order Maintenance Policing New York Style*, 97 MICH. L. REV. 291, 292–389 (1998); Toni Massaro, *The Gang's Not Here*, GREEN BAG 2D, Autumn 1998, at 25, 29–34. The broken windows theory recently may have suffered a fatal constitutional blow when the Supreme Court struck down Chicago's gang loitering ordinance in *City of Chicago v. Morales*, 119 S. Ct. 1849, 1852 (1999). In any event, one would think that drug courts would have generated more than anecdotal evidence supporting broken windows-style claims. I am unaware of any such evidence.

47. *See* William J. Stuntz, *The Uneasy Relationship Between Criminal Procedure and Criminal Justice*, 107 YALE L.J. 1, 25–26 (1997).

48. *See* Denver Drug Court Statistics Sheets for 1997 & 1998 1–2 [hereinafter Drug Court Statistics Sheets] (on file with the *North Carolina Law Review*).

49. In the Denver District Court, judges in the criminal divisions of traditional courts typically set aside one or two days each week for "docket" or "board" days. During these days, all manner of miscellaneous criminal matters are taken up—reviews of doctors' reports regarding a defendant's competence or regarding mental defenses, probation revocation hearings, pleas, trial settings, sentencings, motions hearings—pretty much everything a criminal court does other than trials. In the three years I was in the criminal division, I set aside Mondays and Fridays as my docket days, and we averaged anywhere from 40 to 60 cases on our dockets each week, which, had we spread it over the whole week, would have translated to 8 to 12 per day.

50. Denver's four county misdemeanor criminal courts handle roughly 70 cases per judge per day. *See* Interview with Robert L. Patterson, Presiding Judge, Denver County Court, in Denver, Colo. (May 27, 1999).

51. *See infra* text accompanying notes 56–59. . . .

52. *See id.*; Interview with Gregory F. Long, Chief Deputy District Attorney, in Denver, Colo. (May 19, 1999).

53. In fact, two of the three domestic judges have volunteered to set aside one afternoon every week to do nothing but hear drug court motions. *See* Interview with J. Stephen Phillips, Chief District Judge, in Denver, Colo. (Jan. 27, 2000).

54. *See infra* text accompanying notes 77–84.

55. Our clerk's office did not keep track of the number of drug cases tried prior to the 1994 adoption of the drug court. But I cannot imagine that the plea bargaining rate in the drug court is so much higher than in traditional court (where it is already awfully high) that any increase in the disposition rate could overcome the doubling or tripling of cases filed.

56. *See* Interview with John N. McMullen, District Judge, in Denver, Colo. (Apr. 6, 1999). Judge McMullen served as our Chief Judge from August 1988 through December 1993. During that time period, he kept statistics on transfers—the total numbers of transfers sought and the total number of transfers accepted—and announced those statistics each year at our annual Term Day. Although such transfer statistics are not kept currently, they can be derived from monthly transfer records that we do keep. For purposes of transfers, our court is divided in half—north and south—and each month two courtrooms (one courtroom from each half) are designated as the transfer courts. Those courts receive all the transfer requests from all the courts in their half of the building, and then attempt to locate transfer courts, first in their half then in the other half. Each transfer court keeps a log of the transfer requests—called Case Transfer Forms—by date, requesting court, case number, type of matter (court trial, jury trial, motions hearing), anticipated length, and whether any court accepted the transfer and if so, the identity of the accepting court. The kinds of statistics mentioned earlier, *see infra* note 57, are derived from these monthly Case Transfer Forms.

57. For the six months between November 1, 1998 and April 30, 1999, there were a total of 22.6 transfer requests made formally in our court. *See* Transfer Request Forms for Denver District Court, Nov. 1, 1999–Mar. 31, 1999 (on file with the *North Carolina Law Review*). Of these 226 requests, transfer courts accepted 121, or 53.5%. Not surprisingly, of these 226 transfer requests a whopping 105, or 46.5%, came from the drug court. In a bit of surprise, however, of these 105 requests for transfers from the drug court only 46, or 43.8%, were accepted. Thus, during this six month period at least, it was less likely that a judge on our court would accept a transfer from the drug court than from a non-drug court.

58. *See* Interview with H. Jeffrey Bayless, Presiding Criminal Judge, District Court, in Denver, Colo. (Jan. 24, 2000). The new system of assigning drug court trials to criminal courtrooms should help insulate the civil and domestic divisions from the drug court's mess, but, of course, it will only increase the stresses in the regular criminal courtrooms. Before this change, the criminal judges, just like the civil and domestic judges, retained their right to refuse to accept drug court transfers, and, as discussed in the previous footnote, all judges in all divisions became increasingly reluctant to take drug court transfers. Now, the criminal judges have no choice but to take drug court trials because they get assigned directly to them (on a rotating basis) once no disposition is reached. Of course, if criminal judges cannot conduct their newly assigned drug trials because of regular caseloads, then they can try to get a criminal, civil, or domestic court to take the transfers.

59. *See* COLO. REV. STAT. ANN. §§ 16-11-201(2), (4)(a)(II) (West 1998). Actually, under these statutes the district attorney may waive this so-called two-felony rule and instead consent to a probationary sentence, but only if the current offense is non-violent and none of the prior offenses was a crime of violence, manslaughter, second-degree burglary, robbery, certain kinds of theft, or a crime against children. *See id.* § 16-11201(4)(a)(II).

60. *See* Memorandum from Robert J. Whitley, Deputy District Attorney, to Gregory F. Long, Chief Deputy District Attorney (Oct. 15, 1997) (on file with the *North Carolina Law Review*).

61. *See* Criminal Filings Statistics for 1991–98, *supra* note 40, at 1. Filings dropped from a peak of 3017 in 1996 to 2825 in 1997 and then dropped even further to 2585 in 1998. *See id.*

62. The Denver Drug Court's continuing realization that two-time felons are not necessarily inappropriate for drug court treatment is reflected in several unwritten policies. For example, if a single drug case involves multiple defendants, some of whom have two or more prior felonies and some of whom do not, the case remains in drug court. Similarly, there is a kind of one-way trap door feature to the new exclusion. If a two-time felon's case accidentally slips into drug court (which can happen fairly easily at the beginning of a case when there may be uncertainty about a defendant's record), the unwritten rule is that the case stays in drug court even after the mistake is discovered. Finally, as a practical matter, it is often the case that the drug court judge does not discover that a defendant has

two or more prior felonies until after that defendant has already negotiated a disposition, has begun some pre-disposition treatment, and is appearing for approval of that disposition. When that happens, it is simply easier on all concerned to proceed with the disposition instead of sending the case to a traditional criminal court. *See* Interview with Joseph E. Meyer III, District Judge, in Denver, Colo. (May 18, 1999).

63. *See supra* note 9 at 21.

64. *See* OFFICE OF PLANNING & ANALYSIS, COLO. DEP'T OF CORRECTIONS, DENVER DRUG COURT CONVICTIONS: D.O.C. SENTENCED OFFENDERS FISCAL YEARS 1993 THROUGH 1997 1 (1998) [hereinafter SENTENCE STUDY] (on file with the *North Carolina Law Review*). In particular, there were 309 drug convictions in the Denver District Court in fiscal year 1993 and 265 prison sentences imposed for drug convictions in that same year. Of course, the comparison between the convictions in a given year and the prison sentences in that given year suffers from the fact that there is a delay between conviction and sentence and therefore from the fact that we are not talking about all the same defendants in any one year. Indeed, many of the prison sentences for drug offenses, and probably the lion's share of them, are not initial prison sentences, but are instead sentences imposed after deferred judgments or probationary sentences have been violated. Thus, the remarkably high and consistent percentage of prison sentences meted out each year is actually a gross measure of probation recidivism, and the fact that that percentage has stayed just as high after the implementation of the drug court is a rough confirmation of the dismal treatment results being achieved there. . . . It is no defense to say that the Denver Drug Court routinely imposes very short (120-day) prison sentences on a large category of defendants. Although that is true, the average length of prison sentences meted out by the Deliver Drug Court (54.6 months in 1995) is actually substantially greater than the average length of prison sentences meted out in Denver before the drug court (42.7 months in 1993). *See* OFFICE OF RESEARCH & STATISTICS, COLO. DEP'T OF PUB. SAFETY, CASE PROCESSING EVALUATION OF THE DENVER DRUG COURT 60, tbl.23 (1999) (on file with the *North Carolina Law Review*).

65. *See* SENTENCE STUDY, *supra* note 64, at 1. The numbers for fiscal year 1995 were 539 drug convictions and 434 prison sentences.

66. *See id.* The numbers for fiscal year 1997 were 776 drug convictions and 625 prison sentences.

67. The effect at the county jail level appears to have been less drastic. Indeed, the director of that facility reported to me that although they do not keep statistics segregated by offense, his intuition was that the Denver Drug Court was *reducing* total jail time for drug defendants because it was reducing disposition time, and a significant component of jail resources are consumed by defendants awaiting trial who cannot make their bonds. See Interview with John Simonet, Director of Corrections, City and County of Denver, in Denver, Colo. (Apr. 4, 1999). He also indicated that he believed county jail populations were being relieved because more drug defendants were going to prison, and going there more quickly. *See id.* The speedier deportation of drug defendants also has undoubtedly contributed to any decrease in total county jail time. . . .

68. *See* supra text accompanying notes 59–61.

69. There is no written policy fixing the levels of "personal use." In general, however, one or two rocks of crack (less than one tenth of a gram) is treated presumptively as being for personal use. *See* Interview with Gregory F. Long, Chief Deputy District Attorney, in 'Denver, Colo. (June 18, 1999). *But see* Interview with Andre L. Rudolph, Magistrate, in Denver, Colo. (June 22, 1999) (indicating that when Rudolph was a drug court public defender, he understood that two grams was the presumptive personal use cutoff for both crack and powdered cocaine). In any event, there is no presumptive level for other drugs; prosecutors look at all of the surrounding circumstances to determine whether the drugs were for personal use, including the method of packaging and the magnitude of the particular defendant's drug habit. *See* Interview with Gregory F. Long, *supra*; Interview with Andre L. Rudolph, *supra*.

70. *See* Gregory F. Long, *Denver Drug Court: New Approaches to Old Problems*, COLO. LAW., Apr. 1996, at 29, 30; Interview with Gregory F. Long, *supra* note 272. Actually, there is a fourth dispositional track—prison—but initial prison sentences on possession convictions are rare in the Denver Drug Court, particularly now that two-time felons are no

longer eligible. *See* Long, *supra,* at 30; Interview with Gregory F. Long, *supra* note 52.

71. Unpublished internal statistics of the Denver District Drug Court suggest that the graduation rate is somewhere near 55%. *See* Interview with Adam Brickner, Denver District Drug Court Coordinator, in Denver Colo. (June 25, 1999). Even if this 55% figure were accurate, one must keep in mind that it is a measure of program retention and not of ultimate success in terms of no recidivism. *See supra* text accompanying notes 9–12.

72. *See* Drug Court Clearinghouse and Technical Assistance Project, U.S. Dept. of Justice, LOOKING AT A DECADE OF DRUG COURTS, (1998) (Sup Docs. No. J1.2:C83/7) at 1–2. [hereinafter A DECADE OF DRUG COURTS].

73. The magistrates do a wide variety of drug court tasks, including initial advisements, bond settings, preliminary hearings, compliance reviews, revocation hearings(on misdemeanors), and guilty pleas. *See* Interview with Lynn E. Martinelli, Magistrate, in Denver, Colo., (June 14, 1999), where her guilty plea advisements take 5–10 minutes. Interview with Andre L. Rudolph, *supra* note 69. Prior to January 1. 2000, however there was considerable uncertainty about whether the magistrates had the authority to take guilty pleas. Before that date, Rule 6(b) of the Colorado Rules for Magistrates set forth a laundry list of the powers of district court magistrates sitting in criminal cases, and those powers did not include taking guilty pleas. *See* COLO. R. MAGIS. 6(b). Effective January 1, 2000, that Rule was amended to authorize guilty pleas by district court magistrates with the consent of the defendant. *See* Memorandum from Steven V. Berson, State Court Administrator (Oct. 13, 1999) (attaching the amended Colorado Rules for Magistrates) (to be codified as COLO. R. MAGIS. 6(a)(2)(A)) (on file with the *North Carolina Law Review*).

74. These figures do not include eight district attorneys, one investigator from the district attorney's office, five public defenders, one investigator from the public defender's office, and ten probation officers—all assigned exclusively to the drug court.

75. *See supra* text accompanying notes 72 at 1–2.

76. Long, *supra* note 70, at 29.

77. Boldt makes this point in the context of defense counsel:

[D]efense counsel [in the drug court] is no longer primarily responsible for giving voice to the distinct perspective of the defendant's experience in what remains a coercive setting. Rather, defense counsel becomes part of a treatment team working with others to insure that outcomes, viewed from the perspective of the institutional players and not the individual defendant, are in the defendant's best interests.

Boldt, *supra* note 1, at 1245.

78. A criminal defendant has a Sixth Amendment right to counsel at all "critical stages" of a criminal prosecution. *Eg.,* Powell v. Alabama, 287 U.S. 45, 68–71 (1932).

79. Only those defendants who meet the criteria as good candidates for treatment, or in drug courts like Denver's, those fortunate enough not to be subject to arbitrary exclusions designed to cut down on case filings, qualify for drug court.

80. *See infra* text accompanying notes 92–95.

81. *See* MARK A. R. KLEIMAN, *Against Excess: Drug Policy for Results* 253 (1992), at 146–49, 192–99.

82. *See supra* text accompanying notes 64–67.

83. For example, I doubt that even the most strident drug court proponents, or other "therapeutic jurisprudence" do-gooders, would favor rounding up all suspected drug addicts in the absence of proof rising to the level necessary for criminal conviction and forcing them to undergo treatment, any more than they would favor rounding up all bickering spouses and forcing them to undergo marriage counseling.

84. Prosecutorial discretion—the right of prosecutors to decide when to charge and what to charge free from judicial intervention—is a fundamental principle inherent in the doctrine of separation of powers. *See, e.g.,* Wayte v. United States, 470 U.S. 598, 607–10 (1985) (discussing the government's power regarding who to prosecute). In Wayte, the Court stated the following:

This broad discretion [afforded the executive branch] rests largely on the recognition that the decision to prosecute is particularly ill-suited to judicial review. Such factors as the strength of the case, the prosecution's general deterrence value, the Government's enforcement priorities, and the case's relationship to the Government's overall enforcement plan

are not readily susceptible to the kind of analysis the courts are competent to undertake.
Id. at 607.

85. *See supra* text accompanying notes 68–70.
86. *See supra* text accompanying notes 68–71.
87. *See supra* text accompanying notes 76–78.
88. It is no answer to say that every prosecutor's office has internal standards that guide their formulation of plea offers in traditional courts. First, those standards are seldom ironclad. More importantly they are standards formulated by the district attorney, not imposed structurally by the way a particular court is designed. They are an institutional expression of the very prosecutorial prerogative forfeited when drug courts are formed.
89. However, the INS situation discussed above is such a blatant example. . . .
90. *See* DRUG COURTS PROGRAM OFFICE, U.S. DEP'T OF JUSTICE, DEFINING DRUG COURTS: THE KEY COMPONENTS (1997) (Sup. Docs. No. J12:99009370).
91. This institutional criticism of drug courts meshes with broader criticisms about the federalization of state criminal law. *See generally* Kathleen F. Brickey, *Criminal Mischief, The Federalization of American Criminal Law,* 46 HASTINGS L.J. 1135, 1148–65 (1995) (discussing the impact of the federalization of drug-related crimes); Steven Chippendale, Note, *More Harm Than Good, Assessing Federalization of Criminal Law,* 79 MINN. L. REV. 455, 467–74 (1994) (explaining the negative impact that federalization of criminal law has on law enforcement costs). Chief Justice Rehnquist raised this issue at a speech in May 1999 before the American Law Institute:

[M]atters that can be handled adequately by states should be left to them; matters that cannot be so handled should be undertaken by the federal government. Reasonable minds will differ on how this very general maxim applies in a particular case, but the question which it implies should at least be asked.

Chief Justice Raises Concerns on Federalization, THIRD BRANCH, June 1998, at 1, 1–2 (quoting Chief Justice Rehnquist). After citing several examples of federal legislation that encroaches upon state powers, Chief

Justice Rehnquist went on to state, "[O]ne senses from the context in which they were enacted that the question of whether the states were doing an adequate job in this particular area was never seriously asked." *Id.* (quoting Chief Justice Rehnquist).

92. *See supra* text accompanying notes 80–83.
93. *See, e.g.,* Belenko, *supra* note 9, at 21–22.
94. *See supra* text accompanying notes 14–15.
95. *See supra* text accompanying notes 48–51, . . . Belenko and Dumanovsky offer tips to administrators to attract and keep reluctant drug court judges:

Incentives for judges to preside over the special drug court may need to be created by the judicial administrators if a highly skilled volunteer judge cannot be found. This assignment may be viewed as boring and repetitive, a certain route to frustration and burnout. . . . Therefore, it may be necessary to create incentives for judges to staff the drug court. For example, the drug court judge might be selected from among municipal, misdemeanor, or county court positions and be appointed an acting superior or circuit court judge. Or, a term on the drug court might provide a step up in seniority status for a felony trial assignment. Similar incentive issues may apply to the prosecutor's and public defender's offices.

BELENKO & DUMANOVSKY, *supra* note 16, at 7–8. Translation: if we cannot bribe qualified felony-level judges into acting like cogs in the drug court case-processing machine, we might as well use non-felony judges, who are already used to being cogs in a case-processing machine.

96. Other reasons include keeping judges fresh and humble.
97. *See supra* text accompanying notes 48–51. . . .
98. KLEIMAN, *supra* note 81, at 4–5.
99. *Id.* at 3 (quoting the American philosopher George Santayana without citing the original source of publication).

ISSUE XI

The Public as Thirteenth Juror: Should Cameras Be in the Courtroom During Criminal Trials?

Following the O. J. Simpson trial, television shows like *Court TV*, *The People's Court*, and *Judge Judy* have become increasingly popular to depict the real-life process of criminal courts. Some of the shows aim to educate members of the general public by having lawyers serve as newscasters and case commentators. *Court TV* began in July of 1991, selecting cases to televise on the basis of "how important and interesting the issues in the cases are, newsworthiness, and quality and educational value of the trial" (<http://www.courttv.com/about/ctvfaq. html>) Journalists strongly believe that they should be able to report the news as it happens. At the same time, many journalists gravitate toward sensational cases that will grab viewers' attention. Some defense attorneys, judges, and prosecutors fear that cameras will interfere with courtroom proceedings. *Court TV* conducted a survey of 278 state judges in 1995 regarding the civil and criminal cases that the program had televised between 1991 and 1995. The survey found that 71 percent of judges responded affirmatively to the presence of video cameras in the courtroom and 65 percent reported that cameras helped to communicate a better understanding of the court process (Goldfarb 1998). The issue at hand is whether to continue to allow video cameras into the courtroom to show court proceedings live on television, or whether video cameras should be banned from courthouses altogether.

In *Chandler et al. v. Florida* (1981), the Supreme Court held that allowing electronic media and still photography of public court proceedings does not violate a defendant's right to a fair trial and that states are free to set their own guidelines. Video cameras resurfaced as a major concern during the O. J. Simpson trial in 1996, and this matter remains unresolved by many state courts. Currently, the federal court system and the states of Indiana, Mississippi, and South Dakota do not allow cameras in the courtroom under any circumstances. For the other states, the decision is ultimately left to judges on a trial-by-trial basis (Cohn and Dow 1998). No court has yet ruled that a public trial automatically means that the trial can be televised. The real conflict at issue is the freedom of the press versus the defendant's right to a fair trial. Because this issue strikes at the heart of two Constitutional amendments—the First Amendment's freedom of the press and the Sixth Amendment's right to a fair trial—the answer is not straightforward.

Samuel H. Pillsbury, who served occasionally as a television commentator during the O. J. Simpson case, believes that video cameras should be allowed not only during trial proceedings, but during pretrial proceedings as well. He advocates a broadcast delay as a logical step to placing video cameras in the courtroom, since the delay would not impinge on the defendant's right to a fair trial. Pillsbury believes that a delay of up to

24 hours is the best compromise between total abolition and live coverage. The success of the delay depends on the public's level of trust in the media to accurately report the trial without editing out too many key parts. He argues that broadcasters can remain impartial in their role.

Taffiny S. Stewart considers that video cameras have no place in the courtroom because cameras distract and trivialize the process. Participants (jurors, witnesses, attorneys, and even judges) may alter their behavior with the presence of the camera, and rules of evidence will more likely be violated as a result. Furthermore, live television coverage has no educational purpose in teaching people about trial proceedings; more importantly, television creates distortions and biases even before the trial begins. Stewart would thus say that video cameras affect the defendant's right to a fair trial and should be banned from all court proceedings.

References

Cohn, Marjorie, and David Dow. 1998. *Cameras in the Courtroom: Television and the Pursuit of Justice.* Jefferson, North Carolina: McFarland.

Goldfarb, Ronald L. 1998. *TV or Not TV: Television, Justice, and the Courts.* New York: New York University Press.

Chandler et al. v. Florida, 449 U.S. 560 (1981), 337, 362.

<http://www.courttv.com/about/ctvfaq.html> *Court TV* web page. Accessed January 7, 2002.

Critical Thinking Questions

1. Does the media exist merely to inform the general public, or should it play a more active role (e.g., to ensure that justice is served in the trial)?

2. Should the court have the right to control the editing process of the broadcast if television cameras are allowed in the courtroom?

3. Would allowing cameras in all courtrooms decrease the sensationalism currently present at some felony criminal trials?

4. Do cameras ensure fair trials by making the proceedings open to public scrutiny, or do they distract the process and interfere with the defendant's right to a fair trial?

Internet Websites

Court TV Homepage. <http://www.courttv.com>

Journal of Information Law and Technology—articles about cameras allowed/banned. <http://www.elj.warwick.ac.uk/jilt>

Contains articles from the American Bar Association about the scrutiny placed upon courtroom cameras. <http://bailwick.lib.uiowa.edu/journalism/medialaw/index.html>

An article discussing status of cameras in the courtroom following the O. J. Simpson trial. <http://www.rny.com/archive/opinion/1997/februar...ecourtroom.html>

Requirements for cameras in the courtroom in the Arizona Supreme Court. <http://www.supreme.state.az.us/media/cameras.html>

Cameras in the Courtroom Fact Sheet. <http://searchpdf.adobe.com/proxies/2/64/95/1.html>

Associated Press article "NY Lawmakers say cameras in courtroom not a high priority" <http://www.freedomforum.org/press/1998/5/20cameras.asp>

Article discussing whether or not the media should be permitted to cover criminal trials. <http://library.thinkquest.org/2760/press1.html>

The Radio-Television News Directors Association discusses cameras in the courtroom. <http://www.rtnda.org/news/cameras.htm>

State Bar of California is considering cameras in the courtroom. <http://www.calbar.org/2rel/3nr6/3rel0415.html>

"The Tension Between the 1st and 6th Amendments" <http://www.emunix.emich.edu/~jcooper/emlaw/units_fpft.html>

Pro camera in the courtroom article. <http://www.freedomforum.org/press/news/980202b.asp>

Article from Thomas Mitchell, "Judges and Lawyers contend people are stupid," *Las Vegas Reader's Journal.* <http://www.lvrj.com/lvrj_home/1997/Jun-10-Tue-1997/opinion/5519215.html>

NACDL News Release, "Cameras in the courts of criminal cases?" <http://notes.nacdl.org/MEDIA/pr000006.htm>

Article by Bruce Sanford that analyzes cases (e.g., *Estes v. Texas* and *Nebraska Press Association v. Stuart*) and reflects how the court has decided. <http://www.mediastudies.org/courts/sanford.html>

TV Jury Forum—Public Opinion on the *Jim Lehrer Newshour.* <http://www.pbs.org/newshour/forum/january98/tvcourt3.html> ✦

21

Time, TV, and Criminal Justice

Second Thoughts on the Simpson Trial

Samuel H. Pillsbury

The O. J. Simpson murder trial tested many faiths. In a nation already skeptical about its criminal justice system, the case led some to question a basic legal institution—the unanimous citizen jury—and prompted others to doubt the possibility of justice in a multiracial society. But the most immediate effect of the case has been to raise questions about televising criminal proceedings.[1]

Following the Simpson verdict, judge after judge across the nation barred cameras from the trials of well-publicized cases, fearing that television would obstruct the pursuit of justice.[2] In California the legislature and the judiciary have considered a variety of restrictions on televised proceedings, including a complete ban.[3] Reviews of camera rules are underway in many other jurisdictions.[4]

Following years of laudatory studies on cameras-in-the-court experiments, in a nation with an unparalleled tradition of free press and open government, the recent surge in anti-camera sentiment represents a striking change of opinion.[5] One might ask why. What was it about the Simpson case that prompted this sudden antipathy toward the dominant media of our age? Why in a time of public skepticism about the legal system, do so many believe that restricting courtroom access will improve public confidence? Most important, is there any principled, practical way to reconcile the apparently conflicting needs of broad public access and criminal justice?

The issue of cameras in the courtroom is at bottom an issue of modernity. How much can—how much should—the legal system change to accommodate modern times? Should the legal system alter its media rules in order to restore a measure of public accessibility lost over the last century because of changes in demographics, the economy, and the legal process? How much should the legal system consider the effect of access rules on legal journalism? How much should the normally insular, deliberative processes of the legal system accommodate the public's desire for quick, open decision making? These questions have been asked for a long time, but they have taken on new urgency in the wake of the O. J. Simpson murder trial.

Joining the Circus

On a hot July morning two years ago I drove to downtown Los Angeles to do commentary for "Court TV" on the Simpson preliminary hearing. As a former newspaper reporter and federal prosecutor, I had witnessed media scenes before. This was different.

The entrance to the Criminal Courts Building was mobbed with media, interested bystanders, and trial lawyers arriving for work. A long line of prospective jurors, who had been called for other cases, lined up around the block, awaiting security checks to enter the building. I pushed my way to the back of the building where the patio had been transformed into a makeshift, outdoor television studio. Lights and cameras stood pointed at anchors and commentators who perched precariously on the patio's balcony. The whole scene overlooked a parking lot filled with trailers and satellite trucks for national and international media. The "Court TV" trailer stood next to that of ESPN, not far from that of the E! Entertainment Network. Soon the thunder of helicopters overhead signaled the approach of O. J. Simpson's van from the jail. The helicopters belonged to the local television stations, each of which wanted to broadcast live shots of Simpson's short journey from jail to courthouse.

Later the media scene—Camp O. J. as it became known—moved to the parking lot of the former state courthouse across the street. Two and three-story structures of metal scaffolding rose above the trailers and trucks to create stages for reporters and anchors so they could be photographed with the Criminal Courts Building in the background. At street level, entrepreneurs sold buttons, T-shirts, and other trial paraphernalia. Every day the defense team entered and exited in a flurry of celebrity worship, with pictures, waves, sound bites and sometimes handshakes and autographs.

The scene at the courthouse represented but the tip of the cultural iceberg. In the media the case grew to unprecedented proportions, pushing stories of wars and international peace agreements off the air or to the back pages.[6] Journalists repeatedly referred to it as the "trial of the century"; on the eve of the trial, writer Dominick Dunne dubbed it the "Superbowl of murder trials." Meanwhile the public consumed it all and came back asking for more. Shows about O. J. earned higher ratings; magazines and newspapers that trumpeted O. J. stories sold more copies. From the preliminary hearing to the verdict, the Simpson trial dominated much casual conversion in the United States and was discussed throughout the world.[7] The case took the cult of celebrity to new heights.[8]

I started the case excited to be involved and a true believer in full television access to the courtroom. I finished with mixed feelings. On the one hand the reporters and anchors with whom I worked at "Court TV" were thoroughly professional: always well prepared and careful to avoid sensationalism.[9] The questions put to me were usually intelligent and insightful. On the other hand, the format of live coverage created its own limitations and emphasis. I often had to speak spontaneously about what occurred, or was going to occur in the courtroom, based on minimal information. Inevitably much of the on-camera discussion con-

cerned strategy and inevitably much constituted second-guessing of the lawyers and judge. I was, after all, a kind of color commentator. As much as I tried to relate the case to the criminal justice system as a whole, as much as I tried to give historical perspective, the presentness of the case proved overwhelming. What counted was the issue in the courtroom, now.

I sensed a similar ambivalence in the journalists who covered the case—a pride in their professionalism, but also a disquiet about the phenomenon that was "O. J." Most of the actual trial coverage was soberminded, careful, and informative. As a group, the reporters assigned to primary coverage were far better informed on both the facts and the law than such reporters are in most criminal cases. Nevertheless even veteran journalists were troubled by the dimensions of the coverage, by the media desperation to feed the public's hunger for information, or even speculation, about the trial. There was a sense that the case had become a cultural juggernaut, a natural force that no individual, and perhaps no institution could resist.

The Spotlight Effect

In one sense, the media circus that surrounded the Simpson case is irrelevant to the question of cameras in court. Only if the circus was caused by the courtroom camera and only if it affected the in-court proceedings do we have reason to limit electronic coverage. Given Simpson's celebrity status and the sensational nature of the crime, we would certainly have had a media circus without cameras in the courtroom. Camera exclusion probably would have made the scene outside the courthouse even wilder. But the daily, up-to-the-minute, direct-from-the-courtroom coverage probably contributed to the public's mania about the case. Assuming such an effect on the public, did the broadcasts affect the chances of obtaining a just result in the Simpson case? This question remains difficult to answer, because it requires us to judge the nature and importance of a variety of interrelated factors in a unique case. We cannot hope for a definitive answer, but we must do our analytic best, for the issues are too important to ignore.

Every case that attracts significant public attention has a dynamic that distinguishes it from the general run of criminal cases. Media interest in any case creates what may be called the spotlight effect. Media attention casts a bright public light on witnesses, jurors, lawyers, and judge, turning them into public figures at least for a while. In most cases the spotlight effect is small and probably beneficent. Like children who behave better in public than at home, those participating in a trial will generally become more conscientious when they become aware of public interest in the case. Thus a modest degree of media attention in a case may well improve the justice process.[10]

The spotlight effect in a case like Simpson is an entirely different thing. The live television camera picked out courtroom participants from their previously ordinary existence and spotlighted them for global celebrity. Live broadcasts of the Simpson case converted a small downtown courtroom into an amphitheater of unimaginable proportions, with all the participants projected to giant size, like rock stars on the screen at a concert. The lead lawyers became celebrities, commanding large lecture fees, winning television talk show appearances and million-dollar book and movie contracts. Several of the witnesses—Kato Kaelin and Rosa Lopez—even became internationally famous (or infamous) as a result of their appearance in Judge Ito's courtroom.

Most in the legal system have focused on the camera's effect on lay participants—witnesses and jurors. Many have worried that in-court cameras will make witnesses more reluctant to come forward and less candid when they do.[11] By inducing dreams of celebrity riches, it may affect the judgment and behavior of jurors. There is evidence that all these things occurred in the Simpson case, but again it is hard to link the effect to the in-court camera. The most serious instances of media interference were probably the large-sum payments by tabloids to several potential prosecution witnesses, and the publication of a book by a potential witness.[12] How-

ever, none of these events were tied to in-court television.[13]

In general we worry less about the spotlight effect on the professional participants in a trial—the police, lawyers, and judge—but the problem may be even greater here than with nonprofessionals. Many have complained that during this highest of high-profile trials, lawyers on both sides played to the camera, making the proceedings longer and more rancorous than necessary. I'm sure this happened. How else do we explain arguments on procedural motions made outside the presence of the jury that turned into heated rhetorical exchanges between the lawyers, complete with rival slogans?[14] But this problem has a remedy. Whatever attorney dramatics the camera inspired in the Simpson case could have been curbed by a less-tolerant judge.[15] The more serious concern is that the super-bright spotlight of the in-court camera might affect the professional judgment of the lawyers involved.

We like to think that the law stands above, or at least apart from media depictions and all the vagaries of public opinion, but in real life the people who make the law, lawyers and judges, care a great deal about their public reputations. They read newspapers and watch television like everyone else, and like everyone else they care about what is said about them in print and on the screen.[16] Indeed, trial lawyers and trial judges may care more about public opinion than most; the chance to impress a public audience represents one of the biggest thrills of trial work.

We all swim in a sea of public opinion. To believe that judges, lawyers, or police involved in the legal process can stay above and apart from the vicissitudes of public opinion in a case as high-profile as Simpson is to disregard human nature. In a case like this, the spotlight effect can be enormous.[17]

None of this tells us very much about the effect of in-court television, though. The most important effects will likely remain hidden from public view. No judge, for example, will likely admit that he or she changed a ruling for fear of how the alternative would play on the evening news. No lawyer will concede that he modified an argument to please the viewing public. There is one way, however, that we can track in-court television's impact on the legal process. We can analyze its effect on legal journalism.

Judging in-court television by its impact on out-of-court journalism may seem a strange way to approach the issue. Our main concern remains safeguarding justice in the courtroom and our main threat would seem to come from journalists. Yet journalists represent both problem and solution. Legal journalism will always play a critical role in shaping public perceptions of any given case, and those perceptions will always have a great potential for influencing in-court events. Simply put, what affects legal journalism also affects criminal justice.

Live Broadcasts and the News Economy

The live television broadcasts in the O. J. Simpson case simultaneously boosted public interest in the case and deprived traditional legal journalism of its main work, providing a simple, coherent narrative account of the trial. Live broadcasts fundamentally recast the news economy by making Simpson the overwhelming priority for all major media outlets and by forcing most of those outlets to go outside the courtroom to satisfy the demand for Simpson news.

News is the currency of the journalistic economy. News outlets must constantly find fresh stories to sell their audiences. When the stories concern a legal case, they usually come straight from the courtroom. Television, radio, and print reporters covering a trial normally present the important events in the courtroom since the last story or news cycle. When a significant portion of the public views the trial live on television, however, a simple report of courtroom events will not suffice. Live television thus creates competitive pressure for other kinds of stories: for stories about events outside the courtroom, and new angles on courtroom events.[18] Live broadcasts also create competition in quantity.[19] With so much material going out over the airwaves live, other media feel compelled to produce proportionately large stories of their own.

The *Los Angeles Times* coverage may illustrate this phenomenon. The paper gave the trial unprecedented space, usually playing the trial story on the front page and often including an entire page or more of coverage within. Featured prominently in the stories, sidebars and in a separate column known as "The Notepad," were the comments of a host of "legal experts" on the day's developments in the trial. The paper assigned its veteran City Hall reporter, Bill Boyarsky, to write a column entitled "The Spin," in which he covered the way the lawyers and others tried to "spin" their accounts to the jury and the public. The paper's coverage featured a large amount of strategic analysis, examining the way the prosecution and defense were trying to present their cases and how Judge Ito was trying to maintain control of the courtroom.

Perhaps the most obvious journalistic product of live broadcasts was the expert legal commentator. The academic or trial lawyer who could provide instant analysis and commentary became a staple not only of live TV coverage, but of local news hours, late night talk shows, tabloid shows and, as the *L. A. Times* coverage illustrates, print reportage as well. The legal commentator became a hot item in the new journalistic economy, supplying credibility and a new angle (or at least the appearance of a new angle) for extremely low cost, more often than not for free.[20]

The need for fresh stories in addition to straight courtroom reporting made coverage of the Simpson trial more like political or sports reporting than standard legal journalism.[21] Like political reporting, much of the coverage was cynical and strategic, reporters emphasizing who was ahead and who was behind, who was successfully manipulating the judge, the jurors, or the law.[22] As often happens in contemporary political reporting, the competitive aspects of journalism frequently overwhelmed the substantive issues. Guilt or innocence seemed less important than legal gamesmanship. As in sports reporting, journalists and their commentators often promoted the drama played out every day in the case. This was no ordinary case, this was the "trial of the century." When the case took an unexpected turn, it was always "extraordinary," "unprecedented," "incredible," or just "unbelievable."[23]

Meanwhile the tabloid enterprises, both print and electronic, pounded at the Simpson story by chasing everyone even tangentially involved, on occasion producing scoops that the rest of the media then chased. The talk shows sought guests with a relationship, close or otherwise, to the case. The frequent result of this journalistic fervor was a surrealistic Mobius strip whereby yesterday's out-of-court story—what someone said on "Nightline"—became today's in-court controversy. Journalists and newsmakers constantly shifted places.

But how much can we blame all this on live television? The trial would have attracted sensationalized coverage anyway. Once more we cannot be certain, but the dynamics of the coverage suggest that live coverage made a real difference in the quantity, intensity, and style of case coverage. Listen to the words of a "leading network news executive" about the network's coverage of the Simpson criminal trial, which was televised, and the depositions in the Simpson civil case, which were not:

> All through our coverage of the Simpson trial, we wrestled on a daily basis with the question of whether we were doing the right thing? Was our coverage being driven by a tabloid sensibility? We never answered that question to anyone's satisfaction and I think everyone's glad to have the pressure off and get back to business as usual.... And without television inside the deposition on a daily basis, there's no magnetic pull to keep us focused on this event as opposed to all the others vying for our attention.[24]

The Time Dimension

Much of the legal system's resistance to cameras in the courtroom has a curmudgeonly, even reactionary, quality to it. We hear judges say, in effect: "Maybe we're old-fashioned, but the courtroom is an old-fashioned place. Television and other newfangled media have no place here." In a nation that normally views new technology as the source of salvation, this argument sounds hollow. Yet, slightly reconstituted, it

expresses the central challenge presented by television coverage.

The courtroom is an old-fashioned place in the sense that it operates at a slower pace than most of our frenetic world. Justice requires patience, often a great deal of patience. By contrast live television is the most impatient of media, demanding constant action to satisfy a fickle audience. Television programmers live in terror of the viewer's remote control.

It's not that live television rushed the proceedings in the Simpson case. Actually the proceedings dragged on too long even according to the patient norms of the law. The important effect was indirect. Live television created a daily public fervor about the case that infected and perhaps corrupted the deliberative process in the case.

In television, the word "live" is magical. The history of television news may be told in significant measure by episodes of live reporting—from President Kennedy's assassination to the first landing on the moon, to Watergate and Iran-Contra, the Gulf War, and the Clarence Thomas confirmation hearings. Live television events of this magnitude create Marshall McLuhan's global village, where the audience experiences important events together, though physically apart.[25] In an effort to create this magical experience, news broadcasts tout the fact that a report comes "live from the scene" whenever possible. The fact that live reports are more likely to be jumbled and misleading matters little; they're exciting.

Live television reporting represents the latest example of journalism's never-ending search for the new. All journalists work in a highly perishable present. All strive to witness and then convey those electrifying moments when we feel entirely engaged. Yesterday and tomorrow count only as they affect today. Live television simply takes this drive to a new level. With live television, what counts as "new" may be a matter of minutes or seconds, not hours or days.

The law operates in a different time dimension. Justice requires deliberation; it takes time. Lawyers and judges need time to prepare for hearings and trials, time to consider the issues, time to debate, time to cool off and reconsider. The law puts no time limits on jury deliberations. We expect that appellate courts will produce opinions in a matter of months rather than days and that their holdings and reasoning will remain valid for years to come. We recognize that the wheels of justice may grind slowly in order to grind true. And while justice delayed may be justice denied, justice does not respect deadlines.

Sometimes the time differences between law and journalism are obvious. While trials produce daily news, the trials themselves often last weeks or months.[26] A frequently cited example in the Simpson case of the time gap between journalism and law was the much-hyped cross-examination of Detective Mark Fuhrman by famed defense attorney F. Lee Bailey. At the time the confrontation seemed to be won by the detective, who maintained his calm while the attorney blustered. Nevertheless Bailey pushed Fuhrman to make the surprising claim—given his personal history—that in the last ten years he had never uttered a certain racial epithet. This contention gave the defense team an opportunity at impeachment that led to the hidden treasure of the Fuhrman tapes.[27]

Live broadcasts of trials exacerbate the impatience of the media and the public, putting additional pressures on participants. How many trial lawyers, knowing their careers depend significantly on their public reputations, can put aside a day's bad reviews, knowing that the longer-term goal is more important?[28] How many judges can do the same, day after day?

But the real problem with live television in high-profile trials is simply that it works too well as drama. It is exciting. With its real life what's-going-to-happen-next suspense, its treatment of serious issues along with petty squabbles among the lawyers, and its many personal dramas, live coverage of criminal trials can bring entertainment-size crowds to the courthouse. At least in a case like Simpson, live television creates a mass interest that places huge and often unpredictable pressures on all participants in the legal process. The virtual presence of not hundreds or thousands, but millions and even hundreds of millions of interested spectators, constitutes an unprecedented challenge to the independence of the legal process. The time difference between live television and other media may only be a matter of degree, but it is an important matter.

Value of Broad Access

The Simpson case suggests that cameras in the courtroom can create serious problems for the law. Why not just ban the camera and be done with it? Why make this odd distinction between live and other television broadcasts? The reason lies in the other half of the cameras-in-the-courtroom equation, not the problems caused by the cameras, but the benefits generated. We need to recall why public access to the courtroom has always been central to American criminal justice.

The Simpson case notwithstanding, the public probably sees less of its criminal courts today than at any time in the nation's past. In the early days of the republic, criminal courts provided entertainment for many in the community, and significant portions of the public attended high-profile trials.[29] Today's criminal courtrooms tend to be physically smaller than those of the past and are located further from the workplace.[30] Modern work patterns make court attendance more difficult. In an agricultural society, many might attend court on market day, or by rearranging their labor schedule, but in a nation where most work for others according to a fixed schedule, opportunities to view trials in person are rare. Finally, criminal trials take much longer than they once did. An observer cannot hope to see a significant trial complete in one day or two as was the norm in the early nineteenth century. Today major trials last two to four weeks, with many going on much longer.

Some will question the significance of this change in access. After all, the great majority of courtrooms remain open to the casual passerby and we have a vigorous press to report on important legal events. I think it matters a great deal.

Americans' traditional distrust of government has grown in recent years. A disturbing number believe the legal system is fundamentally corrupt. Such distrust makes it difficult to find conscientious and reliable jurors. Thus, distrust inspires extreme legislative changes that wreak havoc on the criminal justice system.[31] Perhaps most important, the power of law lies primarily in its moral authority, an authority severely diminished by public distrust.

What is the legal system to do about this crisis in public confidence? How can judges and lawyers persuade the public of the basic integrity of criminal justice? Increasing public access to the system represents one of the simplest and cheapest means of reaching a skeptical public. By itself, access will not prove sufficient, though. The public, after all, has many good reasons for believing our criminal justice system to be deeply flawed. But increased access represents a vital corrective to the belief that the legal system is an anti-public conspiracy operated by an elite group, lawyers and judges.

Public access also operates as an important corrective to the legal system's natural tendency to insularity. Lawyers speak a language and follow a set of customs that set them apart from fellow citizens. Even when lawyers and courts consciously work in the public interest, that interest tends to be defined in lawyerly ways. Courts and lawyers set their own timetables and priorities according to the values of the legal profession. Public access will permit direct critique of the legal structure. The public must see the system in action in order to challenge the basic assumptions of the legal community.[32]

Public access to the courtroom is a fundamental good. We should provide maximum access consistent with the demands of justice. Access should be limited only as needed to address the particular, demonstrated problems created by nontraditional media, that is, live television broadcasts, in very high-profile cases.

The Proposal

Criminal courtrooms should be presumptively open to all media that can be physically accommodated, with the lone exception of live television broadcasts. In the great majority of cases, live broadcasts should

present no serious problem. Trial courts though should have the discretion to impose special rules on broadcasts if the danger of extreme spotlight effect looms. Under such circumstances, live broadcasts might be barred, but cameras should still be permitted to tape proceedings for later broadcast. The broadcast delay might be as short as four to six hours or as much as twenty-four hours. Even modest delays should significantly reduce the special pressures on the system exerted by live television in high-profile trials.

The question of how much delay is a difficult one. . . . The delay should be long enough to prevent the camera from dominating the public's view of the proceedings; in other words, long enough to dissipate the special power of live television. Twenty-four hours should be the delay allowed, for by this time the basic story of the day in court will be widely-disseminated by other media and the video broadcast would no longer dominate coverage. A longer delay would unnecessarily destroy the remaining news value of the courtroom video. The aim of the broadcast delay is not to relegate courtroom video to the historical archives, but to change its news role, from provider of suspense to provider of context.

The mechanics of the video delay should prove manageable. As with previous electronic coverage, electronic media would have to make special arrangements with the court. Media representatives would have to prove to the trial judge that no-cost, unobtrusive equipment could be installed and that the tape of proceedings would remain in the control of the court until the delay period ends. At the end of the delay period the court would release the tape for media duplication. None of this would be unprecedented in the media world.[33]

A delay order should be very much the exception. The vast majority of live broadcasts of criminal cases made to date have not generated the problems seen in the Simpson case. Only when there is a high-profile case of this dimension, when the public becomes obsessed with courtroom events, do we have the preconditions for a delay ruling.

Nor do the special problems of live television in certain high-profile cases extend to coverage by other nontraditional media. We have no experience of major problems with live radio or with still cameras. Given our commitment to broad access and lacking proof of a problem, these media should be given broad access to the courtroom. Photographers with modern cameras and film can work as quietly and unobtrusively as courtroom sketch artists. That photography may be more revealing of the participants should not argue against it.[34] And while we can imagine that live radio broadcasts might cause pressures similar to those of television, in this visually dominant age, they will be of a lesser degree.

Impact of the Proposal

Although the proposed rule would give courts a new tool in regulating access, the proposal would, overall, dramatically increase public access to the courtroom. At present courts effectively bar all electronic media from all criminal trials of major public interest.[35] Horrified by the Simpson experience, and without clear authority to allow the approach advocated here, courts have chosen to close the doors to video cameras. The proposal, with its presumption of electronic access, would make the nation's criminal courts a far more familiar place to the average citizen than they are today.

In terms of audience size, however, the delay rule would reduce public access from the levels achieved during the Simpson case. We would no longer have tens or even hundreds of millions watching a single courtroom proceeding.[36] For those who believe access is a good determined according to quantity, this audience reduction will count as a strong negative. If the point of courtroom access is to foster greater understanding of the legal system, though, we should be satisfied with a procedure that, in effect, limits its numbers but improves comprehension.

Make no mistake here: The broadcast delay will work largely *because* it reduces audience size. For true believers in political and marketplace democracy this is heresy. But justice depends on different principles than do partisan politics or media competition. As judges frequently remind us: The court system is not in the entertainment business.[37] When it comes, to courtroom access, we should not mourn too much the loss of the Monday Night Football and "As the World Turns" audiences.[38] If the courts can improve overall public access and safeguard the deliberative process through modest limitations on nontraditional media, we all have reason to celebrate.

The broadcast delay would create a new opportunity for in-depth coverage of the legal system. The delay requirement would reduce the tension between the time dimensions of broadcasting and justice, and permit a kind of legal reporting rarely seen in television today. In the news economy the delayed broadcast would have two selling points: (1) direct visual and aural access to the courtroom and (2) context. Television would have to attempt what the print media has done to compete with electronics: concentrate on the long-term story. Television producers would have the opportunity to edit the broadcasts, not just for the ten-second clip, but for the five-minute clip. Viewers could see a witness's testimony whole, not broken up by objections and other delays. Meanwhile legal commentators could provide background and further context. Instead of incessant questioning about "Who's winning now" or, "What happens next," television commentators might answer questions such as, "How does this all fit together?"

The proposal should not be oversold. As with any form of video, tapes of legal proceedings may be edited to give a superficial and misleading presentation of events. A heated exchange between lawyers and the court over a minor issue may be preferred to critical scientific testimony on grounds of drama. Testimony may be presented out of sequence and out of context. Arguments and rulings may be distorted. In short, the proposal does nothing to cure the standard ills of bad journalism. But then bad journalism was not the problem we set out to address.[39]

Constitutionality

Much of the discussion so far will strike lawyers as constitutionally suspect. Surely the First Amendment prevents the government from deliberately manipulating the media this way, prevents it from privileging one form of expression over another in order to influence the nature of coverage. The delay itself sounds like a prior restraint on publication, usually a core violation of the First Amendment.[40] Here appearances deceive. The U.S. Supreme Court has carved out a wide space for judicial and other government regulation of electronic access to the courtroom. The proposal, with its restriction closely tailored to the well-recognized problems of courtroom video broadcasts, should pass constitutional muster.

The Supreme Court has held that the press and public share a First Amendment right of access to criminal trials.[41] The press component of the right may be fulfilled by nonelectronic access, however; the First Amendment contains no mandate for cameras in the courtroom.[42] The Court's view of the camera issue has been permissive: The federal Constitution allows states to invite or to bar cameras in state courtrooms.[43] The Court's pronouncements suggest that electronic access is a matter largely committed to state courts and legislatures. Yet constitutional concerns remain.

Much rests on how the problem is categorized. Does the delay rule trigger some form of heightened scrutiny, or must it pass some lesser test? We begin with the possibility that it constitutes a prior restraint, a category of conduct subject to the most searching judicial scrutiny.[44] Although the delay acts as a temporary restraint on a form of publication, prior restraint doctrine should not apply. The rule does not restrict publication generally as does a prior restraint order.[45] Even under the delay rule all media outlets, including television, remain free to report on courtroom events without restriction. Instead the broadcast delay distinguishes one form of publication—television broadcast—from others, based on the impact that publication has on the state's critical interest in just and efficient courtroom procedures.

Under the Court's permissive approach, the delay rule may well be deemed a time, place, or manner regulation, subject to lesser scrutiny.[46] One circuit court has held that restrictions of television access to the criminal courtroom should be judged by whether they "promote significant government interests" and do not "unwarrantedly abridge . . . the opportunities for the communication of thought."[47] There can be little doubt that the government's interest in fair and efficient criminal adjudication is significant. Nor would there seem to be a serious problem with unwarranted abridgment of communication, for the proposed scheme would actually increase the amount of electronic access to the courts.[48]

The most serious constitutional questions concerning the proposal involve the potential for discrimination in implementation of the delay rule. In cases arising outside the courtroom context, the Supreme Court has struck down government restrictions on access to nontraditional speech forums when there is evidence of discrimination or excessive discretion in the restriction process.[49] The most serious discrimination problems come with viewpoint discrimination—where the government's action favors or disfavors a particular set of ideas—or discrimination between journalistic outlets. These concerns suggest some important limitations on courts ordering a broadcast delay. If a delay rule is to be constitutional, it must be uniformly applied throughout a case. All electronic outlets must have equal access to the courtroom.[50] Nor should the delay rule vary from the start of a case to its end in order to preclude a claim of advantaging one side, or one viewpoint.[51]

But what of the idea that in deciding on a delay restriction, courts rule on the anticipated content of courtroom communication, that courts are in effect given discretionary, editorial powers? After all, only cases that touch a public nerve, that arouse public interests and passions, should be subject to the delay rule. To determine the effect on the public, courts must look at least in part to the communicative content of the trial. This sounds like a violation of the separation that the First Amendment attempts to erect between media and government. To put this more concretely, we can certainly imagine a case where the court might be asked to engage in a form of communication limitation in order to further state interests. For example, a police corruption and beating trial might present testimony the government would like to soft-pedal. In this case the government might argue that the public outrage generated by the trial testimony supports a broadcast delay; thus the government's interest in avoiding embarrassment and criticism would be consonant with the reasons for electronic access restriction.[52]

We could solve the discrimination problem, of course, by eliminating all discretion. Simply make all courtroom television broadcasts subject to the same delay period. This would avoid discrimination, but at a high cost. In the vast majority of televised cases the delay would be unnecessary. The public would suffer a significant diminution in access for a limited benefit of relating discrimination in the implementation of the delay rule.

To gain a better perspective on the discrimination problem, and assess the proposal more broadly, we should compare the proposal with the current all-or-nothing schemes (live television or no television) that also depend on trial court discretion. In terms of access to the courtroom, the proposal represents a major improvement. More Americans would see more of the legal system under the proposal than they do under the all-or-nothing plans now in force in most jurisdictions. In terms of discrimination possibilities, the danger from the proposal is far less than with current schemes, which usually offer virtually absolute discretion to the trial court. Under the proposal, discretion is limited to whether there should be a delay and to the length of the delay, up to twenty-four hours. By contrast, current schemes usually present a sufficiently broad range of factors to consider, that trial courts have the power to bar television cameras from any case, even when the real reason is to prevent embarrassment to the judicial system. Finally, the proposal takes seriously the justice costs of electronic access to the criminal courtroom. It represents a major improvement in every way.

Rethinking the Debate: Defining the Public Interest

Having set out the merits and legality of the proposal, I must confess a certain pessimism about its chances for adoption. Regardless of its virtues, the proposal lacks an ingredient vital to successful reform: the support of the politically powerful. In the debate over cameras in the court, we find a struggle between two political heavyweights: the courts and the media. Neither group is likely to endorse the proposal. Judges will dislike the presumption of openness; the media will dislike the idea of courts exercising control over the timing of any publication. The true public interest in courtroom access may be lost in the conflict of two powerful public institutions.

For two groups so frequently at odds, the judiciary and the media share some striking characteristics. Each enjoys a wide degree of independence within its sphere of operation, based on long tradition and constitutional law. Each subscribes to a distinctive, deeply held view of the public trust in whose name the institution acts. Each wields a great deal of direct power and indirect influence over a wide variety of public and private matters. Each, when challenged, fiercely defends its independence, ideals, and influence. We see all of these traits displayed in the cameras-in-court debate.

In the months since the Simpson verdict, the discussion about in-court cameras has followed a predictable pattern, with courts and media staking rival claims to represent the public interest. The media has spoken loudest, arguing that free access is a good in and of itself, a vital part of open, democratic government.[53] Media defenders tend to dismiss the Simpson case as aberrational, and largely the fault of a too lenient Judge Ito. The media did not lose control; the lawyers did.[54]

Meanwhile the judiciary speaks softly but carries a big gavel, closing courtrooms to cameras in the name of dignity and due process. Many judges across the nation point with horror to the Simpson case and say, "See what happens when you let in cameras." Those who favor cameras in the courtroom usually condition that support on virtually unlimited judicial discretion: Trial judges must have complete control of electronic access.

Few participants in this debate acknowledge any self-interest in the outcome, though self-interest lies just below the surface, the tidal force beneath the rhetorical white caps. For the television news media, access to the courtroom involves ratings; for the judiciary, television access involves a serious question of turf control and public prestige. Not surprisingly, both tend to see the public's interest as consistent with their own.

An example of the way the media judiciary conflict may distort the real public interest in electronic access came in California with the post-Simpson reexamination of the issue by the state's Judicial Council.[55] After holding several hearings and collecting material from many journalists, judges, and lawyers, a subcommittee of the Council recommended that cameras be barred from all pretrial proceedings in criminal cases. From the judicial point of view the merits of this change appear substantial. Perhaps most important, prospective jurors are less likely to hear of evidence that will be excluded at trial. Meanwhile trials could be televised, subject to trial court discretion.[56]

Media reaction to the proposed pretrial ban was critical, but muted.[57] Steven Brill, founder of "Court TV" and vocal media proponent of broad television access, noted that the proposal would not impede his network's operations significantly because it rarely shows pretrial proceedings.[58] Nor was there any great outcry from other media outlets. Self-interest provides a ready explanation: Trials can be great television shows; by contrast, pretrial proceedings usually lack drama.

In terms of public understanding of the system, though, access to pretrial proceedings is much more important than trial access. Most criminal cases end with a guilty plea, not a trial verdict. Most critical judicial decisions in criminal cases, such as whether

a motion to suppress evidence should be granted, occur pretrial. As a result, the public needs electronic access to pretrial proceedings far more than it does access to trials. Fortunately, when the Judicial Council made its final recommendation on the issue, the complete pretrial ban was eliminated, in favor of a multi-factor approach that gives trial courts a great deal of leeway in deciding whether to permit cameras at either pretrial or trial proceedings.[59]

The media-versus-judiciary conflict has also led to a certain inflexibility in the debate. Both sides tend to view the access issue in absolute terms—either cameras are allowed or not—instead of considering various intermediate positions. Accustomed to First Amendment absolutism, few in the media have seriously considered the need for restrictions on electronic access. Meanwhile the judiciary engages in turf wars, seeking protection from legislative and media interference with rules giving trial courts nearly complete discretion. We can do better than this.

Conclusion

The Simpson case did not go well for many different reasons. Live television was one of them. The Simpson case showed that, at least with a celebrity trial, live television has the power to seriously threaten the deliberative processes of the law. It can bring forces to bear on legal institutions and individuals that neither can reliably withstand.

But for all its problems, the camera also presents the legal system with a major opportunity to improve access to the courts and confidence in the law. Whether we realize this opportunity depends on our confidence in handling change. Does the legal system have the confidence to contemplate increasing electronic access in the face of the Simpson experience? Will the media and its advocates be willing to set aside traditional views and consider a different way of approaching the issue?

Perhaps because ours is a time of great change, we approach it with great anxiety. Fearful of losing hard-won gains, we pit tradition against innovation. But sometimes the only effective defense of the old is by the new. The best defense of traditional criminal justice values in America may be in the judicious use of electronic technology. The video camera gives us a chance to return to the time when virtually all Americans could witness the legal process in important criminal cases. To realize this opportunity, the halting efforts made by many legislatures and courts during the last two decades to open courtrooms to the viewing public should be expanded. We need only to ask television broadcasters, in a few cases, to take a little more time.

Notes

1. See Phil Kloer, "The Simpson Verdict: The Impact: Backlash Against Cameras In Court Feared," *Atlanta Constitution*, Oct. 4, 1995; Stephen Labaton, "Lessons of Simpson Case Are Reshaping the Law," *NY Times*, Oct. 6, 1995, at A1; Lyle Denniston, "Camera's Eye On Blind Justice; Simpson Trial Spells Trouble for Cause of TV Coverage in Court," *Sun* (Baltimore), Oct. 1, 1995 . See also S. L. Alexander, "The Impact of *California v. Simpson* on Cameras in the Courtroom," 79 *Judicature*, 169 (1996).

2. Chailey Roberts, "Simpson Leads to Rethinking of Cameras in Courtrooms," *LA Daily J.*, Nov. 8, 1995, at 1, citing refusals to permit cameras in the trial of Richard Allen Davis for the kidnapping and murder of 12-year-old Polly Klaas, the murder retrial of Erik and Lyle Menendez (whose first trial was shown on "Court TV"), the murder trial of rap star Snoop Doggy Dogg, the trial of the Texas woman charged with killing singer Selena, and the South Carolina murder trial of Susan Smith, among others.

3. See infra notes 48–51 and accompanying text.

4. For example, Massachusetts. Carolyn Ryan, "Lawmakers Propose Ban on TV Coverage of Trials," *Patriot Ledger*, Nov. 1, 1995. For an overview of various jurisdictional approaches and the impact of the Simpson case, see Alexander, "The Impact of *California v. Simpson*," supra note 1. The trend toward camera restriction should not be exaggerated, however. Indeed, it may be temporary phenomenon. A legislative proposal to ban cameras in California's courts was easily defeated in the State Assembly this spring. Associated Press, "Assembly Rejects Proposed Curbs on Cameras in

Court," Apr. 26, 1996. See also infra. note 51. The U.S. Judicial Conference has decided to let each federal circuit decide for itself whether to permit television coverage. This represents a loosening of its previous position, which banned all television coverage. Charges Finnie, "Circuits to Set Own Rules on Camera Bans," *LA Daily J.*, Mar. 13, 1996, at 1. The Ninth Circuit has decided to allow some television coverage of oral arguments of civil appeals, habeas corpus, and death penalty appeals but not direct criminal appeals. All television coverage at the trial level remains prohibited. Philip Carrizosa, "9th Circuit to Allow Cameras Back Into Courtroom for Oral Arguments," *LA Daily J.*, Mar. 25, 1996, at 3. Meanwhile a variety of courts across the country have permitted television coverage of less high-profile cases. John North, "Cameras Permitted During Huskey Trial; Judge Says No to Attorney's Request," *Knoxville News-Sentinel*, May 8, 1996; Deborah Pines, "TV Cameras Allowed in U.S. Court: 'Presumptive Right' Seen in Constitution,'" *NYLJ*, May 1, 1996 at 1; Melinda Wilson, "Cable Network Puts Detroit Court in the Legal Limelight," *Detroit News*, Apr. 21, 1996.

5. For an overview of the studies, see Susanna Barber, *News Cameras in the Courtroom* (1987); Susan E. Harding, Note, "Cameras and the Need for Unrestricted Electronic Media Access to Federal Courtrooms," 69 S. Cal. L. Rev. 827, 834–850 (1996). Similar studies done internationally have been favorable as well. See David. Stepniak, "Forum: Televising Court Proceedings," 18 *Univ. New S. Wales LJ* 488, 490 (1995). For a recent history of the issue, see Ruth Ann Strickland & Richter H. Moore Jr., "Cameras in State Courts: A Historical Perspective," 78 *Judicature* 128 (1994). For a detailed overview of various jurisdictions' approaches to television coverage before the Simpson case, see Carolyn Stewart Dyer & Nancy P Hauserman "Electronic Coverage of the Courts: Exceptions to Exposure," 75 *Geo. LJ*, 1633 (1987).

6. As of late September, 1995, the major networks had devoted 1,392 minutes of their nightly news broadcasts that year to the Simpson case versus 762 to the war in Bosnia and 530 to the bombing in Oklahoma. Peter Johnson, "Other News Stories Suffer During Simpson Coverage," *USA Today*, Sept. 27, 1995.

7. The trial became an international media *event*, covered extensively in Canada, Latin America, Britain, Europe, Australia, and other nations.

Barry James, "Trial on the Tube Fascinated, and Appalled, Most of the World," Int'l *Herald Tribune*, Oct. 4, 1995; Chris Cobb, "For Canadians, Trial Was Highly Entertaining, Even Educational," *Ottawa Citizen*, Oct. 4, 1995; Anne Thompson, "The Simpson Verdict: The Media Trial Affects Courtrooms, Newsrooms; Worldwide Coverage Spurs Poor View of U.S.," *Atlanta J.*, Oct. 3, 1995.

8. On the celebrity aspect of the case, see Thomas Morawetz, "Fantasy, Celebrity, and Homicide," 6 *Hastings Women's LJ* 209 (1995).

9. For me the network's most impressive moment came early in the trial, when the network inadvertently showed a juror's face for a moment, violating its agreement with the court. Judge Ito cut off the television feed. The network quickly acknowledged its mistake, network head Stephen Brill personally apologized to the court, and the network sought to devise ways it would not recur. Based on "Court TV"'s representations, the judge then restored the courtroom feed. For background on the network, see David A. Harris, "The Appearance of Justice: "Court TV", Conventional Television, and Public Understanding of the Criminal Justice System," 35 *Ariz. L. Rev.* 785, 797–807 (1993); see also Paul Thaler, *The Watchful Eye: American Justice in the Age of the Television Trial*, 55–72 (1994).

10. Reporters and trial lawyers commonly note this phenomenon in the courtroom. See Gerald Uelmen, *Lessons From the Trial* 96 (1996). Author Paul Thaler recounts an instance from the televised Steinberg case in which a television report about Judge Harold Rothwax's volatility triggered a warning from his wife and apparently caused the judge to act more temperately in the courtroom. Thaler, *The Watchful Eye*, supra note 8 at 170–171.

11. Prosecutors in the televised murder case of Joel Steinberg reported that a number of witnesses had expressed reluctance to testify because of the broadcasts, but all eventually did. See Thaler, *The Watchful Eye*, supra note 8 at 125. Even expert witnesses the case reported, added pressure from television. *Id.* at 126–130.

12. See Christopher A. Darden, with Jess Walter, *In Contempt*, 235–237 (1996).

13. A ban on in-court cameras might actually increase the demand for behind-the-scenes books about the case and for the stories of would-be witnesses.

14. A fellow prosecutor has reported that Marcia Clark said the prosecution in the case was forced to make lengthy arguments against defense motions to avoid the appearance of "rolling over." Charley Roberts, "Court Cameras a Touchy Issue to Some Jurists," *LA Daily J.*, Apr. 30, 1996, at 1. Co-prosecutor Darden makes a similar point in his recent book: "Cameras caused all the lawyers to change our approach and our style. Everyone became long-winded and abrasive. Often without meaning to, we tailored our arguments to the millions of people watching and the experts second-guessing our every move. . . . I tried to ignore the cameras; I didn't watch TV and tried to shut out what the pundits and experts were saying. But it was like walking past a funhouse mirror, over and over, a mirror that distorts your appearance so that you look taller and fatter than you really are. It isn't long before your very identity is in doubt: 'Is that really how I am?' " *In Contempt*, supra note 12 at 260, 261. For allegations that the defense played to the cameras in the televised Steinberg case, see Thaler, *The Watchful Eye*, supra note 9 at 132.

15. Several critics noted that defense attorneys made presentations to Judge Ito that seemed designed to generate headlines, perhaps with the intent of influencing the families of jurors and eventually the jurors themselves. David Shaw, "The Simpson Legacy: Did the Media Overfeed a Starving Public?" *LA Times*, Oct 9, 1995. See Darden, supra note 12 at 357 (alleging that several jurors received news of the case from family members).

16. One judge in the courthouse I covered was reputed to hand down harsh sentences whenever a reporter was present but would then privately signal the defense attorney to come by chambers to make a motion for reduction of sentence that would be favorably received. During the Simpson case, Judge Ito regularly received celebrity visitors to the trial in his chambers. In a small courtroom where seats were at a premium and controlled by the judge, famous authors, newscasters and celebrities seemed to have priority. The judge granted a lengthy interview to a local television station about his personal background on the eve of trial. Prosecutor Darden wrote about the judge at a pretrial, in-chambers hearing: "I sensed that Ito craved the ceremony of this trial. He seemed infatuated with the idea of being the judge in the 'trial of the century.' It was a show to him, and he was acting unlike any judge I'd ever seen." *In Contempt*, supra note 12 at 216. Darden also observed, "Once, after throwing a fit about the

cameras, he (Judge Ito) posed for pictures with twenty-one boxes of mail, from letter writers who agreed he should turn the cameras off. It was a strange response for someone supposedly concerned about the media to then pose for the media with fan mail." *Id.* at 261. Some judges are truly oblivious to the media. For example, Oliver Wendell Holmes Jr. gave up reading newspapers at an early stage in his public career, a practice that probably assisted him in avoiding the conventional assumptions of the day, and so enhanced his independence as a thinker. Holmes's insulation from popular debate may also have contributed to the worst opinion he ever authored, his notorious forced sterilization decision in *Buck v. Bell,* 274 US 200 (1927). See William E. Leuchtenburg, "Mr. Justice Holmes and Three Generations of Imbeciles," *Supreme Court Reborn,* 3 (1995).

17. Sometimes the effect is simply to make participants feel great pressure. David Bruck, who represented Susan Smith, the South Carolina woman who drowned her two young children, reported the following reaction after hearing that the judge would not allow the proceedings to be televised. "Once the motion was granted and the cameras were unplugged, I felt like someone had pumped air back into the room. I had no idea until the cameras were gone of the effect they were having on everyone." Alexandra Marks, "O. J. Simpson Case Puts Courtroom Cameras on Trial," *Christian Science Monitor,* Sept. 19, 1995, at 10.

18. On the competitiveness of television journalism, see Matthew C. Ehrlich, "The Competitive Ethos in Television Newswork," 12 *Critical Studies in Mass Communication,* 196 (1995). On the effects of in-court television on legal journalism, see Thaler, *The Watchful Eye,* supra note 9 at 45 (effect on print coverage of the William Kennedy Smith rape trial), 148, 197–200 (similar effects in the Steinberg case).

19. Thaler, *The Watchful Eye,* supra note 9 at 198.

20. Many media outlets did pay commentators, however. On the phenomenon generally, see Maura Dolan, "Simpson Case Creates TV Job Openings for Lawyers," *LA Times,* July 5, 1994. For an excellent overview of the benefits and problems of legal commentating, see Erwin Chemerinsky & Laurie Levenson, "The Ethics of Being a Commentator," 69 *S. Cal. L. Rev.,* 1303 (1996).

21. For especially thoughtful critiques along these lines, see Lincoln Caplan, "Sport TV," *New Republic,* Oct. 23,1995, at 18; "Why Play-By-Play Coverage Strikes Out For Lawyers," 82 *ABA J.,* 62 (1996). Or this from the Boston Globe's ombudsman, Mark Jurkowitz: "Let's first acknowledge that the Simpson trial was a television-driven story, with the print media relegated to a peanut gallery role. And though I'm not unalterably opposed to cameras in the courtroom, the relentless punditry generated by the live coverage trivialized and distorted the proceedings. With this trial the obsessive TV culture of instant analysis has now moved from sports (where John Madden explains how the tackle screwed up on the previous play) to politics . . . to the criminal justice system (where commentators were picking winners and losers at every trial break)." "A Guilty Verdict for the O. J. Press," *Boston Globe,* Oct. 16, 1995.

22. For a critique of political reporting along similar lines, see James Fallows, *Breaking the News: How the Media Undermine American Democracy* (1996).

23. As two media critics put it, once television commits to live coverage of an event, "television is protective of the event. It makes clear the event's absolute priority and, in particular, its precedence over other news of all sorts." Daniel Dayan & Elihu Katz, *Media Events: The Live Broadcasting of History,* 79 (1992).

24. Tim Rutten & Jane Hall, "Is the Public Still Hungry for Simpson News?" *LA Times,* Jan. 28, 1996 at A1, A27.

25. Marshall McLuhan & Bruce R. Powers, *The Global Village* (1989).

26. This same tension exists between journalists and legal academics who act as legal commentators. Law teachers think in terms of months and semesters. As scholars, law teachers characteristically take the long view, trying to relate the present to events distant in both past and future. But in commentating, legal academics are called upon for instant answers about the present situation.

27. See Charley Roberts, "Lawyers Split on Their Verdict Of Cameras in the Courtroom," *LA Daily J.,* Nov. 9, 1995, at 1.

28. The defense lawyers in the Joel Steinberg case used television coverage to gauge their own efforts. "They're like film dailies, you know, the day's rushes, and we'd get a sense on the six major channels as to how they were responding, and it gave us a clue how we were coming across." Thaler, *The Watchful Eye,* supra note 9 at 167 (quoting Ira London, lead defense counsel). The defense team in the Simpson case also took careful note of all coverage in

the case. See Robert L. Shapiro, with Larkin Warren, *The Search for Justice*, 23–24 (1996).

Christopher Darden notes in his book about the experience of being a prosecutor in the Simpson case, several occasions when reaction to the day's televised events had a major impact on him personally. The most prominent involved a televised pretrial hearing in which he alleged that Johnnie Cochran's characterization of his (Darden's) arguments over the admissibility of a detective's use of a racial epithet, subjected Darden to enormous personal hostility from the black community. *In Contempt*, supra note 12 at 201–206.

29. For example, one of the most sensational trial in early Massachusetts was the murder trial in 1850 of Harvard professor Dr. John W. Webster. So many wished to attend the trial that spectators were allowed in for only ten minutes at a time. This permitted an estimated 60,000 people to see some part of the proceedings. Leonard W. Levy, *The Law of the Commonwealth and Chief Justice Shaw*, 218–220 (1957). In the first half of the eighteenth century, the Philadelphia criminal courts were often crowded with spectators who expected entertainment from the lawyers and witnesses. Allen Steinberg, *The Transformation of Criminal Justice: Philadelphia 800–1880*, 17–24 (1989). For brief accounts of particularly sensational trials and their audiences, see Lawrence M. Friedman, *Crime and Punishment in American History*, 252–255, 397–401 (1993).

30. This not because courthouses have moved but because workplaces have dispersed from town and city centers.

31. Here in California, the governor signed into law the broadest and least flexible version of three-strikes legislation that reached his desk. See Victor S. Sze, Note, "A Tale of Three Strikes: Slogan Triumphs Over Substance As Our Bumper-Sticker Mentality Comes Home to Roost," 28 *Loy. LA L. Rev.* 1047, 1051–1057 (1995). A direct result has been a great increase in criminal trials, especially in Los Angeles County, delaying the criminal process, for many, delaying or effectively precluding civil trials, and creating dangerous overcrowding in county jails and the under-prosecution and under-punishment of other felons and misdemeanants. Perhaps the most dramatic result has been that, because of three-strikes, prisoners crowding the county jail in combination with a continuing budgetary crisis, misdemeanant prisoners in the county have been serving only a quarter of their sentences. Paul Feldman & Eric Lichtblau, "L. A. County Jail Inmates Serve Only 25% of Sentences," *LA Times*, May 20, 1996, at A1.

32. Ira Reiner, the former L. A. District Attorney and a frequent television commentator on the Simpson case made the same point this way:

Professionals tend to have a guild mentality, and we lawyers are no different. Without being consciously aware of it, most of us have absorbed, with our law school training, an insular, self-protective conviction that only the initiated can judge our activities. How, we think, can layfolk—lacking our expertise, training and experience—truly understand why things are the way they are and why they must be that way? . . . To put it another way, some folks feel that people should not see how sausages and laws are made. But they should. What they see, in either case, may shock or sicken them, but the end result may be better laws and healthier sausages.

"Cameras Keep Justice System In Focus," *Nat'l LJ*, Oct. 23, 1995, at A23.

33. Public figures and institutions sometimes release news subject to a time embargo, a promise by journalists and editors that the story not go out until a specified time. In a recent insightful essay about journalism and the U.S. Supreme Court, *New York Times* reporter Linda Greenhouse describes a process used by the Court in the release of an important decision concerning New York City's financial crisis in which reporters were allowed to read the Court's opinion an hour before its official release, but were not allowed to report it until the release time. Reporters who came to a room at the Court to read the opinion early were not allowed to leave until the official release time. "Telling the Court's Story: Justice and Journalism at the Supreme Court," 105 *Yale L.J.* 1537, 1544 (1995).

34. This states a general presumption concerning witnesses, parties, and lawyers. Restrictions on photographing jurors and particularly vulnerable witnesses remain appropriate.

35. See supra note 2.

36. Estimates on the size of the audience for the Simpson case vary considerably. The largest audience was certainly for the verdict. Estimates of this audience range from 150 to 200 million. Steve McClellan, "All Eyes On O. J.: Verdict In Murder Trial Estimated to Have Been Seen by More than 150 Million," 125 *Broadcasting & Cable*, Oct. 9, 1995. Coverage

of the Simpson case constituted the most successful show of the fall 1995 television season, disrupting traditional viewing patterns. Joe Mandese, "O. J. Skewing New-Season Results," *Electronic Media*, Oct. 16, 1995, at 28.

37. For example, a judge wrote in a recent federal survey: "The basic purpose of the courts is to render justice. The basic purpose of TV is to entertain. There are many detriments to TV courtrooms and no corresponding benefits to the judiciary. Courts should not compete with soap operas, at least not in the name of promoting justice." Lyle Denniston, "Camera's Eye on Blind Justice," *Sun* (Baltimore), Oct. 1,1995. Yet the criminal courts have historically provided public entertainment, see supra note 29, and the drama of crime remains an important part of criminal justice in a democratic society. See Samuel H. Pillsbury, Book Review, "The Challenge of the Dramatic: Crime Journalism," 29 *Loy. LA L. Rev.*, 847 (1996).

38. *Washington Post* television critic Tom Shales compared the verdict in the Simpson case to "finding the one-armed man on "The Fugitive," except this was real, a lot more exciting and, a lot more people were fascinated by it." Steve McClellan, "All Eyes On O. J.," *Broadcasting & Cable*, Oct. 9, 1995.

39. The success of the delay rule also depends on the public's trust in the television media. If viewers believe that all delayed broadcasts of proceedings are distorted by media editing, then such broadcasts will do little to improve public understanding and appreciation of the legal system. I am grateful to my research assistant Karen Cox for pointing out this problem. Perhaps I am naive but I do not see the public's distrust of the media as this severe at present. Even if it is, I believe that in the few cases like Simpson where live broadcasts cause serious problems, a delay rule remains the best compromise between access and restriction.

40. See *Nebraska Press Ass'n v. Stuart*, 427 US 539 (1976).

41. On the First Amendment right of access generally, see *Richmond Newspapers, Inc. v. Virginia*, 448 US 555 (1980); *Press-Enterprise Co. v. Superior Court*, 464 US 501(1984).

42. *Nixon v. Warner Communications, Inc.*, 435 US 589, 610 (1978): "[T]here is no constitutional right to have testimony recorded and broadcast. . . . Nor does the Sixth Amendment require that the trial—or any part of it—be broadcast live or on tape to the public. The re-quirement of a public trial is satisfied by the opportunity of members of the public and the press to attend the trial and to report what they have observed." See also *Westmoreland v. Columbia Broadcasting Sys., Inc.*, 752 F2d 16, 20-23 (2dCir. 1984); *United States v. Hastings*, 695 F2d 1278, 1280 (11th Cir. 1983); *Combined Communications Corp. v. Finesilver*, 672 F2d 818, 821 (10th Cir. 1982).

43. *Chandler V. Florida*, 449 US 560 (1981).

44. See *Near v. Minnesota*, 283 US 697 (1931).

45. *C. F. Globe Newspaper Co. v. Superior Court*, 457 US 596 (1982) (unconstitutional to exclude press from trial of sex offense involving minor victim).

46. See *Globe Newspaper Co. v. Superior Court*, 457 596, 607 n. 17 (1982); *United States v. Hastings*, 695 F2d 1278, 1282 (11th Cir. 1983).

47. *Hastings*, 695 F2d at 1282 (quoting *Young v. American Mini Theatres, Inc.* 427 US 50, 63 n. 18 (1976) and *Richmond Newspapers Inc. v. Virginia*, 448 US 555, 581, n. 18 (1980).

48. The scheme might even pass strict scrutiny. For an example of a more far-reaching broadcast time-restriction that passed constitutional muster, see *Action for Children's Television v. Federal Communications Comm'n* 58 F3d 654 (DC Cir. 1995). . . . The Second Circuit has suggested a more deferential standard should apply to television access to the courtroom questions, holding that courts have general powers to regulate media coverage, including plenary power over television access. "[T]elevision coverage of federal trials is a right created by consent of the judiciary, which has always had control over the courtrooms, a consent which the federal courts . . . have not given." *Westmoreland v. Columbia Broadcasting Sys., Inc.*, 752 F2d 16 (2d Cir. 1984).

49. *Rosenberger v. Rector & Visitors of the University of Va.*, 115 S. Ct. 2510 (1995). See also *Cornelius v. NAACP Legal Defense & Educ. Fund, Inc.*, 473 US 788 (1983); *Legi-Tech, Inc. v. Keiper*, 766 F2d 728, 734–735 (2d Cir. 1985); David W. Burcham, "High-Profile Trials: Can Government Sell the 'Right' to Broadcast the Proceedings?" 3 UCLA Ent. L. Rev. 169 (1996).

50. *American Broadcasting Cos. Inc. v. Cuomo*, 570 F2d 1080 (2d Cir. 1977) (unconstitutional to discriminate between media outlets); *Quad-City Community News Serv., Inc. v. Jebens*, 334 F. Supp. 8 (SD Iowa 1971) (same).

51. See generally *Carey v. Brown*, 447 US 445 (1980) (unconstitutional to selectively pro-

hibit residential picketing based on content of protest); see also *KFMB-TV v. Municipal Court*, 221 Cal., App. 3rd 1362, 271 Cal. Rptr.109 (1990) (trial court's decision to allow taping of criminal proceedings but conditioning broadcast of the tapes on the court's approval reversed as beyond the authority granted the court under the state's rule concerning cameras in court).

52. I am grateful to Chris May for suggesting this example.

53. For example, Editorial, "Judges Should Retain TV Option; They, Not Sacramento Should Decide Camera-In-Court Issues," *LA Times*, Feb. 14, 1996; Cathy Young, "Don't Blame Cameras for O. J. Case," *Detroit News*, Oct. 3, 1995; Walter Goodman, "Television View; The Camera as Culprit? Look Again," *NY Times*, July 9, 1995; Kelli L. Sager, Karen N. Frederiksen & Barbara Wartelle Wall, "The Case For Cameras in the Courtroom," 9 Cal. Litig. 11 (1996). There were some surprising dissenters in the media, though, including Don Hewitt, long-time producer of CBS's "60 Minutes," and Max Frankel, of the *New York Times.* Hewitt, "Pencils, Yes; Camera, No," *NY Times*, June 20, 1995 (" 'Open to the public' doesn't have to mean 'open to cameras.' " . . . "[L]etting cameras in can turn a courtroom into a movie set."); Frankel, "World and Image; Out of Focus," *NY Times*, Nov. 5, 1995 ("The camera corrupts not because it lies but because it magnifies images and issues a millionfold until they are hopelessly and often willfully distorted.").

54. For example: "Whatever negative impressions of the criminal justice system in general, or lawyers in particular, came out of the Simpson case, they were not caused by the presence of a television camera in the courtroom." Sager, et al., supra note 51 at 15.

55. The Council is a body chaired by the Chief Justice of the state's Supreme Court, and comprises primarily judges, along with four attorneys and two representatives from the state legislature. The Council acts to provide policy direction to all branches of state government on court issues.

56. Meanwhile many judges supported a complete ban on courtroom cameras. A survey of judges in the state indicated that a majority supported a ban. Task Force on Photographing, Recording and Broadcasting in the Courtroom, Report, Feb. 16, 1996 at 24. See also David Minier, "Keep Cameras Out of Court," *LA Daily J.*, June 20, 1996.

57. The *Los Angeles Times* criticized the proposal as part of a trend to protect the legal system from public scrutiny. "Banning Cameras in Court Won't Cure What's Wrong," Feb. 26, 1996, at B4. The strongest criticism came from lawyers interested in free speech issues. William Bennett Turner, "Strict Scrutiny: Judicial Council Should Reject Proposal to Curtail Court Coverage," *LA Daily J.*, May 9, 1996, at 6; Douglas E. Mirell, "Short-Sighted: Proposal on Cameras in the Courts Overlooks Key Judges' Views," *LA Daily J.*, Mar. 5, 1996, at 6.

58. Maura Dolan, "Courtroom Camera Plan Called Compromise," *LA Times*, Feb. 24, 1996, at A22 (describing Brill as more relieved than disappointed by the proposal). Brill had earlier presented a proposal to the Judicial Council that contemplated a number of limitations, such as requiring gavel-to-gavel coverage, which would have allowed only the kind of coverage in which "Court TV" specializes. Other media representatives opposed Brill's plan. See Henry Weinstein, ""Court TV" Founder Defends Live Coverage," *LA Times*, Jan. 18, 1996, at B 1, B6; Mike Lewis, "Broadcasters, "Court TV" Split Over Proposal," *LA Daily J.*, Jan. 4, 1996, at 1.

59. See Maura Dolan, "State Panel Puts Partial Ban on Court Cameras," *LA Times*, May 18, 1996. The revised California Rule of Court 980 places a complete ban on televising of proceedings in chambers, jury selection, jurors, courtroom spectators, bench conferences, and lawyer conferences. 980(e)(6). Permission for other courtroom broadcasts depends on the trial court's evaluation of nineteen factors ranging from the "[I]mportance of maintaining public trust and confidence in the judicial system" to the "privacy rights of all participants, in the proceeding, including witnesses; jurors, and victims" and including "[a]ny other factor the judge deems relevant." Rule 980(e)(3)(i-xix).

22

The Distortion of Criminal Trials Through Televised Proceedings

Taffiny S. Stewart

Despite popular thinking, the presence of cameras in criminal trials received criticism long before the O. J. Simpson trial. The first main challenge concerning televised coverage of criminal trials surfaced over sixty years ago in the highly publicized trial of Bruno Hauptmann who was charged with kidnapping and murdering the Lindbergh baby.[1] The disruptions in the courtroom caused by the presence of 120 cameramen led the American Bar Association to change the Canons of Judicial Ethics to prohibit televised court proceedings.[2]

That prohibition no longer exists. Today, forty-seven states allow cameras in their trial or appellate proceedings.[3] With the admission of cameras into the courtroom, the media has offered the public an opportunity to view several criminal trials in the past few years. A national survey conducted by Times Mirror Center for the People and the Press indicated that the public has accepted the media's offer.[4] Prior to the Simpson murder trial, forty-three percent of the public viewed at least four out of the five recent sensational trials aired on television.[5] Sixty-two percent watched the trial of Lorena Bobbit for mutilating her husband; fifty-three percent followed the first trial of the Menendez brothers for killing their parents; eighty-one percent watched Rodney King's trial; and

fifty-five percent watched the trial of William Kennedy Smith.[6] Though the viewing audiences for these trials were large, they cannot compare to the enormous viewing audiences of the O. J. Simpson murder trial.

For almost a year, the public focussed on the seemingly never-ending O. J. Simpson murder trial. The media had a field day with its nonstop coverage of the trial. In the midst of all the publicity, the controversy over cameras in the courtroom grew.

The Simpson murder trial was the catalyst for the National Conference on Media and the Courts Working Together to Serve the American People in 1996.[7] Delegates to the conference consisted of several well known members of the media and the judicial system including the O. J. Simpson murder trial veterans, Linda Deutsch of the Associated Press, and Jim Newton and Bill Boyarsky of the *Los Angeles Times*.[8] The people attending the conference separated into small groups to discuss the effects of televising criminal trials.[9] Among the criticisms were the media's transformation of the public into the thirteenth juror and its concentration on entertaining the public at the expense of reporting accurate information.[10]

The media circus ignited by the Simpson murder trial forces the system to rethink the effectiveness of cameras in the courtroom. This Article focuses on the disruptive effects of televising criminal trials. The media's extensive coverage distorts various aspects of the trial through the application of technical devices used by the cameraman. With the implementation of these devices, the media creates biases within the public before actual coverage of the trial begins. In addition, the cameras adversely influence the behavior of the courtroom participants.

[The next] part explores the conflict between the First and Sixth Amendments. The media's right to inform the public about courtroom proceedings falls within the parameters of the First Amendment's guarantee to freedom of the press. However, the media's right to televise the proceedings is not guaranteed especially when balanced against a defendant's right to a fair trial. The right of the defendant to receive a fair trial by an impartial jury cannot be preserved when the media produces unfair biases and contaminates the jury pool in its production of a criminal trial. The public views the trial with premature opinions caused by the media's distortion of the proceedings. Therefore, televising trials serves no educational purpose.

The Production of a Criminal Trial

Before permitting the media to televise a criminal trial, a court should consider the inevitable disruptive effects that the presence of the camera will have on the judicial proceedings. The strategic tools used by the cameramen in filming the participants of the trial create biases that permeate through the camera into the living rooms of the public. These biases are injected into the minds of the viewers before the presentation of the trial. In addition, cameras can negatively impact the participants the trial unfolds. Appearances may be deceiving because constant observation will change a person's behavior to benefit his case. The Menendez brothers first appeared in stiff double-breasted suits in their televised trial. Their appearances were criticized by the public as looking too harsh. Immediately their attorney instructed them to wear sweaters so that they would have a softer appearance in the eyes of the viewing public. Criminal proceedings are undeniably affected by the public's opinion created by the presence of cameras in the courtroom.

Setting the Stage for the Public

Proponents of cameras in the courtroom argue that television is merely a medium used to inform the public about the functions of the court system and the law.[11] Even though television is considered to be one of the most potent sources of information and news in our society, it is also one of the most manipulative.[12] What is produced on the television screen is the end result of a series of technical modifications that are within the scope of the discretion of editors and the cameraman. Editors may eliminate or cut

certain scenes of the trial in order to appeal to a mass audience. Cameramen manipulate what the public sees by limiting the public's perception for them. Advocates argue that the camera simply mirrors events. However, in nationally televised criminal trials, intricate devices are used to cater to a mass appeal.[13] Space, camera angles, lighting, juxtaposition, and editing are tools used by cameramen that affect how images appear on the television screen.[14] In essence, the public's perception is manipulated prior to the coverage of a trial. Most members of the public lack an understanding of how these tools work; thus, the public never realizes the distorting effects of the devices executed by an experienced cameraman.

The cameras allow the public to formulate premature opinions that originate from the simple focus of the camera lens. Various camera angles are techniques used to establish intimacy between the trial participants and the audience. The most intimate camera angle, the close-up shot, is used to show sympathetic witnesses.[15] For lawyers, a three-quarter shot is used to suggest emotional detachment.[16] Cameramen film the defendant with a profile shot in order to portray remoteness.[17]

Consequently, of all the participants, the defendant appears to be the most vulnerable in the eyes of the camera. Thus, the camera's focus may cause the television audience to infer that the defendant is blameworthy prior to presentation of the testimonies at trial. These techniques introduce unfair biases in the minds of the public before the trial. The media's electronic coverage of the case does not support the vital premise that an individual is innocent until proven guilty.

Casting the Courtroom Participants

The simple presence of the camera has a profound effect upon the participants of the trial. The threat of self-conscious performance emerges when trials are televised to millions of viewers. The courtroom participants lose their anonymity.[18] As a result, the participants alter their behavior to satisfy the large viewer audience. They know that their actions and testimony in a televised trial will extend far beyond the confines of the courtroom and into the homes of millions of spectators.[19] Consequently, the participants will scrutinize their remarks and body language for their performances.[20] The weight and interpretation that witnesses, lawyers, and jurors give their roles before the camera correlates to their behavioral judgments in the courtroom.[21]

The marketing consciousness of witnesses increases with the awareness of being on national or global television.[22] There is a risk that a witness will alter his story in order to appeal to the television audience instead of fulfilling his evidentiary role.[23] His testimony becomes more important for its entertainment value which may cause embellishment of certain aspects of his testimony.[24] Many people dream of becoming a celebrity, and for many witnesses, this may be their only opportunity to shine in the limelight. This consciousness poses a danger of improper and inaccurate testimony. Kato Kaelin's testimony in the Simpson criminal trial is an excellent example of the effects of marketing consciousness.[25] Kaelin's ambiguous testimony aided neither the defense nor the prosecution. Kaelin did not supply the defense with an alibi for Simpson when his vague testimony resulted in a window of time establishing uncertainty of Simpson's whereabouts.[26] In sharp contrast to the testimony of several other key witnesses, Kaelin destroyed the prosecution's hope of securing a motive when he testified that Simpson did not exhibit any anger in the hours prior to the murders.[27] In addition, Kaelin's testimony had a high entertainment value. He subsequently appeared on numerous talk shows providing different descriptions of the events prior to the murders than his testimony at trial had indicated.

In addition, cameras pose a risk that lawyers will modify their roles. In a televised trial, the public becomes an extrajudicial audience that they must persuade.[28] Lawyers may become preoccupied with the cameras which interferes with their devoting full attention to the fact-finder at trial.[29] As a result, some lawyers direct at least part of their case to the television viewers instead of fully representing their clients to the presiding judge and the jury.[30] Lawyers are motivated to present themselves well in the eyes of the public. In a highly televised trial, the marketing consciousness of the participating lawyers may be affected. There is a danger that the media's production of the trial may transform into an excellent opportunity for the lawyers to gain free personal advertisement.

Televising a criminal trial is evidence of the notoriety of the case.[31] This intense media coverage impacts the jury's determination of the verdict.[32] After the prosecution and defense present their sides of the case, the fate of the defendant lies within the power of the jury. In an ordinary case, rendering a verdict is a heavy responsibility. Televising criminal proceedings adds to this burden by indicating that the jury is involved in a celebrated case. This enlargement of the jury's responsibility places undue pressure on its decision-making processes.[33] The effects of the intense publicity of the trial may dissuade jurors from rendering unpopular verdicts.[34] Thus, the realization that the court proceedings are broadcast can irreversibly contaminate the jury pool.

Leveling the Constitutional Conflict: Free Press v. Fair Trial

The United States Constitution embodies several inalienable rights that are guaranteed against infringement. The drafters did not intend any particular right to be measured as more important than another. However, when controversies arise involving constitutional issues, resolving the conflict often rests upon balancing constitutional rights against one another. Televising criminal proceedings sparks an ongoing conflict between the media's right to freedom of the press and a defendant's right to a fair trial which are both fundamentally insured by the Constitution. In a 1941 opinion, Justice Hugo Black stated that "free speech and fair trials are two of the most cherished policies of our civilization, and it would be a trying task to choose between them."[35] Even though it is impossible to determine which right is more valuable, the constitutional controversy surrounding the debate between the media and the courts cannot be ignored.

In 1965, the Supreme Court first attempted to address the free press versus fair trial issue in *Estes v. Texas*.[36] In Estes, the Court concluded that television cameras should not be permitted in the courtroom because of their distracting effects on the judicial process.[37] The Court's underlying reason was not the physical presence of the cameras, but the awareness felt by the participants in the trial.[38] Though the media has an accessible right to courtroom proceedings, it is doubtful that this right mandates its ability to televise criminal trials.

Courts have an obligation to be accessible to the public because they are a branch of the government.[39] The courts usually fulfill this obligation by allowing a public presence and representatives of the media within the courtroom.[40] However, the decision to allow the public and the media within the courtroom is discretionary. A court has the inherent right to close its doors. The public has no inherent right to hear or learn of proceedings until a judgment has been made and the proceedings are part of the public record. In addition, this right may be limited if the court chooses to close the records of a particular case. The admission of television cameras into judicial proceedings is within the discretion of the courts. Because a court has the discretion either to eliminate or to limit public access to its courtroom, the television media does not have an absolute right to be present at criminal trials.

The United States Supreme Court held in *KPNX Broadcasting Co. v. Arizona Superior Court* that courts "may insist that the only performance which goes on in the courtroom is the trial of the case at hand."[41] The Court said further that "the fact that media coverage has transformed events such as professional sports contests into a framework designed to accommodate that coverage does not mean that the First Amendment requires criminal trials to undergo the same transformation."[42] In making these conclusions, the Court addressed the importance of a trial with no outside distractions. While the Court recognizes the media's right to freedom of the press within the First Amendment, it also recognizes the right of a court to close its doors. The Court condemns the transformation of a criminal trial into a spectacle created by intense media coverage.

The Freedom of the Press

The Constitution does not contain an express provision allowing cameras in the courtroom, yet the media claim that its right to televise trials lies within the parameters of the First Amendment. The First Amendment guarantees the freedom of speech and the freedom of the press.[43] The press has an undeniable right to be present at criminal trials and to report their findings to the public. However, the Supreme Court concluded in *Richmond Newspapers, Inc. v. Virginia* that the media's right of access is not absolute and is subject to reasonable limitations.[44] Moreover, the rights of the electronic media can be distinguished from the rights of the print media.[45]

Beyond the obvious physically disruptive effects of cameras, other significant differences exist between electronic and print media. Historically, Constitutional law has protected the printed press.[46] In 1791 the drafters of the First Amendment could not have envisioned the technological advances of modern day television, and certainly a global audience viewing a criminal trial was not considered. History indicates that electronic media is not afforded the same legal rights as print media.[47]

Another important distinction between print and electronic media is that television is a licensed industry that is regulated by the Federal Communications Commission (FCC).[48] The FCC defines the legal limits of television; therefore, the camera has no inherent constitutional right to be in a court of law.[49] Moreover, the electronic media is not absolutely banned from all criminal trials. They can seek access through a legislative or judicial decree pursuant to the procedural rules within the particular jurisdiction.

Media supporters also argue that the First Amendment encompasses the public's right to know about the actions of the government.[50] This argument has less clout when applied to the judicial branch than to the legislative branch.[51] First, courtrooms focus on personal lives more than on governmental abuse.[52] A fair trial necessitates the intense scrutiny of extremely intimate details of the individual participants.[53] Television cameras exercise discretion while they graphically expose these private matters.[54] Second, cameras interject biases into the public by implementing certain camera angles which disrupt neutrality.[55] The public's right to know beyond the reaches of print media must be balanced with the inevitable biases caused by television.[56]

The Right to a Fair Trial

The Sixth Amendment guarantees the right to a fair trial.[57] One of the purposes of this guarantee is to protect the defendant. Also encompassed within the Sixth Amendment is a defendant's right to a public trial.[58] Media advocates claim that televising the trial ensures that justice is served.[59] This argument has several problematic factors. First, the media is not the fourth branch of government.[60] The role of the media is to inform the public, not to police the system. Second, with increased coverage, the media becomes less of a defensive force against injustice and more of an offensive force by intimidating witnesses and jurors, distracting the lawyers, and "distorting the unfolding drama in the courtroom."[61] Third, television coverage of even preliminary hearings creates a bias within the general population.[62] The jurors, the fact-finders in a criminal trial, are chosen from the general population, and they bring these biases with them to the proceedings.[63] This impartiality diminishes the fairness of the jury's findings. Fourth, televising criminal proceedings significantly expands the risk that jurors will be exposed, whether intentionally or not, to information about the case outside of the courtroom.[64] Televising a case simply causes a ripple effect. The print media increases its coverage as the electronic media televises. Fifth, television gives rise to prejudicial opinion and publicity by creating an unwanted thirteenth juror consisting of the television audience.[65] If a trial verdict against the defendant is overturned, the prejudicial publicity attached to the case by the television coverage makes it virtually impossible for a defendant to receive an impartial new trial.[66] If a new trial is warranted, the

jury is chosen from the general public which has been polluted with the biases produced by the media coverage of the defendant's first trial. Sixth, jurors are often harassed by members of the media in a sensationalized trial. The media may not only expose private details about their personal lives but also may probe the jury members for details about their deliberation. The Federal Rules of Evidence preclude jurors from relating matters that are intrinsic to the jury's deliberation.[67] The purpose of these rules is to promote the finality of the verdict and to prevent a chilling effect on the jury process.[68] Most state courts have adopted rules similar to the federal rules. The media attention given to televised trials raises the risk that evidentiary rules will be violated.

The Educational Controversy

Defenders of cameras in the courtroom assert that televising trials serves an educational purpose. Proponents contend that coverage of criminal trials expands the public's knowledge of judicial proceedings. In making this argument, the media misinterprets the role of the judiciary. The purpose of a public trial is to effectively administer justice. The job of the judiciary is not to teach the public of its inner workings but to preserve fairness within the system.

No empirical evidence exists which indicates that televised criminal proceedings broaden the public's understanding of the judiciary.[69] New York University conducted a study following an enactment of legislation prescribing an eighteen-month experimental period of televising criminal trials.[70] The researchers performed the study on the same participants before and after the experimental period.[71] The results indicated that viewing criminal trials had virtually *no effect* on the level of the public's understanding of even the most rudimentary aspects of court proceedings.[72]

[Former] United States Attorney General Janet Reno stated in a Justice Department briefing that cameras in the courtrooms give an opportunity to the public to see "justice in action."[73] Reno believes that, if used in a fair manner, cameras can be an invaluable tool in ensuring defendant's rights, the accountability of the system, and public confidence.[74] Satisfaction of Reno's ideals would place a heavy burden on the media to establish that cameras can be used in a fair manner. In order to meet the burden, the media would have to remain impartial throughout the proceedings. With presently used techniques, the media could not achieve this objective. Failure to use cameras in a fair manner leads to inaccuracies and misinterpretations of the issues at trial. The public's knowledge should not be expanded with false information.

Ethical Differences

Members of the media are not bound by the same professional standards as lawyers.[75] Lawyers are bound by rules of ethics that establish fiduciary duties of loyalty with their clients. Journalists have no similar duty concerning the subjects of their stories. The main duty of members of the media is to obtain information and determine what sells.[76] After making this determination, the media then continues to deliver what the public wants to hear. For example, prior to the O. J. Simpson case, CNN formulated an internal task force to determine the cause of declining ratings.[77] Once the Simpson trial began, the task force became largely unnecessary because the ratings sky-rocketed.[78] The electronic media wants continued access to sensationalized criminal trials because coverage of the proceedings boosts its ratings. The underlying motive behind the media's fight for cameras in the courtroom is money. Our justice system abhors financial benefit at the expense of the victims or the criminal defendants.

Conclusion

The judiciary's role in our society is to prevent injustice. The system carries out this role by guaranteeing to a defendant a fair trial by a jury. As the courtroom door is opened to the endless reaches of the media, the dignity of the proceedings simultaneously begins to falter. Cameras trivialize the proceedings by placing the crucial issues of a criminal trial into a tabloid-like atmosphere with the result of sensationalizing certain aspects of the trial instead of focusing on the administration of justice. Cameras thwart the dignity of the proceedings by causing witnesses and jurors to focus more on their actions than the issues at band. Cameras produce biases within the television audience that have profound effects upon the defendant. If a verdict is overturned, the jury pool will be contaminated from the biases that developed in the original trial. Until the media can eliminate these adverse effects, television should remain outside of the courtroom.

Notes

1. Richter H. Moore Jr., *Cameras in State Courts: A Historical Perspective*, 78 JUDICATURE 128, 130 (1994).
2. *See id.*
3. Christo Lassiter, *Cameras in the Courtroom? A Fair Trial is at Stake*, TRIAL, Mar. 1995, at 68.
4. Harvey J. Sepler, *Where Do We Stand on Cameras in the Courtroom?* 70 FLA. B.J. 113 (Jun. 1996).
5. *See id.*
6. *See id.*
7. M. L. Stein, *Unique Gathering, Remarkable Results: Judges, Lawyers, Journalists Agree on a Number of Issues Concerning Media Coverage of Courts*, EDITOR & PUBLISHER, Jun. 29, 1996, at 12.
8. *See id.*
9. *Id.*
10. *See id.*
11. Paul Thaler, *The Watchful Eye: American Jurisprudence In The Age of The Television Trial* 7 (1994).
12. *See id.*
13. Lassiter, *supra* note 3, at 68.
14. *See id.* at 8.
15. *See id.* at 9.
16. *See id.*
17. *See id.*
18. Lassiter, *supra* note 3, at 89.
19. *See id.*
20. Thaler, *supra* note 11, at 16.
21. *See id.* at 15.
22. Lassiter, *supra* note 3, at 71.
23. *See id.*
24. *See id.*

25. Michael D. Harris, *Kaelin Helps, and Hinders Prosecution; Clark Says Others Will Say Simpson Was 'Angry, Yelling'; Window Established*, L. A. DAILY J., Mar. 24, 1995 at 1, 9.
26. *See id.*
27. *See id.*
28. Lassiter, *supra* note 3, at 71.
29. *See id.*
30. *See id.*
31. *See id.* at 68.
32. *See id.*
33. Lassiter, *supra* note 3, at 71.
34. *See id.* at 68.
35. *Bridges v. California*, 314 U.S. 252 (1941).
36. *See Estes v. Texas*, 381 U.S. 532 (1965).
37. *See id.*
38. *See id.*
39. Thaler, *supra* note 11, at 87.
40. *See id.*
41. *KPNX Broadcasting Co. v. Ariz. Super. Ct.*, 459 U.S. 1302, 1306 (1982).
42. *Id.* at 1306–1307.
43. U.S.C.A. Const. amend. 1.
44. *See Richmond Newspapers, Inc. v. Virginia*, 448 U.S. 555 (1980).
45. Thaler, *supra* note 11, at 86.
46. *See id.*
47. *See id.*
48. *See id.*
49. *See id.*
50. Lassiter, *supra* note 3, at 71.
51. *See id.*
52. *See id.*
53. *See id.*
54. *See id.*
55. Thayer, *supra* note 11, at 71.
56. *See id.* at 72.
57. U.S.C.A & Const. amend. 6.
58. *Id.*
59. Lassiter, *supra* note, at 72.
60. *See id.* at 68.
61. *Id.* at 72.
62. *See id.* at 71.
63. *See id.*
64. Sepler, *supra* note 4, at 113. *See also State v. Menendez*, No. BA06880, slip op. at 2 (Super. Ct. Oct. 6, 1995).
65. Thaler, *supra* note, at 88.
66. *See id.*
67. FED. R. EVID. 606.
68. FED. R. EVID. 606 advisory committee's note.
69. Thaler, *supra* note 11, at 81.
70. *See id.* at 79. *See also* William Petkanas, *Cameras on Trial: An Assessment of Educational Effects of News Cameras*, in TRIAL COURTS (1990) (Ph.D. dissertation, N.Y. Univ.).
71. *See id.*
72. *See id.*
73. Janet Reno, *Judges Support Cameras in Courts*, THE NEWS MEDIA & THE LAW, Sept. 1995 at 44.
74. *See id.*
75. Tony Case, *O. J. Trial and the Press; The Debate Continues*, EDITOR & PUBLISHER, Mar. 4, 1995 at 11.
76. James Martin, *Meta-Coverage*, AMERICA, Mar. 4, 1995, at 25.
77. Alan Bash, *Moving on: CNN and Court TV Contemplate Life After Simpson*, THE SEATTLE TIMES, Oct. 5, 1995, at G7.
78. *See id.*

Reprinted from: Taffiny S. Stewart, "The Distortion of Criminal Trials Through Televised Proceedings." *Law and Psychology Review*, 21 (Spring): 257–269. Copyright © 1997 by Taffiny S. Stewart. Reprinted by permission. ✦

Part Four

Punishment of Offenders

The correctional system carries out the sentence imposed by the courts by incarcerating offenders or by punishing them in the community. Over the last two decades, it seems that U.S. citizens have become less tolerant of offenders and have demanded that more lawbreakers be imprisoned for longer periods of time in the name of community safety. The basis of the "new politics" of criminal punishment is, in part, affected by the public's lack of trust in government officials—police, judges, parole boards, and so forth—to harness the crime problem (Zimring 2001). The rate of release on discretionary parole has significantly decreased, and many people returning to prison have violated conditions of their parole or probation. For these reasons, growth in the jail and prison population has outpaced the number of beds available to those incarcerated within our Constitutional requirements.

The United States has 6.3 million persons, or nearly 3 percent of the total adult population, under correctional supervision. Of this number, more than 2 million offenders are incarcerated in local, state, and federal prison and jail institutions (Beck 2000). Some commentators have said that corrections is one of the fastest-growing industries in the country—its costs outpacing budgets for education, medical care, and other social service programs. In 1999 alone, a total of $32.7 billion was spent on adult state and federal prison institutions, averaging $630.7 million per state. Out of the total amount, $3.3 billion was allocated for new prison construction or other building improvements (Camp and Camp 1999, 85). The $32.7 billion does not include the operational budgets for the thousands of city and county jails.

This section focuses on five controversial issues related to correctional expansion and decreased public tolerance of certain types of criminal activity. The first issue asks whether we overuse imprisonment as a punishment strategy. In thinking about this issue, bear in mind the following questions: Does our crime rate necessitate a high imprisonment rate, higher than that of other countries? Do all felony offenders deserve incarceration? Would some offenders benefit from other types of community supervision?

Two issues in this section, privatization and restorative justice, are reactions to the rate of correctional expansion. The privatization issue asks whether private for-profit companies should be in the business of punishing offenders. Private companies have contracted to provide extra bed space and thus have saved some states from pending lawsuits stemming from crowded institutions. Critics contend that this relationship between public and private spheres is a conflict of interest, doing more harm than good.

Restorative justice is both an emerging paradigm—a new way of thinking—as well as a practice meant to permeate the entire criminal justice system. Some of the principles surrounding this perspective include the idea that crime is more than breaking the law—it disrupts and harms both individuals and community relationships. The primary goal, then, should be for the offender to take responsibility and to repair this harm. The victim, offender, and the community should participate together in the response to crime (Kurki 1999). Restorative justice programs have already begun emerging in a piecemeal fashion throughout the United States. The idea has been embraced as a positive step forward. The question to be considered is whether the implementation of restorative justice will achieve its intended goals.

Finally, two issues are related to decreased public tolerance of certain types of criminal activity. The first type of criminal activity in question is serious crime committed by juveniles and its punishment. The recent trend towards trying youths as adults for serious crimes stems from the public's perception that the juvenile justice system has not been punishing children severely enough. There is some agreement that these children should be punished in accordance with the seriousness of the harm caused by their crimes. The debatable issue is whether

youths tried as adults should be incarcerated alongside adults in the same jails and prisons.

The final issue in this section questions the practice of notifying communities of the arrival of sex offenders after the offenders have been released from prison and have completed their punishment. Sex offenders are currently the only ones who must register with local law enforcement agencies. The personal demographics and whereabouts of sex offenders are made available by statute, by law enforcement discretion, or by a completed risk assessment. It is unclear whether this practice will be extended to other types of offenders in the future.

References

Beck, Allen J. 2000. *Prisoners in 1999*. Washington, DC: U.S. Department of Justice, Bureau of Justice Statistics.

Camp, Camille Graham, and George M. Camp. 1999. *The Corrections Yearbook, 1999*. Middletown, CT: Criminal Justice Institute.

Kurki, Leena. 1999. "Incorporating Restorative and Community Justice into American Sentencing and Corrections," Paper #3 from *Sentencing and Corrections: Issues for the 21st Century*. Washington, DC: U.S. Department of Justice.

Zimring, Franklin E. 2001. "The New Politics of Criminal Justice: Of 'Three Strikes,' Truth-in-Sentencing, and Megan's Laws." Pp. 1–22 in *Perspectives on Crime and Justice: 1999–2000* Lecture Series (Research Forum, Volume IV). Washington, DC: National Institute of Justice. ✦

ISSUE XII

Lock 'Em Up: Do We Overuse Imprisonment as a Punishment Strategy?

Arrest and conviction trends in the last decade show that the criminal justice system is responding differently to criminals than in the past. For example, the war on drugs has changed the way that drug offenders are processed and punished. More drug offenders are behind bars than ever before. In addition, mandatory sentencing laws and sentencing guidelines for some crimes require incarceration, reducing the choices that judges have for alternative sentences.

It is a well-known fact that the number of people under correctional supervision in the United States has reached a record high—the second highest in the world next to Russia (Austin and Irwin 2001). To absorb these growing numbers, new prison units are being built at an unprecedented rate, yet institutional crowding remains a problem. At the same time, fewer treatment and recreational programs are available for prisoners to better themselves while incarcerated (Silberman 1995). The question remains: Are sentencing policies and imprisonment rates achieving their intended purpose of controlling crime? In other words, do we overuse imprisonment, or is our high level of imprisonment necessary to control the high level of crime in the United States?

Franklin E. Zimring authored the first article with guidance and information supplied by his colleague, Professor Gordon Hawkins. Zimring argues that Americans overuse imprisonment for nonviolent and drug offenses relative to the crime and incarceration rates of other countries. He agrees that prison is appropriate for violent offenders and should be reserved for them. Incarcerating nonviolent offenders to prevent future acts of lethal violence is more effective when the capacity of prisons is limited because judges are forced to make hard decisions about which offenders will occupy a prison bed. Zimring states that incarcerating violent and nonviolent offenders together does not distinguish lethal violence from less serious forms of crime. He would agree with others that confinement does not significantly reduce the crime rate, and it has little positive effect on recidivism (Austin and Irwin 2001). One of the reasons for the latter is that long prison terms are more often enforced on people who are already "aging out" of crime (decreasing the propensity at which they commit crime), while much of the predatory crime is committed by younger individuals who may be less likely to receive long prison terms (Petersilia 1994).

Michael K. Block, on the other hand, is convinced that our crime rate is high because we don't incarcerate enough criminals. He demonstrates his point by mathematically calculating that the chance of going to prison for committing a serious crime is extremely low. In addition, Block believes that the chance of going to prison has more deterrent value than the threat of long prison sentences. Thus, it seems that Block favors incarcerating more offenders—both violent and nonviolent—while Zimring supports incarcerating fewer nonviolent offenders.

References

Austin, James, and John Irwin. 2001. *It's About Time: America's Imprisonment Binge* (3rd ed). Belmont, CA: Wadsworth.

Petersilia, Joan. 1994. "Debating Crime and Imprisonment in California." *Evaluation and Program Planning* 17(2): 165–177.

Silberman, Matthew. 1995. *A World of Violence.* Belmont, CA: Wadsworth.

Critical Thinking Questions

1. Are U.S. sentencing policies and imprisonment rates achieving their intended purpose of controlling crime?

2. Do we overuse imprisonment, or is our high level of imprisonment necessary to control the high level of crime in the United States?

3. Assume for a moment that it is your responsibility as newly appointed "Crime Czar" to reduce our national prison population by *half* its current size and to process newly convicted criminals at the same time. Your job is to think of as many creative ways as possible to accomplish this goal.

4. How do other countries in the world handle criminal behavior?

Internet Websites

U.S. incarceration rate soon to surpass Russia. <http://www.pubdef.state.mn.us/homepages/statepd/us_incarceration_vs_Russia.htm>

U.S. incarceration rate second highest in the world. <http://cipherwar.com/news/00/prisons.htm>

The Sentencing Project's information on prison populations. <http://www.sentencingproject.org/brief/prisonpop.pdf>

CNN Story, March 14, 1999, about the U.S. imprisonment rate doubling within 12 years. <http://www.cnn.com/US/9903/14/us.prisons/>

U.S. Department of Justice, Bureau of Justice Statistics Corrections Statistics. <http://www.ojp.usdoj.gov/bjs/correct.htm>

Bureau of Prisons, National Institute of Corrections Webpage. <http://www.ojp.usdoj.gov/bjs/correct.htm>

Families Against Mandatory Minimums, a nonprofit group against sentencing laws requiring offenders to serve a mandatory number of years in prison before becoming eligible for release. <http://www.famm.org/fammgr97/p25c.html>

Proposition 36 in California: Substance Abuse and Crime Prevention Act mandating treatment over prison for people in possession of drugs to avoid the overuse of prison. <http://www.pacificnews.org/jinn/stories/6.20/001009-getting.html> ✦

23

Lethal Violence and the Overreach of American Imprisonment

*Franklin E. Zimring
(with the collaboration of
Gordon Hawkins)*

The purpose of this paper is to provide a brief summary of my views on two of what [NIJ Director] Jeremy Travis has called "core topics" for the plenary session:

1. What are the differential merits of incarceration as a sanction with respect to property, violent, and drug offenses?

2. Does current sentencing policy confine too many or too few offenders in the United States?

My answers to these two questions are linked. The serious problem in the United States is not crime but lethal violence. We have about the same rate of theft and burglary as other developed nations in the 1990s but very high rates of those offenses that put life in jeopardy. At current levels, property crime is not a serious problem in a wealthy nation that has insurance and other loss-spreading devices. Life-threatening violence creates fear because government and insurance can do little to ameliorate the harm that life-threatening assault and rape produce. Life-threatening violence should be a special priority for criminal sanctions, and prison should be mainly reserved for these most serious threats.

Instead, the huge escalation in rates of imprisonment during the past two decades has reduced the share of prison population represented by persons convicted of violent crimes. No matter what the question in American criminal justice, prison has been the answer. From an incapacitation standpoint, this does not reduce the prevention of violence. But the system's sense of proportionality and the moral and educative emphasis on violence as particularly disapproved have suffered as a wider variety of offenses are routinely sanctioned with prison. And deterrent incentives to avoid life-threatening violence are reduced when property crime routinely leads to prison.

So American criminal justice systems are overimprisoning in a quantitative and a qualitative sense. Restoring the proper priority to life-threatening violence will mostly require nonprison sanctions for auto thieves and housebreakers.

The following two sections outline the evidence on crime and lethal violence and show how broadening the range of prison offenses has shifted the focus of penal policy away from appropriate priority.

Most Americans believe they are the victims of crime far more often than the citizens of other developed nations. With one important exception, this is not the case. . . . [P]olice statistics for Los Angeles and Sydney, Australia [indicate that] the two cities have similar levels of nonviolent property crimes but vastly different levels of robbery and criminal homicide. In Sydney, victims are angry about housebreaking but not terrified. Fear is the more common reaction in Los Angeles. Living in a city with 20 times the homicide rate, the citizens of Los Angeles have a specific worry the citizens of Sydney do not have.

. . . [C]rime rate comparisons for New York City and London [show that] rates of nonviolent theft offenses were higher in London than in New York in 1990. Because larceny and burglary are high-volume offenses, this meant that the aggregate rate of what we call "index felonies" was higher in London in

1990 than in New York. There were more crimes and more criminals in London, but the homicide rate was more than 10 times higher in New York.

Gordon Hawkins and I sought out data on the homicides that resulted from victims of robbery and burglary being killed by the offender in these two cities in 1992. A total of 212,000 incidents in London caused 7 deaths. But the 191,000 burglaries and robberies in New York caused 378 victim deaths, a total 54 times as great as in London.

A series of new victimization surveys asking the same question in many different countries confirms that U.S. crime rates are not much higher than crime rates in other industrial nations. Rates of theft, burglary, and even nonaggravated assault reported in the United States are rarely more than 30 percent above those of many Western nations (Zimring and Hawkins, 1997, at chapter 3). But the rates of killing are 4 to 18 times those of other developed countries (Zimring and Hawkins, 1997, at figure 1.5 and chapter 3).

For offenses of violence, the United States ranks second to Australia but has a rate close to the rates reported by Canada, Poland, and New Zealand. Eight of the seventeen nations have violent crime rates within 30 percent of the U.S. rate. The U.S. rate for lethal violence is a high multiple of rates in other developed countries.

Why Fear Lethal Violence?

The offender who kills his victim takes something from that victim and the victim's family that cannot be given back. By contrast, a compensation program can make the victim whole in the theft of the person's BMW with insurance or other loss-spreading devices. So interests in life and bodily security are not just more important than property interests; they also cannot be compensated in a truly commensurate fashion. When modern states make property hard to steal and when they facilitate insurance, they all but guarantee that lethal violence will be the citizen's major worry about crime, even in settings where homicide is low. In the United States, however, where rates are quite high, the fear of lethal violence is debilitating.

The rational response of a criminal justice system to the special importance of lethal violence would be to make the prevention of serious violence the dominant priority in criminal justice. Because prison is our most serious available criminal sanction, such a focus would create a strong link between life-threatening violence and the available sanction of greatest seriousness. That has not, however, been the trend in American criminal justice lately, as the next section demonstrates.

U.S. Imprisonment Rates

We begin our discussion of U.S. imprisonment rates in familiar statistical territory, with data about rates of imprisonment per 100,00 population. . . . The data . . . support the now familiar litany of the grandiose levels of imprisonment in America. As *The Economist* puts it, "America now imprisons seven times as many people (proportionately) as does the average European country largely as a result of get-tough-on-crime laws."

Even more impressive than the current level of American imprisonment is the rapidity with which levels of imprisonment have risen in recent years. There were more than five times as many people in prison in the United States in 1996 as there were in 1973. The growth in American imprisonment has been greater and more sustained during the past two decades than in any prior period (Zimring and Hawkins, 1991).

This discussion adds two new twists to the familiar complaints about high rates of imprisonment in the United States. The first additional item we would add to the data on imprisonment rates and comparison countries is the information about reported crime rates. . . . It would be one thing if America's sevenfold advantage in rates of imprisonment paralleled a sevenfold higher crime rate. But this is clearly not the case for the most common forms of index crime. It appears that the English have just as many thieves as can be found in American cities and a larger number of burglaries. Thus, rates of common crime do not begin to explain the large difference in American rates of imprisonment.

But what about the large difference among American rates of homicide, life-threatening assault, and robbery? The much larger rate of lethal violence in the United States probably explains one-quarter to one-third of the difference in rates of imprisonment between the United States and other countries. The reason lethal violence differences do not explain a larger proportion of the difference in imprisonment is that serious-violence offenders represent a modest and declining share of the American prison population. Prior to the huge expansion in American imprisonment, the concentration of violent offenders in American prisons was much more substantial than in current circumstances.

In California, for example, about 60 percent of all prisoners in 1979 reached the prison system because they were convicted of violent crimes. That was the distribution of offenders in a prison system with an inmate population under 25,000. For the 80,000 prison spaces added to the penal system during the next decade, the concentration of violent offenders was much smaller. If the 1979 population is held constant and if the criminal records of the offenders occupying additional capacity are separately analyzed, only 27 percent of the new space has been allocated to persons convicted of offenses of violence.

So if lethal violence is the problem, the mechanism of imprisonment has become less efficient as the prison population has expanded. This was to be expected because the most serious offenses produce imprisonment decisions even when prison populations are relatively low. The system is not inclined to put Charles Manson or Willie Horton on probation in any event. Adding dramatically to prison numbers means pushing into prison many more people at the margin between prison and nonprison sanctions. Expanding prison numbers means imprisoning larger numbers of housebreakers and car thieves to join the armed robbers already incarcerated under prior policy. Sure enough, as the rates of imprisonment mush-roomed in California during the 1980s, the number of burglars in prison grew more than three times as fast as the number of convicted robbers, and the number of car thieves grew six times as fast (Zimring and Hawkins, 1992:39). There can be no doubt that one natural result of sharp increases in imprisonment is the watering of the stock by increasing the proportionate share of less serious offenders behind bars.

Does this massive addition to a prison population of offenders not convicted of violent crimes reduce the capacity of the system to prevent violence? There are three functions of imprisonment as a criminal sanction to be considered separately in addressing this question: (1) incapacitation, (2) the educative or moralizing function of the threat of imprisonment, and (3) general deterrence. Considering only incapacitation, the imprisonment of large numbers of nonviolent offenders does not reduce the amount of violence prevented by incapacitation as long as there are no practical upper limits on the amount of prison space available in the criminal justice system. If extra nonviolent offenders are imprisoned but no violent offenders avoid imprisonment as a result, the net amount of violence prevented by imprisonment will probably be larger as a result of the prison expansion. Thus, the prison system in California, which held more than 100,000 prisoners in 1991, probably prevented a larger number of life-threatening acts of violence than the prison system of fewer than 25,000 a decade before. How many extra acts of life-threatening violence were prevented is not known, however, and there are indications that the number was relatively small (Zimring and Hawkins, 1995, at chapter 6; Cohen and Canela-Cacho, 1994). But even if the marginal returns from extra imprisonment are very low, the absolute number of violent offenses prevented should increase.

If the amount of prison capacity available for incapacitation is limited, using that limited capacity for those convicted of nonviolent offenses can reduce the amount of life-threatening violence prevented if future life-threatening violence is more common among persons already convicted of violent offenses. So a huge increase in imprisonment risk for thieves and drug sellers would reduce the net amount of violence prevented by imprisonment if nonviolent and violent offenders are in a zero-sum competition for scarce prison space. But if the scale of imprisonment can be expanded indefinitely, even a large increase in the proportion of nonviolent offenders imprisoned will not lead to a palpable reduction in deaths and injuries prevented.

The period 1980–1994 appears to have been a time when additional prison space for nonviolent and drug offenders could be provided without diminution of the penal resources available for persons convicted of life-threatening violence. In the more crowded and resource-competitive conditions of the late 1990s, however, the prospects for prison expansion may not be unlimited, and locking up a large proportion of those without previous records of violence could reduce the amount of violent crime restrained by penal confinement.

The American criminal justice system may already be shooting itself in the foot with respect to the educative and moralizing influence of criminal punishments generally and imprisonment specifically. When 60 percent of a prison population is serving time because of a conviction for violent crime, the criminal justice system is drawing a clear boundary between serious violence and other types of crime. That is an environment where armed robbery and housebreaking are regarded as very different types of crime. Vastly expanding the imprisonment of housebreakers and car thieves blurs the distinction between crimes that involve the risk of injury to the victim and those that do not.

There are a number of indicators that the educative and moralizing influence of criminal sanctions can be a significant influence on the behavior of potential criminals. In areas as diverse as drunk driving and domestic violence, changes in criminal justice policy that emphasized the seriousness of driving after drinking and willful domestic injury played a major role in reducing death rates from automobile accidents and intimate homicide. Blurring the distinction between robbery and burglary in American criminal justice is unwise because the risk of death in the average robbery is 50 times as great as in the average burglary in the United States (Zimring and Hawkins, 1997, at chapter 4).

And an imprisonment policy that treats the robber and the burglar in a similar fashion mutes more than the educative and moralizing influence of the criminal law. Reducing the difference in the threat of punishment for armed robbery and housebreaking reduces the incentive for the potential criminal to choose the less serious of the two methods of obtaining property. Thus, a large increase in imprisonment that reduces the gap between burglary and robbery may produce more armed robbery as a result of the smaller gap between the burglary and robbery punishment, even if the threatened punishment for robbers is expanded. To the extent that the relative magnitude of punishment threats influences the choice of crime, general crackdowns on criminality could produce higher rates of lethal violence. Indeed, if a general crackdown on crime has to deter 50 additional burglaries for every burglar it converts to robbery to break even on crime victim deaths, the impact of such a policy on the death rate from crime may well be undesirable.

There is one other casualty worthy of mention when a war on crime greatly extends the range of offenses to be punished with imprisonment, and that is the sense that the punishments meted out by the system are proportionate to the seriousness of the crimes committed (Allen, 1996:43-46). The diverse offenses found in a modern penal code involve not only many different kinds of harm but also substantially different degrees of social cost. Policies that tend to homogenize punishments and spread them evenly over offending populations are not only problematic because potential offenders may miss important differences in culpability—this is the earlier point about the educative and moralizing influence of punishment—but also misleading because citizens and those who enforce the law may regard all criminal harms as morally indistinguishable.

The principal recent misadventure in American criminal justice that tended in this direction was the "War on Drugs" in the mid-1980s. Making prison the presumptive punishment for an ever-widening list of offenses is a significant symptom of a diminished sense of penal proportion. In this sense, too, large increases in imprisonment obscure the moral differences between different types of crime.

References

Allen, Francis A. (1996). *The Habits of Legality.* New York: Oxford University Press.

Cohen, Jacqueline, and Jose Canela-Cacho. (1994). "Incapacitation and Violent Crime." In Albert J. Reiss, Jr., and Jeffrey A. Roth, eds., *Understanding and Preventing Violence,* Volume 4, pp. 296–388. Washington, D.C.: National Academy of Sciences.

"Crime in America: Violent and Irrational—and That's Just the Policy." *The Economist* (June 8, 1996), pp. 23–24.

Jones, Michael A., and James Austin. (1995). *The 1995 NCCD National Prison Population Forecast.* Washington, D.C.: National Council on Crime and Delinquency.

Mauer, Marc. (1994). *Americans Behind Bars: The International Use of Incarceration, 1992–1994.* Washington, D.C.: The Sentencing Project.

New South Wales Bureau of Criminal Statistics. (1992). Personal communication.

United Kingdom Home Office. (1990). *Criminal Statistics in England and Wales.* London.

U.S. Department of Justice, Federal Bureau of Investigation. (1993). *Uniform Crime Reports, 1992.* Washington, D.C.: U.S. Government Printing Office.

U.S. Department of Justice, Federal Bureau of Investigation (1991). *Uniform Crime Reports, 1990.* Washington, D.C.: U.S. Government Printing Office.

van Dijk, Jan, and Pat Mayhew. (1992). *Criminal Victimization in the Industrialized World.* The Hague: Ministry of Justice.

Zimring, Franklin E., and Gordon Hawkins. (1997). *Crime Is Not the Problem: Lethal Violence in America,* New York: Oxford University Press.

———. (1995). *Incapacitation: Penal Confinement and the Restraint of Crime.* New York: Oxford University Press.

———. (1992). *Prison Population and Criminal Justice Policy in California.* Berkeley, California: Institute of Governmental Studies.

———. (1991). *The Scale of Imprisonment.* Chicago: University of Chicago Press.

Reprinted from : Franklin E. Zimring (with the collaboration of Gordon Hawkins), *Two Views on Imprisonment Policies: Lethal Violence and the Overreach of American Imprisonment.* Presentations from the 1996 Annual Research and Evaluation Conference, Washington, DC (NCJ 165702; Washington, DC: U.S. Department of Justice Office of Justice Programs, National Institute of Justice, July 1997). ✦

24
Supply Side Imprisonment Policy

Michael K. Block

Editor's Note: Throughout the paper, the author refers to "elasticities" which are statistical probability estimates that, for the purposes of this paper, are calculated based on how much one or more conditions need to change (e.g., the likelihood of imprisonment, or sentence length) in order to produce a significant change in the desired condition (e.g., decrease in the crime rate).

My hypothesis about how imprisonment affects public safety is quite straightforward. I am one of those few but growing number of academics who believe that threatening and, not too infrequently, actually imposing noticeable prison sentences helps to control crime. Moreover, I think the empirical evidence, such as it is, supports this position.

I am convinced that there are too many prisoners and prisons in the United States today not because we overuse imprisonment but, quite the contrary, because in major part in the past we have not been willing enough to imprison serious offenders. There are too many prisoners because there are too many criminals committing too many crimes, and we find ourselves in this predicament at the turn of the century because, for most of the last half of the 20th century, sentencing practices have not been harsh enough.

This is by no means the conventional wisdom among my colleagues. More common is the assertion that we overuse imprisonment. The unflattering comparison of the ratio of prisoners to population in the United States with the ratios in other major industrial powers is adduced as evidence of our wrongheadedness on this score.[1] Even if one ignored the empirical evidence on the disincentive effects of imprisonment, the ratio of prisoners to population would not be particularly informative. Only if the propensity to commit crime and the costs of controlling crime were similar in all of the industrial nations would this comparison of per capita imprisonment be relevant. Casual empiricism suggests that this precondition is not even roughly satisfied. Why this is the case is not well understood, but even a brief treatment of the issue is well beyond the scope of this paper.

It is also quite conventional to argue that we have tried getting tough on criminals and have failed. The refrain here is that the ratio of prisoners to population has increased dramatically since 1980, but the crime rate, particularly the violent crime rate, has not fallen appreciably. In actuality, violent crime is down quite substantially of late, but, again, this comparison of ratios of prisoners to population only makes sense to the extent that the propensity to commit crime—or, in the vernacular, the "criminal element"—has remained relatively stable over time. The empirical evidence suggests that this is not the case. Moreover, if we focus on the more relevant ratio of imprisonment to crime, the trends since 1980 are not unambiguously upward.[2]

Instead of comparing per capita imprisonment across countries or even over time, a more reliable comparison to judge imprisonment policy would be one between the costs and benefits of changing that policy. As shown in the work that follows, such a comparison generally indicates that our imprisonment policy has not been harsh enough and that the threat of additional imprisonment would reduce crime and might actually reduce the number of individuals in prison.

Crime and Punishment in Modern America

. . . According to the most recent National Crime Victimization Survey, almost 35 million index crimes (homicide, rape, robbery, assault, burglary, auto theft, and larceny) were committed in 1994.[3] According to the Federal Bureau of Investigation (FBI), about 14 million of these crimes were reported to them by police departments around the country. In terms of arrests, these same police departments made almost 3 million arrests for index crimes in 1994. . . . [O]nly about 1 in 5 reported crimes (or about 1 in 12 actual victimizations) are cleared by an arrest.

What is perhaps most striking . . . is the enormous falloff between arrests and convictions. While there were almost 3 million arrests for index crimes in 1994, there were only about 375,000 felony convictions for such crimes in State courts during the same year. Only about 13 percent of the arrests for index crimes actually ended in a conviction for a felony. Even for crimes like murder and rape, the ratio of convictions to arrests was remarkably low—only slightly over 55 percent in both cases. Undoubtedly, plea agreements muddy the water here. A number of those arrested for one crime were convicted of or pled guilty to another. When we look at the violent crime category as a whole, fewer than 1 in 5 of those arrested for a violent crime were actually convicted of a violent crime.

To account for convictions and pleas to a lesser offense and to obtain a more precise idea of conviction probabilities, data from the National Pretrial Reporting Program were used to estimate the likelihood that an offender arrested for a specific crime was convicted of any crime. . . . [W]hen we use this additional information, the conviction risk for murder reached a more respectable 71.5 percent. (The conviction risk for rape . . . is quite unreliable because of the differences in definitions of the crime between data sources.) However, even when all conviction offenses are accounted for, the overall conviction risk for violent crimes as a group is still quite modest (27.6 percent) and for all index crimes as a group it is even less impressive (17.3 percent). If an offender is arrested, and this is by no means a high-probability event, the likelihood of actually being convicted of the crime that he/she was arrested for (or, for that matter, any crime) is remarkably low.

Given the fact that the likelihood of being arrested and convicted for an index crime serious enough to be reported to and by the police is only about 3 percent or 4 percent, the consequences after conviction are enormously important in determining the expected punishment.[4] . . . [M]y estimate of the likelihood of being sent to prison after conviction . . . for an index crime . . . is about 52 percent. For an offender convicted of a violent crime, the offender's chance of being sent to prison is estimated to be about 63 percent. Of course, these ratios misstate the likelihood of imprisonment for an offender arrested for a specific crime to the extent they ignore the real possibility that he/she may be convicted of a less serious crime than that for which he/she was arrested. . . . [T]he estimates of imprisonment risk are recalculated to reflect these conviction outcomes. This recalculation, as expected, substantially lowers all of the imprisonment risks.

Using my estimates of arrest, conviction, and imprisonment risks, the probability of imprisonment was calculated for the various index crimes. . . . What is obvious from the calculations . . . is just how hard it is to get into prison in the United States. Only about 1 in 100 index crimes reported to the police actually result in imprisonment for an index crime. Even for violent crimes, only about 5 in 100 such crimes result in imprisonment. The ratio varies from 1 in 3 for murder to about 3 in 100 for aggravated assault. Overall, the likelihood of going to prison for committing an index crime is surprisingly low. And this does not change appreciably when convictions for lesser offenses are considered. As I will argue below, increasing the probability of imprisonment for these crimes by even modest amounts will pay handsome dividends.

Although it is true that imprisonment is not the only possibility for incarceration after conviction (the individual could be sent to a county jail), and that incarceration is not the only form of punishment, imprisonment is clearly the most severe sanction. Even when jail time is given for an index offense, it tends to be much shorter than a prison term. And although probation, especially the more recent intensive probation programs, imposes some punishment, it is usually not comparable to prison. Because prison is still by far the most severe form of punishment that is used on a regular basis, it is of special interest to those interested in the disincentive effect of punishment.[5]

Up to this point, I have concentrated on the likelihood of being punished for committing a serious crime. However, in analyzing the disincentive effect of imprisonment policy, it is also important to consider the severity of the punishment. As noted above, the most severe punishment regularly imposed is prison. As a practical matter, the only method of increasing the severity of a prison sentence is to increase its length. Given the propensity of most offenders to think only over the short term, this turn of events is quite unfortunate. Recent jurisprudence on the rights of prisoners and the standards of confinement appear to leave policymakers with only the weakest instrument (sentence length) for increasing the severity of punishment. Policy initiatives aimed at increasing the unpleasantness of prison life would likely be a cost-effective method of fighting crime. . . .

What is quite apparent is how the length of prison sentences has been increasing in recent years, especially for some violent crimes. The average prison time just to first release for those convicted of murder in 1992 is almost 70 percent longer than the time served by all those released in 1992 who were convicted of murder. For index crimes as a whole, time to be served in 1992 was 31 percent longer than the time actually served for those released in 1992.

Notwithstanding the recent trend of increasing sentence length, imprisonment is still very rare relative to crime. . . . The "probability of imprisonment" and the average "time to be served" estimates are combined to get expected months per criminal and reported crime.

Reported index crimes, which are arguably the most serious crimes, have an expected sentence of 18 prison days. In other words, if all of the prison time given out in a year for index crime is totaled, it averages out to 18 prison days for every reported index crime. What this means is that a criminal committing a number of index crimes can expect to spend 18 days in prison for every crime he/she commits. This overall average for all index crimes hides a good deal of variation. Performing the expected prison time calculation by type of crime produces averages that vary from nearly 40 months for every murderer to 3 days for every petty thief. Nevertheless, it is clear . . . that very little prison time is delivered relative to the volume of serious crime.

Is Imprisonment an Effective Crime Control Strategy?

Over the past several decades, a number of efforts have been made to quantify the deterrent effects of both the severity and certainty of punishment. In the mid-1980s Lewis (1986) reviewed most of the econometric evidence on the deterrent effect of increases in the length of imprisonment published up to that time. His review and analysis of the literature were clearly supportive of the hypothesis that an increase in the length of prison terms reduces crime. His results suggest that longer prison sentences have a deterrent effect and that these effects are statistically significant at high levels of confidence for many crimes and categories of crimes.

The studies that Lewis (1986) summarized all derive their estimates of the deterrent effect of imprisonment by attempting to statistically control for nondeterrence-related changes in the environment. Most include some control for changes in demographic factors over time or differences between areas at a point in time. Some studies attempt to control for changes (or variations) in economic conditions over time or between different areas at the same time. The elasticities that result from these studies are intended to provide information on how crime rates would change if only deterrent variables, such as the likelihood and severity of punishment, change. To the extent that other factors are also changing, crime rates will reflect changes in both deterrent levels and demographic and economic variables.

Lewis finds that in the studies he reviewed, the mean elasticity of sentence length (for index crimes) was -0.468. Translated from "econospeak," this means that, on average, a 10 percent increase in the sentence length for index crimes is estimated to result in a 4.68 percent decrease in such crimes. For homicide he finds that, on average, the studies he reviewed suggest that a 10 percent increase in sentence length will result in a 2 percent decrease in the murder rate, a 7 percent decrease in the rate for rape, about a 4.7 percent decline in the robbery rate, and a 6 percent decrease in the rate for aggravated assault.

Because there is nothing like the Lewis (1986) survey currently available for the econometric estimates of the likelihood of imprisonment, Block and Herbert (1994) adopted his methodology to assess the effectiveness of increasing the certainty of imprisonment. The same approach was used to prepare a similar but much abridged study for this report. To produce estimates of the deterrent effect of the certainty of imprisonment comparable to Lewis' findings on the deterrent effect of the length of imprisonment, the elasticity-averaging technique employed by Lewis was also used in this study. . . .

Lewis' (1986) estimates of sentence length elasticities were contrasted with my estimates of the certainty elasticities. Overall, the results suggest the existence of deterrent effects for both severity and certainty. However, with the exception of larceny, it appears that for most crimes there is a greater deterrent effect for an increase in the likelihood of imprisonment than for an increase in sentence length. Moreover, the results of both analyses (with the exception of murder in Lewis' analysis) indicate that the effects of the severity and certainty of punishment are greater for individual violent crimes than for individual property crimes.

The findings comport well with conventional wisdom (it is reassuring that such

"wisdom" is not always wrong) and is buttressed by my experimental findings on deterrence. In a series of economic experiments that included monetary payoffs and penalties, convincing evidence was obtained that prisoners are much more powerfully deterred from criminal acts by an increase in the likelihood that the penalty will be imposed than by an increase in the severity of the penalty (see Block and Gerety 1995).

More Cops, More Prosecutors, More Prisons?

In the last several years, a number of econometric studies have appeared that concentrate on directly measuring the impact on crime rates of increasing the prison population and suppress the distinction between the certainty and severity of punishment. The most recent of these studies, "The Effect of Prison Population Size on Crime Rates," was authored by Levitt and appeared in the May 1996 *Quarterly Journal of Economics.* Using a somewhat different approach than the econometric studies of deterrence summarized above, Levitt finds that a 10-percent increase in the prison population leads to between a 3-percent and 4-percent decline in index crimes. Levitt's estimates are significantly higher than the elasticities obtained by Marvell and Moody (1994) in their study—summarized in "Prison Population Growth and Crime Reduction" in the *Journal of Quantitative Criminology*—that also directly addressed the impact of imprisonment on crime. It should be noted however, that Marvell and Moody did not employ as sophisticated an estimating technique as Levitt, who used information on prison litigation to obtain more reliable estimates of the impact of imprisonment on crime.

Although the results of these studies are comforting because they both suggest that imprisonment works to control crime, and the implication of Levitt's estimate is that additional imprisonment is likely to be warranted, the blending of the deterrent effects of certainty and severity has a cost. Specifically, these studies—relating increases in the prison population to crime rates—are not very informative about what is the most effective way to increase the prison population.

In the short run, prison populations will increase as a consequence of changes in either the likelihood of imprisonment or the length of prison sentences. One relevant question that previous studies addressed but that more recent studies do not is whether one of these approaches is better than the other.

The implication of comparing the empirical estimates of the elasticities is that change in the certainty of imprisonment is a more effective approach to controlling crime, especially violent crime. However, when comparing the efficacy of increases in the certainty of imprisonment with the increases in the length of prison terms, the point has traditionally been made that increases in certainty may be even more expensive than increases in prison terms. Even if increases in certainty are more powerful than increases in severity, cost considerations may be offsetting. Whatever the merits of this argument in general, and clearly there is a strong presumption in its favor, in the current environment it is unlikely to be true.

Although increasing arrest rates and conviction rates may be resource consuming, they are not the only, or, for that matter, the most direct, method of increasing the probability of imprisonment. With the likelihood of being sentenced to prison after conviction at only about 52 percent for index crimes and 62 percent for violent crimes, changes in sentencing practices could deliver a fairly substantial increase in the likelihood of imprisonment with costs comparable to simple increases in sentence length. The quickest and least expensive way to increase the certainty of imprisonment is simply to change sentencing policy.

Costs and Benefits of Changes in Imprisonment Policies

One clear way to illustrate the relative attractiveness of increases in sentence length (average time served) and imprisonment risk is to present these alternatives in a cost-benefit framework. . . . The benefits are the crimes averted and they are valued at the total costs that each type of crime imposes on victims. These estimates are those used by Levitt (1996) and include both estimates of the pecuniary and nonpecuniary losses resulting from each of the index crimes. The costs of changing either of these imprisonment policies (length of time served and sentencing practices) are basically the costs associated with adding additional prisoners. To err on the conservative side, an estimate of the full cost of imprisonment of $2,765 per month per prisoner was used.

Because the monthly cost of other common sentencing outcomes such as probation or jail are not zero, the appropriate cost for the analysis of increasing imprisonment risk should be the net cost, or the difference between the cost of other options such as probation or jail and prison. Likewise if an increase in sentence length comes at the expense of parole time, the costs of the longer prison terms should reflect an offset for parole expense avoided. By ignoring these refinements, the results are biased against finding a positive benefit-cost ratio of any policy change that leads to more prison, and, in particular, an increase in imprisonment risk.

Increasing the risk of imprisonment has an unambiguously favorable benefit-cost ratio in all cases except burglary and larceny. For victimization data the case is similar for increases in the length of prison terms. However, for reported index crimes, increases in the length of sentences have marginal benefit-cost ratios for robbery and rape. Overall, as one would predict from the relative elasticities, increases in imprisonment risks are more attractive policy options. Increasing the likelihood of imprisonment following conviction produces benefit levels substantially in excess of costs for all violent crimes and auto theft. . . .

Getting Tough and Getting It Wrong

What this exercise highlights is the finding that there are substantial gains to revamping the sentencing structure so that more criminals, especially violent criminals, are sentenced to prison rather than to probation or jail. These benefit-cost results clearly indicate that too few violent criminals are imprisoned in the United States.

As noted above, recent attempts at "getting tough" appear to have taken the form of longer prison sentences and not higher levels of imprisonment risk. . . . In fact, if any trend is observed, it is a downward trend. The benefit-cost results imply that this concentration on increasing sentence length in recent years is not particularly good public policy.

Do a Violent Crime, Do Time: A Supply Side Imprisonment Policy

One simple modification of the sentencing structure that would be consistent with the benefit-cost analysis above would be to adopt a practice of sentencing all offenders convicted of violent crime to prison. This would change the sentencing system so that probation and/or jail were no longer sentencing options for offenders convicted of violent crimes.

To see how a "prison only" approach to sentencing for violent crime would fare in terms of benefit-cost analysis and prison populations, a rough cost-benefit analysis was conducted for the case where all offenders convicted of homicide, rape, robbery, and aggravated assault are sentenced to prison for the current average time served.

To construct this hypothetical case, the percentage change in imprisonment risk implied by a policy of making prison a certainty for all violent crime convictions was first calculated. Since the imprisonment risk for violent crime is currently 61.84 percent, it would take an approximately 62 percent increase in the risk of imprisonment to make imprisonment a certainty for all offenders convicted of a violent crime.

Using this 62 percent change in the probability of imprisonment, the year-by-year path of crimes and prisoners as well as costs and benefits were estimated for implementing the prison-only sentencing scheme for violent crime. In these calculations it was assumed that the representative construction cost was $40,000 per bed and that all cells were paid for in the year they were built. The annual cost of keeping an inmate, exclusive

of interest, was assumed to be $2,500 per month.

Again, to err on the conservative side, it was assumed in each of these examples that the deterrent effect did not begin until the fifth year and that it did not reach its full effect until the eighth year after the sentencing reform was instituted. Even with these unfavorable behavioral assumptions and the fact that the prisons had to be fully paid for in the year they went into service, the policy had a positive benefit-cost ratio by the sixth year, and every violent crime had a positive total benefit-cost ratio by the eighth year. This is without considering the reduction in expenditures for arrests and convictions that will also result from this imprisonment policy.

Not only does this example have favorable total discounted benefit-cost ratios, it will also eventually induce a lower prison population. Although the benefit-cost ratio for the policy turns positive before the prison population stabilizes, it will stabilize at a level lower than the level it would have been had there been no change in imprisonment policy. For all types of violent crime, the initial increase in imprisonment rates results in a lower prison population as well as a lower crime rate. It will also eventually result in fewer arrests and convictions.

A Prison-Only Approach in a Less Accommodating World

There is, however, one factor discussed above that may act to reduce the power of imprisonment and, thus, the benefit-cost ratio. Because the elasticities were calculated by averaging studies conducted using data between 1940 and 1970—to the extent that there is a downward trend in these elasticities, possibly resulting from the increase in the level of social pathology since 1960—the elasticities may overstate the impact of increases in the likelihood of imprisonment on crime rates. Although there is some evidence that the elasticities, at least for violent crimes, have declined in recent years, there are not enough studies to adequately explore this issue empirically.

We can, nevertheless, provide some perspective on this potentially important point by asking what the benefit-cost pattern of the prison-only policy for violent crime would be if the elasticities were only half of those reported. What is observed is that, if the elasticity with respect to the likelihood of imprisonment is now substantially less than an estimate based on historical data, the benefits of a prison-only policy for violent crime are still likely to outweigh the costs of such a policy. However, in this case the eventual prison population, while lower than the population level immediately after the intervention, will not dip below its original level.

Real Offense Sentencing for Violent Crime

An important aspect of the implementation in a prison-only policy for violent crime not explicitly accounted for in the analysis is the change in plea practices such a policy might induce. Mandatory prison sentences for any serious violent crime convictions might, by their effect on plea practices, increase the number of violent charges that result in nonviolent convictions. This would reduce somewhat the deterrence yield of the imprisonment-only policy for violent crime, but the existing elasticity estimates are not up to the task of modeling this type of feedback. One way to avoid some of this undercutting of the deterrent effect of a prison-only approach is to adopt "real offense" sentencing, i.e., sentencing based on offense behavior and not on the offense of conviction.

Conclusion

Although the benefit-cost calculations in this report, especially those involving hefty changes in imprisonment risks, stretch the empirical estimates of deterrence elasticities to their breaking point, the examples do make a point. Specifically, there is credible argument that the excessive levels of crime and imprisonment in society have as their cause a sentencing structure that is not harsh enough. There is evidence that instituting a more Draconian sentencing structure, i.e., one that involves imprisonment for essentially all convictions for violent crimes, is likely to be cost justified and may actually reduce the prison population. Imprisoning additional offenders is expensive and society has to sacrifice current consumption to build and operate prisons. However, the evidence suggests that the costs are worth it, at least for violent crimes. Making imprisonment a certainty for violent crimes will make society much better off.

Endnotes

1. "[T]he evidence is that we are quite harsh, in general harsher than other modern industrial nations, and that we have gotten strikingly harsher in recent years. . . . In 1988, the U.S. rate of incarceration (in jails and prisons) was 388 prisoners per 100,000 people. . . . For the same year, the rate for the United Kingdom was 97.4 per 100,000, for West Germany it was 84.9, for Belgium it was 65.4. The rate for Canada, with a society in many ways much like our own, was about 110 persons for every 100,000 inhabitants." (Jeffrey Reiman, *The Rich Get Richer and the Poor Get Prison: Ideology, Class, and Criminal Justice*, 4th ed., Boston, Massachusetts: Allyn & Bacon, 1995, p. 18.)

2. In particular, if we consider the ratio of new prison commitments to crime, we find that in 1980 the ratio was approximately 1 in 100 for index crimes and 4 in 100 for violent crimes. Both ratios were essentially unchanged in 1992. It is true that the average time served has been increasing of late, and, hence, there have been some increases in the ratio of prison population to crime. But the willingness to use prison as a sanction, which is probably best measured by the new commitment rate, has not changed appreciably in recent years.

3. Here . . . the term index crime is used to refer to the crimes of homicide, rape, robbery, aggravated assault, burglary, auto theft, and larceny. In actuality, the FBI uses the term "modified index crime" to refer to this group of crimes because "index crime" now also includes the crime of arson.

4. If we ignore the punishment that results simply from being arrested and assume that imprisonment is the only substantial punishment, the expected punishment (EF) can be expressed as $[EF = p_A * p_C * p_I * F]$ where p_A is the probability of arrest, p_C is the probability of conviction, p_I is the probability of imprisonment given conviction (imprisonment risk), and F is the average time served.

5. While conviction itself imposes a reputational penalty, this is most relevant for offenders who commit white-collar crime, and such crimes are not a very significant proportion of the index crime figures used in this report.

References

Avio, K., and C. Clark. (1978). "The Supply of Property Offenses in Ontario: Evidence of the Deterrent Effect of Punishment." *Canadian Journal of Economics*, Vol. 11, pp. 1–19.

Bartel, A. (1979). "Women and Crime: An Economic Analysis." *Economic Inquiry*, Vol. 17, pp. 29–51.

Becker, G.S. (1968). "Crime and Punishment: An Economic Approach." *Journal of Political Economy*, Vol. 76 (March/April), pp. 169–217.

Block, M.K., and V.G. Gerety. (1995). "Some Experimental Evidence on Differences Between students and Prisoners Reactions to Monetary Penalties and Risk." *Journal of Legal Studies* (January).

Block, M.K., and C.L. Herbert. (1994). "Deterrence: What We Know." University of Arizona. Unpublished working paper.

Blumstein, A., J. Cohen, and D. Nagin. (1978). *Deterrence and Incapacitation: Estimating the Effect of Criminal Sanctions*. Washington, D.C.: National Academy of Sciences.

Chamlin, M.B., H.G. Grasmick, R.J. Bursik, Jr., and J.K. Cochran. (1992). "Time Aggregation and Time Lag in Macro/Level Deterrence Research." *Criminology*, Vol. 30(3), pp. 377–395.

Cohen, M.A. (1990). "A Note on the Cost of Crime to Victims." *Urban Studies*, Vol. 27(l), pp. 139–146.

——. (1988). "Pain, Suffering, and Jury Awards: A Study of the Cost of Crime to Victims." *Law & Society Review*, Vol. 22(3), pp. 537–555.

Ehrlich, I. (1981). "On the Usefulness of Controlling Individuals: An Economic Analysis of Rehabilitation." *American Economic Review*, Vol. 71,pp.307–322.

——. (1973). "Participation in Illegitimate Activities: A Theoretical and Empirical Investigation." *Journal of Political Economy*, Vol. 82, pp. 521–565.

Ehrlich, I., and R. Mark. (1977). "Fear of Deterrence: A Critical Evaluation for the Report of the Panel of Research on Deterrent and Incapacitation Effects." *Journal of Legal Studies*, Vol. 6, pp. 293–316.

Grogger, J. (1991). "Certainty vs. Severity of Punishment." *Economic Inquiry*, Vol. 29 (April), pp. 297–309.

Levitt, S.D. (1996). "The Effect of Prison Population Size on Crime Rates: Evidence From Prison Overcrowding Litigation." *Quarterly Journal of Economics*, Vol. CXI (May), pp. 319–351.

Lewis, D.E. (1986). "The General Deterrent Effect of Longer Sentences." *British Journal of Criminology*, Vol. 26(l), pp. 47–62.

Marvell, T.B., and C.E. Moody, Jr. (1994). "Prison Population Growth and Crime Reduction." *Journal of Quantitative Criminology*, Vol. 1(2), pp. 109–140.

Mathur, V. (1978). "Economics of Crime: An Investigation of the Deterrent Hypothesis for Urban Crime." *Review of Economics and Statistics*, Vol. 60, pp. 446–459.

Miller, T.R., M.A. Cohen, and S.B. Rossman. (1993). "Victim Costs of Violent Crime and Resulting Injuries." *Health Affairs* (Data Watch) Winter, pp. 186–197.

Myers, S. (1982). "Crime in Urban Areas: New Evidence and Results." *Journal of Urban Economics*, Vol. 11, pp. 148–158.

——. (1980). "Why Are Crimes Underreported? What Is the Crime Rate? Does It Really Matter?" *Social Science Quarterly*, Vol. 61 (1), pp. 23–43.

Nagin, D. (1981). "Methodological Issues in Estimating the Deterrent Effect of Sanctions." In *Models in Quantitative Criminology*, J. Fox (ed.). New York: Academic Press, pp. 95–139.

Sjoquist, D. (1973). "Property Crime and Economic Behavior: Some Empirical Results." *American Economic Review*, Vol. 63, pp. 439–446.

Wahlroos, B. (1981). "On Finnish Property Criminality: An Empirical Analysis of the Post War Era Using an Ehrlich Model." *Scandinavian Journal of Economics*, Vol. 83, pp. 553–562.

Wolpin, K. (1980). "A Time Series-Cross Section Analysis of International Variations in Crime and Punishment." *Review of Economics and Statistics*, Vol. 62, pp. 417–423.

——. (1978). "An Economic Analysis of Crime and Punishment in England and Wales, 1894/1967." *Journal of Political Economy*, Vol. 86, pp.815–840.

Zedlewski, E.W. (1985). "When Have We Punished Enough?" *Public Administration Review*, Vol. 45, pp. 771–779.

Excerpts from: Michael K. Block, *Two Views on Imprisonment Policies: Supply Side Imprisonment Policy*. Presentations from the 1996 Annual Research and Evaluation Conference, Washington, DC (NCJ 165702; Washington, DC: U.S. Department of Justice Office of Justice Programs, National Institute of Justice, July 1997). ✦

ISSUE XIII

Beyond Revenge: Will the Restorative Justice Paradigm Achieve Its Intended Goals?

Restorative justice is a victim-centered philosophy that punishes the offender within the community by requiring him or her to restore the victim's losses. This way of thinking focuses on the harm done to people and relationships rather than on the offense committed (Zehr 1990). Restorative justice combines mainstream U.S. criminal justice with indigenous justice practiced by Native Americans, long before European settlers colonized North America. In contrast to mainstream criminal justice that focuses on the punishment of the offender, restorative justice is centered on the victim throughout the whole process. Restorative justice emphasizes that offenders should take responsibility for their actions and repair the injustices and wrongs they caused the victim (Cromwell, del Carmen, and Alarid 2002).

The philosophy behind restorative justice is that when a crime is committed, the offender harms both the individual victim and the community at large. Through shaming, mediation, and face-to-face meetings with the individual victim, restorative justice attempts to strengthen community life by drawing on the strengths of the offenders and the victim instead of focusing on their deficits (Umbreit 1999). Local volunteers and the faith community typically agree to mentor or assist in the supervision of the offender's reparation. The offender remains in the community and performs community service, provides the victim with restitution, and participates in victim impact panels, mediation groups, and other educational programs. Restorative justice programs have shown to reduce victim fear, increase the rate of restitution payments, and decrease the rate and severity of future criminal acts. This approach seems to be more effective for property crimes, particularly those committed by juveniles or first-time adult felony offenders, and less likely to be endorsed by victims of violent crimes (Cromwell, del Carmen, and Alarid 2002).

It is important to note a few points of agreement by authors on both sides of the issue. First, restorative justice is perceived as a good idea. Both sides also recognize the intended positive consequences of restorative justice. Finally, both sides acknowledge that a paradigm shift needs to occur in criminal justice for restorative justice to be embraced fully. The controversy, then, is a question of *implementation* of restorative justice within a pre-existing paradigm of retributive justice.

Eduardo Barajas believes that there are two philosophical camps in the correctional policy arena: Those that believe in punishment and incarceration as a crime solution and a second group that believes in rehabilitation and alternatives to imprisonment. He seems optimistic that both camps can be collectively convinced of the usefulness of restorative justice through the use of prevention strategies in the community. Barajas provides specific examples of how police, community courts, and community corrections officers could collaborate with community organizations to address quality of life and disorder.

Sharon Levrant and her colleagues believe that the idea of restorative justice is an excellent one, but the restorative justice movement will not reach its intended goals. Due in part to the political climate, the implementation of restorative justice will become more symbolic than meaningful and it will be yet another means for "getting tough" on convicted offenders. The authors believe that restorative justice may ultimately do more harm than good.

References

Cromwell, Paul, Rolando V. del Carmen, and Leanne F. Alarid. 2002. *Community-Based Corrections* Fifth Edition. Belmont, CA: Wadsworth.

Umbreit, Mark S. 1999. "Restorative Justice: What Works." In Patricia M. Harris (Ed.), *Research to Results: Effective Community Corrections,* (pp. 273–315). Lanham, MD: American Correctional Association.

Zehr, Howard. 1990. *Changing Lenses: A New Focus for Crime and Justice.* Scottsdale, PA: Herald Press.

Critical Thinking Questions

1. What obstacles may interfere with the transformation to a restorative justice-centered system? What could be done to minimize these obstacles?

2. Will restorative justice bring more harm than good?

3. Will the good ideas inherent in restorative justice be implemented correctly in practice?

Internet Websites

Center for Restorative Justice and Peacemaking, University of Minnesota, School of Social Work. <http://ssw.che.umn.edu/rjp/>

Fresno Pacific University's Center for Peacemaking and Conflict Studies provides links to other websites dealing with restorative justice. <http://www.fresno.edu/pacs/links.html>

Restorative justice online. <http://www.restorativejustice.org>

General information on restorative justice. <http://www.restorativejustice.com>

Friends Committee on Restorative Justice homepage. <http://www.quaker.org/fcrj>

U.S. Department of Justice online restorative justice notebook. <http://www.ojp.usdoj.gov/nij/rest-just/>

Minnesota Department of Corrections, Community and Juvenile Services Division. <http://www.corr.state.mn.us/organization/commjuv/restorativejustice.htm> ✦

25
Moving Toward Community Justice

Eduardo Barajas, Jr.

A revolution is occurring in criminal justice. A quiet, grassroots, seemingly unobtrusive, but truly revolutionary movement is changing the nature, the very fabric of our work. Many theories on crime and criminal behavior have been advanced throughout the history of criminal justice. The criminal justice system has in turn developed and implemented changes based on some of those theories. Although these changes have led to creative innovations, they have seldom changed the basic nature of the business of criminal justice. What is occurring now is more than innovative, it is truly inventive. A "paradigm shift" is changing the focus of the work of criminal justice away from the offender and toward the community and victims of crime.

Because crime continues to plague our society, we need something beyond the scope of a new theory—we need a new paradigm. As John Dilulio states:

> ... a paradigm is broader than a theory. A theory is a statement about a relationship between two or more variables that is supposed to hold under specific conditions. A new paradigm orients general understanding to historical, empirical, or nonnative realities that a prevailing paradigm has arguably de-emphasized, devalued, or simply ignored. In essence, to call for a new paradigm is to appeal for new concepts and categories of thinking about a given subject.

The call for a new paradigm is being spearheaded by citizens and victims who feel left out of the criminal justice process. Citizens might not articulate their frustration in terms of a need for a "paradigm shift," but at the heart of their anger and dissatisfaction is the feeling that the criminal justice system does not represent their interests.

Criminal justice professionals often express an equal frustration with the public's "hysteria" that has resulted in "get tough" legislation related to crime control. The public is often viewed as an outside obstruction that must be "sold" on new policies by criminal justice "experts." When the public fails to buy into such policies, the rift between the public and criminal justice increases.

The rift exists not only between the public and the criminal justice system, but also within the criminal justice profession. We must address these issues in order to move forward, rather than remaining in a "system" that is fragmented, lacks a clear mission, and seems to provide little value to the public it is sworn to protect. In order to solve the problem, we should understand its nature and source.

Toward a New Paradigm of Justice

The current paradigm of criminal justice is focused on the offender. Multiple, contradictory, and competing purposes of the work are each expressed in terms of things to be done to or for offenders. This offender focus is at the core of the public's frustration. The frustration is manifested in statements that the criminal justice system is aptly named, because it represents the interests of the criminal rather than the public or victim. Unfortunately, the present design and operation of the system lend credence to this perception.

... The current criminal justice paradigm ... is based on the traditional purposes of punishment, deterrence, incapacitation, and rehabilitation, each of which is focused on the offender. In this model, these purposes compete for prominence as politicians posture in response to the public's mood shifts. The confusion created by such competitive and contradictory purposes, in the context of a fickle public and political climate, has resulted in calls for reform based on rationality. We speak of creating a "rational" system of sanctions, making "rational" policy decisions to determine a scale of sanctions within a jurisdiction, and "rationally" choosing the sanctions to be imposed on an individual offender.

In addition, the pressure of results-oriented work creates a sense of urgency to determine what works in corrections/criminal justice. Recidivism is the primary measure of success. The overwhelming majority of research in the "what works" area is firmly rooted in the traditional criminal justice model, rather than a community justice model, and is focused almost exclusively on rehabilitation. The emphasis is on long-term behavioral changes in individual offenders through effective treatment.

Competition between rehabilitation and other work purposes is intense. "What works" advocates bemoan the fact that rehabilitation has been relegated to the lowest rung of the ladder and punishment is at the top. A primary task, in their view, is to convince policymakers, practitioners, and the public that rehabilitation should receive new priority because of better results in terms of recidivism. Those who advocate punishment, incapacitation, or deterrence are equally adamant that their views should prevail.

What is needed is a paradigm that is noncompetitive and non-contradictory, that strives primarily for harmony among the aims of the criminal justice system. The way to achieve harmony in the system is to focus on the community, rather than the offender, as the center of our efforts. Rather than asking what to do to or for offenders, we must ask, "How can we best protect and serve the community?" Once we have asked that fundamental question, we find that the traditional purposes of criminal justice work become equally worthy mean to an end rather than independent ends competing for prominence.

. . . This community focus is at the core of the community justice paradigm. In this model, the criminal justice system derives its identity in terms of the *value* of the work it performs rather than the *purpose* of the work. More specifically, the [community justice] model identifies four civic ideals or values that drive the work. These ideals, which were formulated by the [Bureau of Justice Statistics] BJS-Princeton Study Project, are:

- Doing justice,
- Promoting secure communities,
- Restoring crime victims, and
- Promoting non-criminal options.

The traditional purposes of punishment, rehabilitation, and so on operate in conjunction to move the work forward. The community is the focus of the work, rather than being left out of the process and in an adversarial position with the system. The community is viewed as the ultimate customer, and its citizens are recognized as "co-producers of justice." The system, in turn, provides value to the community in return for its investment.

What This Means in Terms of Policy

The traditional criminal justice model is reactive and adversarial. It responds after a crime occurs, and corrections reacts with a series of punitive and/or therapeutic interventions directed at offenders after they are in custody. The offender is the primary client or customer of services provided by the agency. The community may benefit, but only as an indirect consequence of the services provided to offenders. In response to political pressure from victims and other groups, agencies may develop one or more specialized programs emphasizing restitution or victim service. Merely creating programs does not constitute real change, however, if the focus of the agency's work and mission remains unchanged. Victims continue to lose if an agency's ultimate customer is the offender.

Within the criminal justice system there is an adversarial and competitive atmosphere among groups of policymakers and consultants regarding the primary purpose of the system. The long-standing debate is between those who favor punishment versus those who favor rehabilitation. The debate is focused on imprisonment as a *solution* to crime, and whether imprisonment is effective or ineffective. Ironically, the debate is between two sides of the same coin. Both sides attempt to demonstrate effective offender-focused interventions, whether they are based on imprisonment or "alternatives."

This conflict within the system creates disunity and a vague sense of mission, and it is ultimately counter-productive. Nowhere is this better illustrated than in the public relations attempts of some criminal justice "progressives." According to Philip Harris and Stephen Smith:

> . . . the problem over the past two decades for those seeking to reduce America's dependency on imprisonment has been a reliance on strategies that are based on a reaction against something, namely prisons. . . . Unfortunately this reactive view cannot be translated into a comprehensive picture of corrections around which key system actors can rally.

When crime rates were rising, a case was made for "alternatives" based on the fact that increased imprisonment had failed to stem rising crime rates. As crime rates fell or stabilized, the argument became that we didn't need more imprisonment in view of falling crime rates. Is it any wonder that the public is confused and holds in low regard a system suffering from such an identity crisis? True progressive change requires an internal shift of mind, rather than reactions that try to change the external environment.

The community justice model is proactive and emphasizes crime prevention and collaboration. Community justice begins with the premise that the community is the ultimate customer of the system. This is not to say that the community is the only customer or even the primary customer. An agency's primary customer, for example, may be the district's chief judge—approval from this person is of primary importance to that agency. The agency's work, however, must *ultimately* have a positive impact on and provide value to the broader community in terms of safety and well-being.

Community safety and well-being can be improved through a variety of efforts. In the community justice paradigm, imprisonment (or any other sanction) is not viewed as a *solution* to crime but as one of several equally worthy and legitimate responses to crime. The idea is that each component of the system holds a piece of the solution. By coordinating actions within a problem-oriented strategy, solutions can be achieved. This opens up possibilities for agencies to expand the boundaries of their practice and break down the barriers separating them from other components and organizations within and outside the criminal justice system.

New viewpoints, frameworks, and practices in turn require new measures of success. Recidivism, as the primary measure of success, compels the system to validate its efforts to address the universal problem of crime in terms of the success or failure of individuals. In traditional thinking, if a batterer is caught and revoked after violating a "no contact" order, the case is considered a failure because of the offender's recidivism. This is so despite the fact that, through the revocation, a life may have been saved or the cycle of abuse broken.

Community justice addresses a universal problem by investing its efforts in what is best for the safety and well-being of that "universe"—the community and victims. This involves balancing short- and long-term interventions and strategies, as well as focusing on prevention. Short-term interventions, such as imprisonment or surveillance, focus on *controlling* offender behavior and activities. Long-term interventions, such as substance abuse treatment or cognitive restructuring, focus on *changing* offender behavior.

Prevention is a major effort of community justice work. In 1990, the Crime Prevention Coalition formulated the following definition of crime prevention:

> A pattern of attitudes and behaviors directed at both reducing the threat of crime and enhancing the sense of safety and security, to positively influence the quality of life in our society and to de-

velop environments where crime cannot flourish.

This definition clarifies the importance of community as a base for prevention. It also recognizes that there is a dual task: reducing crime's threats to the community, and developing communities that discourage crime.

For several years, corrections has had a practical working model that uses these principles of crime prevention: the direct supervision jail. The direct supervision jail focuses its efforts on the "community" environment of the jail rather than on the inmates. This focus in turn influences the quality of life in the jail and creates an atmosphere in which violence and other disorders cannot flourish. Such a climate enhances the chance that other correctional goals, such as rehabilitation, will be met.

The principles of prevention can and should be translated into community supervision strategies. Jeffrey Roth describes a diversified problem-solving method of violence prevention in the community that calls for:

. . . problem-solving initiatives aimed at sources of violence in several areas: childhood development; 'hot spot' locations, routine activities, and situations; illegal markets, especially for drugs, guns and prostitution; firearms, alcohol, and drugs; bias crimes, gang activities, and community transitions; and relationships between intimate partners.

Such an approach would require community corrections officers to work collaboratively with police, community organizations, and social service agencies. They would proactively address various social disorders and illegal activities. How these efforts affect the quality of life in the community would become the basis for new measures of success.

Some Practical Examples

Community policing, community prosecution, and community courts are three examples of the elements of community justice. Community corrections, in the non-traditional sense, is a fourth example. Traditionally, community corrections is correc-

tions as practiced in the community rather than in a corrections facility. The non-traditional view of community corrections is corrections that is practiced *with* and *for* the community.

Community justice practice has two primary components. The first is problem solving. Staff are trained and encouraged to be problem-oriented—for example, to get city agencies to remove abandoned cars or to close down bars that sell to intoxicated customers or minors. They try to rescue people from abusive domestic relationships in order to break the cycle of abuse.

The second component of community justice is creating community partnerships. Staff are trained to work with other agencies and with the community to identify and solve problems that cause social disorder, such as public intoxication, prostitution, and open air drug markets. For example, the establishment of community courts makes it possible to arrest, prosecute, and sentence an offender, all within the same neighborhood. While the sentence may be determined by the court, in some cases it falls to a citizen board to determine the specifics of the sanction. Further, the sanction is reparative in nature—it is designed to restore the victim and the community.

Such problem solving partnerships are already being formed in this country:

- Vermont's new Reparative Probation system puts low-risk probationers directly under control of a board of community members. This is contrary to the practice in many agencies of reserving resources solely or primarily for high-risk offenders. The board determines reparations to the community and to the victim. Offenders may be ordered to pay restitution, work in community service, or participate in other reparative projects. Offenders and victims may also participate in victim-offender mediation. Violations are reported to the court for further action.

- The probation department in Quincy, Massachusetts regards domestic violence victims as important customers. The agency's domestic violence program is dedicated to breaking the cycle of violence and protecting the victim. Domestic violence is considered not only a crime against a specific victim, but a crime against the community. Batterers may be sentenced to community work service and to batterer-specific treatment. Probation works collaboratively with the police and other agencies to identify and respond to instances of domestic violence. Probation officers do not hesitate to revoke batterers who violate "no contact" orders, even for the slightest infraction. This helps to guarantee that the batterer will not manipulate or intimidate his way back into the home to repeat the cycle of violence.

• Operation Nitelite, in the Roxbury section of Boston, MA, is a joint venture of the Boston Police Department and the Probation Department of the Dorchester Court. Police and probation officers work jointly to address community concerns related to youth violence. Joint patrols check for curfew and other violations of probation. Officers work with parents to help them reassert parental control. Schools, churches, and other community institutions also help to supervise juvenile offenders.

These are only three examples of agencies that have focused their efforts on the community and victims of crime. Many other agencies in the country are turning toward such community-focused missions and work practices. At this time, however, there are no examples of jurisdictions transforming their entire system into a community justice model. For the sake of a more prosperous future for criminal justice, the time is right to consider making such bold and expansive changes.

The Importance of Systems Thinking

In his book, *The Fifth Discipline,* Peter Senge describes the "systems thinking" that is vital to what he calls "the learning organization." This type of thinking requires:

. . . a shift of mind from seeing parts to seeing wholes, from seeing people as helpless reactors to seeing them as active participants in shaping their reality, from reacting to the present to creating the future. Without systems thinking, there is neither the incentive nor the means to integrate the learning disciplines once they have come into practice.

An old Hindu parable tells of some blind men touching an elephant. Each touched a particular body part and perceived the elephant according to that part of the whole. For one man, the elephant was like a rope (tail). Another declared the elephant was like a snake (trunk). Another disagreed, stating the elephant was like a tree (leg). Each man was correct, yet none perceived the entire creature.

For too long, our perception of criminal justice and corrections has been like the parable of the blind men touching an elephant. We tend to view the individual components as independent of the others and serving different, competing purposes. We need to learn to see the overall system. "Systems thinking" lets us see that we are all interconnected, interdependent parts of the whole, working for a common, greater good. No one component of the system is better or worse than the others, but each serves a specific function.

We in community corrections have continued to play "ain't it awful" as we face declining prestige in the eyes of a dissatisfied public. As victims may, we tend to see the problem as "out there" rather than within ourselves. Our continual failure to change the external environment has made some of us increasingly frustrated and reactive.

Yet only by changing ourselves can we hope to grow as a profession and increase our esteem among ourselves and among those who should support us. Community justice should give us an optimistic path into the next millennium and a new framework for our profession.

References

Dilulio, John. 1993. "Rethinking the Criminal Justice System: Toward a New Paradigm." In J. Dilulio (ed.) *Performance Measures for the*

Criminal Justice System. Washington, D.C.: U.S. Department of Justice, National Institute of Justice.

Harris, Phillip W., and Smith, Stephen H. 1993. "Developing Community Corrections: An Implementation Perspective." Paper presented at the conference What Works in Community Corrections: A Consensus Conference, of the International Association of Residential and Community Alternatives, Philadelphia, Pennsylvania, November 3–6, 1993.

Roth, Jeffrey A. 1994. "Understanding and Preventing Violence." *National Institute of Justice Research in Brief,* February 1994.

Senge, Peter M. 1990. *The Fifth Discipline: The Art & Practice of The Learning Organization.* New York: Doubleday.

National Crime Prevention Council. 1994. *Uniting Communities Through Crime Prevention.* Washington, D.C.: The Council.

Reprinted from: Eduardo Barajas, Jr., "Moving Toward Community Justice," pp. 1–7 in *Community Justice: Striving for Safe, Secure, and Just Communities.* Washington, DC: U.S. Department of Justice, National Institute of Corrections, 1996. ✦

26

Reconsidering Restorative Justice

The Corruption of Benevolence Revisited?

Sharon Levrant
Francis T. Cullen
Betsy Fulton
John F. Wozniak

. . . According to Bazemore (1994), this widespread acceptance of restorative justice can be attributed to its underlying values, which provide common ground for parties who have historically disagreed about criminal justice policy. Conservatives and liberals alike support the emphasis on addressing the needs of crime victims and holding offenders accountable for the harm they cause (Clear 1994; Zehr 1990). Liberals, however, are most attracted to restorative justice because of its potentially humanistic and balanced approach to justice. Restorative justice moves away from a state-centered definition of crime to a definition that accounts for the injuries suffered by victims and communities (Van Ness 1986). Thus rather than blaming or punishing the offender through incarceration, it focuses on repairing the harm done to victims and communities through a process of negotiation, mediation, victim empowerment, and reparation (Bazemore and Maloney 1994). In its ideal form, restorative justice balances the need to hold offenders accountable for their wrongdoing with the need for their acceptance and reintegration into the community (Braithwaite 1989; Zehr 1990). It broadens the focus of justice from offender-oriented penal harm to community-oriented peacemaking and only considers justice to be achieved when the suffering of offenders, victims, and communities has ended and crime has been reduced (Pepinsky and Quinney 1991). For all of these reasons, progressives are casting skepticism aside and readily accepting restorative justice as a viable alternative to the get tough policies now in place.

Restorative justice appeals to conservatives for different reasons. Conservatives see restorative justice as an extension of the victims' rights movement that seeks to involve victims in the criminal justice process and to compensate victims for the losses incurred from crime (Schafer 1976; Van Ness and Strong 1997). Rather than the balanced approach to justice advocated by liberal proponents, conservatives endorse restorative justice as a means of securing more justice for victims. In so doing, they often attempt to increase the punishment of offenders at the expense of restoration.

In the middle of these conflicting perspectives, restorative justice is trying to find a place in correctional policy. The question remains whether, as liberal advocates believe, restorative justice ultimately will prove to be a truly progressive reform. This article addresses this question through a critical analysis of the restorative justice movement. Two central issues are explored. First, commentators have pointed out that correctional reforms implemented with good intentions often have been corrupted to serve less admirable goals and interests (see, e.g., Cullen and Gilbert 1982; Rothman 1980). Thus, despite its benevolent possibilities, will restorative justice programs be corrupted and have untoward, unanticipated consequences? Second, given the current knowledge about changing offender behavior, there is little reason to conclude that restorative justice can have a meaningful effect on recidivism. This latter issue is critical given that a perceived failure to reduce recidivism contributed to the decline of rehabilitation and boosted the legitimacy of punitive correctional policies in recent years (Cullen and Gilbert 1982; Hahn 1998). Although not fully dismissing the potential of restorative justice, we believe that there is danger in the impetuous adoption of this model without further examination of these issues and more rigorous research on restorative justice outcomes.

. . . In this context, this section explores four potential unanticipated consequences of restorative justice: (1) it will serve as a means of getting tough on offenders; (2) it will not be restorative for victims, offenders, or communities; (3) it will be more of a symbolic than a substantive reform; and (4) it will reinforce existing race and class biases besetting the criminal justice system.

Getting Tough Through Restorative Justice

According to progressive advocates, restorative justice policies offer potential benefits to offenders, including the opportunity to reconcile with their victims, a more lenient sentence, and the chance for reintegration into society. It remains to be seen, however, whether conservatives will endorse these goals and work with liberals to create a balanced reform or whether they will use restorative justice as yet another opportunity to impose more punishment on offenders. Six considerations suggest that the restorative justice movement may not achieve its progressive goals and, in fact, may increase the extent and harshness of criminal sanctions.

First, Brown (1994) notes that restorative justice systems lack the due process protections and procedural safeguards that are awarded to offenders in the more formal adversarial system. Although programs vary, counsel are generally discouraged from attending mediation hearings because they create barriers for a smooth mediation process. Furthermore, the informality of the system contributes to more lenient rules of evidence. Information presented at conferences also can be used in a formal trial if the offender fails to reach an agreement with the victim during mediation. Restorative justice

advocates believe that the cost of diminished offender rights is outweighed by the benefits of accountability (Berzins and Prashaw 1997; Van Ness 1986). Brown (1994) argues, however, that the loss of rights can result in an offender receiving more severe punishment than he or she would receive through the adversarial process.

Second, despite the progressive rhetoric of restoration, offenders may be coerced into participating in the mediation process because of perceived threats of a harsher punishment if they refuse to do so (Brown 1994; Van Ness and Strong 1997). According to Brown (1994), in certain jurisdictions, prosecutors and judges can consider offenders' refusal to participate in VOM conferences in their charging and sentencing decisions. The problem of coercion can be exacerbated if people who normally would not be subjected to state controls through the formal criminal justice process are coerced into participating in restorative justice programming.

Third and relatedly, restorative justice programs can potentially widen the net of social control (Bazemore and Umbreit 1995; Umbreit and Zehr 1996; Van Ness and Strong 1997). The increased influence that the community has in sanctioning can lead restorative justice programs to target offenders who commit minor offenses and are at a low risk of reoffending. For example, market research in Vermont revealed that citizens wanted the criminal justice system to take minor offenses more seriously (Walther and Perry 1997). Thus, instead of diverting offenders from intrusive forms of punishment (e.g., electronic monitoring, intensive supervision probation, incarceration), restorative justice may place more control over the lives of nonserious offenders who may have otherwise received no formal supervision.

Fourth, Bazemore and Umbreit (1995) contend that if broad changes do not take place to make the system restorative, then restorative justice sanctions will likely increase the supervisory requirements that offenders must satisfy. A survey of offenders participating in Vermont's Reparative Probation Program revealed that offenders perceived the program to be much more demanding than regular probation (Walther and Perry 1997). Furthermore, it was discovered that contrary to the program's design, offenders were subjected to both reparative conditions and traditional probation supervision. Until a complete paradigm shift has occurred, restorative justice policies will potentially inflict additional punishment on offenders.

Fifth, as conditions of probation expand through restorative justice programs, the potential that offenders will not meet these conditions also increases. This higher level of noncompliance, combined with heightened public scrutiny and a demand for offender accountability, will likely result in the revocation of more offenders. Other community corrections reforms have experienced a similar phenomenon. For example, the closer surveillance of offenders in intensive supervision programs has led to the increased detection of technical violations (Cullen, Wright, and Applegate 1996). Because of an emphasis on stringent responses to noncompliance, detected violations in these programs have often been followed by the revocation of probation and incarceration (Petersilia and Turner 1993). Thus, restorative justice programs may not only increase social control within the community but may also result in more offenders being sent to prison because they fail to comply with the additional sanctions imposed within the restorative justice framework....

Sixth, restorative justice may increase punishment if reforms fail to develop policies and programs that are able to reintegrate offenders into society. Karp (1998) notes, however, that shaming penalties are gaining popularity because they can fulfill the retributive aims of the public. Lawrence (1991) also sees a danger in advocating shaming activities. He suggests that they may be wrongly interpreted as a revival of support for public shaming practices, such as the ducking stool and the scarlet letter, without an emphasis on the reintegrative element of community acceptance and support.

In summary, although restorative justice policies are being advocated as a benevolent means of addressing the crime problem, they may increase the punitiveness of the so-

cial control imposed on offenders in several ways: offenders may lose certain rights and privileges that they are granted through the current adversarial process, offenders may be coerced into participating in restorative justice programs because of formal pressures from practitioners within the criminal justice system, restorative justice may widen the net of social control by targeting low risk offenders, offenders may be subjected to greater levels of supervision, offenders may have a greater likelihood of incarceration for technical violations because of the increased probation conditions and scrutiny they face, and, finally, restorative justice programs may not achieve their goal of offender reintegration and therefore fail to restore fully the harmed relationships that result from the crime. This propensity for getting tough with restorative justice creates doubt about the restorative capacities of current practices. . . .

Are Programs Restorative for Victims?

Making victims whole again involves redressing their monetary losses, giving them a voice in the justice process, and reducing their fears regarding future victimization (Center for Restorative Justice and Mediation 1996). Several methods have been developed to restore the victims of crime. Restitution is the oldest and most familiar method of victim restoration (American Probation and Parole Association [APPA] 1994). In addition to redressing victims' monetary losses, restitution offers a means of restoring the relationship between the victim and the offender (Galaway 1977). It provides one of the few tangible ways to compensate crime victims.

Other popular methods of victim restoration include VOM programs, family-group conferences, and various forms of community-sentencing panels—all of which bring offenders, victims, and/or communities together to resolve the conflict created by crime. Research suggests that these programs have some restorative value. Evaluations of VOMs have revealed high rates of victim and offender satisfaction with resulting reparative agreements (Marshall 1992; Niemeyer and Shichor 1996; Umbreit 1994; Umbreit et al. 1997), perceptions of fair treatment (Umbreit et al. 1997), reduced fear and anxiety among crime victims, and an increased likelihood of offenders completing the restitution agreement (Umbreit 1994). Victims participating in family-group conferences have stated that the conferences provided them with a voice in the justice process, an improved understanding as to why the crime occurred, and a chance to assess the likelihood of recidivism (Maxwell and Morris 1997). Clearly, the potential exists for achieving victim restoration. Several considerations, however, may limit the restorative capacities of current victim-oriented programs.

The Limits of Restitution

Although restitution provides a concrete method to compensate crime victims, there are limits on the extent to which victims are fully restored. First, according to Ferns (1994), it is the victim's perspective regarding the extent of losses that must be considered when assessing whether restitution occurs. Because the financial losses experienced by a victim may exceed those stipulated for by court orders, full monetary restoration may not be achieved (APPA 1994). Even if the victim receives financial satisfaction, if the offender remains hostile toward the victim, the latter may remain emotionally dissatisfied and not be restored (Brookes 1998). Second, although all states have made some type of provisions for victim restitution, much of the restitution ordered by the court is never collected (Seymour 1996). Third, the common practice of using an intermediary to collect restitution from offenders and disburse it to crime victims (APPA 1994) would appear to limit the degree to which a relationship between the two parties is either understood or repaired.

Limits to Victim-Offender Conferencing

Marshall (1992) suggests that the effectiveness of mediation programs depends on the involved parties being open and active during the resolution process, using the mediation to solve problems rather than to as-sign blame, and ensuring that the needs of all parties are heard. This implies, first and foremost, that the parties must be present and, second, that the mediator, victim, and offender possess the competencies needed for a successful mediation.

Research indicates that the rate at which offenders and victims participate in victim-offender conferences is influenced by several factors. One factor is the type of crime involved: Studies have found that victims and offenders are most likely to appear at mediations for minor personal and property crimes and least likely to appear for serious personal crimes (Niemeyer and Shichor 1996; Umbreit 1994). Another factor is the nature of the victim-offender relationship; absent a continuing relationship with the offender, the victim may be less inclined to participate (Lindner 1996). Finally, according to Maxwell and Morris (1997), many victims do not attend family-group conferences because they are not invited or are not given adequate notice. Seymour (1996) suggests that regardless of the reason, victims too often are left out of the restorative justice equation, which limits the extent to which restoration can be achieved.

Even if victims and offenders do make it to the "restorative justice table" (Seymour 1996), what evidence would indicate that community members, offenders, and victims possess the requisite skills for an effective mediation? Often, community volunteers are responsible for facilitating mediations (Dooley 1996; Ruddell 1996). Although careful screening and training are important safeguards, it is questionable whether citizen volunteers have the capacity to effectively mediate conflict between a potentially emotional victim and a resistant offender. Walther and Perry (1997) found that Vermont's reparative board members were reluctant to involve victims in the mediation process. They speculated that this reluctance stemmed from a lack of knowledge about how to deal with victims' emotions or from a fear that victims will view the board meetings as a forum for seeking retribution.

Victims and offenders may be equally unprepared for mediation. Lindner (1996) has suggested that a face-to-face meeting with the offender could be traumatic for the victim rather than restorative. Furthermore, Maxwell and Morris (1997) found that about 25 percent of the victims participating in family-group conferences reported feeling worse after attending a conference because of their personal inability to express themselves adequately, the offender's lack of sincerity, and the family's inability to make reparation. Given these findings, it appears that inadequate attention to the competencies required for effective mediation can potentially undermine the goal of victim restoration.

Are Programs Restorative for Offenders?

As indicated previously, restorative justice practices emphasize the importance of holding offenders responsible for restoring victims of crime. Another commonly stated objective, however, is to ensure that offenders entering the criminal justice system exit the system more capable of being responsible and productive citizens (Center for Restorative Justice and Mediation 1996; Maloney, Romig, and Armstrong 1998; Zehr 1990). This objective is achieved, it is argued, by teaching offenders right from wrong through various corrective techniques and through their reintegration into the community.

Corrective Techniques

Restorative justice advocates suggest that, when rooted in a restorative justice philosophy, restitution and community service can serve corrective purposes for offenders by helping them to recognize the harm that they caused to victims (Bazemore and Maloney 1994; Galaway 1977; Lawrence 1991). Berzins and Prashaw (1997), however, question the degree to which this corrective aspect of restorative justice programs can be achieved within the existing adversarial justice system. For example, the majority of criminal cases are resolved through a guilty plea process that lessens the severity of the charge and encourages the offender to evade responsibility for the real damage done to victims and communities

(Center for Restorative Justice and Mediation 1996). The goal of offender correction also may be undermined by the retributive nature of many restitution and community service programs (Shapiro 1990). Within a retributive model, the goal of offender correction is likely to be displaced by the goal of offender compliance. If so, offenders may identify themselves as "victims of the justice system" and identify the victims as "privileged avengers" (Brookes 1998).

Reintegration

Restorative justice recognizes the need to ensure that offenders are given the opportunity for forgiveness after they have been held responsible for their actions (Van Ness 1986). According to Braithwaite (1989), effective "reintegrative shaming" requires the expression of disapproval for the purpose of invoking remorse, followed by gestures of forgiveness designed to accept the offender back into the community. Absent community acceptance and opportunities for change, offenders may be stigmatized, encouraged to participate in criminal subcultures, and become reinvolved in criminal activity (Braithwaite 1989). Thus, successful reintegration requires changes in the offender and in the community. Consistent with this view, Byrne (1986) suggests that a primary role for probation and parole officers should be to work with communities in an effort to increase acceptance, support, and opportunities for offenders. Similarly, Clear (1996) argues for a movement toward a "corrections of place" that broadens the role of corrections beyond the supervision of offenders to organizing community groups and developing crime prevention strategies.

This community focus, however, is potentially problematic. Similar to attempts to implement community policing, this revised focus would alter the contemporary roles and responsibilities of corrections personnel and thus would require major changes in agency operations, including the decentralization of activities and facilities, new training, and revised schedules (Community Policing Consortium 1994). Given the resource constraints currently experienced by community corrections, these changes would be difficult to achieve. Although community corrections agencies are responsible for supervising 75 percent of the correctional population, they only receive one tenth of every dollar spent on corrections (Petersilia 1996). Officers typically are burdened with unmanageable caseloads and struggle to keep up with current supervisory responsibilities. Facing these realities, how can probation officers be expected to expand their role to include community mobilization?

Aside from various corrective techniques and reintegration, the role of rehabilitation in offender restoration is seldom discussed by restorative justice proponents. If rehabilitative programming is incorporated into reparative agreements, it is often done so as an afterthought rather than as a carefully conceived plan for addressing the factors that contribute to an offender's criminal behavior. This shortcoming will ultimately affect the degree to which communities can be restored through restorative justice practices.

Are Programs Restorative for Communities?

Community restoration involves strengthening community bonds in a way that minimizes fear of crime and fortifies informal social controls (Center for Restorative Justice and Mediation 1996; Pranis 1996). Practices designed to restore communities range from community service projects by offenders to grassroots approaches that engage citizens in collective action against crime (Pranis 1996).

Community service by offenders provides the community with the tangible benefit of work and offers much needed resources to the government and to other nonprofit service organizations (Maloney and Umbreit 1995; Van Ness 1986). Engaging offenders in community service also may improve public safety by limiting offenders' opportunities for crime (Maloney and Umbreit 1995) and by developing skills and attitudes conducive to prosocial behaviors. Although a worthy starting point, a simple program of community service cannot begin to achieve true community restoration. Putney (1997) thus argues for a broader grassroots approach to

restorative justice that engages communities in owning and resolving problems that reintegrates offenders and that establishes lines of mutual accountability.

The effectiveness of both narrow and broad restorative methods is bounded, however, by two factors: the degree of community interest in participating in restorative justice initiatives and the range of opportunities available to offenders (e.g., social programs, employment, education). Organizing and maintaining community involvement has been cited as one of the most perplexing implementation problems faced by community policing programs (Grinc 1994). Studies of crime prevention programs suggest that neighborhood organizations are difficult to sustain in disadvantaged communities (Garafalo and McLeod 1986; Silloway and McPherson 1985; Skogan 1990, 1996). Skogan (1996) contends that in these communities, crime and fear stimulate withdrawal from community life and limit the ability to collectively respond to local problems. Furthermore, Currie (1985, 1998) argues that without government policies that invest in poverty-stricken communities by providing support in the form of welfare, health care, and early childhood intervention programs, piecemeal restorative justice practices are not likely to reverse the structural inequality that contributes to crime. Based on the difficulties associated with changing community characteristics, community restoration appears to be a utopian goal within the restorative justice framework.

Substantive or Symbolic Reform?

Zehr (1990) contends that a paradigm shift occurs when reformers are frustrated by an existing model's inability to solve a problem. He argues that the retributive justice system is failing to solve the crime problem and needs to be replaced by programs that are better able to address issues of crime. The question remains whether the reforms that are being put forth as restorative are part of a true paradigm shift that is redefining the crime problem and responses to it or whether they are symbolic reforms that simply rename components of the current retributive justice paradigm. Three key issues are integral to determining whether an agency will achieve substantive or symbolic reform.

First, the substance of restorative justice reforms depends on the degree of staff commitment to a new philosophy of justice. Dooley (1996) recognized that the success of Vermont's Reparative Probation Boards was hindered by staff resistance to philosophical changes and subsequent changes in operations. Second, even if the staff is committed to restorative justice goals, to move toward these goals, staff members must be willing to change their roles from that of service provider to community justice facilitator (Bazemore and Day 1996). This alteration in job orientations has been difficult to achieve (Bazemore and Day 1996). For example, most community corrections agencies have had difficulty getting staff to focus on restoring victims of crime (Bazemore 1994). Immarigeon and Daly (1997) caution "that it is naive to suppose that restorative justice processes and outcomes will entirely replace those of traditional criminal justice in the foreseeable future" (p. 16). Third, organizations must secure sufficient human and financial resources to operate quality programs that are capable of achieving restoration.

The resource and organizational obstacles faced by agencies may create incentives to abandon substantive reform and merely to label current sanctioning schemes as restorative while retaining their retributive focus. The appeal of resorting to such a euphemism may be heightened because programs with restorative aims are better able to gain public support (Colson and Van Ness 1989). In the end, symbolic reform may accrue the desired organizational benefits without having to tackle the challenges of substantive reform.

Race and Class Effects

Despite their progressive underpinnings, restorative justice programs may have unintended class and racial biases that work to the disadvantage of poor and minority offenders. First, advocates have given little thought to how the quality and harshness of restorative justice will vary by the economic status of communities. Although speculative at this point, it is likely that affluent communities will have the resources to develop programs that are more integrative because they offer a greater number of quality services to offenders.

Second, within the restorative justice process, might affluent offenders be treated more favorably? In victim-offender mediation conferences, for example, it is possible that offenders who are more educated, better dressed, and more skilled verbally will negotiate more favorable sanctions. It is instructive that mediators in VOM programs tend to be White, male, and better educated—traits that may converge with those of more affluent offenders (Walther and Perry 1997). More generally, the informal, individualized nature of restorative justice provides few guarantees that racial and class inequities will be easily detected.

Third, there may be class and thus racial differences in the ability of offenders to meet the conditions of restorative sanctions and therefore to avoid harsher penalties, including the revocation of probation. The most obvious example is the requirement of providing victims with restitution—a common feature of restorative sanctions—which may be difficult for disadvantaged offenders to fulfill (Hahn 1998). On a broader level, however, it seems likely that affluent offenders will be more able to draw on family supports (e.g., private drug treatment, parental monitoring) to meet the conditions imposed by restorative sanctions. If so, then larger inequalities in society are likely to be reproduced within the framework of restorative justice.

In summary, restorative justice remains an unproved movement that risks failure and perhaps does more harm than good. Its attractiveness lies more in its humanistic sentiments than in any empirical evidence of its effectiveness. Evaluating restorative justice becomes further complicated when the issue of recidivism is considered. Bazemore and Day (1996) argue that a true assessment of restorative justice programs must involve more than examining how well they reduce recidivism. Although this may be so, the survival of a correctional philosophy is influenced by its ostensible ability to control crime (as the popularity of the get tough movement amply shows). Thus, the next section of this article will evaluate the capacity for restorative justice policies to decrease offender recidivism based on the growing body of literature about what works to change offender behaviors.

Changing Offender Behavior: The Utilitarian Challenge

Many correctional reforms over the past 20 years have developed in response to correctional crises and political pressures rather than from a careful evaluation of policy options and empirical evidence of effectiveness (Cochran 1992). In fact, the very argument that contributed to the demise of rehabilitation—that it failed to reduce recidivism and protect public safety—has been all but ignored in recent progressive reforms. Instead, liberals have tried to promote reforms that promised to reduce the use of incarceration and to advance the legal rights granted to offenders. Whatever the value of these reforms, the result has been that correctional policy has largely been forfeited to conservatives who boldly claim that crime can be reduced by locking up more offenders (Cullen, Van Voorhis, and Sundt 1996). By failing to critically evaluate the capacity for restorative justice practices to lower crime, liberal advocates are in danger of experiencing another setback in their quest for a more progressive system of justice.

Restorative justice proponents, either explicitly or implicitly, argue that crime can be lessened through restorative practices. Pranis (1996) asserts that programs rooted in a restorative justice philosophy decrease crime by strengthening community bonds and enhancing informal mechanisms of social control. Braithwaite (1989) argues that the reintegrative aspect of restorative justice policies reduces recidivism by allowing an offender to remain a part of society and to avoid the criminal subcultures and the labeling process that perpetuate delinquency.

Still others claim that specific restorative justice programs have the capacity to change offender behavior. For example, it is argued that victim-offender mediation can facilitate changes in offenders' behavior by forcing them to recognize the harm that their criminal behavior causes to victims and communities (Ruddell 1996; Umbreit 1994). Bazemore and Maloney (1994) suggest that community service would be more rehabilitative in nature if it was guided by a restorative justice philosophy.

These claims, however, seem more based on wishful thinking than on a systematic understanding of how to change the conduct of offenders. Although programs with a restorative orientation may occasionally reduce recidivism (see, e.g., Umbreit 1994), the current knowledge base on offender change would suggest that restorative interventions am likely to have effects on recidivism that are modest, if not inconsequential. In the following section, we elaborate this point by assessing the extent to which restorative programs have features that coincide with the principles of effective treatment.

Effective Correctional Interventions

. . . Three principles of effective intervention address the importance of matching offenders to services based on their risk, need, and personal characteristics (Andrews and Bonta 1994; Andrews, Bonta, and Hoge 1990). The risk principle suggests that levels of service should be matched to the risk level of the offender (Andrews and Bonta 1994). This principle is based on several studies that have found that intensive services are necessary to achieve a significant reduction in recidivism among high-risk offenders, but that when applied to low-risk offenders, intensive services have a minimal or positive [increase] effect on recidivism (Andrews, Bonta, et al. 1990). . . .

The need principle suggests that changes in recidivism are dependent on changes in the criminogenic needs of offenders (Andrews and Bonta 1994). Criminogenic needs are dynamic factors that are potentially changeable and that are associated with recidivism, such as antisocial attitudes, substance abuse, poor family communication, and antisocial peer associations (Andrews and Bonta 1990). Thus, when these factors are reduced, there is a decreased likelihood of recidivism. The responsivity principle suggests that in addition to matching services with an offender's risks and needs, the learning styles and personality characteristics of offenders can influence treatment effectiveness (Andrews and Bonta 1990; Van Voorhis 1997). For example, high anxiety offenders do not generally respond well to confrontation (Warren 1983), whereas offenders with below-average intellectual abilities do not respond to cognitive skills programs as well as do offenders with above average intellectual abilities (Fabiano, Porporino, and Robinson 1991). . . .

The most effective interventions possess other similar characteristics. First, they occupy 40 percent to 70 percent of high-risk offenders' time (Gendreau 1996). Second, they last at least 23 weeks (Lipsey and Wilson 1998). Third, they employ service providers who relate to offenders in interpersonally sensitive and constructive ways and who are trained and supervised appropriately. Fourth, they use relapse prevention techniques to monitor and to anticipate problem situations and to train offenders to rehearse alternative behaviors. Last, effective interventions link offenders to other services in the community that are relevant to their needs.

Meta-analyses of correctional interventions have found that programs that meet these principles are achieving, on average, a recidivism reduction of 50 percent (Andrews, Zinger, et al. 1990). Interventions that depart from these principles have a dismal success rate. . . . Given the increasing knowledge base on what works to change offender behavior, to what extent can we expect restorative justice programs to reduce recidivism? In addressing this question, the next section will examine the degree to which restorative justice programs reflect these principles.

Assessing Restorative Justice Programs

As currently implemented, most restorative justice programs fail to incorporate the principles of effective intervention, particularly as they relate to the risk, need, and responsivity principles. In restorative justice, the primary criterion for matching sanctions to offenders is the nature and extent of the harm caused by the crime. The seriousness of the offense, however, is not consistently related to an offender's risk of recidivism (Correctional Service Canada 1989; Goldkamp and Gottfredson 1985). Thus, restorative justice programs run the dual risks of producing an interaction effect in low-risk offenders and of underservicing high-risk offenders.

Traditionally, restorative justice programs have targeted low-risk nonviolent offenders for participation (Dooley 1996; Ruddell 1996). These offenders typically are unlikely to recidivate. If subjected to unnecessary sanctions and services, however, their chances for noncompliance, and hence revocation, are increased (Clear and Hardyman 1990). The opposite problems exist for high-risk offenders who increasingly are being included in restorative justice programs. Given research findings that suggest that intensive services are required to reduce recidivism among high-risk offenders, it is unlikely that, for example, a one-hour victim-offender mediation session will lessen criminal propensities among these offenders. Thus, the restorative approach runs the risk of becoming the progressives' equivalent of conservative Scared Straight programs, which attempt to shock youth into positive behavior by subjecting them to an afternoon in prison (Finckenauer 1982).

It is also highly unlikely that restorative justice programs will, as currently implemented, produce lasting changes in an offender's criminogenic needs. As discussed previously, restorative justice programs are currently implemented in a piecemeal fashion and are focused primarily on victim restoration. The only criminogenic need that is even remotely targeted by these practices is lack of empathy or sensitivity to others—a part of many offenders' antisocial values system (Gendreau, Andrews, Goggin, and Chanteloupe 1992). Victim-offender mediation and victim-impact panels are common approaches to developing an offender's empathy toward victims of crime. However, they lack the behavioral framework and re-lapse-prevention component needed to rein-force improved attitudes in a manner that leads to internalization and continued im-provements. Instead, they provide only short-term confrontations with victims that may re-sult in more punishment for the offender. Furthermore, these victim-oriented pro-grams fail to help offenders make generaliza-tions about how their behavior influences others over the long-term or fail to teach of-fenders alternative ways of behaving.

Findings from a study of a restitution pro-gram demonstrate the limitations of restor-ative justice programs that do not abide by the responsivity principle. Van Voorhis (1985) found that low-maturity offenders, as measured by Kohlberg's stages of moral de-velopment, were more likely than high matu-rity offenders to view restitution as a means of obtaining a lenient sentence and were sig-nificantly less likely to provide restitution to their victims. Thus, restitution does not ap-pear to be a viable mechanism for changing the antisocial attitudes of low-maturity of-fenders and, more important, for reducing the likelihood of their future criminal behav-ior.

More generally, meta-analyses conclude that restitution programs have modest, if not weak, effects on recidivism. In a meta-analy-sis of 10 restitution interventions with seri-ous, noninstitutionalized juvenile offenders, Lipsey and Wilson (1998) found that the mean effect of restitution on recidivism across the studies was .17. Although not in-consequential, this result is modest when compared with behaviorally oriented and in-dividual counseling programs that had an ef-fect size in Lipsey and Wilson's analysis of .43. Even less promising results were found in Gendreau et al.'s (forthcoming) meta-analy-sis of 16 studies of restitution programs. They found that the mean size of the effect of resti-tution on recidivism was only .04.

Community service programs also have failed to incorporate the principles of effec-tive intervention. Bazemore and Maloney (1994) suggest that to achieve the full poten-tial of community service, the assigned activ-ity should "bring the offender and conven-tional adults together" and "provide for a sense of accomplishment, closure, and com-munity recognition" (p. 30). Programs designed in this manner would provide of-fenders with the modeling and positive rein-forcement that are needed to motivate prosocial behavior. However, because com-munity service has historically been im-posed as an additional punishment or condi-tion of probation supervision, little attention has been paid to such treatment goals and re-lated practices. In fact, the image of offend-ers in bright orange jumpsuits picking up trash on the side of the road suggests that some community service assignments may be stigmatizing. In these instances, the ex-tent to which offenders learn attitudes and skills conducive to prosocial behavior is likely to be limited.

In contrast, victim-impact classes con-ducted by the California Youth Authority may prove more effective. The primary goal of these classes is to make offenders under-stand the devastating effects of crime (Sey-mour 1996). Youth participate in a six-week course that teaches alternative ways to re-solve conflict. According to Seymour (1996), the curriculum is an educational model that is culturally sensitive and appropriate for the offenders' age and cognitive development. Although too brief in duration for high-risk offenders, this curriculum appears to in-clude the behavioral and cognitive compo-nents required to change offender behavior.

Until more programs operating within the restorative justice framework incorporate the principles of effective intervention, the likelihood of producing reductions in recidi-vism is limited. This, in turn, will compro-mise the extent to which other restorative goals can be achieved because victims and communities will continue to suffer from the criminal behavior of these repeat offenders. A truly restorative program will be rooted in empirical evidence on what works in chang-ing offender behavior.

Conclusion: Restorative Justice and Rehabilitation

Restorative justice is increasingly em-braced—by criminologists and by policy makers—as an alternative correctional paradigm to the prevailing view that penal harm is the solution to crime. By offering something to everyone—victims, offenders, and the community—restorative justice is, at first glance, seemingly deserving of the excitement that it is generating. Our essay, however, is a cautionary reminder that jumping on this bandwagon may be premature, if not risky. Regardless of the benevolent rhetoric that is often used to describe the goals of restorative justice (e.g., peacemaking, communitarian), there is reason to believe that this paradigm will be corrupted and may do more harm than good.

Our goal, however, is not simply nay-saying. By illuminating potential problem areas, we hope that those implementing restorative justice programs will not oversell the intervention or be blind to its dangers. We also recognize that restorative justice potentially avoids a crucial weakness in other progressive policy agendas: the charge that the intervention is a form of entitlement to offenders. This problem is readily seen in the traditionally progressive approach of rehabilitation. Given the principle of less eligibility, any provision of treatment services to offenders is open to attack because such social welfare is undeserved. In contrast, restorative justice demands a certain level of accountability from offenders. Their reintegration depends on their willingness to make efforts to restore victims and the community. Accordingly, the paradigm moves away from entitlement to the principle of social exchange.

As noted, however, a fundamental weakness of restorative justice is its failure to provide a plausible blueprint for how to control crime. This failure is critical because the substantial hegemony of the penal harm or get tough movement has been due to the compelling promise that this strategy will protect society by locking up as many wicked people as possible. In contrast, restorative justice provides few answers for how to deal with serious and persistent offenders. It is especially disturbing that advocates of restorative justice have ignored the research on the behavioral change of offenders in favor of the hope—based on a new and unproved criminological theory—that brief in-

terludes of public shaming will change deeply rooted criminal predispositions. No progressive policy agenda will take hold, we argue, unless citizens are convinced that it will not jeopardize their safety. The failure to control crime inevitably will lead to a new round of penal harm.

Although a marriage may prove uneasy, an alternative approach is to explore bringing together the ideals of restorative justice and rehabilitation. If rehabilitation were seen as part of a process that held offenders accountable and tried to restore victims (e.g., through public service, working to pay victim restitution), then it would be less vulnerable to the criticism that it is only concerned with the welfare of offenders. Alternatively, if restorative justice embraced the logic and knowledge of the rehabilitative ideal, it would have a scientifically informed approach of how to change offenders' behavior. In short, restorative justice transforms rehabilitation from an entitlement or welfare paradigm to an accountability paradigm, whereas rehabilitation transforms restorative justice from a paradigm that speculates in questionable ways about changing offenders to one that can be the conduit through which effective services can be transmitted.

Merging these two correctional paradigms undoubtedly would be a daunting task and would not obviate the need to address other problems relating to these two paradigms. Even so, the dual concepts of restoration and rehabilitation are powerful ideas that can challenge the view that harming offenders is the only and best solution to crime. It is instructive that the public continues to support rehabilitation as an important goal of corrections (Applegate et al. 1997), and it seems likely that this support would increase if offenders, as part of their correctional service, were working to restore victims and the community. In short, beyond pure altruism or benevolent sentiments, why should citizens want to invest in or do good for offenders? One potentially compelling and progressive answer is that doing so will allow offenders to restore those that they have harmed and will make them less likely to harm again.

References

American Probation and Parole Association (APPA). 1994. *A Guide to Enhancing Victim Services Within Probation and Parole.* Lexington, KY: American Probation and Parole Association.

Andrews, D. A. and James Bonta. 1994. *The Psychology of Criminal Conduct.* Cincinnati, OH: Anderson.

Andrews, D. A., James Bonta, and Robert D. Hoge. 1990. "Classification for Effective Rehabilitation: Rediscovering Psychology." *Criminal Justice and Behavior,* 17: 19–52.

Andrews, D. A., Ivan Zinger, Robert D. Hoge, James Bonta. Paul Gendreau, and Francis T. Cullen. 1990. "Does Correctional Treatment Work? Clinically Relevant and Psychologically Informed Meta-Analysis." *Criminology* 28: 369–404.

Bazemore, Gordon. 1994. "Developing a Victim Orientation for Community Corrections: A Restorative Justice Paradigm and a Balanced Mission." *Perspectives* Special Issue: 19–25.

Bazemore, Gordon and Susan E. Day. 1996. "Restoring the Balance: Juvenile and Community Justice." *Juvenile Justice* 3: 3–14.

Bazemore, Gordon and Dennis Maloney. 1994. "Rehabilitating Community Service: Toward Restorative Service Sanctions in a Balanced Justice System." *Federal Probation* 58 (1): 24–35.

Bazemore, Gordon and Mark Umbreit. 1995. "Rethinking the Sanctioning Function in Juvenile Court: Retributive or Restorative Responses to Youth Crime." *Crime & Delinquency* 41: 296–316.

Berzins, Lorraine and Rick Prashaw. 1997. "A New Imagination for Justice and Corrections." *The ICCA Journal of Community Corrections* 8 (2): 22–25.

Braithwaite, John. 1989. *Crime, Shame and Reintegration.* New York: Cambridge University Press.

Brookes, Derek R. 1998. "Evaluating Restorative Justice Programs." *Humanity and Society* 22: 23–37.

Brown, Jennifer G. 1994. "The Use of Mediation to Resolve Criminal Cases: A Procedural Critique" *Emory Law Journal* 43: 1247–1309.

Byrne, James M. 1986. "Reintegrating the Concept of Community Into Community-Based Corrections." *Crime & Delinquency* 35: 471–499.

Center for Restorative Justice and Mediation. 1996. *Restorative Justice: For Victims, Communities, and Offenders.* Minneapolis: University of Minnesota, Center for Restorative Justice and Mediation.

Clear, Todd R. 1994. *Harm in American Penology: Offenders, Victims, and Their Communities.* Albany: State University of New York Press.

Clear, Todd R. and Patricia Hardyman. 1990. "The New Intensive Supervision Movement." *Crime & Delinquency* 36: 42–60.

Cochran, Donald. 1992. "The Long Road from Policy Development to Real Change in Sanctioning Practice." Pp. 307–318 in *Smart Sentencing: The Emergence of Intermediate Sanctions,* edited by J. Byrne, A. Lurigio, and J. Petersilia. Newbury Park, CA: Sage.

Colson, Charles W. and Daniel W. Van Ness. 1989. *Convicted: New Hope for Ending America's Crime Crisis.* Westchester, IL: Crossway.

Community Policing Consortium. 1994. *Understanding Community Policing: A Framework for Action.* Washington, DC: U.S. Department of Justice, Bureau of Justice Assistance.

Correctional Service Canada. 1989. "What Does Type of Offense Tell Us About Recidivism?" *Forum on Corrections Research* 1(2): 3–4.

Cullen, Francis T. and Karen E. Gilbert. 1982. *Reaffirming Rehabilitation.* Cincinnati, OH: Anderson.

Cullen, Francis T., Patricia Van Voorhis, and Jodie L. Sundt. 1996. "Prisons in Crisis: The American Experience." Pp. 21–52 in *Prisons 2000: An International Perspective on the Current State and Future of Imprisonment,* edited by R. Matthews and P. Francis. New York: St. Martin's.

Cullen, Francis T., John P. Wright, and Brandon K. Applegate. 1996. "Control in the Community: The Limits of Reform?" Pp. 69–116 in *Choosing Correctional Interventions That Work: Defining the Demand and Evaluating the Supply,* edited by A. T. Harland. Newbury Park, CA: Sage.

Currie, Elliott. 1985. *Confronting Crime: Art American Challenge.* New York: Pantheon.

——. 1998. *Crime and Punishment in America.* New York: Metropolitan.

Dooley, Michael J. 1996. "Reparative Probation Boards." Pp. 185–192 in *Restoring Hope Through Community Partnerships: The Real Deal in Crime Control,* edited by B. Fulton. Lexington, KY. American Probation and Parole Association.

Fabiano, Elizabeth, Frank Porporino, and Dave Robinson. 1991. "Canada's Cognitive Skills Program Corrects Offenders' Faulty Thinking." *Corrections Today* 53 (August): 102–108.

Ferns, Ray. 1994. "Restorative Case Management: The Evolution of Correctional Case Management." *Perspectives* 18 (Summer): 36–41.

Finckenauer, James O. 1982. *Scared Straight! and the Panacea Phenomenon.* Englewood Cliffs, NJ: Prentice Hall.

Galaway, Burt. 1977. "Restitution as an Integrative Punishment." Pp. 341–347 in *Assessing the Criminal: Restitution, Retribution, and the Legal Process,* edited by R. E. Barnett and H. Hagel III. Cambridge, MA: Ballinger.

Garafalo, James and Maureen McLeod. 1986. "Improving the Effectiveness and Utilization of Neighborhood Watch Programs." Presented to the National Institute of Justice from the Hindelang Criminal Justice Research Center, State University of New York at Albany.

Gendreau, Paul. 1996. "The Principles of Effective Intervention With Offenders." Pp. 117–130 in *Choosing Correctional Options That Work,* edited by A. T. Harland. Thousand Oaks, CA: Sage.

Gendreau, Paul, D. A. Andrews, Claire Goggin, and Francoise Chanteloupe. 1992. "The Development of Clinical and Policy Guidelines for the Prediction of Criminal Behavior in Criminal Justice Settings." Department of Psychology, University of New Brunswick, St. John. Unpublished manuscript.

Gendreau, Paul, Betsy Fulton, and Claire Goggin. Forthcoming. "Intensive Supervision in Probation and Parole Settings." In *Handbook of Offender Assessment and Treatment,* edited by C. R. Hollin. Chichester, UK: Wiley.

Goldkamp, John and Michael Gottfredson. 1985. *Policy Guidelines for Bail: An Experiment in Court Reform.* Philadelphia: Temple University.

Grinc, Randolph M. 1994. " 'Angels in Marble': Problems in Stimulating Community Involvement in Community Policing." *Crime & Delinquency* 40: 442.

Hahn, Paul H. 1998. *Emerging Criminal Justice: Three Pillars for a Proactive Justice System.* Thousand Oaks, CA: Sage.

Immarigeon, Russ and Kathleen Daly. 1997. "Restorative Justice: Origins, Practices, Contexts, and Challenges." *The ICCA Journal on Community Corrections* 8(2): 13–19.

Karp, David R. 1998. "The Judicial and Judicious Use of Shame Penalties." *Crime & Delinquency* 44: 277–294.

Lawrence, Richard. 1991. "Reexamining Community Corrections Models." *Crime & Delinquency* 37: 449–464.

Lindner, Charles. 1996. "VORP: An Unproven Fringe Movement." *Perspectives* 20 (Winter): 15–17.

Lipsey, Mark and David Wilson. 1998. "Effective Intervention for Serious Juvenile Offenders: A Synthesis of Research." Pp. 313–345 in *Serious and Violent Juvenile Offenders: Risk Factors and Successful Interventions,* edited by R. Loeber and D. P. Farrington. Thousand Oaks, CA: Sage.

Maloney, Dennis, Dennis Romig, and Troy Armstrong. 1998. *Juvenile Probation: The Balanced Approach.* Reno, NV, National Council of Juvenile and Family Court Judges.

Maloney, Dennis and Mark Umbreit. 1995. "Managing Change: Toward a Balanced and Restorative Justice Model." *Perspectives* 19(2): 43–46.

Marshall, Tony F. 1992. "Restorative Justice on Trial in Britain." Pp. 15–28 in *Restorative Justice on Trial: Pitfalls and Potentials of Victim-Offender Mediation-International Research Perspectives,* edited by H. Messmer and H. U. Otto. Boston: Kluwer.

Maxwell, Gabrielle and Allison Morris. 1997. "Family Group Conferences and Restorative Justice." *The ICCA Journal on Community Corrections* 8(2): 37–40.

Niemeyer, Mark and David Shichor. 1996. "A Preliminary Study of a Large Victim/Offender Reconciliation Program." *Federal Probation* 60 (3): 30–34.

Pepinsky, Harold and Richard Quinney, eds. 1991. *Criminology as Peacemaking.* Bloomington: Indiana University Press.

Petersilia, Joan. 1996. "A Crime Control Rationale for Reinvesting in Community Corrections." *Perspectives* 20(2): 21–29.

Petersilia. Joan and Susan Turner. 1993. "Evaluating Intensive Supervision Probation/Parole: Results of Nationwide Experiment." *Research in Brief,* National Institute of Justice, Washington, DC.

Pranis, Kay. 1996. "A Hometown Approach to Restorative Justice." *State Government News* 39(9): 14–16.

Putney, Bart. 1997. "A Grassroots Approach to Restorative Justice." *The ICCA Journal on Community Corrections* 8(2): 20–21.

Rothman, David J. 1980. *Conscience and Convenience: The Asylum and Its Alternatives in Progressive America.* Boston: Little, Brown.

Ruddell, Regina. 1996. "Victim Offender Reconciliation Program." Pp. 171–172 in *Restoring Hope Through Community Partnerships: The Real Deal in Crime Control,* edited by B.

Fulton. Lexington, KY: American Probation and Parole Association.

Schafer, Stephen. 1976. "The Victim and Correctional Theory: Integrating Victim Reparation With Offender Rehabilitation." Pp. 227–236 in *Criminal Justice and the Victim,* edited by W. F. McDonald. Beverly Hills, CA: Sage.

Seymour, Anne. 1996. "Putting Victims First." *State Government News* 39(9): 24–25.

Shapiro, Carol. 1990. "Is Restitution Legislation the Chameleon of the Victims' Movement." Pp. 73–80 in *Criminal Justice, Restitution, and Reconciliation,* edited by B. Galaway and J. Hudson. Mousey. NJ: Willow Tree Press.

Silloway, Glenn and Marlys McPherson. 1985. "The Limits to Citizen Participation in a Government Sponsored Community Crime Prevention Program." Presented at the annual meeting of the American Society of Criminology, San Diego, CA.

Skogan, Wesley G. 1990. *Disorder and Decline: Crime and the Spiral of Decay in Urban Neighborhoods.* Berkeley: University of California Press.

——. 1996. "The Community's Role in Community Policing." *National Institute of Justice Journal* (August): 31–34.

Umbreit, Mark S. 1994. "Victim Empowerment Through Mediation: The Impact of Victim Offender Mediation in Four Cities." *Perspectives* Special Issue: 25–30.

Umbreit, Mark and Howard Zehr. 1996. "Restorative Family Group Conferences: Differing Models and Guidelines for Practice." *Federal Probation* 60(3): 24–29.

Van Ness, Daniel W. 1986. *Crime and Its Victims.* Downers Grove, IL: InterVarsity Press.

Van Ness, Daniel W. and Karen H. Strong. 1997. *Restoring Justice.* Cincinnati, OH: Anderson.

Van Voorhis, Patricia. 1985. "Restitution Outcome and Probationer's Assessments of Restitution: The Effects of Moral Development." *Criminal Justice and Behavior* 12: 259–287.

——. 1997. "Correctional Classification and the 'Responsivity Principle'." *Forum on Corrections Research* 209 (1): 46–50.

Walther, Lynne and John Perry. 1997. "The Vermont Reparative Probation Program." *The ICCA Journal on Community Corrections* 8(2): 26–34.

Warren, Marguerite. 1983. "Application of Interpersonal Maturity Theory to Offender Populations." Pp. 23–49 in *Personality Theory, Moral Development, and Criminal Behavior,* edited by W. Laufer and J. Day. Lexington, MA: Lexington Books.

Zehr, Howard. 1990. *Changing Lenses.* Scottdale, PA: Herald Press.

ISSUE XIV
For Profit or Punishment: Should Jails and Prisons Be Privatized?

When a judge pronounces a prison sentence, the convicted defendant is placed in the care and control of the government through the federal bureau of prisons or a state department of corrections. Some jurisdictions allow for early release via a parole board, although some sentences are mandatory, in that a specified number of years must be served before an offender is eligible for release. The significant increase in mandatory sentences in the mid-1980s diminished the choices left for state and federal agencies. The number of prisoners exceeded available space, and prisons have become crowded. To alleviate crowded correctional institutions, governments have increasingly elected to use privately owned facilities to house prisoners.

Private businesses are able to construct new facilities and own the buildings, leasing out space to government tenants for a contracted daily fee per person. While the state must request voter approval to build a new prison, private prisons do not need public consent and therefore take less than half the time to build a new facility. There are currently 158 privately operating facilities housing 116,626 prisoners in 30 states, Puerto Rico, and the District of Columbia (Austin and Coventry 2001).

Most private facilities are concentrated in the southern and western portions of the United States. The most extensive research to date on private prisons examined 65 private institutions operated by 7 different companies and compared to them to nationwide data for minimum- and medium-security state and federal prisons operated by the government. The study was conducted by the National Council on Crime and Delinquency (Austin and Coventry 2001). The researchers found that ". . . it cannot be concluded that a private or a public prison is superior to the other . . . with one major exception: in this comparison, the privately operated facilities have a much higher rate of inmate-on-inmate and inmate-on-staff assaults and other disturbances" (Austin and Coventry 2001, 52). The researchers mentioned that private facilities had an "impressive record of programming activities" for inmates (p. 43) and that over 95 percent of the prisoners were classified as minimum- or medium-custody level. Such prisoners pose less risk to the security of the community and are therefore less expensive to house because less staff is needed than for prisoners in maximum security. In terms of cost savings, research found that private prisons saved an average of only 1 percent compared to public institutions housing prisoners of equivalent custody level. Cost savings were achieved primarily through having fewer staff working for less pay and fewer benefits than government institutions (Austin and Coventry 2001).

Analysts predict that larger private companies, such as Corrections Corporation of America and Wackenhut Corrections Corporation, will buy out the smaller private companies because daily operating costs and competition have increased, forcing smaller firms to consolidate (Austin and Coventry 2001). Although the private sector has expanded into juvenile facilities (Moore 1999), county jails (Sechrest and Shichor 1997), and halfway houses, it is predicted that private prisons are unlikely to be a focus for high-security prisoners. Rather, Austin and Coventry (2001) predict that private prisons will grow at a slower rate than in the past and will continue to house minimum- and medium-security prisoners. Private companies may increasingly draw from elderly prisoners and those with medical and mental health problems who pose less risk to the safety of the community.

Charles W. Thomas supports privatization for its ability to save money, be more efficient and flexible, generate competition, and encourage providers to improve the quality of their services. These abilities result in enhancing the conditions inside prisons and reducing legal costs and liability. Thomas makes two points clear. First, *courts* decide whom to punish and for how long—private firms cannot make these decisions. Second, private firms are not the only ones profiting from the building of new prisons. Many small rural communities have lobbied hard to convince the government to build state-run prisons nearby because the institution would give them much-needed jobs.

Richard G. Hogan gauges private prisons using Logan's (1990) categories of propriety, cost, quality, security, quantity, flexibility, accountability, liability, dependency, and corruption. Among his assertions, Hogan states that private prisons decrease service quality and underpay their staff in the name of saving money. Private prisons are thus understaffed with low-paid officers, and treatment of prisoners and prison conditions suffer as a result. Hogan shows that private prisons are politically and economically linked and maintain relationships that have a conflict of interest. Hogan supports his assertions using both current and historical research and concludes that privatization may cause more harm than good.

References

Austin, James, and Garry Coventry. 2001. *Emerging Issues on Privatized Prisons.* Washington, DC: Bureau of Justice Assistance, U.S. Department of Justice.

Logan, Charles H. 1990. *Private Prisons: Cons and Pros.* New York: Oxford University Press.

Moore, Jacqueline. 1999. "Juvenile Corrections: A Public View of the Private Sector." *Corrections Management Quarterly* 3(3): 43–56.

Sechrest, Dale K., and David Shichor. 1997. "Private Jails: Locking Down the Issues." *American Jails* 11(1): 21–36.

Critical Thinking Questions

1. Assume that you are a business owner of Profit-Prison, Inc., and that your company wants to build and operate a private jail or prison in a nearby community. What are the questions that you as a business owner may need to ask before making your decision?

2. What role do you believe that private facilities *should* have in the future of corrections?

3. What role do you believe that private correctional facilities *will* have in the future?

Internet Websites

Emerging issues of privatized prisons. (NCJ 181249) <http://www.ncjrs.org/pdffiles1/bja/181249.pdf>

Correctional Services Corporation homepage. <http://www.correctionalservices.com/>

Database of articles on private prisons by Oregon AFSCME corrections. <http://www.oregonafscme.com/corrections/private/aprivatearticlesholding.htm>

Database of Charles Logan, Professor of Sociology, comparing public and private prisons. <http://www.ucc.uconn.edu/~wwwsoci/nmexsum.html>

Smith, Phil. 1993. "Private Prisons: Profits of Crime," *Covert Action Quarterly.* <http://www.mediafilter.org/MFF/Prison.html>

Thomas, C. W. (1999, October). Chart showing the numbers of private facilities by geographical location. <http://web.crim.ufl.edu/pcp/census/1999/Chart3.html>

An article titled: "The promise and peril of private prisons". <http://www.gomemphis.com/newca/special/import/import3.htm>

Wackenhut Corporation homepage. <http://wackenhutcorp.com/> ✦

27

Correctional Privatization

The Issues and the Evidence

Charles W. Thomas

Criminologists behave prudently if they respond cautiously to the type of "should we" questions that Professors Decker, Alarid, and Katz posed when they selected the topic of correctional privatization for this book. It is inherent in the nature of such questions that the response, whether overtly or by some more subtle implication, will reflect a value judgment. There is little reason to believe, however, that the value judgments of criminologists or other behavioral scientists are superior to those of anyone else.

This having been said, it is also the case that I have been publishing research on a broad array of topics of criminological relevance for more than three decades and on the economic, legal, and public policy dimensions of correctional privatization for roughly half of that time (Lanza-Kaduce, Parker, and Thomas 1999; Thomas 1991a, 1991b, 1992, 1997; Quinlan, Thomas, and Gautreaux 2001; Thomas, Lanza-Kaduce, Calvert, Hanson, and Duffy 1988; Thomas and Hanson 1989). The position I will advance here in favor of correctional privatization is one that flows from thirty years of personal research experience in both traditional and privatized correctional facilities.

Making the Value Choice Clear

Second only to the continuing controversy about capital punishment, the highly politicized debate about correctional privatization ranks at the top of any list of the con- tentious topics that attracted the interest of criminologists during the twentieth century. The debate is unlikely to become either less passionate or more objective in the foreseeable future. Further, those on both sides of the often-strident debate speak as though someone had granted them a strange species of immunity from the influence of evidence, logic, and reason. The irony deepens when it is recognized that many, if not most, of those who leaped into the ideological debate have never set foot into a privatized facility. Indeed, more than a few have never gotten closer to any type of correctional facility than the television screens in their living rooms.

Because there continues to be more ideological smoke than objective research on correctional privatization, it is necessary that this discussion begin with some introductory comments regarding two issues. One of these is closely linked to such cute alliterative phrases as "dungeons for dollars" (Robbins 1989). The core but also misguided notion is that it is morally improper for one group of persons to derive a financial benefit from the punishment of their fellow citizens (Logan 1987, 1990, 1996).

This notion is plagued by at least two fundamental flaws. The first of these is the implication that private management firms determine who will be punished and, for those who are confined, decisions regarding such issues as the place and the duration of their confinement.

The implication is demonstrably false. It is government that invariably defines crimes, types of punishment, and sentence lengths. It is government that invariably establishes the place of confinement for those who are confined. It is also government that invariably has the power to release offenders prior to the expiration of their court-imposed sentences via, for example, conditional release on parole.

In short, the fact of the matter is that private management firms lack—and for both moral and constitutional reasons should lack—the power to punish. This means that another alliterative phrase we often hear being chanted almost as a mantra by privatization critics—punishment for profit—is really quite irrelevant to the privatization debate. Private management firms do not punish. Their exclusive role is to maintain custody of persons *the State* has chosen to confine for the period *the State* chooses to confine them and to provide the programs and services *the State* has deemed to be in the public interest during the term of their confinement.

The second fundamental flaw I alluded to earlier is closely related to the first. It flows from the notion that only private management firms make a profit from punishment. I earlier noted that private management firms lack the power to make the critical "in and out" decisions that determine who will be confined, the place of confinement, and the duration of confinement. Still, it is the case that private firms seek a financial gain from the array of services they provide. Thus, even if privatization critics were to accept the fact that the private sector does not have the power to punish, their fallback position would be that it is morally reprehensible for any person to derive a financial benefit from the management of a jail or a prison.

This fallback position is indefensible to the point of being ludicrous. Do private firms, their employees, and their shareholders have a profit motive? Of course they do. But does it logically follow from such a matter-of-fact stipulation either that those on the private sector side are sinners who are doomed to an eternity in a hot spot or that those on the public sector side are exemplars of virtue who are destined to a loftier fate?

Of course not. Public employees, after all, are compensated for their services, so the existence of some people deriving a financial benefit from the punishment of other people is a reality quite without regard to whether correctional facilities are or are not privatized. The antiprivatization position is not strengthened by the fact that private firms are motivated to earn a profit for their shareholders. Because we all are taxpayers, we all have what amounts to a shareholder interest in our public agencies. Thus, we expect and often demand that improvements in the economic efficiency of those agencies yield dividends for us in the form of reduced taxes, enhanced services in other areas of value to us, or a combination of reduced taxes and improved services.

In Search of a Rational Bottom Line for Public Policy

At this point in the discussion it should be clear that, first, privatization decisions do not delegate the power to punish to a private entity and that, second, the existence of financial motivations does not distinguish between public and private providers of correctional services. Further, various derivative arguments one encounters in debates over privatization are similarly unpersuasive in their rhetorical effort to depict one group as saints and the other as sinners. For example, it has become common for privatization critics to contend that private firms may some day lobby for sentencing policies that would enlarge our prison population and thus expand their markets. No credible evidence has ever been offered to prove that private firms have engaged in this type of lobbying behavior. Still, it is possible that, absent a constitutional amendment that prohibits corporations and their employees from participating in the democratic process, the private sector might engage in lobbying activities intended to advance its economic interest.

The flip side of this involves what *is* happening rather than what *might* happen in the lobbying trenches. It is undeniably true that aggressive lobbying is already taking place aimed at "toughening" our sentencing policies by, for instance, some of the most powerful public employee unions in the nation (e.g., the California Correctional Peace Officers Association). To be sure, some readers will agree with the CCPOA's advocacy of tougher sentencing. My judgment being that we confine too many offenders for too long a period of time already, I happen to disagree. The point, however, is that some public employee unions and also some public agencies already are lobbying for public policies whose adoption would clearly be to their financial benefit. It is their constitutionally protected right to support whatever public policy they favor, and the right does not lose that protection merely because it advances their economic or political self-interest. At the same time, it is amusing that those who actually *are* lobbying for sentencing policies that advance their self-interest are so piously willing to criticize private firms on the grounds that they *might* engage in precisely the same conduct.

In any event, once one accepts the reality that privatization conveys no inherently governmental powers to private entities and the fact that the delivery of correctional services unavoidably entitles both the public and the private service provider to financial benefits, it becomes necessary to focus on other issues if the development of prudent public policy is our goal. My judgment is that this quest for fair and reasonable public policy standards is a far less daunting task than the on-going privatization debate implies.

First, sound public policy in corrections requires that we devise means of protecting the public safety interest by designing correctional facilities and delivering correctional services in ways that meet or exceed all applicable constitutional, legal, and professional standards. Too often we have failed to implement such policy. Before the first jail or prison was privatized, our state and especially federal court dockets for decades were clogged with tens of thousands of cases in which prisoner plaintiffs confined in publicly managed facilities litigated their claims of official misconduct. The result was reams of legally adequate proof of prisoners having been treated in an unconstitutional and too often in an outrageously brutal fashion (e.g., Cohen 1995).

Second, public funds obviously being a limited resource, it is necessarily the case that a dollar expended in one area of governmental responsibility is a dollar that cannot be made available to meet pressing needs elsewhere. Sound public policy in corrections must reflect an awareness of this reality by achieving cost savings whenever doing so is possible.

So what does all of this tell us about whether we should or should not privatize jails and prisons? I think it tells us a lot. To begin with, I think this image of sound public policy making urges us to disregard *both* those who argue that privatization is the equivalent of original sin *and* those who argue that privatization is somehow inherently a panacea for the many ills of the nation's correctional systems. Only a fool would argue that privatization is intrinsically either good or evil—just as only a fool would argue that maintaining the historical monopoly government has had with regard to managing jails and prisons is intrinsically either good or evil.

A more thoughtful person would begin by conceptualizing his or her public policy objective. I believe corrections has three main objectives:

1. to protect the public safety interest, which is a goal that demands rehabilitative programs aimed at reducing recidivism;

2. to design and operate jails and prisons in such a way as to meet or exceed all applicable constitutional, legal, and professional standards;

3. to do what is in need of being done at as low a cost to taxpayers as is possible.

To the degree that this statement of the public policy objectives of our correctional system is viable, then the focus should be on what is done and how well it is done rather than on the public or private identity of those on whom we rely to advance the public interest. Further, this focus on the pursuit of value—which may be defined as a quest for the highest quality services at the lowest possible cost—cannot possibly be criticized for being biased in favor of either public or private providers of correctional services.

The Proof Is in the Evidence, Not the Rhetoric

Thus far I have done little more than defend the proposition that fair competition between alternative public and private providers of correctional services aimed at obtaining the best professional services at the lowest cost may serve the public interest—and also, I should add, the interests of the confined persons who are the most direct beneficiaries of high caliber correctional services. Thus stated, the proposition defends itself. The alternative would be to favor the preservation of the traditional governmental monopoly even if doing so yields something less than the best possible services and does so at a higher than necessary cost. Even the most zealous of the public employee unions—groups which have defended a status quo that accords them access to substantial economic benefits and political power as they loudly but wrongly proclaim that their self-interest and the public interest are one and the same thing—would hesitate to advance so absurd a position as what this alternative leaves open to them.

Importantly, even if the debate rhetoric of privatization critics fades to insignificance when it is placed under even a low-power microscope, it does not logically follow that correctional privatization necessarily provides a sound public policy option. On the abstract level of public policy theory, a favorable case is not hard to state. Sound public policy, however, cannot be allowed to live or die because of its theoretical appeal. It must prove its value in the real world. This point was made succinctly by none other than Professor Marvin E. Wolfgang when he wrote, "The privatization of criminal justice from crime reporting to enforcement, mediation, prosecution, and prison management should be seriously considered, empirically evaluated, and if found to be positive, implemented" (Wolfgang 1998).

This reality is of vital importance to the on-going privatization debate. Twenty years ago there were no privatized jails or prisons in the United States or elsewhere in the world. Thus, there was no evidence of the success or failure of correctional privatization. There was no evidence of value even when the initial management contracts were awarded by local, state, and federal agencies in the early 1980s (Logan 1990; Thomas and Logan 1993; Thomas 1996). Time must pass before credible evidence of the success or failure of any public policy initiative can be collected. Today, however, more than 110,000 prisoners are housed in privatized facilities in the United States, and an additional 30,000 prisoners are in private facili-

ties in Australia, Canada, Great Britain, and South Africa (Thomas 2002). This robust growth in the appeal of privatization has stimulated the publication of quite a voluminous body of research (Quinlan, Thomas, and Gautreaux 2001).

It is unfortunate that both advocates and critics of correctional privatization are guilty of focusing attention only on the evidence that is favorable to their contrary interests. Not at all amazingly, both advocates and critics make sweeping assertions about the bias and ineptitude of anyone who is bold enough to publish research that contains conclusions that fail to support their position. This is to be expected. Shooting messengers who deliver unwelcome messages in the form of research reports continues to be a fashionable and sometimes entertaining indoor sport. Those who do public policy research must accept "being shot at" as an unavoidable occupational risk. Indeed, speaking as one who has been shot at more often than most, I believe the absolute certainty of being targeted by one species of zealot or another whenever I put pen to paper has had the altogether desirable result of improving the quality of my research.

This is not the place for me to shoot back at my various antiprivatization opponents. Further, space limitations will preclude me from providing a detailed assessment of the research literature. Instead, I have made a good faith effort to sort through the dozens of studies that have been published. My goal was to identify patterns or themes in those studies that are relevant to reaching an informed judgment about whether the privatization of jails and prisons makes good public policy sense. I will refer to those patterns and themes as advantages of privatization. Before discussing those advantages, however, one general point should be put forward with some emphasis.

Specifically, there is nothing magical about decisions to privatize correctional facilities. Just as the historical record in corrections chronicles the failures of many public correctional agencies, so too does the far briefer record of contracting with private management firms reveal results that fell far short of success. On the other hand, however, the very same historical record also documents numerous settings within which both public agencies and private management firms have confronted challenging and often dangerous situations to which they have responded successfully and sometimes with distinction. Thus, a key to making prudent public policy choices is to avoid focusing on isolated evidence of either success or failure and, instead, to emphasize whatever patterns or common denominators the evidence reveals.

I say this with emphasis because the heated privatization debate often finds its participants trying to bury their opponents with carefully selected anecdotal evidence of their failures. For example, I regularly stumble across websites on which privatization critics gleefully post news items regarding any negative incident involving a private facility but include not a single item regarding either positive news from private facilities or negative incidents involving public facilities. The effect of the extremes the debate sometimes reaches is that we are encouraged to imagine a world within which either public agencies or private firms are always demons and within which those on the opposing side are always saints. This, of course, is a false dichotomy. Both public agencies and private firms have successes—and both have failures.

Advantages of Privatizing Jails and Prisons

The advantages of privatization are shaped by the particular circumstances within which public policy decisions are made. Some advantages to which a very high priority might be assigned in one setting might be of no relevance in another. For example, construction cost savings would be irrelevant in a context that involved privatizing an existing facility. Similarly, improving the caliber of management would be irrelevant in a well-managed public system. Finally, in communities within which one finds facilities that are privately owned as well as privately operated, an economic advantage of privatization at the local level is the significant flow of property tax pay-

ments, but this is irrelevant when privatized facilities are publicly owned and are for that reason exempt from paying taxes. Thus, what follows is a largely unranked identification of advantages of privatization that appear with sufficient frequency in a combination of court decisions, experience, and published research as to warrant the attention of policy makers.

Competition

The least often discussed or researched but perhaps also the most powerful single advantage of correctional privatization is its ability to generate competition between alternative providers of correctional services and thereby to motivate public agencies both to improve the quality of the services they provide and to control or reduce costs (Harding 1997). Arguably one of the most fundamental problems of a government monopoly is the absence of incentives that encourage them and their employees to become more efficient and effective (Kettl 1993; Logan 1990).

Not surprisingly, government agencies and public employees often are the most outspoken opponents of privatization. Their desire to preserve a relatively comfortable status quo is not hard to understand. Although our everyday life experience provides unequivocal proof that we perform better in competitive settings, there also is a lazy bone or two in all of our bodies that makes noncompetitive settings appealing. Nonetheless, a growing body of evidence coming, for example, from Arizona, Florida, Tennessee, and the Federal Bureau of Prisons provides persuasive evidence that privatization can be a powerful stimulus for change in how public agencies perform.

Construction Time and Cost Savings

Despite the testy nature of the privatization debate, no informed person on either side of the issue would deny that one benefit of privatization is the ability of the private sector to move far more swiftly with the construction of new correctional facilities and to do so at a substantially lower cost. New privatized facility construction times are generally 50 percent or more below those of government projects. Construction cost savings of 15 to 25 percent are quite typical.

One recent example of this dual cost and time benefit is provided by a case study of a fairly large facility in Delaware County, Pennsylvania, that was published by Kengor and Scheffler (1999). Prior to the decision to privatize, construction costs had been estimated at $93 million. The Wackenhut Corrections Corporation received a contract to design, construct, and manage the needed facility and did so at a cost of $55.84 million. Further, observe Kengor and Scheffler, when "Wackenhut broke ground for the new facility, a similar state prison in Chester County was over a year-and-a-half underway, yet Delaware County completed its prison before the government finished its facility" (Kengor and Scheffler 1999, 9).

Research reports containing comparable conclusions of construction cost savings appear to have become routine. For instance, the Florida Office of Program Policy Analysis and Government Accountability, the research arm of the Florida Legislature, published a detailed statistical analysis in March of 2000 on the construction cost savings achieved by the Wackenhut Corrections Corporation (Florida Office of Program Policy Analysis and Government Accountability 2000). Here it was possible to make a direct comparison between the costs of constructing the 1,318-bed private prison and a nearby traditional state prison of equivalent size and mission. The total construction and financing costs of the private prison was $69.9 million; the comparable cost of the traditional public prison was $85.7 million.

Access to Construction Capital

The construction of new correctional facilities places a substantial burden on government. Construction costs expressed on a per bed basis are quite commonly at or above $50,000. Thus, the capital outlay for a 1,000-bed jail or prison can easily exceed $50,000,000. Government must either divert the needed funds from its present-year budget or arrange for the sale of bonds that, in a manner rather like a home mortgage, allows the construction cost burden to be spread over a period of twenty or more years. How-

ever, much like ordinary citizens, government agencies sometimes find themselves in the awkward position of confronting pressing needs for new jails or prisons at the very same time that existing levels of debt undermines the ability to borrow more capital through the sale of tax-exempt bonds.

Suffice it to say that many jurisdictions favoring privatization have placed the burden of obtaining construction capital on private management firms (e.g., Arizona, Colorado, Georgia, Kentucky, Oklahoma, North Carolina, and the Federal Bureau of Prisons). Although the private firms certainly hope to recapture their investment of capital, I am not aware of any contract that includes a guarantee that this hope will be realized. Nonetheless, it clearly is the case that many government agencies define the ability and willingness of the private sector to commit large amounts of private capital to the construction of new facilities as a significant advantage of privatization.

The benefits of this advantage can be multifaceted. In 1998, for example, the Corrections Corporation of America (CCA) assessed the need for prisoner housing space for either state or federal prisoners in California to be so great that it committed more than $100 million of private capital to construct a 2,304-bed medium-security prison located in California City, California. The commitment was made without any contract that guaranteed the utilization of the facility. Importantly, not a penny of public capital was put at risk by CCA's decision to move forward with the project prior to a contract award. Soon after the construction was completed, however, the largest prisoner housing contract ever awarded by the Federal Bureau of Prisons was announced. The net effect of this was that the Federal Bureau of Prisons was able to gain access to a new state-of-the-art facility almost immediately following the contract award, to do so at a construction cost far below the norm for the agency, and to achieve significant daily operating cost savings for federal taxpayers.

Other illustrations of the access to capital advantage the private sector has provided are easily identified. In 1999, for instance, Cornell Companies, a rapidly growing management firm which has significant experience in community corrections and juvenile corrections as well as in the management of jails and prisons, committed more than $30 million of private capital to the construction of the New Morgan Academy in New Morgan, Pennsylvania. This modern 214-bed facility was constructed in only eighteen months and today provides intensive programs and services for some of the most difficult juveniles in the nation. Although the corporate decision to move forward with the project was based on its internal assessment of government needs rather than a preconstruction contract award, the fact that the facility is already operating at very close to its design capacity offers evidence of prudent risk-taking by the private sector yielding a tangible benefit to government.

Operating Cost Savings

Everyday operating cost savings achieved by privatized facilities is routinely found to be between 10 to 15 percent. For example, a few years ago I received a contract from the Arizona Department of Corrections for the purpose of evaluating whether its first privatization initiative in 1994, which involved a management contract award to Management and Training Corporation, had yielded cost and performance benefits (Thomas 1997). The overall conclusion, which was endorsed by the Department of Corrections, was that cost savings of no less than 13.8 percent had been achieved and that the quality of the services provided by Management and Training Corporation had been either equivalent or superior to the services provided in public prisons housing inmates with comparable security classifications. Unsurprisingly, various opponents of privatization, including the Office of Research and Evaluation of the Federal Bureau of Prisons, were quick to criticize my research (Gaes, Camp, and Saylor 1998).

The criticism of my research notwithstanding, my results regarding cost savings and performance were recently cross-validated by a two-year study that recently was conducted by the Arizona Department of Corrections (Arizona Department of Corrections 2000). This study broadened the focus

of the comparisons to include both the Management and Training Corporation facility and two newer facilities that are being operated by the Correctional Services Corporation. The three private facilities were compared with fifteen public facilities that house prisoners with comparable security classifications. The report concluded that "the private prisons performed at or above the aggregate performance of Level 2 public prisons 62.3 percent of the time" (Arizona Department of Corrections 2000, 2) and did so at a cost per prisoner per day of "less than $41.00 versus a comparable public prison cost of $46.72 in 1998 and $45.85 in 1999." This translates into an average operating cost savings of 13.62 percent in fiscal year 1998 and 10.84 percent in fiscal year 1999 (Arizona Department of Corrections 2000, 46–47).

Because the provisions of many state laws flatly require evidence of consequential cost savings as a precondition for any contract award, findings of the type that I reported in my Arizona research and that were reinforced by the more recent analysis should hardly be a shock to anyone. Still, this often-demonstrated advantage of privatization has been the subject of far more controversy than the construction cost savings. Although the vast majority of the published cost comparisons in the United States as well as those coming from Australia and Great Britain document attractive cost savings (Brown 1994; Crants 1991; Dunmore 1996; Florida Office of Program Policy Analysis and Government Accountability 2000; Gold 1996; Kengor and Scheffler 1999; Logan 1989; Logan and McGriff 1989; Loux 1999; McDonald 1990; Moore 1998; Texas Sunset Advisory Commission 1991; Thomas 1997), privatization critics continue to contend either that the documented savings are unpersuasive or that they will diminish over time (Gaes, Camp, and Saylor 1998; United States General Accounting Office 1996). Despite this criticism, the same body of evidence as well as other studies that focus only on the quality of services provided in privatized facilities make it equally clear that cost savings do not come at the expense of the caliber of the correctional services that are provided

(Brakel 1988; Logan 1992, 1996b; Thomas 1997; Quinlan, Thomas, and Gautreaux 2001).

Quality of Service Enhancements

To achieve cost savings through privatization is a meaningful public policy objective, but to blindly pursue those savings in the absence of clear evidence that the precontracting quality of services is being preserved or enhanced achieves no productive purpose whatsoever. In recent years, for example, I watched closely as two states—Arkansas and North Carolina—ineptly privatized two state prisons. Both either knew or reasonably should have known that the services required by their contracts could not be delivered at the prices they agreed to pay. All four initiatives failed, which many suspect was the intended purpose of the weaknesses in the procurement processes and contracts in both states. Now, however, the operating budgets for all four facilities will be significantly and unapologetically pushed higher as they return to the publicly managed side of the ledger. Fortunately, those responsible for more thoughtful privatization initiatives have recognized the distinction most of us make between "good value" and "cheap" in our everyday economic lives (e.g., Alaska, Arizona, Florida, Hawaii, Oklahoma, Wisconsin). Policy makers in those states had the sophistication to pursue reasonable cost savings but to do so at the same time that they demanded solid programs and services.

The bottom line is that the research evidence quite clearly shows that government agencies that qualify as being what Kettle (1993) refers to as "smart buyers" can and do obtain enhanced correctional services by privatizing. Many of the individual research studies that support this conclusion were identified during the previous discussion of cost savings, and there is other evidence that improved services made possible by privatization may yield meaningful long-term benefits. Indeed, the results can be dramatic. Recent research in Florida, for instance, compared recidivism among prisoners released from a medium-security prison operated by the Corrections Corporation of America and a similar facility operated by the Wackenhut Corrections Corporation with recidivism among a closely comparable group of releasees from prisons operated by the Florida Department of Corrections (Lanza-Kaduce, Parker, and Thomas 1999). Recidivism was measured in terms of differentials in rearrest, technical violations of the conditions of release, and resentencing for postrelease criminal. The research results revealed significantly lower recidivism among the releasees from the private prisons. For example, releasees from the private prisons were more than 28 percent less likely than releasees from the public prisons to be returned to prison following their release (Lanza-Kaduce, Parker and Thomas 1999, 36).

The Florida study is certainly not the only published research that demonstrates that sophisticated programs in privatized settings can yield impressive recidivism results. An interesting additional illustration is provided by longitudinal research being conducted by the Institute of Behavioral Research at Texas Christian University on the Dallas County Judicial Treatment Center (DCJTC) in Wilmer, Texas, that is operated by Cornell Companies. The DCJTC provides a 300-bed residential treatment program for offenders with histories of substance abuse and addiction, an offender group that typically has a high risk of recidivism. The research findings revealed that only 11 percent of program "graduates" were re-arrested within a year of their program completion. By contrast, 21 percent of those removed from the program as a result of misconduct or other program infractions had re-arrest records during the same time period (Knight and Hiller 1997; Residential Directors Council of Texas and the Community Assistance Division of the Texas Department of Criminal Justice 1999).

Heightened Accountability

Debate rhetoric to the contrary notwithstanding, it is impossible for any reasonable person to argue against the position that enhanced accountability is an important benefit of privatization (Harding 1997). The reason is simple. The legal link between government policy makers and private management firms is a management contract. The performance requirements in such contracts are quite specific with respect to numbers of employees the private firm is obliged to hire, the training standards those employees must meet, the array of programs and services the private firm agrees to provide, the fraction of the prisoner population that must be involved in programs, and so on. Private firms risk significant financial performance penalties if the terms and the conditions of their contracts are violated, and either serious or chronic contract violations justify contract terminations. Further, most contracting agencies are sophisticated enough to appreciate the value of full-time contract compliance monitors whose presence in private facilities serves as an additional guarantee of contract compliance. Nothing similar to such contracts and fully independent contract monitors exists when facilities are managed by public agencies.

Heightened accountability, of course, is a means to an end and should not be viewed as an end in and of itself. Still, much experience gained since the first management contracts were awarded in the mid-1980s offers persuasive proof that the prospects for the success of privatization initiatives is greatly enhanced by the dual accountability mechanisms of properly drafted contracts coupled with fair but firm contract compliance monitoring.

Reduced Legal Costs and Liability Exposure

Correctional privatization is an especially useful means by which the considerable legal liability risks associated with the operation of jails and prisons can be transferred from government to independent contractors. It is widely recognized that prisoners are an unusually litigious group. To be sure, sometimes they initiate civil actions in state or federal court that have real merit. Often, however, the frequency with which they push frivolous or trivial suits before the courts suggests that litigation is something of an indoor sport.

Mounting a legal defense against prisoner-initiated suits is both time consuming and costly, and tens of thousands such suits are filed each year. This imposes a double

burden on policy makers. First, it is not uncommon for successful prisoner suits, most particularly those filed as class actions whose outcome includes court-imposed requirements for sweeping change, to yield multimillion-dollar price tags. Second, budgetary planning to cover legal liability risks is almost impossible. The year-on-year trends in litigation costs, settlement costs, damage awards, and so on are simply too erratic.

Privatization shifts these burdens from the public to the private sector. The legal boilerplate in facility-management contracts routinely requires that private firms indemnify and hold harmless the contracting agency and its employees against any and all sources of legal liability. Importantly, I am not aware of any incident in the history of correctional privatization that found a private management firm being unable to meet the hold harmless guarantees of its contract with government.

Operational Flexibility

Change and flexibility are two concepts that are difficult to translate into meaningful action in government agencies. Absent a meaningful ability to implement change swiftly and to respond flexibly to changing circumstances, virtually any private corporation would fail to survive. This general weakness of government and this general strength of private firms that have any rational hope of surviving establishes flexibility as yet another advantage of correctional privatization.

Private management firms, for example, regularly add, significantly modify, or replace various educational, vocational, and treatment programs. It is difficult and often simply impossible for government agencies to be as open to change or as flexible in their operations. Although part of this flows from bureaucratic habit, a large part is tied to civil service job security guarantees. To be sure, it is at least theoretically possible to eliminate a government program, but the general effect of this is merely to transfer all of the involved employees to some other government program. The consequence, therefore, is far too often change without either cost savings or program improvements being achieved.

Enhanced Protection of the Legal Rights of Prisoners

After years of teaching and publishing research in the area of correctional law, I must confess that the single most perplexing source of opposition to privatization that I continue to encounter comes from academics and even some civil rights attorneys who are concerned about the possibility that privatization might undermine the legal rights of confined persons. On this topic the law is clear; the United States Supreme Court has spoken more than once, and there simply is no room for debate. First, the constitutional rights of prisoners change not at all if they are housed in a privatized rather than a public facility (see *Payne v. Monroe County* 1999; *Skelton v. Pricor, Inc.* 1992; *Street v. Corrections Corporation of America* 1996; *West v. Atkins* 1988). Second, the legal barriers to cases brought by prisoner plaintiffs are lower if they are housed in a privatized rather than a public facility (*Richardson v. McKnight* 1997). Third, the legal remedies (e.g., compensatory and punitive damage awards) available to prisoner plaintiffs are greater if they are housed in a privatized rather than a public facility (Thomas 1991b). To be sure, some political conservatives are of the opinion that prisoners should have less and not more of an opportunity to litigate their claims. However, for those holding positions to the left of the political center to oppose privatization because they believe it might undermine the legal rights of prisoners strongly implies their ignorance—or what a lawyer might consider to be a willful ignorance—of the law.

Conclusions

The rhetoric of the privatization debate remains as testy today as it was when I first joined it some fifteen years ago. I must admit that some of the by-products of the debate that I have experienced personally in the form of occasional death threats and more carefully organized but equally personalized efforts at character assassination have not been the high points of my career. Here, however, I would like to conclude by taking a moment to put the debate into a somewhat broader context.

The context can be summarized fairly easily. Today our jails and prisons house more than 2,000,000 pretrial detainees and sentenced offenders at an annual cost of more than $40 billion. Our incarceration rate, which is a measure of the number of confined persons per 100,000 people in our general population, is approximately 690 and thus is higher than it has been at any earlier point in our history (Beck 2000). Most of our prisoners already are housed in facilities that are at or above their maximum rated capacities. For example, recent statistics show that California, Illinois, and New York are operating between 25 and 50 percent above what their system capacities were designed to handle. California had a design capacity of 80,272 and an actual population of 163,067 prisoners. Illinois was designed to hold 27,529 but has an actual population of 44,660. New York was designed for 53,815 but incarcerates 72,896 (Beck 2000, 8).

This means that we have far, far too many dangerously overcrowded facilities within which idleness and violence are much more familiar than meaningful rehabilitative programs. Thus, it should come as no great surprise to learn that 206,751 of the 565,291 prisoners admitted to state prisons in 1998 were parole violators rather than new court commitments (Beck 2000, 11). Despite all of this, recent population trends suggest that our jail and prison population will increase by at least an additional 50,000 to 80,000 more prisoners during 2001.

These statistics outline the contours of a national disgrace and, I fear, what amounts to a national accident waiting for a place to happen. Is there evidence that our public correctional agencies can diminish the magnitude of the disgrace and reduce the likelihood of the explosion I fear is on the horizon? Of course there is. Can private corrections management firms act as productive partners of those public agencies? Of course they can. Can both public agencies and private management firms do a better job than they are doing today? Of course they can—and, of course, they must.

Although what must be done would challenge the combined resources and creativity of both the public and the private sectors, there is something very wrong or at least very misguided about us remaining locked in a debate about privatization. To me, it is the correctional equivalent to fiddling while Rome burns.

To be sure, I fully understand the fact that we live in a time when the politics of self-interest often dominate. I fully understand that elected officials are fearful of the effects on their political careers that might flow from their supporting sound public policies that are stridently opposed by, most obviously, powerful public employee unions. These political realities aside, surely there can be such a thing in corrections as prudent public policy that is formulated by political leaders whose focus is on the goal of protecting the public safety interest, delivering correctional services that meet or exceed all applicable legal and professional standards, and expending scarce resources in an appropriately frugal manner.

The achievement of this goal recommends and requires that we define the public or private identity of the providers of correctional services as being irrelevant. To the degree that this happens—to the degree that public policy fosters and requires fair competition between alternative service providers—then the recent history of correctional privatization provides persuasive evidence that the role of the private sector in American corrections will continue to grow.

References

Archambeault, William G. and Donald R. Deis. 1996. *Cost Effectiveness Comparisons of Private versus Public Prisons in Louisiana.* Baton Rouge, LA: Louisiana State University School of Social Work.

Arizona Department of Corrections. 2000. *Public-Private Prison Comparison.* Phoenix, AZ: Arizona Department of Corrections.

Beck, Allen J. 2000. "Prisoners in 1999." Washington, DC: Bureau of Justice Statistics.

Brakel, Samuel J. 1988. "Prison Management, Private Enterprise Style: The Inmates' Evalua-

tion." *New England Journal of Civil and Criminal Confinement* 14: 175–244.

Brown, Allan. 1994. "Economic and Qualitative Aspects of Prison Privatization in Queensland." In Paul Moyle (ed.), *Private Prisons and Police: Recent Australian Trends,* pp. 194–218. Annandale, New South Wales: Pluto Press.

Cohen, Fred. 1995. "Pelican Bay: Excessive Force; Mental and General Health Care So Deficient as to Show Deliberate Indifference." *Correctional Law Reporter* 6: 81–82, 88–93.

Crants, Doctor R. III. 1991. "Private Prison Management: A Study in Economic Efficiency." *Journal of Contemporary Criminal Justice* 7: 49–59.

Dunmore, James. 1996. *Review of Comparative Costs and Performance of Privately and Publicly Operated Prisons.* London: Her Majesty's Prison Service.

Florida Office of Program Policy Analysis and Government Accountability. 2000. "South Bay Correctional Facility Provides Savings and Success; Room for Improvement." Tallahassee, FL: Office of Program Policy Analysis and Government Accountability.

Gaes, Gerald G., Scott D. Camp, and William G. Saylor. 1998. "The Performance of Privately Operated Prisons: A Review of Research." Appendix 2 in Douglas McDonald, Elizabeth Fournier, Malcolm Russell-Einhorn, and Stephen Crawford (eds.), *Private Prisons in the United States: An Assessment of Current Practice.* Cambridge, MA: Abt Associates, Inc.

Gold, Martin E. 1996. "The Privatization of Prisons." *The Urban Lawyer* 29: 359–399.

Goodstein, Linda and Doris Layton MacKenzie (eds.), *The American Prison: Issues in Research and Policy.* New York: Plenum Press.

Harding, Richard W. 1997. *Private Prisons and Public Accountability.* Buckingham, U. K.: Open University Press.

Kengor, Paul and Mark Scheffler. 1999. *Prison Privatization in Pennsylvania: The Case of Delaware County.* Pittsburgh, PA: Allegheny Institute for Public Policy.

Kettl, Donald F. 1993. *Sharing Power: Public Governance and Private Markets.* Washington, DC: The Brookings Institution.

Knight, Kevin and Matthew L. Hiller. 1997. "Community-Based Substance Abuse Treatment for Probationers: 1-Year Outcome Evaluation of the Dallas County Judicial Treatment Center." *Federal Probation* 61: 61–68.

Lanza-Kaduce, Lonn, Karen F. Parker, and Charles W. Thomas. 1999. "A Comparative Recidivism Analysis of Releasees from Private and Public Prisons." *Crime and Delinquency* 45: 28–47.

Logan, Charles H. 1987. "The Propriety of Propriety Prisons." *Federal Probation* 51: 35–40.

Logan, Charles H. 1989. "Proprietary Prisons." In Lynn Goodstein and Doris Layton MacKenzie (eds.), *The American Prison: Issues in Research and Policy,* pp. 45–62. New York: Plenum Press.

Logan, Charles H. 1992. "Well Kept: Comparing Quality of Confinement in Private and Public Prisons." *Journal of Criminal Law and Criminology* 83: 577–613.

——. 1990. *Private Prisons: Cons and Pros.* New York: Oxford University Press.

——. 1996a. "Objections and Refutations." Pp. 127–138 in Stephen T. Easton (ed.), *Privatizing Correctional Services.* Vancouver, British Columbia: The Fraser Institute.

——. 1996b. "Public vs. Private Prison Management: A Case Comparison." *Criminal Justice Review* 21: 63–84.

Logan, Charles H. and Bill W. McGriff. 1989. "Comparing Costs of Public and Private Prisons: A Case Study." *National Institute of Justice Research in Action* 216. Washington, DC: National Institute of Justice.

Loux, Steven. 1999. *Prison Privatization in Pennsylvania.* Harrisburg, PA: The Commonwealth Foundation.

McDonald, Douglas C. 1990. "The Costs of Operating Public and Private Correctional Facilities." In Douglas C. McDonald (ed.), *Private Prisons and the Public Interest,* pp. 86–106. New York: Rutgers University Press.

Moore, Adrian T. 1998. *Private Prisons: Quality Corrections at a Lower Cost.* Los Angeles: Reason Public Policy Institute.

Quinlan, J. Michael, Charles W. Thomas, and Sherril A. Gautreaux. 2001. "The Privatization of Correctional Facilities." In Deborah Ballati (ed.), *Privatizing Government Functions,* pp. 10.1–10.75. New York: Law Journal Press.

Residential Directors' Council of Texas and the Community Assistance Division of the Texas Department of Criminal Justice. 1999. "Community Corrections Facilities Outcome Study. Austin: Texas Department of Criminal Justice.

Robbins, Ira P. 1989. "The Legal Dimensions of Private Incarceration." *American University Law Review* 38: 531–854.

Texas Sunset Advisory Commission. 1991. Recommendations to the Governor of Texas and Members of the 72nd Legislature.

Thomas, Charles W. 1991a. "Correctional Privatization: How It Redefines the Legal Rights of Prisoners." *Privatization Review* 6: 38–58.

——. 1991b. "Prisoners' Rights and Correctional Privatization." *Business and Professional Ethics Journal* 10: 3–45.

——. 1992. "Resolving the Problem of Qualified Immunity for Private Defendants in Section 1983 and Bivens Damage Suits. *Louisiana Law Review* 53: 449–493.

——. 1996. "Issues and Evidence from the United States." In Stephen T. Easton (ed.), *Privatizing Correctional Services,* pp. 15–61. Vancouver, British Columbia: The Fraser Institute.

——. 1997. *Comparing the Cost and Performance of Public and Private Prisons in Arizona.* Phoenix: Arizona Department of Corrections.

——. 2002. Website on private prisons. University of Florida, Center for Studies in Criminology and Law: <http://www.crim.ufl.edu/pcp>.

Thomas, Charles W., Lonn Lanza-Kaduce, Linda S. Calvert Hanson, and Kathleen A. Duffy. 1988 "The Privatization of American Correction: An Assessment of Its Legal Implications." A report prepared for the Florida House Committee on Corrections, Probation, and Parole. Gainesville: Center for Studies in Criminology and Law, University of Florida.

Thomas, Charles W. and Linda S. Calvert Hanson. 1989. "The Legal Implications of 42 U.S.C. Section 1983 for the Privatization of Prisons." *Florida State University Law Review* 16: 933–961.

Thomas, Charles W. and Charles H. Logan. 1993. "The Development, Present Status, and Future Potential of Correctional Privatization in America." In Gary W. Bowman, Simon Hakim, and Paul Seidenstat (eds.), *Privatizing Correctional Institutions,* pp. 213–240. New Brunswick, NJ: Transaction Publishers.

United States General Accounting Office. 1996. *Private and Public Prisons: Studies Comparing Operational Costs and/or Quality of Service.* Washington, DC: U.S. General Accounting Office.

Wolfgang, Marvin E. 1998. "Foreword." In Bruce L. Benson (ed.), *To Serve and Protect: Privatization and Community in Criminal Justice,* pp. xiii-xvii. New York: New York University Press.

Cases Cited

Payne v. Monroe County, 779 F.Supp. 1330 (S.D. Fla. 1999).

Richardson v. McKnight, 117 S.Ct. 2100 (1997).

Skelton v. Pricor, Inc., 963 F.2d 100 (6th Cir. 1991), cert. denied, 503 U.S. 989 (1992).

Street v. Corrections Corporation of America, 102 F.3d 810 (6th Cir. 1996).

West v. Atkins, 487 U.S. 42 (1988).

28
McPrisons Are McFailures by Most If Not All Objective Measures

Richard G. Hogan

The number of people incarcerated in the United States rose significantly from 501,886 in 1980 to 2,026,596 by 1999 (Beck and Gilliard 1995; Beck 2000, 1). This dramatic expansion continues, with predictions for the rapid growth of those incarcerated in the United States failing to keep pace with the actual growth of inmate populations. Prison systems that were already scrambling to adjust to court ordered standards prohibiting overcrowding were generally unprepared for this unprecedented growth in the convict population (Lemov 1993, 45). Meanwhile, rapidly expanding convict populations continue to put stress on the budgets of many prison systems (Logan 1990, 9; Selke 1994, 44–45; Durham 1994, 45–46; Currie 1998, 71).

A few prison systems have attempted to address overcrowding by contracting with various re-emerging private prison providers (Logan 1990; Thomas 1994). Although prison systems had previously contracted for some services ranging from food service to health care, the first modern day contract that transferred total custody and control of prisoners from a local governmental entity to a private corporation was awarded to Corrections Corporation of America (CCA)

(Marquart, Marianos, Hebert, and Carroll 1997, 202; Logan 1990, 31). On October 15, 1984, CCA took control of the Silverdale Detention Facility in Hamilton County, Tennessee (Logan 1990, 31). This local contract award to CCA and the first state level contract awarded to U.S. Corrections Corporation (USCC) in Kentucky signaled the rebirth of the private prison industry in America.

The re-emergence of prisons for profit sparked considerable debate among criminologists and others (Adams 1996; Brakel 1992; DiIulio 1990; Durham 1994; Geis 1986; Hogan 1999; Hunzeker 1991; Lemov 1993; Logan and McGriff 1989; Logan 1990; Press 1990; Robbins 1994; Shichor 1995; Thomas 1994; Walzer 1991; Yu 1995). Much of this debate is drawn along ideological lines between opponents of private prisons and proponents of private prisons. The concerns of many critical criminologists are expressed by Gil Geis (1986) in his assertion that

> . . . prison privatization calls for giving the private sector enormous direct control over the lives of a captive human population. Prisoners cannot walk away, cannot resign, from a situation they find abhorrent. They did not elect to be where they are (unless we presume that by their behavior they asked for it), and they certainly cannot elect to go elsewhere because they want to. (Geis, 1986)

Critical criminologists continue to argue that one of the primary goals of incarceration must be rehabilitation, while proponents of private prisons, such as Charles H. Logan (1990), embrace a very different ideal for prisons.

Logan (1996) proposes that prisons and any evaluation of prison operations should be "based on fairly consistent adherence to a purely retributive philosophy of punishment" (p. 1). In other words, Logan advocates what he refers to as the "confinement model of imprisonment." The confinement model is defined in the following way:

The mission of a prison is to keep prisoners—to keep them in, keep them safe, keep then in line, keep them healthy, and keep them busy—and to do it with fairness, without undue suffering, and as efficiently as possible. (Logan 1992, 580)

Across this ideological divide proponents and opponents of prisons for profit have raised numerous issues.

The purpose of this paper is to provide an overview of the issues that Logan (1990) asserts define the public versus the private prison debate. Private prison entrepreneurs and their proponents (Logan 1990; Thomas 1994; Harding 1997) claim that private prisons can deliver better quantity and quality of service at a lower cost than the public prisons. Logan, using the confinement model to establish goals for prisons, then asserts that the "full range" of issues can be grouped into ten general categories: propriety, cost, quality, security, quantity, flexibility, accountability, liability, dependency, and corruption (p. 38). The following critically evaluates these issues.

Propriety

Propriety is concerned with whether private prisons are proper instruments for fulfilling the incarceration function of the criminal justice system. The argument surrounding this issue has been partially ideological, questioning the morality of private prisons. However, propriety also has a legal dimension that addresses whether it is proper to delegate governmental power, the incarceration of offenders, to private individuals.

The words of Gil Geis, quoted earlier, add voice to the moral dimension. This concern is heightened by the egregious history of the nineteenth- and early twentieth-century private prisons (Ayers 1984; Cable 1885; Lichtenstein 1996; Mancini 1996; Oshinsky 1996; Taylor 1993; Walker 1988). Convicts given over to the total custody and control of private prison entrepreneurs worked in coal mines, constructed railroad roadbeds, worked in the fields, and performed many of the same tasks as slaves.

However, the similarities do not extend much past the type of work performed. Convicts were leased from the state unlike slaves that were purchased. There was no investment (purchase price) in leased convicts, only a rental fee. If convicts died as a result of malnutrition, exposure, beatings from overseers, or accidents, there was no resultant monetary loss to the private prison entrepreneur. The title of one of the books about the period, *Worse Than Slavery*, provides insight into the conditions suffered by convicts at the hands of private prison overseers (Oshinsky 1996). Overall, private prison entrepreneurs and the state adopted a cavalier attitude toward the lives of convicts, which is reflected in the assertion of a South Carolina warden that "casualties would have been far less frequent if convicts were property having a value to preserve" (Adamson 1984, 450).

An example of how lethal nineteenth-century private prisons were comes from Alabama state records for the year 1870. Those records report a 41 percent death rate among state convicts leased to Tennessee Iron and Coal, the entity that leased Alabama's entire convict population (Cable 1885, 170). Assessments of private prison operations of the period covered a wide range—from reports of death rates, to such descriptive comments as "[a]n epidemic death rate without the epidemic" and in an *Arkansas Gazette* headline of the period referring to the private prison at Coal Hill as, "A Hell in Arkansas" (Mancini 1996, 131, 121).

The exploitation of convict labor under the guise of punishment for crimes made former Georgia Governor Brown, the "cotton king" Edmund Richardson from Mississippi, and others extremely wealthy (Taylor 1993, 35–36). William Taylor, at the University of Southern Mississippi, summarized his assessment of private prisons of this era stating, "[S]eldom in American history has a branch of public administration been more baldly exploited for private gain" (p. 54). This history should stand as a warning that the primary goal of private prisons is the production of private profits, placing the performance of the public service function, at its maximum, as a secondary goal.

Still, the moral concerns and those directed toward convict welfare and the exploitation of convict labor are generally restricted to Eighth Amendment challenges predicated on allegations of cruel and unusual punishment. Such challenges balance on a fulcrum of humanitarian concerns that in the current political environment effectively limits debate on this issue to its legal dimension. The legal issue is whether governmental agencies may make such a delegation of governmental power.

Ira P. Robbins (1988), an attorney, addressed the delegation of governmental power to private prisons in *Legal Dimensions of Private Incarceration*. His analysis identified three aspects of delegation of governmental power as they apply in a prison setting; delegation of management authority, rule-making authority, and adjudicative power. The delegation of management authority is a purely administrative function supported by case law on both a state and a federal level (Robbins 1988).

On the federal level, the delegation of rule-making authority and adjudicative power (i.e., award or removal of good time) raises legal issues in which case law is silent. Delegations of rule-making authority and adjudicative powers, necessary functions of prison management, might withstand constitutional review if the government entity (e.g., Federal Bureau of Prisons) required review and approval before implementation of rules and adjudication. However, because prisons are such a unique environment in which virtually every action of the staff is intentionally coercive and affects liberty interest, the courts should hold that it would be impossible to operate a prison exercising only administrative authority.

On the state level, the delegation of rule-making authority and adjudicative power is supported by case law if all such actions are subject to review by the contracting state agency. However, case law addresses only private entities functioning in a regulatory capacity who do *not* have a pecuniary interest in the outcome. But, private prisons could benefit substantially from the application of adjudicative power. An example of such potential benefits comes from Texas where, at one private prison, a manufacturing plant was constructed at a cost of $200,000, which was $300,000 under the estimate of the private prison's usual contractor. The warden gave the convicts high praise, stating that "he [the warden] made the inmates, who often worked from 6 a.m. until midnight, take daily breaks for lunch and dinner" (Yu 1995, 9–10). Some inmates at this facility have received as much as 3-year reductions in sentences, called "set offs" (Yu 1995, 9–11). Whether there was any impropriety in this instance is not the issue. What is important is that it illustrates the potential for abuse of rule-making and adjudicative power by private prisons, who may benefit substantially from those delegations of power.

The issue of propriety, as discussed, illustrates that for analytical purposes we may separate morality and the law; but in application, these dimensions of propriety remain inseparable. The danger of the improper use of delegated powers escalates as states' budgets falter under the weight of correctional costs.

Costs

The costs to incarcerate a growing convict population continue to strain the budgets of most states. For this reason cost is the primary issue for administrators searching for methods to cope with budget constraints. This is apparent in the literature and research concerning private prisons.

For example, Charles H. Logan and Bill W. McGriff (1989), the county auditor and the contract monitor for Hamilton County, Tennessee, conducted what they assert "to be the first published study comparing the actual costs of public and private operation of a prison facility" (p. 1). Logan and McGriff concluded that "contracting out prison management generated annual savings of at least 4 to 8 percent—and more likely in the range of 5 to 15 percent—compared to the estimated cost of direct county management" (Logan and McGriff 1989, 1). This is the most often cited and perhaps the most influential early research reported in the literature (Logan 1990, 105–118; Thomas 1994, 11–12; Shichor 1995, 210–211; McDonald 1990, 89–90).

Subsequent studies devoted to the cost analysis of private prison operations did not generally reach similar conclusions. This may be attributed to the number of different methods developed to compare private and public operation of prison facilities. For instance, Logan and McGriff (1989) adopted a what-if model in the Silverdale study, using the actual cost of private operation compared with estimates of costs projected for continued operation by Hamilton County.

The majority of private prison operations have been in new facilities with no public operation history. Therefore, studies devoted to cost analysis have generally been conducted using either the comparison of private operation costs to nonexistent facilities, such as the Texas Sunset Advisory Commission (TSAC, 1991) study, or the comparison of privately operated facilities with comparable publicly operated facilities.

The TSAC study (1991) concluded that ". . . as of the end of fiscal year 1990, the cost of operating the private prisons was close to ten percent less than the cost if the state were to operate equivalent facilities" (p. 9). What-if calculations that compare privately operated facilities with hypothetical nonexistent state prisons would intuitively appear to be the least accurate method, while at the same time being the most supportive of the cost savings claims of the private prison industry. However, governmental studies (e.g., the Florida Department of Corrections (FDC) in 1997 and the Florida Office of Program Policy Analysis and Governmental Accountability (OPPAGA) in 1996 and 1998) that compared private prison operations with actual comparable state-operated facilities generally found private prison costs *higher* than those of comparable state-operated facilities (FDC 1997; OPPAGA 1996, 1998).

The General Accounting Office (GAO) in 1996 performed a meta-analysis of the five major existing studies: TSAC (1991), New Mexico (1991), California (1994), Tennessee (1995), and Washington (1996). Its response concluded that "the studies reported little difference and/or mixed results in comparing private and public facilities" (GAO 1996, 7). The GAO meta-analysis and the continuing reports by the Florida OPPAGA suggest that claims made by the private prison industry about lower cost of operation are often unrealized by the governmental entities they serve (GAO 1996; OPPAGA 1998).

In other words, the cost savings claims of the private prison industry are not supported by the existing research. Moreover, that research has focused on costs and has universally failed to address the interrelated issues presented here, even those issues that are inseparable from costs, except for analytical purposes, such as quality.

Quality

Quality is so interrelated with cost that the two are complementary in many ways. For example, if additional services are provided, it is a normal expectation that costs will increase and, conversely, if services are reduced, costs will decrease. The process of examining costs/quality related to private prison operations necessitates the breakdown of cost into two categories; fixed and variable costs. Fixed costs represent those costs over which management has little direct control and that do not vary in any substantial amount. For example, the cost to construct a facility with a rated capacity of 1,000 prisoners is the same whether it houses 10 prisoners or 1,000 prisoners. In contrast, management decisions may substantially impact variable costs.

The largest items of variable cost in the normal operation of a prison are security personnel (approximately 80 to 85 percent), kitchen operation, and medical care for prisoners (Hanson 1996, 7, 10). These services encompass the basic necessities of human existence: safety, food, and health care. The costs of these necessities are the most controllable by prison management. In the past, some of the methods employed by private prisons to control such costs have been reducing security personnel to dangerously low levels, feeding prisoners a minimal or substandard diet, and creaming (Sullivan and Purdy 1995; Hanson 1996; John T.

Vernon, personal communication, March 12, 1998). *Creaming* refers to the practice of accepting only prisoners without health or disciplinary problems. This practice relegates the higher-cost prisoners, those with health or disciplinary problems, to the public facilities, artificially inflating their average costs per prisoner compared with those of private prisons.

Equally problematic are the additional needs of persons incarcerated in prisons for services and programs beyond the basic necessities for human existence, such as counseling, skills training, and education. Denied these additional services, convicts often feel that time spent in prison is wasted time and become resentful. On release, convicts adopting such an attitude are bitter towards the prison administration, guards, and society in general, enhancing the probability of their re-offending. However, it is unreasonable to expect additional programs from private prison operators when they fail to provide even minimal services, such as security for prisoners and the surrounding community.

Security

Prison security personnel serve to maintain order within the prison. Correctional officers are there to inhibit acts by prisoners who intend to injure others or, in some instances, themselves. Furthermore, the presence of physical barriers and personnel prevent prisoners from escaping the institution. Decreasing operational costs by reducing the number of security personnel is a safety hazard affecting the safety of prisoners, prison workers, and the community at large.

The existing research indicates that efforts by the private prison industry to reduce operating costs have also reduced security (Hanson 1996, 10; Sullivan and Purdy 1995, 2). In an attempt to reduce costs, the private prison industry has tried to supplement staff with facility design and technology (i.e., cameras and electronically controlled doors). Nevertheless, private prisons may still attempt to operate without any design or technological enhancements that would reduce staffing requirements. For example, in

Florida where state standards require one correctional officer for every eight prisoners, Wackenhut Corrections Corporation (WCC) was operating the Monroe County Jail with one officer for every thirty prisoners (Hanson 1996, 10). And, in New Jersey at the Elizabeth Detention Center, understaffing directly contributed to a detainee riot (Sullivan and Purdy 1995, 2).

A recent survey that examined public and private facilities with comparable security levels revealed that "private prisons had fifty percent more inmate-on-staff assaults and two-thirds more inmate-on-inmate assaults" (Greene 2000, 5). In New Mexico at WCC facilities, assaults and deaths are becoming routine with four prisoners and one guard killed in the first nine months of 1999 (Tangley, Pethokoukis, Shapiro, Gest, and Couzin 1999, 10). The reduction in staffing or understaffing to dangerously low levels clearly jeopardizes the safety of both prisoners and prison staff.

A reduction in staffing or understaffing also affects the protection of society through the prevention of escapes. Logan (1992) asserts that "escapes are an obvious indicator of a lack of security . . . " (p. 582). Escapes from public prisons do occur, but they remain a fairly rare occurrence. In addition, public facilities almost always report escapes to law enforcement agencies and the media. This is not the case with private prisons. Often private prisons do not report escapes in a timely manner or fail to report escapes at all until escapees are discovered by law enforcement agencies. In one incident at the Northeast Ohio Correctional Center operated by CCA, six prisoners escaped in broad daylight. The escape was finally reported to authorities, not by CCA staff, but by inmates from within the facility who called the county sheriff themselves (Oregon AFSCME 2000). In addition, security often suffers when private prisons attempt to expand beyond their capacity and open new facilities without experienced personnel.

Quantity

Quantity in this instance refers to the ability to rapidly provide additional bed space as needed by the prison system. Proponents of private prisons suggest that the industry can provide additional prison capacity faster than government (Logan 1990, 42). This is certainly true assuming that governmental entities must approve the design of the facility, appropriate funds for the construction of the facility, request bids for construction, construct the prison, and finally staff the facility. Logan offers the Houston Processing Center as an example of how quickly the private prison industry can respond to increasing demand. This facility was site selected, financed, designed, and constructed in "just seven months" (Logan 1990, 23).

If quantity alone composed the entire criteria for assessment, then private prisons would score a victory on this issue. However, quantity is also inseparable from other issues, such as security. For example, during construction of the Houston Processing Center, "CCA leased a former motel to house 140 aliens temporarily" (Logan 1990, 23). Other interrelated issues beyond mere security have been raised by research references to this facility. A publication of the British Police Officers Association asserted that the Houston Processing Center "demonstrated what are possibly the worst conditions we have ever witnessed in terms of inmate care and supervision" (Walzer 1991, 172).

The issue of cost as it relates to quantity was also raised by Aric Press (1990) when discussing the Silverdale study. Press pointed to the increase in the inmate population from 240 to 340 primarily due to the county taking a "sterner line" on drunk driving cases. The "sterner line" resulted in the county running $200,000 over budget for the Silverdale facility (Press 1990, 29). Quantity at the expense of cost, quality, and security cannot be viewed as beneficial. However, proponents of private prisons see the ability for rapid expansion as desirable and indicative of the industry's flexibility.

Flexibility

Logan (1990) suggests that private prisons have greater flexibility than public prisons. Flexibility for Logan is the ability to respond to changing prison conditions and to act faster to correct mistakes based on faulty predictions (Logan 1990, 162). In addition, Logan asserts that minus the bureaucratic constraints of the public prison system, private prison flexibility "promotes innovation, experimentation, and other changes in programs, including expansion, contraction, and termination" (Logan 1990, 43). This suggestion, that there is greater innovation or experimentation (i.e., flexibility as per Logan) in private prisons as compared with public prisons is not apparent from the literature. Correctional literature in general supports philosophy (e.g., confinement model, rehabilitative model) and not flexibility as the determining factor contributing most to innovation or experimentation. A strict adherence by private prisons to the confinement model which posits that the "essential purpose of imprisonment is to punish offender[s] . . ." (Logan 1992, 580), suggests that innovation and experimentation is undesirable except in the areas of confinement.

Flexibility as applied to contraction and termination of contracts is virtually untested. There has been no substantial contraction in the number of those to be confined per any private prison contract. The termination of contracts for adult facilities that have occurred (e.g., Monroe County Jail, Florida; Elizabeth Detention Center, New Jersey) have all been the result of performance violations (Hanson 1996: Sullivan and Purdy 1995), which were discovered only when the private prison operators were monitored and held accountable.

Accountability

Generally, accountability refers to being liable or responsible for actions or services. Logan (1990) suggests that "contracting increases accountability" (p. 44). Ideally, contracts between government entities and private prison providers would specify in clear terms what services the private prisons would provide. The private prison would then, during the contract period, be closely monitored by a representative of the contracting governmental body, ensuring strict contract compliance. However, the brief history of the re-emerging private prison industry does not support any claim that effective monitoring of contracts by governmental representatives actually occurs.

For example, a riot at the Elizabeth Detention Center occurred after Immigration and Naturalization Service (INS) contract monitors ignored numerous complaints, which ranged from guards robbing inmates to denial of basic necessities, such as sanitary napkins and toilet paper (Dugger 1996; "Immigration Center" 1995). Shortly after the riot, an "assessment team found numerous contract deficiencies," which were apparently ignored by in-house INS employee monitors (Florida Corrections Commission 1996, [on-line]). This example suggests that in some cases, no accountability requirement exists until conditions degenerate to the point of discovery by law enforcement agencies or the media (Hogan 1999, 73). In this case, the discovery of "numerous contract deficiencies" did not cause INS to terminate its contract with Esmor. Instead, INS allowed a contract novation where Esmor transferred the contract to CCA, avoiding almost all losses or liability (Hogan 1999, 73).

Liability

Civil suits filed by prisoners or their representatives alleging violations of their rights or indifference to their welfare represent the majority of liability issues of concern to prison administrations. Logan (1990) asserts that contracting with the private prison industry provides an extra layer of protection for contracting governmental entities (p. 181). According to Logan, this additional protection results from private prison operators "running prisons better," obtaining certification, "carrying adequate and cost-effective insurance," settling lawsuits (where appropriate) prior to going to trial at lower costs, and through providing contract provisions in which governmental entities are indemnified against legal damages (p. 188). This would indeed reduce the liability of contracting jurisdictions if Logan's bold assertions were accurate. Unfortunately, there is little support for the argument that private prison operators "run prisons better," "carry adequate and cost-effective insurance," set-

tle lawsuits prior to going to trial at lower costs, or effectively indemnify contracting entities against legal damages.

The experience of Missouri in contracting to place prisoners in the Brazoria County Detention Center in Texas, which was operated by Capital Correctional Resources, Inc. (CCRI), is just one example that contradicts the assertions of Logan. On September 18, 1996, Missouri prisoners were assaulted by CCRI guards using dogs, stun guns, tear gas, mace, fists, and feet. The evidence in the case was overwhelming. The most important evidence came from CCRI guards videotaping the assaults. Adding to the prisoner's case was information that at least one of the CCRI guards who participated in the assaults was a former department of corrections officer with a prior conviction for beating a prisoner (*Kesler v. King*, 29 F.Supp.2d 356). The lawsuits growing from this and other alleged violations of Missouri prisoner rights were finally consolidated into a class action suit encompassing "2,100 prisoners sent from Missouri to Texas from 1995 through 1997 under the Texas Cell Lease Program" (Dana Fields 2000, [online]). The final settlement approved by the court amounted to $2.2 million with $2.1 million coming from CCRI, "the limit of its insurance coverage" (Dana Fields 2000, [online]).

The assertions regarding reductions in liability, initially made by Logan in 1990, are not supported by this instance or by other experiences reported in the literature over the past decade (Logan 1990, 188; Dana Fields 2000, [online]). In fact, the lawsuits stemming from the transfer of Missouri prisoners to private prisons in Texas exposed the Missouri Department of Corrections to other possible liability. Fortunately, Missouri had no real dependence on private prisons and was able to bring all their prisoners quickly back to Missouri public facilities.

Dependency

As it is used here, dependency refers to an over-reliance by some contracting governmental entities on the services of private prisons. For example, a contracting entity, such as the Tennessee Department of Corrections (TDC), could cease to operate prisons by relying completely on the services of private prisons (CCA has offered to operate all the prisons in Tennessee). In such a scenario, the TDC would become totally dependent on the services of private prisons by effectively eliminating the ability of the TDC to relocate prisoners from private to public prisons within the state. Logan (1990) suggests that some critics are concerned with just such a scenario in which private prisons would obtain contracts by "low-balling" (p. 221). This practice could, over time, create a prison system dependent on the services of the private prison operator.

Once the contracting entity becomes dependent on the services of the private prison operator, *per diem* rates would escalate. This is a very unlikely scenario for a number of reasons. The private prison industry is still extremely competitive with CCA and WCC struggling to be both profitable and able to garner market share. This alone effectively limits any escalation of pricing. In addition, there are a substantial number of smaller operators (i.e., Cornell Corrections, Inc., Correctional Services Corporation) that would welcome an opportunity to enter into additional prison contracts.

The Elizabeth Detention Center contract transfer from Esmor to CCA may indicate some dependency by INS on the private prison industry. If a dependency on private prisons does exist for any contracting entities (and it seems not to exist) it would be difficult to accurately assess that level of dependency. In fact, in the cases where adult facilities were taken back from private prison operators by contracting authorities, there have been no major problems (Hogan 1999, 69). This may in the future become an issue, but with the current level of market penetration, dependency on the private prison industry is not a serious issue. What *is* a serious issue for the private prison industry is its apparent ability to foster corruption.

Corruption

Corruption alone is a strong argument against contracting with the private prison industry. However, Logan (1990) asserts that such an argument is illogical because "political corruption is a corollary of government, not just of governmental contracting" (p. 211). The counter argument presented here is that the criminal justice system exists based on the public's belief in its legitimacy. Continuing with that argument, engaging in any activity that calls into question that legitimacy constitutes bad public policy.

Historical records of the private prison industry in the South during the nineteenth and early twentieth centuries contradict Logan's assertion that private prisons do not foster corruption more than public prisons (Ayers 1984; Cable 1885; Hogan 1999; Mancini 1996; Oshinsky 1996; Taylor 1993). For example, from the history of early private prisons, Edward L. Ayers (1984) reveals that conflicts of interest often occurred where "the same name played the roles of both [private prison] entrepreneur and [public] officeholder" (p. 195).

Similar conflicts of interest are apparent in the modern day history of the private prison industry. In Tennessee, the political elite are investors in CCA, which operates all the state's private prisons (Hogan, 1999). CCA also employs the wife of the speaker of the Tennessee House of Representatives as a lobbyist. In New Mexico, the president pro temp of the Senate is employed as a lobbyist by WCC (Greene 2000, 7).

Among academics, cries of conflict of interest arose when it was discovered that a professor once referred to as "the nation's leading expert on prison privatization" was a highly paid consultant for CCA. At the same time, the professor was a consultant for the Florida Correctional Privatization Commission (CPC), thus advising both for the contractor and the contracting governmental entity (Geis, Shichor, and Mobley 1999, 378).

In addition, this professor was the director of the Private Correction Project (PCP) established in 1988 in the Center for Studies in Criminology and Law, University of Florida, which was widely regarded as the leading academic and primary source of information about private prisons. According to its director

The Private Corrections Project was established in 1988 for the purposes of conducting policy-oriented research on and serving as a clearinghouse for information about correctional privatization. The Project also provides technical assistance to governmental agencies that plan to contract for the full-scale management of secure adult correctional facilities. (Thomas 1995, 1)

The suggestion appears to be that PCP was established to assist the public sector in making decisions about whether to contract with private prisons. The PCP was allegedly there to help public entities with technical assistance in contract construction and implementation vis-à-vis private prisons. However, reality may be much different from perception, as in this instance. Even though the PCP seemed to be funded by the university, in fact the operating budget came from funds contributed by the private prison industry (Hogan 1999, 65–66).

Of critical importance is whether these conflicts of interest amount to a lack of judgment or a criminal act on the part of those involved. Modern day incidents of corruption, like other forms of white-collar crime, are difficult to detect. Once detected, however, they are generally either not prosecuted or carry penalties so minor that they fail to deter either the perpetrator or others. Political corruption may be a corollary of government, as Logan suggests, but such an assertion does not carry with it any obligation to offer additional opportunities for the corruption of government officials.

Conclusions

Corporate officers have a fiduciary responsibility to their stockholders to maximize profits. Those same officers operating private prisons are contractually obligated to provide certain minimal services to contracting entities. Therefore, the corporate officers of these private prison corporations are simultaneously trying to accomplish two conflicting goals. Historical evidence, starting with the first nineteenth-century private prisons and culminating with modern day private prisons, clearly indicates that the conflict between these competing goals is al-

most always resolved in favor of reducing services (convict care) and increasing profits. In fact, this chapter's discussion of the issues of propriety, cost, quality, security, quantity, flexibility, accountability, liability, dependency, and corruption clearly demonstrates that these services are often not provided in an effort to maximize corporate profits.

Considered separately or as a collective whole, this overview of the issues finds no support for the private prison industry and their proponents' assertions that they can deliver the same or better service at a reduced cost. There is no consistent verifiable data that support these assertions. If only the issues that are most touted by proponents (i.e., cost, quality, and security) are analyzed, the private prison industry not only fails, but fails miserably.

Private prisons bring more problems than solutions to the criminal justice system. The private prison industry may continue to make unsupported claims that it can deliver the same or better service at a lower cost. However, that argument is beginning to lose all credibility given the early nineteenth-century history of the industry and its failure to demonstrate any verifiable success in its current re-emergence.

References

Adams, K. 1996. "The Bull Market in Corrections." *The Prison Journal* 76, 461–467.

Adamson, C. 1984. "Toward A Marxian Penology: Captive Criminal Populations as Economic Threats and Resources." *Social Problems* 31, 435–458.

Ayers, E. L. 1984. *Vengeance & Justice: Crime and Punishment in the 19th Century American South.* New York: Oxford University Press.

Beck, A. J. 2000. *Prisoners in 1999* (NCJ-183476). Washington, DC: Bureau of Justice Statistics.

Beck, A. and J. Gilliard, D. K. 1995. *Prisoners in 1994.* (NCJ-51654). Washington, DC: Bureau of Justice Statistics.

Brakel, S. J. 1992. "Private Corrections." In Gary W. Bowman, Simon Hakim, and Paul Seidenstat (eds.) *Privatizing the United States Justice System: Police, Adjudication, and Corrections Services from the Private Sector* (pp. 254–274). Jefferson, NC: McFarland & Company, Inc.

Cable, G. W. 1885. *The Silent South, Together with the Freedman's Case in Equity and the Convict Lease System*. New York: C. Scribner's Sons.

Currie, E. 1998. *Crime and Punishment in America*. New York: Henry Holt and Company.

DiIulio, J. J., Jr. 1990. "The Duty to Govern: A Critical Perspective on the Private Management of Prisons and Jails." In D. C. McDonald (ed.), *Private Prisons and the Public Interest* (pp. 155–178). New Brunswick, NJ: Rutgers University Press.

Dugger, C. W. 1996, September 11. "A Refugee Escapes from Togo, Body Intact but Family Torn." *New York Times*, p. A1.

Durham, A. M. III, 1994. *Crisis and Reform: Current Issues in American Punishment*. New York: Little, Brown and Company.

Fields, D. 2000. "Judge Approves $2.2 Million Deal for Inmates in Jail Shakedown." *Digital Missourian* [on-line]. Retrieved January 21, 2000. Available: <http://www.digmo.org/news/local/premium/0121local12552.htm>

Florida Corrections Commission. 1996. *1996 Annual Report* [on-line]. Retrieved June 23, 1998. Available: <http://www.dos.state.fl.us/fgils/agencies/fee/reports/final96/app5-5.html>

Florida Department of Corrections. 1997. *1996-97 DC Annual Report: The On-line Guidebook to Corrections in Florida* [on-line]. Retrieved June 23, 1998. Available: <http://www.dc.state.fl.us/executive/research/annual/9697/>

Geis, G. 1986. "The Privatization of Prisons: Panacea or Placebo?" In B. J. Carroll, R. W. Conant, and T. A. Easton (eds.), *Private Means Public Ends: Private Business in Social Services Delivery*. New York: Praeger Publishers.

Geis, G., Shichor, D., and Mobley, A. 1999. "Private Prisons, Criminological Research, and Conflict of Interest: A case study." *Crime & Delinquency* 45, 372–389.

Greene, J. 2000, May. "Prison Privatization: Recent Developments in the United States." Paper presented at the International Conference on Penal Abolition. Toronto, Canada.

Hanson, R. A. 1996, September. "The Failure of Privatization in the Monroe County Jail: An Exception or the Rule?" Paper presented at the Midwest Criminal Justice Association Meeting. Indianapolis, IN.

Harding, R. W. 1997. *Private Prisons and Public Accountability*. Brunswick, NJ: Transaction.

Hogan, R. G. 1997, November. "Exploiting and Profiting from the Poor: Private Prisons and Convict Labor." Paper presented at the American Society of Criminology Meeting, San Diego, CA.

Hogan, R. G. 1999. *A Comparison of Modern Day Private Prisons and Those of the Nineteenth and Early Twentieth Century*. Unpublished master's thesis, University of Missouri–Kansas City, Kansas City, MO.

Hunzeker, D. 1991. "Private Cells, Public Prisoners." *State Legislatures* 17, 24–27.

Immigration Center. 1995, July 22. *The Kansas City Star*, p. A10.

Kesler v. King, 29 F.Supp.2d 356 (S.D. Texas 1998).

Lemov, P. 1993, May. "Jailhouse, Inc." *Governing* 5, 44–48.

Lichtenstein, A. 1996. *Twice the Work of Free Labor: The Political Economy of Convict Labor in the New South*. New York: Verso.

Logan, C. H., and McGriff, B. W. 1989. *Comparing Costs of Public and Private Prisons: A Case Study*. (NCJ 119964). Washington, DC: U.S. Department of Justice.

Logan, C. H. 1990. *Private Prisons Cons and Pros*. New York: Oxford University Press.

———. 1992. "Well Kept: Comparing Quality of Confinement in Private and Public Prisons." *The Journal of Criminal Law & Criminology* 83, 577–613.

———. 1996. *Well Kept: Comparing Quality of Confinement in a Public and Private Prison* [on-line]. Retrieved June 11, 1999. Available: <http://www.ucc.uconn.edu/~wwwsoci/nmexsum.html>

Mancini, M. J. 1996. *One Dies. Get Another: Convict Leasing in the American South, 1866–1928*. Columbia, SC: University of South Carolina Press.

Marquart, J. W., Merianos, D. E., Hebert, J. L., and Carroll, L. 1997. "Health Condition and Prisoners: A Review of Research and Emerging Areas of Inquiry." *The Prison Journal* 77, 184–208.

McDonald, D. C. 1990. "The Cost of Operating Public and Private Correctional Facilities." In D. C. McDonald (ed.), *Private Prisons and the Public Interest* (pp. 86–106). New Brunswick, NJ: Rutgers University Press.

Office of Program Policy Analysis and Government Accountability. 1996. *Performance Audit of the Gadsden Correctional Institution*. Tallahassee, FL: Office of Program Policy Analysis and Government Accountability.

Office of Program Policy Analysis and Government Accountability. 1998. *Review of Bay Correctional Facility and Moore Haven Correctional Facility*. Tallahassee, FL: Office of Program Policy Analysis and Government Accountability.

Oshinsky, D. M. 1996. *"Worse Than Slavery": Parchman Farm and the Ordeal of Jim Crow Justice*. New York: The Free Press.

Oregon AFSCME. 2000. *Recent Escapes from Private Prisons* [on-line]. Retrieved June 28, 2000. Available: <http://www.oregonafscme.com/corrections/private/recent_escapes_from_private_pris.htm>

Press, A. 1990. "The Good, the Bad, and the Ugly: Private Prisons in the 1980s." In D. C. McDonald (ed.), *Private Prisons and the Public Interest* (19–41). London: Rutgers University Press.

Robbins, I. P. 1988. *Legal Dimensions of Private Incarceration*. American Bar Association: Washington DC.

Selke, W. L. 1993. *Prisons in Crisis*. Indianapolis: Indiana University Press.

Shichor, D. 1995. *Punishment for Profit: Private Prisons/Public Concerns*. Thousand Oaks: Sage Publications.

Sullivan, J., and Purdy, M. 1995, July 23. "A Prison Empire: How It Grew." *New York Times* Special Supplement.

Tangley, L., Pethokoukis, J. M., Shapiro, J. P., Gest, T., and Couzin, J. 1999, September 13. "Private Prisons Suffer a Blow." *U.S. News & World Report* 127, 10.

Taylor, W. B. 1993. *Brokered Justice: Race, Politics, and Mississippi Prisons 1798–1992*. Columbus, OH: Ohio State University Press.

Texas Sunset Advisory Commission. 1991. *Contracts for Correctional Facilities and Services* (staff report). Austin, TX: Texas Sunset Advisory Commission.

Thomas, C. W. 1994. *The Transformation of Correctional Privatization from a Novel Experiment into a Proven Alternative*. Gainesville, Florida: University of Florida, Center for Studies in Criminology and Law.

Thomas, C. W. 1995, March 1. *Private Adult Correctional Facility Census* (8th ed). Gainesville, Florida: University of Florida, Center for Studies in Criminology & Law, Private Corrections Project, University of Florida.

U.S. General Accounting Office. 1996. *Private and Public Prisons: Studies Comparing Operational Costs and/or Quality of Services*. Washington, DC: Government Printing Office.

Vernon, John T. 1998, March 12. Personal communication at Western New Mexico State Correctional Facility, Grants, New Mexico.

Walker, D. R. 1988. *Penology for Profit*. College Station: Texas A&M University Press.

Walzer, M. 1991. "Private Prisons Are Unjust." In S. L. Tipp (ed.), *America's Prisons Opposing Viewpoints* (pp. 168–173). San Diego: Greenhaven Press, Inc.

Yu, K. S. 1995. "High Tech, Hard Labor." *The Texas Observer*, 9–11.

ISSUE XV

Is It a Good Idea to House Juveniles in Adult Correctional Facilities?

Violent juvenile crime continues to be a pressing issue in our society. The public has become outraged at seemingly endless incidents of youth violence reported in the media. In reality though, most juvenile offenders are nonviolent or petty offenders, and most cases are adjudicated in juvenile courts under a more informal process than that for adult offenders. For the small number of juveniles who do commit serious or violent crimes, many states have created more options for prosecutors or judges to "transfer," "waive," or "certify" a juvenile as an adult. These are the cases that capture the media's attention.

The waiver process varies widely by state. Generally speaking, a juvenile waiver means that a transferred juvenile is tried and sentenced in an adult criminal court. In 1998, for every 100 juvenile offenders who were formally adjudicated in juvenile court, one juvenile was waived to an adult criminal court (Stahl 1999). Some states even have certain crimes (e.g., first-degree murder) in which a juvenile is automatically charged (no discretion) as an adult because of the nature of the crime committed.

Most states create a range of punishment options for certified juveniles. For example, approximately half of all waived juveniles receive probation. For juveniles who are sentenced to jail or prison, most states hold one or more hearings at different stages to determine whether to retain the waived juvenile in a juvenile detention facility or to transfer the juvenile to an adult prison. Age and demeanor are among the factors that define if and when a certified juvenile is physically transported from juvenile detention to an adult prison. For example, the oldest age for which the juvenile justice system may retain jurisdiction over a waived juvenile varies from 17 to over 24 years of age. Thus, some states may retain waived juveniles in juvenile detention until they reach the limit and must be transferred to adult prison. Five states do not even require a waived juvenile to serve any time in an adult institution (Altschuler 1999). On the other hand, some states do not allow waived juveniles to be housed with other juveniles. Thus, a juvenile who is convicted as an adult of a violent crime must be transferred directly to an adult prison even if he or she has not yet reached the age of 18. For example, "Georgia's 1994 law requires mandatory transfer of juveniles 13 and older charged with specified serious crimes. If convicted, juveniles face a minimum 10-year term in Georgia's (adult) Department of Corrections" (Parent et al. 1997, 3–4).

Consequently, a very small number of all formally adjudicated juvenile offenders age 17 and younger actually serve time with adults in an adult institution (0.25 percent). In the year 2000, there were about 9,100 juveniles held in adult *jails* and 5,400 juveniles from 44 states under the age of 18 in adult *prisons*. In the jails, 5,475 juveniles were sentenced as "adults" while 3,625 were either pretrial detainees or were being held as juveniles. Note that juveniles who have *not* been sentenced as adults *cannot* be integrated with adults.

The ages of juveniles upon being admitted to adult state correctional facilities were as follows:

79 percent were 17 years old,

18 percent were 16 years old,

3 percent (162 juveniles) were between 13 and 15 (Austin, Johnson, and Gregoriou 2000).

Most of the offenders ages 13 to 15 were convicted in Arkansas, Florida, Georgia, and North Carolina (Parent et al. 1997, 4). The constant admission and release of offenders means that the number of juveniles actually admitted each year is much higher. In 1997 alone, 13,876 juveniles were admitted to an adult prison. Over half (57 percent) of juveniles were admitted to adult prisons for a violent crime, while 22 percent were admitted for a drug offense, and 21 percent for a property crime (Austin et al. 2000). Finally, there are housing differences within adult penitentiaries. In 1994, only six state prisons housed waived juveniles separately from adults. However, nine states housed transferred juveniles with adults ages 18 to 21, and the remaining 36 states housed juveniles with adults of any age. In a more recent nationwide study, Austin and his colleagues (2000) reported that one-third of juveniles in adult institutions are in protective custody (single-cell), while the vast majority of juveniles (51 percent) are housed in dormitories, and a small number (18 percent) share a cell with one cellmate.

An interesting observation is that most waiver policies were created by public demand on public officials, not by sound empirical research (Schwartz et al. 1996). Keep these facts in mind as you read the arguments for and against housing juveniles in adult correctional facilities.

References

Altschuler, David M. 1999. "Trends and Issues in the Adultification of Juvenile Justice." In Patricia M. Harris (Ed.), *Research to Results: Effective Community Corrections* (pp. 233–271). Lanham, MD: American Correctional Association.

Austin, James, Kelly Dedel Johnson, and Maria Gregoriou. 2000. *Juveniles in Adult Prisons and Jails: A National Assessment.* Washington, DC: U.S. Department of Justice.

Parent, Dale, Terence Dunworth, Douglas McDonald, and William Rhodes. 1997. *Transferring Serious Juvenile Offenders to Adult Courts.* Washington, DC: U.S. Department of Justice.

Schwartz, Ira M., Chang-ming Hsieh, and Gretchen P. Kenagy. 1996. *Juveniles in Adult Prisons.* Philadelphia, PA: Center for the Study of Youth Policy.

Stahl, Anne L. 1999. *Delinquency Cases Waived to Criminal Court, 1987–1996.* Washington, DC: U.S. Department of Justice.

Critical Thinking Questions

1. Are juveniles actually *committing* more serious crimes today than in the past, or is the criminal justice *response* to the same juvenile crimes more severe?

2. Can punishment be counterproductive?

3. What will it be like for juveniles once they are returned back to society from adult prison?

4. What are prevention strategies that could be used to entirely avoid the situation of juveniles in the adult system?

Internet Websites

April 1999 issue of *Corrections Today*—articles about juveniles in adult courts and adult prisons. <http://www.corrections.com/aca/cortoday/april99/index.html>

The impact of the Kansas Juvenile Justice Reform Act—juveniles in adult prisons. <http://www.jrsainfo.org/pubs/reports/sjsreport/kansas.html>

Increase of juveniles of minority groups held in adult prisons. <http://www.apbnews.com/cjsystem/justicenews/2000/02/27/juveniles0227_01.html>

Juvenile justice database of resources and links. <http://www.lib.msu.edu/harris23/crimjust/juvenile.htm>

PBS Forum: On-Line News Hour: Kids and Crime. <http://www.pbs.org/newshour/forum/january00/kids_crime4.html>

Talbot, Margaret. September 10, 2000. "What's become of the juvenile delinquent?" *The New York Times.* <http://www.newamerica.net/articles/Talbot/mt-NYTimes9-10-00.htm> ✦

29

The House of Last Resort

Incarcerating Juveniles in Adult Prisons

David L. Myers

Treating juvenile offenders as adults currently is a popular approach for dealing with serious and violent youthful offending. By the mid-1990s, in response to nearly a decade of rising juvenile violent crime rates and increasing concern about a large generation of young people expected to grow over the next 10 years, most states acted to facilitate the process of "transferring" or "waiving" adolescent offenders to the adult criminal justice system (Sickmund, Snyder, and Poe-Yamagata 1997; Torbet et al. 1996; Griffin, Torbet, and Szymanski 1998). It was anticipated that in the adult system, juveniles would receive more severe sanctions than those imposed by juvenile courts. Subsequently, this harsher treatment would have a beneficial impact on juvenile crime, by providing both greater deterrence and lengthier incapacitation. Moreover, policymakers were fueled by strong public support of this strategy (Feiler and Sheley 1999; Meddis 1993; Swartz, Guo, and Krebs 1993; Sprott 1998).

Despite the popularity of transferring juveniles to adult court, arguing in favor of housing them in adult prisons is no easy task. Over the past two decades, research (including some of my own) has been steadily building that questions the effectiveness of this practice. Studies suggest that, as compared to similar youths in juvenile institutions, adolescents in adult facilities experi-ence greater victimization by both inmates and staff (Forst, Fagan, and Vivona 1987) and also exhibit higher suicide rates (Flaherty 1980). Furthermore, expanded juvenile transfer laws have not been found to produce a general deterrent effect on aggregate adolescent crime rates (Jensen and Metsger 1994; Singer and McDowall 1988). Other recent research indicates that rather than providing a specific deterrent effect, transferring juveniles to the adult system may actually increase the likelihood and seriousness of future recidivism (Bishop, Frazier, Lanza-Kaduce, and Winner 1996; Fagan 1995; Myers 2001; Podkopacz and Feld 1996). Finally, nearly all studies that examine the race of transferred youths find strong disproportionate minority confinement, as African Americans generally constitute a large majority of all waived offenders (DeFrances and Strom 1997; Thomas and Bilchik 1985; Myers 2001).[1]

Although the evidence mentioned above does not support widespread efforts to send as many adolescents as possible to the adult system, it appears unlikely that transfer trends will be reversed in the near future. As long as there is a separate system of justice for dealing with juveniles, there will probably be a need and desire to treat some of them as adults. Few would argue that there are not certain chronic or violent young offenders who, for the sake of public safety, should be removed from society for long periods of time. Although some authors have suggested that the juvenile court should be completely abolished (Feld 1993, 1998) or at least reconceptualized as a court for "bankrupt families" (Moore and Wakeling 1997), overall support for a separate system of juvenile justice still seems strong enough to prevent a complete move toward a unified system. Therefore, for policy purposes it may be most practical to specify which juvenile offenders should be transferred to the adult system and to clarify what should be done with them once they get there. The issue, then, is not simply whether juveniles should be housed in adult prisons, but rather *which* juveniles should be placed in these facilities and how should they be treated during their period of incarceration.

Who Should Be Housed in Adult Prisons?

To begin, research shows that age is an important factor in the waiver process, as older youths are more likely to be transferred to adult court (Eigen 1981; Fagan and Deschenes 1990; Feld 1989; Podkopacz and Feld 1996; Poulos and Orchowsky 1994). This practice of transferring older juveniles is undoubtedly influenced by a perceived need for longer sentences than are available in the juvenile system. Some have argued that waiver should occur only when an appropriate term of confinement greatly exceeds the period available to a juvenile court judge (Feld 1989; Zimring 1991). However, this may still allow younger adolescents to be eventually placed in the company of older, more experienced adult prison inmates, setting the stage for a criminal learning process, violent victimization, or both.

To prevent these potential negative consequences, younger offenders should not be placed in adult prisons. A minimum age of 16 (or higher) would seem appropriate for adult correctional intervention. For younger juveniles, raising the maximum age at which the juvenile system can maintain custody and supervision (e.g., from age 18 to age 21 or 24) or creating a "blended jurisdiction" between the juvenile and adult systems[2] would allow for lengthy confinement without the risks associated with the presence of adult inmates.

Along with only placing older youths in adult facilities, sufficient attention should be given to the offense and offending history of these juveniles. If public safety is a key concern, then certain violent offenders with more serious prior records should be considered for longer-term incarceration. Interestingly, prior to the 1990s, research indicated that property offenders made up the largest percentage of waived juveniles (Bishop, Frazier, and Henretta 1989; Bortner 1986; Champion 1989; Hamparian et al. 1982; Thomas and Bilchik 1985). More recent research shows a change in this pattern, as youths charged with personal or violent offenses now make up the largest percentage of those transferred (DeFrances and Strom 1997; Sickmund et al. 1997). Violent adolescents should continue to be the central focus in placing juveniles in adult prisons.

More specifically, an emphasis on firearm use and an established pattern of violent behavior appears justified. Firearm use was a key factor in the surge in youth violence that took place from the mid-1980s to the mid-1990s (Blumstein 1995; Cook and Laub 1998; Fagan and Wilkinson 1998; Greenbaum 1997), particularly with regard to the rapid increases that occurred in the juvenile murder arrest rate and juvenile murder victimization rate (Sickmund et al. 1997). Research suggests that violent juvenile gun users receive the most severe sanctions in adult court, and that justice system officials believe waiver laws should target cases involving a firearm (Myers 2001). In addition, youths exhibiting a history of violent behavior would appear to pose a greater risk to community safety and to be more appropriate choices for lengthier adult correctional intervention.

If the above recommendations were followed, juveniles in adult prisons would be older and more violent offenders. This would reduce the likelihood of negative experiences among younger and less serious offenders (who would stay in the juvenile system) and increase public safety by incapacitating those youths who pose the greatest risk. This approach contrasts with many current waiver laws (*see* Griffin et al. 1998) that encompass broad categories of potentially younger, less serious, and lower risk youths, but it still allows for longer-term incarceration in adult facilities of juveniles who present the greatest public threat.

How Should Juveniles Be Treated in Adult Prisons?

Identifying which juveniles are most appropriate for placement in adult prisons is an important first step, but further clarification is needed with regard to how these youths should be treated within adult facilities. As mentioned earlier, research suggests that adolescents housed in adult prisons may experience a variety of negative consequences, which can have both an immediate and long-term impact on their attitudes and behavior. In particular, consistent findings of greater and more serious recidivism on the part of transferred juveniles, as compared to similar youths retained in the juvenile system, raise substantial concerns and deserve discussion of possible explanations (Myers 2001; Podkopacz and Feld 1996).

First, it is possible that more effective treatment services are offered in the juvenile correctional system. Research to date indicates that juveniles in adult prisons and jails receive inferior treatment services as compared to similar youths in juvenile facilities (Forst et al. 1989; Reddington and Sapp 1997). A second possible reason for the findings of greater recidivism by transferred juveniles is that these youths are victimized by (Forst et al. 1989) or learn from other adult criminals. In other words, the adult court, incarceration experience, or both may breed or serve as a training ground for future criminality. Some might argue that by placing violent youths in the company of older and more seasoned offenders, a forum is provided that serves to enhance the very behavior that is hoped to be prevented.

Third, being sent to adult court and labeled a criminal may produce a variety of negative consequences for adolescent offenders: (a) public identification as a criminal (*see* Paternoster and Iovanni 1989), (b) exclusion from conventional activities, such as jobs, school, and other social functions (see Braithwaite 1989; Freeman 1992; Link 1982; Link et al. 1989; Paternoster and Iovanni 1989), (c) a perception of unfair treatment (*see* Lanza-Kaduce and Radosevich 1987; Paternoster, Brame, Bachman, and Sherman 1997; Sherman 1993; Tyler 1990), and/or (d) an alteration of personal identity toward a criminal self-image (see Paternoster and Iovanni 1989). These factors, in turn, may lead to worsened future behavior.

Although all of the above explanations for the findings of greater recidivism among transferred youths are plausible, the possibility cannot be ruled out that juvenile courts and waiver laws are simply successful in identifying and transferring the most chronic offenders who have the greatest likelihood of subsequent criminal behavior. Although researchers have made great effort to identify and control for variables that may influence and predict the future behavior of violent youths (e.g., prior offending, age of onset, firearm use), it is possible that other relevant factors have not been considered. Therefore, although the evidence to date suggests that treating juvenile offenders as adults may make things worse, potential problems with "selection bias" preclude anyone from drawing a final conclusion (*see* Smith and Paternoster 1990).

At this point, it is important to note that none of the explanations discussed above, including the possibility of selection bias, support a practice of placing waived youths in the presence of adult prison inmates. In this setting, adolescents may receive inadequate treatment services, be trained or victimized by more veteran offenders, experience the negative consequences of a criminal label, or all three. Therefore, for the older, more violent juveniles who are deemed appropriate for placement in adult prisons, special provisions should be met. At a bare minimum, they should be segregated from the rest of the inmate population, at least until the age of 18.[3] A much better approach would be to provide separate adult correctional facilities and treatment services for these adolescents.

Benefits of Longer-Term Incarceration and Treatment

The main advantage that adult prisons possess in housing older and more violent youths is in the length of incarceration and treatment that potentially can be provided. Beyond the greater incapacitation that lengthier confinement provides, research suggests that for the most serious and chronic youthful offenders, longer-term institutional confinement reduces the likelihood of recidivism (Gottfredson and Barton 1993; Murray and Cox 1979; Myers 2001; but *see* Schneider and Ervin 1990 for contradictory findings). This may be due to a greater deterrent, rehabilitative, or combined effect from longer periods of incarceration. However, providing long-term custody and treatment to serious and violent youthful offenders in the juvenile system is often problematic. Juvenile correctional resources are often limited, leading some juvenile courts to "wash their hands" of offenders who are the most in need. Unfortunately, while lengthier periods of confinement are commonly imposed on violent juveniles in adult court (Barnes and Franz 1989; Bishop et al. 1996; Fagan 1990, 1995; Myers 2001; Podkopacz and Feld 1996; Rudman et al. 1986),[4] adult correctional systems have not always been ready to receive these youths. There are indications, though, that this situation is changing.

One very encouraging sign concerns the overall effectiveness of correctional treatment programs. During the past 15 years, a variety of criminologists have examined the effectiveness of correctional rehabilitation, and many have offered much more optimistic assessments than those of the 1970s (*see*, e.g., Andrews et al. 1990; Gaes, Flanagan, Motiuk, and Stewart 1999; Gendreau and Ross 1987; Howell 1997; Lipsey 1992; Lipsey and Wilson 1999; Sherman et al. 1997). Although no specific treatment program has been found to work effectively for all types of offenders, a consistent conclusion from recent meta-analyses and literature reviews is that some programs do work, at least for some offenders and under certain conditions.

As suggested by Andrews and his colleagues (1990) and discussed in a variety of other works (e.g., Gaes et al. 1999; Gendreau, Little, and Goggin 1996; Lipsey and Wilson 1999; Sherman et al. 1997), a number of guiding principles provide for effective rehabilitation. First, there should be an emphasis on assessing and subsequently addressing "criminogenic needs." These are factors that appear directly related to an offender's propensity to commit crime and include "procriminal attitudes, procriminal associates, impulsivity, weak socialization, below average verbal intelligence, a taste for risk, weak problem-solving and self-control skills, early onset of antisocial behavior, poor parental practices, and deficits in educational, vocational, and employment skills" (Gaes et al. 1999, 363).

Another principle of effective treatment involves matching offenders with programs that will not only consider their criminogenic needs, but also their risk of reoffending. To achieve a measurable improvement in behavior, programs must target offenders who are at a sufficient or high risk for reoffending. In general, offenders with the greatest risk of recidivism are typically those with the most criminogenic needs. Treatment programs that target lower-risk offenders with few needs cannot be expected to produce substantial improvements in behavior, as many of these individuals would not recidivate even without the benefit of the program. Therefore, programs offering the most intensive and comprehensive treatment (i.e., those longest and strongest in dosage) should be used for higher-risk offenders.

In addition to needs and risk assessment, program matching should also be based on the learning styles and abilities of offenders. For example, "more effective programs follow a cognitive behavioral and social learning approach rather than nondirective relationship-oriented counseling or psychodynamic, insight-oriented counseling" (Sherman et al. 1997). Overall, effective correctional treatment interventions, both within institutions and in the community, usually employ behavioral modeling and reinforcement of prosocial attitudes and behavior, while also teaching offenders skills that allow them to understand and resist antisocial attitudes and behavior.

Finally, the available evidence strongly suggests that researchers should be involved with treatment program development, implementation, and evaluation (Gaes et al. 1999; Sherman et al. 1997). Recent meta-analyses and literature reviews reveal that programs directly involving researchers in these processes attain greater effects. Although experimenter bias is a major concern (i.e., the success of a program could be an artifact of researcher participation), it appears just as likely (if not more so) that researchers can enhance the integrity of a program. Furthermore, allowing researchers to participate in program development and implementation can contribute to the creation of stronger scientific knowledge about treatment effectiveness.

The information discussed above points to the potential that adult prisons have for housing and treating older, violent juvenile offenders. Longer-term confinement is more likely in the adult system, and the principles for effective rehabilitation seem tailor-made for these youths. Violent adolescents are likely to exhibit a variety of criminogenic needs, present a high risk for reoffending, and be responsive to a cognitive behavioral or social learning approach to treatment (Lipsey and Wilson 1999). Finally, studies on the effectiveness of treating juvenile offenders as adults have steadily grown in number along with the popularity of this policy option, meaning that researcher involvement in adult correctional treatment programs directed at violent youths is likely.

Prospects for Juveniles in Adult Prisons

As a result of contemporary legislative efforts to increase the number of juveniles transferred to adult court, adult correctional facilities are being required to handle greater numbers of youthful offenders, particularly those who have committed violent acts. Although various studies have questioned the effectiveness of this practice, it seems likely that certain adolescents will continue to enter adult prisons. The argument presented here has been that efforts should be made to target the most appropriate juveniles for placement in these facilities (i.e., older, more violent youths), and that further attention should be paid to the treatment they receive during their period of incarceration (i.e., long-term, rehabilitative services).

Of course, critics could point out that in today's "get tough" society, many or most juveniles sent to the adult system may not receive segregated or separate facilities that offer treatment suited to violent adolescent needs. However, many others have questioned whether the juvenile system, with its generally limited resources and jurisdiction,

can be expected to provide longer-term incarceration, rehabilitation, and public safety. It seems, then, that model approaches for dealing with this problem should be identified and evaluated before forming a conclusion on whether juveniles should be placed in adult prisons.

To illustrate, the state of Pennsylvania has decided to build a special facility and provide unique treatment services for violent youthful offenders who are transferred to the adult criminal system. As a result of a change (known as "Act 33") in Pennsylvania's juvenile code in 1995, since March 1996 certain violent juvenile offenders have been sent directly to adult criminal court for prosecution.[5] Some of these transferred youths eventually receive a state prison sentence. A new prison, known as the Pine Grove State Correctional Institute (SCI Pine Grove), opened in January 2001 to house inmates of this type. This facility appears very unique in terms of its target population, treatment philosophy, and accessibility for researchers (Zimmerman et al. 2000).

The basic mode of treatment planned for the SCI Pine Grove Program is behavioral modification. The program will be offered through a multiphase system and is designed to take place within a safe, highly structured therapeutic community. Inmate responsibilities and privileges are to increase as progress is made within the therapeutic community. Integration of the various parts of the program (e.g., education, recreation, and counseling) is a major goal, through the use of a multidisciplinary team approach to unit management and program delivery. Finally, researchers from Indiana University of Pennsylvania (IUP) have established a collaborative relationship with the administration and staff in an effort to link research and practice for the creation of stronger scientific knowledge about violent offending and promising strategies for changing this behavior.

Overall, SCI Pine Grove's program appears to be supported by the recent literature on correctional rehabilitation. Undoubtedly, other similar adult prisons either have opened or will open in the near future to house and treat serious and violent youthful offenders. These facilities will provide opportunities for further research on violent adolescent behavior and hopefully will allow for a better understanding of the effectiveness of adult correctional intervention.

Notes

1. Although African Americans are highly overrepresented among transferred youths, recent research employing multivariate statistical techniques to control for critical legal variables (i.e., offense seriousness and prior record) has failed to find evidence of direct racial bias toward these offenders (Fagan and Deschenes 1990; Fagan, Forst, and Vivona 1987; Podkopacz and Feld 1995, 1996; Poulos and Orchowsky 1994). Still, based on probable differential treatment earlier in the juvenile justice process (e.g., at the time of arrest or intake; *see* Smith 1986; Leonard, Pope, and Feyerherm 1995), it appears that the effect of race on the transfer decision may be more indirect than direct.

2. In general, "blended sentencing" seeks to achieve proportionality and heighten formal control by combining juvenile and adult court sanctions. In sentencing youthful offenders, several states allow adult criminal courts to impose a sanction involving either juvenile or adult correctional services, or both in some states (DeFrances and Strom 1997; Feld 1998; Sickmund et al. 1997). Other states have enabled juvenile courts to identify certain offenders for special processing and sanctioning, which may or may not include relocation to adult correctional facilities at some future point.

3. The age of 21 may be more appropriate, particularly for young offenders who likely will be released from prison sometime between the ages of 18 and 21.

4. Some early research on juveniles prosecuted in adult criminal courts found evidence of a "leniency gap" for these young offenders, who seemed to appear relatively less criminal than their older and more experienced adult counterparts. These youths typically were not imprisoned and appeared to receive more lenient sentencing than they would have in juvenile court (Bortner 1986; Champion 1989; Emerson 1981; Gillespie and Norman 1984; Hamparian et al. 1982; Royscher and Edelman 1981; Sagatun, McCollum, and Edwards 1985). However, more recent research assessing this situation has found higher incarceration rates and lengthier periods of incarceration in adult criminal court than in juvenile court, particularly for violent offenders (Barnes and Franz 1989; Bishop et al. 1996; Fagan 1990, 1995; Myers 2001; Podkopacz and Feld 1996).

5. The revised juvenile code excluded from juvenile court jurisdiction any youth charged with murder or any of the following violent offenses, when the offender was between 15 and 18 years of age at the time of the alleged offense and a deadly weapon was employed: rape, involuntary deviate sexual intercourse, aggravated assault, robbery, robbery of a motor vehicle, aggravated indecent assault, kidnapping, voluntary manslaughter, or an attempt, conspiracy, or solicitation to commit murder or any of these other listed offenses (Pennsylvania Juvenile Court Judges' Commission 1996, 2–3). The new act also excluded any youth between 15 and 18 years of age at the time of the alleged offense who was charged with any of the above listed crimes, except for aggravated assault, after previously being adjudicated delinquent on the basis of any of these offenses. Aggravated assault was intentionally omitted from this repeat violent offender clause, apparently based on the belief of policymakers and practitioners that aggravated assault without a deadly weapon could encompass too many violent but less-serious acts (e.g., a fist-fight at school).

References

Andrews, D. A., Zinger, I., Hodge, R. D., Bonta, J., Gendreau, P., and Cullen, F. T. 1990. "Does Correctional Treatment Work? A Clinically Relevant and Psychologically Informed Meta-Analysis." *Criminology* 28, 369–404.

Barnes, C. W., and Franz, R. S. 1989. "Questionably Adult: Determinants and Effects of the Juvenile Waiver Decision." *Justice Quarterly* 6(1): 117–135.

Bishop, D. M., Frazier, C. E., and Henretta, J. C. 1989. "Prosecutorial Waiver: Case Study of a Questionable Reform." *Crime and Delinquency* 35(2): 179–201.

Bishop, D. M., Frazier, C. E., Lanza-Kaduce, L., and Winner, L. 1996. "The Transfer of Juveniles to Criminal Court: Does It Make a Difference?" *Crime and Delinquency* 42(2): 171–191.

Blumstein, A. 1995. "Youth Violence, Guns, and the Illicit-Drug Industry." *The Journal of Criminal Law and Criminology* 86(1): 10–36.

Bortner, M. A. 1986. "Traditional Rhetoric, Organizational Realities: Remand of Juveniles to Adult Court." *Crime and Delinquency* 32(1): 53–73.

Braithwaite, J. 1989. *Crime, Shame, and Reintegration.* Cambridge: Cambridge University Press.

Champion, D. J. 1989. "Teenage Felons and Waiver Hearings: Some Recent Trends, 1980–1988." *Crime and Delinquency* 35(4): 577–585.

Cook, P. J., and Laub, J. H. 1998. "The Unprecedented Epidemic in Youth Violence." In M. Tonry, and Mark H. (eds.), *Crime and Justice: A Review of Research* (Vol. 24, pp. 27–64). Chicago: The University of Chicago Press.

DeFrances, C. J., and Strom, K. J. 1997. *Juveniles Prosecuted in State Criminal Courts.* (Report No. NCJ-164265). Washington, DC: Bureau of Justice Statistics/Office of Juvenile Justice and Delinquency Prevention.

Eigen, J. P. 1981. "Punishing Youth Homicide Offenders in Philadelphia." *The Journal of Criminal Law and Criminology* 72(3): 1072–1093.

Emerson, R. 1981. "On Last Resorts." *American Journal of Sociology* 87, 1–22.

Fagan, J. 1990. "Social and Legal Policy Dimensions of Violent Juvenile Crime." *Criminal Justice and Behavior* 17(1): 93–133.

Fagan, J. 1995. "Separating the Men from the Boys: The Comparative Advantage of Juvenile Versus Criminal Court Sanctions on Recidivism Among Adolescent Felony Offenders. In J. C. Howell, B. Krisberg, J. D. Hawkins, and J. J. Wilson (eds.), *A Sourcebook: Serious, Violent, and Chronic Juvenile Offenders* (pp. 238–260). Thousand Oaks, CA: Sage Publications, Inc.

Fagan, J., and Deschenes, E. P. 1990. "Determinants of Judicial Waiver Decisions for Violent Juvenile Offenders." *The Journal of Criminal Law and Criminology* 81(2): 314–347.

Fagan, J., and Wilkinson, D. L. 1998. "Guns, Youth Violence, and Social Identity in Inner Cities." In M. Tonry, and M. H. Moore (eds.), *Crime and Justice: A Review of Research* (Vol. 24, pp. 105–188). Chicago: The University of Chicago Press.

Feiler, S. M., and Sheley, J. F. 1999. "Legal and Racial Elements of Public Willingness to Transfer Juvenile Offenders to Adult Court." *Journal of Criminal Justice* 27(1): 55–64.

Feld, B. C. 1989. "Bad Law Makes Hard Cases: Reflections on Teenaged Axe-Murderers, Judicial Activism, and Legislative Default." *Journal of Law and Inequality* 8(1): 1–101.

Feld, B. C. 1993. "Criminalizing the American Juvenile Court." In M. Tonry (ed.), *Crime and Justice: A Review of Research* (Vol. 17, pp. 197–280). Chicago: University of Chicago Press.

Feld, B. C. 1998. "Juvenile and Criminal Justice Systems' Responses to Youth Violence." In M. Tonry, and M. H. Moore (eds.), *Crime and Justice: A Review of Research* (Vol. 24, pp. 189–261). Chicago: University of Chicago Press.

Flaherty, M. 1980. *An Assessment of the Incidence of Juvenile Suicide in Adult Jails, Lock-Ups, and Juvenile Detention Centers.* Champaign, IL: Community Research Forum.

Forst, M., Fagan, J., and Vivona, T. S. 1989. "Youths in Prisons and Training Schools: Perceptions and Consequences of the Treatment-Custody Dichotomy." *Juvenile and Family Court Journal* 40, 1–14.

Freeman, R. B. 1992. "Crime and the Employment of Disadvantaged Youth." In G. Peterson, and W. Vroman (eds.), *Urban Labor Markets and Job Opportunity* (pp. 201–238). Washington, DC: Urban Institute Press.

Gaes, G. G., Flanagan, T. J., Motiuk, L. L., and Stewart, L. 1999. "Adult Correctional Treatment." In M. Tonry, and J. Petersilia (eds.), *Crime and Justice: Prisons* (Vol. 26, pp. 361–426). Chicago: University of Chicago Press.

Gendreau, P., Little, T., and Goggin, C. 1996. "A Meta-Analysis of the Predictors of Adult Offender Recidivism: What Works!" *Criminology* 34(4): 575–607.

Gendreau, P., and Ross, R. R. 1987. "Revivification of Rehabilitation: Evidence from the 1980s." *Justice Quarterly* 4(3): 349–407.

Gillespie, L. K., and Norman, M. D. 1984. "Does Certification Mean Prison: Some Preliminary Findings from Utah." *Juvenile and Family Court Journal* 35, 23–34.

Gottfredson, D. C., and Barton, W. H. 1993. "Deinstitutionalization of Juvenile Offenders." *Criminology* 31(4): 591–607.

Greenbaum, S. 1997. "Kids and Guns: From Playgrounds to Battlegrounds." *Juvenile Justice, III(2): 3–10.*

Griffin, P., Torbet, P., and Szymanski, L. 1998. *Trying Juveniles as Adults in Criminal Court: An Analysis of State Transfer Provisions.* Washington, DC: US Department of Justice, Office of Justice Programs, Office of Juvenile Justice and Delinquency Prevention.

Hamparian, D., Estep, L. K., Muntean, S. M., Prestino, R., Swisher, R. G., Wallace, P. L., and White, J. L. 1982. *Youth in Adult Court: Between Two Worlds.* Columbus, OH: Academy for Contemporary Problems.

Howell, J. C. 1997. *Juvenile Justice and Youth Violence.* Thousand Oaks, CA: Sage Publications, Inc.

Jensen, E. J., and Metsger, L. K. 1994. "A Test of the Deterrent Effect of Legislative Waiver on Violent Juvenile Crime." *Crime and Delinquency* 40(1): 96–104.

Lanza-Kaduce, L., and Radosevich, M. J. 1987. "Negative Reactions to Processing and Substance Use Among Young Incarcerated Males." *Deviant Behavior* 8, 137–148.

Leonard, K. K., Pope, C. E., and Feyerherm, W. H. 1995. *Minorities in Juvenile Justice.* Thousand Oaks, CA: Sage Publications, Inc.

Link, B. 1982. "Mental Patient Status, Work and Income: An Examination of the Effects of a Psychiatric Label." *American Sociological Review* 47, 202–215.

Link, B., Cullen, F. T., Struening, E., Shrout, P., and Dohrenwend, B. P. 1989. "A Modified Labeling Theory Approach to Mental Disorders: An Empirical Assessment." *American Sociological Review* 54, 400–423.

Lipsey, M. W. 1992. "Juvenile Delinquency Treatment: A Meta-Analytic Inquiry Into the Variability of Effects." In D. T. Cook, H. Cooper, D. S. Cordray, H. Hartman, L. V. Hedges, R. J. Knight, T. A. Louis, and F. Mosteller (eds.), *Meta-Analysis for Explanation* (pp. 83–127). New York: Russell Sage Foundation.

Lipsey, M. W., and Wilson, D. B. 1999. "Effective Intervention for Serious Juvenile Offenders: A Synthesis of Research." In R. Loeber, and D. P. Farrington (eds.), *Serious and Violent Juvenile Offenders: Risk Factors and Successful Interventions* (pp. 313–345). Thousand Oaks, CA: Sage Publications, Inc.

Meddis, S. V. 1993, October. "Poll: Treat Juveniles the Same as Adult Offenders." *USA Today,* pp. A1, A11.

Moore, M. H., and Wakeling, S. 1997. "Juvenile Justice: Shoring Up the Foundations." In M. Tonry (ed.), *Crime and Justice: A Review of Research* (Vol. 22, pp. 253–301). Chicago: University of Chicago Press.

Murray, C. A., and Cox, L. A. 1979. *Beyond Probation: Juvenile Corrections and the Chronic Delinquent.* Beverly Hills, CA: Sage Publications, Inc.

Myers, D. L. 2001. *Excluding Violent Youths from Juvenile Court: The Effectiveness of Legislative Waiver.* New York, NY: LFB Scholarly Publishing, LLC.

Paternoster, R., Brame, R., Bachman, R., and Sherman, L. W. 1997. "Do Fair Procedures Matter? The Effect of Procedural Justice on Spouse Assault." *Law and Society Review* 31, 163–204.

Paternoster, R., and Iovanni, L. 1989. "The Labeling Perspective and Delinquency: An Elaboration of the Theory and an Assessment of the Evidence." *Justice Quarterly* 6(3): 359–394.

Pennsylvania Juvenile Court Judges' Commission. 1996. *The Juvenile Act.* 42 PA C.S. Sec. 6301 et seq. Harrisburg, PA: Juvenile Court Judges' Commission.

Podkopacz, M. R., and Feld, B. C. 1995. "Judicial Waiver Policy and Practice: Persistence, Seriousness and Race." *Journal of Law and Inequality* 14(1): 73–178.

Podkopacz, M. R., and Feld, B. C. 1996. "The End of the Line: An Empirical Study of Judicial Waiver." *The Journal of Criminal Law and Criminology* 86(2): 449–492.

Poulos, T. M., and Orchowsky, S. 1994. "Serious Juvenile Offenders: Predicting the Probability of Transfer to Criminal Court." *Crime and Delinquency* 40(1): 3û17.

Reddington, F. P., and Sapp, A. D. 1997. "Juveniles in Adult Prisons: Problems and Prospects." *Journal of Crime and Justice* 20(2): 139–152.

Royscher, M., and Edelman, P. 1981. "Treating Juveniles as Adults in New York: What Does It Mean and How Is It Working?" In J. C. Hall, D. M. Hamparian, J. M. Pettibone, and J. L. White (eds.), *Major Issues in Juvenile Justice Information and Training: Readings in Public Policy* (pp. 265–293). Columbus, OH: Academy for Contemporary Problems.

Rudman, C., Hartstone, E., Fagan, J., and Moore, M. 1986. "Violent Youth in Adult Court: Process and Punishment." *Crime and Delinquency* 32(1): 75–96.

Sagatun, I., McCollum, L. L., and Edwards, L. 1985. "The Effect of Transfers From Juvenile to Criminal Court: A Koglinear Analysis." *Journal of Crime and Justice* 8, 65–92.

Schneider, A. L., and Ervin, L. 1990. "Specific Deterrence, Rational Choice, and Decision Heuristics: Applications in Juvenile Justice." *Social Science Quarterly* 71(3): 585–601.

Schwartz, I. M., Guo, S., and Krebs, J. J. 1993. "The Impact of Demographic Variables on Public Opinion Regarding Juvenile Justice: Implications for Public Policy." *Crime and Delinquency* 39(1): 5–28.

Sherman, L. W. 1993. "Defiance, Deterrence, and Irrelevance: A Theory of the Criminal Sanction." *Journal of Research in Crime and Delinquency* 30(4): 445–473.

Sherman, L. W., Gottfredson, D., MacKenzie, D., Eck, J., Reuter, P., and Bushway, S. 1997. *Preventing Crime: What Works, What Doesn't,*

What's Promising. Washington, DC: US Department of Justice.

Sickmund, M., Snyder, H. N., and Poe-Yamagata, E. 1997. *Juvenile Offenders and Victims: 1997 Update on Violence.* (Report No. NCJ-165703). Washington, DC: Office of Juvenile Justice and Delinquency Prevention.

Singer, S. I., and McDowall, D. 1988. "Criminalizing Delinquency: The Deterrent Effects of the New York Juvenile Offender Law." *Law and Society Review* 22(3): 521–535.

Smith, D. A. 1986. "The Neighborhood Context of Police Behavior." In A. Reiss, and M. Tonry (eds.), *Crime and Justice: An Annual Review of Research* (Vol. 8, pp. 313–341). Chicago: University of Chicago Press.

Smith, D. A., and Paternoster, R. 1990. "Formal Processing and Future Delinquency: Deviance Amplification as a Selection Artifact." *Law and Society Review* 24(5): 1109–1131.

Sprott, J. B. 1998. "Understanding Public Opposition to a Separate Youth Justice System." *Crime and Delinquency* 44(3): 399–411.

Thomas, C. W., and Bilchik, S. 1985. "Prosecuting Juveniles in Criminal Courts: A Legal and Empirical Analysis." *The Journal of Criminal Law and Criminology* 76(2): 439–479.

Torbet, P., Gable, R., Hurst, H. I., Montgomery, I., Szymanski, L., and Thomas, D. 1996. *State Responses to Serious and Violent Juvenile Crime.* (Report No. NCJ-161565). Washington, DC: Office of Juvenile Justice and Delinquency Prevention.

Tyler, T. R. 1990. *Why People Obey the Law.* New Haven: Yale University Press.

Zimmerman, S., Myers, D. L., Giever, D., Dandeneau, C., Gido, R., Kiehl, K., Komorosky. 2000, March. *Establishing a Research Institution: The Partnership Between IUP and the Pine Grove Prison for Violent Youthful Offenders.* Paper presented at the annual meeting of the Academy of Criminal Justice Sciences, New Orleans, LA.

Zimring, F. E. 1991. "The Treatment of Hard Cases in American Juvenile Justice: In Defense of Discretionary Waiver." *Notre Dame Journal of Law, Ethics and Public Policy* 5, 267–280.

30

Arguments Against the Confinement of Juveniles with Adult Offenders

David W. Roush
Earl L. Dunlap
Jill Rinella

The January 2001 U.S. Surgeon General's comprehensive report on youth violence examines the factors that lead young people to violence, reviews the factors that protect youth from perpetrating violence, and identifies effective research-based preventive strategies (Satcher 2001). The report also challenges false notions and misinterpretations about youth violence and debunks myths about violence, including the following:

> *Myth:* Getting tough with juvenile offenders by trying them in adult criminal courts reduces the likelihood that they will commit more crimes. (*Fact:* Juveniles transferred to adult criminal court have significantly higher rates of re-offending and a greater likelihood of committing subsequent felonies than youth who remain in the juvenile justice system.)

The report shows the ineffectiveness and subsequent dangers associated with the tools of juvenile justice adultification,[1] such as the legislative and prosecutorial transfers of youthful offenders to adult court and the incarceration of youth with adult offenders.

When the authors first expressed their opposition to the incarceration of juveniles with adult offenders, they believed it to be such a bad idea that it was hardly worth discussion (Roush and Dunlap 1997). However, the past four years indicate that the idea continues to grow in popularity. At the same time, opposition to the incarceration of youth with adult offenders also continues to grow. The National Juvenile Detention Association (NJDA) passed a resolution opposing the confinement of juveniles with adults in the absence of or prior to a hearing before a judge. The National Commission on Correctional Health Care (NCCHC) pronounced the incarceration of youth in adult facilities to be "detrimental to the health and developmental well-being of youth" (NCCHC 1998, 115). The American Correctional Association (ACA) ratified a public policy statement opposing the incarceration of youth with adult offenders (Branham 2000). The U.S. Surgeon General attacked as ineffective the theoretical assumptions of the practice (Satcher 2001). And, most recently, the media has started to criticize the practice (Pelley 2001).

This is not, however, a commentary on prisons; this is a question of how best to protect society from our most troublesome juvenile offenders. Several principles apply: (a) there are significant differences between adults and juveniles; (b) certain juveniles require secure incarceration, but this incarceration is wrong for both juveniles and society if it occurs with adult offenders; and (c) public safety is best served by correctional interventions that restore youthful offenders to a healthy, law-abiding lifestyle. The adult correctional system, as presently defined by politicians, the public, the courts, and most practitioners, is at odds with these principles.

Why Are More Juveniles Being Placed in the Adult System?

There are several explanations for the increased incarceration of more youth in the adult system, but none is very appealing. The complexity of youth crime combined with weapons-related increases in juvenile violence forces a legislative and public policy quest for the "silver bullet" or a definitive solution (Soler 1997). Finding no "quick fix" or cheap alternatives, a bit of creative reframing occurred—such as changing the definition of "juvenile" so that more youth qualify for the adult criminal justice system. If "do the crime, do the time" can be the maxim, the expense of dealing with the most troublesome juveniles becomes no more costly than adults. And, if most of these "bad" juveniles are "youth of color," the highly rational and dispassionate nature of offense-driven decisions can deflect accusations of racism. What then would be the best mechanism to transform juveniles into adults for purposes of trial and incarceration? The answer came in the form of new transfer or waiver laws that lowered the age of transfer and removed control of the process from judges by making transfer automatic (a legislative transfer) or by giving the prosecutor the option of which court would hear the case (prosecutorial transfer).

Description of Waivers

The waiver of juvenile court jurisdiction or "transfer" is the vehicle for adjudicating the most dangerous juveniles in the criminal court (Snyder and Sickmund 1999; Snyder, Sickmund, and Poe-Yamagata 2000). The greatest numbers of juveniles waived to adult court and incarcerated in adult facilities are property offenders (Godinez 1999; Mendel 2000). In 1993, 46.6 percent of juveniles waived to the adult court committed property or public order offenses, not serious or violent crimes (Champion 1998, 207). Older juveniles with a prior record, especially blacks and males of any race, are more likely to be waived to criminal court (Snyder, Sickmund, and Poe-Yamagata 1996). The research on transfers indicates that Florida waives the greatest number of juveniles to the criminal court and has the highest number of juveniles in adult prisons (Frazier, Bishop, and Lanza-Kaduce 1999). Florida transferred between 6,000 to 7,000 cases annually during the past 10 years. Every state experienced an increase in juveniles waived

to the criminal court. However, there is no reliable information on the long-term impact on juvenile's behaviors by transferring juveniles into the adult criminal court.

The Myths

Incarceration of youthful offenders in adult prisons incorporates some or all of seven myths. Many politicians, policymakers, media personnel, talk-show hosts, and members of the public continue to believe these myths. The following describes each myth and presents a response to its faulty assumptions:

The No Difference Myth: Serious Juvenile Offenders Are No Different than Adult Prisoners

This myth presents the argument that the large, physically mature juvenile is equivalent to an adult. Furthermore, criminal thinking is criminal thinking, and victims are victims regardless of the offender's age. This seems to translate into: If youth are old enough to do adult crimes, they are old enough to do adult time *with adults*.

The problem is that physical maturity does not equal social, emotional, or cognitive maturity. The differences between adults and juveniles are so numerous and profound (Glick, Sturgeon, and Venator-Santiago 1998) that their denial portends pathology. The claim that differences do not exist reveals a naivete about human development. More importantly, practitioners have no trouble explaining the differences (Smith 1996).

The National Institute of Corrections (NIC) and the Office of Juvenile Justice and Delinquency Prevention (OJJDP) recently surveyed juvenile justice administrators to identify the characteristics of juveniles that make them different from an adult population. Many youths have experienced previous abuse and are vulnerable, yet malleable to change. Some of the most important needs of juvenile offender populations are as follows:

- Individual mentoring and higher staffing ratios than with adult facilities.

- Smaller living units (8 to 20 beds, compared with 50 to 100 in adult units).
- Peer interaction and active recreation.
- Counseling services and other programmatic requirements.
- Full-scale educational programming, including intensive remedial education within a structured learning environment (Zavlek and Barron 2000).

The Effectiveness Myth: The Adult System Is Better Equipped to Handle These Youth

Is the adult system better equipped for young criminals? In reality, the adult corrections system is overworked, overcrowded, and overwhelmed. Despite the overcrowding in adult jails, the numbers of youth placed in these facilities rose 35 percent from 1994 to 1997 (Snyder and Sickmund 1999).

There is evidence that the adult system makes juveniles more criminal (National Coalition of State Juvenile Justice Advisory Groups 1993; Redding 1999; Snyder and Sickmund 1999). The longer a juvenile is incarcerated in any facility, especially an adult facility, the greater the chance the juvenile will re-offend following release (Gross 1999; Mendel 2000; Snyder et al. 2000). Youth in the adult system have higher recidivism rates than comparable youth incarcerated in the juvenile system for the same offense (Redding 1999; Snyder and Sickmund 1999). Some possible reasons to explain the higher recidivism include stigmatization, humiliation, loss of self-respect, attenuation of guilt or shame, hardening of the delinquent self-concept, weakened ties to families and peers, diminished job and educational prospects, and retaliation (Redding 1999).

How has the adult corrections system prepared to assume responsibility for juveniles? A major problem with the incarceration of juveniles in the adult system is its lack of preparation. There is scant evidence of comprehensive planning, research, or training on managing juveniles. New training materials include a correspondence course (Jepsen 1999) and a text for program and staff development (Glick, Sturgeon, and Venator-Santiago 1998). For the most part, however, the adult system is far less prepared than the juvenile system to address the safe physical management and aftercare services needs of serious and violent juvenile offenders (Altschuler and Armstrong 1995; Howell 1997). The result will be increased warehousing, crowding, and harm to youthful offenders and staff. Warehousing (the incarceration of large numbers of inmates in dorms or barracks without programs or services) symbolizes (a) the "adultification" of juvenile institutions and (b) the failure of the juvenile justice system to make a compelling argument that addresses community protection, accountability, and competency development. Warehousing is the outward and visible sign of a system that has abandoned the notion of accountability for the offender, as has happened in the adult departments of corrections.

Glick (1998) notes that many adult correctional officers find that the interventions that control adult behavior do not work on juveniles. Without formal training on how to deal with a juvenile population, staff may view adolescent behavior in adult institutions as bizarre, unpredictable, without basis, and extreme. In reality, these behaviors are completely normal for juveniles who have just lost their freedom (Glick 1998).

Most sheriffs and prison administrators do not want juveniles in their facilities. Juveniles *are different* than adults and are therefore perceived by the adult system as more difficult to manage. However, the adult system is either slow to understand the differences or slow to make changes to address these differences. This assumes, of course, that the adult system has not summarily ruled out an acknowledgement of the differences. For example, a western state medical director (a pediatrician) asked an assembly of the state's sheriffs how many calories per day they feed their jail inmates. The responses ranged from 1800 to 2500 calories per day. The pediatrician stated that when the average adolescent experiences a normal growth spurt, he or she burns more than 5000 calories per day. He then asked the sheriffs what would happen to their inmate population if they reduced the daily caloric intake by over 60 percent. Many sheriffs responded that there would be a riot; others said that their adult detainees would be irritable, cantankerous, restless, fidgety, and angry (Owens 2000). These were similar characteristics used earlier by the sheriffs to describe the behavior of the juvenile offenders in their jails.

The placement of juveniles in adult correctional facilities warrants an increase in the number of correctional officers assigned to their supervision (Godinez 1999; Gover, MacKenzie, and Armstrong 2000; Zavlek and Barron 2000). Considering the significant stress that the juvenile experiences when placed in an adult facility, constant supervision is needed to prevent major psychological damage or suicide (Godinez 1999). However, close supervision is not occurring.

The primary goal of adult corrections is the efficient management of a secure prison, not the long-term rehabilitation of the adult prisoner. The inmate's needs are subservient to the most cost-efficient ways to protect public safety. Therefore, a certain amount of intimidation and violence among inmates and between staff and inmates is tolerated, so long as the levels of harm and intimidation between inmates do not threaten a substantial breakdown of control in the facility. This is the mini-max principle; the minimum expenditure of resources for the maximum level of security.

Juvenile offenders are easy prey in the adult prison, which makes them difficult to protect both physically and mentally. Juveniles are five times more likely to be sexually assaulted and two times more likely to be beaten in prison than in a juvenile institution (National Coalition of State Juvenile Justice Advisory Groups 1992). Placement of juveniles in adult prisons is thus an act of pessimism, an acknowledgment of defeat, and a denial of hope. It does, however, satisfy Dunlap's definition of the "political id" and expresses his 3R's of contemporary politics: Revenge + Retribution = Re-election (Roush and Dunlap 1997).

Finally, there is no evidence that the adult system can rehabilitate juveniles (McMillen and Hill 1997). Placement in adult facilities does not restore the victim, the community, or the offender. It expresses no concern for the future well being of the victim, the community, or the offender. It simply reinforces the notion of "out of sight, out of mind."

Problems with Juveniles Tried in Criminal Courts

Waiving juveniles to the criminal court does not have the deterrent effect that was originally expected (Pelley 2001; Redding 1999):

1. A sentence of incarceration in prison is longer in adult court than in the juvenile court (Gross 1999). In the cases of juveniles waived for murder, those who do not receive the death penalty receive a longer sentence than those tried in juvenile court by an average of just over two years (Snyder and Sickmund 1999). Younger and younger juveniles are now being placed in adult correctional facilities (Glick 1998).

2. Waived juveniles are more likely to receive incarceration than a community sentence. Criminal courts imposed community sanctions for one out of every four juvenile offenders (Snyder and Sickmund 1999). In 1993, 77 percent of Florida juveniles in criminal court received sentences to jail (34 percent) or prison (43 percent) (Bishop, Frazier, Lanza-Kaduce, and White 1999). Redding (1999) speculates that juveniles receive more time in incarceration because criminal court judges are not as experienced with the unique problems and developmental needs of juveniles.

3. Most statutes prevent juveniles from subsequent trial in juvenile court once they qualify for a transfer to adult court. Also, as a result of a felony conviction in criminal court, they lose the right to vote and the right to serve in the military (Redding 1999).

The Ineffectiveness Myth: The Juvenile System Is Ineffective

Placement of juveniles in adult correctional facilities mistakenly presumes the failure of the juvenile justice system at a time when juvenile crime is the lowest in decades.

Yet, juvenile justice brought much of this harsh criticism upon itself. In the 1980s, politicians questioned the credibility of juvenile corrections. There was a huge gap between the public's outcry for answers to juvenile violent crime (e.g., gang violence, homicides, and drive-by shootings) and the juvenile justice community's "soft" assessment of the problem (e.g., the breakdown of the family, the hopelessness of urban poverty, and institutional overcrowding). Instead of presenting hard empirical evidence about what works and fixing what doesn't work, the juvenile justice system took a defensive and apologetic stance. This has changed dramatically in the past decade. Recent innovations and improvements in the juvenile justice system indicate that now may be the worst time to assert the ineffectiveness of juvenile justice.

The literature is replete with resources that show promising strategies in juvenile justice (American Correctional Association 1996; APA Commission on Violence and Youth 1993; Bilchik 1995b; Butts and Snyder 1992; Elliot 1998; Glick and Goldstein 1995; Howell 1995b; Rhine 1998; Roush and Wyss 1994; Sherman et al. 1997). OJJDP Administrator Shay Bilchik (1998) called the recent declines in arrests for juvenile violent crimes and murders a "promising sign." This cautious optimism belies a host of other "promising" indicators:

1. A coherent, rational, accountability-based theory of juvenile justice called the Balanced and Restorative Justice (BARJ) model (see Bazemore and Umbreit 1994, 1995; Bazemore and Washington 1995; Umbreit 1995; Umbreit and Carey 1995; Zehr 1990).

2. The dissemination of a body of scientific knowledge that guides the development of effective interventions (Altschuler and Armstrong 1995; Dobbin and Gatowski 1996; Howell 1995a, 1997; Howell et al. 1995; Leffert et al. 1996; Lipsey 1992; Loeber and Farrington 1997, 1998; Parent et al. 1994).

3. A proliferation of user-friendly resources in the areas of statistical information (Snyder and Sickmund 1995), staff training and technical assistance

(Blair et al. no date; National Training and Technical Assistance Center 1997, 1998; Roush 1996a); and specialized efforts related to disproportionate minority confinement, gangs, gender-specific programming, and crowding.

Reversing the national trends in juvenile violence, juvenile victimization, and family disintegration required both a change in national priorities and an unprecedented commitment by public and private agencies, institutions, organizations, and individuals. The juvenile justice system reform instituted in Jefferson County, Kentucky, under the leadership of U.S. Senator Mitch McConnell, then county executive, remains an excellent model of system transformation (Dunlap 1986; McConnell 1986; Roush 1996b). One of McConnell's main reform points was that "youth should not be placed in detention facilities with adults" (p. 3–4).

Again, the signs are clear that change in the juvenile justice system is happening. Research has begun to identify the obstacles to success facing youth, families, communities, agencies, and institutions (Bilchik 1998). From a logical and empirical perspective, this is the worst time in twenty years to assert that the juvenile justice system is ineffective.

Placement of juveniles in adult prisons denies the juvenile justice system an opportunity to adjust to the needs of the most violent offenders. Abandoning the goal of rehabilitation of troublesome young offenders is shortsighted and unnecessary (Carter 1997). Placement of juveniles in adult prisons ignores factors that contribute to violence, such as family dysfunction, poverty, access to hand guns, gang involvement, drug use and sales, teen pregnancy, inadequate prenatal health care, illiteracy, lack of job skills, fetal alcohol syndrome, fetal drug exposure and addiction, physical abuse, sexual abuse, emotional abuse and neglect, learning disabilities, negative peer involvement, lack of positive role models, and lack of attachments to community, school and religion (Howell, 1997).

Benefits of Cases Tried in the Juvenile Court. Juvenile court stands on a foundation that juveniles are fundamentally different from adults. It safeguards American principles of justice by addressing these differences as follows (Champion and Mays 1991):

1. Most juvenile proceedings are civil, not criminal; there is no criminal record. There is more public sympathy and less labeling for those youth processed in the juvenile court. Youth labeled as "criminal" may be more likely to adopt a life of crime (Funk and Polsby 1998; Redding 1999).

2. Juveniles tried in the juvenile court are also less likely to be placed in detention or any sort of out-of-home placement. Probation, community service, and counseling are common sentences for juveniles that do not sacrifice public safety (Champion and Mays 1991).

3. The presiding judge is an expert in juveniles, families, and their misbehaviors (Champion and Mays 1991). The juvenile court judge is the most important factor in the success of the local juvenile justice system (DeMuro and Dunlap 1999; Forrester 1999).

The Offense-Driven Decision-Making Myth: The Best Model of Justice Eliminates Discretion and Shifts the Basis for Decisions to the Nature of the Offense and Away from the Individual

Placement of juveniles in adult prisons is an outgrowth of the offense-based decision-making fallacy. Offense-based decisions eliminate the discretion needed for individual justice, a principle at the very heart of the juvenile court. Thus, in the absence of offender-based considerations, age becomes less of a factor in fairness. If this continues, there may be no need for separate juvenile systems of justice and institutions. The nationwide lowering of the age at which juveniles can be tried as adults threatens to reduce juvenile court cases to only misdemeanor charges and dependent and neglect issues (Soler 1997).

At what age do youth possess the ability and culpability to appreciate the consequences of their actions, to take responsibility for these actions, or to participate meaningfully in their defense? Steinberg (2000)

argues that juveniles usually have a general sense of right and wrong by the age of nine. However, youths under the age of 13 lack the mental capacities to be held completely accountable for their actions. By the age of 17, youths should be held fully accountable as adults for purposes of trial and incarceration.

Though age is an important factor in adjudication and sentencing, Steinberg (2000) believes that pinpointing a certain, definite age when a youth has the emotional, cognitive, and moral maturity of an adult is not possible.

Prosecutors. An offense-driven system helps prosecutors erode the distinction between juveniles and adults. If the distinction disappears, a prosecutor could charge a child of any age with an offense that carries a mandatory prison term, or life without parole.

In-depth news documentaries may be the only way for the public to understand fully the problems associated with prosecutorial transfers and incarcerating youthful offenders with adults. Most recently, *60 Minutes*, a CBS News Magazine, was very critical of these practices in a program aired in February 2001. Reporter Scott Pelley (2001) confronted a Maricopa County, Arizona, prosecutor who charged a 14-year-old with a crime punishable by 30 years in adult prison because the youth pointed an unloaded shotgun at a group of kids who had beaten him up. "In the end, I have an obligation to protect the community," prosecutor Richard Romly responded. Juvenile Court Judge William Gladstone then cited this kind of thinking as the reason why prosecutors should not be responsible for the decision of charging a juvenile as an adult. Before the end of the broadcast, Pelley noted that Romly had dropped the charges.

Judge Gladstone believes that prosecutors are too susceptible to "the hysteria whipped up by politicians after high-profile juvenile crimes." As a result, "decisions regarding youth become purely political when left in the hands of prosecutors." No one has more experience with Florida juvenile crime than William Gladstone, the senior juvenile judge and the former chief of the juvenile court in

Miami. He believes that the incarceration of juvenile offenders with adult offenders causes public safety to suffer. According to Judge Gladstone, "Instead of treating them, we put them into prisons where, of course, we make them worse and more dangerous to you and me." When asked about Florida's role as the nation's leader in juvenile transfers, Judge Gladstone responded, "Shame on us" (Pelley 2001).

An offense-based system may be acceptable for adults, but it reduces the ability to respond effectively to a juvenile's problems. An offense-based system enforces a "one-size-fits-all" strategy of decision making. It is retributive; it encourages the punishment of juveniles; and it perpetuates the dehumanizing forces by discounting individual factors. An offense-based system for juveniles further aggravates disproportionate minority confinement. It compounds the mounting empirical evidence of racial bias in the juvenile justice system (Bilchik 1999). In 1998, 7 out of 10 transfers to the criminal court were black males arrested for personal offenses (Snyder and Sickmund 1999). Black and Hispanic juveniles were more likely than whites to be transferred to criminal court for the same crimes (Steinberg 2000).

The Public Opinion Myth: The Public Favors Punishment Over Treatment for Juveniles

Advocates for placing juveniles in adult prisons often assert that it clearly reflects public opinion. A desire exists among the public that juveniles be held to the same legal standards as adults, or that they should be "treated as adults." However, when asked about "how" that treatment should be implemented, over 75 percent believe that the incarceration of a juvenile should be for rehabilitation purposes, a finding that has remained consistent over time and across jurisdictions (Schwartz 1992).

The public reacts quickly and strongly to what it learns from the electronic and print media. Public opinion seldom includes a thorough understanding of facts, and the media often perpetuates the myths about juvenile crime. As of 1998, the homicide rate for juveniles had declined by 52 percent.

However, Vincent Shiraldi of the Washington-based Justice Policy Institute reported that the coverage of juvenile homicides on ABC, CBS, and NBC evening news increased by 721 percent (Toner 2000). Also, the combined rates for serious crimes, between 1994 and 1998, declined 32 percent for youth ages 15 to 17 and 27 percent for youth 14 and under. Very young offenders get a lot of media attention, but they account for only a small, stable percentage of juvenile crime (Mendel 2000). Crime data consistently show that less than one half of one percent of all juveniles are involved in serious crime (Loeber, Farrington, Rumsey, Kerr, and Allen-Hagen 1998; Snyder and Sickmund 1997).

The media also suggests a violent crime spree in the nation's public schools. However, the numbers of people killed in schools in the last six years has declined by 50 percent. With 50 million juveniles in school, 26 died from school violence during the 1998–1999 school year. Admittedly, school violence is a terrible tragedy. But, nearly three times that number of Americans die annually by lightning (Mendel 2000).

This is the tyranny of small numbers. Many statewide arrest statistics show increases in small numbers that are reported by the media as huge percentage increases. Although increases in serious crime are unacceptable, there are many ways to report the data. Consider the following headlines. Both refer to the same change in murder data but convey an entirely different meaning: "Juvenile Murders Up 100 Percent" or "Juvenile Murders Increase by One." In both cases, the number increases from one to two murders. This manner of reporting enflames societal fears about all juvenile offenders, and it is also the logical outcome of the scapegoating of juveniles (Males 1996).

After a 1993 series of tourist killings by minority youths, the Florida Secretary of State Jim Smith stated, "We should shoot them down like the mad dogs that they are" (Frazier, Bishop, and Lanza-Kaduce 1999). Inflammatory rhetoric aggravates legislative and prosecutorial interests in public displays of "get tough" action. It also encourages media attention and officially sanctions the dehumanizing of minority youth.

Placement of juveniles in adult prisons reflects a "quitter's" mentality. Since the solution to serious juvenile crime is not a simple and "quick fix," politicians give up. By throwing all the "little bastards" in prison, do politicians believe they have solved the problem? Or is *Newsweek* correct and have we created a "prison generation" (Cose 2000)?

The 'Get Tough' Myth: A Punitive Approach Can Be Made More Effective by Increasing Its Intensity

While incarcerated in adult facilities, juveniles receive less age-appropriate rehabilitative, medical, mental health, and educational services than they would in a juvenile facility and are at far greater risk for physical or sexual abuse and suicide (Redding 1999). After spending months or years living only with criminals, juveniles incarcerated with adult offenders return home better educated in how to commit bigger crimes without being caught. Incarceration does not change much except prison bed counts and the length of death row (Arthur 2000).

Placement of juveniles in adult prisons reflects a disregard for history. History is replete with examples of how "get tough" and "scared straight" approaches fail. Classical criminology established the axiom that when sanctions are swift and certain, they need not be lengthy or severe to be effective. Is the placement of youth in prison a reflection of frustration with the inability to deliver swift and certain sanctions under the present system?

Nationally respected juvenile court judge Lindsay Arthur (2000) maintains that incarceration suppresses behavior; it does not change or improve behavior. Behavior reoccurs when the punishment is removed. Increased intensity or severity does not increase its effectiveness. Rather, punishment frequently fails to achieve the goals of retribution and revenge. Politicians increase the severity of sanctions in small increments in hopes that more punishment will solve the crime problem.

The desire to "get tough" is a thinly veiled desire to "get even." But, as Youth Law Center attorney Sue Burrell questions, who "gets even" and how is public safety protected when these young offenders come out of prison at age 25 or 30 with inadequate educational, social, and vocational skills, filled with anger and contempt for society after just having spent their formative years locked in a crowded cement box? If incarcerated juveniles do not acquire the proper skills, receive the proper education, learn the difference between right and wrong, and if they are not treated with basic dignity, they run huge risks of committing further crimes, and being jobless and a burden to society (Rosenbaum 1999).

The Ethical Fallacy: Treating Youth Like Adults Is Right

Regardless of the evils committed by serious juvenile offenders, their placement in adult prisons is wrong. Placement of juveniles in adult prisons continues the process of dehumanizing the juvenile offenders. "Those youth" and "their kind" deserve prison, in part, because they are "superpredators," "punks," the "new breed," or the "wild and savage" (c.f., Satcher 2001). In all instances, these words serve to lessen the value of human worth of youth. The more that dehumanization occurs, the easier it is to inflict punishment. Placement of juveniles in adult prisons negates the standard that a society is judged by how well it treats the least of its population; and it denies the use of youth as a resource. It is the antithesis of the positive youth development model (Brendtro, Brokenleg, and Van Bockern 1998).

Criminal justice professionals and practitioners frequently use "good versus evil" metaphors to describe the profession. In these instances, they also refer to various religious beliefs as the philosophical and spiritual justifications for their actions. However, which religion, theology, or system of values omits the forgiveness and redemption of the sinner? Which one advocates the use of malice to conquer evil?

Policy Implications

For many reasons, the direction of juvenile justice has taken some unusual turns. The movement toward a more punitive, "get tough," adult-oriented strategy culminated in the passage of statutes that waive juveniles to adult court and incarcerate them in adult correctional facilities. In many ways, juvenile justice permitted this to happen because of its silence. Juvenile justice has been remiss in establishing, stating, promulgating, and advancing its mission and vision. Moreover, it has failed to use the abundant empirical research findings to do mortal combat against the forces that think that it is beneficial to lock up youth with adult offenders. Mark Soler (1997), president of the Youth Law Center, set forth six action strategies to address the "adultification" of youth: (1) Fight fear with facts, (2) keep the danger in perspective, (3) do not let fear control behavior, (4) publicize and celebrate successes, (5) keep in mind the human face of juvenile justice, and (6) work together. Juvenile justice professionals must take a stand on these issues, and practitioners look to the professional correctional associations and organizations to articulate public policy statements that can be used to guide and direct correctional practice.

The American Correctional Association and Public Correctional Policy

The failure of the American Correctional Association (ACA) to send a consistent message to the field represents a major obstacle to preventing the incarceration of juveniles in adult prisons. University of Illinois law professor Lynn Branham (2000), a member of the ACA Commission on Accreditation for Corrections and ACA's Standards Committee, notes that the ACA Public Correctional Policy on Youthful Offenders Transferred to Adult Criminal Jurisdictions (ratified by the Delicate Assembly in January of 1999) restricts the confinement of youthful offenders to juvenile detention and juvenile corrections systems or confinement systems distinct from the adult correctional system. However, ACA refused to make this restriction meaningful by incorporating it into its accreditation standards. With no consequences for failing to comply with its official correctional policy, ACA renders its actions meaningless and undermines the credibility of the policy.

Responsible Interventions

There is a need for responsible and early interventions rather than a strengthening of punishment. Community-based early interventions, strategies common to juvenile justice, continue to demonstrate notable reductions in recidivism (Parks 2000). Many other programs reduce juvenile delinquency (Mendel 2000). These programs treat the juvenile in the home or the school; they include the family, the community, and the school; and they begin when the juvenile is demonstrating at-risk behaviors (Loeber et al. 1998). The emphasis on community-based programs is even more important following release from a juvenile court program. As Michigan State University's Professor Vince Hoffman asks juvenile justice students, "Isn't it foolhardy to treat a cancerous organ, put it back in a cancer stricken body, and believe it will stay healthy?" Is it not then equally ridiculous to treat an individual, place him or her back in the same environment, and believe that youth will remain cured?

Juveniles do not become serious violent offenders overnight. There are early signs and warning symptoms (Johnson 1999). Howell (1997) describes the case for developmental criminology, including a delineation of the "stepping stones to criminality," the "stacking" of problem behaviors, and the three pathways to problem and delinquent behaviors. The majority of serious and violent offenders start their criminal careers at an early age and typically display behavioral problems as early as seven years old (first grade) (Loeber et al. 1998). The pathways to delinquency start with behavioral problems and progress and branch through several stages, such as property offenses, conflicts with authority, and bullying, before resulting in a serious, violent offenses (Loeber et al. 1998).

Many offenders will simply "age-out" of crime (Steinberg 2000). Three significant factors associated with aging-out of crime are marriage, military service, and employment. Once the juvenile develops stakes in conformity, crime declines. Public policy should look into ways to increase this type of conformity, since most delinquent careers are relatively short-lived and generally confined to the period of adolescence and young adulthood (Brezina 2000).

Public policy should emphasize and promote parenting education or parenting skills because maltreatment has been highly correlated with crime and delinquency (Brezina 2000; Kelley, Thornberry, and Smith 1997). Attorney General Janet Reno (1998) asked why parenting skills were not as important as bilingual education. Parents, especially young or single parents, need education about the time and attention youth need and deserve (Kelly, Thornberry, and Smith 1997). Parents also need to know the problem issues and the many strategies that lower frustrations and increase patience levels with their youth. Parents also need to be educated in their youth's need for constant supervision. In the event that the parent cannot be present, some responsible adult needs to be supervising the youth (Kelley, Thornberry, and Smith 1997).

Conclusion

Certain juveniles require extensive and secure incarceration, and juvenile justice has many effective strategies to identify and intervene with these serious, violent, and chronic offenders. However, the incarceration of juveniles in adult prisons is wrong for both youth and society. Research indicates that treating juveniles as adults is more detrimental than beneficial. To give up on the juvenile justice system at a time when its accomplishments are overwhelmingly more effective than the adult criminal justice system is to (a) choose the politically expedient path over one that reflects a rational and caring society's concern for "human rights," (b) debunk and deny the same data that started the "get tough" movement, and (c) abandon, in part, the hope and value of the next generation.

This is an ethical question. Legislatures have failed to produce systems that effectively identify and transfer to adult criminal court youth who present the greatest dangers to society. Although there are, indeed, examples of just and equitable transfer decisions, the data show that these examples of success are not indicative of the vast majority of the cases. As a result, other factors, particularly race, emerge as empirically substantiated explanatory factors in waiver decisions. Waivers of youth to adult court, as currently practiced, are flawed, and the wrong youth end up in prison. It is wrong, therefore, to withhold the programs and services of the juvenile justice system because of inefficiency, color, or crime committed. The right choice calls for more attention to the individual youth when considering adult trial and incarceration. In the past, juvenile justice did just that; now, we do less when we need to do more. Archbishop Desmond Tutu (Hope for the Future 1996) articulated the ethical position when addressing our role in the futures of the most troubled and at-risk youth:

> If we don't do all we can to salvage [them], it is almost like spitting in the face of God. (p. 60)

Note

1. The term used to describe the movement of the juvenile justice system toward the adult criminal justice system (c.f., Soler 1997).

References

Altschuler, D. M., and Armstrong, T. L. 1995. "Managing Aftercare Services for Delinquents." In B. Glick and A. P. Goldstein, (eds.), *Managing Delinquency Programs That Work*. Laurel, MD: American Correctional Association.

American Correctional Association. 1996. "A Directory of Programs That Work." *Corrections Today* (August), 124–136.

APA Commission on Violence and Youth. 1993. *Violence and Youth: Psychology's Response*. Washington, DC: American Psychological Association.

Arthur, L. G. 2000. "Punishment Doesn't Work!" *Juvenile and Family Court Journal* 51(3): 37–42.

Bazemore, G., and Umbreit, M. 1994. *Balanced and Restorative Justice: Program Summary.* Washington, DC: Office of Juvenile Justice and Delinquency Prevention, U.S. Department of Justice.

——. 1995. "Rethinking the Sanctioning Function in Juvenile Court: Retributive or Restorative Responses to Youth Crime." *Crime and Delinquency* 41, 296–316.

Bazemore, G., and Washington, C. 1995. "Chartering the Future of the Juvenile Justice System: Reinventing Mission and Management." *Spectrum* Spring, 51–66.

Bilchik, S. 1995, November. *Delinquency Prevention Works: Program Summary.* Washington, DC: U.S. Department of Justice, Office of Juvenile Justice and Delinquency Prevention.

——. 1998, May. "A Juvenile Justice System for the 21st Century." *OJJDP Juvenile Justice Bulletin.* Washington, DC: U.S. Department of Justice, Office of Juvenile Justice and Delinquency Prevention.

——. 1999, December. "Minorities in the Juvenile Justice System." *OJJDP Juvenile Justice Bulletin.* Washington, DC: U.S. Department of Justice, Office of Juvenile Justice and Delinquency Prevention.

Blair, J., Collins, B., Gurnell, B., Satterfield, F., Smith, M. G., Yeres, S., and Zuercher, R. (n.d.) *Guidelines for Quality Training.* Ithaca, NY: Juvenile Justice Trainers Association.

Branham, L. S. 2000. "In Hot Water: ACA Standards on the Confinement of Youthful Offenders in Adult Correctional Facilities." *Corrections Today* (December), 16, 18, 20–21.

Brendtro, L. K., Brokenleg, M., and Van Bockern, S. 1990. *Reclaiming Youth at Risk: Our Hope for the Future.* Bloomington, IN: National Educational Service.

Brezina, T. 2000. "Delinquent Problem-Solving: An Interpretive Framework for Criminological Theory and Research." *Journal of Research in Crime and Delinquency* 37(1): 3–30.

Butts, J. A., and Snyder, H. N. 1992, September. "Restitution and Juvenile Recidivism." *OJJDP Juvenile Justice Bulletin.* Washington, DC: U.S. Department of Justice, Office of Juvenile Justice and Delinquency Prevention.

Carter, B. 1997. "Comprehensive Strategies for Juvenile Violent Offenders." *Alternatives to Incarceration* 3(6): 3.

Champion, D. 1998. *The Juvenile Justice System: Delinquency, Processing and the Law.* Upper Saddle River, NJ; Prentice Hall.

Champion, D. J., and Mays, G. L. 1991. *Transferring Juveniles to Criminal Courts: Trends and Implications for Criminal Justice.* New York: Praeger Publishers.

Coordinating Council on Juvenile Justice and Delinquency Prevention. 1996, March. *Combating Violence and Delinquency: The National Juvenile Justice Action Plan.* Washington, DC: U.S. Department of Justice, Office of Justice Programs, Office of Juvenile Justice and Delinquency Prevention.

Cose, E. 2000. "The Prison Paradox." *Newsweek,* November 13, 40–49.

DeMuro, P., and Dunlap, E. L. 1999, December. "A Reasonable Alternative to Locking Up More Kids: The Development of Jurisdictional Core Groups." In D. W. Roush, (ed.), *Crowding In Juvenile Detention Centers: Practitioner Perspectives on What to Do About It.* Richmond, KY: National Juvenile Detention Association & Youth Law Center.

Dobbin, S. A., and Gatowski, S. I. 1996. *A Guide to Research on Juvenile Violence.* Reno, NV: State Judicial Institute and the National Council of Juvenile and Family Court Judges.

Dunlap, E. L. 1986, Winter. "Perspectives on Institutional Change." *The Rader Papers: A Journal of Juvenile Detention Services* 3, 5–14.

Elliot, D. E. 1998. *What Makes a "Best Practice?" Proceedings of the 1998 Governor's Juvenile Justice Summit.* Columbus: Office of Criminal Justice Services.

Forrester, F. L. 1999, December. "Gee, Officer Krupkee!" In D. W. Roush, (ed.), *Crowding in Juvenile Detention Centers: Practitioner Perspectives on What to Do About It.* Richmond, KY: National Juvenile Detention Association & Youth Law Center.

Frazier, C. E., Bishop, D. M., and Lanza-Kaduce, L. 1999. "Get-Tough Juvenile Justice Reforms: The Florida Experience." *Annals of the American Academy of Political and Social Science* 564, 167–184.

Funk, T. M., and Polsby, D. D. 1998. "The Problem of Lemons and Why We Must Retain Juvenile Crime Records." *Cato Journal* 18(1): 75–83.

Glick, B. 1998. "Kids in Adult Correctional Systems." *Corrections Today* 60(5), 96–99.

Glick, B., and Goldstein, A. P. (eds.). 1995. *Managing Delinquency Programs That Work.* Laurel, MD: American Correctional Association.

Glick, B., Sturgeon, W., and Venator-Santiago, C. R. 1998. *No Time to Play: Youthful Offenders in Adult Correctional Systems.* Lanham, MD: American Correctional Association.

Godinez, S. 1999. "Managing Juveniles in Adult Facilities." *Corrections Today* 60(5): 96–99.

Gover, A. R., MacKenzie, D. L., and Armstrong, G. S. 2000. "Importation and Deprivation Explanations of Juveniles' Adjustment to Correctional Facilities." *International Journal of Offender Therapy and Comparative Criminology* 44(4), 450–467.

Gross, B. H. 1999. "The Fitness of Juvenile Court." *Journal of Forensic Sciences* 44(6): 1199–1203.

"Hope For the Future: An Interview With Archbishop Desmond Tutu." 1996. *Reaching Today's Youth*, Fall, 58–60.

Howell, J. C. 1995a. "A National Perspective." In B. Glick and A. P. Goldstein, (eds.), *Managing Delinquency Programs That Work*. Laurel, MD: American Correctional Association.

Howell, J. C. (ed.). 1995b, May. *A Guide to Implementing the Comprehensive Strategy for Serious, Violent, and Chronic Juvenile Offenders*. Washington, DC: U.S. Department of Justice, Office of Justice Programs, Office of Juvenile Justice and Delinquency Prevention.

———. 1997. *Juvenile Justice and Youth Violence*. Thousand Oaks, CA: Sage.

Howell, J. C., Krisberg, B., Hawkins, J. D., and Wilson J. J. (eds.). 1995. *Serious, Violent, and Chronic Juvenile Offenders: A Sourcebook*. Thousand Oaks, CA: Sage.

Jepsen, B. 1998. *Supervising Youthful Offenders* (Correspondence course). Lanham, MD: American Correctional Association.

Johnson, D. 1999. "Rehabilitating Criminals Before They Grow Up." *The Futurist* 33(10): 11–12.

Kelly, B. T., Thornberry, T. P., and Smith, C. A. 1997, August. "In the Wake of Childhood Maltreatment." *OJJDP Juvenile Justice Bulletin*. Washington, DC: U.S. Department of Justice, Office of Juvenile Justice and Delinquency Prevention.

Leffert, N., Saito, R. N., Blyth, D. A., and Kroenke, C. H. 1996. *Making the Case: Measuring the Impact of Youth Development Programs*. Minneapolis: The Search Institute.

Lipsey, M. W. 1992. "Juvenile Delinquency Treatment: A Meta-Analytic Inquiry Into the Variability of Effects." In T. D. Cook, et al. *Meta-Analysis for Explanation: A Casebook*. New York: Russell Sage Foundation.

Loeber, R., and Farrington, D. P. (eds.). 1997. *Never Too Early, Never Too Late: Risk Factors and Successful Interventions for Serious and Violent Juvenile Offenders* (Final Report of the Study Group on Serious and Violent Juvenile Offenders). Washington, DC: U.S. Department of Justice, Office of Justice Programs, Office of Juvenile Justice and Delinquency Prevention.

Loeber, R., and Farrington, D. P. (eds.). 1998. *Serious and Violent Juvenile Offenders: Risk Factors and Successful Interventions*. Thousand Oaks, CA: Sage.

Loeber, R., Farrington, D. P., Rumsey, E., Kerr, C. A., and Allen-Hagen, B. (eds.). 1998, May. "Serious and Violent Juvenile Offenders." *OJJDP Juvenile Justice Bulletin*. Washington, DC: U.S. Department of Justice, Office of Justice Programs, Office of Juvenile Justice and Delinquency Prevention.

Males, M. 1996. *The Scapegoat Generation: America's War on Adolescents*. Common Courage Press.

McConnell, M. 1986, Winter. Keynote address. *The Rader Papers: A Journal of Juvenile Detention Services* 3, 3–4.

McMillen, M. J., and Hill, J. 1997. "Jadults and Adulniles: Housing the New Breed of Youthful Offender." *Corrections Today* 59(2): 100–104.

Mendel, R. A. 2000. *Less Hype, More Help: Reducing Juvenile Crime, What Works—and What Doesn't*. Washington, DC: American Youth Policy Forum.

National Coalition of State Juvenile Justice Advisory Groups. 1993. *Myths and Realities: Meeting the Challenge of Serious, Violent, and Chronic Juvenile Offenders*. (1992 Annual Report to the President, the Congress, and the Administrator of OJJDP). Washington, DC: Author.

National Commission on Correctional Health Care. 1998, Spring. "Position Statement: Health Services to Adolescents in Adult Correctional Facilities." *Journal of Correctional Health Care* 5, 113–117.

National Training and Technical Assistance Center. 1997. *Training and Technical Assistance Resource Catalog*. Washington, DC: U.S. Department of Justice, Office of Justice Programs, Office of Juvenile Justice and Delinquency Prevention.

———. 1998. *OJJDP Training and Technical Assistance Protocols: A Primer for OJJDP Training and Technical Assistance Providers*. Washington, DC: U.S. Department of Justice, Office of Justice Programs, Office of Juvenile Justice and Delinquency Prevention.

Owens, Jim, Doctor of Medicine, personal communication.

Parent, D., Leiter, V., Kennedy, S., Livens, L., Wentworth, D., and Wilcox, S. 1994, April. *Conditions of Confinement: Juvenile Detention and Corrections Facilities* (Research report). Washington, DC: Office of Juvenile Justice and Delinquency Prevention.

Parks, G. 2000, October. "High/Scope Perry Pre-school Project." *OJJDP Juvenile Justice Bulletin*. Washington, DC: U.S. Department of Justice, Office of Justice Programs, Office of Juvenile Justice and Delinquency Prevention.

Pelley, S. 2001. "Adult Time: More Teens Are Serving Time in Adult Prisons." *60 Minutes II*, February 6. New York: CBS Worldwide Inc. (Transcript by Burrelle's Information Services).

Redding, R. E. 1999. "Examining Legal Issues: Juvenile Offenders in Criminal Court and Adult Prison." *Corrections Today* 61(2): 92–95+.

Reno, J. 1998. "Taking America Back for Our Children." *Crime and Delinquency* 44(1): 75–82.

Rhine, E. (ed.). 1998. *Best Practices: Excellence in Corrections*. Lanham, MD: American Correctional Association.

Rosenbaum, S. H. 1999. "Civil Rights Issues in Juvenile Detention and Correctional Systems." *Corrections Today* 61(6): 148–156.

Roush, D. W. 1996a, April-June. "A Comprehensive Strategy for Implementing the NJDA Careworker Training Curriculum." *JERITT Bulletin* 7(2): 1–4.

——. 1996b. "Chapter 3: A Juvenile Justice Perspective." In C. M. Nelson, R. B. Rutherford, and B. I. Wolford, (eds.), *Comprehensive and Collaborative Systems That Work for Troubled Youth: A National Agenda*. Richmond, KY: National Juvenile Detention Association.

Roush, D. W., and Dunlap, E. L. 1997. "Juveniles in Adult Prisons: A Very Bad Idea." *Corrections Today* June, 21.

Roush, D. W., and Wyss, T. (eds.). 1994, August. *Effective and Innovative Programs: Resource Manual*. Washington, DC: U.S. Department of Justice, Office of Juvenile Justice and Delinquency Prevention.

Satcher, D. 2001, January. *Youth Violence: A Report of the Surgeon General*. Washington, DC: Department of Health and Human Services, Office of the Surgeon General. <http://www.surgeongeneral.gov/library/youthviolence.htm>

Schwartz, I. M. 1992. "Juvenile Crime-Fighting Policies: What the Public Really Wants." In I. M. Schwartz (ed.), *Juvenile Justice and Public Policy: Toward a National Agenda*. New York: Lexington Books.

Sherman, L. W., Gottfredson, D., MacKenzie, D., Eck, J., Reuter, P., and Bushway, S. 1997. *Preventing Crime: What Works, What Doesn't, What's Promising*. Washington, DC: U.S. Department of Justice, Office of Justice Programs.

Smith, J. S. 1996. "Adolescent Development." In D. W. Roush (ed.), *Desktop Guide to Good Juvenile Detention Practice*. Washington, DC: U.S. Department of Justice, Office of Juvenile Justice and Delinquency Prevention.

Snyder, H. N., and Sickmund, M. 1999. *Juvenile Offenders and Victims: 1999 National Report*. Washington, DC: U.S. Department of Justice, Office of Justice Programs, Office of Juvenile Justice and Delinquency Prevention.

Snyder, H. N., Sickmund, M, and Poe-Yamagata, E. 1996. *Juvenile Offenders and Victims: 1996 Update on Violence: Statistics Summary*. Washington, DC: U.S. Department of Justice, Office of Justice Programs, Office of Juvenile Justice and Delinquency Prevention.

——. 2000, August. *Juvenile Transfers to Criminal Court in the 1990s: Lesson Learned from Four Studies*. Washington, DC: U.S. Department of Justice, Office of Justice Programs, Office of Juvenile Justice and Delinquency Prevention.

Soler, M. I. 1997. "The Changing Faces of Juvenile Offenders: Meeting the Challenges of the Adultification of Juvenile Detention and Corrections." *Journal for Juvenile Justice and Detention Services* 12, 38–44.

Steinberg, L. 2000. "Should Juvenile Offenders Be Tried as Adults?" *Joint Center for Poverty Research*2(3).

Thomas, C. W., and Bilchik, S. 1985. "Prosecuting Juveniles In Criminal Courts: A Legal and Empirical Analysis." *The Journal of Criminal Law and Criminology* 76, 439–479.

Toner, M. J. 2000. "Telling Our Stories in Juvenile Court." *Juvenile and Family Justice Today* 8, 10–11.

Umbreit, M. 1995. "Holding Juvenile Offenders Accountable: A Restorative Justice Perspective." *Juvenile and Family Court Journal* 46, 31–42.

Umbreit, M., and Carey, M. 1995. "Restorative Justice: Implications for Organizational Change." *Federal Probation* 59(1): 47–54.

Zavlek, S. and Barron, D. D. 2000. "Teamwork: National Workshop Addresses Planning Strategies for Juvenile Justice System." *Corrections Today* December, 145–151.

Zehr, Howard. 1990. *Changing Lenses*. Scottdale, PA: Herald Press.

ISSUE XVI
Megan's Law: Should Neighbors Be Notified When a Sex Offender Is Released Into Their Community?

Imagine that you have just received a flyer informing you that a sex offender has moved into your neighborhood and lives only three blocks away. Is this something you need to be concerned about?

In 1990 Washington became the first state to require that all sex offenders register with local law enforcement agencies; other states subsequently followed suit. These are the first formal attempts to require that offenders make their whereabouts known for years after they have completed their sentences, on the basis of the type of offense they committed. At this time, no other types of offenders are required to register. This seems to indicate that the due process rights of sex offenders are a low public priority (Gallagher 1997). Sex offender registration statutes were initially enacted with the goals of enabling parents to protect their children's safety and to improve the ability of police to investigate future sex crimes. These statutes came to be known as "Megan's Law"—named after one of the children who was brutally victimized by a repeat sex offender (Finn 1997). The basis for the law also includes a characteristic of sex offenders— their persistence in the behaviors.

All fifty states now require that sex offenders (on or off correctional supervision) register annually with the local authorities, usually within one month after release from prison. Some states, such as Missouri, have expanded the sex offender registration law to include convicted misdemeanor sex offenders. The registration must continue for a period of 10 years, and some states require annual registration indefinitely. Sex offenders, both adult and some juveniles, must provide name, address, date of birth, social security number, vehicle registration, place of employment, fingerprints, and a recent photo. Some states also collect blood or DNA samples. The constitutionality of the public's notification via the Internet has been upheld by federal court as long as public access is restricted to people who are likely to encounter the offender (Oakes 1999).

Because sex offenders pose different levels of risk to the community depending on the nature and prevalence of their crimes, three risk levels exist. In many states, an offender is classified as fitting into one of the levels, and the higher the risk, the more proactive and extensive the notification guidelines. Higher risk levels typically permit proactive dissemination of information about the offender (knocking on doors, flyers, etc.). Information about lower-risk sex offenders will be shared only in response to individuals who initiate contact with their local police department or to agencies, such as child care centers, schools, and summer camps (Campbell 1995).

Authors on both sides of the issue acknowledge that community notification is not a panacea for solving or eliminating sex offenses. Mary Ann Farkas asserts that community notification of sex offenders is a good idea because it will raise community

awareness of sex offenders who live nearby
and assist police in solving future sex offenses if they do occur. Furthermore, some
sex offenders will be inhibited from future
sex offenses if others are aware, and this will
further assist the offender in taking responsibility for his or her crimes. Community notification will help educate the public about
the nature of sex crimes.

Lisa L. Sample and Anthony J. Streveler
argue against community notification. They
believe it provides a false sense of safety and
also ignores sex offenders who have not yet
been detected by the criminal justice system.
Since many sex offenders are family members known to the victim, these laws may discourage victims from reporting the crime if
they know that their family member will be
exposed to the whole community. Sample
and Streveler also predict that notification
laws will do little to deter future sex offenses—crime will be displaced to areas
where the identity of the sex offender is unknown. A willing sex offender will simply
drive farther from home to commit a crime.

References

Campbell, Sheila A. 1995. "Battling Sex Offenders: Is Megan's Law an Effective Means of
Achieving Public Safety?" *Seton Hall Legislative Journal* 19: 519–563.

Finn, Peter. 1997. *Sex Offender Community Notification*. Washington DC: National Institute of
Justice.

Gallagher, Brian D. 1997. "Now That We Know
Where They Are, What Do We Do with Them?:
The Placement of Sex Offenders in the Age of
Megan's Law." *Widener Journal of Public Law*
7: 39–85.

Oakes, Susan. 1999. "Comment: Megan's Law:
Analysis on Whether it is Constitutional to
Notify the Public of Sex Offenders Via the
Internet." *The John Marshall Journal of Com-
puter and Information Law* 17: 1133.

Critical Thinking Questions

1. What assumptions (correct or incorrect) do sex offender notification laws
make about the notion of sex offending
relative to: (a) victim/offender relationships, and (b) where and when the offenses occur?

2. Will sex offender notification laws increase or decrease the rate at which sex
offenses are now reported to the police?
Why?

3. Will sex offender notification laws displace sex crimes (meaning, will sex offenders commit crimes in a different location)? Why or why not?

4. Should notification statutes be expanded for other types of crimes? If so,
which ones? If not, why not?

Internet Websites

Adams, Devon. 1999. *Summary of State Sex Offender Dissemination Procedures*. Washington, DC: U.S. Dept. of Justice. <http://
www.ojp.usdoj.gov/bjs/pub/pdf/sssorst.pdf>

Center for Sex Offender Management. <Wysi-
wyg://19/http://www.csom.org>

National Center for Missing and Exploited
Children. <http://www.missingkids.org>

NOTE: The following websites originate
from the State Database Registry Website
<http://www.sexoffender.com> to pro-
vide states that maintain a database or
provide information on how to obtain
registry information.

Alabama <http://www.gsiweb.net/so_doc/so_in-
dex_new.html>

Alaska <http://www.dps.state.ak.us/nsorcr/asp/>

Arizona <http://www.azsexoffender.com>

Arkansas <http://www.acic.org/registration/reg-
istration-main.html>

Connecticut <http://www.state.ct.us/dps/
Sor.htm>

Delaware <http://www.state.de.us/dsp/sexoff/in-
dex.htm>

Florida <http://www.fdle.state.fl.us/sexual_pred-
ators>

Georgia <http://www.ganet.org/gbi/sorsch.cgi>

Guam <http://jisweb.justice.gov.gu/sor/>

Idaho <http://www.isp.state.id.us/htmldocs/reg-
istry.html>

Illinois <http://samnet.isp.state.il.us/ispso2/sex_
offenders/frames.htm>

Indiana <http://www.state.in.us/serv/cji_sor>

Iowa <http://www.iowasexoffender.com/de-
fault.asp>

Kansas <http://www.ink.org/public/kbi/
kbiregoffpage.html>

Kentucky <http://kspsor.state.ky.us/>

Louisiana <http://www.lasocpr.lsp.org/socpr/>

Maryland <http://www.dpscs.state.md.us/sor/>

Michigan <http://www.mipsor.state.mi.us>

Minnesota <http://www.dps.state.mn.us/bca/invest/documents/page-07.html>

Mississippi <http://www.sor.mdps.state.ms.us>

Montana <http://svor2.doj.state.mt.us:8010/index.htm>

Nebraska <http://www.nsp.state.ne.us/sor/find.cfm>

Nevada <http://www.state.nv.us/ag/agpub/offender.htm>

New Mexico <http://www.nmsexoffender.dps.state.nm.us/servlet/hit_serv.class>

New York <http://criminaljustice.state.ny.us/nsor/index.htm>

North Carolina <http://sbi.jus.state.nc.us/sor/maintext.htm>

Ohio <http://www.drc.state.oh.us/cfdocs/inmate/search.htm>

South Carolina <http://www.sled.state.sc.us/sled/default.asp?Category=SCSO&Service=SCSO_01>

Tennessee <http://www.ticic.state.tn.us/sex_ofndr/search_short.asp>

Texas <http://records.txdps.state.tx.us/so_search.cfm>

Utah <http://www.udc.state.ut.us/asp-bin/sexoffendersearchform.asp>

Vermont <http://www.dps.state.vt.us/cjs/s_registry.htm>

Virginia <http://sex-offender.vsp.state.va.us/static/search.htm>

West Virginia <http://www.wvstatepolice.com/sexoff/>

Wisconsin <http://www.wi-doc.com/offender.htm>

Wyoming <http://www.state.wy.us/~ag/dci/so/so_registration.html>

The following states do *not* maintain an on-line sex offender registry or information about how to access information: California, Colorado, District of Columbia, Maine, Massachusetts, Missouri, New Hampshire, New Jersey, North Dakota, Oklahoma, Oregon, Pennsylvania, Puerto Rico, Rhode Island, South Dakota, Virgin Islands, Washington. (Hawaii is off-line per the state government.) ✦

31
Community Notification

A Valuable Strategy for Managing Sex Offenders in the Community

Mary Ann Farkas

On July 30, 1994, the body of seven-year-old Megan Kanka was found in a wooded area in a New Jersey park. She had been raped, beaten, and murdered. The perpetrator was a twice-convicted sex offender named Jesse Timmendequas. He had been previously convicted of sexually assaulting a five-year-old girl and later a seven-year-old girl. Timmendequas lived across the street from Megan with two other convicted pedophiles. He had apparently lured Megan into his house with the promise of seeing his puppy. One of the most disturbing aspects of the case was how these three convicted sex offenders could live anonymously in a neighborhood filled with families and their children. None of the residents in that neighborhood knew about the sex offender trio living in close proximity.

What happened to Megan touched a nation and fueled a movement calling for the public notification of sex offenders. The community agonized over the question of whether Megan Kanka would be alive today had her parents been armed with the vital information that three sex offenders lived across the street. Just three months after the body of Megan Kanka was found, Governor Christine Todd Whitman signed "Megan's Law." Although the state of Washington was the first to pass a notification law in its Community Protection Act of 1990, community notification laws came to be known collectively as "Megan's laws." In 1994, Congress passed the Jacob Wetterling Act (Title XVII of the Federal Violent Crime Control and Law Enforcement Act of 1994) mandating states to establish registries for offenders convicted of sexually violent crimes or crimes against children (Matson and Lieb 1997, 3). The act was later amended in May 1996 with a community or public notification provision.

Under these provisions, states were afforded the discretion to determine if disclosure information about a specific person required to register is necessary for public protection. Three types of notification are used by states: (1) broad community notification, (2) notification to individuals and organizations at risk, and (3) access to registration information (Matson and Lieb 1997). Broad notification is the broad dissemination of relevant information to the public regarding designated sex offenders. In some states, this applies to all sex offenders convicted of specific offenses with no discretion used by public officials. Other states use notification based on potential risk that the sex offender may recidivate, or return to criminal behavior. Notification to individuals and organizations at risk concerns the release of information based on a *need to protect an individual or vulnerable organization*, such as a child care facility or public school, from a specific sex offender. Local law enforcement generally makes this determination. The third notification type, access to registration information, allows access to information by citizens or community organizations through local law enforcement.

In some states, all sex offenders convicted of certain offenses are eligible for notification. Many other states, though, rely on a three-tiered system for releasing information on sex offenders based upon the amount of risk the offender poses to the community (Farkas and Zevitz 2000).

That system is summarized as follows:

Level I: Limited to Law Enforcement—Offenders are assessed to present minimal risk with no aggravating factors. Information is maintained within the police department and disseminated to other appropriate law enforcement agencies.

Level II: Targeted Notification—Individuals who present a moderate number of aggravating factors and/or equal number of mitigating factors. Notification is beyond law enforcement, but limited and targeted to specific groups and organizations including schools, day care providers, and neighborhood organizations. These groups are responsible for dissemination to their constituents.

Level III: Expanded Notification—Highest level of notification, which includes those individuals who present a significant number of aggravating factors. Methods of expanded notification include door-to-door notification, informing the public through specific media releases, and conducting community meetings.

The three-tiered system used in sex offender community notification is "intended to provide a reasonably valid method for using critical data that will result in acceptably accurate predictions" (Brooks 1996, 61). However, this classification scheme has been criticized because it is based on predictions of risk. Steinbock (1995) claims that it is difficult to predict which sex offenders will reoffend and which ones will not. Methods for reoffense predictions, though, have become far more accurate with the use of actuarial methods (Quinsey, Rice, and Harris 1995).

Actuarial assessments offer the most empirically valid way to classify offenders according to risk. Criteria can be set in such a manner that the most dangerous sex offenders can be identified as dangerous with very few false positives (i.e., persons incorrectly identified as dangerous). (Harris, Rice, and Quinsey 1989, 107)

The community notification laws themselves have also raised numerous constitutional challenges. My position is not to debate the legality or, constitutionality of Megan's Law, which is a task for legal schol-

ars, but rather, to argue for the right of the public to know about a serious potential risk to its safety and the safety of its children. The critical issue is whether the public should be notified of a sex offender in the community who has been convicted of a repeat offense, an offense involving a child, or an offense involving the use of force. "The solution of the past, of releasing sex offenders quietly and hoping for the best, has been tried, with imperfect and sometimes terrible consequences" (Lieb 1996, 300). In essence, notification is actually a response to the failure of other efforts, such as treatment and incarceration, as a long-term strategy to manage sex offenders (Simon 1998, 461).

The appeal of community notification as a solution is evident in the fact that it took only twenty-two months for the federal government and all fifty states to pass a version of Megan's Law (Gallagher 1997). Notification laws are indicative of the views of society toward sex offenders who use coercion and manipulation to violate and defile their victims. The philosophical meaning of notification is that it defines the boundaries of behavior for society and declares what conduct society will tolerate. The molestation of children, in particular, draws the condemnation of society. Denouncing sex offenders satisfies the community's social and emotional need to define itself in a way to exclude these offenders (Telpner 1997). Community notification also lessens the fear that what happened to Megan Kanka could happen in other communities. "Whatever the real levels of risk may be of becoming a crime victim, particularly, a victim of a sex crime, risk and its attendant fear become all encompassing and begin to order the conduct of one's ordinary life" (Pratt 2000, 148). So in a very real sense, notification is more about the community, its values and its sense of safety than about sex offenders.

Notification laws inform the public about the presence of a sex offender in the community so that neighbors are able to use this information to take protective action for the safety of themselves and their children. Although some sex offenders choose their victims indiscriminately, most others select a victim who meets their criteria of attractiveness and who is available and vulnerable. Although sex offenders have strong urges for a particular type of victim, they do not victimize in every instance in which they encounter potential victims (Garafalo 1987). That is, other aspects of the situation must be conducive to offending. For example, sex offenders must believe that they can complete the crime successfully with a minimal amount of risk of being detected (Garafalo 1987, 28). The victim must be accessible and vulnerable, such as a young child who is left in the offender's care. Both the child and the parents need to trust the offender. The sex offender must groom the guardian in order to win trust and have access to the child. Foremost, the offenses usually occur at times and places in which guardians are absent and unable to intervene (Felson 1997). Thus, the chance to be alone with the child in a private setting and to physically touch the child provides the opportunity for the victimization.

Public notification of sex offenders inhibits their opportunities for offending, particularly for offenders classified as Level III. These offenders are subject to expanded notification, which means the entire community may be notified, and that is likely to impact heavily on the sex offenders (Brooks 1995, 13). They can no longer hide behind a cloak of anonymity and groom children and parents for their intended sexual victimization. Offenders who victimize children have a known proclivity to assume occupational and volunteer positions that involve contact with children. Because of their notoriety, these offenders are prevented from access to child victims in organized children's groups and schools or places where children congregate. Public notification identifies a person's past behavior and *modus operandi,* which may introduce an external control or obstacle in the way of further offending. Having one's behavior watched closely and the fear of "getting caught" weighs heavily in the calculus of whether to offend or reoffend. Notification may provide the external control necessary to inhibit or control the sexual urges and impulses. Both compulsive and opportunistic sex offenders are keenly sensitive to external controls (Herman 1990, 188).

Evidence suggests that sex offenders are substantially more likely than other violent offenders to be rearrested for a new violent sexual offense (Greenfeld 1997). Those with multiple prior sex offense convictions are at relatively high risk to reoffend (Quinsey, Rice, and Harris 1995). Recidivism rates for repeat offenders have been estimated between 33 percent to 71 percent, whereas for first offenders the rates were 10 percent to 21 percent (Marshall, Jones, Ward, Johnston, and Barbaree 1991). And, it is important to bear in mind that most measures of recidivism underrepresent the true offense rates of sex offenders because of the need to rely on arrest and conviction rates for sex offenses (Furby, Weinrott, and Blackshaw 1989). Sex offenses are seriously underreported and sex offenders may commit several offenses prior to "getting caught." In short, we may not even have an accurate representation of the rate of sex offending in our society.

In treatment, sex offenders learn to identify their deviant thought patterns, cognitive distortions, and offense precursors. They learn to develop internal controls over risk situations. Nonetheless, Herman (1990) asserts that one cannot assume that a sex offender has any reliable internal motivation for change. Sex offenders are known to deceive and manipulate, and this must always be a consideration. She contends that external motivation for change must be provided.

Critics of community notification express the concern that it may be antitherapeutic and interfere with treatment. However, not all treatment will work for all sex offenders. For some, no treatment will be effective. They may have a compulsion to offend and are incapable of self-control. For example: studies of humanistic and psychodynamic treatments show no reduction in sexual offending by rapists and child molesters (Harris, Rice, and Quinsey 1998). Similarly, the effectiveness of cognitive-behavioral treatment for sex offenders has yet to be demonstrated (Furby, Weinrott, and Blackshaw 1989; Quinsey, Harris, Rice, and Lalumiere 1993). The use of drugs combined with treatment shows reoffense rates are lower among child molesters (Harris, Rice, and Quinsey 1998), yet the success of the drug treatment is dependent on the ongoing medication compliance of the sex offenders (Becker and Murphy 1998).

Pullen and English (1996) state that *"the immense value* of the community notification law is that the *threat* of notification can act as a catalyst for sex offenders to actively participate in treatment, remain employed, and comply with the special conditions of their supervision." Notification may enhance an offender's internal control. In a study by Zevitz and Farkas (2000a), one sex offender reported that community notification furthered his progress in treatment by helping him to fully understand and take responsibility for his offense, while another offender stressed how it facilitated openness and honesty in treatment. Other research has found that sex offenders who were previously resistant to treatment acknowledged their deviant behavior and attended and worked harder in treatment in order to demonstrate that they did not need to be subjected to notification (Finn 1997, 12). The threat of notification may be the greatest contribution as a tool for managing sex offenders in the community (Pullen and English 1996).

Community notification of sex offenders also augments police surveillance, making it more difficult for the sex offender "to escape into anonymity under hundreds of watchful eyes" (Bedarf 1995, 906). Law enforcement's efforts to protect communities, conduct investigations, and quickly apprehend sex offenders is enhanced by information supplied by community residents. Public safety is improved when citizens are able to identify and report risky behaviors by sex offenders that might escalate into criminal behavior if ignored (Finn 1997, 2). The risks that their offending behavior will be detected is increased substantially (Zevitz and Farkas 2000b). Neighbors are more likely to observe and then notify law enforcement and corrections authorities of suspected violations or suspicious behavior. Megan's laws reflect a new involvement of the public in the process of social control by enlisting community members to be a part of the supervision network to manage the behavior of sex offenders (Zevitz and Farkas 2000b). Thus, notifi-

cation empowers the community to avert the risk of future victimization by these known sex offenders.

Another benefit of community notification is its important education component. Mailings and community notification meetings have been used by law enforcement and corrections not only to alert the public to a specific sex offender, but also to educate about the nature of sex offending. Knowing the predatory behaviors of the sex offenders allows individuals to assess their lifestyle, behaviors, and associates for situations that make them or their children more vulnerable. It alerts the community to be more careful in interactions that may avert the risk of future victimization. Families look at the description of the sexual offense (e.g., a babysitter molesting his charge) and become more cognizant of just who is watching their child. Everyone is informed of *known* offenders and further cautioned to be vigilant concerning inappropriate or suspicious behavior from offenders not yet identified. The community receives the critical information that most sexual victimization is perpetrated by individuals *familiar* to the victims. Parents are encouraged to teach their children general safety rules, such as always informing them where they are going and asking permission first.

Criticisms of notification surround its core tenet—community protection. Opponents question the effect of notification on sex offending. Only one study has actually examined this issue. Schram and Milloy (1995) compared the number of arrests for new sex offenses among 90 sex offenders who had experienced community notification with arrests for sex offenses among 90 offenders not subject to notification over a 54-month period. They found no statistically significant difference in the arrest rates for sex offenses between the two groups; however, findings indicated that notification had an effect on the duration between the next arrest for any type of offense. In other words, sex offenders subject to notification were arrested for new crimes much more quickly than offenders not subject to notification (Finn 1997, 11). This suggests that notification, with its attendant surveillance and intensive supervision of sex offenders, may result in offenders' behavior being more closely watched, and thus serve a critical law enforcement function.

Steinbock (1995) argues that notification laws focus on only a tiny percentage of those who commit sex crimes against children—dangerous strangers. Moreover, she believes that the laws fail to protect children from the most common type of sexual abuse—that which is inflicted by friends and relatives. Notification targets all types of sex offenders based on risk factors. The sex offenders who she refers to are the dangerous, repeat sex offenders classified as risk level three, the highest level of notification. Prior to the notification laws, there was NO mechanism to alert the public to the reentry of these high risk individuals. We now have access to vital information that can protect the safety of our children. And to the extent that treatment and incarceration have failed to reduce recidivism, external forms of control, including notification and supervision, are added to our arsenal of solutions.

The notification provision of the law also gives the criminal justice system another option than simply releasing these individuals back into the community to further victimize. Criminal justice agents have a means to register and track sex offenders. They can increase their powers of surveillance with the help of an alert, informed public. Collaboration, increased communication, and information sharing among criminal justice agencies are also fostered, which furthers the goals of surveillance and management of sex offenders in the community. Law enforcement, corrections, and other agencies collaborate to review, plan, and make decisions regarding the extent of notification, as well as to plan and conduct community notification meetings if expanded notification is chosen (Farkas and Zevitz 2000). Studies on the effect of community notification on law enforcement and corrections have reported enhanced community surveillance of sex offenders due to this collaboration among criminal justice agencies (Matson and Lieb 1996; Zevitz and Farkas 2000c, Farkas and Zevitz 2000).

Another concern with notification is that it will incite widespread vigilantism. The fear is that citizens will rise up against the sex offenders and harass or harm them. There is no empirical data to support this. Studies in New Jersey, Oregon, Washington, and Wisconsin reported only a small percentage of notification cases that resulted in harassment of the offender (Matson and Lieb 1997; Zevitz and Farkas 2000a). Even with many cases of notification, the incidence of harassment is minimal. And only a very few cases of harassment involved extreme behavior. In their study, Matson and Lieb (1997) reported a sex offender threatened at gunpoint, another sex offender's tires slashed, and threats of arson to the house of still another sex offender. One case, however, is typically used to point out the inflammatory nature of notification. A sex offender had his house burned down to the ground. This incident occurred in the first year that the Washington law was passed. Since then, law enforcement has learned how to notify people in a less provocative manner and the public has learned that if they *abuse* the law, they will *lose* the law. Notification laws typically contain a penalty provision for anyone who harasses or in any other way harms a sex offender.

Longer prison terms and lifetime supervision on parole have been suggested as alternatives that would eliminate the need for public notification of sex offenders. The average time served for rape is five years and for sexual assault just under three years (Greenfeld 1997). Despite the "get tough" legal and public policies toward sex offenders, the actual reality is that sex offenders really do not serve long sentences in prison. The likelihood of them serving longer terms does not seem probable because of the expense and overcrowding in our correctional system. In any case, the concept of longer sentences for sex offenders is riddled with dubious assumptions. First, there is an assumption that a long prison term will somehow change the offenders and that they will come out different than when they went in. Does a longer prison term necessarily translate into less risk? Even presuming that a person undergoes sex offender treatment, this doesn't guarantee "rehabilitation." Would he or she remain in sex offender treatment for the full length of a term, and would this even be effective? Hence, the prison term is only a temporary solution postponing the inevitable, the release of the sex offender from prison into the community—then what?

Lifetime supervision with sex offenders under the supervision of a probation/parole agent with a small caseload is another proposed alternative. Yet, community corrections is stretched beyond its capacity, having over 3.9 million offenders on probation or parole (Bureau of Justice Studies 1997). With increasing numbers of sex offenders being released from prison, how likely is it that correction caseloads will grow smaller? And how likely is it that supervision of sex offenders will remain close and intense for a *lifetime?*

In closing, is sex offender community notification the panacea for the complicated social problem of sex offending? No. It is only one tool in managing and controlling the behavior of convicted sex offenders returning to the community. Legal and public policy regarding sex offenders must allow for a comprehensive plan of community supervision and treatment. English (1998) calls for a "containment approach," which involves control of the sex offender's behavior through supervision and surveillance, sex-offense–specific therapy for the offender, and polygraph examinations. "Notification becomes one more tool along with curfews, the polygraph, and special restrictions to manage sex offenders in community settings" (Pullen and English 1996, 5). Community notification is therefore a valuable strategy of surveillance and a source of information for both corrections and law enforcement.

Notification creates social awareness and cohesiveness surrounding a threat to community safety. It empowers citizens to be active participants in protecting themselves and their children from an identified threat. It also helps the community protect their children through the awareness that children are victimized most often by *known* perpetrators. The public education efforts

incorporated into notification programs have also helped the community in this realization. In the final analysis, the true value of community notification may lie more in its effect on the community than on the criminal (Telpner 1997).

References

Becker and Murphy, W. D. 1998. "What We Know About Assessing and Treating Sex Offenders." *Psychology, Public Policy and Law* 4(1/2): 116–137.

Bedarf, A. 1995. "Examining Sex Offender Community Notification Laws." *California Law Review* 83(3): 885–939.

Brooks, A. D. 1995. "Megan's Law: The Legal Issues." *Criminal Justice Ethics* 14(2): 12–16.

——. 1996. "Megan's Law: Constitutionality and Policy." *Criminal Justice Ethics* 15(1): 56–67.

Bureau of Justice Statistics. 1997. *Corrections Populations in the United States.* Washington, DC: U.S. Department of Justice.

English, K. 1998. "The Containment Approach: An Aggressive Strategy for the Community Management of Adult Sex Offenders." *Psychology, Public Policy, and Law* 4(1/2): 218–235.

Farkas, M. A. and Zevitz, R. 2000. "Sex Offender Community Notification: Assessing the Impact on Law Enforcement: A Research Note." *Journal of Crime and Justice* 23(1): 125–139.

Federal Violent Crime Control and Law Enforcement Act of 1994, Pub. L. No. 103–322, §170101 (f)(2)(A) and §170101 (d)(3), U.S.C.C.A.N. (108 Stat.) 1796, 20380–42.

Felson, R. B. 1997. "Routine Activities and Involvement In Violence as Actor, Witness or Target." Violence and Victims,*12(3), 209-222.

Finn, P. (1997). *Sex Offender Community Notification. National Institute of Justice: Research in Action,* 1–19.

Furby, L., Weinrott, M. R., and Blackshaw, L. 1989. "Sex Offender Recidivism: A Review." *Psychological Bulletin* 105, 3–30.

Gallagher, B. D. 1997. "Now That We Know Where They Are, What Are We to Do With Them? The Placement of Sex Offenders in the Age of Megan's Law." *Widener Journal of Public Law* 7, 39–85.

Garafalo, J. 1987. "Reassessing the Lifestyle Model of Criminal Victimization." In Gottfredson, M. R. and Hirschi. T. (eds.), *Positive Criminology.* Newbury Park, CA: Sage Publications.

Greenfeld, L. A. 1997. *Sex Offenses and Offenders: An Analysis of Data on Rape and Sex-*

ual Assault. Washington, DC: U.S. Department of Justice, Bureau of Justice Statistics.

Harris, G. T., Rice, M. E., and Quinsey, V. L. 1998. "Appraisal and Management Risk in Sexual Aggressors: Implications for Criminal Justice Policy." *Psychology, Public Policy, and Law* 4(1/2): 73–115.

Herman, J. L. 1990. "Sex Offenders: A Feminist Perspective." In Marshall, W. L., Laws, D. P. and Barbaree, H. E. (eds.), *Handbook of Sexual Assault: Issues, Theories, and Treatment of Sexual Assault*. New York: Plenum Press.

Lieb, R. 1996. "Community Notification Laws: A Step Toward More Effective Solutions." *Journal of Interpersonal Violence* 11, 298–300.

Marshall, W. L., Jones, R., Ward, T., Johnston, P., and Barbaree, H. E. 1991. "Treatment Outcome With Sex Offenders." *Clinical Psychology Review* 11, 465–485.

Matson, S. and Lieb, R. 1996. *Community Notification in Washington State: A 1996 Survey of Law Enforcement*. Olympia: Washington State Institute for Public Policy.

——. 1997. *Megan's Law: A Review of State and Federal Legislation*. Washington: Washington State Institute for Public Policy.

Megan's Law of 1994 New Jersey Stat. Ann. §§ 2C: 7–1 to 2C: 7–11 (West 1987 & Supp. 1995).

Pratt, J. 2000. "Sex Crimes and the New Punitiveness." *Behavioral Sciences and the Law* 8, 135–151.

Pullen, S. and English, K. 1996. "Managing Adult Sex Offenders: A Containment Approach." In English, K., Pullen, S., and Jones, L. (eds.), *Managing Adult Sex Offenders: A Containment Approach*. Lexington, Kentucky: American Probation and Parole Association.

Quinsey, V. L., Harris, G. T., Rice, M. E., and Lalumiere , M. L. 1993. "Assessing Treatment Efficacy in Outcome Studies of Sex Of-

fenders." *Journal of Interpersonal Violence* 8, 512–523.

Quinsey, V. L., Rice, M. E., and Harris, G. T. 1995. "Actuarial Prediction of Sexual Recidivism." *Journal of Interpersonal Violence* 10, 85–105.

Schram, D. and Milloy, C. 1995. *Community Notification: A Study of Offender Characteristics and Recidivism*. Seattle, WA: Urban Policy Research.

Simon, J. 1998. "Managing the Monsters: Sex Offenders and the New Penology." *Psychology, Public Policy, and the Law* 4(1/2): 452–467.

Steinbock, B. 1995. "Megan's Law: A Policy Perspective." *Criminal Justice Ethics* 14(2): 4–9.

Telpner, B. J. 1997. "Constructing Safe Communities: Megan's Laws and the Purposes of Punishment." *Georgetown Law Journal* 85, 2039–2067.

Washington State Community Protection Act of 1990, Was. Rev. Code Ann. § 9A.44.130 (West Supp. 1997).

Zevitz, R. and Farkas, M. A. 2000a. "Sex Offender Community Notification: Punishing High Risk Offenders or Exacting Further Vengeance?" *Behavioral Sciences and the Law* 18(2/3): 375–391.

——. 2000b. "Sex Offender Community Notification: Examining the Importance of Neighborhood Meetings." *Behavioral Sciences and the Law* 18(2/3): 393–408.

Zevitz, R. and Farkas, M. A. 2000c. "The Impact of Sex Offender Community Notification on Probation and Parole in Wisconsin." *International Journal of Offender Therapy and Comparative Criminology* 44(1): 8–21.

32
Latent Consequences of Community Notification Laws

Lisa L. Sample
Anthony J. Streveler

In October of 1989, Jacob Wetterling, 11, was abducted near his home in Minnesota by an armed masked stranger. To date, he has still not been found. His case resembled that of a boy in a neighboring town who was abducted and sexually attacked earlier in the year. Both incidents are believed to have been committed by the same man (The National Criminal Justice Association 1997). These cases brought nationwide attention to a growing public fear—that of child sexual victimization at the hands of repeat offenders. In an effort to address public concern, the Jacob Wetterling Crimes Against Children and Sexually Violent Offender Registration Act was passed in 1994. This act mandates that 10 percent of a state's funding under the Edward Bryne Memorial State and Local Law Enforcement Assistance grant program be used for establishing a statewide system for registering and tracking convicted sex offenders (The National Criminal Justice Association 1997).

However, the year the Wetterling Act was passed, 7-year-old Megan Kanka was reported missing from her New Jersey home; she was later found sexually assaulted and murdered. It was determined that she had been killed by a previously convicted sex offender who had been released from prison.

Megan's parents believed that if they would have known a convicted sex offender was living in their community, they might have been able to prevent the death of their daughter. They, along with other parents of murdered children, lobbied Congress for the right to be notified of a convicted sex offender's residence within the community. The result of these efforts was the passage of "Megan's Law" in 1996. As an amendment to the Wetterling Act, Megan's Law requires states to make sex offender registry information available to the public. As of January 2001, all fifty states had made some provision to comply with Megan's Law by having law enforcement agents go door-to-door to inform communities of a sex offender whereabouts, take requests for sex offenders' addresses over the phone, post listings of registered sex offenders in libraries and police departments, or place registration information on the Internet (Adams 1999).

On the surface, community notification laws hold much value in that they may bring about closer supervision of children, reduce child sexual victimization, deter future incidents of sex offending, and reduce public fear of sex crimes. However, these laws have a potential for unintended ramifications that must be understood by policy makers, those administering the law, and the public at large. Without this understanding, the act of notification may result in creating more harm than good.

Latent Consequences of Community Notification Laws

Displacement of Offenders

Notification laws mandate that sex offender registry information be made available to the public; they do not, however, prohibit the movements of sex offenders. Sex offenders remain free to leave their community of residence for employment, entertainment, and other activities such as crime. To this end, notification laws may do little to deter future acts of sexual violence. Rather, they may simply displace sex offending to unsuspecting communities in which offenders' identities are not known. A statement from an interviewed sex offender provides examples:

> Are you going to notify the whole city of Milwaukee? If two-thirds of my victims are more than a mile away and you're going to notify one block, where do you stop? I have a problem with the notification law because in my case, if I wanted to, I could beat it without even trying. I could groom the grandkids. They live 10 miles away. (Zahn 1998)

> When Scott Lee Stoller was released from prison in 1996, Seattle police notified neighbors with a community meeting and a flier that indicated he was "a high risk to re-offend." A few months later, he drove 10 minutes to Redmond, where parents hadn't been notified, and molested two girls ages 5 and 6 (Shenk 1998).

These cases suggest that notification laws will do little to curb sex offenders' behavior. In a world filled with automobiles and mass transit alternatives, motivated offenders will simply travel to other communities that have not been notified of their status as convicted sex criminals. There they retain the anonymity needed to seek out victims and perform criminal acts. In essence, notification laws may then do nothing more than encourage mobility among sex offenders, thereby making it more difficult to monitor their activities and to find and apprehend offenders.

False Sense of Community Safety

As residents review registration listings and find that no convicted sex offenders live in their community, they are likely to conclude that their neighborhood is safe. Community members can acquire a sense of security because no police officer has gone door-to-door to inform them of a sex offender's presence. However, simply because sex offenders are not listed as residents within the community does not mean that they are not present.

In many states, community notification occurs upon a conviction for a sex crime regardless of whether the offender receives a sentence of probation or imprisonment. In Illinois, for example, the names and addresses of all convicted sex offenders are placed on the sex offender registration Website. Those who receive prison sentences are listed as DOC (Department of Corrections) residents until such time that they are paroled and adopt an address in the community. However, in other states, notification involves informing the community of only those offenders who are approaching release or have been released from prison, and the type of notification enacted varies by the offenders' predicted risk of re-offending. For example, offenders judged to be at a low-risk for re-offending are subject to Level I notification, which involves maintaining sex offender information within local law enforcement agencies and disseminating the information only to other appropriate criminal justice entities. Offenders with a greater risk of re-offending are subject to Level II notification, which includes disseminating sex offender information to community groups and schools. Those with the highest risk of re-offending are subject to Level III notification, and offender information is delivered to the general public via special bulletins in the form of flyers, press releases, or door-to-door visits (Poole and Lieb 1995). The problem is that most persons convicted of sex crimes are not sentenced to prison and, in these states, are often not subject to notification beyond Level I.

About 60 percent of all offenders convicted of sexual assault are under probation or parole supervision in the community (Greenfield 1997). Only a small percentage of offenders are actually subject to community notification. From 1990 to 1996 in the state of Washington, for example, it was estimated that only 11 percent of registered offenders were subject to Level II and III notification (Matson and Lieb 1996). In Wisconsin, Level II and III notifications represent approximately 4 percent of the total number of sex offenders in the registry (Wisconsin Department of Corrections 2000). In accordance with the notification laws of these states, the public is informed of the whereabouts of only a small proportion of the sex offenders living within the community.

More importantly, notification laws assume that the public knows all persons who engage in sex offending and where they reside. Sex offender registration lists include only those offenders who have come to the attention of the police and been successfully prosecuted for their crimes. Undoubtedly, many sex offenses remain unreported to police. Therefore, more sex offenders live within the community than are listed in sex offender registries and subject to any level of notification. Notification can alert residents to the presence of a *convicted* sex offender and can help the residents of a community avoid that particular individual. However, by its very nature, the act of notification does little to protect community residents from the *first-time* offender and ensure complete safety and security of a neighborhood.

Given these facts, we must be careful not to mislead the public into believing that "because there is no notification held in my community, it means that sex offenders do not live here." Notification can empower people with information on which they can judge their risk of victimization and take the appropriate steps to avoid it. However, the omission of a community from notification procedures can make parents, children, and the public believe that their neighborhood is safe and protective measures are unnecessary. Under this false sense of security, parents may supervise children less stringently and monitor neighborhood activities less closely. Notification may then facilitate sex offending within communities as residents are less prepared for sexual attacks.

Impact on the Public's Fear of Sexual Victimization

Some evidence of notification laws' ability to reduce the public's fear of sexually violent crime has been documented in the state of Washington (Phillips 1998). Four hundred residents, from both urban and rural environments, were surveyed to discern their thoughts on notification. Nine out of ten males indicated that notification had no effect on their likelihood of going outdoors alone, and males were less fearful of sex of-

fenders and offending after learning of their presence in the community (Phillips 1998). However, this reduction in fear was dependent on the gender and age of respondents.

More than eight out of ten females indicated that they were at least somewhat frightened by learning that convicted sex offenders resided in their communities (Phillips 1998). The majority of respondents 51 to 65 years old stated that they were frightened upon learning the residence of convicted sex offenders, and over three-quarters of the respondents 30 to 40 years old reported the same. In the short term, the fear generated by notification laws may reduce sexual victimization as people come to take more safety precautions, restrict the outdoor activities of children, and limit their social interactions with strangers. To the extent that sex offenders are strangers to their victims and attacks occur outside the home, these preventative measures could reduce the number of victims from which offenders can draw, thereby reducing incidents of offending. On the other hand, preventative behavior that leads to a reduction in social interaction among community residents could have negative consequences on a community in the long term.

In their classic formulation, Cohen and Felson (1979) suggest that the convergence in space and time of motivated offenders, suitable targets, and the absence of capable guardians is the cause of criminal offending. The fear generated by notification laws can lower the number of capable guardians within communities and damage relationships among neighborhood residents—both of which can allow offending to occur. Fear can cause people to speak less to strangers, remain in their homes, and reduce their social interactions. This decrease in interaction could diminish the guardianship residents exert over neighborhood activities and public spaces, which may encourage sex offending and other criminal behaviors. Moreover, some scholars suggest that much of the variance in crime rates across neighborhoods can be explained by the level of cohesion among community members (Lee 2000; Sampson, Raudenbush, and Earls 1997). Cohesion among residents enables them to control the behavior of community members and strangers within the neighborhood. As people shut themselves in their homes and remain strangers to their neighbors, they have no communication with fellow residents, thus discouraging the relationships needed to exert control over people and behaviors in the community.

Notification has been found to increase people's awareness of sex offending (Phillips 1998). Although this heightened awareness can empower people and help them prevent victimization, it can also lead to misplaced suspicion and increased fear, which can be detrimental to the relationships within the community that are needed to supervise public domains and monitor behavior. In this way, the fear generated by notification may appear to be a positive consequence of the law, but, over time, notification may harm community relations and actually create neighborhoods conducive to offending.

Impact on Reporting Sex Crimes

Most sexual offenses occur between victims and perpetrators who are known to each other. As reported, almost 7 in 10 rape or sexual assault victims knew the offender as an acquaintance, friend, relative, or intimate (Rennison 2000). More than 90 percent of the cases involving sexual abuse of children are perpetrated by someone the child knows, not strangers (Association for the Treatment of Sexual Abusers 2000). Notification, through the act of providing information to the community about the offender, can result in identifying the victim(s) of the crime. This is particularly true when notification results in widespread media attention and involves incest or intrafamilial cases. To avoid public ridicule and further the harm done to children, family members may be less inclined to report sex offenses to police because they know that, upon conviction, their family member's name will be released to the public (Edwards and Hensley 2001).

Intuitively, this concern has merit. Envision the child who is living the nightmare of sexual abuse and is torn between the pain and degradation of the acts, their desire to let someone know, and the fear and shame they have about reporting the crime. Then envision that child watching the 6 o'clock news showing members of a community picketing the residence of a released sex offender and hearing angry people shout, "Back to prison," "Castrate him," "He ought to be shot." This scenario is not atypical after many Level II and III notifications. Since the majority of the children molested are abused by someone they know, the child is aware that if the incidents of incest or abuse are reported, this scenario may be played out in front of a friend's or family member's home. Through the eyes of the unknown victim, it is easy to see where he or she may be less likely to report the crime, potentially undermining years of effort by victim advocacy and service agencies to encourage the reporting of sexual victimization.

There is concern that community notification can further result in decreased reporting of sexual victimization by encouraging trials for sex crimes rather than plea bargains. Given what is at stake upon conviction for a sex crime—the possibility of a prison term, registration for anywhere from ten years to life, and community notification—those accused of sexual misconduct or assault would most likely *not* accept a plea bargain that essentially convicts them of a sex crime. Accused offenders would most likely want to see their guilt proven in court beyond a reasonable doubt. Notification laws may then encourage offenders to elude conviction by forcing victims to face the embarrassment and trauma of testifying at trial. Although this is not a unique defense tactic, laws such as community notification, registration, and chemical castration may encourage this practice beyond its current use because there is more at stake upon a conviction for a sex offense that includes penalties *after* the initial punishment has been served.

In principle, notification may be intended to prevent sexual victimization and deter sex crimes, but in practice, it may only reduce the number of sex offenses reported to the police. To this end, any decline in the rates of sex offending observed after notification laws are enacted may not be a function of the laws' ability to deter offending. Instead, the rates may reflect the reluctance of victims to report the crime, subject themselves to the humiliation of a trial, and force family members or friends of the family to endure public harassment and degradation. Rather than suppressing sex offending, notification may simply keep incidents of the behavior hidden from public view.

Impact on Offenders and Their Families

Although the U.S. Supreme Court has not ruled that community notification laws are unconstitutional, many suggest that notification may violate sex offenders' civil rights under the Fifth, Eighth, and Fourteenth Amendments. The double jeopardy clause of the Fifth Amendment disallows being punished twice for the same crime. Critics of notification argue that the increased surveillance of sex offenders brought about by notification laws is a form of punishment, which is placed on sex offenders after they have already been punished for their crimes (News Media and the Law 1999a).

Also, opponents of notification have asserted that the way in which sex offenders are singled out under notification laws violates their rights under the Fourteenth Amendment's equal protection clause. In many states, sex offenders are the only category of offenders subject to notification. Differential treatment of criminal offenders is typically based on the elements of the crime—murderers traditionally have been given harsher sentences than burglars, robbers, or thieves—but even convicted and released murderers have not, as a category, been subject to notification laws upon release from prison. Just as we would not accept laws that require notification for only black or Hispanic offenders, some attorneys believe we should not accept laws that discriminate against people based solely on their offense type. The critics suggest that, at the very least, sex offenders should not be treated more harshly than people who have served time for murder.

Lastly, notification has been challenged under the Eighth Amendment on the basis that it is a "cruel and unusual" punishment. According to critics of notification, the cruel and unusual aspects of the law are its ability to invoke long-standing public ridicule, shame, isolation, and even violence (News Media and the Law 1999b). U.S. Courts of Appeals have held that sex offender registration and community notification are not forms of punishment; therefore, notification cannot be seen as either cruel or unusual. There is some evidence, however, that would suggest otherwise.

One of the more blatant outcomes of notification laws has been incidents of vigilantism as a result of the release of offenders' residential and offense information. For example, in California, a paroled sex offender, Michael Patton, was found hanging from a tree five days after the police went door to door to alert neighbors of his release and residence (Purdam 1998). However, offenders are not the only people that have been harmed by acts of vigilante justice. Hanley (1998) reported that the home of a neighbor of a paroled rapist was the target of vigilante gunfire by outraged New Jersey citizens. The sister of a convicted sex offender was the victim of an arson attack against her home after her brother was placed on Kansas' sex offender registry—even though he did not reside with her (Campbell 1998). The address listed in the directory was incorrect. Stories such as these have been reported across the country where community notification laws have been enacted. Although few people are likely to care much about the plight of sex offenders under notification laws, should their families be made to suffer for their transgressions? In many cases, people have endured harm at the hands of fellow citizens, yet they have been guilty of nothing more than living near or sharing a genetic link with offenders.

A less obvious consequence of notification laws is the impact they may exert on offenders' behavior. Notification laws can negatively affect an offender's ability to successfully reintegrate into the community (Edwards and Hensley 2001). They can also hamper an offender's chances of finding shelter and employment. For example, Zevitz and Farkas (2000) found out the following:

> Shortly after the offender was placed, he was evicted from his apartment. There was a media onslaught, with most information being negative. . . . All landlords

subsequently contacted denied residence, mostly out of fear from media attention. When a residence for the offender was found in another police jurisdiction, residents in that area started a rally and the plan for placement was not followed.

This type of treatment within the community can create stress and isolation for sex offenders and promote feelings of rejection and low self-esteem, all of which can make re-offending more likely (McAlinden 1999).

Adequate community supports, particularly in the area of housing, employment, and treatment, are critical to the effective transition of sex offenders, or any offender, from prison to the community. Thus, notification laws can hamper community support. It is not popular to talk about the difficulties that exist for persons who have committed such horrendous crimes. Most citizens likely feel "they get what they deserve." However, from a public protection standpoint, it is necessary to acknowledge the potential impact of notification as it relates to re-offending. Setting up the offender for failure only puts the community at greater risk. In essence, we must acknowledge the possibility that notification laws may exacerbate the emotional "triggers" seen as responsible for the behavior that they are trying to suppress.

Impact on the Criminal Justice System

Implementation of notification laws has resulted in substantial time and staff costs to an already overburdened criminal justice system. It has impacted all aspects of the criminal justice system, from law enforcement officials conducting door-to-door notifications, to parole agents attempting to find housing for offenders, to the courts addressing the multitude of legal challenges associated with the law (Adams 1999).

An example of the resources needed to implement and enforce community notification can be found in Illinois. In 1999, the Illinois State Police received approximately $500,000 from the legislature to maintain the sex offender registration database and place this information on the World Wide Web. These funds did not fully cover the costs of the computer mainframe, software, servers and printers, personnel salaries, training, and research needed at the Illinois Sate Police to support registration and community notification laws. Moreover, no funds were distributed to law enforcement agencies across the state to hire additional officers to receive the daily alerts of offenders who were not in compliance with registration laws, investigate where offenders may be, and apprehend those who failed to register. Officers simply performed these duties in addition to the community service and crime-fighting tasks they are already expected to perform.

Notification has also overwhelmed parole officers involved in community supervision (Poole and Lieb 1995). Notification laws tie up huge amounts of parole agents' time going to meetings with people throughout the community in order to find shelter and employment for released offenders. There has been no corresponding increase in funding to hire additional agents; therefore, they now have significantly less time to supervise offenders. Poole and Lieb (1995) suggest, "The large investment of time and energy on [sex offender] cases often means less attention paid to other cases." One parole agent explained to these authors, "The rest of your caseload has to be put on hold . . . because your time is totally consumed by the release of the SBN [special bulletin notification] sex offender" (Poole and Lieb 1995, 3).

Notification laws have also diminished court resources. To the extent that notification results in fewer plea bargains and more trials, the cost of adjudicating sex offense cases will significantly increase. Beyond the salaries of judges, prosecutors, and public defenders, jurors will have to be reimbursed for their time, court recorders must be employed, and administrative staff must be retained. As with other criminal justice agencies, it is unlikely that budgets will be increased, and additional personnel will be hired to compensate for the additional time and expenses incurred by resolving sex offense cases with trials rather than pleas.

To the extent that notification laws prevent harm to victims, their costs are naturally justified. However, to date, the deterrent effects of notification laws have yet to be determined. To this end, we must ask what community needs are not being met or what other crimes are allowed to flourish while police officers, courts, and probation and parole agents spend increasing amounts of time trying to reintegrate sex offenders into the community and monitor their whereabouts, as they are free to move about the country at will.

Impact on Sex Offending

More than six in ten respondents surveyed in the state of Washington believed that notification makes released sex offenders' behave better than if no one knew of their background (Phillips 1998). The thought underlying this belief is that while sex offenders are under an almost constant state of formal and informal surveillance from law enforcement agents and community residents, they are less likely to offend. Their actions will be monitored, so they will have few opportunities to commit acts of sexual violence without the possibility of being detected. The increase in surveillance of sex offenders, coupled with any preventative measures community residents may take, should make sex offenders feel less free to offend and deter their behavior. To date, however, little empirical evidence has been offered to support this belief.

We know of only one study that directly investigated the ability of notification laws to deter the behavior of sex offenders. Schram and Milloy (1995) monitored the offending patterns of 14 adjudicated juvenile sex offenders and 125 convicted adults released from correctional facilities from 1990 through 1993. All offenders were subject to the highest level of notification (Level III). These authors found that most juveniles re-offended during the follow-up period. Seventy-nine percent were arrested for another offense of any type, and 43 percent were re-arrested for a new sex crime. Of the adults, 42 percent were re-arrested for some type of crime from 1990 through 1993, and 14 percent were re-arrested for a new sex offense. Most importantly, the majority of the new sex offenses for adult offenders occurred in the same jurisdiction where Level III notifi-

cation took place. From these findings, it seems that notification laws do not preclude re-offending among convicted sex offenders. What is not known from this study is the ability of notification laws to deter the first-time sex offender.

In the last decade, reports of sexual victimization have declined. In 1998, the estimated rate of victimization for rape and sexual assault was 1.5 per 1,000 persons age 12 or older—a 40 percent decline from the rate of 2.5 per 1,000 persons in 1993 (Bureau of Justice Statistics, 1998). Given that this time period encompasses the years following the implementation of notification laws, some may suggest that this decline can be correlated with the increased knowledge and surveillance of released sex offenders. However, there were comparable decreases in the rates of other violent and nonviolent offending over this period as well. Given that most other violent and nonviolent offenders are *not* subject to notification, it would seem irresponsible to conclude that these laws are solely responsible for the decline in rates of sexual victimization. Moreover, the rate of sexual victimization for children ages 12 to 15 rose slightly from 3.1 per 1,000 persons in 1994 to 3.5 in 1998. From these data, one could surmise that the implementation of notification laws in 1996 actually served to increase sexual victimization among youths. Again, this would most likely be an inaccurate conclusion.

At this time, the best that can be said about the deterrent effects of notification laws on sex offending is that we simply do not know what the effects may be. From the evidence available, these laws do not seem to prevent convicted sex offenders from re-offending, but researchers have yet to determine the effect notification laws have on those that have not yet come to the attention of law enforcement. Given the possible latent consequences associated with community notification laws, it is imperative to determine if any gains have been made in deterring sex offending and preventing victimization. If notification has only negligible effects on offending, these laws may simply be creating more problems than they solve.

Conclusion

Community notification laws, on the surface, appear to be a reasonable response to the problem of sex offending. By providing people with the knowledge of who sex offenders are, where they live in the community, and what types of crimes they have committed, these laws are intended to prevent the sexual victimization of children and deter future incidents of offending. However, it does not appear that this well-intended legislation has reduced incidents of re-offending. Instead, it may simply displace sex offending to unsuspecting communities, create a false sense of security among community members, decrease the likelihood of reporting sex crimes, and diminish the resources of criminal justice agencies. Moreover, notification has resulted in physical harm to sex offenders and their families and may actually exacerbate the very factors believed to be the cause of sex offending.

Community notification laws highlight two specific problems that have remained a constant struggle in our society, recognizing both the intended and latent consequences of public policies and maintaining a reasonable balance between the rights of individuals and the protection of the public. All too often, criminal justice policies are enacted as knee-jerk responses to public fear, and little thought is given to the costs of enacting the policies or the long-term consequences of their implementation. These policies may appear to solve the problem they are meant to address, yet often they carry with them outcomes that create other problems or make the problem they are trying to solve worse. Notification laws provide proof of the need to anticipate the unintended and spend more time investigating the variety of outcomes that can occur when policies are enacted.

Notification also brings to light the difficulties in ensuring the protection of society while preserving the rights of individuals. Citizens have a right to protect themselves from crime. It logically follows that they also have the right to the information needed to do so. On the other hand, released sex offenders have already been punished for their crimes and should have the right to live free from continual threats and persecution. Moreover, sex offenders' families and friends have committed no crimes at all. Like any other citizen, they should not be subjected to harassment and physical harm. In order to derive balance between the rights of citizens and the rights of offenders and their families, the concepts upon which notification laws are based need to be examined.

Community notification laws are based on the notion that if we know who sex offenders are and where they reside, we can keep our children out of their reach. Therefore, inherent within these laws is the assumption that pedophiles and child molesters are usually strangers to their victims. Yet, empirical evidence indicates that most incidents of child sexual victimization are committed by people known to their victims (Rennison 2000). Given this finding, notification would likely be more effective at preventing child victimizations if it was carried out within the home rather than in the community at large.

Notification laws also intimate that sex offenders repeat their crimes more frequently than other categories of violent offenders. This intimation is witnessed in the fact that other types of violent offenders, such as murderers, robbers, and people who commit nonsexual assault, are rarely subject to notification laws. To some degree, these assumptions are justified in that recidivism among sex offenders has been well-documented (Furby, Weinrott, and Blackshaw 1989). Yet, reported levels of re-offending among treated and untreated sex offenders range from 3.8 percent to 55.6 percent, so clearly not all sex offenders re-offend. Moreover, recidivism has been documented among violent nonsex offenders as well (Sample 2001; Sipe, Jensen, and Everett 1998; Wright and Decker 1997). When compared, sex offenders exhibit lower rates of sexual and nonsexual re-offending than both robbers and those who commit nonsexual assault, even after taking into account offenders' time spent in custody (Sample 2001). To the extent that notification is based on the inevitability of re-offending among sex offenders, this finding would suggest that other types of violent offenders may be better candidates for notification laws.

Community notification appears to strike a balance between community needs and the rights of offenders, but given the evidence currently available, these laws appear to weigh heavily on the side of the public's right to information at the expense of offenders' and their families' rights to privacy and their liberty to live free from harassment and assault. These laws then highlight the difficulty in achieving equilibrium between the protection of society and the rights of individuals, the need to investigate the assumptions underlying public policies, and the need to explore all the possible consequences of policies before they are enacted.

In sum, notification can be a powerful tool for the community, but a tool is all it can be. Notification laws do not seem to prevent sex offending. They cannot ensure that no sex offenders live in the community, that risk of sexual victimization is reduced, or that no harm will befall children. Instead, it is possible that notification laws have no effect on the problem of sex offending whatsoever. It is also possible that notification may actually exacerbate that which it is trying to suppress. Until such time that more research on the effects of notification is performed, we can only speculate as to the desired and unintended consequences of these laws. These speculations should be kept in mind when a sex offender list is viewed at the library or on an Internet site, or if you receive a flyer to inform you that a released sex offender is living in your community.

References

Adams, Devon B. 1999. *Summary of State Sex Offender Registry Dissemination Procedures.* Washington DC: Bureau of Justice Statistics.

Association for the Treatment of Sexual Abusers. 2000. <http://www.atsa.com.>

Bureau of Justice Statistics. 1998. Washington DC: U.S. Department of Justice.

Campbell, Matt. 1998. "Lists Tell Names, Addresses, of Sexual Offender Information Publicized in the Area Under a New Missouri Law." *Kansas City Star,* (February 4): A11.

Cohen, Lawrence E. and Marcus Felson. 1979. "Social Change and Crime Rate Trends: A Routine Activities Approach." *American Sociological Review.* Vol. 44 (Aug.): 588–608.

Edwards, William, and Christopher Hensley. 2001. "Contextualizing Sex Offender Management Legislation and Policy: Evaluating the Problem of Latent Consequences in Community Notification Laws." *International Journal of Offender Therapy and Comparative Criminology*" 45(1): 83–101.

Furby, Lita, Mark R. Weinrott, and Lyn Blackshaw. 1989. "Sexual Offender Recidivism: A Review." *Psychological Bulletin* 105(1): 3–30.

Greenfeld, Lawrence A. 1997. *Sex Offenses and Offenders. An Analysis of Data on Rape and Sexual Assault.* Washington DC: Bureau of Justice Statistics, U.S. Department of Justice.

Hanley, Robert. 1998 "Neighbor Accused of Firing at House of Paroled Rapist." *New York Times,* (July 1): A17.

Lee, Matthew R. 2000. "Community Cohesion and Violent Predatory Victimization: A Theoretical Extension and Cross-National Test of Opportunity Theory." *Social Forces* 79(2): 683–707.

Matson, Scott, and Roxanne Lieb. 1996. *Community Notification in Washington State.* Olympia: Washington State Institute for Public Policy. <http://www.wa.gov>

McAlinden, A. M. 1999. "Sex Offender Registration: Some Observations on 'Megan's Law' and the Sex Offenders Act 1997." *Crime Prevention and Community Safety: An International Journal,* p. 41–53.

The National Criminal Justice Association. 1997. *Sex Offender Community Notification.* Washington DC: National Criminal Justice Association.

News Media and the Law. 1999a. "Privacy Argument Insufficient to Defeat 'Megan's Law' Requirements" 23(2): 12–13.

——. 1999b. "Judges Cannot Rule that Sex Offender Information May Not Be Discloseable." 23(2): 13–14.

Phillips, Dretha M. 1998. *Community Notification as Viewed by Washington's Citizens.* Olympia WA: Washington State Institute for Public Policy.

Poole, Carol, and Roxanne Lieb. 1995. *Community Notification in Washington State: Decision-Making and Costs.* Olympia, WA: Washington State Institute for Public Policy.

Purdam Todd S. 1998. "Death of Sex Offender Is Tied to Megan's Law." *New York Times,* (January 9): A13.

Rennison, Callie Marie. 2000. *Intimate Partner Violence*. Washington DC: U.S. Department of Justice, Bureau of Justice Statistics.

Sample, Lisa L. 2001. *The Social Construction of the Sex Offender*. Dissertation. St. Louis, MO: University of Missouri-St. Louis.

Sampson, Robert J., Stephen W. Raudenbush, and Felton Earls. 1997. "Neighborhoods and Violent Crime: A Multilevel Study of Collective Efficacy." *Science* 277(5328): 918–924.

Schram, Donna D., and Cheryl Darling Milloy. 1995. *Community Notification: A Study of Offender Characteristics and Recidivism*. Seattle, WA: Urban Policy Research.

Shenk, Wolf J. 1998. "Do 'Megan's Laws' Make a Difference?" *U.S. News & World Report*, March 9.

Sipe, Ron, Eric L. Jensen, and Ronald S. Everett. 1998. "Adolescent Sexual Offenders Grow Up: Recidivism in Young Adulthood." *Criminal Justice and Behavior* 25(1): 109–124.

Wisconsin Department of Corrections. 2000. *Agency Report*. Unpublished.

Wright, Richard T., and Scott H. Decker. 1997. *Armed Robbers in Action, Stickups and Street Culture*. Boston: Northeastern University Press.

Zahn, Mary. 1998. "They Share Shame, Guilt and a Monstrous Deed." *Milwaukee Journal Sentinel*, (March 29): 9.

Zevitz, R., and Farkas, M. A. 2000. "The Impact of Sex Offender Community Notification on Probation and Parole in Wisconsin." *International Journal of Offender Therapy and Comparative Criminology* 44(1): 8–21.